REHEARSALS

*To the memory of the Belgian civilians killed in 1914
and to those among their descendants
who have not forgotten them.*

*And to Rita and Celeste and
in memory of Rita and Morey.*

REHEARSALS
The German Army in Belgium, August 1914

Jeff Lipkes

The Brabant Press

2014

Typesetting: Diane Collins

Cover design: Kachergis Book Design

Cover illustration: Richard Jack, *De burgers op de vlucht voor de invasie in 1914* (1915, Oil on canvas, inv. 804238, © KLM-MRA, Belgium)

Table of Contents

Acknowledgments

I'm grateful for the help I've received from various archivists and their staffs. I'd especially like to thank Pierre-Alain Tallier of the General State Archives in Brussels, Dr. Françoise Peemans of the Ministry of Foreign Affairs, Manuel Duran, Sandrine Smets, Luc Vandeweyer, and Roger Vranken of the Royal Museum of the Armed Forces and Military History, Father Wally Platt of the American College of Leuven, and the late Abbé André Deblon of the Diocesan Archives of Liège. The staffs of the National Archives of the United Kingdom, the Imperial War Museum, particularly Anthony Richards, Stephen Walton, and Jenny Wood, and the manuscripts departments of the Bodleian Library and the British Library were also most helpful. I'm especially grateful to two archivists who offered assistance well above and beyond the call of duty, Canon Daniel Meynen of the Diocesan Archives of Namur and Gerrit Vanden Bosch of the Archdiocesan Archives of Mechelen. The latter translated several documents in Dutch and provided valuable guidance. Professor Francis Balace of the University of Liège, Dr. Alan Kramer of Trinity University Dublin, and Professor Laurence van Ypersele of the Université catholique de Louvain also offered useful suggestions, and Col. Bruce Vanderwort, editor of *Journal of Military History,* answered a quick question promptly. Professor Martin Swartz and Father Paul Janssens also kindly provided some information. I'd like to acknowledge as well the staffs of the Library of the Katholieke Universiteit Leuven, the Sterling Library at Yale University, the British Newspaper Library, and the Library of the University of South Florida, especially the interlibrary loan department of the latter.

Bruce Kinzer, Sally Marks, and Ken Rasmussen have read and commented on individual chapters. Mark Derez, archivist of the library of the Katholieke

Universiteit Leuven, has read the book in its entirety with scrupulous care and has provided enormously helpful corrections and comments. If I've negotiated the minefield of Belgian orthography successfully, it's thanks to him and to Beatrice Van Eeghem, my meticulous and hard-working editor at University of Leuven Press. I'm extremely grateful to all of the readers, and especially to Mark. The usual caveat – that they are not responsible for what follows – should perhaps be italicized and underscored.

My intellectual debts are acknowledged in the footnotes, but I would like to recognize a few Belgians and two Netherlanders who were especially zealous in gathering testimony about the events of August, and did so at some risk to themselves. They are, first and foremost, Canon Jean Schmitz and Father Norbert Nieuwland, along with Gustave Somville, Hervé de Gruben, Bart Mokvelt, and Lodewijk Grondijs. Each was also, in his own way, a notable stylist. It would have been a privilege to have had a chance to meet any of them.

I did meet plenty of helpful Belgians. I would like to thank the many individuals who shared with me the reminiscences of relatives who witnessed the events of August 1914, or provided other information. These include Father René Obbels of the Damiaan Instituut, Aarschot, and Simon Alexandre of Namur, who were particularly helpful, Dr. Robert Mordant, Ivo and Tom van Hees, M. Igual, Abbé Maurice Leonard, Patrick de Wolf, Staf Floridor, Gaby Lens, Bart Hendrickx, Jozef Hendrickx-Delvaux, Luc Devos, and Piet Reynaert. There were many more individuals whose names I unfortunately neglected to write down or misplaced, along with those of the staff members of tourist bureaus and communal archives who responded to emailed queries. The Premonstratensian Father in Leffe, the *échevin* in Dinant, and a number of others I met fortuitously, particularly in Aarschot, Dinant, and Leffe, shared interesting and useful information. Members of the online community of Great War aficionados at the listserve hosted by University of Kansas (wwi-l@listproc.cc.ku.edu) generously offered their expertise, including Leslie Graham, Daniel Ross, Colin Fenn, David Heal, the late Ted Rawes, and the moderator, Dr. Geoffrey Miller. I'd like to thank also the following members of Veterans of the Battle of the Bulge for information on the invasion of Germany: Richard Glunt, Gerald Myers, and Wayne Pierce. Juliana Cooper worked hard to make my conversational French less amusing, and Koen Janssens and Gaby Lens did some translating of documents in Dutch. Dick Gilbreath of University of Kentucky provided the map on p. 12 on very short notice, and cheerfully made several revisions. I'm indebted to Willy Schroeven and, again, Mark Derez for assistance with the illustrations, and to the Hertogelijke Aarschotse Kring voor Heemkunde, the Katholieke Universiteit Leuven, and the Leuven Stadsarchief for permission to reproduce photos in their collections. I appreciate as well the help of Rita Ciresi and Celeste Lipkes in revising the index.

I'd especially like to thank Hilde Lens-Gielis, Marike Schipper, Beatrice Van Eeghem, and Ineke Deckers of Leuven University Press for their support and encouragement. I began this book in the summer of 2000 and Hilde's interest in the project five and half years later enabled me to conclude it at long last, for which my family and I are profoundly grateful. It has been a real pleasure working with Marike since she assumed the directorship in May, 2006, as well as with Beatrice and Ineke.

Perhaps I should mention why an historian of British economic thought strayed into the August 1914 combat zones of eastern Belgium. In the late 1990s I was asked to teach a number of classes on European and World History in the 20th century by departments perhaps hoping to capitalize on fin de siècle nostalgia. *Rehearsals* is one of a great many books, I imagine, that is a response (at far greater length than they or I anticipated) to questions posed by students, in this case about the fate of civilians in World War I. The book should probably be dedicated to those students everywhere who sit in the front row and raise their hands.

I occasionally told friends half-jokingly that the working title of the book was The Huns of August, but I truly hope I won't be accused of any animus towards Germany or Germans. When I was in graduate school, I spent a summer in Bavaria and, like most Americans (including soldiers after both World Wars), found the people I encountered congenial, sympathetic, *gemütlich*, and easily the most "American" of any European nationals, for better or worse. It should go without saying that no German alive today bears any responsibility for crimes committed during the first half of the 20th century. Unfortunately, the charge of "racism" is issued so promiscuously that what should go without saying sometimes needs to be said.

Finally, I read a great many fascinating and heart-rending accounts that I was unable to include, and, among other regrets, I'm sorry about this second injustice done to some of the victims of 1914.

-<-->-

Note: I refer to all towns, villages, and streets in Flemish-speaking regions by their Dutch names (though Leuven was, in 1914, a bilingual city). However, I have not altered the titles of books, articles, or chapters, nor, generally, without some evidence, the first names of individuals. I've used the English names for Belgium and for Brussels and Antwerp, and have opted for the modern spelling of all other places. I have anglicized "franc-tireur," so that term is not italicized and the plural is "franc-tireurs" rather than *"francs-tireurs."* An *échevain* is not an alderman (the usual translation), in so far as he has administrative responsibilities, something like a municipal cabinet minister, so I have retained the Belgian word.

Preface
to the Second Edition

Chapters 14 and 15 and several sections of Chapter 2 have been cut in this abridgement. Additional paragraphs and a number of sentences have been eliminated as well from the second and other chapters, and errors and stylistic infelicities corrected. The two omitted chapters surveyed the history of the denial of the August massacres, Chapter 14 in Germany and Chapter 15 in Britain and America. Whatever interest this depressing story may have for students of ideology or historiography, it is secondary to the chief purpose of the book, which is to describe in detail, relying on eyewitness accounts, what actually happened in Aarschot, Andennes, Tamines, Dinant, and Leuven and some of towns and villages of Liège province. Because some readers might be interested in how the victorious Allies dealt with those who had committed war crimes in August 1914, I've included as Appendix II a short section of Chapter 14 summarizing the Leipzig Trials.

The chapter on denials in Britain and the U.S. began with the war-time writings of Bertrand Russell and G. B. Shaw and continued down to the present. I kept encountering fresh examples and dutifully added the more egregious to the final footnote. It would be gratifying if the publication of the first edition has resulted in fewer recitals of the revisionist case—that the "atrocities" were the invention of British propagandists, or at least were gross exaggerations of harsh, but legitimate, reprisals for guerilla attacks. I don't think this is likely.[1]

The omissions, revisions, and additional material are also not likely to satisfy the book's critics among academic reviewers. Its title was intended to be provocative, of course, and I ought not to have been surprised that some reviewers found it provoking. The title undoubtedly influenced their read-ing of the text, and occasionally their misreading.[2]

There are obvious differences in the conduct of the German armies between the two World Wars, and perhaps I ought to have mentioned them in pass-ing in the original Prologue. However eloquently Pan-German professors and publicists proclaimed that their country was engaged in a "racial" war pitting Germans against Latins and Slavs,[3] the OHL had other priorities. Undoubtedly it was long-standing perceptions of the enemy that helped give credence to the belief in franc-tireurs and that justified the campaign of terror that was waged against civilians, along with convictions about German rights and privileges. But even before the front stabilized along the Yser, the killings diminished, if the condescension did not disappear. The subsequent occupation of Belgium cannot be compared to that of Eastern Europe a quarter of a century later. The Flemish population was ardently, though unsuccessfully, wooed—even Walloon nationalism was encouraged—and the opinion of neutrals conciliated. Particularly striking was the government's concern about American sensibilities, in contrast to its National Socialist successor.

The fact that the regime the Germans installed east of the military zone in Flanders was called the *Generalgouverment* underscores the contrast: this was the name given to occupied Poland in 1939. After the massacres of August, 1914, fewer than 500 Belgians were killed by German troops, apart from those executed as spies or shot or electrocuted as they attempted to cross into the Netherlands. Some three million Poles and three million Pol-ish Jews lost their lives between 1939 and 1945. The Germans conscripted around Belgian 120,000 workers after October 1916, a move long resisted by the Governor General, Moritz von Bissing. Some 12 to 15 million slave laborers worked in the mines, factories, and fields of the Third Reich. The Germans had many more scruples in 1914 than they would have twen-ty-five years later.

Though officers occasionally declared that they were engaged in a war of annihilation[4] and Belgians compared the conscripted workers to slaves, the First World War was not waged to exterminate and enslave enemies of the Reich, but to consolidate German hegemony in Europe.

Nonetheless, there are important ways in which the events of August anticipated the behavior of German armies in Eastern Europe during the Second World War, and were in turn anticipated by campaigns in China and Southwest Africa, and the government's response to events in Alsace. These are explored in the Afterword. Michael Geyer, in his Foreword to the book based on the controversial exhibit that toured the Federal Republic in the late 1990s, "The German Army and Genocide," concludes that the Wehrmacht's crimes were the result of "a shared sense of German superiority and the imagined bestiality of the enemy."[5] These beliefs do not date from 1933.

⤙⤚

Critics of the first edition were both offended by the book's conclusions and disliked its approach.

References to differences between European nationals are sure to rile most intellectuals in the 21st century. Needless to say, I do not believe in a German "national character," let alone an unchanging one.[6] At the same time, if we are convinced of the importance of history and geography in shaping values, we should hardly be surprised that, given their very different experiences between 43 AD and 1914, people inhabiting the regions that became Britain would feel differently about many things on the eve of the war than people who inhabited the lands that became Germany.[7]

Scholars today prefer an anodyne relativism. John Horne and Alan Kramer think the behavior of German troops in August 1914 was much like that of French peasants in 1789. The AHR reviewer believes it was similar to that of American soldiers at Abu Ghraib in 2003 and 2004.[8] *Plus ça change*. I don't think these analogies are helpful, and Chapter 13 attempts to explain why.

⤙⤚

Second, though narrative history was supposed to have begun a comeback a generation ago, what was meant by "the new narrative history," in Lawrence Stone's influential analysis, was, it turns out, the study of *mentalités* and the adoption of the approach of anthropologists rather than that of economists.[9] The attitude toward actual narrative history on the part of academics is still something like that described by Stone: the historian's "friends tend to apologize for him, saying: 'Of course, he only did it for the money.'"[10] This seems to be the feeling of at least one of the book's critics, who suggested that "the book was rushed into print to capitalize on a renewed interest in First World War atrocities"—an interest, regrettably, I've seen no evidence of.[11]

Post-structuralist assumptions have added to the animus Stone noted. Narrative history betrays a profound naïveté about the past. There is no one story to tell. There are, rather, multiple points of view on a given historical "event" and one has to make heroic efforts to avoid "privileging" those of the dominant race, class, or gender, or, in wars, the triumphant nation or colonizing power.

Thus it is no surprise that Horne and Kramer are more interested in the way the executions, arson, and looting were represented by intellectuals and journalists on both sides during and after the war, than in the "atrocities" themselves. "The heart of the matter," they argue, "is to be found in subjective perceptions. What each side thought was going on–the stories it told–shaped what happened."[12] As a result, they devote only 51 of 431 pages to the actual events in Belgium.

While I share an interest in perceptions of the killings—two chapters, after all, examined in detail the ways in which the war crimes were rationalized or denied in Britain, the U.S., and Germany—*Rehearsals* is mostly, unabashedly, an account of the events themselves, largely from the standpoint of the victims.[13]

As I understand narrative history, it is a detailed reconstruction of an event as it unfolded, moment by moment. In E. M. Forster's famous distinction, it is "showing" rather than "telling." While the accumulated weight of such anecdotal evidence can naturally support an argument, the objective of a narrative is not merely to defend a thesis, but to enable readers to share in the experience to some degree, to relive a moment in the past charged with drama. This happens to be why many non-academics enjoy history.

In the case of the events in Belgium, there is a good reason for adopting such an approach. As I mention in the Prologue, and demonstrated at length in the omitted chapters, the war crimes of August 1914 have been dismissed decade after decade, down to the present. While World War I scholars today are not likely to repeat the claims made by Jay Winter in the 1996 PBS documentary *The Great War and the Shaping of the Twentieth Century*, books by non-specialists and journalists continue to treat the stories of killings, rapes, and arson as outright fabrications, or, at best, exaggerations of a few inevitable excesses.

-<-->-

Abbreviations

DVF — Imperial War Ministry, Imperial Ministry of Foreign Affairs, *Die völkerrechtswidrige Führung des belgischen Volkskriegs* (Berlin, 1915)

FR — Fonds Rutten, Diocesan Archives of Liège

FSN — Fonds Schmitz-Nieuwland, Diocesan Archives of Namur

GSA — Inventaire 298: Inventaire des archives de la Commission d'Enquête sur la Violation des Règles du Droit des Gens, Des Lois et des Coutumes de la Guerre (1914–1926), General State Archives, Brussels

IWM — Imperial War Museum, London

MFA — Ministry of Foreign Affairs, Brussels

NA — National Archives of the United Kingdom (formerly Public Records Office)

PRW — Parish Reports on World War I, Archdiocesan Archives of Mechelen

RBC — British Committee on Alleged German Outrages, *Report of the British Committee on Alleged German Outrages* (Sydney, Australia, 1915)

RDE — Commission d'Enquête sur les Violations des Règles du Droit des Gens, des Lois et des Coutumes de la Guerre, *Rapports et Documents d'Enquête*, premier vol., (Brussels, 1922–3), 1 (tome I), 2 (tome II)

Reply — Kingdom of Belgium, Ministry of Justice and Ministry of Foreign Affairs, *Reply to the German White Book of the 10th May, 1915* (London, 1918)

RMAF — Royal Museum of the Armed Forces and Military History, Brussels

RVR — Official Commission of the Belgian Government, *Reports on the Violation of the Rights of Nations and of the Laws and Customs of War in Belgium* (London, 1915), 1 (vol. I), 2 (vol. II)

SN — J. Schmitz and N. Nieuwland, *Documents pour servir à l'histoire de l'invasion allemande dans les provinces de Namur et de Luxembourg* (Brussels, 1919–1925)

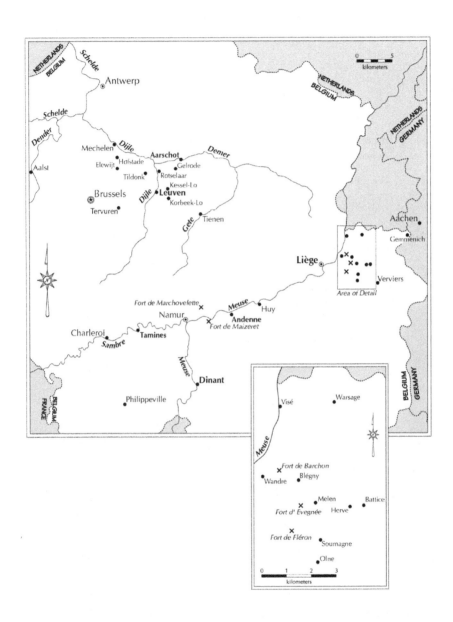

Prologue

"The truth transcends the limits of the probable."
Cardinal Désiré-Joseph Mercier

"What a vast difference there is between the barbarism that
precedes culture and the barbarism that follows it."
Friedrich Hebbel

This book describes what happened when three German armies invaded Belgium in August 1914. In district after district, troops looted and burned homes and murdered the inhabitants. By the end of the month, nearly 6,000 Belgian civilians were dead, the equivalent of about 230,000 Americans today. The worst of the carnage took place during an eight-day period between August 19th and 26th.[1]

To anyone familiar with activities in Nazi-occupied Eastern Europe, there will be a sense of déjà-vu. In a series of organized manhunts, residents were chased out of their homes at gunpoint, the men herded to isolated fields or, more often, to town and village squares, and then gunned down, without the pretense of a trial. Others – including women and children – were forced into cattle-cars and, under deplorable conditions, transported east to concentration camps, where they were held for months. Still other captives were forced to march for days in the sweltering August heat, with little or no food or water, before being herded to Belgian lines or dispersed. Whenever residents were removed from their villages and towns, the homes were systematically looted and then set on fire. The stolen goods selected by officers were shipped back to Germany. Some 25,000 homes and other buildings in 837 communities were burned to the ground. About one and a half million Belgians fled the country, 20% of the population. The suffering was without precedent in modern Europe. For over two hundred fifty years civilians had not fled en masse before invading armies. They had not been targeted by the invaders. As in the 1940s, the German advance was preceded by endless columns of refugees, caked with dust, shuffling along under heavy bundles, feet bleeding, staring blankly ahead, numbed beyond despair.

Yet even today, particularly in the U.K. and the U.S., reports of German crimes in Belgium are frequently dismissed as Allied propaganda. Historians and popular writers treating the subject concede that the Germans retaliated harshly for attacks by "franc-tireurs" (guerilla snipers), but the stories told by survivors of murder, arson, rape, and pillage have generally been regarded as gross exaggerations, if not wholesale inventions.

Typical is the treatment in the 1996 PBS series "The Great War and the Shaping of the Twentieth Century." In terms of audience size, this is perhaps the most influential recent account of World War I. Sections of it are replayed in high school and college history classrooms throughout the U.S. each semester.[2]

The film approaches the subject from the point of view of German soldiers. "To their surprise, Belgian snipers known as franc-tireurs began shooting," the narrator declares. A German solider is then quoted: "The war became a hideous experience, because the population took part in the fight. Whenever they had a chance, they shot down German soldiers."

After briefly mentioning that "hundreds" of Belgian civilians were executed, the narrator informs viewers that "with each retelling, [the tales] became more vicious. Exaggerated stories were taken as fact." Host Jay Winter then discusses "the first substantial propaganda campaign in history," by which he means the attempt to tell the world about the massacres of Belgian civilians. The campaign freely indulged in racism, Winter claims. The image of "'poor little Belgium'" – the irony is unmistakable – "would haunt the Germans for years to come," the narrator concludes.[3]

In the most recent history book to make the *New York Times* bestseller list, apart from biographies of America's founders, readers are assured that "in fact, Belgium was not neutral at all; it had agreements with France and Britain, and forts dotted its border with Germany (unlike its border with France, which had none)." All of these statements are false. "After the war," the author continues, "it was well established that the Belgian atrocities were largely fabricated, but the lies did their damage."[4]

So why the unwillingness to acknowledge that war crimes took place in Belgium in 1914? There is, in the first place, a problem with the term adopted in Britain and America to describe the mistreatment of civilians. During the first two months of the war, stories were told of sadistic maimings both of Belgian civilians and German soldiers, though to an extent much exaggerated subsequently. (There are very few references to such crimes in the leading British newspapers in August and September: only three in the *Daily Mail,* where one might expect to find more, and just one in the *Times,* along with a letter to the paper forwarded from a soldier at the front. The paper with the most "atrocity stories," seven, was, interestingly, the Liberal *Daily News.* Correspondents in all cases clearly indicated that these reports were not first-hand. The "atrocities" receiving the most extensive coverage were genuine: at least twenty-five articles in the *Times, Daily Mail, Telegraph, Evening Standard, Morning Post,* and *Daily News* were devoted to the destruction of Leuven, some on the front page. In second place was the shelling of Rheims Cathedral. A distant third was the bombardment of Dendermonde.) Rumors circulated nonetheless that hands and fingers had been severed, eyes gouged out, breasts and genitals cut off. There were also reports of grisly executions: soldiers and civilians crucified on barn doors; infants roasted on spits or speared by bayonets, etc. Germans seemed to be particularly fascinated by gouged eyes, Belgians by severed hands, the British by severed breasts and by crucifixions. Though many hundreds of Belgians civilians were stabbed or slashed by bayonets, the stories of gratuitous cruelties were mostly without foundation. No cases of gouged eyes or severed hands were ever substantiated.[5]

Unfortunately, the term "atrocities" came to be applied both to these grisly allegations and to the more prosaic crimes that the German Army indubitably committed. The sack of Leuven and the massacres of civilians and the burning of villages in the provinces of Liège, Namur, and Brabant were all "atrocities." So were the sinking of the *Lusitania* and the execution of Edith Cavell. That nearly all of the sensational stories of sadistic mutilations were discredited permitted partisan historians to dismiss the mass executions, arson, looting, abuse of "hostages," and rapes for which there is abundant and persuasive documentation. No one familiar with the history of the 20th century needs to be reminded about how easy it is to murder innocent civilians without recourse to the particular refinements of cruelty that captivated gullible audiences in 1914. I will use the term "atrocities" to refer exclusively to the latter.

In addition to dismissing massacres because there were no maimings or dismemberments, those attempting to justify the behavior of German troops in Belgium during the first weeks of the war have insisted that the executions and burnings were legitimate reprisals for guerilla attacks by Belgian civilians. The existence of a "franc-tireur" army, however, is as much a myth as the claim that German troops systematically hacked the hands off of Belgian children. There are only a few instances of trials of any kind, and these were farcical. The official defense of the conduct of the German Army in Belgium published no transcripts or summaries of such trials. Only two alleged franc-tireurs are identified by name – both incorrectly. No burgomaster, communal official, village priest, or *Garde civique* officer imprisoned in Germany was prosecuted for organizing resistance.

This is not to insist (as did the Belgian government) that not a single civilian fired on passing troops. It is conceivable that in the opening days of the war in eastern Liège province, Belgian gamekeepers and peasants fired on lone uhlans or small parties on patrol, though Belgian Army units were also operating east of the Meuse. There is simply no credible evidence, however, of the organized resistance the Germans claimed to have encountered repeatedly: townspeople shooting suicidally from their homes on battalions marching down the main street, with predictably disastrous results. The franc-tireur legend will be taken up in detail, but for any impartial observer, the only question that remains is whether the stories flared up spontaneously, fed by fears and inexperience, or whether they were deliberately contrived to foster the brutality considered necessary for a rapid passage through Belgium.

⊰⊱

However, I believe the underlying reason for the continued unwillingness of journalists and popularizers to acknowledge what happened in Belgium in August 1914 has to do with the seductive appeal of revisionism. Views inspired by the bitter reaction to the Great War during the 1920s and early '30s, though long rejected by most scholars, have retained their grip on public opinion. Briefly, revisionists believe that all the nations that went to war in 1914 were equally to blame. They "slithered into war," in Lloyd

George's unfortunate phrase. Nonetheless, at the war's close, the victorious Allies imposed a draconian peace on Germany – which led inevitably
to World War II. The fact that thousands of innocent civilians had been
butchered during one week by an invading army violating international
law and treaty obligations was simply not compatible with the appealing
myth of collective guilt in 1914 and Allied vindictiveness in 1919.

World War I was the first total war. Entire populations were mobilized
to support the armies; immense sacrifices were demanded. The killing
could not have been sustained for four years, the argument goes, unless
people in all the warring nations had not been manipulated by their governments, whipped into a patriotic frenzy over the enemy's vileness. Hate
is a more effective stimulant than pride, and easier to induce. Stories of
German "atrocities" were especially useful in the recruitment campaigns in
Britain and the Empire, and to seduce America into abandoning neutrality.

The history of the denial of the Belgian massacres is fascinating in its
own right. The bulk of the book, however, simply chronicles in detail the
systematic killing carried out in August 1914. The worst of the massacres
took place between August 19th to 26th in the towns of Aarschot, Andenne,
Tamines, Dinant, and Leuven, successively. There are chapters on events
in each of these locations, preceded by a chapter on the killings in the towns
and villages in Liège province just east of the forts, and in the city of Liège.

The accounts draw on published and unpublished testimony by eye-
witnesses. When appropriate, I've let individuals tell their stories in their
own words. The chapters consist mostly of a series of vignettes. Some are
only a couple of paragraphs in length, and recount particularly vivid or
revealing moments. Others provide fuller descriptions of what particular
individuals and families experienced. Still other sections offer overviews
of what transpired in each location, or summarize the military actions that
preceded the killings.

The witnesses range widely in age, background, and perspective, and
include Dutch, American, Australian, and British observers, as well as Belgians. I've made some use as well of captured German diaries and letters,
and sworn depositions by German soldiers and prisoners of war. The witnesses told their stories in testimony collected by two Belgian commissions
and a third investigation by the Ministry of Foreign Affairs, by two committees in Britain, in interviews with numerous journalists and historians, and

in their own written accounts. I have drawn on a large body of published and privately published narratives, and have consulted original material in six archives in Belgium. I have also spoken and corresponded with some descendants of survivors and victims in Aarschot, Dinant, and Leuven.

Those who deny massacres took place in Belgium in August 1914 seldom fail to mention the unreliability of refugees. Uprooted from their homes, exhausted, hungry, badly frightened, those who had fled occupied Belgium, the argument goes, had already given credence to all kinds of irresponsible rumors, which now they, in turn, exaggerated with each retelling. "Truth is the first casualty of war," we are repeatedly reminded, and though, unlike their governments, most refugees did not intentionally lie, critics concede, their accounts are no more to be trusted than Foreign Office press releases. The only appropriate response to this claim is that it is precisely the task of the historian to distinguish false or implausible stories from accounts that are likely to be credible. That the attorneys working for the Committee on Alleged German Outrages did not always do so, unlike, by and large, their counterparts on the Belgian *Commission d'Enquête,* is regrettable, but is no reason for historians to despair of accurately describing the transgressions of the German Army. In any event, given the long antipathy to Belgian testimony on the part of British and American historians, I have used all sources I've mentioned with caution. The majority of the evidence, in any case, comes not from refugees, but from eyewitnesses who did not flee the country and who wrote or were interviewed after the war. Naturally, I would not wish to claim that there is not a single misrepresentation or exaggeration in any of the testimony I've drawn on, but I trust the inevitable inaccuracies are few and slight.

⋖⋌⋅⋋⋗

A couple of questions may occur to readers at this juncture. It has been asked for at least a generation, and not only by Germans, how long citizens of the Federal Republic must be made to feel guilty for the murders committed under the Nazi regime. Is it not unsporting to now add war crimes committed by soldiers of the *Kaiserreich* to the burden of German guilt? Scrupulous historians can only answer that the feelings of the descendants of the individuals whose actions they describe cannot be any of their concern. But it is also safe to say that few historians, unlike commanders ordering executions in 1914, believe in collective guilt, and fewer still in transgenerational guilt. Nonetheless, the actions of the German Army in Belgium are part of the historical record, and anyone wishing to explain German history between 1871 and 1945 needs to account for them.

It is hardly surprising that the three major conflicts roiling the historical profession in Germany between 1961 and 1988 – the Goldhagen controversy of 1996 makes a fourth – all had to do with continuities in German history.[6] Despite the outcome of the latter, when the dust settled, no informed writer would wish to make the case that Adolf Hitler was a great aberration in German history. *Der schlechte Österreicher* (the wicked Austrian), as one of my German teachers invariably referred to him, did not seduce an unwilling nation, nor did he turn to mass murder under the inspiration of Lenin in an attempt to pre-empt a Bolshevik threat. But antisemitism played a comparatively small role in the seduction. The Nazi revolution was also a restoration. Bethmann Hollweg, Chancellor in 1914, certainly bore no resemblance to Hitler – though in some respects he anticipated Goebbels.[7] However, a predisposition to force and fraud and a contempt for the rights of civilians and for due process characterized German polity decades before the Nazi era.[8] "Necessity knows no law," the Chancellor proclaimed to the *Reichstag* on August 4, 1914. For some influential Germans, "necessity" had come to be defined as German hegemony in Europe with, ultimately, a great global empire, though the final reckoning with Britain to acquire the latter was not to have taken place until the former was achieved. The Belgians were the first victims of German lawlessness. They were not the last.

The invasion of Belgium precipitated a long chain of events that resulted in the murders of untold millions of civilians.[9] One of the most chilling facts about the 20th century is that we cannot estimate the death toll worldwide of those murdered by government order even to the nearest ten million.[10] Six thousand deaths is hardly a drop in the bucket. But it was the first drop. The staggering scope of the massacres that followed is precisely the reason to examine in detail what happened in the provinces of Liège, Namur, and Brabant during the German invasion.

CHAPTER I
An ultimatum

Sunday, August 2, 1914, was not an auspicious day in the career of Karl-Konrad von Below-Saleske, German Minister to Belgium.[1] Suave and polished, recruited from the ranks of the aristocracy, like nearly all pre-war diplomats save those of the two republics, the forty-eight-year-old envoy had served the German Empire in Turkey and China before assuming his position in Brussels in October, 1913. After the war broke out, Brand Whitlock, Below's American counterpart, recalled an encounter with the German diplomat earlier that summer. It had been at the end of a formal reception at the German Legation, the last of the season.

"Well, thank God it's over," Below had confided. "We can be tourists now, go where we please, do what we please."[2]

As the two men chatted, the American noticed that the silver bowl he had been using as an ashtray had a bullet hole in its side. Did it have a history? It did indeed.

"'In China,'" Below explained,

> it stood on my desk, and one day during the riots a bullet came through the window and went right through it."
>
> Several of the guests pressed up to see;...the German Minister had to recount the circumstances several times.
>
> "I have never had a post," he said, "where there has not been trouble; in Turkey it was the Revolution, in China it was the Boxers. I am a bird of ill omen."
>
> He laughed, standing there very erect and tall and distinguished, with his pointed black moustaches, raising his cigarette delicately to his lips with a wide and elegant gesture, while the guests purred about, examined the silver bowl, thrust their fingers into the bullet hole.
>
> "But now," he went on, "I have the most tranquil post in Europe; nothing can happen in Brussels."[3]

On Thursday, July 31, Below had received a sealed envelope from a special messenger dispatched from the German Foreign Office in the Wilhelmstrasse. He was told not to open it until he was so instructed by telegram. Below was one of the rare diplomats not to leave a written account of his activities on the eve of the war, but he must have been apprehensive. The Austro-Hungarian ultimatum was delivered to Serbia on July 23, four weeks after the assassination of Archduke Francis-Ferdinand in Sarajevo. Every professional diplomat understood that it was the prelude to a declaration of war; the Austrian ambassador to Serbia, indeed, barely glanced at the Belgrade government's conciliatory reply before breaking off relations. What was not clear was how members of the two great alliances would respond to Austria's transgression of international law.

The German High Command was parsimonious in the information it communicated to civilians in the Foreign Office and the Willhelmstrasse was itself not very forthcoming with its ambassadors, so it's unlikely Below knew much about the Schlieffen Plan, the grand strategy to launch an end-run around the French fortresses and take Paris from the west, flooding the Belgian plain with over 750,000 troops.[4] Nonetheless, Below must have guessed that the sealed envelope contained some unwelcome requests of Belgium, whose neutrality Germany had pledged to observe.

Whatever Below surmised about the contents of the envelope, he was obliged to put up a good front; this was precisely why the envelope had been sealed, of course. Called to the Foreign Office in the evening of July 31, he reassured Baron Léon van der Elst, the Secretary General, that he was aware of the solemn declaration his predecessor had made three years earlier that the *Kaiserreich* would respect Belgian neutrality. Van der Elst, regarded as sympathetic to Germany, reminded Below of similar commitments made even more recently, by the Chancellor in private and by the Foreign Minister in an open session of the *Reichstag's* Budget Committee. Below replied that he was certain that the sentiments expressed on those occasions had not changed.

Later that night, at 10:30 p.m., the Belgian government learned that the British Foreign Secretary, Sir Edward Grey, had telegraphed Paris and Berlin asking if they intended to respect Belgium's neutrality. The French Minister showed up promptly the next morning to assure Count Julien Davignon, the stout, professorial Foreign Minister, that his country had immediately and unequivocally replied in the affirmative.[5] Davignon was regarded by foreign diplomats as a rather quaint character, overly sanguine and not especially energetic or effectual. He was, recalled the French envoy,

> very much an *honnête homme*, as they used to say in the eighteenth century, of extreme rectitude and imperturbable placidity. I enjoyed his company. In his room the sounds of the outside world seemed to arrive hushed and muted... In his charming optimism, M. Davignon must, I imagine have held the view that things have only the importance one attaches to them... In the anxious period we were passing through, which shook him somewhat out of his usual habits, his final remark invariably was: "Let us hope it will turn out all right in the end."[6]

The Foreign Ministry was actually run by Baron van der Elst, it was widely believed.

Germany's silence began to weigh heavily on Davignon and van der Elst. Count Albert de Bassompierre, Secretary to the Belgian Minister of Foreign Affairs, was dispatched to the German Legation to inform Below of the French response and to see what he had to say.

After he had delivered his message, the Secretary recalled, Below leaned back in his armchair, looked at the ceiling through half-closed eyes, and recited back to Bassompierre exactly what he had just said, word for word. The Belgian diplomat was impressed by the performance, but perplexed as to its significance. Below then thanked the Secretary for sharing the information with him. Another moment elapsed before the German Minister, looking directly at Bassompierre for the first time, stood up and offered him a cigarette. Officially, he told the Secretary, he could say nothing, but personally he was confident Belgium had nothing to fear from Germany.[7]

Increasingly concerned, Davignon invited Below to the Foreign Ministry the next morning. Again the German Minister regretted he could still say nothing officially, but Davignon, he was sure, knew very well his own feelings on the issue of Belgium's security concerns.[8] This was not especially comforting. Distinguishing their own feelings as honorable gentlemen from what they were obliged to communicate officially became something of a habit among German diplomats during the days just before the outbreak of the Great War.

The following morning, Below offered the Brussels *Soir* a less guarded response. While he could not declare officially that Germany would respect Belgium's borders, his government, he said, firmly believed that its neighbor's neutrality must not be violated. "Grave events are about to take place. Your neighbor's roof may go up in flames, but your house will be spared."9

The Sunday edition of the *Soir* hit the streets around 3:00 p.m. Half an hour earlier, Below received the message he must have anticipated with mounting curiosity and dread. He was to open the sealed envelope. Below was still shaken when he presented the ultimatum to Davignon at 7:00 p.m. that evening, as the telegram had requested. (When Below had asked for the appointment half an hour earlier, Davignon and his aides were delighted. The Germans, they were confident, were now at last ready to confirm officially that they would observe Belgian neutrality.)

Ushered into Davignon's office, Below staggered in, ashen-faced. He may have experienced momentary heart palpitations, because he clutched his chest with one hand and slumped against a table. Davignon was alarmed. "What's the matter?" he asked. "Are you ill?" 10

The German ambassador struggled to regain his composure. "I came up the stairs too quickly," he replied after a moment. "It's nothing."

Before Davignon could invite him to be seated, Below told him, "I have a most confidential communication to make to you on behalf of my government." He pulled an envelope out of his pocket and handed it to the Foreign Minister.

Unnerved by Below's demeanor, Davignon tore open the envelope. The document inside was handwritten. It would have been considered uncivilized to have presented a typed communication. The agitated Foreign Minister read it through several times.

Davignon's German was very poor. Perhaps his eye traveled naturally to point one, with its ominous opening, "Germany intends no hostile act against Belgium." Or he may have deciphered the single sentence comprising point two: "Germany undertakes under the previous condition to leave the Kingdom as soon as peace is concluded."

Once he had registered its import, Davignon turned pale. "No, surely?" he gasped. "No, it's not possible!' His hand trembled and he dropped the paper. It fluttered to the floor between the two men.11

The sheet of paper lying on the parquet floor in the magnificent office on rue de la Loi represented one of the most fatal blunders in human history. Purporting to have "reliable information" about French preparations to invade Belgium en route to Germany, it announced that German troops were about to advance into Belgium. It urged the Belgians to adopt a "benevolent neutrality," permitting the German Army to pass through the Kingdom unhindered. In return, Germany promised to guarantee the country's "integrity and independence," to purchase all supplies in cash, and to make good any damages caused by troops. Then came the stick. If Belgium resisted, the Kingdom would be regarded as an enemy and "relations between the two states would be decided by the sword."

The carrot had originally been juicier. In the version actually sent to Below, the *Kaiserreich* had offered "compensation at the expense of France." However Chancellor Bethmann-Holweg had just promised Britain that Germany, in exchange for British neutrality, would leave France in tact (though not France's overseas possessions). That offer had been rejected, but the Chancellor still hoped to induce Britain to stand aside.[12]

Below was asked to introduce still another change in the document he was sent. The Belgian government had originally been given twenty-four hours to respond. But either the exigencies of the Army's timetable necessitated a more rapid response, or Foreign Ministry tacticians decided that it would be useful to keep members of the Belgian government up all night. Darkness, fatigue, and the ticking clock might make the ministers more malleable. And so a response was demanded of the Belgians by 7:00 a.m., twelve hours after the demands had been presented.[13] The ultimatum, moreover, was written in German. French was the language of diplomacy, as well as the native tongue of most of the ministers. As the Wilhelmstrasse had no doubt hoped, one of the allotted hours was spent translating the note.

⊰⟶⊱

Without the invasion of Belgium, Britain would not have entered the war when it did. If Germany had refrained from invading France as well, it's highly unlikely Britain would have entered the war at all. In the event, the three German armies that remained on the defensive in the west, some 545,000 men, stopped cold the French offenses into Alsace and Lorraine between August 10 and 28, then drove the French Army out of the provinces. Meanwhile, the German Eighth Army in the East, about 225,000 troops, annihilated the invading Russians under Samsonov between August

26 and 30, then turned on the Russian First Army under Rennecamp, routing it by September 9th. These were crushing defeats for the Allies. Had
the 750,000 men who invaded Belgium been ordered instead to amuse
themselves in cafés, bars, and restaurants along the Rhine during August,
it is conceivable that Germany would have won a war against France and
Russia, possibly by Christmas, 1914. It's not likely we'd have heard of Hitler, Lenin, and Stalin. Tens of millions of Europeans, starved, shot, gassed,
blown apart, and incinerated, would have survived into the second half of
the 20th century.[14]

-<->->-

Perhaps it was during the moment that Davignon stooped down to retrieve
the paper that Below recovered his poise, recalling who he was and who
he represented. In any event, the German Minister detailed the arguments
of the memorandum and elaborated on its sugary reassurances. Germany
had the highest regard for Belgium, but had to act in its own defense in
light of the impending French offensive through the Meuse valley. (Either
because he thought it ill-advised, given Davignon's reaction to the ultimatum, or because he simply forgot, Below neglected to propose, as he'd
been instructed to, that the Belgian government retire with its army to Antwerp. The Germans would take care of any internal disturbances.)[15] By the
time Below had finished, Davignon's shock and chagrin had quickened into
anger. "In an agitated and vehement tone, he poured out his indignation,"
according to one account. The idea of a French assault on Namur was a
shameful lie. It was the Germans who were launching a sneak attack on
their enemy, and in doing so were violating international law and their own
repeated promises.[16]

　　The international law the Germans were abrogating was Article 7 of
the Treaty of London, signed on April 19, 1839 by Britain, France, Prussia,
Austria, and Russia. This imposed permanent or "perpetual" neutrality on
Belgium (as opposed to "occasional" neutrality, a temporary, pragmatic
expedient). The Great Powers had not bothered to obtain the consent of
the Belgians themselves, but there was nothing inappropriate in this, in
their view. Permanent neutrality was intended not so much to safeguard the
existence of the neutral itself as to preserve peace in Europe by removing a
centuries-old casus belli. Since the time of Caesar, as schoolchildren once

were taught, Belgium had been "the cockpit of Europe." Either to seize the wealth of the inhabitants of the Schelde or Meuse valleys or en route to conquests east or south, European armies had trooped across Belgium's plains for two millennia. A cardinal principle of British foreign policy in particular had long been that no Great Power should occupy the European coast from Oostende to the North Sea islands.[17]

Davignon's protests may have been offered sotto voce. Other Foreign Office officials, on tenterhooks, listening intently, did not know what had transpired. As soon as they saw Below cross the courtyard and enter his car, once again haughty and impassive, they rushed to Davignon's office for news.[18] Whatever remonstrations he offered the German emissary, Davignon promised that the Cabinet would immediately consider the document.

◂┄▸

The ultimatum accomplished what eighty years of royal cajolery had failed to achieve. It united all Belgians. Next morning, everyone in the Kingdom would share Davignon's outrage. But the unanimity was preceded by two acrimonious meetings of Belgium's highest ranking officials.

The document was carefully translated and read to the Prime Minister, Baron Charles de Broqueville, who had been summoned to the Foreign Ministry.[19] He listened intently, arms crossed, one hand supporting his chin. "Are we ready?" someone asked. De Broqueville also served as Minister of War.

Speaking slowly and calmly, he assured the Foreign Ministry officials that mobilization had gone well and was nearly complete. "But," he added, "there is a 'but': we don't have any heavy artillery."[20]

King Albert was then notified, and the Belgian Cabinet summoned for a 9:00 p.m. meeting. An emergency session of the Crown Council was to follow at 10:00. In addition to the ministers with portfolios, the Crown Council was comprised of individuals who had been named by the King "ministers of state," and included senior diplomats and leading members of Parliament. Two generals attended both meetings as well.

At 8:30 de Bassompierre grabbed a hasty meal by himself at a restaurant in la Place Royale. Later, he vividly recalled studying the diners at neighboring tables in the brightly lit room.

They knew nothing. They had read the afternoon papers, the *20ième Siècle, Le Soir,* containing the reassuring declarations made that morning by M. de Below-Saleski... They were happy, carefree... And I, I was crushed by the weight of what I knew, by the secret that would be revealed the next day and would prove such a cruel awakening to those surrounding me. I wondered if I were in the grip of a nightmare, or if I were truly awake.[21]

⊰⊹⊱

Exactly what transpired at the two meetings was the subject of dispute for decades. There were no official minutes and it was thought, until 1958, that no one had taken notes. In fact Georges Helleputte, Minister of Agriculture and Public Works, had jotted down extensive, if rather cryptic and not very legible, notes in pencil while the meetings were in progress.[22] Indeed, there was confusion even as to what was discussed at each meeting. The first, the Cabinet meeting, which began about 9:15 and lasted only 30 or 40 minutes, focused on the military situation and included a sharp disagreement between Belgium's two leading generals as to what strategy to pursue. It was only at the second meeting, of the Crown Council, that the ministers discussed how the government should respond to the ultimatum.[23]

At the Cabinet meeting, with the King presiding, Davignon described Below's visit and then read the translation of the ultimatum. A brief discussion followed. There were, no doubt, expressions of incredulity and outrage, but the conversation was quickly diverted by de Broqueville to a consideration of the country's military situation. Perhaps he thought that the larger, more representative body should determine the government's response. In any event, the Crown Council was bound to discuss the ultimatum, and there would be no point in soliciting opinions that would have to be repeated within an hour.

The King, whose efforts both to modernize the army and to prepare it for a German invasion had been frustrated for years, bitterly reproached the ministers for the woeful state of the country's military forces. For over four decades, his blistering remarks were suppressed in all published accounts of the meeting.

Announcing that the ultimatum was unacceptable, the King turned to the Army's Chief of Staff, General Antoine Selliers de Moranville. According to Selliers, there was no discussion of strategy. He was simply asked a number of questions about the capabilities of the army. His answers were not reassuring. The army had no chance of stopping the enemy. Its reorganization (begun only the year before) was incomplete; there were insufficient numbers of officers, especially reserve officers. The field artillery was inadequate and there was no heavy artillery. The mobilization, however, was proceeding well and Liège and Namur might hold out for a month. With the full deployment of the field army, Antwerp could withstand a siege, despite the fact that some of its fortresses were unfinished.[24]

At this point, according to Selliers, the King called on the army's second in command, General Louis de Ryckel, who, in what the Chief of Staff characterized as a brief outburst, urged that the army should move east immediately after concentrating, cross the Rhine and attack Köln. "We've mobilized before anyone else," De Ryckel claimed. "If we cross into Germany, we can scatter the first enemy concentrations and disrupt mobilization throughout the Rhineland."[25] Selliers was horrified. He immediately pointed out that this strategy posed grave risks: the field army could be cut off from the Antwerp forts and face annihilation. The King listened in silence.

De Ryckel naturally tells a different story. The discussion, according to him, focused on where the army would be situated. Rather than await the enemy behind the Velpe, the army should march to the Meuse, Belgium's natural line of defense in the east, he argued. But only if the Germans disengaged from that front would the army proceed to Aachen, not Köln. His long speech, drawing on a memorandum he had drafted in January, was, according to de Ryckel, "listened to with rapt attention by the Ministers. 'I think, gentlemen,'" said the King, "'that there can be no hesitation. We can do nothing but follow this plan which as been so wisely devised.'"[26]

While its stirring denouement makes the account suspect, and four of the ministers queried seven years later supported Selliers' version (one, de Broqueville, claiming that Ryckel's narrative was "completely at odds with reality"), Helleputte's notes lend some credence to the Second-in-Command's recollections. Strategy was, indeed, discussed, and the King wound up over-ruling Selliers. The Chief of Staff had planned that Namur and Liège be defended only by the fortress garrisons and that the field army should give battle in the center of the country before retiring on Antwerp. Instead, the 3rd Division was deployed along the Meuse to support Liège, while the 4th was retained at Namur. The King, De Ryckel, and Albert's able and outspoken former fellow-student and Military Advisor, Captain Emile Galet, had had no doubts that the threat would come from the east. They had tried repeatedly and unsuccessfully to push through a war plan that would concentrate the entire army behind the Meuse, if a German invasion were imminent – a deployment, Galet was convinced, that would have thwarted von Emmich's forces.[27] For Belgian civilians in the eastern provinces, the Cabinet's decision was disastrous. The Germans were not stopped in front of the Liège forts, but they were engaged by Belgian forces – the worst of both worlds. In at least some locations, the casualties these encounters inflicted on the Germans led directly to savage reprisals against villagers and peasants.

-<--->-

One of the many myths about the war holds that the Crown Council, when it convened at 10:00 p.m., spoke with one voice. As Galet writes, "On hearing the Imperial demands, the meeting was swept by such a wave of patriotic indignation that in spite of the gloomy outlook for the future there was an immediate and impassioned expression of unanimity."[28] This was not the case. Charles Woeste, leader of the Catholic Party that had governed Belgium for a generation, did not wish to resist the German invasion. He was supported by an influential senior diplomat, his brother-in-law Baron Jules Greindl, for twenty-five years Belgium's Minister in Berlin.

In the version of the events that acknowledges Woeste's reservations, the Catholic leader's assent is made all the more dramatic by his doubts. Minister of Justice Henri Carton de Wiart describes him as speaking "with great calm." "'We will lose. It will be terrible. There can be no doubt our army will sacrifice itself, our country will experience frightful ruin.' But he concluded: 'It doesn't matter. Despite what will happen, there can be no hesitation over the response.'"[29] (In another account, Woeste, "dry, sharp, precise and clear, as usual," after going over the consequences of the decision, hesitated for a long moment, and then said, "'We have to say *no*.'")[30] In fact Woeste and Greindl thought that the government should merely inform the Wilhelmstrasse that its information was incorrect. French troops had not entered Belgium. Woeste was very concerned that the government "not raise the German's hackles."[31] After asking several questions about the state of the army, he concluded, "The situation is very grave. We face a formidable power. Belgium is a small country. We can protest and invoke the treaties Germany herself has signed. We can fire on them. But after this demonstration...we must retire to Antwerp and do nothing."

Greindl repeatedly expressed his disbelief that Germany was preparing to invade Belgium. He had been assured many times of Germany's excellent intentions and "the Kaiser is a very honest man." The former ambassador worried about the possibility of Belgium's annexation by France if the Brussels government were to make common cause with its southern neighbor.[32]

At this point several ministers heatedly disagreed with the two Catholic leaders. Paul Hymans, the sole Liberal on the Crown Council, told Woeste that what he advocated was treachery toward Europe. Belgium was obliged to do its duty. Louis de Sadeleer, former President of the Chamber of Deputies and the future defense attorney for Edith Cavell, was angrier still. The German demand was "an abomination, a felony." Belgium should defend every square metre of its territory from the criminals. The enraged de Sadeleer began pounding the table with his fist. "It's a shameful act," he yelled. "I'm going to tell the Kaiser. I know him and I'm going to tell him what I think of him!"[33]

Such displays were not going to move Woeste. Frans Schollaert, former Prime Minister, reverted to the moral high ground, repeating that Belgium had no choice but to defend its honor. Antwerp was intended only to be "the refuge after a storm." His successor De Broqueville added a dash of realpolitik: "Let's not kid ourselves. If Germany wins, Belgium, whatever its attitude, is going to be annexed by the Empire. It's necessary then, if we want to survive, to fight with all our strength." But he, too, invoked moral imperatives: "And if despite our loyalty, our bravery, our heroism, Belgium is vanquished, the whole world will regard its death as an eternal symbol of Duty and Honor."[34]

Others appealed to Woeste on legal grounds. A neutral nation defending itself, argued one minister, was not in a state of war. Jules van den Heuvel, an eminent jurist, a professor at Leuven University and former Minister of Justice, who rushed back from Gent to attend the meeting, pointed out that to retire to Antwerp would be to violate the 1839 Treaty. Belgium was not only defending its own rights, but those of its guarantors.

He had not suggested that the army retreat immediately to Antwerp,

Woeste pointed out. But faced with dire prospects – France would be beaten, England would not be able to offer much help – the government, he argued, should merely deny the allegations contained in the ultimatum. Here Helleputte's notes end. At some point Woeste must have abandoned his objections to armed resistance, or else yielded to the majority under protest.

Another critical issue arose at this juncture: what should be requested of the other guarantors of Belgian neutrality. Some ministers, including several who urged that the ultimatum be rejected, still hoped that Germany might not invade. Perhaps the request was a Machiavellian bluff. Strategists at the Military College believed that Germany's best bet in a war with France was to penetrate its enemy's right wing, as it had done so successfully in 1870, pinning the French to the coast and the Belgian border. A sweep around the north of the line of forts would allow the French ample room to regroup and resupply. Thus the ultimatum might be a feign to draw the French northward, and perhaps induce them to violate Belgian neutrality and antagonize the British.[35]

Some ministers, in addition, shared Woeste's fear that allies might turn into occupiers. Belgian independence would have to be guaranteed by France and England, some Council members demanded, and its army remain autonomous. The King insisted on the second point. At this juncture, Hymans objected heatedly, "When one is drowning, one does not ask the rescuer for his credentials."[36]

Van den Heuvel proposed a compromise. Until German troops actually crossed the Belgian border, the government would request only diplomatic assistance from Britain and France. (The scrupulous observance of Belgium's neutrality was indeed carried out. Until the moment the Germans crossed the frontier at Gemmenich at 8:00 a.m. on August 4, troops of the 4th Division were ordered to fire on any armed French soldiers entering the Kingdom.)[37]

Around midnight, a committee was selected to draft a response. The three men chosen, Carton de Wiart, Van den Heuvel, and Hymans, labored away at a large table in the corner of the Council chamber. They were repeatedly interrupted, however, by others seeking to add their two centimes. The trio retreated to the Ministry of Foreign Affairs, where they found that the Political Director, Baron Gaiffier de Hestroy, had already prepared a draft. After some emendations by the Ministers, an eloquent response emerged, all the more forceful for its restraint. "No strategic interest justifies such a violation of law," it proclaimed, and concluded that "Were it to accept the proposals laid before it, the Belgian Government would sacrifice the nation's honor while betraying its duties toward Europe."[38]

While the committee polished the reply, Belgium's military situation was again discussed. When it was proposed to blow up the Meuse bridges, the impulsive De Ryckel leapt to his feet. "Oh no," he protested. "We need to drive the Germans back to where they came from."[39]

The King was more realistic. After dismissing the rumor that the French would at once dispatch five army corps to Belgium, Albert told the ministers that the war would be "long, harsh, and relentless. We cannot be lulled into foolish illusions. I know Germany. Its army is formidable. We'll need to fight with all our strength if we don't want to be conquered."[40]

Blind as they were about Germany's intentions, Woeste and Greindl nonetheless saw the disaster that Belgium confronted with greater clarity than did some of their idealistic colleagues. When the meeting broke up at 2:30 a.m., Greindl emerged pale and disheveled. He walked down the stairs with great difficulty, leaning heavily against his brother-in-law for support.[41]

⧫⟵⟶⧫

Before he adjourned the meeting, the King, seeing the sky growing light behind the steeple of St. Jacques, observed, "Gentlemen, this is the dawn of a dark day." After a pause, he added, "However it promises to become brilliant." Then he said, as if speaking to himself, "If we had been weak enough to yield, tomorrow the people would have hanged us in the streets of Brussels."[42]

While this account may have been embellished, the King's words no doubt reflected a reality that must have weighed on all the ministers. Public opinion would countenance only one response to the ultimatum.

⧫⟵⟶⧫

Back at the German Legation, Karl-Konrad von Below, if he'd been able to fall asleep after delivering the ultimatum, was roused some time after midnight by an urgent telegram from the Wilhelmstrasse. He was ordered to the Foreign Ministry, where he showed up at 1:30 a.m., just after the reply to the German demands had been completed. Von Below had been instructed to announce various breaches of international law by the French, including an air attack, a border crossing by cavalry, and "eighty French officers in Prussian uniforms heading for Germany in twelve motor cars." These were all fabrications. Baron van der Elst, who received von Below, icily inquired where these alleged incidents had taken place. The German Minister was caught off-guard. "In Germany," he replied.

"In that case," said Van der Elst, "I do not understand the object of your call."[43]

Von Below attempted to explain that these activities might be a prelude to other border violations and in any case revealed the duplicity of the French.

The indignant Van der Elst cut him off and began berating Germany. His angry words could be heard in Davignon's office at the end of the corridor.

Outside the Ministry of War down the street, groups of civilians and soldiers gathered, anxious that the lights were still blazing in the building's windows. Rumors spread rapidly, and the crowd began scanning the sky for German dirigibles.[44]

Von Below motored back to the embassy. He had already told his superiors, after delivering the ultimatum, that "the Foreign Minister could not conceal his painful surprise at the unexpected communication."[45] Now, in a message dispatched at 3:50 a.m., he laconically observed that, though he had duly reported the incidents, "I do not believe this will influence the Belgian reply, which, according to my impression, is likely to be in the negative."[46]

Von Below received his answer promptly at 7:00 a.m. It was copied, and the original taken by the military attaché to Aachen, where General von Emmich impatiently waited with his invading force.

Several hours elapsed before von Below was able to telegraph the full text of the reply to the Wilhelmstrasse. Ever the master of understatement, he added the terse comment: "Feeling against Germany strong."[47]

⊰⊱

At about 2:00 p.m. on Tuesday, August 4th, Brand Whitlock received the

Secretary of the German Legation, Herr von Strum. Whitlock had just returned from a very emotional session of Parliament, addressed by the King.[48] The Secretary had come to ask that the Americans represent German interests until diplomatic relations were restored.

> Herr von Strum was nervous, agitated, and unstrung; I suppose that he, too, had been without sleep for nights on end. Tears were continually welling into his eyes, and suddenly he covered his face with his hands, leaned forward, his elbows on his knees, an attitude of despair. Presently he looked up.
>
> "Oh, these poor, stupid Belgians!" he said. "Why don't they get out of the way! I know what it will be. I know the German Army. It will be like laying a baby on the track before a locomotive!"
>
> He bent over, stretching his hands towards the floor as though to illustrate the cruel deed.
>
> "I know the German Army," he repeated. "It will go across Belgium like a steam-roller; like a steam-roller!"
>
> He liked the phrase, which he must have picked up in America – he had an American wife – and kept on repeating it.[49]

Later that afternoon, when a legal document had been drawn up, Whitlock walked across the street to the German Legation. Von Below was stretched out on a low chair, smoking a cigarette, a cup of tea at his side. "When I had seen him last, the night of his formal dinner, he had been so happily looking forward to a peaceful, idle summer. At the sight of me he flung up his hands, shrugged his shoulders and made a little moue, as though he too remembered, as though words were unnecessary – or inadequate."[50] After signing the *procès-verbal*, the two diplomats watched in silence as an elderly clerk sealed the oak file cabinets with red wax.

-‹-·-›-

Herr von Below's counterpart in Berlin was Baron Napoléon Eugène Louis Beyens. He had a somewhat less sanguine view of Germany than did most of his colleagues in the rue de la Loi.

In Berlin, he recalled, during the years before the war,

> the air that one breathed was strangely oppressive; the ground quaked beneath one's feet, as in the neighborhood of a volcanic eruption. One never ceased gazing anxiously at the horizon, now towards the Vosges, now towards the Balkans, wherever the storm-clouds, charged with electricity, were gathering at the moment. A gust of fresh wind would scatter these clouds, but they would gather again after the briefest interval.[51]

Beyens was well aware of explicit threats that had been made to King Leopold II and to King Albert about Germany's intention to invade France, and the implicit threat made to both monarchs and to the Belgian military attaché, as well as the secret warning provided by the Kaiser's kinsman, King Carol of Rumania, as to the German Army's route into France – it would pass through Belgium.[52]

He himself had been warned several times. On one occasion, a friend, a colonel in the Potsdam Guards, though half-Belgian, remonstrated with Beyens after Brussels introduced universal military service in 1913. "'What is the good of enlarging the number of your troops? With the small number that you had before, you surely would never have dreamt of barring the way to us in a Franco-German war. The increase...might inspire you to resist us. If a single shot were fired on us, Heaven knows what would become of Belgium.'"

Beyens assured the colonel that, whatever the size of her army, Belgium was prepared to resist any invader.

"I had occasion to repeat this phrase several times to other Germans. They listened with smiles, but they did not believe me."[53]

Yet despite the many warnings, Beyens found himself "dumbfounded" when he learned by telegram on August 3rd of the German ultimatum.

Prewar diplomats kept bankers' hours, even in crises. The Foreign Ministry in Wilhelmstrasse was deserted when Beyens arrived at 9 a.m. the next day, but Gottlieb von Jagow, the Foreign Secretary, was busy at work and seemed eager to see him.

Before Beyens could launch into his protests, von Jagow interrupted.

"Believe me that it is with acute grief that Germany decides to violate the neutrality of Belgium, and personally I feel the most profound regret on that account. But there is no help for it. It is a question of the life or death of the Empire. If the German armies do not wish to be caught between the hammer and the anvil they must strike a severe blow in the direction of France, in order that they may afterwards turn their arms against Russia."

Beyens pointed out that it was not necessary to cross Belgium to attack France. The French frontier, von Jagow replied, was too strongly fortified. "And what are we asking of you?" he added reproachfully. Only to use your roads, bridges, tunnels, and railroads, and to occupy your fortresses.

There is only one response, Beyens told the Secretary of State. "Imagine that France had addressed to us the same invitation and that we had accepted it. Would not Germany have said that we had betrayed her in a cowardly manner."

Von Jagow did not reply.

The Belgian Minister persisted. "Have you anything with which to reproach us? Have we not always, for three-quarters of a century, fulfilled...all the duties of our neutrality? Have we not given Germany tokens of loyal friendship? How does Germany propose to pay us for that? By making Belgium a European battle-field. And we know what devastations and calamities modern war brings in its train...."

"Germany has nothing with which to reproach Belgium, and the attitude of Belgium has always been perfectly correct."

"You must recognize then," replied Baron Beyens, "that Belgium cannot give you any other reply than that which she has now given you without losing her honor. It is with nations as with individuals: there are not different codes of honor for peoples and for private persons..."

"As a private person I do recognize it, but as Secretary of State I have no opinion to express." There was no trace of irony in von Jagow's expression.

The conversation was at an end. But when Beyens mentioned that he would shortly be asking for his passports, von Jagow seemed genuinely upset. "Don't go yet. Perhaps we shall still have reason to talk." At the Wilhelmstrasse and at Potsdam hope remained that after a taste of war, the Belgians would be able to convince themselves that they had honored their pledges and the government would capitulate. Were there no pragmatists in Brussels?

As he was leaving, Beyens observed, with some malice, that the violation of Belgian neutrality would certainly mean a war with England.

Von Jagow just shrugged his shoulders.[54]

CHAPTER 2

Liège

GEMMENICH: CROSSING THE RUBICON The first Belgians to encounter the invaders were two border guards at Gemmenich, on the route to Visé, officers Thill and Conard. They were approached by about twenty-five uhlans at 8:05 on the morning of August 4th. The gendarmes ordered the patrol to halt. "Belgian frontier!" they announced.[1]

"I'm perfectly aware of that," said the officer commanding the squadron, "but the French have crossed the border and we're going to continue on our way." The lieutenant had with him a proclamation that officers had been instructed to read in the villages along the frontier. "To the Belgian People," it was entitled.

> It is with the greatest regret that the German troops find themselves forced to cross the frontier of Belgium. They are impelled by inevitable necessity, the neutrality of Belgium having already been violated by French officers who in disguise crossed Belgium in a motor to enter Germany.
>
> Belgians! It is our greatest wish that there may yet be found a way of avoiding a combat between two nations who have hitherto been friendly and at one time even allies. Remember the glorious day of Waterloo, when the German armies helped to found and establish the independence and prosperity of your country.
>
> But we must have a free road. The destruction of bridges, tunnels, and railways will be regarded as hostile acts. Belgians! It is for you to choose.
>
> I therefore trust that the Army of the Meuse will not be compelled to fight you. All we wish is to have a free road to attack the enemy who wanted to attack us.
>
> I give a formal guarantee to the Belgian people that they will not suffer from the horrors of war; that we will pay in money for the provisions that must be taken in the country; that our soldiers will show themselves good friends of a people for whom we feel the utmost esteem and greatest sympathy.
>
> It depends on your discretion and wisely conceived patriotism to save your country from the horrors of war.
>
> Von Emmich
> General Commander in Chief,
> Army of the Meuse[2]

The proclamation had been printed at a time when Germany still hoped Belgium would yield to its ultimatum, and was concerned that the country's communications network remain intact. But it's unlikely anyone hearing the announcement believed that French officers, in disguise or otherwise, were motoring through Belgium (what would they have done when they crossed into Germany?) or was persuaded that even if this were the case, it was legitimate grounds an invasion, or that von Emmich's troops should be welcomed out of gratitude to Blücher's a hundred years earlier.

Watching the encounter from a concealed position was a third gendarme, Sergeant Béchet, the head of the station, who immediately phoned his superiors in Liège. "A platoon of cavalry crossed the frontier and is descending into Gemmenich," he told the officer monitoring communications in Liège.

In the Belgian "Grey Book" *(Diplomatic Correspondence Respecting the War)*, the thirtieth document is the most laconic. Sergeant Béchet's message was communicated to Army Headquarters at Leuven and from there relayed to the Foreign Ministry in Brussels. Foreign Minister Julien Davignon immediately cabled the Belgian embassies in London and Paris: "The General Staff announces that Belgian territory has been violated at Gemmenich." The two Belgian ambassadors at once phoned the British and French Foreign Ministries with the news.[3]

⊰⊹⊱

Some of the Gemmenich gendarmes decided, rather quixotically, to pursue the uhlans, and at once set off on motorbikes. The two cavalry platoons that had been sent out by General Leman to monitor the invasion had been given strict instructions not to engage the Germans. The border guards reached Visé around noon, and were fired on by German sentries who had just arrived. Sergeant Boucko was hit in the head and killed instantly, the second combat fatality on the Western Front.[4] The gendarmes returned the fire and the sentries retired. However, a party of German cyclists arrived moments later, alerted by the shots. Sergeant Thill was killed, one guard was captured and two, though wounded, escaped. There were apparently no German casualties. About twenty minutes later, Belgian troops entrenched on the far side of the Meuse opened fire on soldiers approaching the river, and the Imperial Army suffered its first losses.

LIÈGE PROVINCE: OVERVIEW The province of Liège, where the first mass executions took place, has been relatively neglected in the literature on German war crimes. The victims, by and large, were not middle-class townspeople, let alone professors and scholars with international reputations. (The crime of sacking Leuven was compounded by the folly of imagining that the world would not immediately receive graphic and credible accounts of the event.)[5] There was no outpouring of articles, pamphlets, and books describing the nightmare. The one exception was the searing *Vers Liège*, published in 1915 by a courageous journalist, Gustave Somville. He clandestinely toured the devastated region in the fall and winter after the massacres, collecting evidence from survivors and recording his impressions of the devastated towns.[6] The wartime Belgian Commission of Inquiry was unable to gather much evidence about the province; the investigation of events in Liège does not appear to have been a priority. Though the burning of Visé was mentioned in the Commission's third report, it was not until May 20th 1915, in their seventeenth report, that the members got around to describing the various massacres in the province. (The Commission claimed to have collected more than 600 depositions from Liège, mostly given under oath, but nowhere near this number remain in its archives. Testimony about the great massacres in front of Fort Fléron is particularly sparse.) The evidence published by the second, post-war Commission was also meager, given the scope of the killings. There are, for instance, only two depositions from Melen, where 108 residents were killed, including thirteen children under the age of 16, and only one of these describes any of the mass executions. When it comes to Liège, the double theft of the Commission's depositions is particularly devastating. Fifteen were in fact collected from residents of Melen, and another fourteen from civilians in Soumagne.[7]

In 1919, Mgr. Martin-Hubert Rutten, the Bishop of Liège, like his colleagues, asked each curé within the archdiocese to submit a report on events in his parish during the war. Two of the ten questions the Bishop asked concerned the treatment of civilians, but the responses were often cursory. Partial exceptions in the extensive deanery of Soumagne include the abbé Joseph Hardy from the parish of Melen, the curé of Chênée, and abbé Oscar Madenfacher, curé of Retinnes.

The fullest published account of the killings remains volume two of *Liège pendant la Grande Guerre,* by two enterprising Liège journalists, Jules de Thiers and Olympe Gilbart. But while more thorough and systematic, though no less impassioned, than Somville's survey, and reproducing excerpts from some interesting written accounts – the journal of the curé of Blégny, abbé Remy-Joseph Labeye, the accompanying narrative of the Mother Superior of the convent of Blégny (also reprinted in Somville), the memoir of the feisty burgomaster of Warsage, Ferdinand Fléchet (which appeared as well in the Belgian government's 16th Report and its *Reply to the German White Book*), and a heartbreaking report by a young school-mistress from St. Hadelin, Berthe Warnier – the descriptions are seldom as vivid and detailed as Somville's, or those provided by chroniclers of the great urban massacres.

-<-·->-

The worst of the killings in the province of Liège took place in a semicir-cular swathe just beyond the eastern forts, between Sprimont in the south and Blégny in the north. The savagery was most intense along a 4-mile arc facing Fort Fléron, running from between 6 to 8 miles east of the city of Liège. In the villages around Olne, Soumagne, and Melen, approximately 290 civilians were killed, along with an additional 22 who were marched from Herve to a meadow outside Melen. A total of seventy-five civilians from Battice and Herve were murdered as well; the towns lie just east of the semicircle.

In some locations the violence began on the night of the 4th, but most of the killings took place on the 5th and 6th. The massacres were clearly a response to a decisive and unexpected German defeat. The commanders of the Army of the Meuse had anticipated that a frontal assault on the forts by massed infantry would rout the defenders. They underestimated the num-ber of defenders as well as their resolve, imagining only about 6,000 garri-son troops would be facing them.[8] The Belgian 3rd Division and the troops manning the forts stood their ground, and their rifle fire and machine guns, and the forts' 15 cm canons and 21 cm mortars, decimated the invaders. (The total number of Germans killed in the taking of the forts has been variously estimated at between 30,000 and 45,000. There are no German casualty figures on the operation.) As the survivors retreated back to the villages they'd passed through en route to the forts, they looted, burned, and murdered indiscriminately.

In some cases there was not even the pretext of franc-tireur gunfire. In St. Hadelin, outside Olne, the Warnier family was massacred because a shell from Fort Fléron hit a German field hospital outside the family's residence. Victor Warnier pointed out in vain that as he had been in the Germans' presence for the past 48 hours, he could hardly have revealed the location of the installation to the fort, two miles away, even if he'd wanted to. In Labouxhe, a village of thirty dwellings outside Melen, homes were attacked and inhabitants slaughtered at 3:30 a.m. on the morning of the 6th. As at St. Hadelin, the executioners did not bother to claim they'd heard "franc-tireur" gunfire prior to their exploits. German investigators returning to the scene months later tried to get some of the widows to testify that there had been a dispute during one of the card games villagers had been invited to play with the soldiers the evening of the 4th, as if this might justify the killings.

In other instances, however, encounters with Belgian companies defending the gaps between the forts, or with reconnaissance patrols, provoked the massacres. This was the situation near Soumagne, where a Belgian machine gun, hidden behind a hedge in the hamlet of Les Viviers, panicked the Germans and was the pretext for the execution of forty-eight men in a meadow called Fond-Leroy.

A second wave of killings in Liège followed later in the month. Belgian commentators made much of the fact that it appeared to commence following the rejection of a second German demarche on August 12th, urging the Belgians to cease hostilities, and that there was a hiatus in the violence as the Germans awaited the Belgian response.[9] Belgian writers emphasized the warning about "the horrors of war" in the proposal (which repeated a threat already issued twice in Von Emmich's original proclamation), as well as a prediction in the Kaiser's cable to President Wilson of August 14th that the war would soon assume "a cruel character." There was indeed a lull in the killings. It ran, with a few exceptions, from the 9th (when the German communication was sent) through the 14th. While any connection with the overture to the Belgian government must remain speculative, circumstantial evidence supports the assumption that a halt was ordered. The point of the Belgian critics was naturally that the brutalities had been approved by the highest authorities, and did not represent spontaneous outbreaks of violence. They could be terminated and resumed at will. There is indeed

substantial evidence of premeditation in the massacres after the 14th, notably in the city of Liège, as well as Visé, Barchon, and Blégny.

≺-≺--≻-≻

For reasons having to do sometimes with their uniqueness, sometimes with
their representativeness, but also with the quality and quantity of the surviving testimony, I've included accounts of events in the following towns
and villages, all from the northern part of the devastated region of the
province: Blégny, Warsage, Visé, Wandre, and Liège. The events occurred
in the second phase of violence in the province, after all of the forts east of
the Meuse had surrendered. These are preceded by descriptions of events
in Olne, Soumagne, and Melen, where the first mass executions of civilians
in western Europe in over one hundred years took place.

First, however, the franc-tireur question has to be addressed. It's appropriate to deal with it in the chapter on Liège province because it was here, it
was widely assumed, that hot-headed peasants, villagers, and gamekeepers,
inflamed by patriotic ardor and by drink, and totally oblivious to the scope
of the invasion and awesome firepower of the enemy, could not resist taking pot-shots at uhlan patrols as they passed down country roads.

FRANCS-TIREURS Were there not any franc-tireurs? Abbé Guillaume Voisin
of Battice addressed that question in a letter to the Minister of the Interior.

> I have often heard it said: "there were francs-tireurs, because it is the most natu-
> ral thing in the world for the inhabitants of an invaded country to resist the enemy.
> Francs-tireurs are the best patriots." So people argue at a safe distance and a *priori*. But
> I was living on this side of the Meuse during the early days of the war, and I can say as
> a fact that the inhabitants did not consider it natural to resist that swarm of formidably
> armed soldiers who were spreading over the country. Certainly patriotism was not
> wanting. But it manifested itself only in the wish to see our soldiers greet the invaders
> with the welcome they deserved…. Yet they realized that to commit acts of violence
> would merely mean the sacrifice of one's life for nothing. In truth the dominating
> feeling was terror, especially in the countryside, where one felt oneself isolated and
> at the mercy of the soldiery; one was almost grateful to the enemy for allowing one
> to live.[10]

While there are numerous reports of "franc-tireur" gunfire in the German
White Book (*Die völkerrechtswidrige Führung des belgischen Volkskriegs*),
with only a couple of exceptions, no franc-tireur is identified by name, and

these are incorrect.[11] If the guerilla attacks were organized or coordinated by the government, as many German depositions allege, logic dictates that the captured franc-tireurs be identified and closely questioned, if only to thwart future operations. Transcripts of a legitimate courts martial would also have made excellent propaganda.

There were rare occasions when victims appeared before some kind of military tribunal, but these hearings as a rule consisted simply of charges being read to the victim. Only in a few instances are there reports of civilians being questioned, and, needless to say, the accused never had the opportunity to cross-examine the German soldiers who claimed that they had fired.[12] In the case of mass executions, ad hoc death sentences were often read out to the victims prior to their being shot, but this was the extent of the legal niceties. More significant, no judicial proceedings were taken against any of the thousands of "francs-tireurs" deported to Germany. These included Civic Guard officers and communal officials in towns where the Germans claimed the Belgian government had carefully orchestrated attacks on troops. After the killings were halted, German investigators, over a period of six months, could come up with no Belgian or neutral witnesses who could provide details of a franc-tireur attack, though there was widespread collaboration with the occupiers during this period. And though it insinuated repeatedly that the "People's War" was organized by the Belgian Government, the White Book failed to document this claim. The machine guns and hand grenades so promiscuously distributed to civilians left no paper trail.

The many books written by apologists for the German Army after 1915 relied primarily on testimony from the German White Book for evidence of franc-tireur activity.[13] In lieu of additional reports from eyewitness, writers attempting to prove the existence of francs-tireurs frequently cited Belgian, Dutch, and French newspaper accounts from the opening days of the war. However, when these are examined critically, they turn out to be long on patriotic ardor, but short on hard evidence. The reporters are never at the scene of the alleged incident. Typical is an article of August 5th from the Amsterdam *Telegraaf* quoted by Raf Verhulst, a particularly vitriolic proponent of the franc-tireur thesis: in Visé "women and children fired upon the Germans." The correspondent "was quite near the Liège frontier," Verhulst assures readers, and indeed, the story is filed from Maastricht.[14] This town, however, is more than seven miles away, and no testimony is cited from anyone closer by. Evidence of this quality can be multiplied endlessly, and was. "The fury also seized a certain portion of the country populace where peaceful labor in the fields was disturbed. They were mad to defend the native soil against the treacherous Prussian... From cellar-windows, roof-apertures, made by removing tiles, from private houses, farms and cottages, a furious fire was opened on the onrushing uhlans and Sleswickers."[15] "At Bernot, advance parties came into conflict with the townspeople who fired like madmen on the invaders from the windows and roofs of houses. Even women took part in the firing."[16] Again, no dispatch originates from a reporter on the scene. There is no doubt a correlation between the paucity of evidence for franc-tireurs and the ferocity of the sarcasm of those arguing that there was assuredly a "People's War" in Belgium.[17]

Seemingly oblivious to the implications for their argument, apologists for the German Army sometimes quoted newspaper accounts suggesting the Germans were on the point of surrendering: "The Germans are dying from starvation and are giving themselves up to village policemen, gamekeepers and even to peasants. We are taking an enormous number of prisoners in this fashion."[18] "Show to the soldiers of the Kaiser a loaf of bread and a can of coffee and they will surrender."[19] They cited these and similar quotations to condemn the Belgian government for inciting resistance by permitting them to be published. However, apart from the fact that censorship was imperfectly enforced in the opening days of the war, after decades in which Belgium had enjoyed the freest press in Europe, the tales of German desperation at the very least call into question the veracity of reports by the same journalists about the suicidal tactics of the valiant francs-tireurs. Bart Mokveld, a correspondent for the Amsterdam newspaper *De Tijd*, who was the only European journalist to travel extensively in Belgium during August, concluded that Belgian reporters, "in their nervous, over-excited condition...sat at their desks and listened to the gossip of refugees about civilians taking part in the struggle. In their imagination they saw hordes of barbarians overrun their native soil, saw man and man, woman and woman, shoulder to shoulder, resisting the invader without regard for their own life." Mokveld, who witnessed the destruction of Visé and Leuven, testified that he had:

1. Never seen any sign of a franc-tireur guerilla.
2. Never seen anyone who was arrested as a franc-tireur.
3. Never heard any German soldier, of whatever rank, assert that he himself had witnessed any action by a franc-tireur, although I questioned such soldiers times without number. They always mentioned others, who had left days ago, and were said to have gone through the miserable experience!
4. Never heard the name of any franc-tireur in answer to my question.[20]

In a book written expressly to prove the existence of franc-tireurs, Raf Verhulst could come up with nothing better in the way of direct testimony than a single third-hand account. A journalist told him that a friend of his had had to flee the country because his gamekeepers killed three uhlans on his property near Liège.[21] (The author cited another acquaintance who mentioned encountering a weeping young German cavalryman, who told him *"Kameraden all tot."* In lieu of any evidence that the comrades were not in fact killed by Belgian soldiers, Verhulst speculated that "if by any mischance this young fellow met any franc-tireurs...the probabilities are that he was shot down" – just as he might have been eaten had he encountered a party of cannibals.)[22]

If there is no clear evidence of franc-tireurs operating on Belgian soil, apologists for the German Army were on slightly firmer ground when they criticized the Belgian government about the activities of the Boy Scouts and the *Garde civique.*

It is quite probable that Boy Scouts accompanied a few regiments and may have assisted troops engaged in combat on at least one occasion. There is one credible report to that effect, though there is no evidence that they were not in uniform or that they participated in guerilla activities.[23]

As for the *Garde civique,* there were, in the first place, two organizations, an "active" and a "non-active." The former served in towns of over ten thousand, wore full uniforms (which they were obliged to purchase) and drilled regularly. The non-active *Garde* was expected to perform police functions during emergencies, and only when it was activated by the King. It was to play no military role. In the chaotic days just before the invasion, the government called up about 100,000 non-actives, but failed to mobilize the 46,000 active *Garde* members, though it sent detailed descriptions of their uniforms to the German General Staff on August 8th. The non-active *Garde civique* was inundated with applications the first days of the war, and the new recruits, who normally wore a short blue tunic, were required, as of August 5th, to put on an arm-band and a cockade with the national colors and to bear their arms openly. Three days later, a blue shirt was required as well. Though some guarded bridges, railroad lines, and other sites of strategic importance in the opening days of the war, there is no credible evidence that any non-actives took part in combat.[24]

The role of the active *Garde civique* varied considerably. A few units did participate in the fighting. In Tamines, for example, a detachment from Charleroi gathered behind a cemetery wall beside French troops and fired on patrols approaching the town. Guards in Liège served under General Leman and defended the forts alongside units of the 3rd Division. In Sint-Truiden, the *Garde civique* fired on approaching cavalry. Frightened refugees told an English headmistress of a nearby school that the *Garde civique* killed an uhlan outside Linsmeau.[25] More typical were the activities in Brussels, where members of the *Garde* dug trenches and set up barricades, and then dismantled them. Whatever they were up to, active *Garde* members were required to wear their uniforms; there was no mistaking them for franc-tireurs. Most *Garde* detachments were disarmed and disbanded by August 18th. This was the case in Leuven, where those members who still hoped to take part in the fight against the invaders made their way to Antwerp.[26]

-<-+->-

It would be rash to claim that there was not a single franc-tireur in Belgium. Some of the White Book accounts of gunfire in towns east of the Meuse are plausible. An anonymous German sergeant, in a book published in France in 1918, actually provided the name and details of the trial of a would-be assassin, a policeman in Arlon named Louis Empereur. According to the *feldwebel*, the man, though a father of four, defied his German defense lawyer and proudly owned up to having fired at an officer, regretting only that he hadn't killed him. And a deserter with no axe to grind believed he saw gunfire coming from a home in Bertrix, near Bouillon; five men emerged after grenades were hurled in, and were promptly executed.[27] In the first case, however, the second Belgian Commission of Inquest reported that Emile Lempereur, an assistant police commissioner, was executed, without histrionics, as a reprisal for shots fired by soldiers who were amusing themselves by shooting off guns stored in the town hall. As for the incident in Bertrix, French troops were in the vicinity, and Belgian witnesses deny the men fired on the Germans.[28] The German claims in the White Book would be more convincing if one were not familiar with the extent to which German witnesses misrepresented events in Andenne, Aarschot, Dinant, and Leuven – where, unlike in the case of many of the villages of Liège, very extensive and damning Belgian testimony is available. Particularly in the eastern provinces during the opening two or three days of the war, it is conceivable that individual cavalrymen and small patrols were ambushed by civilians. But Belgian patrols were also operating in Liège for two days, until they fell back to the other side of the Meuse. When the outrage over the invasion was replaced by fear of the invaders, when vast columns of heavily armed troops began moving toward the Meuse, it is unlikely that any sniping continued, especially after reports of the killing, burning, and looting began to be given credence. What is clearly the case is that in those towns where the worst massacres occurred, there is simply no credible evidence of franc-tireur activity. Troops were taking revenge on residents either for the stiff resistance of Belgian or French forces or for the panic and casualties that resulted either from friendly fire or from random shooting by undisciplined troops – or by agents provocateurs.

‹‹-›-›-›

The franc-tireur stories that circulated throughout Germany from the opening day of the war, however, generally did not describe bands of armed irregulars shooting at patrols or harassing the flanks and supply lines of the advancing armies. Rather, they were lurid accounts of gruesome, barbaric acts frequently committed by women and children against wounded soldiers. Mutilations of all kinds were a recurring motif. Fingers and genitals were chopped off, though never hands, and, more frequently, eyes were gouged out. The treacherous Belgians poisoned wells, passed out exploding cigars, and shot or stabbed generals with whom they were about to dine. (This latter exploit was frequently the handiwork of the burgomaster or his son or daughter.) Bernhard Duhr, a German Jesuit working for the Köln organization Pax, collected thirty-three stories that implicated priests or nuns. While these generally concerned espionage activities and incitements, Duhr also tracked down nine variants of the frequently-repeated tale of Belgian civilians gouging out the eyes of wounded soldiers. In each case he contacted the hospital where the victims were supposedly seen, and

in each case the claims proved groundless. "There was certainly a mania
for witnessing atrocities involving the putting out of eyes. Innumerable
tales of this kind were spread around, and finally guaranteed as absolutely
authentic – and yet they were all fairytales."[29] The unmistakable hostility to the Church coloring so many of the stories made Catholic authorities suspicious, and on August 16th, the influential *Kölnishche Volkzeitung*
denounced atrocity propaganda, after having initially published several
dubious stories.[30] On August 24th, *Vorwärts*, the national paper of the
Social Democratic Party, also expressed skepticism. Karl Liebknecht, the
left-wing SPD deputy whose outspoken criticism of the war would eventually land him in jail, visited Belgium in September 1914, and concluded
that the idea that Belgian civilians were waging war was a myth. Atrocities
were being committed, but it was by Germans.[31] Bethmann Hollweg himself toured Leuven in November, and not long after conceded privately
that the German Army had indeed committed atrocities in Belgium.[32]

-<-->-

Only sixteen accounts of sadistic mutilations of German soldiers by Belgian civilians made their way into the White Book. But the descriptions of
franc-tireur attacks that comprise the bulk of the volume are scarcely more
plausible. Unlike their counterparts in other times and places, the Belgians
seldom ambushed troops from concealed positions in woods or ravines
or from behind hedges. The modus operandi of the guerillas, stubbornly
adhered to despite its obvious disadvantages, was to shoot down on large
bodies of German troops from their homes. Even in Dinant, with the Citadel at their disposal, the franc-tireurs apparently preferred to fire on the
invaders from the comfort of their living rooms. But when their homes
were broken into, the reckless desperados never fired on the Germans, let
alone held out to the last man. In town after town, seemingly oblivious to
the lethal consequences of being caught, they meekly walked out of their
homes, hands held high. Perhaps they were buoyed by the knowledge that
they had managed to make their weapons disappear.

Some Germans, including even Major von Manteuffel in Leuven, were
astute enough to recognize the implausibility of this scenario, and instead
claimed that Belgian soldiers disguised as civilians had forced their way
into homes and fired on soldiers. Needless to say, the notion that residents

would quietly submit to this, and then breathe not a word about it subsequently, is hardly more plausible than that they themselves would fire from their residences.

No less suspicious are the insignificant German casualties. Witnesses in the German White Book repeatedly express their amazement that the aim of the franc-tireurs was so poor, even when the Germans were convinced the guerillas were wielding machine guns. In the heart of Leuven, according to the testimony of the *Kommandant*, the franc-tireurs succeeded only in shooting three men in the legs and killing a horse.[33] The authors of the White Book wisely made no attempt to tally the German dead and wounded from the "Belgian People's War."[34]

-<·->-

No informed writer now argues that franc-tireur attacks preceded the massacres of Belgian civilians. The issue that remains for historians is why German soldiers made such claims. Was it simply a case of spontaneous paranoia, or was the paranoia deliberately fostered?

A number of Belgian, French, and British intellectuals and eye-witnesses to the depredations in August were convinced that certain highranking commanders, if not the General Staffs of the First, Second, and Third Armies, intentionally deceived their troops in order to facilitate a speedy passage through Belgium. If German soldiers were taught to regard Belgians of all ages as potential murderers, they would not hesitate to treat the civilian population with a brutality that would discourage actual resistance. As the message that was read in the villages of Liège province on the first day of the campaign made clear, the German Army viewed with great alarm the prospect of its advance being delayed by destruction of bridges, tunnels, railway lines, and other acts of sabotage. The Schlieffen timetable was unforgiving. Paris had to be taken within six weeks if the Army was to stop the Russian "steamroller" before it approached Berlin; Moltke's anxieties on this score are well known. Corps and division commanders had demanding assignments.

Accusations that atrocity stories originated with officers implied, of course, that the massacres of civilians were premeditated. The killings, in this view, were an essential part of the Army's war plan, not "collateral damage." As the Report of the British Committee on Alleged German

Outrages concluded, "The excesses recently committed in Belgium were...
too widespread and too uniform in their character to be mere sporadic outburst of passion or rapacity. The explanation seems to be that these excesses
were committed – in some cases ordered, in others allowed – on a system
and in pursuance of a set purpose. That purpose was to strike terror into
the civil population and dishearten the Belgian troops, so as to crush down
resistance and extinguish the very spirit of self-defence."[35] Gruesome tales
of outrages perpetrated by civilians simply hardened troops to carry out
this terrorist campaign.

The fact that the massacres of civilians appeared to have been suspended
between August 9th and 14th added credence to this claim. As mentioned,
Allied writers argued that the hiatus coincided with a period when the Germans were awaiting the Belgian response to a communiqué urging the government to cooperate with the invaders. When it was rejected, the killings
resumed with new ferocity, suggesting that the terrorism was controlled by
the *Oberste Heeresleitung* (OHL).

Clearly, tales of franc-tireur outrages also helped solidify support
for the war at home. Despite the display of solidarity in the *Reichstag* on
August 4th and the *Burgfrieden*, there was some lingering doubt about the
willingness of socialists to support a war they had for so long vowed to
resist. Stories of barbarities by treacherous Belgians nicely complemented
the strategy of presenting the war as an act of self-defense and deflected
concerns about violating the territory of a peaceful neutral nation. Demon-
izing the Belgians was not only an adroit propaganda ploy; clearly, it also
relieved the guilt of those who had engineered the war and those who were
now devastating the small country. "We were forced to do this," German
soldiers repeatedly told Belgian witnesses.

⤙⤚

A more benign interpretation of the franc-tireur legends also emphasizes
psychological factors, like analyses suggesting the stories represent an
attempt to assuage guilt and evade responsibilities. However, this approach,
associated with Fernand van Langenhove, a Solvay Institute sociologist,
begins by acknowledging the sincerity of many of the soldiers testifying in
the White Book. It seeks to explain the grip the franc-tireur stories exercised on the imaginations of Germans by adopting the methodology of

studies of the origins and survival of myths. Much as secular 19th century intellectuals tried to explain the success of Christianity in terms of the needs it fulfilled, rather than to dismiss it as a conspiracy of priests, like their 18th century predecessors, so this functionalist take on the franc-tireur stories sought to account psychologically for what Van Langenhove regarded as a singular episode of mass hysteria. Franc-tireur legends, he argued, were the result of the stresses of modern warfare, the surprising and disturbing resistance of the Belgian Army – including the use of isolated detachments roaming outside the battle lines – and the memory of the French franc-tireurs of 1870.[36] Further inflaming the imagination of the ordinary soldier were the exaggerated claims of abuse reported by German residents of Belgium who had fled during the opening days of the war. Rather than originating the legends, the State simply gave its imprimatur to stories that began spontaneously. The myth trickled up, rather than down.[37] Van Langenhove clearly felt he was taking the scientific high road in interpreting the phenomenon as he did. Collective beliefs "differing from historical truth," as he delicately put it, needed to be explained, not condemned.[38]

He is followed by two recent scholars, John Horne and Alan Kramer, who emphasize and elaborate upon the importance of the Prussian experience of French resistance during 1870 and 1871. The guerrilla campaign claimed the lives of about one thousand soldiers, and seemed to epitomize the horrors of republicanism for the Prussian officer corps. Raised by a levée en masse, without the uniform and discipline of a professional soldier, the French franc-tireurs not only disdained conventional tactics, but repeatedly engaged in what seemed to the Prussians dishonorable practices. They would fire on troops from concealed positions, then remove their armbands, hide their weapons, and assume the guise of innocent peasants or laborers.[39] To Van Langenhove's discussion of the franc-tireur "myth cycle" theory, Horne and Kramer add insights from George Lefèbvre's 1932 analysis of the Great Fear of summer, 1789.[40] (This was a widespread panic that bands of "brigands," supported by the aristocracy and foreign monarchs, were roaming the French countryside killing, looting, and burning crops.) This collective delusion was brought about by "auto-suggestion" – the fact that attacks were feared led to the belief that they were actually taking place. Thus was born what Horne and Kramer label a "myth-complex," colored as well by animosity toward civilians in general and Catholics in particular, frustration over the resistance of the Belgian Army and the pace of the German advance, and re-enforced by fatigue, disorientation, and the firepower of modern weaponry.[41] (The latter promoted the myth in two ways: the high velocity of bullets fired by French Lebels and Belgian Mausers (over 2,000 feet per second) mis-led troops into imagining that a shot fired at a great distance came from nearby, the report arriving simultaneously with the bullet. Also, high explosive shells sometimes mutilated victims in ways that suggested the handiwork of barbaric civilians.)[42] The presence of so many men in the countryside was also disturbing to soldiers from a nation that knew only universal conscription; mobilization had left few twenty-to-forty-year-old men in German towns and villages.

While they acknowledge that the "myth-complex" may have been exploited by officers, Horne and Kramer emphasize the fear and anger of ordinary soldiers, rather than manipulation.[43] They follow Van Langen-hove in believing that "the complex was generated essentially from below during the first phase of the invasion, by soldiers in the field...," while only during "the main invasion" did "the part played by the military command [become] much more pronounced."[44]

The relative merits of these two interpretations – that of Belgian and British investigators, on the one hand, and Van Langenhove and his successors on the other – will be discussed in Chapter 13. In any event, whether German soldiers were deliberately misled or whether the franc-tireur myths took on a life of their own, the conviction that they faced a vicious and unscrupulous civilian population undoubtedly contributed to the viciousness and unscrupulousness of German behavior in Belgium.

VON SCHLIEFFEN, VON EMMICH The Schlieffen Plan had called for a wide sweep through the Netherlands.[45] Troops were to cross the lightly defended border and march along the flat, straight roads into Western Belgium, bypassing the Liège fortresses. It made excellent sense, strategically. But German planners were convinced that though the British might con-nive in a violation of Belgium's neutrality, they would be less inclined to overlook the tens of thousands of grenadiers whose right sleeves would be sweeping along the length of the North Sea coast opposite East Anglia. A neutral Netherlands, the Germans also believed, would give them access to the shipping of other neutrals. (Both assumptions would prove wrong. Britain would not countenance the attack on Belgium and it would eventually deny the Germans shipping through Dutch ports.) And so Schlieffen's plan was scaled back. Additional troops, Moltke was also convinced, would be needed elsewhere, a still more compelling reason for narrowing the front and altering its trajectory.

But if the arc was flattened, the blow would have to come more quickly. Moltke's modification of his predecessor's plan meant that the Liège fortresses had to be captured in six days if the army was to keep to its timetable – defeat France within six weeks and entrain east before the Russian steamroller gathered momentum.

Liège's importance was obvious: it commanded the railroad network linking Germany with the plains of Brabant and northern France. But long before this major European trunk line was laid down, armies had appreciated the strategic significance of the city. It straddles the Meuse where the river turns northward and it guards the southern end of the basin which fans out above the Ardennes forest. The forest was hardly impenetrable in 1914 – two major roads cut through it – but it was difficult to haul heavy artillery across and not where you'd chose to march soldiers with 66-pound packs if time were of the essence. Below these two roads, which ran from Malmédy through Stavelot southeast and from Trier through Luxembourg to Longwy – was the heavily fortified French border, with intentional gaps left between the fortresses of Toul and Epinal and above Verdun to "canalize" invading German forces. The Metz Gap, the most likely route into France, was only 30 miles wide.

Another road led out of the Ardenne forest northward to Liège, from Malmédy over the Hautes Fagnes to Spa. But three roads led directly to Liège from Aachen, where the First and Second Armies were massing – one ran south to Verviers and then northwest down the valley of Vesdre, another straight across the open fields of eastern Wallonia to Visé, just below the Dutch border, and down the Meuse to the forts. Still another ran between these two, dipping south from Aachen just inside the Belgian border, and then running due west through Battice and Fléron. It was over these three routes that the main striking force would come, though troops would also sweep up from Malmédy. The invaders were von Emmich's "Army of the Meuse," cobbled together from three corps of von Bülow's Second Army and an additional brigade – about 130,000 soldiers in all.

Von Emmich's strategy was an imperfect microcosm of the Schlieffen Plan itself. The guns of the northern Liège forts guarding the Meuse did not cover the entire 8.6 miles to the Dutch frontier. A strong, rapidly moving force was to seize Visé, the northernmost Belgian town on the Meuse, penetrate the 5-mile gap above the range of the guns of Fort Pontisse, and then swing south and attack the western forts and invest Liège. With Visé taken and its bridges secured, cavalry units could also fan across the plains of southern Limburg and mask the movements of the invaders. The two cavalry divisions under von Emmich's command were thus dispatched directly to Visé. At the same time, other brigades of the VIIth Army Corps were to attack the eastern forts, Barchon and Fléron, and the "fortins" of Evegnée and Chaudfontaine. Fléron was particularly vital: it commanded the railroad link with Aachen. Waiting impatiently in and around Aachen were von Kluck's First Army and most of the remainder of von Bülow's Second Army. Additional brigades from the Xth Army Corps (von Emmich's own) were to attack the ring of forts from the south. They would cross the Vesdre at Verviers and proceed over the rolling hills between that river and the Ourthe.

The German Army had begun concentrating along the Belgium frontier on July 29. On August 1 they received the green light from Potsdam to implement the German War Plan. Then the marching order was abruptly canceled by the Kaiser an hour later. A telegram from Lichnowsky in London had convinced him that Britain might guarantee French neutrality, and spare Germany a western front. Lichnowsky corrected the impression with a second telegram and the armies were unleashed.

-<-->-

Until the morning of August 3rd, von Moltke thought the chances very good that Belgium would submit, albeit with bad grace, to the German ultimatum. But even after the Brussels government vowed to oppose the march through its territory, the Germans expected to encounter "chocolate soldiers" when they crossed the border. The Army would offer only token resistance, then retire on Antwerp. Certainly once the guns of the Liège fortresses had been silenced, the Belgians would sue for peace.

THE LIÈGE FORTS General Alexis Brialmont was responsible for designing the forts. It galled the general that he had never seen action. This was clearly an occupational hazard for anyone serving in the army of a country consigned to permanent neutrality, but one the general never reconciled himself to. He wrote bitterly to a woman who had witnessed the *Théatre Français* burn down, "I envy you, Madame: luckier than I, you have seen fire." In compensation he churned out some thirty-five books, seventy-four pamphlets, and innumerable designs for forts.

Work started on his final plans in June of 1888 and was completed by the end of 1891.[46]

Though trained in France, Brialmont had early in his career rejected the French star-shaped design, with its high, bastioned ramparts providing wide firing angles, and supplemented by extensive outworks. Instead, recognizing the ability of long-range guns firing high-explosive shells at steep angles to decimate the walls of conventional forts, Brialmont adopted the stark German model.

The Liège forts were a series of detached concrete bunkers buried under mounds of earth. Piston-like gun turrets slid up and down cylindrical shafts. A network of underground chambers housed machinery for maneuvering the guns, stores of ammunition and supplies, electric generators and ventilating fans, and living quarters for the garrison.

The entire system consisted of twelve such forts encircling the city of Liège, six principal forts and six smaller *"fortins."* Each of the former contained eight or nine cupolas, large and small, arrayed in a pentangular formation, their guns ranging from 21 cm howitzers (of which each fort had two) to rapid-firing 5.7 cm guns, ten of which were also placed on the parapet of each fort. The triangular *fortins*, situated between the large forts, also bristled with guns. Each had seven or eight cupolas with a smaller complement of weapons.

They were spaced less than 1,220 yards apart on average, so that if one were to fall into enemy hands, it would come under fire from both of its neighbors. The forts averaged about four miles from the city center, and formed a defensive perimeter with a circumference of over thirty-two miles.

What may have been state-of-the-art in 1891 was no longer so on the eve of the war. The forts were engineered to withstand barrages from 22 cm guns. But bigger guns were being turned out from the late 1890s. At around the same time, an effective method of reinforcing concrete with steel was finally perfected by Gustav Wayss. The aggregate for the forts, moreover, was not cleaned, crushed, and graded as it would have been a quarter century later. The forts' vulnerability was increased by a structural design flaw: at their center was a large hall with an unsupported roof.[47]

-<-->-

Commanding the Liège garrisons in 1914 was General Gérard Leman, an engineer, a professor at the Belgian Military Academy, and, fittingly, Brialmont's foremost living disciple. A somber, taciturn man, he inspired respect rather than devotion. His task, he knew, was not to hold off the enemy indefinitely, but to delay the German army as long as possible until French and British troops could reinforce the Belgians. While the forts were certainly formidable obstacles, Leman commanded only about 25,000 soldiers in addition to the 4,500 garrison troops, a force not sufficient to defend the Liège perimeter against the 130,000 invaders. (The entire Belgian Army consisted of only 117,000 men in August 1914, of whom 93,000 were combatants.) Worse, the 3rd Division and the mixed brigade from the 4th that augmented it had only twenty-four machine-guns, not even a quarter of the Belgian Army's meager arsenal, though it did have 500 sabres. How much time could Leman buy? Everyone looked anxiously westward. "Two questions recurred perpetually. 'Where are the Allies?' 'When will the great battle take place?'"[48]

Most Belgians did not doubt that the Allies would come soon. And perhaps the great battle might take place in front of Liège. Few Belgians, however, were aware of the existence of certain squat behemoths from the Krupp works at Essen – siege guns with a 42 cm bore through which a 2,535-pound shell three feet long could be blasted nearly 8 miles.[49]

The Krupp monsters, however, were not yet ready when war broke out. The chief technical difficulty to be overcome – apart from making the short-barreled, unrifled howitzer accurate – was to make the guns mobile. The original 1909 model had to be transported by rail and embedded in concrete before it was fired, so powerful was its recoil. A road model was tested in February 1914, but further refinements were necessary and the motor-driven version was not scheduled to be delivered until October 1914.[50] As the July crisis approached its climax, the Krupp plant, working twenty-four hours a day, managed to convert two of the *Dicke Berthas* into road-trans-portable models and rapidly trained the 280-man crew the two-gun battery required. But the howitzers would not be ready until August 10th.

Von Emmich didn't wait. He was convinced his crushing numerical superiority would enable his troops to penetrate the gaps between the forts and overwhelm the garrisons. On the morning of the 5th, after a sustained barrage with 15 and 22 cm guns, the Germans attacked the eastern forts with massed infantry. The chocolate soldiers mowed them down. From their positions behind the parapets, it seemed to the Belgian machine-gun-ners that the German soldiers were advancing on parade. Column suc-ceeded column. Men trampled over the piles of corpses. Such prodigality amazed the defenders of Fléron, Barchon, and Evegnée. Still the waves of infantry swept forward. As many as forty-three thousand Germans were to die before the last Liège forts surrendered, according to one estimate.[51]

At one point below Fort Barchon the Germans penetrated the barbed wire and broke though the Belgian lines north of the fort. They were repulsed by a bayonet charge from the 11th and 35th regiments of the 16th brigade. Across the entire front the Germans fled back to the villages on the 5th that they had passed through peacefully the day before. And then the massacres began in earnest.

MELEN: "IL PLEUT, IL PLEUT BERGÈRE" After Battice and Herve, the next town on the road to Liège is Melen, about equidistant from the forts of Barchon and Fléron, and just less than a mile in front of the fortin of Eveg-née. Lining the road to the east of the town is the little village of Labouxhe, consisting in 1914 of about thirty homes. Soldiers of the 165th regiment lodged there on the 4th. As elsewhere, the troops seemed well disposed toward the civilians on day one of the invasion. Soldiers invited some men of the village to play cards that first evening. The next day the guns of Fléron decimated the invaders as they attacked the forts, and the soldiers returned in a very different mood. At 11:00 p.m. residents were ordered into their cellars; they were told to expect "serious events."[52]

At about 3:30 a.m. on the 6th, intense firing broke out. Residents assumed that the Belgian army had launched a counterattack. The firing ceased. Germans entered the ground floor of most of the houses, shouting

"Draussen, schlechte Franzosen!" As soon as the men emerged from their homes, they were gunned down at point-blank range. The males of at least ten households were slain. Women and children were driven into the street with blows from rifle butts. The houses were ignited and several soldiers yelled in schoolroom French, "Bad French women, you, alive into the fire." (Only a few days later soldiers would be told horrific tales of Belgian franc-tireurs. But on August 4, some companies among von Emmich's forces were led to believe they had invaded France.)[53]

Not all of the women and children were so fortunate. Entire families were massacred in the early morning onslaught and in a second round of killings on the 8th: the Benoits, a father, three sons ages 19, 18, and 16, and his 12-year-old daughter Marie; the Cresson family, André and Marie and their four children, Guillaume, 16, Gilles, 13, Thérèse, 11, and Cathérine 7; the Brayeuxs, Joseph, Marie, and their twelve-year-old daughter Anna; the Lorquets, a father and four sons; the Weerts, the Weyenbergs, and the Wislets. Marie Wislet and her daughter Marguerite, 20, were handsome women. Perhaps her good looks and poise would enable Marguerite to leave her tiny village for Liège. But the mother and daughter were raped repeatedly in their basement by the rampaging troops in the early morning of the 6th, after Louis Wislet was butchered as he defended them. When they were finished, the Germans stabbed them in the chest, smashed in the women's skulls with rifle butts and then shot them several times for good measure.[54]

After the Thursday morning butcheries in Labouxhe, the troops swarmed into Melen proper. The residents were driven out into the street, and the Germans entered their homes, claiming they were searching for weapons. After allowing the inhabitants to re-enter their dwellings, soldiers once again forced them out at gunpoint. No weapons had been confiscated; no accusations were made. This time they were told that they would be marched toward Fort Fléron. Instead, about forty men were bound together and taken directly to a meadow belonging to the Falla family. Here they were lined up, with a soldier stationed two or three yards behind each victim. Among those selected were Henri Defooz and his two sons Guillaume, 20, and François, 18. The order was given; the shots rang out. Defooz was hit in the stomach and left arm, but survived. He lay perfectly still, pretending to be dead, listening intently for any sign of life from either of his sons. Soldiers approached, patted his pockets, and relieved him of 2,080 francs. Defooz held his breath and remained limp. Other groups of prisoners were marched out to the meadow and despatched. A total of one hundred eight men, women, and children were murdered in Labouxhe and Melen, forty-eight from neighboring farms and villages. This does not include the twenty-two residents of Herve massacred at Labouxhe.[55]

Among the first to fall were the husband and daughter of Elizabeth Lambert Degueldre. On the 4th, the day of the invasion, she was walking with her family in a meadow behind their farm. They had gone to milk the cows. Eighteen-year-old Marie Degueldre became very apprehensive and wanted to return to the house. Suddenly, Elizabeth spotted a German soldier crouched in the meadow, his gun leveled. The next instant, shots rang out. Her husband and daughter fell. Marie, hit in the chest, died in half an hour. Olivier was badly wounded in the thigh. Neighbors helped carry the dying girl to a stable. But more Germans began firing when they returned for Olivier. Elizabeth, concerned that the soldiers might finish him off if they found him, decided to leave him in the meadow and attend to him there. He slowly bled to death, over a period of nine and a half hours. His final words: "Bernard will avenge me." His son was serving in the Belgian Army.[56]

Stunned by the gratuitous murders, Elizabeth focused on providing her husband and daughter with proper burials. In a peasant village in 1914, the rituals surrounding burial and mourning still had a sanctity and inviolability the war was to do much to erode. But the Germans had installed themselves in the Degueldre home, compelling the distraught widow to feed them and wait on them, and they forbade her from bringing the bodies back to the house for burial. On Saturday, the 8th, they finally gave their consent. Apparently, there was some entertainment value to be derived. After her neighbors helped Elizabeth Degueldre retrieve her husband and daughter, the soldiers compelled the neighbors' children to dance in front of the corpses and sing, *"il pleut, il pleut bergère,"* a popular tune. The men did not appear to be drunk at the time, Degueldre testified. They also stole 400 francs and made off with several animals. As she watched, the soldiers amused themselves by beating the pigs until the animals fell dead. Further entertainment was on its way.

Two undertakers arrived from Herve with coffins to bury the father and daughter. No sooner had the two men entered the house than they were set upon by the soldiers, who battered them to death with their rifle butts. The terrified women were ordered into the cellar. Then the Germans lit the curtains of the living room, and the women and children raced upstairs and out into the meadow, the neighbor dragging her hysterical five-year-old. Threatened repeatedly, the women were marched to the Polinard Cross outside the village, loaded into a cart and taken to Herbesthal. En route, the cart halted and the women and girls were raped over and over. After a brief interrogation at Herbesthal, Degueldre and her neighbor's family were escorted to a town near the Dutch border and told, "You are free."

Five years later, after offering a laconic account of the nightmare, the woman recalled an important omission: "I forgot to tell you that the bodies of my husband and daughter were consumed by the flames. I was not permitted to bury them."

⋖⋯⋗

On February 16th, 1915, the Germans re-entered Melen. This time they didn't molest the inhabitants. Two officers had been sent by the *Kommandantur* of Liège, and their mission was to come up with some plausible pretext for the slaughter. The Germans were increasingly anxious about public opinion in the U.S. Seventeen witnesses were interviewed. By necessity, they were almost entirely women. The officers tried to get the women to concede that they were "not absolutely certain civilians did not fire; it is possible that they did so."[57] The witnesses steadfastly refused to lie. The investigators then focused on the card games. Was it not possible that some dispute over cards could have precipitated the violence? – as if accusations of cheating at vingt-et-un could justify the slaughter of over one hundred civilians. In the end, the Germans decided that the inventiveness required to vindicate the killings was beyond their capacities. The German White Book makes no mention of Melen and Labouxhe.

SOUMAGNE: "WE WERE NOT ACCUSED OF ANYTHING" Also unmentioned in the White Book is the village of Soumagne, about 4 miles south of Melen, on the picturesque road winding from Verviers to Liège via Fléron. This was the site of the worst single massacre in the province. One hundred seventeen people from the town and surrounding villages and farms were butchered here on August 5th and 6th, fifty-five in the meadow of

Fond-Leroy. As at Melen, the soldiers were from the 165th and also the 27th regiment.

At Melen it was the hamlet of Labouxhe where the worst massacres occurred; at Soumagne it was the little village of Fécher, just north of the commune, that bore the brunt of the assault.

The killing commenced early Wednesday morning when several farmers attempted to return to their homes. They'd driven their cattle into Liège the previous afternoon and had been detained by Belgian troops securing the forts. The men were shot as they re-entered the village. No questions were asked, no inquiries made.[58]

Later that day, around 4 p.m., a large group of soldiers who were marching down the Bas Bois road toward the center of the village were targeted by a Belgian machine-gun hidden behind a hedge in the hamlet of Les Viviers. The Germans fled back to a colliery, regrouped, and were given orders. They marched back down the chemin de Bas Bois, raiding all the homes en route. Some three hundred residents were rounded up and placed at the head of the battalion. The Belgian machine-gun was silent when they arrived in its vicinity. Either it had already been withdrawn or the gunners chose not to jeopardize the lives of their compatriots. But instead of releasing the hostages, the Germans selected some forty-eight men and forced them along route de Fecher to a meadow called "Fond-Leroy." Thirty-two others were rounded up in Les Viviers itself. Luckily, a shell from Fléron hit this column of captives as it approached the meadow. One prisoner was killed, but thirteen men at the rear escaped in the confusion, including the burgomaster. A young boy managed to untie himself, and freed the rest with a pocket knife that had not been confiscated, as the men crouched behind a hedge.[59]

In the meadow, the prisoners were made to stand in two rows. The soldiers were lined up eight or nine yards in front of the men. No charges were read out. Two men, Léon Jerome, 48, and Joseph Lejeune, 33, whispered to a teenager, Joseph Dedoyard, to stand directly behind them. The two men moved together, shielding him with their bodies, and then fell on top of him. None of the three was killed, but Jerome and Lejeune were finished off with bayonet thrusts and blows from rifle butts. Dedoyard would have survived unscathed had he not imprudently raised his head. He, too, was stabbed several times in the back, but survived.[60]

A number of other captives were only wounded in the initial volley, especially those standing at the far end of the lines, furthest from the captain barking the orders. Some of the soldiers were apparently more merciful than their officers, firing high or wide when their actions couldn't be detected. But another order was shouted and a group of soldiers charged the victims. Those not dead were stabbed with bayonets, pummeled with rifle-butts, or whacked with hatchets. Nevertheless, eleven other besides Dedoyard survived by feigning death.

Dedoyard, or possibly another badly injured young man, Joseph Daniel, noticed, as he slowly inched away from the row of corpses, that seventeen-year-old Pierre Germay was still alive. He urged Germay to follow. "Impossible," the teenager whispered. "I'm suffering too much." But he was able to crawl as far as a hedge at the far end of the meadow, where his body was discovered two days later.[61]

Not all the men who survived the fusillade and the hatchets and bayonets were able to make their way from the meadow. On Thursday morning villagers continued to hear the moans of the wounded. But German sentries would let no one near the victims. It's not difficult to imagine the anguish of the women and children, not knowing if their husbands, sons, or fathers were still alive and in excruciating pain – and not being able to find out or to help them in any way. It was only on Friday that the Germans allowed the villagers to return to the fields. By this time, all the men were dead. An accurate count of the victims was only possible when exhumations and reburials were permitted the next year.

Similar scenes were enacted at other meadows – Chession, where nineteen were killed, Nevray, where eighteen were slaughtered. At the latter, the Germans were particularly vicious. The wives of the victims were permitted to accompany them. Some were crying and pleading with the soldiers, some hysterical with grief, others, aware of the futility of begging, shouted farewells or words of encouragement. The soldiers tormented the women: "Is that him, your husband? Well, then look!" And then they opened fire.[62]

-<-·->-

"On ne nous a rien reproché et nous n'avons jamais été interrogés" – we were not accused of anything and never questioned – one of the survivors of the

Fond-Leroy massacre recounted.[63] The following day, however, the Germans thought it desirable to correct at least the former oversight. As René Varlet and his German-born maid Bertha Fraurenbath watched, an open car full of officers drove slowly down the road toward Herve. One officer fired a single shot in the air. Immediately, as if on cue, soldiers raced out from the houses where they were billeted, screaming theatrically, "Someone has fired on our wounded officers!"[64] This was the pretext for a few more murders and the burning of several more homes.

The German maid reproached several soldiers who were about to kill an old man. He was trembling like a leaf. How could he possibly have fired on troops? she demanded. The soldiers let him go, though they killed his son and burned his house down. Like so many other witnesses who hoped vainly for some redress after the armistice, she tried to provide what information she could for Belgian prosecutors. She didn't know the soldiers' regiment, but two of the men had told her their names – Godeker and Flechtener. She'd served the troops hot drinks the afternoon before. They had just come from Fond-Leroy.

⊰⟶⊱

SOUMAGNE: EXPATRIATES As in the towns close to the border, there were a number of German families in and around Soumagne. They fared no better than their neighbors at the hands of their former countrymen. Even a record of military service was of no help, as so many Jewish veterans were shocked to learn twenty-five years later. Jacob Rotheudt had served in the 1870 invasion of France. About to be executed as a franc-tireur, this former Prussian soldier identified himself and held aloft his discharge papers. His executioners hesitated; soldiers approached to take a closer look. An officer intervened. "Ta-ta-ta!" he said, dismissing the appeal. He then gave the order to fire.[65]

Nor were German women always treated more kindly. A Soumagne widow, Mme. Gorrès, sheltered her two daughters and a daughter-in-law. Everyone was driven out of the house and the sons-in-law shot on the spot. The women, hysterical with grief, were ordered to leave at once. One of the daughters was disabled and Gorrès helped her by taking her two-month-old son, Pierre. Moments later an enraged soldier killed the grandmother with a bayonet thrust. Pierre Gorrès was yanked out of her arms and hurled to the ground. He died instantly. The child's mother was also knocked to the ground and beaten. Grief-stricken, she raced to the river and threw herself in. She was rescued and taken to the church.[66]

Soldiers killed two other children of German descent, thirteen-year-old Anna Ernestine Kramer and her ten-month-old brother Marcel. The boy was shot as his mother held him in her arms. Crazed with despair and terror, she refused to put her dead son down after she was thrust into the packed church.[67]

And among the residents of Soumagne who were shot in Micheroux, the next village on the road to Fléron, there were several Germans, including a young girl named Elsa Goebels. On the same day, soldiers murdered still another German child in nearby Riessonsart, eleven-year-old Bette Schwiez. Not long afterward, a Micheroux resident who'd been born and raised in Germany bitterly admonished his former compatriots. "You kill more civilians than soldiers. This is not war."

"True," a soldier acknowledged, "but if we had carried out our orders to the letter, not a living person would be left where we have passed, nor one stone lying upon another."[68]

SAINT HADELIN AND RIESSONSART: VIVE LA BELGIQUE! About one and a half kilometers south of Soumagne is Olne. Sixty-eight Belgians were murdered in the villages around this town, the highest death toll for any commune in the province, after Soumagne, Melen, and the city of Liège. Among the unlucky villages was St. Hadelin, lying in a picturesque valley just below Olne, its houses situated along both banks of the little Magne river as it winds towards the Vesdre. As the Germans marched through the hamlet on the morning of August 5th, rumors circulated about the killings in nearby villages. At 4:30 p.m. a shell exploded just outside town, killing six soldiers and wounding ten, mostly Poles. The latter were carried to several buildings by the side of the road, and a Red Cross flag was hoisted. According to witnesses, a German gun began firing from behind the buildings. A shell from Fléron hit the improvised hospital. Angry soldiers swarmed through the village, pillaging all the homes. As always, the wine cellars were the first target. Most of the population, sensing that worse violence was imminent, took refuge either in the church or in an old weaving shed.

Troops eventually began deploying along the bank opposite these buildings, in a field planted with beech trees, known as the "Faweu," where they thought they'd have more cover from the fire of the fort. At one end of the field was the village school and the homes of the schoolmaster, Victor Warnier, and the constable, Jean Naval.

Warnier's two oldest daughters were schoolteachers and the younger son, Edgard, was studying to become one. The oldest boy, Victor Jr., was a clerk in a registrar's office; the youngest girl was only two. "There were seven in our family," recalled Berthe Warnier after the war, "happy, full of vigor and courage and faith in the future. Alas, only three of us remain now, miserable, without any means of support, without even a roof to shelter us. This was the work of the barbarians! And why such cruelty? Why? Who knows."[69]

On the first day of the war, cavalry troops knocked on the door and politely asked for detailed maps of the area, for which they offered to pay. Warnier informed them that he didn't have any and they rode off.

On the 5th, following the shelling of the field hospital, about a thousand soldiers camped in the woods in front of the family home. The Warniers busied themselves attending to the Germans. Edgard took some men around the village to purchase sheep for dinner, while Victor, who spoke German, chatted with a lieutenant. Nelly brewed pots of coffee for the troops and Bertha and her mother prepared a meal. The soldiers broke up benches in the school so there would be sufficient fuel for the stove.

After Edgard had been gone an hour, Mme. Warnier began to grow anxious. A French-speaking major reassured her: "You're being foolish. Don't worry. Your son is going to come back. We're not barbarians. I'll go myself to find him. Calm down."[70] The officer returned with Edgard a few minutes later.

Around 10:30 p.m. the family, and the six officers who were sleeping in the entry hall, sheltering from a storm, were awakened by the crash of a shell in front of the home.

> The officers, frightened, rose and left, telling us to shut the door. I ran to get my little sister from her cradle and we descended once again into the cellar. Hardly had we arrived when a second shell struck. Then began a spectacle more terrifying than anything one is capable of imagining. Howling like enraged beasts, the soldiers battered down our door with rifle butts, rushed en masse into the house, knocked over my

mother and brothers in the entry hall, broke the doors to the salon and dining room, doused the furniture with benzine and lit it. At the same time they shattered mirrors, the piano, knick-knacks, and slashed wall hangings. They raced up to the second floor and down into the cellar, their way illuminated by pieces of wood soaked in benzine.

Having ransacked the house, they made us leave.

Their hideous faces, the gleaming bayonets, our house in flames made an unforgettable tableau.[71]

The family was divided up. The brothers' hands were tightly bound. They briefly kissed their parents goodbye and were hustled off. "Have courage, children," Mme. Warnier called out after them. "We're prisoners, but we'll see each other again." Soldiers then forced the rest of the family forward, beating them with rifle butts. Berthe's arm was broken in two places from the blows. Horses galloped by pulling field guns, and the children lost sight of their parents. As she strained to look for them, Berthe suddenly noticed that soldiers were taking aim at her. She was hit in the head and passed out.

When she regained consciousness, she was lying face down in water in a pit twenty yards from the house. But she was soaked in something besides water. Blood was seeping over her – from her sister's body, lying on top of her. She heard some agonized groans and the savage cries of the German troops as they filed past, occasionally pausing to kick one of the victims. For three hours Bertha pretended to be dead, until it was quiet. Suffering terribly, she dragged herself along a hedge to a neighboring home that had been spared. Victor's body lay near by, along with Naval's, but she knew nothing about the fate of her parents or other siblings.

She learned later that her father and mother, still holding Andrée, had been made to stand side-by-side in a little street a hundred yards from the home. But this execution squad was more humane, firing only at the father, who was killed instantly. The next day, Edgard was found behind the school, shot in the head, his hands bound so tightly that there were blackened ridges around his wrists.

The Germans, as usual, provided fanciful excuses. Berthe Warnier was told that the family had been attacked because the father had refused to provide maps to the uhlans and had struck and killed a soldier. But clearly, as other witnesses testified, the Warniers and Nevals were blamed for the two shells from Fléron that hit the Germans encamped in the field in front of the school. Victor Warier and Jean Neval tried to point out to the Germans that there was no way they could have alerted the gunners at Fléron as to the presence of enemy troops, even if they'd wanted to. The fort was two miles away; both men had been in their homes all day, surrounded by troops. The shells that crashed into the troops in the beech grove, though they wounded a number of soldiers, had killed only a horse.[72]

⤙⤚

For good measure, three other prisoners were shot as well, seized arbitrarily earlier in the day and tethered like animals. After still more murders, including a sixty-six-year-old paralytic, Mme. Desonay, and her daughter Joséphine, the Germans headed for the weaving shed. They drove off the women, who pleaded and cried, and marched the men toward the village of Riessonsart. When several people from this hamlet came forward with provisions, naively hoping to appease the Germans and secure the release of their neighbors, they, too, were seized and condemned to death. Among them was Jacques Maguet, "the model of the village, a man of generous and worthy character," and the Dewandres, "handsome young men noted for their good hearts and obliging natures."[73] Making allowances for eulogistic excesses, it was, given the circumstances, the more generous and courageous of this tiny hamlet who were made prisoner.

The executions began in small batches, at a site known as the Ash Tree. Somville reconstructed the event from survivors.

> One of the doomed men, Victor Polet of Ayeneux, a retired schoolmaster, a man of high character, was revolted by the cowardice of the executioners. When he was ordered to take up his position for execution, the old man refused with disdain; he was shot on the little hillock on which he stood, in an attitude full of dignity and courage.
>
> Survivors report that before the shooting began, Jacques Maguet, turning to the whole group of prisoners, recited in a loud, firm voice the act of contrition, which all repeated, sentence by sentence. Then, when his turn had come, and he was being pushed, with others, toward the place of execution, Maguet raised his hat and shouted: *"Vive la Belgique!" "Vive la Belgique!"* repeated his companions, as though electrified. And the patriotic cheer was raised again.
>
> "Listen to your companions cheering!" said an officer, who stood some distance away; he was greatly moved. But the demonstration merely increased the rage of the other Germans; they began to bawl insults at the Belgians.
>
> "Ah!" said one of the survivors, "when we heard that shout, *Vive la Belgique!* we felt a shiver run through our whole being; we plucked up courage, feeling that we, too, like our brave soldiers, were dying for our country."[74]

But they were not. They were only civilians guilty of living in a town shelled by Belgian artillery.

The massacre was halted dramatically when a cavalry officer came galloping up with orders that the soldiers were to depart immediately. Thirty-three men had been shot. The remainder were kept prisoner for sixteen more hours, hauling German guns toward Magnée, between Fléron and Chaudfontaine."[75]

AFTERMATH In most accounts, the grisly and agonizing process of identifying the remains and burying the victims is passed over in silence. But the burgomaster of Olne dwelt at some length on this task in his testimony before the Commission of Inquiry. It was not until the 8th that the residents of the town were permitted to proceed with the burials. The stench was intense. The curé, M. Alers, presided, supervising twelve workers. Seven or eight butcher's and baker's carts were requisitioned. The victims were first placed against a wall to be identified. It wasn't always easy to determine who was who. "The heat was overwhelming. Since the morning of the 6th, the unfortunate victims had been left in the sun, lying in their blood. It is futile to describe the atmosphere in the cemetery. Days like that are unforgettable."[76]

THE CURÉ OF BLÉGNY Blégny, just under two miles north of Melen, sits at the top of the arc of villages stretching from a little below Fort Fléron to just above Fort Barchon, where the worst atrocities in the province took place. Nearly fifty people were killed in and around Blégny and nearby Barchon. There were actually more murders at the latter, but a more vivid and complete record remains of the events at Blégny.[77] The massacres in both villages, like those in the city of Liège, Wandre, and elsewhere, took place after the hiatus in the killing between August 9 and August 14, while the Germans waited for a response to their appeal for a Belgian surrender. In Blégny there was a large religious house, the Blégny Institute, where the sisters cared for over seventy German wounded. After the war, the nuns collaborated on a detailed account of their experiences – comprising nearly twenty closely printed pages in the official *Rapports et Documents d'Enquête*. In addition, the much beloved curé of Blégny, sixty-two-year-old Remy-Joseph Labeye, kept a journal, which was carried off to the Netherlands and preserved. A schoolteacher also wrote an account of the events in Blégny. Not many of the depositions have the immediacy of these texts. And they clearly reveal the animus against Catholicism that surfaced so frequently in August. They also provide conclusive evidence that the execution of four leading citizens, without any legitimate pretext, was ordered by German authorities.[78]

Nearly everyone in Belgium had vivid recollections of the moment their village or town was abandoned to the invaders. The schoolteacher, Théophile Ghuysen, recalled seeing a group of Belgian riflemen on their knees in the middle of the road, facing the curé of Blégny, who was performing an absolution. "It's impossible to describe this scene, at once moving and majestic: the confession on a public route of young men full of life and vigor, whom death was watching over, like a hawk preparing to swoop down on its helpless prey."[79] A little later Ghuysen watched as an order was received by a young lieutenant on Place de l'Église. The detachment stationed in Blégny were told to resist à *l'outrance*. The officer drew his sword and announced to his men, with a smile, that they had been condemned to death. Moments later three strapping German prisoners were marched across the square, a scary-looking lot. But soon after, a sergeant up in the church tower observed masses of infantry descending from the north, and the platoon abandoned Blégny. From behind shuttered windows, residents soon heard the heavy tramp of boots in the streets. When an officer yelled *"Halt,"* Ghuysen briefly imagined that it was the French who had arrived. He was disillusioned a moment later.[80]

The attacks on civilians in Blégny took place in two phases. Not long after the Germans entered the town on the 5th, the first victim lay dead, Joseph Smeets. Not surprisingly, in several villages near the forts, and in Liège proper, there were a great many munitions workshops and factories. Like Birmingham, the region was noted for its outstanding gunsmiths. Smeets was himself a teacher in a school of armory at Blégny. Naturally, many of the craftsmen had stockpiles of gun parts in their workshops, and they hastened to get certificates from German commanders authorizing them to keep what had not been requisitioned. The suspicion that Smeets had a cache of arms may have been responsible for his death, but the Germans acted so precipitously it is difficult to say. Smeets's home was invaded, and he was shot with a pistol. His body was tossed onto the road.

His wife had just given birth. The widow and the victim's mother were clubbed with rifle butts and driven from the house. The 82-year old mother was also slashed in the face with a bayonet. Tears and blood streamed down her face, as she kept wringing her hands, crying, "They've killed my son." Soldiers looked on impassively.[81]

As the Germans came under the fire of the Barchon guns, they broke into a number of other homes, though only one additional resident was killed. The terrified residents fled en masse to the Blégny Institute. Soon around three hundred men, women, and children had crammed into its small rooms and corridors, many crying piteously. A sympathetic German soldier witnessing the scene was himself moved to tears. All night long there were prayers and lamentations. Meanwhile, soldiers thoroughly searched the convent for arms. None were found, but the people taking refuge with the nuns, their hands raised while the search was conducted, suddenly noticed flames consuming the buildings on all sides of the Institute. The town had been set on fire. The people sheltering in the Institute had already been ordered to sit down, lie down, stand up, by a malicious officer. He now commanded everyone to stand outside, hands still raised, the better to witness their homes being consumed by flames. Another officer invited several of the nuns to admire the spectacle, "so much more impressive at night." The flames roared, children sobbed and shrieked, their stunned parents tried to console them.[82]

German troops continued moving through town. A howitzer rumbled by with a wretched old man lashed to it. It was the burgomaster of Julémont. A platoon of retreating Germans invaded the Institute, demanding Red Cross armbands.[83] There were more searches for weapons and threats to the Institute and the refugees. *"Demain la maison sera kaputt,"* the nuns were told. And the capricious orders continued: at one point everyone was made to shout *"Vive l'Allemagne!"*[84]

The crowd in the Institute had swollen during the night. Then, at 5:00 a.m., the women and children were released and the men made hostage. The latter were ordered into the church, where they joined a great number of other men who'd taken refuge there with their families. The men were then taken outside and marched toward Battice. Smeets still lay unburied. The contingent passed a second corpse, that of Jules Herman, "the pearl of men, kind and obliging," one witness later recalled. "There was no end to his help for others." Herman had been reluctant to abandon his wife, who was seriously ill. He carried her to the cellar and stayed by her side when everyone else had fled to the Institute or the church. The Germans gunned him down in front of his four children.[85]

The men marching toward Battice were subjected to various indignities en route, but the worst treatment was always reserved for the curé, abbé Labeye. Even the irreligious were appalled. The men repeatedly surrounded him to protect him from the blows and kicks, but the Germans pushed them away and resumed their abuse.[86]

The curé's journal entries are worth recording, as are some of the comments of the nuns who rescued the book, taking it with them when they fled to the Netherlands.

> We pass the night in the church. Ernest Clermont is taken with a nervous attack; so is Léopold Dortu. About 5 o'clock someone comes to make a statement: the women and children can go; the men will remain; they will be sent to Germany... Could I have managed not to be included in this sentence? I doubt it. In any case, I shall not make any request. I'm sure it would be much more useful to accompany the 170 unfortunates.[87]
>
> We leave. Past Gobcé we are made to enter a meadow; first alarm: we're convinced they are going to shoot us. I begin to recite the rosary. ("An eyewitness said that M. le Curé pronounced a general absolution for all the poor people...") After an hour we resume the march. Again we go into a meadow near Battice. We are gathered together in the middle, surrounded by sentinels. We're permitted to lie down, but we remain standing; here we'll spend the night. For food, some bonbons and breadcrusts; in the evening a few swallows of bouillon from some compassionate soldiers. I was the target of much of the bad behavior of the soldiers and subordinate officers; they accused me of having placed a telephone in the church tower (it was installed by the Belgian Army) and of having sent soldiers from there with orders to fire on the Germans. I heard a great many impieties against religion, Jesus Christ, and prayer. They wanted me to admit that I could speak German. As I did not understand, they shook their fists at me, kicked me, threatened me with their rifles, bayonets, with an axe and a dagger. Once an officer spat in my face and threw my hat on the ground and spat on it. Another struck me in the chest with his rifle-butt, and gave me a violent kick on the leg. A soldier pricked me three times with his bayonet and wounded me slightly. Others, in giving some apples to my companions, threw them at my head. Nothing very serious; however, they were so furious that if they had found me alone, I think they would have killed me.
>
> Meanwhile they shot five of our companions: Gérard Custers, Jean Dortu, Godard, Jacques Flamant, and Renard. On two occasions they made us believe that we too were about to be shot. Another time they fired volleys over our heads to frighten us. Then they once more placed in front of us a second series of four men condemned

to die, among others, Noël Nihan. These unhappy creatures had been there since 4 o'clock the previous day, their hands bound, and I know they were still there the day after our departure. What became of them?[88]

Another witness recalled that on the forced march of the men of Blégny and Trembleur to Battice, one of the two mock-executions was staged with genuine dramatic flair, with an officer on horseback riding up at the last minute and countermanding the order. The first of the actual executions also showed some imagination. The seven men selected were bound together. On arriving in Battice, the Germans lined up these men and told the rest of the captives to watch them closely. This time there was no reprieve. But for some reason only the five inner men were then shot. The men on each end were untied and told to rejoin their comrades.[89]

The four prisoners whose fate the curé was unsure of were eventually shot, after being prodded by bayonets and tortured with lighted cigarettes held to their ears and nostrils.

Finally, after twenty-four hours without food and water, a German-speaking doctor among the prisoners was able to buttonhole a German physician. The doctor's protests apparently moved his German counterpart to complain to his superiors. The men were released shortly thereafter.[90] Other witnesses, however, believed they owed their freedom to a captain who had appeared sympathetic to their plight for some time. It was he who approached Father Labeye and told him the men could return to Blégny, but they must go quickly. He accompanied the former captives most of the way back to town, to insure that they would not be rearrested by soldiers.[91]

Around 2:30 in the afternoon someone in Blégny spotted the first of the men trudging back into town. *"Les voilà,"* she cried out. The villagers were delirious with joy. People rushed up to embrace the bleeding curé and the others. Abbé Labeye was himself affected by the extraordinary emotional display and wept freely. But one woman circled frantically among the men. "Where is my son? Why isn't he with you?" she implored. No one could tell the distraught mother the truth, that her son was among those still bound when the others had been released. He'll return later, someone reassured her. As for the men who had been shot, the priest consoled the families and urged everyone to respond to the trials with a renewal of faith.[92]

Things remained quiet until the evening of Saturday, August 15th, Assumption Day. At 6 p.m. a note was left at the curé's home informing him that if there were any firing in the village, he would be shot. Also made hostage were the burgomaster, M. Ruwet and, inexplicably, M. Delnooz, the father-in-law of a local doctor.

An officer ordered, in an ironic voice, that the curé be served "a good supper." Around 9:00 p.m., six officers entered the house to interview the abbé and burgomaster.[93] They brought along a translator, Jeanne Delnooz. "Are you aware of any arms still remaining in the village?" they asked the two men.

When M. Ruwet emphatically denied that there were guns in Blégny, he was told that weapons had been discovered in the basement of the Haikins. The burgomaster pointed out that these arms were unfinished and inoperable, and that the brothers had received permission from a German officer to keep them.

The Haikins were brought forward and flourished their permit. The officer interrogating them pocketed it. The two brothers were also vaguely accused of using the Red Cross flag to disguise their maneuvers against the Germans. No evidence was provided.

In fact the older of the Haikins (sometimes spelled Kaikin or Hackin) owned a thriving arms manufacturing business employing 128 laborers, who worked mostly in their own homes. When the Germans entered the town, he had 15,000 unfinished "Bull Dog" revolvers in his workshop – with no cartridges. A German officer ordered him to nail shut the doors of the workshop, and he complied, in the presence of witnesses.

In addition to his armament business, Haikin had recently purchased a large dance hall. When war broke out, the father of ten converted it into a Red Cross hospital. A number of German wounded were treated there, but these had been evacuated by August 15th.

After the arrival of the Germans, Haikin always carried with him four certificates: one issued by the German officer stating he could pass through German lines to make purchases, another from the same officer permitting him to retain the unfinished revolvers in his workshop, and two testifying that he was serving with the Belgian Red Cross. On August 16th these were only so many scraps of paper for the Germans.

Though all the certificates were missing when a relative was finally permitted to claim the body, he found that the Germans hadn't taken all his money. Perhaps they were satisfied with the 8,000 francs they stole from the man's wife before they burned his house down. In any event, they had taken the precaution of mutilating the arms manufacturer with bayonet slashes after they had shot him. To spare the family the ordeal of seeing the butchered remains, the nuns concealed the brothers' bodies in a packing case.[94]

⋖⋅⋗

Following the cursory questioning of the burgomaster, there was not even the pretense of an interrogation of the priest.

Later that night, August 15th, at about 10:30, a sister who was staying up with a sick woman observed four soldiers furtively leaving the grounds of the Institute. One went barefoot. His boots were later found in the recreation room. A moment later the outside of the Institute and the presbytery were fired on. Soldiers immediately poured out, yelling and shooting. Several times a voice, in heavily accented French, called out, "Let's go, comrades. Jean, keep watch!"[95]

A dead soldier was brought in and the commander turned to several of the sisters and remarked, "You see how the civilians are firing on our poor men!" One of the nuns challenged the officer to surround the francs-tireurs, capture them and bring them back. After all, there were seven or eight hundred German soldiers in the village. But the Institute's physician, Dr. Reidemester, was meanwhile examining the body. There was no bullet wound. A "franc-tireur" had murdered his victim with a blow from a bayonet. When the doctor pointed this out to the commandant, he merely shrugged his shoulders.[96]

A short time later a wounded German was brought in. A soldier who had just been remonstrating with the sisters shouted in French to the young major accompanying the stretcher, "It's civilians who shot him, right?"

"No, it's certainly not the civilians," the officer responded brusquely.[97]

The truth, of course was what the nun had been telling the soldier: "The civilians are filled with terror, they're in hiding, and not one among them would fire on the German army."[98]

More shots were fired at 1:15 a.m. near the curé's house. An officer made a pretense of looking out the window. "They've fired again, the *Schweinehunde!*" he announced.

"There are no guns left in Blégny," the curé's servant responded, exasperated.

At 5:00 a.m., the translator was again sent for.

> The sister begged for mercy. The officer replied, "It is a superior order which must be executed." Then the sister asked permission for the curé to say his mass, which was granted. The priest, having shaved, went to say mass in the chapel of the Institute, accompanied by two soldiers. The vicar served. He was astonished by the curé's calm and serene bearing. The orate, fratres, and the prayers after the mass were recited by him in a particularly moving fashion. After the thanksgiving, he went up to the vicar in the choir and demanded absolution, without saying why; he seemed in no way disturbed... [99]

The priest then left the chapel, blessing the sisters. In the presbytery he had a cup of coffee, but declined food. He also refused some money the servant gave him. "I won't be needing it," he told them, though he took some bread and butter and chocolate the woman had brought him.

> The burgomaster and M. Delnooz had also gone home to dress themselves – accompanied by soldiers. They were convinced that they were going to be taken to Liège. The burgomaster had drafted a letter of defense. He returned alone, M. Delnooz having been pardoned, because – so it was said – he was the father-in-law of a doctor who had tended the German wounded.
>
> The curé asked if he might take a book from his study; he took his breviary and another little book. He was weeping and trembling when he was taking his cup of coffee, making his last recommendations.
>
> The burgomaster and the curé, accompanied by the soldiers, left in the direction of the church, where they were joined by the two brothers Haikin...
>
> Having reached the church, they were told: "The carriage for Liège is about to come past...but you do not need to see which way you go." And the Germans bandaged their eyes, placing them with their backs to the church.
>
> They were shot about half past seven... First the two Haikins were executed, then the curé, then M. Ruwet. The curé fell with his face to the ground, upon the two Haikins, and the burgomaster on the curé. The latter was killed instantaneously; a bullet struck him in the forehead, carrying away a piece of the skull as large as a man's hand. [100]

The curé still clutched his rosary.

The town was so terrified it was three hours before anyone dared to retrieve the bodies.

The curé's journal concludes with notes for a sermon he planned to give on Sunday, the 16th, the day he was executed:

> Hold fast to God: not so much so that He may make an end of your woes, but in order that he may seal you of the number of His elect... What matter though we suffer, what

matter though all we possess is taken from us, what matter though we die, provided we are of His number and are triumphant with Christ Jesus in Heaven![101]

THE BURGOMASTER OF WARSAGE When the Germans entered a village or town, they generally demanded to see the burgomaster and the curé. Sometimes these men were taken hostage immediately. In most places they were initially left at their liberty, the better to secure the provisions the Germans required and to assist with arrangements for quartering soldiers. But in nearly all locations they were made responsible for the good behavior of the residents. Their lives hung on the whims of a drunken soldier, the caprice of an officer – or orders from brigade headquarters.

The burgomasters and priests the Germans encountered in Liège ranged widely. As for the latter, the level of education of the Belgian clergy was high, so that although some pastors undoubtedly resembled the sly, ignorant, and self-indulgent curé of anti-clerical propaganda, others had doctorates of divinity from Leuven and were respected, even revered, by their parishioners. The burgomasters were mostly successful grain merchants and cattle dealers or prosperous farmers, and occasionally country lawyers, doctors, or veterinarians. Though undoubtedly competent and amiable, their experience was likely to be somewhat circumscribed and they were overawed and sometimes unnerved by the massive invasion that turned their provincial world upside-down.

In Ferdinand Fléchet, however, the burgomaster of Warsage, the Germans encountered a rather different character. Worldly, fiercely proud, more than a trifle pompous, occasionally feisty and truculent, Fléchet was a mining engineer who had managed major lead, zinc, and silver mines in Germany for several years, and spoke the language fluently. He had represented his district in the Belgian parliament for a quarter of a century and had served as burgomaster for twenty-seven years.[102]

While directing a mine near Dietz, Fléchet had been befriended by Duke Georg of Oldenburg, who occasionally invited him to his shooting parties. They were joined one day by the future Kaiser, then a student at Bonn. Fléchet, even then a colorful character, was seated next to the Prince Imperial at lunch and dinner.

Warsage, the largest town on the road from Aachen to Visé, lies just two and a half miles to the east of the latter. Residents heard distant explosions on the night of August 3rd. The Meuse bridges were being blown. At 8:00 the following morning, the burgomaster located a detachment of Belgian Lancers two miles from town; they told him to expect German troops by that afternoon. But it was only 11:00 a.m. when a cavalry platoon arrived in Warsage. Waiting for them in the middle of the road, wearing his burgomaster's sash, was Ferdinand Fléchet. "I have not the means of preventing you from passing," the burgomaster announced to the officer in charge of the detachment. While soldiers distributed the proclamation, "To the Belgian People," the officer conversed with the burgomaster. Why, he asked, had King Albert declared war on Germany? The Germans had no grudge against the Belgians and only wanted to proceed to Paris. They would be there in eight days.[103]

An hour later the Germans arrived in force, first cyclists and motorcars, then infantry, artillery, more cavalry. Despite the formidable display of force, the Germans seemed nervous. The cyclists and chauffeurs drove with one hand, a pistol clutched in the other.

Fléchet accommodated 150 German soldiers on his extensive grounds. The five officers of the company lodged with him. The burgomaster was a gracious host, and he was thanked profusely. He even fed a couple of famished chauffeurs who showed up the next morning. One was eventually to save his life.

Soldiers and officers lodged at the other substantial homes in town. The 120 men on a large farm outside town left behind a broken rifle and a few cartridges. This was to cost the farmer his home; he was fortunate he didn't also pay with his life. (Once again a German woman, Fraulein Borgoms, a servant, successfully intervened.)

Still more anxious than the troops that initially passed through Warsage was the infantry company that entered the town mid-afternoon on August 6th, shortly after the men who'd been billeted in town had marched westward. These soldiers, with a carbine in one hand and a pistol in the other, circled warily. They were about three hundred strong, and had just been pillaging and burning the village of Berneau, northeast of Warsage. Some civilians had been shot there, allegedly for poisoning the German wounded.

Soon the troops were firing in Warsage as well. Around 1:30 p.m. residents heard an intense fusillade on the Aubel road, east of town. Soldiers

raced into town, firing at windows and roofs. The cause? An officer had
been killed while leading his troops on horseback.

With the help of Fraulein Borgoms, Julien Drèze, a lawyer and provincial councillor, along with the burgomaster's brother, pointed out to officers that the bullet had obviously been fired from below. The entry wound
was beneath the left eye and the bullet had lodged just below the skull, in
the right side of the brain. The Belgians pleaded for a postmortem exam.[104]

The Germans preferred their own methods. The burgomaster's house,
where a number of residents were sheltering, was invaded. *"Hier hat man
geschossen,"* soldiers shouted. When one of the individuals in the house disputed this, he was shown a broken tile on the roof. "Someone is hidden
up there," he was told. The civilian patiently pointed out that the tile was
broken because the roof had been fired on from the street moments earlier.[105]

Now all the residents were ordered out of their homes and assembled in
the square, where the burgomaster tried to reassure them, at the request of
the captain in command. "The tumult was terrible," Fléchet recalled, "you
could not make yourself heard."[106] A half dozen men were seized, including
the burgomaster, and marched off to the nearby German camp at Mouland.
These were the "franc-tireurs." An officer announced that the men would
be executed "if anyone fired again." Providentially, a shot rang out seconds
later and the men were condemned to death.[107]

Troops passing in the opposite direction of the prisoners, who'd been
placed at the head of the column, heaped abuse on the hapless men. They
urged their captors to execute them on the spot.

When they arrived at Mouland, the "francs-tireurs" were made to kneel
in a semi-circle. Other captives had been added to their ranks en route,
including two young girls, the Grensons, whose father had been killed at
Berneau. He had been desperately searching for a missing third daughter.
Then the executions began.

Reflecting on the experience months later, the seventy-three-year-old
burgomaster, safely in the Netherlands, was still incredulous about the
absence of legal formalities: "I declare we were not questioned; they did
not even tell us of what we were accused. So much so that I was absolutely
ignorant that the officer had been killed... So then there was not the smallest
enquiry; no questioning, no investigation!"[108] Six of the younger men were
selected at random at 5:30 p.m., marched fifty yards off and told to remove

their jackets. Their shirts were opened from behind, baring their backs, and the men were shot – amidst "protestations, cries, lamentations, and groans." One of the condemned, Teheux, was retarded. "Are you going to shoot this man, who is simple-minded?" Fléchet demanded. "What has that got to do with me?" an officer responded.[109]

The others were still compelled to kneel. A soldier who spoke French suggested mockingly that they pray to the Virgin Mary to come rescue them. The condemned men were forbidden to speak. But an exception was made for the burgomaster. Having failed to save Teheux, he was determined to familiarize his captors with the other victims. If he could make them see something of the real individual – rather than the bogus "franc-tireur" – it might calm their rage. He began describing the men. Léon Dobblestein, a baker, had spent the last two days baking bread for the Germans. Nestor Galen had been watering the Germans' horses during the same period. Another man was an exemplary father and husband; he walked every day from Warsage to his factory job in Eijsden. The burgomaster rambled on, telling everything he knew about the condemned and patiently disputing the epithets hurled at him. His pedantry no doubt incited the soldiers to further abuse. But the burgomaster persevered. How could the Germans condemn innocent men to death? And how could they treat old men so inhumanely? Five of the captives were at least seventy.

Fléchet went on to talk about himself, his sundry accomplishments, his acquaintance with eminent aristocrats. When he described the hunting party, an officer muttered, *"Der Kerl kann aber lügen"* – the guy sure knows how to lie. The burgomaster drew himself up as best he could in a kneeling position. "Sir," he proclaimed, "I am seventy-three years old and I have never lied, and in spite of the position in which I find myself today, I have no wish to lie, and I will prove it to you." And he proceeded to rattle off the names and titles of the worthies in attendance that day, the attachés of the Prince Imperial, the *Oberförster* who organized and conducted the hunt. The officers and soldiers seemed to listen respectfully, but did not say anything.[110]

His eloquence undiminished, the burgomaster went on to explain exactly what he had done to insure that Warsage remained tranquil and hospitable, and again remonstrated with his captors. He got into a political discussion with officers. The patriotic burgomaster was shocked at their contempt for

King Albert and for Belgium. "These little countries must all be made to disappear," he was told. The burgomaster overcame his indignation and proceeded to detail all that the communal government had done to insure that one and all would "refrain from any hostile manifestation or act."[111]

The parleying ended; the officers moved off. Soldiers then began torturing one of the old men, a pensioner from Berneau. He was accused of cutting off the ears and gouging out the eyes of wounded soldiers; the charges were amplified with each retelling. The man protested that he hadn't as much as seen a wounded German soldier. Without any orders, seven or eight Germans kicked and stomped on the old man, then bound him to the wheel of an ammunition cart and clubbed him with rifle butts. A horse was brought up and lashed until it kicked him. An officer passing by reproached the soldiers: "Are you not ashamed to maltreat a defenseless old man like that?" As soon as the officer left, the torture was resumed.[112] Fléchet could not bear to look, but he heard the old man's agonized cries and groans.

At dawn on the 7th, the prisoners were marched toward Berneau, where a scaffold had been erected – an iron bar attached to two poplars. Six more of the "francs-tireurs" were hanged, after beatings and other torments. (The men had been given nothing to eat or drink since they were made captives. When one prisoner complained of thirst, the soldiers began to drink water in front of him, without giving him any.) Even the hanging was savage. The first victim was raised and lowered by a pulley seven or eight times, his head banging against the iron bar.

The survivors, jabbed by bayonets, were marched on to another location. Three of the old men couldn't keep up and were eventually killed en route, including the burgomaster of Berneau.

But Fléchet was not among them, nor did he witness the hangings. At around 11:00 p.m. on the 6th, he spotted one of the chauffeurs and called him over. "Mr. Burgomaster! What are you doing here?" the man asked.

"I certainly haven't come here for my pleasure," Fléchet replied.[113] The chauffeur told a friend about the burgomaster's generosity and promised to do what he could. A tall non-commissioned officer who overheard their conversation also vowed to help.

Fléchet, however, resigned himself to being shot. He did not suffer the anguish described in novels, he later recalled. The reality was numbing, though he worried about how his family and friends would take the news.

The chauffeur and the sergeant apparently convinced one of their supe-riors to listen again to the burgomaster, and the loquacious Fléchet obliged with another recitation of his story, the biographical sketches of the others, and his responsible actions as burgomaster. The non-commissioned officer listened attentively a few feet away. However, his commander remained stony-faced and mute. But twenty minutes later the senior officer returned and whispered to Fléchet that he was to be imprisoned in Germany. The man was back in a quarter of an hour, and still more amiable. "Mr. Burgomaster, you are free," he told Fléchet, who headed straight for the Dutch border, three hundred yards away.[114]

The burgomaster never found out how much of his good luck he owed to his kindness to the chauffeur and how much he owed to his acquaintance with the Kaiser and other eminent Germans. Perhaps the officers were sim-ply worn down by Fléchet's monologues.

◄◄·►►

Ironically, on August 7th a party of eminent German aristocrats lodged in Warsage, including Prince Frederick Charles of Hesse, Count Jena, Count Wolff Metternich, and the Duke of Reisnitz. Many of the residents had fled to the Netherlands the day before, but several of those who remained expressed their anguish to these distinguished officers. Twenty-five homes had been destroyed and, they feared, more than a dozen villagers had been killed. With the noblesse oblige that would have gratified Ferdinand Fléchet, Count Jena promptly wrote a safe conduct pass permitting all inhabitants to cross over to the Netherlands and Prince Frederick Charles issued an order that no more homes be burned in Warsage.[115]

VISÉ: "LIKE FURIES" Apart from residents of the city of Liège, most Belgians knew little about the Walloon villages that lay just across the Meuse. Perhaps there had indeed been peasants foolish enough to fire on German troops as they'd marched toward the forts. It was hard to get accurate news, even in Liège. But Visé, less than nine miles from the provincial cap-ital, was well known. This charming town, situated on the right bank of the Meuse, was home to a number of middle class families with ties to Liège, some with businesses or practices in the city, including a handful of univer-sity professors.

At the end of May, 1914, the journalist Gustave Somville had walked down the Meuse to Visé with four friends. He addressed them in a reminiscence. The sun was out, he recalled,

and a breeze rippled the green wheat and made the grass shimmer like silk under newly blossomed apple trees... Following the heights on the left of the Meuse, we stopped at the entrance to a village, where a farmhouse raised its broad square of whitewashed buildings, with their high-pitched roofs of purplish slates, on the summit of which weather-cocks turned against the blue sky. Ah, that was a famous farm! There were forty horses... and countless head of beautiful cattle, grazing in the surrounding pastures.

We chatted with the farmer, a wrinkled, gray-haired old fellow. "I'm getting near fourscore years, you know!" he told us; but he was still astonishingly vigorous and jovial.

And then we went to greet the curé, whom we had often met on other occasions... A fellow-priest was there, from a neighboring parish. We accepted his four o'clock coffee and bread and butter. When we left, his colleague, whose handsome and kindly countenance impressed you, took a detour to show us the right path.

You may still recall the vaulted canopy formed by the branches of the splendid elms bordering the wide road. It descends in a gentle slope, almost parallel to the river, which it gradually approaches. From there we could see, on the steeper hills of the right bank, a few châteaux and villas, buried in verdure, their windows reflecting the fiery light of the setting sun.

Finally we came to Devant-le-Pont, that coquettish suburb. From the bridge itself we admired the river, so wide at this point, and so calm that it reduplicated, as in a mirror, the gardens and verandahs of the little town, which rose tier above tier on the right bank.

Well, my friends, all this no longer exists. A few weeks later, and They came swarming in like bandits.

The great farm was burned down, the farmer hacked to pieces by German bayonets. His son was deported, his horses stolen. The presbytery and village of Hermée were destroyed by fire, the curé exiled, his colleague from Heure-le-Romain massacred.

As for the town of Visé, what a horrible fate! ! Apart from one tiny suburb and a college which served the invaders as a hospital, there is nothing left but ruin and solitude. Its five or six hundred houses, its curious old-fashioned dwellings, its Gothic church, its fifteenth century town-hall, its schools and charitable institutions – all, absolutely all, have perished. And of 3,900 inhabitants, how many have survived? No one knows. Six hundred were dragged away to Germany amid the acts of violence, the pretended executions, the spittings and insults to which the Teutonic race is addicted. The others, after suffering weeks of slavery, forced labor, and privation, fled to other countries.[116]

"The Germans arrived in Visé like furies," Abbé Lemmens, the Dean of Visé, recalled. "They believed all the inhabitants, men and women alike,

were armed and prepared to fire on them." All the Visétois were potential cut-throats. The Germans turned homes inside-out looking for arms.
When officers spoke with the Dean, they did so with their revolvers drawn.
The Dean even observed a doctor making his rounds among the wounded
with his pistol drawn. Still on the first day of the invasion, the Dean was
besieged by tired and thirsty soldiers in the Place de l'Église. He showed
them a fountain two steps away. "This water is poisoned," they told him.
Naturally, the Dean proceeded to drink from the fountain, and the soldiers
cautiously followed suit.[117]

⭠⭢

The Germans arrived in Visé a little before 12:30 p.m. on the 4th. Ten minutes later they'd shot their first civilian. He was a Monsieur Istas, a cashier
at the railway station, gunned down as he returned to work after an early
lunch.[118] Within an hour of their arrival, as German soldiers crowded the
Meuse quays, the Belgian troops stationed on the left bank of the Meuse
opened fire across the river. The Germans retreated, then returned in force.
The Belgians had blown the Meuse bridges, and as the sappers began constructing a pontoon bridge, the guns of Pontisse opened up. The Germans
again withdrew from the river.

As always, civilians paid for the successes of the Belgian Army. By evening, more than a dozen corpses littered the streets.[119] Most of the murders
seemed wholly arbitrary. The townspeople groped for explanations. The
Brouhas, father and son, brewers, were dragged out of their basement and
executed in front of their house. When the Germans had arrived in Visé,
they'd encountered a minuscule barricade, unattended, in front of the gen-
darmerie. Among the planks and barrels that it was constructed of was a little beer cart bearing the proprietor's name – Brouha and Son. This was sufficient reason to execute the pair. The Germans dragged the bodies to the
rue de la Fontaine and compelled a crowd gathered in front of the church
to file past the corpses. "You'll meet the same fate if you don't respect the
German Army," they were told.[120]

Elsewhere in town men were gunned down without any pretext. A barber, Louis Kinable, was shot in front of his shop. This franc-tireur had
been caught red-handed with a pair of clippers. An older man, Honoré
Cosmé, was apprehended with his two sons near the train station. They

were compelled to march, with about fifteen others, to the nearby village of
Berneau. Here at the intersection of four roads some of the men were shot,
others hanged, and still others bayoneted. Two civilians, Cosmé claimed,
were buried alive, Leonard Rion and his son. Cosmé's own son was so
battered by German rifle butts that his body could only be identified thanks
to a card from his middle school proclaiming him an honors student. The
father had been rescued by a Dutchman who drove him to a Red Cross
hospital. He died later the same day, August 5th.

Among those who attended him was eighteen-year-old Joseph Meurice,
the son of Visé's burgomaster, Léon-Joseph Meurice, a professor at the
University of Liège. Cosmé, young Meurice recalled, was worried about
his wife, daughters, daughter-in-law, and grandchildren; his son was dead,
he himself was dying. He entrusted the teenager with a small purse in his
jacket pocket containing 600 francs. But when Meurice and a doctor opened
the purse, they discovered it was empty. To console Cosmé, the doctor pretended the money was still there.[121]

Joseph had watched from a window of the family's home as the
Germans entered Visé. He'd already been warned by a friend that a troop
of Death's Head Hussars had murdered a man behind the hospital, for no
apparent reason. (This was Jean Charlier.) The soldiers moved cautiously,
as the young man watched, firing into houses from behind trees, though
they'd encountered no resistance. Belgian soldiers had vacated the town,
and were waiting across the Meuse.

Joseph's mother begged him to come away from the window. He
obliged her and a moment later the pane was shattered by a bullet. Then,
hearing cries of distress from the street, Joseph raced upstairs again, just in
time to see the wife and daughters of Joseph Brouha screaming in terror.
Hussars were chasing the father and son, yelling and laughing. Abruptly
they aimed their rifles and fired on the two men, killing them instantly.[122]

The second time he'd gone to the window, young Meurice had been
lucky that the Germans in the street below had been distracted. When
August Lieutenant, a colliery agent, had walked to his window after hearing a loud noise outside, an infantryman carefully took aim and ordered
him out into the street. Looking out windows was just the sort of thing
franc-tireurs did. Lieutenant was immediately arrested and marched off,
with about two dozen others, to the stables behind the train station. It was

of no consequence that he was unarmed and there were no weapons in his home. At no time was he interrogated; he was never even asked his name. When he pleaded with a sympathetic officer for a trial, the man consulted his superiors and informed Lieutenant that he had already been judged.[123]

Lieutenant was not the last Belgian who would pay for his curiosity. Nor was his acquaintance Gérard Dubois the last pigeon-fancier who would be executed as a spy. The colliery agent spent a harrowing twenty-four hours, but he survived. He was fed soup into which excrement had been dumped, to the amusement of his jailers, denied water, stabbed with a bayonet and was condemned to die, before managing to escape – while his guards were searching for a cloth to use as a blindfold.[124] Soon after the killing of the brewers, the Germans invaded the Meurice house. Joseph and his father were seized. A revolver was pointed at the burgomaster's head. They were conducted to General von Emmich himself, who was conferring with his staff in a meadow by the road to Berneau.

"Civilians have fired on our troops, and you're responsible," the general told Dr. Meurice. The professor hotly denied the charge. German soldiers had not appeared in the town until moments earlier, and no civilians had fired on them. Neither man was apparently aware of the skirmish that had taken place at the southern end of town between German sentries and cyclists and the Belgian border guards. When Von Emmich insisted that his soldiers had been killed, Professor Meurice pointed out to him that Belgian forces occupied Devant-le-Pont, across the river, and may well have engaged the invaders. Von Emmich didn't press the point, but ordered the burgomaster to issue a proclamation to the residents that if any firing occurred, the town would be set ablaze.[125]

Fires had already been lit, however. When, on their return to town, the Meurices asked where the fire brigade was, they were told it had been forbidden to intervene.

During the first twenty-four hours of occupation, the Germans had succeed in terrorizing Visé. When he was compelled to circulate through the town to reassure the population and urge calm, Dean Lemmens found everyone fearful and depressed. For a gathering he convened at 8:00 that evening, the church was filled to capacity; among the crowd, the Dean could not refrain from observing, were many parishioners that he had not seen there in years.[126]

The violence subsided during the following days. The Germans seemed now to be distinguishing between the actions of the Belgian army, which had pulled back to the center of the country on the 7th, from those of the cowed civilians. In contrast, on the first day of the invasion, upon arriving at the convent of the Sisters of Notre Dame, the Germans had tried to get the mother superior to admit that it was the curé who had ordered the destruction of the bridge.[127] (The Germans were convinced that priests routinely issued orders to soldiers. Father Labeye in Blégny, it will be recalled, was accused of stationing troops in his church and installing a telephone to link up with Army Headquarters.)

There remained a few hostages in Visé, eventually reduced to only the dean and the burgomaster, who were intermittently threatened and abused. And during the first few days, scores of men were compelled to clear roads, fill trenches, and remove barbed wire. A group of captives was told at one point that if the work wasn't completed in twenty minutes, the town would be machine-gunned. Otherwise an uneasy peace prevailed until the 10th, when the church in the center of town was destroyed. Its slender Gothic spire, along with the bulbous clock tower of the Hôtel de Ville, made for a distinctive skyline. Joseph Meurice witnessed the destruction. A soldier rapped on the door of the family home in the afternoon and ordered the burgomaster's son to turn over to him the key to the church, with which he had been entrusted. When the student asked why it was needed, he was told that the tower was going to be blown up. An officer had claimed that the tower was being used by the gunners at Fort Pontisse to direct their fire. The soldier who'd been despatched to get the key expressed his regret; these were his orders. As would happen elsewhere, the operation was bungled. The entire church caught fire and burned to the ground. Some of the contents of the church were saved, and a few German soldiers even assisted the residents in rescuing items.[128]

By the middle of the month the hussars had come and gone, followed by pioneers from Köln. The 15th was the last night in town for the Köln regiment; they were to depart for the front the next morning. That evening there was a great deal of drinking and carousing, and renewed pillaging. At about 11:00 p.m., a furious fusillade rang out. Machine guns briefly opened fire. The barrage lasted only about fifteen minutes, however. Then the *Aktion* commenced.

The two hostages, the Dean and the burgomaster, were housed in a tent, where several officers slept beside them. It was raining that night, and the tent leaked. The water dripping onto Abbé Lemmens's blanket made it impossible to sleep. When the firing began, the officers woke up, but didn't budge; they appeared not in the least alarmed. The gunfire intensified a few minutes later and they sauntered outside, but returned immediately and lay down again.

"What's going on?" asked the Dean.

"They're shooting at us," an officer replied nonchalantly.

Reflecting back on the incident, the Dean had no doubt the "franc-tireur attack" had been prearranged by officers of the Köln regiment.[129]

Meanwhile, residents were chased out of their homes and herded to the square in front of the station. One man recalled what happened after hearing the burst of gunfire.

> I dressed hastily, as did my wife and daughters. While they were doing this, I opened the door to soldiers who were knocking on it with the butts of their rifles. A sergeant told me brutally that I had to leave; they were going to burn my house. I called to my wife and daughter. The moment I came out onto to street, I saw other soldiers shoot one of my neighbors, who fell to the sidewalk. "Why did you kill this good, honest man?" I asked a sergeant.
>
> "Because he fired on us!" the sergeant replied. He appeared very enraged, like all the soldiers.
>
> "He couldn't have fired, because he didn't have a gun." "He's holding a revolver in his hand."
>
> I approached the body and saw that the man was holding a wooden pipe. "Look," I told the sergeant. "It's only a pipe."
>
> This little discussion probably saved my life, because the gunfire continued...

On all sides one heard the victims cry out in anguish and misery.[130]

The women and children were separated from the men and brought to the plaza in front of the College of St. Hadelin. Hearing the cries of the terrified women and children, Abbé Frits Goffin, director of the College, went down to find out what was going on. One of the women, carrying a three-day-old baby in her arms, begged him to intervene with the Germans. Father Goffin, who had been fired on by German soldiers as he attempted to give last rites to the dying border guards, approached an officer and asked if he could offer asylum to the women and children. The officer brusquely refused, and ordered the priest to "Tell those wild beasts that if anyone touches a hair of a German soldier, I'm going to have five hundred men and five hundred women killed."

When Abbé Goffin did not respond, the officer barked, "Didn't you understand?" The priest remained mute, and the officer ordered, "Tell them what I told you to say, or I'll make an example of you."

Father Goffin turned to the women and said, "I'm obliged to warn you that if you fire on German soldiers, measures of reprisals will be taken. But be assured this won't happen."

The priest then went about trying to obtain German approval for the women and children to take refuge in the rooms of the College. When officers turned their backs on him or shrugged their shoulders, he announced that if he didn't receive an authorization within five minutes, he would take upon himself the responsibility for sheltering the refugees.

Five minutes elapsed, and he called out, "*Entrez*!" No one budged. Finally, after several more times, some women began filing into the College. Everyone followed. About fifteen minutes later, the abbé heard the roaring and crackling of an enormous fire. Flames raged around the College. Most of the town, however, would not be set ablaze until the following morning.[31]

Meanwhile, the men who had been gathered in front of the railway station were herded down route de Mouland. But they were returned to Place de la Station early the next morning. They would be interned in Germany, as had been originally planned. But first there would be a lesson.

The assembled men were compelled to watch the execution of Désiré Duchesne, a sixty-six-year-old plasterer, amiable, well liked and respected. He was accused of killing two officers. Duchesne had done no such thing, but the Germans were doubly confused as to his identity. They kept referring to him as "the major." This, in fact, was the soubriquet of a hotel owner named Quaden. However, it was not this individual, but a second hotel owner, Michaux, who the Germans had determined was guilty of the foul deed.

Outside the Hôtel Michaux the Germans had rigged up a device they were quite proud of: a little bell placed on a pole in front of the condemned man. It was to be rung as a signal to the execution squad. Photos were taken of it. In the presence of the men assembled in the square, Duchesne was bound to one of the acacias in front of the hotel, a soldier rang the bell, and the execution squad fired. Duchesne slumped to the ground, riddled by twelve bullets. There had been no trial, needless to say.

The execution squad withdrew and an officer rode up on horseback, drained his champagne bottle with a flourish, and hurled it at the crumpled body. (For many weeks afterward the Germans continued to deny that they had shot Désiré Duchesne. But after several personnel changes in the Kommandantur, abbé Goffin obtained permission to exhume the body, and clearly established the victim's identity.)[132]

Suddenly, just after the antics of the officer on horseback, a shot rang out. Naturally, the unarmed, terrified civilians were accused of firing. Luckily, one soldier indignantly rebuked the soldier standing next to him for having discharged his gun.[133]

Then troops began systematically setting fire to the entire town. The Germans were thorough and efficient.

> I saw commissioned officers directing and supervising the burning. It was done systematically with the use of benzine spread on the floors and then lighted. In my own and another house I saw officers before the burning come in, with their revolvers in their hands, and have china, valuable antique furniture, and other such things removed. This being done, the houses were by their orders set on fire. On the morning of 15th August, two officers inspected my house, and finding there were things worth taking, they wrote and signed a paper directing the house to be spared and pinned it on the door. Then when the valuables had been removed, the place was burned down. I took the paper off the door and preserved it.[134]

Bart Mokveld, a courageous young Dutch journalist, the newly minted war correspondent for *De Tijd,* Amsterdam's Catholic daily, had already visited the town under occupation and had been impressed by the submissiveness of the residents. He returned on the morning of the 16th.

> I shall never forget that sight. The Meuse separated me from the raging blaze on the opposite bank. The flames roared violently, roofs and rafters and walls crashed down, and the wood of living trees was burning and screeching loudly. I saw only a sea of fire, one glaring glow, and the air was scorchingly hot. A light breeze blew through the place, and made clouds of smoke whirl through the streets like avalanches of snow...
>
> The wind seemed to play with the smoke, rolling dense volumes down the slopes, which dispersed only when they reached the bank along the river. While the flames soared high up from the roofs, the walls of the houses still stood erect, and everywhere in the windows one saw those miserable little white flags, symbols of submission, mute prayers that submission should be rewarded by sparing the lives and possessions of the inhabitants...[135]

Undeterred by the smoke and heat, Mokveld decided to return to Lixhe and cross the river on the pontoon bridge to explore the devastated town. En route he encountered a German civilian who identified himself as an editor of the *Kölnische Zeitung*. Like so many of the Germans Mokveld encountered, the editor heaped praise on the Netherlanders, making invidious comparisons with the treacherous Belgians – as if they hadn't desired as fervently as the Dutch to remain neutral. When Mokveld at last turned the conversation to the burning city, the man looked across the river at it casually, then exploded with a torrent of abuse against the population. He had no specific information, the reporter noted. Someone had simply claimed that civilians were shooting, and that sufficed.

Mokveld crossed the river and made his way back down to Visé.

> The whole town was like a sea of fire. The Germans, who are nothing if not thorough, even in the matter of arson, had worked out their scheme in great detail. In most houses they had poured some benzine or paraffin on the floor, put a lighted match to it, and thrown a small black disc, the size of a farthing, on the burning spot, and then immediately the flames flared up with incredible fury. I do not know the constituents of this particular product of "Kultur."
>
> Nor did I see any inhabitants in the burning town. It was practically impossible to stay in the streets; burning walls and roofs and gutters crashed down with a great noise, so that the streets were as much on fire as the houses themselves. Only at the crossings were any soldiers to be seen, who, in various stages of intoxication, constantly aimed at the burning houses, and shot everything that tried to escape from the burning stables and barns: pigs, horses, cows, dogs, and so on.
>
> Suddenly I saw a boy about twelve years old in one of the burning streets. He waved his arms, rushed madly to and fro, calling for his father and mother, and his brother and sisters. He was in danger of perishing in the fire or being killed by the murderous bullet from a rifle. I ran after him, laid hold of him, and in spite of his resistance pulled him back. Fortunately I met a couple of kind, sober soldiers to whom I told the story, and who promised to send the boy away from the burning town.
>
> Shortly afterward I met a Dutch Red Cross motor-car. The male nurses, who had met me already on former occasions during the war, recognized me, rushed up to me, and forced me to come with them to the car. ...They tried to explain, with a torrential flow of words, that I exposed myself to the greatest danger by coming here, as nearly all the soldiers were drunk, shot at every civilian, and so on.
>
> They insisted on my staying near the car...[136]

Mokveld didn't follow their advice. He continued into town and soon encountered a small group of refugees, "carrying as usual their miserable parcels in which they had hurriedly collected the things that had the least value. As they saw me they shuddered and shivered and crept closer together. Most of them wept and sobbed and their faces were twisting nervously."[137] Mokveld explained who he was and urged them to cross over into the Netherlands at Eijsden. They were afraid they would be turned back, as they were penniless, but Mokveld assured them they would be welcomed and cared for. Just then a cavalry patrol approached, "the men tipsy and their seat rather unstable.

Seeing the refugees, they aimed their rifles at them and roared, "Hands up!" The poor creatures not only put up their hands, but fell on their knees, and muttered incoherent words. The women folded their hands, and stretched them out to the cavalry, as if praying for mercy. The soldiers looked at the scene for a moment, burst out in a harsh laughter, spurred on their horses, and raced on without a word. Two of them stopped near me. I gave them, however, no time for threats, but quickly showed them the old pass to Visé. As soon as they saw the German writing they said: "All right!" and went off.

I came now to the western boundary of the town, where the streets slope gently towards the bank of the Meuse. Here I had an atrociously fantastic view of the burning mass of houses. I fell in with a crowd of dead-drunk soldiers, who first handed my papers on from the one to the other, but as soon as they understood that I was a Netherlander they showed no hostility.

They sang and shouted and waved their arms. Most of them carried bottles full of liquor, which they put to their mouths frequently, smashed them on the ground, or handed them to their comrades, when unable to drink any more themselves. Each of a troop of cavalry had a bottle of pickles, and enjoyed them immensely.

Other soldiers kept on running into the burning houses, carrying out vases, pictures, plate or small pieces of furniture. They smashed everything on the cobblestones and then returned to wreck more things that would have been destroyed anyway by the fire. It was a revelry of drunken vandalism. They seemed mad, and even risked being burned alive at this work of destruction. Most of the officers were also tipsy; not one of them was saluted by the soldiers.

The beastly scenes which I witnessed in the glaring, scorching heat benumbed me, and I looked on vacantly for a long time. At last I went back and called at St. Hadelin College, the Head of which I had visited already once or twice. The building was still undamaged.

As soon as the Reverend Head, Dr. Frits Goffin, saw me he burst out sobbing, and, taking me by the hand, speechless, he pressed it a long time. I myself was also quite dumb. At length he muttered:

"Could you ever have thought...that...that...such...a cruel...fate would overwhelm us? What crime did these poor people commit? Have we not given all we had? Have we not strictly obeyed their commands? Have we not done more than they asked for? Have we not charitably nursed their wounded in this House? Oh! They profess deep gratitude to me. But...why then? There is nothing left in the House for the aged refugees whom we admitted, for the soldiers we nurse; our doctor has been made a prisoner and taken away, and we are without medical help. There is nothing for the Sisters and myself, but all these unfortunate creatures... they must have food..."

The excellent man went on weeping, and I was not able to console him and did not know what to say. He took my arm, and led me to the large common hall, where twenty wounded Germans lay, who had been hit in the fight for the forts. He went to one bed after the other, and, with tears in his eyes, asked each man how he felt, and inquired, "Are you...properly...cared for...here? Are you?" The sick men turned round, their eyes beamed, and they stammered words full of gratitude. Others said nothing, but took the Head's hand and pressed it warmly.[138]

While the town burned, most of the men who had been rounded up and made to watch the execution of Duchesne were en route to Germany. They were dispatched in two groups of about three hundred each; 627 Visétois were deported in all. The first group left around nine. They were made to walk to Gemmenich, where they were loaded onto cattle cars and taken to Munsterlager. The second group left in the afternoon and were compelled to walk all the way to Aachen. Here they were taken to the train station, where they were assaulted by a mob of German civilians who had been invited to view the franc-tireurs. They were spat at, slapped, poked, and threatened by the enraged crowd. They were transported to Munsterlager, but then sent back to Celles, eventually being interned at Kassel.[139]

Two of the residents imprisoned in Munsterlager provided detailed descriptions of what they'd experienced.

We were taken away on the 15th of August;[they actually left the following morning] there were three hundred of us, and we did not know what they wanted with us. Three hundred more were to leave the following day. We reached Gemmenich on the evening of the 16th. There the soldiers were ordered to load their rifles. We expected to be shot. We were all seated in a semicircle, in a meadow, with rifles pointed at us. Then they suddenly forced us to stand up, striking us on the head, in the chest, with their rifle butts... It was 9 o'clock. We were taken to the railway station and we left by train at 11 o'clock. We passed through Aachen, Köln, Bochum, Osnabrück... I don't know what other places.

We were on our feet, famished, overwhelmed with fatigue, packed into cattle trucks. The only food we had was a bowl of soup given us in a station near Bremen.

We reached the Munster camp on the 18th, at 4 in the morning. We remained in the station, still without food, until 3 in the afternoon. Finally half of us were given a little coffee, bread, and some potatoes. The distribution of food was not continued: the rest were left hungry. On the 19th, at 7 o'clock in the morning, these last received the same small meal in turn, but the first half were not given breakfast.[140]

The Germans, however, did take care to vaccinate the prisoners.

Then, on the 21st, we were installed in the stables of the camp, where there was a litter of straw which for months was never renewed. There we lived, miserably. We were terribly hungry till the 23rd of September, after which date those whose money had not been stolen could obtain sausages, etc., at a high price, in the canteen. They shared with the others.

In the first barracks were the townsfolk of Leuven; in the second and third, those of Visé; in another, 400 Russian students of the University of Liège, etc.

I remember some of the Visé people died: Urbain Dodémont, Eugène Labeye, Jean Lambrecht. Several became insane.[141]

On October 19, 1914, the older men and children were permitted to return to Belgium. After half a year of imprisonment, it was the turn of the Flemish. One Visé resident remaining in Munsterlager speculated that their release was ordered because the Germans either

wanted to humor the population of the provinces of Antwerp and Limburg, which they hope to retain, or because they hoped to cause dissension between Walloons and Flemings.

The Visé people are often called to the Kommandantur, where they try to make them admit that civilians fired on the troops. To all their denials the commandant replies that the testimony of a thousand civilians would not prevail against that of a single officer. The Germans, however, must have been impressed to see 600 people of all backgrounds resigning themselves to suffer a harsh captivity for eight months, when one word would have set them free...

When a new inquisitor interrogated the prisoners recently, he was surprised to learn that Visé was not destroyed at the time of the invasion, but that the inhabitants had been living for ten days with the soldiers preceding the more than suspicious incident which served as a pretext for the destruction of the town.[142]

Needless to say, no charges were ever filed against any individual for the fifteen-minute barrage of gunfire on August 15th. In finally releasing the captives eight months after their removal to Germany, the Germans were implicitly acknowledging the groundlessness of the accusations.

Even the destruction of Visé, the kidnaping of 627 residents and the dispersal of the remainder, mostly to the Netherlands, did not end the violence in the canton. A credible witness in Devant-le-Pont across the Meuse recounted the following incident:

At the beginning of September, M. Roebroeck, junior, a farmer of Wonk, went with two farm-servants to reap the grain on a hill. The Germans had forbidden access to these elevated points, but the three were unaware of this. They were captured by cavalrymen, who tied their bound hands to their saddles, and made off at a sharp trot. They were seen to go by at Devant-le-Pont, their tongues hanging out, their eyes bulging from their heads, the blood flowing from ears and nose. The prisoners were thus dragged by their executioners, without a halt, as far as Lixhe, where they were shot. The families did not know till long afterwards what had become of them. When the victims were exhumed they could be identified only by their clothing; their faces were unrecognizable...[143]

◄‹··›►

"It might be Pompeii," wrote Brand Whitlock. Somville, too, had titled his chapter on Visé, "A New Pompeii." A friend of the American Minister, born in Visé, had returned to the town after the Germans left, and provided him a detailed description.

> Those ruins might have lain there for centuries. There is not a living thing there. The devastation, the destruction are absolute, the silence complete; it is the very abomination of desolation – a mass of brick and stone and charred beams, crumbling white facades, whose windows, their casements blackened by fire, stare like the hollow sockets of skulls. Of the four thousand inhabitants, not one is there, not a house is standing, not a roof remains. The taverns, where the people used to go in joyous bands to eat of the famous roast goose, are heaps of cinders; the very trees in their gardens, under whose boughs the youth of Liège used to dance the cramignon, have been burned. The scaling walls of the church tremble in the wind, the roof has fallen in; the towers with their bells, the organs, the statues, have tumbled into bits. The work that would have required ages was accomplished by German organization in a night.[144]

"'Since there is nothing left with which to begin life anew,'" Whitlock's friend told him, "'let the city be preserved as it is – a holy necropolis and a shrine; a monument to the implacable ferocity of German "Kultur."'"[145]

Reflecting back on his time in Visè, Bart Mokveld concluded, "I left burning Visè deeply impressed by the savage scenes I had witnessed: men turned into beasts by drink, passion, and anger, doing all manner of wrong to the wretched inhabitants; but the impression became deeper by the great contrast: the perfect, charitable devotion of a virtuous priest... Never have I experienced so many emotions in one day as at Visè."[146]

WANDRE: A GERMAN EMPIRICIST Though Belgium patrols engaged squads of uhlans as they rode westward, only when the Germans approached the Meuse did the Belgium 3rd Division launch counterattacks between the forts. One of the deadliest clashes for the Germans, more costly than the barrage that had welcomed the invaders to Visé, took place at Rabozée, on the heights above Wandre, where troops were attempting to descend along the right bank of the Meuse to Liège. Miners' cottages dotted the slopes behind Wandre, now a suburb of the metropolis. And after the battle of Rabozée ended, it was the miners who paid.

On August 5, as German troops climbed a small hill before the hamlet, they were met by murderous fire from a long trench at right angles to the road. The Germans kept coming, running over and around the dead, then falling in heaps where the machine-guns caught them. Several hundred soldiers were ordered to cross the meadow to the left of the road to enfilade the trench. They were carrying machine guns. The Belgians had anticipated the move. Troops concealed in a second trench at the back of the meadow abruptly opened fire on the swarming Germans. Over 400 were cut down on the meadow alone, where they were eventually buried.[147]

The Belgians fell back on Barchon, leaving behind 135 dead. The curé of the nearby parish of St. Remy, along with a socialist *échevain* from Wandre, Jean Brand, crisscrossed the battlefield, carefully collecting and identifying the personal effects of the Belgian soldiers to send back to their families: papers, photos, medallions, watches, pocket knives, etc. The items were wrapped in the dead man's handkerchief and ticketed. The bundles were carefully packed in sacks and deposited in the Wandre police station with an inventory of the articles. But when the Germans entered the town, they broke into the police station, stole what they wanted from among the bundles, and destroyed the rest.[148]

◄─►

The Germans waited ten days (so often the magic number) to revenge the losses at Rabozée. The attack had nothing to do with the resistance of the eastern forts: Barchon had surrendered on the 8th, Evegnée three days later, and Fléron on the 14th. The 15th, of course, was the day Visé was burned and the curé and burgomaster of Blégny executed. The village of Barchon had been razed the day before – twenty-six men and women had been slaughtered in a place called Les Communes. Five young women were led off to the German camp to be gang-raped. Credible witnesses observed German soldiers firing off their rifles as a pretext to loot, rape, and murder.[149]

On the 15th a new regiment arrived in town, the 52nd infantry. With them was a general and his staff. A tiny, elderly man with spiky moustaches and a choleric complexion, the general demanded fresh requisitions

– there had been two rounds already – and quarter for one thousand men. At around 7:30 p.m., as the burgomaster, forty-year-old Michel Houge, worked to carry out the general's orders, some soldiers rushed into the headquarters and an animated discussion ensued. The general emerged apoplectic with rage. "Our troops have been fired on. Come with me." He shook the burgomaster by the shoulders. "You're going to see that we know how to teach a lesson."[150]

The commander, his staff, the soldiers and the burgomaster strode off to rue Bois-la-Dame, a winding street that climbed a hill on the eastern edge of town. The residents were nearly all miners. Earlier, a woman who lived on the street had observed a soldier furtively squeeze off a shot from his rifle while it was still slung over his shoulder. The houses in the vicinity were immediately sprayed with bullets. Now, as he approached, Houge saw that sixteen men had been lined up against one of the houses, surrounded by soldiers. It was a horrible scene. The wives, mothers, sisters, and daughters of the men had gathered around the troops, some clutching small children. They were crying, praying, and beseeching the Germans. Some grabbed at the soldiers' clothes as they pleaded and were kicked or struck with rifle butts. "Monsieur Burgomaster, we've done nothing," the men shouted at him when they spotted him. The curé, M. Depaquier, was expostulating with the troops.

Houge first asked permission to conduct the women and children to a place where they wouldn't be able to see what was happening. He returned and began arguing heatedly with the Germans. All weapons had been confiscated on the 10th; the Germans themselves had supervised the operation. No one would consider firing on troops after the massacre in Barchon and the killings that had already taken place in town – for several men had been shot at random. And no German soldier had been hit in the "franc-tireur" attack.

In response to the pleas of the burgomaster and curé, two men were released who lived furthest away from the house the Germans claimed the shot had come from. The remaining fourteen were lined up, the general himself shouted the order, and the men were gunned down. As so often happened, whether intentionally or not, the aim of the execution squad was poor. A number of the victims were only wounded. But a group of soldiers rushed up to finish off the survivors. They attacked the wounded with sickening savagery. Men were beaten to a pulp, stomachs were slashed open, fingers cut off.[51]

A second massacre took place the following morning. Eight men were seized at 6:00 a.m. from the village of Chefneux, outside Rabozée. One was released; one was permitted to escape by a soldier who had lodged with him. The remaining six victims were dragged first to a café, then to a meadow called Pré-Clusin, where they were tied to a wire fence – an unusual precaution – and then shot.[52]

⊸⊷⊶

Scenes like these were repeated all over the province during the opening days of the war, and then again after the 14th, but a third mass killing in Wandre two days later, on the 18th, had an unusual outcome.

Houge was again in his office discussing requisitions with still another regimental commander when gunfire erupted outside the building. The burgomaster raced into the street, along with his translator and sometime political rival, Jean Brand. Five men were slumped in front of a gate by the tram stop, and another lay across the road. The men had been taken as hostages by German troops reconnoitering the area. If anyone fired on the troops, the men were told, they would be shot. But no one did, and they were released with a safe conduct pass at the Wandre bridge. However, a patrol on the other side of the bridge immediately re-arrested the men, tore up their passes and proceeded to shoot them on the spot. According to witnesses, one man, Jean Theunissen, made a dash for freedom, but was gunned down in a doorway across the street. Another victim circled round and round until he fell.[53]

Only two of the victims were dead, however, Amadée Crout, 22, and thirteen-year-old Léon Herveaux. But the soldiers were about to finish off the wounded. Houge, vividly recalling the grisly scene in rue Bois-la-Dame, shouted desperately at the troops. And then a miracle happened. A German officer strode up and ordered the soldiers to lower their rifles. He was Lieutenant Welcke of the 77th Infantry Regiment. More remarkable still, he then followed the two Belgians back into the office and began remonstrating with the other officers. He had walked around the town for several days, he told them, armed only with a cane. The population had impressed him with their calmness and dignity. Not content with upbraiding the officers, who were from a different regiment, Welcke went back outside and collared the sergeant who had ordered the shooting. From where had his men been fired on? the lieutenant demanded. The victims were unarmed. The sergeant first pointed to one building, then changed his mind and indicated a second. The lieutenant, accompanied by Brand and Houge, investigated. The house was unoccupied and there was no evidence anyone had been inside recently. Welcke was told by a girl from the neighborhood that some time earlier the house next door to the one the sergeant pointed out had been struck by a bullet fired from the heights above Wandre – but this was hardly grounds to execute six civilians who had been out of town with a German patrol at the time. Accounts are garbled as to what happened next, but apparently the humiliated sergeant ran off. He was from a different regiment, the 110th. Welcke chased after him, yelling, "You need to answer!"[154]

When the three men re-entered the Kommandantur, Welcke was incensed to discover several doctors lounging around. He ordered them to attend to the victims still lying in the street.

While there are other instances of Germans rescuing Belgians during the invasion, there are no reports of any soldier or officer acting as decisively and energetically as Welcke. Who was Welcke? How did he acquire so distinctive a set of values?

WANDRE: THE PIG Nearly every Belgian in the eastern provinces had relatives or friends who had suffered at the hands of the Germans in August. Everyone heard accounts of the tortures, rapes, and killings, of towns destroyed and the men sent off to camps in Germany. The indignation and grief were leavened, however, by stories told at the expense of the Germans – stories that mocked Teutonic obtuseness, paranoia, and vulgarity. The Liégeois made invidious comparisons between the Germans and themselves.

> Physically the two types are familiar: the Liégeois is generally slender, wiry, with the head rather small than otherwise; an obstinate head, with angular features, lit up by the vivacity of the glance and the irony of the smile; while the German is thick-set, powerful, but heavy, his coloring porcine and his features congealed in an expression of incurable pretension. Morally, the contrast is even more marked.[155]

The culinary outrages committed by the Germans were commented on frequently, and were a source of grim amusement. In Herve, villagers spotted a group of soldiers pouring various wines – bordeaux, burgundies, champagne – into a bucket, dipping their bowls in and drinking. Elsewhere in town – and this excited nearly as much indignation – they were seen drinking cognac from the bottle.[156]

Occasionally an individual German came along who was the object of derision. Private Knappmann helped restore a measure of *amour-propre* to Wandre.

> In the beginning, when the nocturnal battle on the Rabozée hillside was being so hotly and murderously contested, he concealed himself in the pigsty of a Madame Gordenne. When the woman came to feed her pigs in the morning, she discovered the German, who addressed her thus: "Me no want fight no more, not go to war no more, take my weapons."
>
> "No thank you!" retorted the woman.
>
> With which she closed the door and pushed the bolt.
>
> Two neighbors, being warned, came to liberate the soldier; he surrendered his arms to them, and informed them that he was wounded in the shoulder; he had, he assured them, tumbled off a wagon, and was suffering acutely.
>
> He was taken to the Red Cross, where the physician discovered that he was absolutely sound. Nevertheless, he somehow contrived to loiter about the hospital and in the village. Later the Germans entrusted him with the task of tending the cattle, which were herded in the meadows in large numbers after the beginning of the siege. And the people of Wandre used to say: "There's our Gordenne's swine – he's been promoted – he's become a cowherd!"
>
> Later on Knappmann was involved in making requisitions. People were at the mercy of the "pig," and it often rested with him whether they were or were not subjected to annoyance. In civil life, he claimed, he had been a law student.
>
> One day, in the café, he began to boast. "What is left you of your Belgium? Three square yards!"
>
> "Why," said an inhabitant of Wandre, "that's just the area of a pigsty!"
>
> Knappmann looked at the clock, and took his departure with the air of a man in a hurry, while the company burst out laughing.
>
> About the 5th of December the Germans began to gather up the shirkers on every side, and our poor Knappmann was sent to Liège. "He'd best look out for himself," said a villager. "This is the season for killing them!"[157]

LIÈGE: THE LIBRARY AND THE JEWS Of all the public buildings in the city of Liège, the Germans perversely picked the university and its surrounding neighborhood to billet most of the troops assigned to the city.

The central building was converted into a dormitory. Straw twenty inches deep covered the floor. Even the library was requisitioned. "One hall served as a boot store; another as a slaughter-house; the periodical room and the photographic studio became stables; urine was trickling everywhere."[158] Bales of straw were stored as well in the library's stacks. The librarian, M. Brassinne, watched in despair as drunken soldiers lit cigarettes as they lounged among the bales. "It was a miracle our rich holdings didn't share the same fate as Leuven's," wrote History Professor Eugène Hubert after the war.[159]

The library contained a valuable collection of art, manuscripts, and incanabula bequeathed by Baron Wittert. The contents were housed in several halls, and the doors were carefully sealed when the Germans entered the city. Soldiers nonetheless contrived to enter the rooms, and officers were appealed to. They promised to protect the collection. However, there were more depredations. Again there were protests, more promises were made, but this time the commander adopted the simpler expedient of denying the staff access to the rooms. Librarians nonetheless managed to enter the hall, and found drawers flung open, the contents ransacked, books and manuscripts flung about and soiled. Furniture, exquisite oriental carpets, rare pieces of glazed pottery, silver and copper goblets, bowls, and candle-holders were all missing. (An inventory of the Wittert Collection later revealed that more than thirty paintings and miniatures had disappeared, along with sixteen porcelain vases, twenty-two bronze vases, four Chinese tapestries, two Oriental carpets – more than one hundred items altogether.)[160] In other parts of the university, valuable laboratory instruments were also stolen, and at least thirty were maliciously destroyed.[161]

A group of professors protested to the authorities. They were received by Counts von Pukler and von Hasfield, who told them that "if articles had been carried off, it could not be by the soldiers, who were not interested in matters of art and science, nor by the officers, who were above suspicion. It must have been the work of the Jewish antiquarian dealers of Liège."[162]

◄◄·►►

The director of the Breslau library had an opportunity to inspect the Liège library in early 1917. Making excuses for the thievery and vandalism to his Belgian hosts, he was nonetheless worried about the bad publicity that had resulted. Writing to his superiors, Dr. Milkau accused the staff of wishing to preserve the library in its present state "as a striking monument to

German barbarism." He suggested that it might not be a bad idea to put things in order and return some of the stolen items.[163]

LIÈGE: PLACE DE L'UNIVERSITÉ German troops first entered Liège on August 7th. The city enjoyed its ten days of relative calm, and then some. Liège residents wondered if the reports they had heard from the eastern part of the province weren't exaggerated. On August 20th, the Germans enlightened them.

Two days earlier, ninety-four soldiers of the 29th reserve regiment had been installed in a building in the middle of the block of houses facing the university, at 16 Place de l'Université.

The first floor of this building consisted of a large hall leased by the Société d'Emulation. Except for the concierge and her two sons, seventeen and twenty, number 16 was otherwise unoccupied. It was owing to the escape of the two young men, Arthur and Marcel Delhougne, and their mother, that it is possible to reconstruct the beginning of the incident, for it was from the Emulation Building that the firing began. Soldiers had been assigned to a couple of other residences on the block, numbers 3 and 5, and to the Communal College on a side street, rue des Croisiers. The bulk of the Germans in Liège, though, were lodged across the triangular-shaped Place, in the buildings of the university itself, and in those of the medical school just across the Meuse.

On the morning of the 20th, six machine guns were brought to the ground floor of the Emulation Building. That evening, many of the soldiers billeted there were listening to a performance by the regiment's head cook, in happier days a tenor with the Imperial Theater of Düsseldorf. Two officers arrived at the end of the concert, and demanded that the program be repeated. Around 9:00 p.m. (Central – German – time), a first lieutenant entered abruptly. The music stopped. The officers present were summoned to an ad hoc conference in the foyer outside the hall.

The soldiers had been drinking heavily the past two evenings. In nearby rue des Croisiers, where another large detachment of troops was lodged, soldiers had looted the wine cellars of two abandoned residences, both owned by doctors. The men fared even better at the mansion of Baron d'Otreppe, in rue des Carmes, where the pillaging was more systematic and supervised by officers. Outside the hôtel d'Otreppe, shortly before

the firing began, witnesses saw several officers so drunk that they were
unable to mount their horses. At the Communal College, where soldiers
and n.c.o.s were drinking around tables at the rear of the building, another
witness heard a German proclaim, "Something is going to happen tonight.
We've got to have women or there'll be trouble." "There's going to be
quite a ruckus this evening," another soldier predicted.[164]

Back in the Emulation Building, the officers returned to the main hall
and, oddly, ordered the men who'd been listening to the concert to remove
their boots and lie down in the large hall. At 10:20, another set of commands
was issued. The soldiers put their boots back on and raced around all the
floors of the building, brandishing hatchets and smashing furniture. Shortly
afterward, about 10:45, a shot rang out from the 2nd floor of the building.
The structure was illuminated, and a witness living in the Place Cockerill,
kitty-corner from the rue d'Université, Charles Marchal, clearly saw a gun
firing out the 2nd floor window. This was followed by a brief fusillade. [165]

Hearing the single shot, Henri Fléron, a waiter at Café des Maraichers
on Place Cockerill, rushed to the window and saw three or four German
soldiers firing at the other restaurant on the block, Café Charpentier. The
square was otherwise deserted; the Liégeois scrupulously observed the
8:00 p.m. curfew.[166]

Moments after the initial gunshot, soldiers poured out of the Emulation
Building and the Communal College. They were joined in the Place
d'Université by troops from the university buildings. An intense barrage
followed the first shots at the windows of Café Charpentier, directed at the
other shops in the row of buildings across from the university, flanking the
Emulation Building. When Fléron went to the window a second time, he
saw soldiers surging through the square, running in all directions, yelling
and firing. Machine guns were set up in the Place and the rue des Croisiers,
and their rapid ticking joined the crackling rifle fire and the shouting of
officers and men. Then the firing stopped, axes were unsheathed and the
troops broke into the houses in the long block they'd just fired on.

One witness heard an officer shout, in French, "The woman and children are to come out. As for the men, they must die by fire or steel." If this
was supposed to provoke some genuine gunfire from the terrified residents
crouched in their basements, it failed to do so.[167]

The row of houses was inhabited mostly by the families of the shopkeepers whose establishments faced the university. In number 20, a Spaniard, Antonio Olivier, lived with his wife and children. Lodging with him were his brother Janos (or Iago) and three employees of the fruit market Olivier owned. The men were led out into the Place de l'Université and ordered to stand at the base of the statue of André Dumont, which is located at the wide, northern end of the square. They were joined by a greengrocer, the owner of an egg and poultry store, a pork-butcher, and a brewer. As always, there was pleading, shouting, screaming. Antonio Olivier and his wife Rose kept yelling at the Germans that they and their employees were Spanish subjects. Their protests were to no avail. The Germans thrust aside their identification papers. Without the least pretense of legal formalities, the men were murdered in front of the statue. The women were driven off and the building set ablaze.

There were, inevitably, diplomatic consequences. The Spanish Minister in Brussels, who had been assisting his American counterpart in overseeing German interests, filed a sharp protest and launched an investigation. Not long afterward, a mysterious telegram arrived in Madrid from Port Said. It read: "I am in good health. Antonio Olivier." This clumsy deception was no more successful than the Wilhelmstrasse's inventions at the beginning of the month, and Rose Vincent Olivier was eventually paid 12,000 francs in compensation.

Enormous chests of the Oliviers' oranges were later dragged into one of the halls housing the Wittner collections. The soldiers ate them with their burgundy. [168]

⊰⊹⊱

Having despatched the shopkeepers of Place de l'Université, the Germans poured into the adjacent Place Cockerill in search of more victims. Again soldiers cried out, *"Man hat geschossen!"* Again the houses were fired upon and the men led off. They were shot one by one in front of the bodies of the earlier victims. As before, there was not the least pretense of an inquiry. As before, women and children implored the Germans to spare their husbands and fathers.

Most of the victims were the owners, relatives, or employees of the two cafés in the square, Café des Maraichers and Café Charpentier. One victim, Paul Smits, a schoolteacher on vacation, happened to be lodging overnight in a room next to one of the cafés. Henri Fléron, the waiter who saw the opening shots from the square, was also not a resident. He had been asked to stay the night by his anxious employer, a widow, Mme. Foullien-Fasssin, though two lodgers and the woman's twenty-one-year-old son and sixteen-year-old daughter also lived on the premises. Fléron, along with one of the tenants and the son, Charles, were forced to flee the wine cellar they were hiding in when the Germans set fire to the building. They were immediately seized by soldiers. Their trial consisted of a single question: had they fired? Fléron assured the officer that no one had fired a single shot from the building, but they were placed, along with two others, in front of a firing squad. Fléron dropped to the ground as he heard the first shot. Though hit by four bullets, he survived, the only one of the sixteen men the Germans arbitrarily condemned to death. (Two women on the square died when they were prevented from leaving the cellar of their burning home.) The waiter was lucky. Other victims who still appeared to be alive were finished off with pistols and bayonets.

Eventually firefighters and Civic Guards were permitted to remove the bodies. Fléron whispered to one of them not to throw him onto the cart too hard; he was still alive, but didn't want anyone to know. When the cart arrived at the makeshift morgue outside the Bourse, Fléron asked the startled Civic Guardsman unloading the bodies to fetch a doctor.[169]

⊰⊹⊱

There was additional evidence of premeditation. As often happened, at least one resident received an urgent warning to leave the area. Three times in the two days before the 20th, a German officer who had made some purchases at her precision-instrument store warned the proprietor, Mme. Wery, to leave her home. Though the officer didn't provide any specifics, something in his tone convinced her. Unfortunately, Mme. Wery moved only as far as the rue des Pitteurs, just across the river, and this neighborhood, too, was burned down the same evening.[170]

A policeman, Officer Van Cauwenbergh, normally passed through Place de l'Université on his nightly rounds. At 9:35 he was prevented from entering the Place by a German soldier. When he returned an hour later, he was again stopped. Shortly afterwards the fusillade commenced.[171]

⊰⊹⊱

At approximately the same time as firing broke out in Place de l'Université, the district across the river received the same treatment. On the Quai des Pêcheurs along the right bank of the Meuse and the rue des Pitteurs which angles off it were located the buildings of the University's College of Medicine and blocks of middle-class residences. At least twenty-seven homes were destroyed. The modus operandi was familiar. Shots were fired into the homes, the doors were smashed with hatchets, the inhabitants driven out into the streets. Seven people were shot as they emerged, or as they sheltered in their cellars. At least one murder may have been preceded by rape. Still other residents were forced back into their burning homes, where their charred remains were not recovered for days. There was widespread pillaging and then systematic arson, with the usual incendiary paraphernalia. A wagon full of benzine and rockets had been parked in the rue des Pitteurs since 8:00 a.m. Several witnesses reported that many of the rampaging Germans appeared to be drunk.[72]

On both sides of the Meuse, German soldiers impeded the firefighters summoned to the scene. Some were reportedly threatened with death if they started up their pumps. Others were lined up against a wall and made to strip. Several were relieved of their wallets.[73]

LIÈGE: COMPASSION Some lives were spared by the actions of individual Germans.

The residents of number 26, Place de l'Université, a musical instrument dealer, Godefroid Framback, and his family, were awakened by the fusillade and fled to the cellar of the adjacent house, joining three other families, the Lejeunes, the Rolands, and the owners of the house, the Franquets. The Germans set the building alight. An officer ordered the women and children out. "What will happen to the men?" Mme. Framback asked.

"They'll be shot or die in the fire," an officer told her, repeating the earlier threat.

"Then we'll all die together," she announced defiantly, and refused to move. The officer left and a second arrived. Mme. Framback threw herself on her knees and begged that he spare the men. Hundreds of women had done this over the previous two weeks to no avail. Hundreds more would go down on their knees during the following week and beg in vain for mercy. But this officer, for whatever reason, responded to the plea.

"I'm taking you under my protection," he assured the families. "I swear to you on my honor as a soldier that the men won't die."

And the officer, despite the attempts of another officer to intervene, conducted the men on a circuitous route to the Palais de Justice, where they were reunited with their wives and children. Everyone was released the next morning.[174]

With less drama, a soldier enabled a young man, Charles Vitot, to flee from the Place Cockerill. Waiting to be shot, the twenty-seven-year-old businessman was kneeling and praying aloud when his eyes met those of a soldier standing nearby. Without saying a word, the German pointed to the rue de l'Étuve. Vitot raced down it. No one shot at him, no one followed him.[175]

Across the river, a German soldier who was one of the guards at the Institute of Zoology, where eight hundred men were billeted, offered to swear under oath that no civilian had fired from the building. The officers he presented himself to were impressed by his earnestness and the building was spared. Three civilians who faced execution were released.[176]

JEWS, AGAIN The Germans, dimly aware of the outrage the killings provoked in Liège, decided it expedient to blame the Russian students they encountered in large numbers. The fact that no Russian lived on Place de l'Université, Place Cockerill, or rue des Pitteurs did not deter them. An organization of Russian Jewish students had occasional meetings in a room on the floor above the Oliviers. However, no students had been in the building for several days prior to the 20th. In fact, the Germans searched the entire floor – and the floor above, where the butcher Degueldre lived – and discovered it was deserted. "It's all shut up," one German was heard to say.[177]

The Germans resolutely hunted down the Russian students over the next two days and posted the following placard throughout Liège:

> Six hundred Russian students, who hitherto have been a burden to the population of Liège, to which they have caused a great deal of trouble, have been arrested and sent back by me.
>   The Lieutenant-General Governor [178]

"This placard contained as many lies as words," Somville bitterly observed. "The Russian students were never a burden to the people of Liège, nor had they given any trouble to anyone; and the Governor did not 'send them back'; he deported them, men and women, to the verminous barracks of Munster."[179]

Among the deportees was a thirty-year-old engineering student from Kishnev, Choulime Bloustein. An officer accompanied by five soldiers appeared at his residence and arrested him. His landlady rushed downstairs in tears, but the officer assured her that Bloustein was not going to be shot. Among the Germans yelling at the Russian students as they were hustled north to gare du Palais was a general – von Kluck himself, Bloustein believed – who brandished a whip and shouted, "On to Siberia, all you *Schweinehunde!*"

From the station, which was littered with smashed suitcases and garments, the students were taken to the old abandoned fortress east of the city, La Chartreuse. Here the women and children were separated from the men. The crowd panicked. Were the men about to be executed? The men were herded into a stable, where they were lined up against a wall. This only confirmed everyone's fears. When every fifth man was pulled from the ranks, those selected were convinced they were about to be shot. Instead, they were stripped and thoroughly searched. The women were also subjected to body searches. Bloustein heard their hysterical cries and glimpsed disheveled hair.

Straw was spread in the stable for the Russian students, but there was no food until the following day, when bread and coffee were distributed. Forty-eight hours later they were shipped off to Celle in Germany.

After two weeks there, three hundred residents from Leuven arrived. Some of the thirty priests among them appeared to have been mistreated – they had cuts and bruises. Several priests asked the Russians if they might borrow some of their clothes. They feared worse abuse if they continued to wear their cassocks.

The violence, indeed, was not at an end. That night the Russians heard gunfire, and later agonized cries and groans. Along with the awful sounds of the wounded and dying, Bloustein and his companions heard the laughter of German soldiers. Some prisoners had apparently been induced to leave the ranks and had headed toward the area where the Russians were housed, without the least thought of escape. Bloustein believed sixteen men were killed.[180]

⊰⟶⟩

Nearly three years later a German military judge, Lieutenant Trumer, arrived in Liège to gather information on the events of August 20, 1914. When the Assistant Commissioner of Police, M. Collet, reminded the judge of the story of the six-hundred Russians who fired on German troops, he dismissed it as a legend. "No one believes that any longer."[181] The German authorities did not share the lieutenant's skepticism. The Russian students remained prisoners at Munsterlager.

LIÈGE: SIGNALING In the hours following the massacre at Place de l'Université, German soldiers roamed through other quarters of Liège looking for signs of "franc-tireur" activity. In the Christian College on the right bank of the Meuse, one of the brothers felt ill during the night and got out of bed to take some medicine. He lit a lamp, but had trouble locating the medicine. In the course of looking he moved the lamp several times. Moments later, Germans were pounding on the door. All of the brothers were arrested and charged with "making signals." The Germans did not indicate who the brothers might be signaling and for what purpose. The monks were taken to the old fortress of La Chartreuse, where they were imprisoned for several weeks.[182]

LIÈGE: PLACE DU PALAIS German violence was not confined to the immediate vicinity of the university. Headquarters for the commandant, Bayer, "Lieutenant-General Governor of the Fortress of Lüttich," was located in the Palais de Justice. These massive buildings had been the seat of the Prince-Bishop of Liège, who for nearly eight hundred years had ruled over a vast territory encompassing slices of Luxembourg, Namur, and Hainaut provinces, as well as present-day Liège. Thirteen hundred soldiers were billeted in the Palais buildings, including the vast Public Record Office and the provincial administrative building. The carefully-preserved state rooms, assembly halls, drawing rooms, dining rooms, and episcopal apartments were ransacked.

On the Place du Palais, directly across from the southern corner of the palace, was a small café owned by Martin Banneux. He and his wife and their two young children, a daughter and a son, occupied the second floor. Above them was the Dewever family, consisting of husband and wife, two sons, Laurent, 23, and Pierre, 17, and two younger daughters, Joséphine and Jeanne.[183]

Both households had retired early on the night of the 20th. At 11:30 p.m. they were awakened by shots. Soldiers broke into the building, searched the three floors for weapons, and, not finding any, nonetheless bayoneted the four men in front of their horrified wives and daughters. Banneaux alone survived. The café's wine cellar was then looted. This, Liègeois were convinced, was the motive for the savage attack. The proprietor had strictly adhered to an order forbidding him to sell drinks to soldiers. German newspaper readers were nonetheless assured that the four franc-tireurs had decided to take on the 1,300 soldiers across the Place du Palais. For good measure a lodger, a teen-aged girl who had been staying with her aunt that night, was gang-raped when she returned the next day for her possessions.[184]

More murders took place when soldiers who had been drinking all evening at another café, in the Cornillon district on the right bank, began firing their rifles in the air. A soldier in a company crossing a bridge above the café was hit, and his comrades returned the fire, fatally wounding one of the revelers. Three civilians were shot in retribution, but not before all residents of the neighborhood, including women and children, were roused from their homes—it was 4:00 a.m.—lined up against a wall, and subjected to two mock executions. Some of the soldiers were apparently convinced that they had been ordered to kill the families. One, directly across from the wife of a journalist, was visibly upset. Her three children, facing the row of leveled rifles, all held up their hands, including the two-year-old.[185]

A total of 67 residents were killed in Liège before dawn on the 21st.

CHAPTER 3

Aarschot

"A VERY KINDLY, GOOD MAN" The Germans approached Aarschot early on the morning of August 19. At 5:30 a.m., their artillery began bombarding Belgian positions east of the town. The 9th Regiment of the 3rd Division, outnumbered by about five to one, was not attempting to hold Aarschot, but was covering the Army's retreat to the Antwerp forts. Before the final assault that carried them into the town, the Germans, according to Captain Georges Gilson, commanding the 4th Company of the regiment's 1st Battalion, drove before them four young women, each holding in her arms a child, along with two little girls. The Belgians ceased firing, but the German machine-guns rattled away. Only one of the women was wounded.[1]

At about 8:00 a.m., the Belgian forces began pulling back. Some soldiers skirted the town; most retreated through it.[2] There was some sporadic firing from behind buildings.[3] Belgian troops may even have fired their rifles at a passing plane from the church bell tower, and possibly on advancing troops,[4] though no German witness makes this potentially damning allegation.[5] (In Schaffen, outside Diest, German troops murdered twenty-three and burned the town to the ground after being strafed by machine-gun fire from Belgian troops in the church steeple.)[6] At least one witness had an even more incendiary story. A Belgian soldier dressed in civilian clothes fired on the Germans from a house in Mechelsestraat, though the civilian did not himself witness this.[7] Another witness thought that retreating soldiers may have fired from homes, but he, too, did not actually observe this. The Germans, once again, seem not to have been aware of any such incident. When Aarschot's troubles began that evening, around 7:00 p.m.,

Aarschot before the war.

Jozef Tielemans, burgomaster of Aarschot.

A notice from Tielemans posted a week before his death urging residents to remain in their homes, to refrain from carrying or, especially, shooting weapons, and to offer the passing troops food and drink.

no accusations were made about franc-tireur activity early in the morning.

Bertha Hubert Tielemans, wife of the burgomaster of Aarschot, had attempted to take her children, Louis and Florence, to church at about 8:00 a.m., but the bullets were still flying in the streets. At about 9:00, some wounded Belgian soldiers limped by, their faces bloodied. Mme. Tielemans flung open one of the windows of the big house on the Grote Markt and asked what was happening. A soldier told her the obvious: "We're retreating. The Germans are pursuing us."[8]

Some Belgian soldiers urged the townspeople to flee. The 3rd Division had defended Liège, and had heard graphic accounts of the German operations in Melen, Soumagne, Olne, and elsewhere.[9]

"The Germans entered the village and broke all the doors and windows and stole everything that came into their hands," one witness recalled.[10] There was widespread looting. Several men unlucky enough to be caught outside were gunned down or bayoneted.[11] According to one witness, six men were stabbed to death in a corridor between two houses.[12] Residents were then evicted from their homes on the main streets. During this process, still more civilians were shot. Guillaume Pauwels, a furniture-maker, watched in horror as his brother-in-law was killed as he emerged from Pauwels' house, just as he'd been ordered to do. The soldiers then shot Pauwels' uncle, who was seated peaceably in a chair in the front room. The old man was 91.[13] As usual, a great number of shots were fired at upstairs windows and, for good measure, several houses were set ablaze.[14]

Of those evicted from their homes, the men were compelled to march, with hands raised, first to the Grote Markt and then on to the Demer. Some time later, the women and children were ordered to follow. The Germans changed their minds once again, and the women and children were freed.[15] The crowd of somewhere between 1000 and 1200 men waited for nearly three hours. Soldiers amused themselves by telling their captives that everyone would be shot. And an officer passing by at the head of a column shouted *"Durch den Kopf schiessen"* and spat at the men nearest him.[16]

At about 11:00 a.m. the burgomaster, Jozef Tielemans, addressed the crowd. He consulted his notes several times. "Every person among you who has weapons must take them to the Town Hall. Any of you poor men who have weapons will be killed by the Germans. I therefore beg all of you to give up your weapons."[17]

As elsewhere in central Belgium, the order was redundant. Guns had been collected at the outbreak of the war. One man, however, had failed to turn in a rifle he used for pigeon shooting, and hastily went off to fetch it. Someone recalled that some ceremonial rifles were hanging in the Garde Civique armory and these were retrieved.[18] Then everyone was dismissed.

The purpose of the exercise was revealed when the residents returned to their homes. The houses in the district around the Grote Markt had been thoroughly ransacked and plundered.[19] For good measure, a few civilians who were not at the meeting were shot as the crowd dispersed.[20] It was soon after this that Frans Thiere, the director of the telegraph office, was warned by a German soldier to flee Aarschot. "The town will be pulverized," he was told. A neighbor received the same advice. The two families fled together.[21]

The burgomaster had been ordered to the Town Hall at 10:00 a.m. He was treated with extreme brutality, according to his wife, repeatedly called a *Schweinehunde*, shoved and kicked.[22] The first order of business was to haul down the national flag. Tielemans, however, didn't speak German, and a local school teacher, Jean van Kerckhoven, was summoned to translate.[23] The burgomaster was instructed to tell all the civilians that they "'must let the German troops pass freely, give them all they requested, not display any hostility and hand in all weapons.'"[24]

When Van Kerckhoven pointed out that there were flyers posted over town communicating these instructions, the commandant dictated a new notice: "If any hostile act is committed against the German army, the town will be destroyed and one inhabitant in three will be shot."[25]

Despite the violence and the threats, the burgomaster remained cautiously optimistic during the early afternoon. Perhaps the Germans had gotten the violence out of their system. Maybe henceforth the occupation would be as peaceable as that of Liège, to date.

Tielemans and his brother Emile owned a brewery and a mill. The burgomaster was well-liked and respected – "a kindly, good man," recalled a shoemaker. "The last man in the world to give provocation."[26] Other witnesses testified to his calm demeanor and his self-possession throughout his ordeal.[27]

Bertha Tielemans, from her exile in the Netherlands, provided a detailed account of what she recalled.

Moments after the retreating Belgians passed by, the Grote Markt in front of the burgomaster's house was filled with German troops. The Tielemans' fifteen-year-old son Louis attempted to lower the blinds. Immediately, a shot was fired through the window. The ricocheting bullet caught him in the foot.

While her husband was parleying with the Germans at the Town Hall, three officers knocked on the door and requested lodging.

They were a general [actually a colonel] and his two aides-de-camp. They were taken to their rooms, which looked out on the Grote Markt. They could watch the troops stationed there from their windows. Shortly afterwards they went out. The house-maid called me to show the condition in which they had left the rooms. The lowest burglar could not have upset the furniture in the way the Germans did. Not a drawer had been left unexamined or a paper intact. I got an explanation of this conduct later on. The General asked me the name of the Belgian colonel who was there the night before, insisting on knowing the branch of the service to which he belonged, etc. I replied: "I no more know his name than I do yours. I don't know whence he came or whither he went, any more than I know where you are going." The German army kept on passing. Then the men were halted. About 4 o'clock my husband returned. He said to me: "up to now all has gone well, but I am anxious." He took some cigars to give to the sentries posted at the house. The position of the street door in the garden enabled us to see the General on the balcony. I said to my husband that what he was doing might displease the authorities. As I went away I glanced at the Grote Markt, and I saw very distinctly two pillars of smoke, followed by a multitude of shots. My courtyard was at once filled with horses and soldiers, who were firing in the air like madmen. My husband, children, servants and myself had only just time to rush into a cellar, hustled by the soldiers who took refuge in our house, still firing their rifles. After a few moments of indescribable anguish, one of the aides-de-camp came down-stairs, calling out: "The General is dead. I want the Burgomaster." The General was hit by a German bullet while he was on the balcony. My husband said to me: "This will be a serious matter for me." I clasped his hand and said, "Courage." The captain handed my husband over to the soldiers, who hustled him and took him away. I threw myself in front of the captain, saying: "Sir, you can prove that my husband did not fire, nor my son either, for they were both here and unarmed." "No matter, madam, he is responsible."

My son made us change our cellar. About half an hour later, he said: "Mamma, I hear them seeking for us. Let us go up and meet our fate bravely." It was the same captain. "Madam, I want your son." He took my son, 15 years old! As my poor child walked with difficulty, because of his wound, he followed, kicking him. I shut my eyes so as not to look. I felt I was dying of grief. It was atrocious. I believe that he had my son taken to his father at the Town Hall.

The rage of the captain was not yet assuaged. He came back and insisted upon my accompanying him from cellar to attic, alleging that there had been firing at the soldiers. He was able to satisfy himself that the rooms were empty and the windows shut. During this inspection he threatened me with his revolver. My daughter placed herself between him and me. This procedure did not make him understand his cowardice. When we reached the hall I said to him: "What is going to become of us?" He replied coldly: "You will be shot with your daughter and servants." Meanwhile, the soldiers were bending their bayonets and showing the terrified servants that they pricked well. When the captain left us, a soldier came up to me and said: "Go into the Grote Markt. They will do nothing to the women." I turned to get a hat and cloak, but all was stolen already. We left our home without anything. When we reached the Square we found all the neighbors in tears. By my side was a young girl dazed with grief. Her father and two brothers had been shot, and she had been dragged from the bedside of her dying mother. She found her dead nine hours later.

We were an hour in the square, surrounded by a cordon of soldiers. All the houses on the right side of the square were in flames. We could notice the perfect order and method with which these bandits set about their task. There was none of the greediness of men left to their own devices. I can state that they worked systematically and under orders. While the houses were burning, we could see the soldiers enter the other houses. Using electric torches, they searched the houses, opened the windows and threw out the mattresses and bedclothes... From time to time they spoke to us, saying, "You are going to be shot. You are going to be shot." In the meantime, soldiers came out of our house with their arms full of bottles of wine. The windows of our rooms were opened and everything in them was thrown out. I turned away so as not to see this pillage. In the light of the burning houses, my eyes fell on my husband, my son and my brother-in-law, with other gentlemen, whom they were taking to the place of execution. Never shall I forget the sight nor the look of my husband casting a last glance at his home and wondering what had become of his wife and daughter. And that I might not make him lose courage, I refrained from calling out to him, "Here I am."

About 2:00 they said to us: "The women can go home." As my house was still full of soldiers, I accepted the hospitality of a neighbor. We had hardly got inside before the Germans came and said that we must leave the town at once. It was going to be bombarded. We had to leave by way of Rillaar. With about 30 women and children, we had to walk along a road, upon which were lying the bodies of poor Belgian soldiers, and civilians and horses, in the midst of burning houses. On the way we met hundreds of motors filled with German officers, whose bravery consisted in pointing revolvers at women who had nothing in their pockets with which to buy bread.

The group finally found refuge on a farm, under German guard. They witnessed several wrenching mock executions. The Germans were looking for her, Bertha Tielemans learned, and she destroyed her passport. She was told later that 10,000 francs was offered as a reward to anyone turning her in. She also learned some details about her husband's final moments. Facing his executioners, he told them that he died in peace, that he had passed his life endeavoring to do all the good he could, that he did not ask for life, but he asked that his son, 15 years of age, should be spared to comfort his mother. He was not answered. My brother-in-law asked that his brother and nephew might be spared. He was not listened to. About 5 o'clock on the 20th of August they were made to kneel, and a moment later the best people in the world had ceased to live.[28]

Vrouw Tielemans appeared to be almost as upset by the accusations against her beloved son as she was by his death. He was, by all accounts, an unusually compassionate boy–*"un garçon doux et timide."*[29] He could not have shot the officer, wrote the Dean of Aarschot, Joseph Meeus: "The boy was incapable of it."[30] He appears to have bourne his ordeal stoically. As he was marched from the Stadhuis toward the Leuvensesteenweg, a school friend shouted out, "Courage, Louis!" "I've got it," the fifteen-year-old replied.[31]

-<--->-

The story of the death of Colonel Johannes Stenger became one of the great German legends of the Belgian campaign. Versions cropped up everywhere. The details varied endlessly. Sometimes the colonel was shot while he dined with a treacherous burgomaster, sometimes moments after he had been greeted by the Belgian official. Frequently it was the burgomaster's son who was supposed to have pulled the trigger. Colonel Stenger was promoted. First he became a general; soon he was declared to be one of Germany's foremost military strategists.

The incident took on a life of its own. It was supposed to have taken place in at least a dozen other localities.[32] No less a personage than the military governor of Brussels, General Arthur von Lüttwitz, assured the American minister to Belgium, Brand Whitlock, that the shooting had taken place in Leuven, and that it provided ample justification for the burning of that city.[33]

-<--->-

Several witnesses were in the Grote Markt at the moment the colonel was shot. Frans Tuerlinckx, a printer, lived across the street from the burgomaster, above his store.[34] A German officer was in the shop when the firing started and Tuerlinckx immediately asked if it was machineguns and what it meant. *"Die Franzosen sind da"* – the French are there, said the officer. Through the shop windows the two men observed German soldiers firing from behind wagons on various buildings in the Grote Markt. Some were simply shooting into the air. Noticing three officers on the balcony of the burgomaster's house across the street, Tuerlinckx remarked to the officer that this was a dangerous place to stand. The officer agreed.

While the printer may have embellished his account, he was certainly not the only witness to observe Colonel Stenger in an exposed position on the balcony at a time when numerous soldiers were firing into the air. No German witness denied that there was indiscriminate gunfire below the balcony.

As one might expect, there is conflicting testimony among Belgian witnesses about the first shot. Even the time is in dispute, though the firing appears to have begun about 7:00 p.m. Belgian time, 8:00 German time. There had been intermittent firing throughout the day. Louis Cresens, a mathematics teacher who acted as a translator for the Germans, was walking with two soldiers and a Belgian government official, René Terweduwe, who had been charged with telling all inhabitants to keep their doors and windows open. The men heard two shots. The soldiers raced over to where the firing originated from, the garden of the former burgomaster. Here they found two German soldiers, who freely admitted having fired. They'd shot off their guns because they'd wanted to, they defiantly told the two soldiers who had rushed over. The soldiers escorting Cresens and Terweduwe reprimanded their comrades, but then proceeded on their mission.[35]

One witness observed the three German officers, moments before the firing began, standing behind the balcony window, drying their hands with towels. She heard a shot from a nearby house, possibly that belonging to a jeweler three doors away. The woman observed a number of drunken Germans in the street at the time, and was convinced that one of them had fired.[36]

Frans Theeuws, watching from behind his home, saw a German soldier racing down the street, and then heard a single gunshot from a café behind the fleeing soldier.[37] Another witness thought the Germans in one café, De Molen, fired on soldiers in another café, De Arend.[38]

A twenty-two-year-old medical student from Leuven was told by a friend, Omer Nijs, who was later executed, that Nijs had heard a "revolver shot" coming from a house belonging to Achille Wygaerts. The house was burned down soon after. Wygaerts dropped his young child out the second floor window, then jumped, breaking both legs. His wife burned to death. Wygaerts himself was subsequently investigated by the Germans and no charges were filed against him.[39]

Captain Hans Karge, who was soon to order the execution of nearly eighty Aarschot residents, originally thought the initial shots came from the rifle of a soldier approaching the Grote Markt.[40]

Perhaps the most damning testimony comes from Thérèse Slaets Nijs. "I live two houses down from the Tielemanses and I clearly saw, on the 19th of August, between 6 and 7 o'clock, six or seven Germans who were at the base of the stairs of the Stadhuis fire in the direction of the burgomaster's house. Immediately afterwards someone fired on my house."[41]

Whoever may have fired the initial shot or shots, there followed an intense fusillade lasting fifteen minutes or so. Along with Tuerlinckx, some witnesses thought they heard a machine gun.[42] Others regarded it as a sham fight intended to frighten the residents.[43] When Tuerlinckx said as much to the officer taking shelter with him, the man didn't dispute this.[44] This is improbable, however. The wild firing was more likely the result of panic. Wagons collided, horses ran loose, and repeated commands to cease fire were ignored.[45] As soon as the firing began, the officers with Stenger, Captain Schwartz and Lieutenant Beyersdorff, rushed out of the Tielemans' house "to establish order among the troops in the marketplace."[46] Similarly, a captain of the 140th Infantry Regiment repeatedly ordered the bugles to sound the cease-fire. "Evidently the officer first wished to stop the firing of our men in order to be able to settle upon a plan of action," a captain in another regiment explained, not recognizing that the other man's behavior discredited his own fanciful account of machine-gun wielding franc-tireurs.[47]

After calm was restored, the Germans went into action. On the Grote Markt and in nearby Peterseliestraat and Kortestraat, every house was broken into and the inhabitants expelled at gunpoint.[48] Though it is nowhere described, it is not difficult to imagine the terror experienced by the Aarschot families: hearing the loud crackling of gunfire in their streets, and the wild shouts of soldiers, seeing their doors and windows smashed, dragged out of their homes at gunpoint by the enraged soldiers, children watching their fathers hit with rifle butts, their wrists bound tightly with copper wire, everyone watching the solid, comfortable homes ignited and thinking rapidly of particular possessions now being consumed by the flames – a wedding dress, the plate and cutlery, a photograph, a chess set, a violin, a leather armchair, an encyclopedia, a volume of poetry, a favorite jacket, a new pair of shoes. And then watching as the men were led off – the mothers consumed with dread but trying to be optimistic, reassuring their hysterical children that their fathers would be back in the morning after the Germans had asked them some questions. After all, they had done nothing.

◂┄▸▸

The executioners proceeded at different rates and with different methods. Men and women driven from the houses on the Grote Markt near the one the Germans believed the franc-tireurs had fired from were assembled in the square. The buildings were set ablaze and the residents captured as they fled. The instigator was a captain in command of a detachment of military police, Hans Karge, who had originally believed a German soldier had fired the first shot. Karge first appealed to a colonel for permission to burn the house of the "ringleaders," but the request was denied. Undeterred, the captain waited until the colonel moved off, then took charge of some soldiers of the 140th Infantry Regiment, broke windows and doors and poured kerosene over the ground floor, taking care to splash some on the steps leading to the basement. Karge's mounted military police unit had now assembled in the square, and the captain assumed command of the prisoners. After he had "discharged" the women and children, he marched the eighty-one men out of town down the Leuven road. He separated out three disabled men, then had the rest shot by the glare of a burning farmhouse.[49]

The captives, who, as usual, had been clubbed and cursed en route, were ordered to form into groups of three. As they moved forward, holding hands, the Germans shot them in the back from about ten yards away. No charges were read, no judgment pronounced.[50]

There were a few survivors. The fusillade failed to hit François de Winter, a thirty-seven-year-old tram machinist. He raced into the darkness as fast as he could. The soldiers fired after him, but only managed to wound him in the left thigh. De Winter was able to drag himself into a garden and conceal himself. The Germans searched for him with a flashlight, but were unable to find him.[51]

Also fortunate was Paul Verlinden, a thirty-year-old merchant. The men on either side of him went down, Professor Joseph-Robert Carette and Hendrik de Vroey, but, miraculously, he wasn't hit. Verlinden pretended to be dead. The seconds ticked by. He heard the order, "Three others!" The next group was shot, then the next. Bodies piled up around him. As the firing diminished, Verlinden crawled into a potato field nearby, and then into a wooded area, where he hid for thirty-six hours. From the woods he was able to observe the Germans finishing off the wounded with bayonets.[52]

A little more consideration was given to the fate of the burgomaster, his son and brother, and the hundred or so other men arrested with them. Among them were many of the town's leading citizens. They were detained for a longer time in the Town Hall. Their wrists were tightly bound with copper wire and they were marched out of the square down the Leuvensesteenweg. They, too, were treated with the customary brutality. A young man, struck hard on the back with a rifle-butt, cried out, "Oh, father!" His anxious father, walking beside him, muttered, "Keep quiet, my boy." Another prisoner was stabbed in the thigh by a bayonet. The gash was more than two inches deep.[53]

The men may have heard the intermittent sound of gunfire from the field where the military police were executing the 78 captives. The column walked another 500 yards down the road and was halted by a potato field outside the farm of Karel Stockmans.[54] Less confident of his duty than Captain Karge, the officer in charge kept the men overnight, still tightly bound. The pain was excruciating: men cried out in agony. One of the prisoners begged to be executed. The men, sprawled flat on the ground, were ordered not to move or to elevate their heads.[55] The men slept as best as they could in the sandy field. The burgomaster and his family were provided with some hay. The captives were not forbidden to talk and he and his brother repeatedly went over the day's events. The behavior of the Germans was incomprehensible. The troops could not have asked for a more peaceable and accommodating reception.

At 5:00 a.m. four or five officers arrived. They conferred briefly in the farmhouse. Among them was an officer who had stayed with Emile

Tielemans the night before, Lieutenant Wolff. He had been chatting with the burgomaster's brother at the time the firing broke out and the younger Tielemans urged him to let the other officers know that he had in no way been involved in the shooting: "You and you alone can be witness to my innocence." "I know it, M. Tielemans," Wolff replied, "and at the appropriate moment I shall testify in your favor." "... All these men as well," Tielemans continued, "could be shot without a word said in their defense." Wolff entered the farmhouse with the other officers, but when they emerged some time later, he was not with them. Some Belgian witnesses were convinced the lieutenant was protesting the decision after he had been overruled. Another officer informed Emile Tielemans that he, his brother and nephew all had to die.[56]

Six soldiers were selected and a proclamation was read in German, announcing the charges and the punishment. "We were accused of breaking a certain law," recalled one witness, straining to understand the orotund German phrases.[57] The two men and the boy were shot first. Tielemans briefly defended himself, reminding the Germans that he had circulated through the town in their company, urging calm. There were no plots against the Germans, he assured his captors. Emile Tielemans added that he had done everything he could to receive the Germans hospitably.[58]

At this point another man spoke up. He was Achille Claes van Nuffel, a political rival of the Tielemans. The sixty-five-year-old merchant offered to exchange his life for theirs, according to at least one witness. For the sake of the town, Tielemans and his son and brother should be spared, Claes argued. "No," an officer replied. "It's the burgomaster we want."

Claes himself testified only that he declared that although he was an opponent of Tielemans, the burgomaster was an honest man and that both by his speeches and the notices he had had posted, he had maintained calm in the town. His behavior had been exemplary. According to Claes, his short speech moved the commanding officer, who announced that an inquest would be conducted. The officers proceeded back to the farmhouse. But just as they reached the road, another officer arrived on horseback with orders to shoot the three Tielemans and one out of three of the other captives.[59]

Another witness, Petrus Bols, also recalled some confusion among the officers. According to the forty-two-year-old butter distributor, it was

Tielemans' own forceful arguments that persuaded the commanding officer. But he was overruled by the officer who arrived on horseback.[60]

The burgomaster now stood up and implored the commanding officer to spare the others. The officer refused. When Tielemans begged that at least his son's life be spared, "so that he might comfort his mother," the officer laughed derisively.[61]

It was Emile Tielemans' turn. He asked the Germans not to kill his brother and nephew, who were entirely innocent of any wrongdoing.[62] The plea was denied. The men and the boy were made to stand ten yards from the execution squad and were shot as they were saying goodbye to each other.[63]

The other prisoners were then lined up and an officer, a fat man in a blue uniform and banded cap, then counted off by threes.[64] It's not hard to imagine the awful suspense as most of the men craned their necks to look down the line and calculate their position, while others waited with eyes shut, silently praying.

Seventeen-year-old Gaston Nijs had unfortunately been standing beside his older brother Omer. Gaston was number two, Omer number three. "Can I take my brother's place?" Gaston asked. "It doesn't matter to you which one you shoot, but my brother has finished his studies, and is more useful to our widowed mother than I am."[65] The officer was unmoved. "Let number three fall out," he said. Other brothers and good friends had stood side by side, as had fathers and sons, including Frans Tuerlinckx and his eighteen-year-old son. The printer watched in horror as the boy was selected.[66]

The officer in charge was willing to exempt at least one of the doomed men, however. A twenty-two-year-old medical student from Leuven, who was the last to be selected, told the officer that he was a member of the Red Cross. He flourished a card identifying him as a student of the Faculty of Medicine. At other times and places that August this would not have worked, but the young man, the last to be chosen, was not made to join the men who were now lined up behind the bodies of the three Tielemans. The remaining prisoners were ordered to turn their backs. Now the squad of six soldiers passed slowly in front of the condemned men, at a distance of ten meters. As their friends and relatives listened intently, the soldiers fired at the men, killing three with each discharge. An order followed, and they moved down the line, executing the next three.[67] The massacre was carried out by daylight, and so this time there were no miraculous escapes.

After the shooting was finished, the survivors were compelled to shake hands with the executioners and the other dozen soldiers.[68] When this grotesque ceremony was completed, the men were told they were now free, but they must return directly to town. No sooner had they arrived back in Aarschot, however, than a number of them were recaptured and marched back down the Leuven road. Here these men, who had so narrowly escaped death earlier in the day, were executed. They were probably shot by the gendarmes under Captain Karge, who reported killing a second batch of prisoners.[69]

Concerned this time with collecting some evidence, Karge selected a man he felt was the most intelligent-looking and offered to spare his life if he would explain how the franc-tireur attack had been organized. Not coincidentally, the man spoke German; he was a teacher at the Aarschot seminary, St. Jozef's College. There was, naturally, a strong incentive to tell the captain exactly what he wished to hear. However, the teacher merely said that it had been a mistake for the residents to have offered refuge to Belgian soldiers and to have supplied them with civilian clothes.[70]

◄--►

The following day, Thursday the 20th, men who had not been seized the evening before were escorted to the two killing fields and ordered to dig trenches to bury the 140 or so dead. (A total of 169 were killed in Aarschot, but as many as thirty were murdered in town.)[71] The job took all day, and was not made easier by intermittent rain. At about 7:00 p.m. five or six of the older men were released, but the others were kept at their grim task until the next morning.[72]

Other civilians, meanwhile, had been required to come out and observe the proceedings. As a precaution, their suspenders, belts, and keys were first confiscated.[73]

Karel Stockmans was one of those selected to bury some of the victims. The bodies, he reported, were arranged in a row, with their faces toward the grey sky.[74]

◄--►

Jean-Jacques-Robert Carette, who was killed in the first mass execution, was one of two priests murdered in Aarschot. Both had arrived from out of town. Carette was a professor at St. Pieter's College in Leuven, and was visiting his parents, who owned a shop off the Grote Markt. The thirty-eight-year-old priest had concealed himself with six other clerics in various places around town, but then had become concerned about his parents and had left to join them. After he was shot, Carette's notebook was discovered by Pastoor van Roey. Among his last entries were the following:

> God is all, man is nothing.
> Pray as if work is useless; work as if prayer is useless. Life is a war, and there is no victory.
> Merciful Jesus, give us eternal rest.[75]

SUCCESSORS, AUTOPSIES Even before they attempted to represent themselves as the liberators of Flanders, the Germans found some collaborators among disaffected or opportunistic Belgians. The military, however, preferred to deal with German or Swiss nationals.

In Aarschot, they turned to Carl Ronnewinckel, owner of a tavern in nearby Hamont, a German subject long resident in Brabant. Characterized as "an intelligent, well-read man of dubious morality and equivocal honesty," Ronnewinckel had been supplying both armies. In October, the Germans declared him the new burgomaster of Aarschot, following a very brief elevation to the position of "acting burgomaster."[76]

The Germans had initially named Julien van Praet to the post. It's not clear why the thirty-seven-year-old teacher was selected. He is not very forthcoming on the subject in his several depositions. The job, in any event, was not particularly gratifying. His first three nights as burgomaster, Van Praet was made to sleep in the office of the communal secretary, guarded by two soldiers. His first task was to circle the deserted town, announce his appointment, and convey the familiar German threat: if there was any more firing, the burgomaster would be shot, followed by the rest of the population. After performing various tasks for the Germans, including supervising some additional burials, cleaning the streets, and requisitioning supplies, Van Praet fled Aarshot when it was liberated by Belgian troops on September 9. He was hauled before a tribunal in Antwerp later that month, but cleared of any wrongdoing.[77] Carl Ronnewinckel took over and served for the duration of the war.

He was able to amass a fortune for himself and his entourage by supplying the German front lines with animals, wood, hay, and straw. He and his cohorts, including a Belgian army deserter, fled to Bavaria when the German Army collapsed in November 1918.[78]

One of Ronnewinckel's responsibilities was to assist in the interrogation of witnesses in the German investigation of the events of August 19th. The new burgomaster became convinced that Colonel Stenger would have survived had his wounds received immediate attention. He professed to be indignant that the two adjutants had rushed out into the street and left him to die. He became quite obsessed by the subject.

◄◄·►►

Indeed, no proper autopsy had been conducted on the colonel. A regimental surgeon the following day had extracted a "deformed lead bullet."[79] The caliber of the bullet suggested only that it was fired by a rifle. The doctor's testimony is nowhere to be found in the German White Book. Needless to say, had he discovered a Belgian bullet, the result would have been publicized throughout the world. Instead, we have only the doctor's observation, as recalled by Captain Folz of the 49th Infantry, that a second, facial wound had not been "caused by an infantry bullet."[80] In fact, the only wound found on Stenger's body when it was exhumed and carefully examined in January 1921 was a large lesion level with the upper right part of the thoracic cage.[81] Folz believed that "the downward direction of the wound" indicated that it had been fired from one of the houses across the street, but Belgian doctors conducting the autopsy were not able to determine the trajectory of the projectile.

"WHY WASTE A BULLET?" Apart from the three mass executions of civilians on Leuvensesteenweg, the Germans massacred over forty-five prisoners of war in Aarschot. In one incident, twenty-three captured Belgian soldiers, along with five or six civilians, were gunned down just outside town, on the banks of the Demer.

Gustave Pierard, a twenty-year-old volunteer with the 6th Line Regiment of the 3rd Division, wounded in the arm, was captured in the

woods outside Aarschot around 8:00 a.m. on the morning of the 19th. He
was attended by a German physician in a nearby field, then moved to one
of the first buildings in Aarschot proper, a bicycle repair shop. The men
were then taken down to the river and driven in front of two German companies. The soldiers were ordered to fire on the prisoners as they trotted
past.

Pierard was only wounded, and slid down the embankment. A soldier rushed over to finish him off, but an officer intervened. "Why waste
a bullet?" he said, and ordered the wounded Belgian to be tossed into the
Demer. Pierard floated down to a shallow, concealed part of the river and
was able to gain his footing by grasping the roots of a bush by the bank.
Standing on rocks, with only his head above the water, he remained in the
river overnight. The next morning he clambered out and took shelter in a
deserted house. He found some civilian clothes and joined the stream of
refugees heading west.[82]

-<-•->-

Seventeen-year-old Joseph van Reusel reported another slaughter of Belgian soldiers taken captive. Van Reusel, along with his parents and sister,
was working as a Red Cross volunteer in a convent that had been converted
into a hospital. The men were taken out, the Red Cross armbands cut off by
an officer, and were made to climb up a hill to a site called Kruisplaats. Here
the prisoners were placed in front of a large bonfire. Their hands were
tightly bound and they were spat at and mocked by the soldiers guarding
them. "We're going to burn you alive," they were told.

On the other side of the fire was a group of Belgian p.o.w.s. These men
were executed one by one, Van Reusel reported, and after each gunshot
there was a sustained burst of applause. The seventeen-year-old counted
eleven shots.[83]

-<-•->-

Eugène de Busschere, Father Hilonius of the Fathers of the Sacred Hearts,
reported still another instance of prisoners of war being executed in and
around Aarschot. De Busschere spoke with some of the Belgian wounded
being cared for at the Damien Institute. They told him that when their platoon had been reduced to twenty and they were surrounded by Germans,

the soldiers had surrendered. They had been relieved of their arms and made to sit down, when a major arrived. *"Töten Sie alle die Schweine!"* he ordered. The execution began at once. Four or five men were only lightly wounded, however, and were able to make their way to the Institute. Perhaps a few sympathetic soldiers intentionally aimed high or wide. De Busschere interrogated the Belgian soldiers carefully and collected detailed depositions. He decided to destroy these, however, shortly before he was imprisoned in the church. "The report could have cost me my life," he correctly observed. It is unlikely these were the same soldiers who were shot with Pierard. The latter were from various regiments and there was only one survivor beside Pierard himself.[84]

A DRUM ROLL The first twenty-four hours of terror would not have been complete without fake executions.

After being conducted on a guided tour of the execution sites beside Leuvensesteenweg, the mathematics teacher Louis Cresens was taken to the house of Aarschot's Dean. About twenty-five men and women were being held captive here, among them several priests and employees of the diocese.[85] The group was made to walk slowly to the Old Cemetery, where they were surrounded by German soldiers with rifles raised. Cresens noticed that a drummer was present. There was a slow, lugubrious drum roll and the soldiers loaded their rifles. The civilians waited. Several extremely tense minutes passed. Then the guns were lowered and the women led off. The men were detained until the evening, but not threatened again. Finally, they were conducted to the church, where Cresens was imprisoned, off and on, until the infamous walk to Leuven on August 28th.

Before being incarcerated in the church, the mathematics teacher, who spoke German, obtained permission to return to his own house. One of the two soldiers assigned to accompany him offered the nearest thing to an explanation for the charade. The priests were responsible for all the cruelties the Belgian civilians had inflicted on German soldiers. The priests were the true masters of Belgium.[86]

A notebook found in the knapsack of a military cyclist stationed in Aarschot elaborates on this motif: "The 6th of September was a day of rest. We only sent 300 Belgians to Germany, among whom were 22 priests.

It was terrible to see the women and children bidding them farewell. All the people are incited by the priests, who have preached in the churches that they should fire upon the Germans and kill them in order to enter Heaven."[87]

‹‹‹·›·›

Father Paul Oscar van Hanke was told much the same thing by a lieutenant on the Leuvensesteenweg. "We've already shot one priest," he assured Father van Hanke. (This was Professor Carette.) "And we intend to shoot you, too." For twenty-four hours the priest was imprisoned with five others in a tiny room. The men were then taken out and placed against a wall. A soldier called out to his comrades to prepare to shoot them. "It was a comedy to frighten us," Father van Hanke wrote.

The priest, however, was not about to take any chances. He yelled out to his captors in English that he was an American. While this was not true, the priest had spent two years there and could do a decent American accent. He was immediately conducted to a superior officer, to whom he mentioned that, apart from being the citizen of neutral country, he was a chaplain at the château de Schoonhoven, in the service of the Duchess of Arenberg, a German subject with extensive holdings in Brabant.

Doubly indemnified, the priest was promptly released.[88]

"THE GOOD WILL PAY WITH THE BAD" Louis Gustave Michiels, head guard at the Aarschot train station, went to work early on the morning of the 19th. However, the trains were no longer running, and he returned home. Waiting for him anxiously was his wife Cécile with their seven month-old child. Shots were ringing out in the street, and the family took refuge in their cellar. German soldiers broke into the home and turned it upside down searching for weapons. The family was ordered out, with hands raised.

Neither Cécile Michiels nor the German White Book makes mention of any gun being found, and no such accusation was made at the time. The couple was taken some two hundred meters down the street. When they attempted to talk, soldiers yelled *"Halt's Maul"* – shut your trap.

At length an officer rode up and addressed Louis Michiels. "Someone has fired in this street."

"Possibly," Michiels replied, "but we haven't done it."

"The good will pay with the bad," said the officer, and rode off. Michiels, who was holding the couple's seven-month-old baby, handed the child to his wife. He was then escorted into a field with three neighbors. From behind a chapel where she had taken refuge, Cécile Michiels heard a number of shots. Not long afterwards, she was discovered there by a soldier. "You can leave," he told her. "Your husband is dead."

But she was detained by other soldiers, who required her to take them to the home of the lock-keeper. Here they shot two other men, one of whom was deaf and did not open the sluice gates quickly enough.

"When all the Germans had gone," Cécile Michiels testified, "I went to where my husband was lying and saw that he had a bayonet wound in the thigh and a bullet in the head. He was already stiff and quite dead. I took his watch, his wallet and wedding ring, and returned home."[89]

"A VERITABLE MARTYRDOM" As Albert, the handsome young king, came immediately to symbolize the resistance of the Belgian Army to the treacherous invasion, so Cardinal Désiré-Joseph Mercier, Archbishop of Mechelen and Primate of Belgium, came to represent the stoicism of the civilian population and its passive resistance to the occupation. Sometimes that resistance consisted merely in bearing witness.

In his famous pastoral letter issued on Christmas 1914, Cardinal Mercier chronicled the suffering his countrymen had endured during the previous four months. When he came to list the priests who had been slain, he singled out the curé of Gelrode. Father Dergent suffered, said the Cardinal, "a veritable martyrdom."[90]

Three times in August the Germans entered Gelrode, a town of just under a thousand, half an hour's walk from Aarschot down the Leuvensesteenweg. Troops of the 149th regiment appeared late in the afternoon of the 19th. They seized between forty and forty-five men and imprisoned them in the church. There was not the least pretext for this: there had been no firing in Gelrode, nor had weapons been found on anyone.[91]

The next morning about twenty-one of the men, the youngest of the hostages, all in their teens and twenties, were marched out of the church. Then the Germans made another selection, choosing every third man. Among them was the sacristan's son, a soloist in the church choir and, according to residents, an exemplary boy. As the men walked through town, a woman standing in the door of her house asked a soldier, "What are you going to do with these young fellows?"

"We're going to shoot them," he replied cheerfully.[92]

The men were indeed executed. They were lined up against a wall and four soldiers were chosen for the task. The officer responsible for arranging the prisoners in a row was clearly not happy with the decision, according to a witness. The officer in charge, however, had no such compunctions. Two of the men, for some reason, were struck with swords before being shot, according to one witness.[93]

The fourteen men not executed were made to dig a pit for the victims. Then they were taken to Leuven, a trial run, of sorts, for the forced march of over a thousand Aarschot residents the following week.

By 3:00 on the 20th, there were no Germans left in the village. Civilians who had not fled at the approach of the soldiers emerged to give the young men a proper burial. Two indeed had had their heads slashed in addition to being shot in the back.[94]

German troops returned over the weekend, but nothing of significance happened.

The Germans re-entered the village a third time on Thursday, the 27th. Again, everyone they could lay their hands on was seized and confined in church. Again there was a pointless march, this time to Wezemaal, an hour down the Leuvensesteenweg. This time the women and children were included. These were released on the 29th, having had no food for forty-eight hours, except what the people of Wezemaal were able to toss to them as they passed. Most of the men, held hostage in yet another church, were sent on to Germany, along with some women. Some ninety-seven residents were forced into the cattle-cars and sent east. All witnesses testified that there was not the least provocation.[95]

When the Germans arrived in Gelrode on the 27th, three men attempting to flee the village were shot. Two were killed outright, but a third, a railroad worker named Vounckx, was badly injured and left lying in the road. There was no hospital or doctor in Gelrode, so the village curé, Pieter-Jozef Dergent, helped him into a cart and set off for Aarschot.[96]

We will never know what so enraged the Germans about the pastor or his charitable mission. One witness claimed he was accused of being an English spy. According to another, his piety upset them.[97] At any event,

Father Pieter-Jozef Dergent, pastor of Gelrode.

The burgomaster's house on the Grote Markt, with the balcony on which Col. Stenger was standing when he was shot.

Father Dergent had come at a bad time. All the remaining population of Aarschot was being held captive in the partially burned church.

The priest first brought the wounded man to the Damien Institute, home of the Fathers of the Sacred Hearts, known as the Picpus Fathers. Like so many other monastic and educational institutions, it had been converted into a Red Cross Hospital at the outbreak of the war. Simon Goovaerts, the Father Superior, whose monks had already been threatened by the Germans, urged Father Dergent not to leave the monastery. The priest, however, insisted on returning to his parish.[98] But as he left town, he and his driver were seized by the Germans. The cart and horse were confiscated, and the two men, after some delay, were hustled off to the church.

En route, the priest was repeatedly struck on the head by soldiers. But instead of being shoved inside, like the driver, Father Dergent was placed against an outer wall. There were more blows to the head. The pastor asked if he might turn and face the wall, and attempted to do so. The Germans stopped him, then changed their minds, pushed his face into the wall and ordered him to hold his hands up. He was then compelled to stand on tiptoe. When he attempted to lower his arms or rock back onto his heels, he was struck by the Germans. They alternately punched him on the head and banged their rifle-butts on his toes, yelling "higher, higher."[99]

At various times over the next two hours, imprisoned civilians who were permitted to go outside to relieve themselves caught glimpses of the priest. They returned horrified. Not content with the rather simple torture they'd devised, the soldiers decided to strip him, and then urinate and defecate on him. He was soon standing, dripping, in a pile of excrement. One woman, permitted to bring a child outside, saw two soldiers urinating on him at the same time, the urine running onto the crumpled soutane at his feet. A third soldier spotted the woman and ordered her back into the church.[100]

Eventually the Germans tired of this game. Four soldiers marched him toward the Demer. He was placed in front of the Van Thielen house and shot, and then thrown into the river. His body floated back to Gelrode, where, badly decomposed, it was spotted and pulled out. Father Dergent was given a church burial.[101]

"I made a pilgrimage to his grave," wrote Cardinal Mercier, "and amid the little flock which so lately he had been tending with the zeal of an apostle, there did I pray to him that from the height of Heaven he would guard his parish, the diocese, the country. We can neither number our dead nor compute the measure of our ruins."[102]

"WHO ARE YOUR HEIRS?" When war was declared, the fathers of the Damien Institute in Aarschot converted the monastery into a Red Cross hospital, as happened all over eastern Belgium. The institute was located on the outskirts of town, on the Herseltsesteenweg. It included two hundred beds and an operating room with surgical instruments and dressings. Three doctors were attached to the hospital.

The war came to Aarschot on August 19th and with it the first patients, twenty Belgian soldiers.

For all of two hours, the hospital operated as it had been designed to. Then, after a brief firefight around the building, the Germans broke in. At once the fathers were accused of having shot at the soldiers. The fact that no weapons were found in the hospital did not give the Germans pause. They ripped bandages off the wounded, but the injuries proved to be all too real.[103] Nonetheless, a major had claimed to have seen three shots fired from the building and so everyone was ordered out of the hospital and lined up against a wall at the front of the institute. The Superior, who spoke German fluently, argued vehemently with the commanding German officer, who kept repeating, *"Der Major hat es gesagt"* – the major said so.

The officer nonetheless began to have some reservations. A superior officer happened to be riding by and the lieutenant eagerly appealed to him for instructions. The fathers held their breath. Perhaps he would be reasonable.

"Shoot them all," the senior officer ordered, and rode off.

This had been a death sentence for Belgian prisoners of war the same day. But Goovaerts vehemently appealed the order, and, finally, after twenty anxious minutes, the lieutenant agreed to consult the general commanding the forces in Aarschot.

No sooner had he set off than the fighting began again. The Belgians returned in force. A machine gun mounted on a car swept the street. The Germans fled. However, the soldiers guarding the priests and the other captives remained. They took shelter, but with menacing gestures prevented the hostages from doing likewise. Exposed in the crossfire, three men were killed.

The Germans surged back into town. Eventually the lieutenant who had gone off to consult the general returned with good news: the fathers were to be spared, at least for the time being. They could perform some useful work for the Germans.

About sixty wounded German soldiers were transferred to the hospital. But after mulling over the treachery of the burgomaster, who had murdered a colonel while they dined together, the Germans thought it advisable to remove their wounded. The fathers, however, were permitted to care for the wounded Belgian soldiers for several more days. During this time the house was invaded repeatedly and the rooms searched. The fathers were accused of being franc-tireurs and threatened with death or deportation to Germany. Several fathers, their Red Cross brassards conspicuously displayed, were shot at, even in the corridors of the hospital. When Goovaerts protested, he was bluntly informed, "We do not recognize the Red Cross in Belgium." It was not clear what in Belgium was recognized. In one of the endless interrogations of the Father Superior, an officer spotted a map of the country on the wall. *"Belgien besteht nich mehr,"* he angrily declared, and ordered a soldier to slash the map with his bayonet.[104]

One night the fathers were commanded to lodge 1,100 men en route to the front. The next morning they collected about 800 empty bottles of wine, champagne, and gin.

During these days, the fathers watched the Germans methodically plunder the town. Empty vans pulled up in front of the houses, everything of value was loaded onto the vans, and the houses were set alight. On the evening of the 27th, the fathers heard firing outside the monastery wall. The next day the Institute was again invaded and all the priests and the Belgian wounded were compelled to assemble in the street – *"schnell, schnell."* One priest, who was saying mass, was permitted to finish because the soldier sent to fetch him defied his orders.

When the Superior asked for an explanation, he was told, *"Sie haben geschossen und Signale gegeben."* Goovaerts heatedly denied this, but the commanding officer brushed him aside. "That doesn't matter. I have my orders and am executing them."

"It was a dirty business," a non-commissioned officer confessed the next day to the Superior. "Our soldiers were firing, but you're being punished for it."[105]

While everyone was standing outside, the entire building was searched again. This time, soldiers claimed to have found a cigar box full of cartridges on top of the Superior's desk. The exasperated ecclesiastic pointed out how unlikely this was. Would he keep cartridges in plain view? Would they not have been discovered on the many other searches the Germans had already conducted? The officer finally conceded that the priest had a point. The cartridges were not mentioned again.

After two hours, everyone was permitted to re-enter the building. The priests were to pack up their clothes and toiletries. They could expect to be gone two weeks – that is, an officer explained, until the end of the war. Each priest was permitted to return to his room for this purpose, accompanied by a soldier. When they returned to their quarters, several of the men noticed that some of their few possessions were missing – watches, chains, shoes, money.

The priests were then surrounded by soldiers and marched to the church. They were relieved to get there. The soldiers kept threatening their hostages and the officer in charge of the escort repeatedly ordered them to be silent. "These people have done nothing," he yelled at one point. "They have been tending our wounded."[106]

Once they arrived at the church, the fathers were searched again, and such dangerous articles as crucifixes and statuettes were confiscated. As before, German soldiers helped themselves to articles they wanted – this time in plain view of the victims.

During this phase of their captivity, the priests' meals consisted of bread and water, their bed the choir stalls or the floor in front of the altar. By this time, the more than one thousand civilians confined to the church were permitted to use the exterior wall of the church as a latrine during the day time. At night, however, they were obliged to use the twenty buckets distributed around the church – the same buckets that were used the next day for drinking water.

After three days the priests were permitted to walk outside for half an hour under armed escort, and shortly thereafter a primitive latrine was constructed in the cemetery.

German paranoia continued unabated. Several days after the priests had been imprisoned, two officers brandishing pistols stormed into the choir and demanded to know which of the priests had fired shots out of a window in Aarschot's convent the night before. They were ultimately convinced of the improbability of anyone escaping from the church, locating weapons, firing them from the convent (without injuring anyone) and surreptitiously returning to the church.

A few days later another officer entered the church and announced that soldiers in town had been fired on and that, if another shot were fired, four hundred men would be selected from among the hostages and executed, the priests first.

At this point, some 6,000 German troops had been in possession of the deserted town for two full weeks.

⊰⊹⊱

On September 6, three hundred men were sent to Germany, the priests among them.

Again they were subjected to threats and insults at nearly every stage of the long journey. The priests were particularly struck by the intensity of the anti-clericism among the soldiers. The hundred or so troops accompanying the prisoners were particularly incensed when the priests were ordered into one of the two third-class carriages instead of the cattle cars. At one point they threatened to execute their hostages on the spot. The commander, Menne, was barely able to restrain them. "I'm master here!" he finally bellowed at them, restoring order.[107]

The commandant knew the priests were innocent. The day before, when he had permitted them to celebrate mass for the first time since their imprisonment, he had told them reproachfully, "You would have been spared all these miseries if you had not fired." When, once again, Goovaerts vigorously objected to the accusation, the commandant hastily corrected himself. "No, not you. But at Leuven priests shot at and mutilated German soldiers."[108]

During the 36-hour train ride, the priests were repeatedly reviled. Crowds of civilians mobbed the platforms in Germany, and seemed to the priests hardly less threatening than the soldiers they'd encountered in Belgium. At one point, enraged Germans tried to break into the compartments. The doors rattled violently, but the locks held.

When the comparatively decent Landsturm soldiers who had been guarding the priests were relieved at Köln, the first concern of their replacements was to have the priests remove their boots in order to check for knives.

⤙⤚

At Sennelager near Paderborn, where the priests were taken, they endured petty tortures and humiliations.

They were given some food, but no utensils to eat it with. They were deprived of water the entire first day; the pump they were denied access to was less than fifteen yards away. After being examined by a doctor, the priests were told they would be given a shower. When they entered the shower room, they were drenched with scalding water, to the great amusement of their guards.

The priests were also compelled the first day to exchange their money at highly unfavorable rates, and to purchase civilian prison clothes at exorbitant prices. The fathers were particularly chagrined at having to give up their habits.

That night, the priests discovered that their sleeping quarters consisted of the bare floor of a stable. The next night a compassionate soldier brought some straw.

Before they were summoned to meet him, then, the priests had deduced that the camp's commandant, Major Bach, was not fond of Catholics. They soon realized that he also had a rather Teutonic sense of humor. When they were taken to see him, with their luggage, he at once ordered their chalices seized.

"Who are your heirs?" he asked one of the fathers who had protested. "I want to be able to send it to them after you're shot."

In the satchel of another priest, Bach discovered a little vase with unction for the dying. "Ah ha!" he joked, "you brought that for yourselves. You knew you were guilty and would be shot."

"No," the father countered, "we use it for your wounded."[109]

Only about three-quarters of the confiscated habits were ever returned to the priests and these were cut up and pierced. A Catholic newspaper charged that they had been used in parodies of religion. Major Bach claimed that the clothes had merely been damaged in storage.

Despite these petty indignities, the priests noted that they were far better treated than the French and English prisoners of war. Two circumstances further improved their situation.

One day a Catholic soldier brought along a German priest from a nearby village, as the fathers had urged him to do. This priest, in turn, informed the Bishop of Paderborn, who, with the Bishop of Münster, evidently exerted some pressure on the German authorities.

Even before the priests had made their presence known to the church leaders, General Moritz von Bissing, then military governor of Münster, had inadvertently encountered the fathers and had quizzed them briefly. Like nearly every officer they conversed with, the general smiled cynically when they protested their innocence. Nonetheless, he ordered an inquiry, telling an aide that he should "try to separate the innocent from the guilty and report back to me."[110] Unexpectedly, the magistrate before whom they appeared took his duties seriously and wrote up a long report clearing the fathers. The Germans, now preparing for the eventual absorption of Belgium into the Reich, felt it expedient to honor the judge's findings. The Fathers of the Sacred Hearts were sent to a seminary in Münster. After three months, they were permitted to cross over into the Netherlands.

"SHE'S OURS" The German penchant for driving groups of civilians hither and yon peaked in the province of Brabant. Usually residents were herded out of town the better to loot. They were often told the town was to be bombarded. It seldom was. So it's not surprising that "the worst of the pillage took place on the 28th and 29th" – the day and the day after the Germans compelled the entire remaining population of Aarschot to walk to Leuven, some nine miles away. And as usual, "what the Germans could not take away, they tore up and soiled."[111]

But the commandant may have been ordered to send everyone east, and was informed that he needed to use the lines running through Leuven. This seems the most reasonable explanation, and a few of the captives were told this. However, the reception the residents received when they arrived at the station casts some doubt on this. Also, the day before, when some 40,000 residents of Leuven had been expelled from their homes, only a few hundred were loaded into cattle cars and transported to Germany, and many of these were sent back after being exhibited for 24 or 48 hours. The German White Book, not surprisingly, is silent on the forced march. Many Belgian accounts of the ordeal survive, naturally.

Residents were evacuated from the church early in the morning on the 28th. They were led to the front of the building and arranged in groups of five. The columns, under armed guards, then began trudging toward Leuven, normally a three to four hour walk for an adult. The old and the sick were piled onto carts, which were pulled by the younger men. When people fell by the side of the road, an officer circling back and forth on a bicycle would yell, "shoot them." These orders seem not to have been obeyed, at least until the civilians entered Leuven. However, one prisoner observed a soldier casually shoot and kill a peasant who was working in his field outside Wilsele.[112]

The day before, men and women who had been permitted to go outside the church to relieve themselves had caught glimpses of the torture inflicted on the priest of Gelrode. That evening, about thirty drunken soldiers had entered the church and briefly fired on the men, women, and children huddled inside. Everyone dove for cover and, miraculously, no one was injured. But the screams and whimpering of the children didn't subside for some time. "The consternation and despair of the mothers with children were indescribable," said one witness.[113] Nobody was inclined to question the expedition to Leuven.

Among the civilians trudging along the highway was Elmire Janssens, a single, middle-aged woman. She owned a wine shop on one of Aarschot's main streets.

She had kept the shop open on the morning of the 19th, naively expecting that there was nothing to fear from the German troops. As soon as the soldiers arrived in town, however, they had smashed her big front window. The bottles on display disappeared in an instant, and the entire contents of the shop was cleaned out within minutes. When soldiers began quarreling over bottles of rum and cognac, an officer strode into the shop. But the man had merely come to appropriate some liquor himself, for which he issued a worthless receipt.[114]

Mejuffrouw Janssens's 74-year-old father had been marched off with the men who had accompanied the burgomaster, but, unable to keep up with the others, had mercifully been sent back. Fearing he might not be so fortunate in any subsequent *Aktion*, Janssens cut off her father's moustache and dressed him in woman's clothes. He walked hunched over, to hide his face. Father and daughter were unable to escape Aarschot, however. The roads were clogged with troops and officers in cars. After spending some time in a hospital and in a neighbor's house, they were seized on the 25th and taken to the teeming church.

The Aarschot civilians reached Leuven between 5:30 and 6:00 p.m. The journey had taken over six hours. They had been menaced repeatedly en route. One witness described the officer in charge as "a veritable bandit" who treated the captives with great brutality.[115]

The civilians were led down Diestsevest to the Stationsplein. Charred ruins still smoldered. Unburied corpses still lay piled alongside the road. On one corner, a soldier was playing an accordion. In front of the train station, knots of armed men glared at them. There were menacing yells: *"Alles kaputt!"* and *"Der Feind!"*[116] And then the soldiers opened fire on the men, women, and children. Unlike in church the day before, they were not all drunk and their aim was better.

Elmire Janssens was holding one of her nephews by the hand. Two bullets tore into her arm, just above the elbow. She fell to the ground, dragging the boy with her. Her sister raced up and gathered her into her arms and attempted to carry her off. German soldiers interceded. "She's ours. She's been hit," one shouted.[117] The sister continued to drag Janssens another twenty yards. Then the Germans fired on the two women. This time Janssens was hit in the stomach. She tumbled out of her sister's arms and lost consciousness.

When she came to, she started screaming and was picked up by a soldier, who carried her into the first-class waiting room in the station. Here she was treated by a German doctor, who cut away her bodice and gave her an injection. "She's a brave lass," Janssens heard him say. "But there's nothing more to be done. She's past help."[118] When the doctor returned some time later, she begged to be taken to the Leuven hospital. He refused. She was to be sent to Aachen and imprisoned, he told her.

She was then carried into the main hall of the station, where about 300 soldiers were quartered. The man who had originally picked her up was among them, and came up to inquire about her. She thanked him.

An hour later the doctor returned with a stretcher. All the soldiers were now asleep, so he grabbed a rifle and banged the butt loudly on the ground. He ordered two of the soldiers to help Janssens into a carriage with German wounded. The men stared at her curiously. She shared a compartment with a man whose chest had been crushed. One soldier assigned to tend to the wounded on the trip was particularly solicitous. He brought her a drink and applied cold compresses to her head.

"You're a brave girl," he told her. "I live in Essen. Come and see me when the war is over. I'm married, but that doesn't matter."[119] The gallant suitor then kissed her hand.

When Janssens was removed from the train at Tienen, the soldier made the same proposition, again kissing her hand. Immediately afterward she noticed that a ring was missing, along with some money she'd hidden in her dress.

At Tienen she was moved to three hospitals before finally receiving treatment, nearly twenty-four hours after having been shot. She spent eleven weeks in the third hospital, at which point she found out she was to be sent to Germany. Janssens was able to contact her family, who succeeded in rescuing her.

At 5:00 a.m. on November 1st, she crossed the Dutch border after an eighteen-hour journey on a cart loaded with furniture.

⤙⤖

No one who lived through the German invasion forgot it. Yet what was recalled was not always what one would expect. In the midst of scenes of unspeakable horror there were odd moments of pleasure – as well as the moments of heroism and self-sacrifice that catastrophes so often call up.

An unmarried daughter dresses her father as a woman and cuts off his moustache. Had he been responsible for her not marrying? She becomes the object of much attention. She is casually propositioned by a German soldier. Yet this suitor, rather than offering a ring, may have relieved her of one.

The relationship of Germany and Belgium during the war was nicely epitomized, for Allied propagandists, by the treatment of Belgian women by German soldiers: posters depicted supplicating women and girls being trampled on or carried off, against a background of flaming buildings. Sometimes "Belgium" was emblazoned on the woman's chemise; usually this was not considered necessary.

A representation of the flirtation and theft on the Tienen platform would not have made for stirring propaganda, even if Mejuffrouw Janssens had been very young and very pretty. But it encapsulates no less the national experience at the hands of the Germans in August 1914.

-<-->-

A less complex story from the late-afternoon shooting in front of the train station:

Thirty-five-year-old Emilie Janssens had also been interned in the Aarschot church, along with her four-year-old daughter. She later described the hellish scene in front of the station. Buildings still smouldered in the square. The troops, their faces distorted with hatred, aimed their rifles at the terrified civilians and opened fire. Down went Vrouw Janssens, hit in the right leg and the back. Her daughter was shot in the left leg. While the firing continued, two chivalrous soldiers carried them inside the station. Shooting went on intermittently for another forty-five minutes, despite repeated cease-fire orders.

Emilie Janssens was then taken to the St. Thomas Hospital, where her leg was amputated. The daughter was more fortunate. She was released after three weeks, with only a slight limp.[120]

-<-->-

Twenty-year-old Célestine Angélique Claes was less lucky. When the shooting began in Leuven, her brother, a school teacher, thinking that only the men were in danger, abandoned his three sisters and hid in a garden. Mejuffrouw Claes, also a schoolteacher, took refuge in the cellar of the Café Vieux Temps, or she may have been seized outside the café and dragged downstairs. A waiter named Vandersteen eventually found her naked body with a deep bayonet slash in the back.[121]

-<-->-

Other captives were killed in the city, including a twenty-six-year-old woman, Alida Sylvia Bruyninck-Marien, shot in the lower back.[122] On the 29th, the survivors were herded back to Aarschot. Some individuals and families managed to escape in the confusion, and joined the hordes of Leuven residents fleeing south.[123]

Back in Aarschot, the men were again confined to the church, but the women, this time, were taken to the large Château Fontaine. They had been given nothing to eat in Leuven, though some children had received drinks. No one explained the purpose of the trip. As for the shooting, "I was informed," said one witness, "that we were fired upon by the German soldiers because the civilians in Leuven had fired upon the Germans."[124]

"IT IS NO LONGER WAR" Almost no civilians were left in Leuven when the Aarschot contingent arrived. Among the few were the doctors and staff of the St. Thomas Hospital, who had chosen to brave a bombardment rather than abandon their patients. As usual, the artillery barrage never materialized; it was merely a pretext to clear out the residents. Hervé de Gruben, a philosophy student turned stretcher-bearer, recalled the event.

> In the evening of Friday, between five and six o'clock, we suddenly heard the crackling of rifle fire in the direction of the station. None of us could imagine the cause of this. The guns had been silent since the preceding day, and the Belgian Army must have retired. Since the expulsion of the inhabitants, there was no one left in town to be massacred. What could the sound of these explosions mean?
>
> An hour later the mystery was explained. Two German soldiers rang the bell at the gate. They had brought on a stretcher a woman of about twenty-five and her little girl of three. One of the men was crying; the other seemed agitated and embarrassed. "It is horrible," said the first. "It is no longer war."
>
> The woman had a bullet in her side and a terrible wound below her right knee; the projectile had torn the muscles and shattered the bone frightfully. The child had a bullet in her knee. The woman, Emilie Janssens, had been driven out of Aarschot with several hundred of her fellow citizens; the German soldiers had told them that they would be placed in a train at Leuven, from where they would be deported to Germany as prisoners of war.
>
> While the human herd was waiting in Stationstraat, suddenly, for no reason at all, the German soldiers began to fire into the crowd. There were several killed and wounded.[125]

By the light of three candles, doctors amputated Emilie Janssens' leg.

⊰⟺⊱

Two German officers provided damning accounts of the incident. According to Lieutenant Paul Telemann, adjutant to the Commandant in Leuven,

> All of a sudden, some shots were fired. There then occurred a general fusillade in which a good part of the men of Battalion Neuss took part... I don't know who fired the first shot; the crowd prevented me from taking note. Shots may have been fired unintentionally. During the general fusillade, there was firing in all directions. I personally observed men firing into the ruins of burned buildings. Apparently they took

the dust raised by the ricochet of bullets for the smoke produced by enemy fire. Others fired on the prisoners who approached, because these were the only civilians they could see. The troops took them for the authors of the outrage, though there was not the least reason to believe that...

Seeing the guns aimed at them and frightened by the din of the fusillade, the prisoners hastily dispersed. But they were driven back toward the station by some of the troops... A good part of the civilians managed to escape, however.

As for me, I ran among the soldiers commanding "cease fire"... Other officers did the same, and after some time – I couldn't say how long – the firing stopped completely. Many women were wounded. Personally, I saw a woman slump to the ground in Stationsplein, hit in the leg. She was holding a child in her arms, or by the hand.[126]

Non-commissioned officer Georg Körber was still more scandalized by the incident. He grabbed the soldier who had fired on Emilie Janssens at close range, but the man got away. A number of soldiers were clearly drunk during the melee, Körber testified. They must have imagined that the unarmed civilians, mostly women and children, approaching the station were a mob of fanatical francs-tireurs launching a frontal attack.[127]

Körber's surmise was correct. In the company's war journal for the 28th of August is the following cryptic entry: "Around 6:00, the inhabitants again attacked the station. They were repulsed by the men who occupied it."[128]

Things were no better on Saturday. "The next day," Körber testified, "I saw soldiers behaving like madmen toward the civilians and their goods. These soldiers were clearly acting under the influence of alcohol and were exasperated by an attack of which they believed themselves to have been the victims."[129]

⊰⊱

There is still another possible explanation for the shooting. Three young diplomats and an American businessman happened to be visiting Leuven late in the afternoon on the 28th. The secretary of the two-man U.S. Legation, Hugh Gibson, and his friend Blount had casually decided during lunch to see for themselves exactly what was going on in Leuven. When they heard about the trip, the Swedish and Mexican chargés d'affaires were anxious to come along. An English-speaking German officer had discovered the men's identities as they were making their way on foot up Stationsstraat toward the Stadhuis. He suavely conducted them back to the station, warning them melodramatically about the perfidious Belgian franc-tireurs, who, he claimed, were still firing on his men.

Outside the station, Gibson noticed a crowd of several hundred civilians, whom he took to be Leuven residents being herded onto trains. The diplomats were taken to the front of the station and seated in armchairs. An orderly was despatched for a bottle of wine. "Suddenly several shots rang out, apparently from some ruins across the street, and the whole place was instantly in an uproar. The lines of civilians were driven helter-skelter to cover..."[130] Gibson and the others took refuge on the tracks of the station, amid some artillery horses tethered there. When two of the party finally crawled over to a place from which they could see the station square, they were greeted by the friendly officer, who "showed us where the attacking force was concealed – at least he told us that they were there and we were willing to take his word for it without going across the street to make a first-hand investigation."[131] Some civilians, Gibson surmised, no doubt "goaded to desperation by what they had seen, had banded together, knowing that they were as good as dead, and had determined to sell their lives as dearly as they could."[132] When Gibson's American friend joked that they'd never gotten their wine, the officer calmly fetched a bottle, walking directly in front of the "franc-tireurs." After it had been emptied, he urged them to lie down among the horses again. "He said it looked as though an attempt would be made to take the station by storm, and that there might be a brisk fight."[133] Other antics followed. No franc-tireurs were captured, naturally.

When Gibson finally returned to the U.S. Legation in Brussels and told his story, the minister, Brand Whitlock, was not amused. He believed that it was entirely probable that the Germans had staged the performance for the benefit of the young secretary, and, despite German pleas, refused to allow him to testify that he had seen Belgian civilians firing on German soldiers. Gibson could not have so testified in any event, Whitlock added tartly, at least "according to our rules of evidence."[134]

There is the possibility, then, that the gunfire that killed and injured several of the Aarschot civilians may have been the consequence of a ruse intended to convince a naive American diplomat that the franc-tireurs of Leuven were no myth, and that he had been fortunate to escape with his life. The refugees may have inopportunely arrived just at the moment when the charade was commencing.

RAPES Historians today are likely to be less confident than were their predecessors in the 1920s and '30s that reports of rapes in the Bryce depositions and elsewhere were wholesale fabrications. "Revisionists" cavalierly assumed, on the one hand, that any invading army was likely to indulge in this practice, however regrettable. But having conceded this point, they warned that reports of rapes could seldom be corroborated, and expatiated on the alleged appetite for salacious tales about the bestial Huns on the part of British and American audiences.

For the victims, the experience was profoundly humiliating, and, for unmarried women, far more consequential than today. The euphemism is revealing: rapes were "violations," and what they violated was something unimaginably sacrosanct in the early 20th century – chastity. Pride, modesty, and self-interest combined to discourage testimony.

Rapes undoubtedly occurred in and around Aarschot between August 19th and the recapture of the town by a Belgian cavalry division on September 9th. In the countryside west of Aarschot and south of Mechelen, the retreating Germans behaved with particular savagery. However, unlike the massacres carried out in the towns, there is no evidence that the rapes on the farms and in the hamlets of northern Brabant were ordered. Nor did the German Army systematically enlist criminals. (A Landsturm officer in Leuven was reprimanded for releasing German nationals from the city's jails, on condition that they enlist.) Nonetheless, there were undoubtedly thousands of criminals among the troops sweeping through Belgium. Entire companies and battalions earned reputations for brutality.[135]

Sometimes there were only threats. While his boot shop was being looted and the windows smashed, George Meyerman reported, his wife was told that she would have to remain there while her husband was taken to the Grote Markt, because "being a young woman they might want her afterward." To reinforce the point an officer jabbed a revolver at Vrouw Meyerman's breast. The couple, however, was able to escape.[136]

Many were not so fortunate. If the testimony of the Belgian soldiers advancing south on September 9th cannot always be relied upon, two reputable residents of Aarschot, Pastoor Arthur Leemans, Professor at St. Jozef's College, and Jeanne Vandemeulebroucke, the wife of a wealthy coal merchant, assured investigators that they knew of numerous girls and women who had been violated. They were not asked for specifics, and didn't provide them.[137] A Leuven magistrate and a justice of peace from Aarschot reported numerous outrages committed against young girls and married women in Aarschot. Many were told to them in confidence, but they named one young victim, Adrienne van de Bempt, whose father and two brothers were killed the night of the 19th.[138] Another woman claimed to have been raped by two soldiers in her home in Gelrode. One knocked her down and knelt on her chest while the other violated her. Then they switched places. The woman recalled staring fixedly at the numbers 4 and 9 on the soldiers' helmets, which they had not bothered removing. In Elewijt, a little over 13 miles east of Gelrode, the communal secretary identified four young rape victims by name.[139]

Then there is the testimony of Belgian soldiers. One, who subsequently escaped to England, reported encountering a mother and her seventeen-year-old daughter. The woman had been wounded and was lying down. The girl told the soldier that she had been raped by German soldiers. She didn't reveal how many. The Belgian was impressed with her calmness.[140] Another soldier, entering Aarschot with an officer, told investigators that he saw the naked, badly bruised body of an eighteen-to-twenty-year-old lying beside a ditch. Her abdomen had been cut open.[141]

Two soldiers, Charles-Louis Vervynckt and Frans Verbiest, offered detailed, signed declarations to a provincial administrator. Both of them heard a sixteen-year-old girl recount her ordeal, in one instance before an entire company. The girl, who sobbed as she spoke, told the soldiers that she was repeatedly raped by eighteen Germans over a period of several days. She was kept captive in a grocery store in the Grote Markt, opposite the burgomaster's house. On the third day, her father was made to witness the violations; he was then taken off to the church. Neither Belgian soldier was told the young woman's last name. Her friends called her Marie; she had blonde hair and lived on the Leuvensesteenweg, Verbiest recalled. Marie told the men that her sister was also raped in front of her husband.

A number of women were seized and forced to "cohabit" with German soldiers for as long as fifteen days, Vervynckt was told. They were permitted to prepare food for their husbands, sons, and brothers who were imprisoned in the church. However, when they brought the meals to the men, nearly all the food was seized and eaten by the guards, who amused themselves by throwing morsels of bread to their captives.

Undoubtedly, some of the second-hand stories the two soldiers were told had no factual basis. "Many women spoke of outrages against the sisters of the Aarschot convent," Verbiest reported. However, there is no evidence that nuns were violated in Aarschot, though not for a lack of trying.[142] And nuns elsewhere in Brabant were compelled to strip in front of soldiers, on the pretext that they were spies or men in disguise.[143]

If some reports of rape were invented, the quantity and quality of testimony on sexual abuse makes it more than likely that women were repeatedly victimized in and around Aarschot between August 19th and September 9th. Rape was nearly as ubiquitous as murder, arson, and looting, if never as visible.[144]

"A RELIGIOUS WAR" One of the first foreigners to arrive in Aarschot was an intrepid Dutch polymath, Lodewijk Grondijs, a teacher of physics at the Technical Institute of Dordrecht and later a professor of Byzantine Art at University of Utrecht. He had immediately recognized the significance of the German invasion – that it inaugurated a new kind of warfare – and, no less curious to investigate the phenomenon than was his countryman Bart Mokveld, had signed on as war correspondent with the *Nieuwe Rotterdamsche Courant*. Like Mokveld, Grondijs discovered that assertiveness, even combativeness, cut more ice with the German authorities than sweet reasonableness. This attitude no doubt accorded with his professorial habits and inclinations. Grondijs had a number of friends at the University of Leuven. His timing was fortuitous. Grondijs descended from the train in Brussels on August 19.

His first day in Leuven, the Dutch professor dined with a well-known priest, Father van Ussel. Joining them was a German Catholic, a sergeant-major who'd been wanting for some time to confide in a priest.

He was the only Catholic in his company, he told the men. As a rule, Protestant units were intentionally sent to Catholic Belgium, while Catholic troops, he claimed, were dispatched to Poland to fight the Eastern Orthodox Russians.

Sergeant Kluck's opinion of the death and destruction the German army had wreaked was identical to that of the university-educated reserve officers Grondijs had already spoken to: "It was a shame, but it was unfortunately necessary."[145] But when Father van Ussel reminded Kluck that his

own regiment had persecuted Catholic clergy, the man began to weep. The
military spirit, he eventually explained, was so ingrained in the troops that
it overwhelmed the scruples of any individual.

When van Ussel mentioned the great sympathy for Germany in Flemish
Belgium that had been dissipated by the German actions, this led to a lively
debate between Grondijs and van Ussel about the treatment of the Church
in Germany versus France. Van Ussel was convinced that a terrible persecution was raging in France, where his co-religionists faced the forces of
secularism at their full strength. But Grondijs argued that the *Kulturkampf*
had been far worse than anything Catholics confronted in Paris. Free-
thinkers might be galling to the Church, he allowed – contempt wounds
lovers more than hatred. But the heretic is the far more dangerous enemy.
Looking back on his off-hand remarks, Grondijs was convinced that they
were prophetic. He had not been aware at the time the strength of the ideological animus driving the Germans.[146]

◄―►

Anxious to see Aarschot after hearing about the atrocities committed there,
Grondijs headed north the day after he arrived in Leuven. Refugees from
the burned villages between Leuven and Aarschot were now returning
to see what they could salvage. Masses of German troops passed them,
marching south. When a column halted, Grondijs watched with incredulity and disgust as the soldiers begged for cigarettes from the passing refugees. Walking through the devastated streets of Aarschot, Grondijs was
particularly struck by the ferocity displayed toward Catholic images. A
home close to the entrance of town had been hastily vacated. The furniture was undisturbed, but two statuettes, one of the virgin and the other
of St. Anthony, had been shattered. Grondijs found evidence of similar
profanations throughout town. "One might take it to be a religious war!"
he observed.[147]

◄―►

Thanks to his friendship with an audacious Red Cross medic, journalist Scott
Liddell arrived in Aarschot on September 11, just after it had been recaptured
by the Belgians. He was appalled by the extent of the devastation. While he
was gaping at the charred ruins, the wind picked up, blowing soot, powdered

plaster, and slivers of glass, which tinkled eerily. Great loops of telephone and telegraph wires hung down over the heaps of bricks and plaster. Proceeding with difficulty down Demerstraat, he arrived at the church.

> On the left-hand side as we entered, we found a little altar which had been destroyed. On the top of this on each side of the altar had stood two wooden saints which had been dressed in costly gaudy raiment. Against these the Germans had heaped chairs, and had then poured paraffin or other inflammatory materials around and set fire to the whole lot. The main altar was also burnt down. The confessionals, pulpits, harmonium, and candlesticks had all been smashed. The offertory boxes had been burst open and robbed. The wooden statues of saints around the pillars of the nave had either been broken up or burnt. Empty wine bottles littered the floor around the main altar.[148]

Outside the church, Liddell encountered a large body of troops marching south. "For the first time I noticed that the faces of the Belgian soldiers were hard and stern. Other times I have seen them go into battle with a smiling face and a wonderful cheerfulness... *'Bonne chance!'* I would have cried, but somehow I remained dumb."[149]

BOTTLES Louise Mack, a popular Australian novelist and poet turned war correspondent, also arrived in Aarschot not long after the Belgians recaptured the town. The only female journalist on the front lines in Belgium, she was covering the war for *The Daily Mail* and *The Evening News*. Mack was conducted through the charred ruins by two young lieutenants from Brussels, formerly, she was told, two of the "smartest young men of the town," but now looking haggard and disheveled.

"'*Toujours les bouteilles,* '" one of them kept repeating, pointing out the hundreds of empty bottles littering each street.

"They took me to the main church," Mack recalled

> and there the little old brown-faced sacristan joined us, punctuating our way with groans and sobs of horror.
>
> This is what I see.
>
> ...On the high altar stand empty champagne bottles, empty rum bottles, a broken bottle of Bordeaux, and five bottles of beer.
>
> In the confessionals stand empty champagne bottles, empty brandy bottles, empty beer bottles.
>
> In the Holy Water fonts are empty brandy bottles.
>
> Stacks of bottles are under the pews, or on the seats themselves.
>
> Beer, brandy, rum, champagne, bordeaux, burgundy; and again beer, brandy, rum, champagne, bordeaux, burgundy.

Everywhere, everywhere, in whatever part of the church one looks, there are bottles – hundreds of them, thousands of them, perhaps – everywhere, bottles, bottles, bottles.

The sacred marble floors are covered everywhere with piles of straw, and bottles, and heaps of refuse and filth, and horse-dung.

"Mais Madame," cries the burning, trembling voice of the distracted sacristan, "look at this."

And he leads me to the white marble bas-relief of the Madonna. The Madonna's head has been cut right off!

Then, even as I stand there trying to believe that I am really looking at such nightmares, I feel the little sacristan's fingers trembling on my arm, turning me towards a sight that makes me cold with horror.

They have set fire to the Christ, to the beautiful wood-carving of our Saviour, and burnt the sacred figure all up one side, and on the face and breast...

"And here, Madame, *voyez-vous*! Here the floor is chipped and smashed where they stabled their horses, these barbarians!" says the young lieutenant on my left.

And now we come to the Gate of Shame. It is the door of a small praying-room.

Still pinned outside, on the door, is a piece of white paper, with this message in German, "This room is private. Keep away."

And inside?

Inside are women's garments, a pile of them tossed hastily on the floor, torn perhaps from the wearers....

A pile of women's garments!

In silence we stand there. In silence we go out. It is a long time before anyone can speak again, though the little sacristan keeps on moaning to himself.[150]

⊰⊱

Scott Liddell was shown the same scene:

> On one side of the church was the vestry. The door was broken down. We went inside. Empty wine bottles lay in great numbers in every corner. On a shelf on our left as we entered and on the floor itself was a quantity of women's clothes: cheap furs such as the peasant women wear, and skirts and underclothes. The latter were bloodstained.[151]

"WHAT WILL I TELL?" On his return trip from Aarschot to Leuven, Lodewijk Grondijs was stopped by a suspicious captain. "Who are you?" he demanded. "I saw you yesterday traveling in the other direction. Why are you returning?"

Grondijs came up with an acceptable pretext and displayed his Dutch passport. He was grudgingly permitted to continue, but was warned not to go to Leuven. Grondijs asked why.

"When you get there, you will tell what you have seen in these villages."

"What will I tell?" the Dutch professor asked innocently.

When he got no response, he repeated the question, glaring at the officer: "What will I tell?"

Earlier in the month German authorities were eager to have refugees spread the word as to what awaited communities harboring "franc-tireurs." *Schrecklichkeit* was useful. As recently as the 22nd, posters in Liège had publicized the Andenne massacre. But the captain was a university-educated reserve officer, Grondijs reckoned, and his conscience was not as clear as that of most of his superiors and subordinates.

"It's for me to speak, not you," the captain finally replied, but he permitted Grondijs to return to Leuven.[152]

"A FRIGHTENED DEER" Alexander Powell, the war correspondent for the *New York World,* accompanied the Belgian Army during its sorties from the Antwerp forts. With the director of the Belgian branch of the British American Tobacco Company, he volunteered on September 10th to drive to Brussels to convey messages from the American government to Brand Whitlock. The American Minister, like the rest of the city, had been entirely cut off from the world after the German occupation. Only with difficulty did Powell secure a laissez-passer from the Belgian authorities. "More work for the undertaker," muttered the Military Governor of Antwerp grimly. But the Americans displayed large flags, wrote *"Amerikanischer Consulardienst"* in white paint on the hood, and armed themselves with great quantities of cigarettes. They did not encounter any Germans until they were just outside Aarschot. Here the car was halted by the officer of a German company concealed behind a hedge. If the car had traveled another ten feet, his troops would have opened fire, he later told the men. The commander, once he assured himself of the nationality of the visitors, proved quite congenial. He had lived in the U.S., and he and Powell compared notes on the best hotels in Atlantic City and discussed the relative merits of the dining car service on the Pennsylvania Railroad and that of the New York Central.[153]

The incongruity of the discussion struck Powell forcibly, but the officer's sense of camaraderie enabled the two Americans became the first foreigners beside Grondijs to see Aarschot or rather what was left of Aarschot since it had been sacked and burned by the Germans. A few days before, Aarschot had been a prosperous and happy town of ten thousand people. When we saw it, it was but a heap of smoking ruins, garrisoned by a battalion of German soldiers, and with its population consisting of half a hundred white-faced women. In many parts of the world I have seen many terrible and revolting things, but nothing so ghastly, so horrifying as Aarschot. Quite two-thirds of the houses had been burned and showed unmistakable signs of having been sacked by a maddened soldiery before they were burned. Everywhere were the ghastly evidences. Doors had been smashed in with rifle-butts and boot-heels; windows had been broken; furniture had been wantonly destroyed; pictures had been torn from the walls; mattresses had been ripped open with bayonets in search of valuables; drawers had been emptied upon the floors; the outer walls of the houses were spattered with blood and pock-marked with bullets; the sidewalks were slippery with broken wine-bottles; the streets were strewn with women's clothing. It needed no one to tell us the details of that orgy of blood and lust. The story was so plainly written that any one could read it.

For a mile we drove the car slowly between the blackened walls of fire-gutted buildings. This was no accidental conflagration, mind you, for scattered here and there were houses which stood undamaged and in every such case there was scrawled with chalk upon their doors *"Gute leute. Nicht ʒu brennen. Nicht ʒu plündern"* (Good people. Do not burn. Do not plunder.)

The Germans went about the work of house-burning as systematically as they did everything else. They had various devices for starting conflagrations, all of them effective...

Despite the scowls of the soldiers, I attempted to talk with some of the women huddled in front of a bakery waiting for a distribution of bread, but the poor creatures were too terror-stricken to do more than stare at us with wide, beseeching eyes. Those eyes will always haunt me. I wonder if they do not sometimes haunt the Germans. But a little episode that occurred as we were leaving the city did more than anything else to bring home the horror of it all. We passed a little girl of nine or ten and I stopped the car to ask the way. Instantly she held both hands above her head and began to scream for mercy. When we had given her some chocolate and money, and had assured her that we were not Germans, but Americans and friends, she ran like a frightened deer. That little child, with her fright-wide eyes and her hands raised in supplication, was in herself a terrible indictment of the Germans.[154]

CHAPTER 4

Andenne

A BAD ATTITUDE Andenne, with a little over 7,900 inhabitants in 1914, sits on the right bank of the Meuse, about one-third of the way from Namur to Liège. It lay in the path of the 28th Regiment of Pioneers and the 81st, 83rd, and 87th Infantry Regiments of the southernmost corps of von Bülow's Second Army, the Reserve Prussian Guard, which was advancing toward Namur from Liège and across the upper Ardennes.

The massacre that took place in Andenne on August 21st was the most savage to date. Andenne also had the distinction of being the first mass execution to be publicized by the Germans: the day after the killings, a new proclamation appeared all over Liège. "The inhabitants of the town of Andenne," it read,

> after having protested their peaceful intentions, made a treacherous surprise attack on our troops. It was with my consent that the commanding General had the whole place burnt down and about one hundred people shot. I bring this fact to the knowledge of the town of Liège, so that the Liégeois may know the fate with which they are threatened, if they take up a similar attitude... The General Commander-in-Chief, Von Bülow.[1]

In fact, a total of 262 men, women, and children were shot, stabbed, hacked to death, or immolated in Andenne and its neighbors directly across the Meuse, Seilles and Landenne-sur-Meuse.[2] Presumably, the Dutch journalist Bart Mokveld surmised, the others were killed without von Bülow's consent.[3] Needless to say, there was no "attack" on German troops.

About 8:30 in the morning of August 19th, shortly after a German reconnaissance plane was spotted soaring above the Meuse, the bridge across the

Armee - Oberkommando

LE 22 AOUT 1914

Abteilung II b. Irn. N. 150.

Aux Autorités communales

DE LA

VILLE DE LIÉGE

Les habitants de la ville d'Andenne, après avoir protesté de leurs intentions pacifiques, ont fait une surprise traitre sur nos troupes. C'est avec mon consentement que le Général en chef a fait brûler toute la localité et que cent personnes environ ont été fusillées.

Je porte ce fait à la connaissance de la Ville de Liége pour que les Liégeois se représentent le sort dont ils sont menacés, s'ils prenaient pareille attitude.

Ensuite, il a été trouvé dans un magasin d'armes à Huy des projectiles « dum-dum » dans le genre du spécimen joint à la présente lettre. Au cas que cela arrivât, on demandera rigoureusement compte chaque fois des personnes en question.

Le Général-Commandant en chef,

von BULOW

Imp. La Meuse

Proclamation from General von Bülow declaring that he personally authorized the killings in Andenne.

river was blown up by sappers from the 8th regiment of the Belgian 4th Division. Soldiers also barricaded a railroad tunnel at Sclaigneux on the outskirts of town.[4] The regiment then retired toward Namur, to defend the gap between Forts Marchovelette and Maizeret. The plane had spotted the bridge intact and Belgian troops retiring. When the first squadron of uhlans arrived at the base of the bridge and found it demolished, residents later speculated, they had blamed the civilian population and decided to punish the town.[5]

There were engagements with uhlan patrols on the outskirts of town that the Germans may have attributed to civilians. Three times on the 19th Belgian rear-guard troops of the 8th regiment clashed with German horsemen, once in the Stud Woods west of town, once by the tunnel, and, at 4:00 p.m., across the river in Seilles, at the far end of the demolished bridge. One German soldier was killed in the last encounter, the commander of the detachment, Lieutenant Friedrich von Bülow, a cousin of the former Chancellor, and several were wounded. Living and dead were abandoned by the remaining cavalrymen, who galloped off. Also abandoned was the wounded commander of the second patrol, Count von Schimmelman. He was carefully carried to a nearby hospital set up in the École de St. Begge. Hours later, when the Germans occupied the town, the doctor who attended him and several officers tried to get the Count to declare that he had been shot by franc-tireurs. Schimmelman vigorously denied this: a Belgian soldier on the opposite bank had fired three shots and hit him with each shot.[6]

Early in the morning of the 20th, the gravedigger of Seilles, Ernest Michel, was ordered to disinter Lieutenant von Bülow's body with his bare hands. When he had finished, one of the officers yelled in French, "Comrade, you will be revenged."[7]

CALVARY Like so many of his counterparts elsewhere in Belgium, the burgomaster, sixty-four-year-old Dr. Jules Camus, had taken great pains to insure that no one would give any provocation to the Germans. Three sets of proclamations had been posted throughout Andenne. The first established a stringent curfew, the second warned of grave consequences for any acts of violence, and the third, on August 13, ordered that all arms be surrendered to the civic authorities. A great number of guns of all types were collected in the communal school, and receipts issued.[8] Telegraphic

*Dr. Jules Camus,
burgomaster of Andenne.*

Andenne was one of the only locations where photos were taken of some of the victims. The man in the lower right is Victor Joseph Davin, an échevin and the town's Police Commissioner. All but one of the men and boys in his and his brother's families were murdered by axwielding soldiers.

equipment was also requisitioned. Accompanied by other municipal officials, the mayor had visited the homes of several individuals considered
likely to cause trouble and had warned them about the terrible consequences of any acts of bravado.[9]

Nonetheless, the destruction of the bridge and attacks on the patrols
apparently infuriated the Germans, and they blamed the burgomaster. A
group of uhlans sought him out at 11:00 a.m. on the morning of the 19th.
"We are in possession of Andenne," he was told. "If anyone shoots at us,
you'll be shot and the village burned." Camus tried to calm the officers. He
would guarantee the behavior of the citizens, he said, and showed them the
placard requiring the inhabitants to bring in their arms. One officer took
the poster and flung it to the ground. "That's just paper and ink," he said
contemptuously.[10]

Camus was made to escort the uhlans on an extended tour of the town.
The first stop was the home of M. Rousseau, Andenne's tax collector,
where the Germans confiscated the communal funds. Camus was returned
to his house about four hours later, bleeding, disheveled and covered with

mud. He'd been beaten and abused, he told his housekeeper. A soldier at one point had thrown him into a ditch and backed his horse over him. He referred to the ordeal as his calvary, perhaps anticipating its denouement. [11]

Camus had done nothing to offend the Germans, apart from questioning the amount of the "ransom" the invaders had demanded from the town. At the town treasurer's office, he had objected to handing over the entire contents of the safe, more than 3,000 francs. A fine of this amount "was not proportionate to the size of the town," he argued. [12]

The next evening, the 20th, he would be shot as he closed his shutters, and then nearly decapitated by soldiers after his housekeeper pulled him into the kitchen. The soldiers would drag him back onto the sidewalk, where he would be again attacked by hatchets and left to die. For good measure, his house would be machine-gunned later that night.

POPPING THE CORK Apart from the abuse of the burgomaster on the previous afternoon, the first full day of the German occupation, August 20th, was otherwise peaceful until about 5:45 p.m. All day troops poured into Andenne from the south and east, along the Ciney and Liège Chaussées. The regiments, belonging to the Prussian Guard Reserve Corps of the Second Army, had expected to march toward the French border, but they had been diverted north to invest the Namur forts above the Meuse. When these capitulated, they would head south across the Sambre.

Buildings in Andenne were occupied and supplies requisitioned, including timber, casks, and girders for the pontoon bridge the engineers were constructing. One merchant was relieved of 20,000 francs worth of wood. [13] Everyone was very accommodating. Wine, tartines, and cigars were handed out to passing troops. "It would hardly be an exaggeration to say that the population fraternized with the invading soldiers," commented the Dean of Andenne, Abbé Louis Cartiaux. [14]

The troops had the day off while they waited for the bridge to be completed. In the morning and early afternoon, soldiers paid for their food and drink, but as more alcohol was consumed, they ceased paying. As usual, droll types offered receipts stating that the debts incurred were "payable by France." Café and shop owners naturally raised no objections. Dozens of witnesses testified to the heavy drinking and the growing rowdiness of the troops. [15]

The bridge was not completed until about 4:00 in the afternoon, and troops did not begin filing across it into Seilles for another hour. The Andennois watched nervously from behind closed doors.

Then, some time between 5:30 and 6:00, shots rang out from the heights of Seilles. Of the thirty-six sworn affidavits collected by the Belgian Commission of Inquiry after the war, the twenty-three that offer testimony as to the origin of the massacre agree unanimously about the shots. All the witnesses interviewed by Schmitz and Nieuwland also concur, as does the German commander, Major-General von Langermann.[16]

The initial shots apparently came not from troops who had just crossed the pontoon bridge from Andenne, but from soldiers who had occupied Seilles most of the day, having begun arriving early in the morning of the 20th from Liège. They included companies from the 28th, 83rd, and 113th regiments of the Guard Corps.

Seilles was known in the region as a distribution center for French wine. There was a large population of boatmen plying the Meuse up to Sedan – and a disproportionate number of bars and cafés.[17] Many witnesses reported heavy drinking during the afternoon. "They had only one word on their lips – champagne," recalled Abbé Thys, the curé of Seilles.[18] The cafés had plenty of burgundy, cognac, and rum as well, and by mid-afternoon residents had become quite disturbed about the drunkenness, especially as the officers themselves were indulging freely at Chez Elias, where the commandant was installed.[19]

Around 5:30 p.m., gunfire was heard from the district called Les Houillères, east of Seilles proper and northwest of the train station that still serves both Andenne and Seilles. The station sits in a little valley at the north end of the bridge to Andenne. Intoxicated soldiers, residents reported, had entered a girls' school and were firing on the houses across the street. Soon several homes had been set on fire. The rumor had apparently spread among the troops that Lieutenant von Bülow had been killed in the neighborhood, and the inebriated soldiers had decided to avenge his death.[20]

Other testimony suggests some premeditation. Some witnesses thought the gunshots came from closer to the station. They believed it was a signal, because a manhunt commenced almost at once. Residents were dragged out of their homes and addressed by a French-speaking officer. "You are going to be shot. Someone has killed a cavalryman." At that very moment a riderless horse with an injured leg was ostentatiously led down to the station from a neighborhood called Thier. The men protested their innocence. A second burst of gunfire came from behind a pharmacy on the square facing the station. "To the wall!" bawled the officer, and twenty-four civilians were lined up against the Hôtel Dethier, opposite the station. A group of soldiers trained their guns on the captives.[21]

Meanwhile, the burgomaster, Xavier Somme, along with a local aristocrat, the Comte de Borchgrave, encountered four tipsy uhlans wending their way up a hill overlooking the station. The cavalrymen invaded the home of Honoré Thys, who had fled with his family that morning. From here they began firing in the direction of Andenne.[22]

Hearing these shots, the troops preparing to execute the civilians were convinced they were coming under fire from the French. Rumors of a French attack had already been sweeping through the ranks. Abbé Thys, fluent in German, testified to the extraordinary fear of the French he overheard among the soldiers. When the firing commenced from above the station, most of the executioners scrambled for safety, abandoning their victims. At least four of the condemned were killed, however, and possibly as many as nine. (It was difficult afterwards to distinguish those shot by the firing squad from those hit in the barrage that followed.) Shouting *"Franzose! Franzose!"* the panicked troops began shooting back at the Thys house. Others fired across the Meuse. Witnesses heard the crackling of machine-guns and the booms of artillery.[23]

Alarmed soldiers rampaging through Les Houillères now opened fire on the franc-tireurs who had apparently seized the train station, as did troops in the hamlet of Nouveau Monde, north of the train tracks. As he passed in front of the presbytery, Abbé Thys saw a cavalry squadron that had just arrived assaulted by a withering barrage coming from the girls' school in Les Houillères. Three horsemen fell. The priest estimated that as many as one hundred Germans were killed, as platoons fired furiously on each other up and down the left bank, testimony corroborated by another witness. But this is undoubtedly an exaggeration. Other civilians were convinced the total was considerably lower. Léon Delvigne estimated that twenty were killed or wounded.[24]

It is as difficult to reconstruct the exact chain of events as it is to determine the number of German casualties. It is possible, for instance, that there

was only one barrage coming from Les Houillères. Clearly, though, gunfire from the heights west of the train station preceded the initial round-up
of men from the buildings around the station, and then disrupted the activities of the firing squad a few minutes later.

The executions re-commenced as soon as order was restored. Seven
civilians were shot in the vicinity of the train station, including a woman
and a child. One man, Henri Kenis, was savagely bayoneted, dragged into
the middle of the street, and left to die. Residents listened helplessly to his
anguished pleas for water. Forty-five residents would be killed by morning.[25] But it was civilians in Andenne, across the Meuse, who would pay the
steepest price for the anarchy in Seilles – or for the charade that went awry.

PORTENTS There were now several thousand troops south of the Meuse,
waiting to cross over to Seilles. When the gunfire erupted from across
the river, some soldiers in Andenne rushed to the quay and returned the
fire. Some appeared to panic, and took off in the opposite direction. If the
troops in Seilles imagined the French were attacking from the west, many
of those in Andenne initially assumed that the Belgian Army had launched
an offensive from the north.[26]

But others acted more mysteriously. An artillery piece was unlimbered
and lobbed three shells in different directions, rather than across the river.[27]
Machine guns were rapidly assembled and fired into rows of homes on the
main streets descending to the Meuse. Soon after the firing commenced,
several witnesses saw soldiers descend into the cellar of a building and fire
out through the ventilator, then rush into the street claiming franc-tireurs
had been shooting.[28] A merchant in rue Brun, Alexandre Wery, watched
with curiosity as a dark blue luxury car made its way slowly down the
street. Four officers sat in the car and leisurely fired over the roofs of the
buildings on both sides of the street. Soldiers on the streets paralleling rue
Brun would imagine the bullets were raining down on them from the rooftops. The car came to a stop in front of the Café Liégeois, and Wery saw
the officers laughing as they heard the volleys of shots hitting the far side
of the buildings in response.[29]

Even before the initial shots rang out from Seilles, there were signs that
something was afoot. A magistrate observed an order being passed along a
column making its way to the improvised bridge. The soldiers immediately

cradled their rifles in their arms. Less than ten minutes later firing broke out from across the Meuse.[30] Dr. Émile Dondenne observed some suspicious troop movements in Place des Tilleuls, prior to and immediately after the shots. The Potsdam Guards were carefully ranged in battle order along the square, facing Seilles, and, fifteen minutes before the fusillade, the officer in command of each group seemed to be transmitting an order. Other witnesses observed "a certain effervescence among the troops."[31]

Additional evidence of premeditation soon surfaced. Undoubtedly, some stories were mere rumors. (A few residents, for instance, claimed to have had overheard the phrase "Andenne massacre" from the Germans who first entered the town.)[32] But a number of reports are more plausible. A dying officer at a hospital in Huy infomed a "trustworthy individual" that not a tenth of what the General Staff had planned for Andenne was actually carried out.[33] Dr. Auguste Mélin was assured on the morning of the 21st by an officer speaking fluent French that there would not be a single man left alive in Andenne by that afternoon. Melin would be spared because he was a doctor.[34] An officer billeted in a house six kilometers from Andenne warned his hostess against going into town. "Terrible things will happen," he told Mme. Schellinx.[35] The mother superior of the Sisters of Providence of Landenne was given a similar warning between 5:30 and 6:00 p.m. by a Dr. Maler and a Westphalian captain. An hour later, she testified, she visited General von Bülow himself in order to get a safe-conduct pass to rescue some nuns from Seilles. When the mother superior repeated what had been told by the officers, the General did not disavow the claim.[36]

Earlier, on the 19th, an officer told Achille Thys that tomorrow the Andennais would pay dearly for the folly of their king. The officer in charge of setting fire to two buildings in the hamlet of Peu-d'eau, just south of Andenne, told Joseph Leflot on the morning of the 20th, "We're only burning these two buildings now, but in the afternoon we'll burn the entire town." Also on the morning of the 20th, Edouard Noël was warned by a soldier that Seilles would burn because someone had fired on the troops. Around 2:00 that afternoon, Captain Junge, who would soon be directing the massacres, told Mme. Roland pithily, "We'll bring fire and blood to your town."[37] The German woman who would confront Junge in the Place des Tilleuls the following day, Eva Comes, was also tipped off about an upcoming bombardment.[38]

Only half an hour before the firing commenced, Junge did something more remarkable, and more significant. Very agitated, he asked the director of the École Sainte-Begge, where he had been lodged, for some writing paper, preferably with the name of the institute on the letterhead. When the director, Georges Belin, Brother Réginald, confessed there was none, Junge wrote the following note in German on a blank sheet: "The Brothers of Charity at Andenne have, from noon August 19th until 6 in the afternoon on August 20th, given food and lodging to five officers and thirty sharpshooters and have conducted themselves in a very hospitable manner."

Having completed the note, he appeared overcome with emotion. Tears filled his eyes. "Hold on to this paper carefully, my brother. You could have great need of it."[39]

MOTHERS AND CHILDREN When the shooting began, terrified residents all over town fled to their cellars. Horrific things began happening right away. Soldiers broke down doors and windows with their rifle butts, shot and stabbed the inhabitants, pillaged their homes and then set them on fire. An extended family and their neighbors were herded into an alley next to their home in Hautebise, a village just south of Andenne. Without any explanation, soldiers began firing at the unarmed civilians. Nineteen-year-old Ida Mauguit was the first to fall. Marie Warzée, daughter-in-law of the head of the family, Honoré Warzée, was nursing her eight-month-old baby, Honoré-Georges. As she raced toward a shed behind her house, she was hit by two bullets. One lodged in her right arm, but the other passed through her engorged left breast and immediately killed the nursing infant. In excruciating pain, she spent the night in the shed with the dead child, fervently wishing, she later recalled, that it was she who had been killed.[40]

Several family members managed to escape. The rest of the group was made to march downhill toward the center of Andenne, but was soon ordered to stop once again. The officer commanding the detachment had spotted the body of a soldier against the wall of a chateau, and was enraged. Again the soldiers were ordered to fire on the group; this time the firing was more prolonged and intense. Twelve of the seventeen civilians died within minutes.

Two young sisters, Marie-Thérèse and Valentine Mauguit, 9 and 11, clung to their mother as she fell. "Maman," cried Marie-Thérèse, and

Mme. Mauguit responded weakly. Then she was silent. But the girl had been heard by German soldiers. She and Valentine were each bayoneted. Marie-Thérèse, lying on a heap of corpses, was aware of being kicked and examined by the soldiers, and then lost consciousness. She and her sister spent the night in the arms of their dead mother, while their neighbor Marie Warzée crouched in her shed, a few hundred meters away, cradling her dead baby.[41]

Neighbors found the two girls the next day and carefully lifted them off the pile of bodies. Dr. Auguste Mélin, who examined them, was amazed at the amount of coagulated blood covering their faces and hair. It was their mother's blood, and it had saved them.[42]

SHOPPING Many of the Andennois killed during the night of August 20 died in their homes, not on the streets. Hermine Blanchaert Froment, the wife of the manager of a large store, Delhaize, Frères, and Co., was serving German soldiers in the store when the gunfire broke out. "Hide," they yelled at her as they rushed outside. At the same time, civilians loitering outside raced into the store for cover, including M. Froment. But husband and wife became separated when Hermine Froment stumbled as she was running upstairs and was knocked unconscious. Slumped behind the kitchen door, she was not spotted by her husband and the others when they scrambled back downstairs and then down to the cellar, where they assumed she was hiding. A moment later, when a neighbor, Jean Noël climbed back up to the kitchen to look for her, the Germans raced in, howling like banshees. The two civilians hid beside a large storage closet, but were discovered immediately. Nöel was shot twice and staggered forward. A soldier leveled his gun at Froment, who begged for mercy. He fired nonetheless, but she instinctively whipped her head away at the last instant, and the bullet hit her hand. A second bullet struck her left side. She fainted. When the woman regained consciousness, she was lying in a puddle of blood. She saw a group of soldiers beating with their rifle butts a fifteen-year-old boy whom they'd tied to the front door. Nöel, meanwhile, writhed in agony a few feet away, sat up briefly, pushed against the wall, then fell again to the floor. Another group of soldiers entered the kitchen. One flipped her over with his rifle and announced, *"Kaputt."* She, too, had been saved by blood on her face.

The Froments lived on the premises of the store, and as she lay next to her dead neighbor, Hermine Froment listened as the soldiers took an informal inventory: "cognac," "malaga." Groups of men returned throughout the night "abominably drunk," yelling like savages, to ransack the shop. At one point she was turned over again by another soldier. He fired into the floor next to her and staggered off. More shots were fired above her, the windows of the store were smashed, and, at around 6:00 a.m., yet another neighbor looking for her was shot by soldiers.[43]

◄‹·›►

What was always distinctive about German pillaging was the sheer amount of wanton destruction. A magistrate who was able to return to his house in Andenne after soldiers occupied it noted the following:

> All the glass of the mirrors was broken or pierced by bullets, the glass of the front door, the large glass over the dining-room chimney-piece, an alabaster clock, the gas fittings, the piano – everything was broken. A mahogany escritoire in the drawing room was broken and forced, and jewelry had been taken. The fireplace, the mirror and the ornaments in the drawing room were broken, and generally everything within reach was smashed. The linen was taken, the curtains pulled down, and everything of value removed.[44]

FIRES About forty-five houses were torched that night in Andenne, and the fires claimed several victims. The Walgraffe's house was the first in Andenne proper to be burned. The family had dashed into the cellar when the shooting began and had listened, terrified, to the shouts and the gunfire. Early in the morning, the Germans entered their courtyard and yelled for all the inhabitants to come out. As Arthur Walgraffe emerged from the house, followed by his ten-year-old son, he was gunned down by a soldier standing three feet away. Behind the German was a car loaded with petrol drums. Soldiers raced over to it and ignited the house. There were ten children under fifteen years old in the cellar; Mme. Walgraffe, was watching her sisters' children as well as her own. After the home was set ablaze, German sentries wearing Red Cross insignias, ignoring the children's pleas, fired pot-shots into the basement.[45] Everyone was rescued when coffee shop owner Alexandre Polet, with the help of his son Léon, was able to lift the grill off the cellar window. Crossing the street after escaping from the burning house, the the family was fired on by soldiers at the top of Rue Bertrand. No one was hit.

The blaze destroyed everything the family possessed, save for a single crucifix, which was discovered intact. Also retrieved from the ashes was the head of Arthur Walgraffe. His sister-in-law brought it in a bucket to the Brothers of Charity, where the family was staying.[46]

The conflagration was even more widespread in Seilles, where over 140 houses were burned, particularly in the vicinity of the station. Several victims suffocated in their cellars. On both sides of the Meuse, residents attempting to escape the fires were shot.[47]

PLACE DES TILLEULS Early next morning a systematic round-up of the population began. Windows, shutters, and doors were smashed, homes invaded, and the Andennois seized and herded at gunpoint to the Place des Tilleuls. Many were beaten with rifle-butts or slashed with bayonets en route. Many never made it to the Place.

The perpetrators had all volunteered for the task, according to the testimony of a German prisoner of war. They were unleashed at 4:30 a.m., with orders to massacre all males in town over seventeen years old, except for the elderly. Originally they had been told to use their bayonets; no one was to be shot. The order was changed, however, when too many soldiers objected.[48]

Alexandre Polet, who had rescued his neighbors, the Walgraffes, was forced into the corner of his living room by soldiers brandishing hatchets. There he was shot in cold blood, along with two friends, while his wife and ten-year-old son watched. The Walgraffe family had left only moments earlier.[49] A Flemish clockmaker and his eighty-year-old father-in-law were ordered out of the house by the Germans. The old man was unable to stand by himself, and when a soldier commanded the clockmaker to raise his hands, he held up only one. He was supporting his father-in-law with his other arm. An infuriated soldier struck him on the neck with a hatchet. The man died in agony on his doorstep. When his wife knelt down to help him, she was driven indoors at gunpoint.[50] Others were conducted not to the Place des Tilleuls, but into back alleys, gardens, or fields, where they were brutally dispatched. Seventeen people were driven into an orchard off rue de l'Industrie, including a family of eight, the children and siblings of Andenne's Police Commissioner Victor-Joseph Davin. The family owned several iron foundries in town. Most of the men were shot, but several were hacked to death with hatchets. A tall, red-haired German with a scar on his face distinguished himself by the ferocity with which he wielded his ax, according to the sole survivor, young Théophile Davin.[51]

The most innocuous remark could be fatal. Jules Laloup and his wife left their house promptly when soldiers appeared at their door and ordered them out. "You've shot at us. You killed our son," declared a soldier in bad French. At other houses along the street, the residents were accused of killing a horse. *"Cheval,"* like *"fils,"* would be a familiar word to someone with a rudimentary knowledge of the language. "If anyone fired on the troops," Laloup responded gallantly, "he was a coward." But Laloup had probably exceeded his captor's vocabulary. The soldier immediately struck him with his bayonet and blood spurted from a long wound. As soon as he and his wife arrived in Place des Tilleuls, Laloup was hauled into a small side street and executed. Anyone who had been wounded was clearly a franc-tireur.[52]

Between 6:00 p.m. on the 20th and late the following morning, when the mass executions began, nearly 150 people were killed, most during the round-ups that had begun around 4:30 a.m.[53]

By mid-morning between 800 and 850 men, and perhaps double that number of women and children, were crowded into the Place.[54] Already the sun was beating down mercilessly, and the thirty-two lime trees for which the square was named offered little shade. A twenty-year-old student made some cryptic notes shortly afterward:

> It was an awful sight. The corpses of an officer or non-commissioned officer and many civilians lying on the ground, debris of all kind, dead horses. The houses riddled with bullets, along with a stained-glass window, doors ripped off. In the square, desperate-looking men, women, and children, more dead than alive, halfclothed. Here a young man, sprawled on the ground, begging for his mother, there a disabled man, carried by his children. Not far away, civilians being manhandled by soldiers. Everywhere terror and brutality.[55]

Two large cars pulled up and disgorged a dozen officers, who, according to one witness, were visibly pleased by the spectacle. They applauded and yelled "bravo." Presiding was Major Bronsart von Schellendorf; assisting was Captain Junge, who spoke French. He pointed to the body of a German sergeant who been killed by a discharge from a German rifle the night before. "This is another one of our men killed by franc-tireurs," Junge announced. "He will be avenged."[56]

Also on display were some of the hunting rifles and cartridges that had been collected at the town hall and local schools, by order of the burgomaster. The Germans claimed the guns had been found in homes. Nearby, two mortally wounded Belgians bled to death on the cobblestones, one shot in the chest, the other bayoneted. Occasionally they called out for water. When a civilian signaled to a sympathetic soldier to bring over his canteen, the man obliged. But an officer snatched the canteen from the soldier's hands and reprimanded him. The officers meanwhile discussed various methods for killing all the people in the square.[57]

Entering Place des Tilleuls, Alexandre Wery, the merchant, saw some acquaintances from the Hautebise district tied together. He also recognized the distinctive cattle ropes that bound them. They had been requisitioned from his cousin's store the day before, while he was there. When the merchant had asked what they were needed for (it was not yet dangerous to ask such questions) he was told that they would be used to help construct the bridge. The soldier, however, had not headed down to the river with the ropes, but toward Hautebise. Wery was now convinced that the actions against the civilian population had been planned well in advance.[58]

After some time, the men were separated from the women. "The goodbyes were heartbreaking," one witness recalled. "A cordon of soldiers armed with guns and hatchets surrounded the men."[59] Then a selection began. All the men would not be killed, apparently. One man, guilty of signaling to his wife, standing across the square, was pulled out of the crowd. Another man innocently asked what would be done with everyone. This was insubordination, and he was condemned to death. The expression on the face of another appeared to an officer to indicate disgust at the proceedings. He was guilty of "insolence toward the German Army," and likewise condemned. One simple young man had picked up some empty Belgian and German cartridges. This was sufficient evidence that he was a franctireur. Several men were condemned to death for having dirty hands or clothes. They were factory workers, they explained, and dirty hands were an occupational hazard. The Germans were not impressed. An unlucky carpenter was caught with a spanner in his pocket. This dangerous implement was confiscated and he, too, joined the ranks of the condemned. More unfairly still, any wound, whether a month old or inflicted by German soldiers the night before or en route to the Place, like Laloup's, was grounds for execution. Several men were chosen on this basis. After about fifty had been selected, the back of each victim was marked with a cross in chalk.[60]

At least one condemned man was able to talk his way out. Because he was wearing a Red Cross arm band bearing the inscription "Namur," Dr. Charles Lehoye was identified as a spy, and faced execution on the spot. Luckily, he had his medical bag with him, and produced a thermometer and some surgical instruments. After a brief discussion with a French-speaking officer, he was permitted to resume his place with the other men. Before long, he would be appointed assistant burgomaster by the mercurial German authorities. He would serve under another man condemned to death prior to his elevation, Émile de Jaer. (In exchange for issuing the numerous proclamations the Germans required, the men's homes were not set on fire.)[61]

Spared as well were three priests. They were isolated in front of the crowd of hostages and the commanding officers were prepared, as usual, to assume they were responsible for the franc-tireur attack on the army. But the abbés Waffard and Polet, it emerged, were retired and could not have inflamed the populace from the pulpit. The wrath of Captain Junge was directed entirely at young Father Delcourt. He was about to shoot the priest with his pistol when he was stopped by Lieutenant von Bunau. This officer reminded his commander that Father Delcourt was the almoner of the Sainte-Begge Institute and had been issued a laissez-passer by Junge, which Bunau himself had delivered. The captain's demeanor changed at once. He became very solicitous. He ordered that the priest be given an escort back to the hospital for his own protection. "The soldiers are very enraged and would do you harm," he confided to Delcourt.[62]

At least one man in the Place was rescued on more capricious grounds. A barber, François Hellings, was standing among the group selected to be shot when he was recognized by a soldier he had shaved the day before. The soldier apparently liked the way Hellings had trimmed his beard. He walked up to the condemned man and pulled him from among the hostages, picking at random unlucky Arthur de Barsy to take his place. No officer intervened.[63]

EVA COMES Eva Comes, a twenty-five-year-old German woman from the Rhenish town of Mayen, near Koblenz, happened to be vacationing in

Andenne. Soldiers invaded the home where she was staying early Friday morning, and she and her hosts were herded into the square. Comes circulated among the officers, pleading for the victims. Few were sympathetic. But several, though they assured her that their troops had been fired on by franc-tireurs, indicated that they were "sad" to have to carry out their orders. Some were more outspoken. "I don't approve of this business," Captain Prey told her. "It's disgusting," Lieutenant Wogge confided. "I don't know how I'm going to be able to watch it." The original order had specified that the soldiers were to use their bayonets to kill their victims, another officer told her. The soldiers had recoiled, he claimed, and the commandant had decreed that the victims would be shot and that the women would be escorted away from the execution site.[64]

Growing increasingly indignant, Comes demanded to be taken to the commandant. She was told it was useless to approach him; he never rescinded an order. But when Captain Junge arrived in the square, the petite young woman – witnesses guessed that she was only eighteen – strode up to him. She flung herself on her knees and pleaded for mercy. Twice Junge told her to go to the devil. A young officer, Lieutenant Schuman, moved by Comes's courage, offered to intercede with Junge, who was a friend of his. At length, the captain permitted her to speak with him. Comes again asked for mercy for the innocent. "Innocents!" Junge cried. "But they've fired on my soldiers. Here's another noncommissioned officer killed by two bullets!" And he gestured at the body of the sergeant that had just been dragged into the square. But Comes persisted. Before the largely uncomprehending but attentive crowd, and several bemused officers, she argued that the townspeople were nonviolent. When Junge claimed priests had incited the people, Comes disputed this. Parishioners had repeatedly been advised to remain calm and show goodwill toward the soldiers. The burgomaster had also insisted that the town receive the Germans hospitably. Arms had been collected in the town hall. Junge objected. Arms had been requisitioned only to be redistributed to franc-tireurs.

"Where were you during the night?" he asked, switching tack. When Comes told him she was in the cellar, he pointed out that she could have observed nothing. "But at least I know those who were with me didn't fire," Comes countered. When Junge asked who was with her, she rattled off the names of everyone she knew in Andenne. Then she challenged the captain to conduct a genuine inquiry. "You think I have time to ferret out the guilty?" he asked scornfully. "The innocent must pay with the guilty." He then promised to pardon members of the family she was staying with, but she was not placated. "What about the others?" she insisted.

We'll never know what Junge made of the intransigent young woman. Her refusal to be bought off no doubt annoyed him. He'd offered to spare her friends; surely that had been her motive in pleading for an inquiry. What hope was there for Alsace and Lorraine if Rhinelanders, after a hundred years of Prussian rule, still possessed such antiquated notions about individual rights and due process? But Captain Junge may have admired Comes's resolve. There was something attractive, perhaps, in her passion and doggedness, despite her subversive ideas. It's also possible that the captain may have considered for the first time the possibility of unpleasant repercussions. Comes was a German subject, with family and friends in the Eiffel region. Undoubtedly she would talk about what she had seen and heard.

In any event, Junge finally promised Comes that he would present her case to Bronsart. After consulting with his chief, he announced that the major had agreed to be merciful. However, two of the men would still be executed, as the German non-commissioned officer whose body lay in the square had been shot twice. A relieved Comes did not dispute the logic of this. She was issued a passport and hustled off to Seilles.[65]

‑‹‑›‑

Bronsart did not keep his word. Nearly all of the fifty men chosen by the officers in Place des Tilleuls were executed. However, they were marched from the square to other destinations. The majority were shot beside the Meuse or in front of the police station.

But while Eva Comes was still in the square, the promised executions were dutifully carried out. For some reason, however, three, rather than two, of the condemned men were pulled from the group and lined up against the wall of the Discry house. By poetic justice, one man, remarkably, survived the shooting, a fifty-seven-year-old merchant named Félix Heurter.

Like nearly all the Andennois, Heurter and his wife had hidden in his cellar when the firing commenced the previous evening. The next morning, he was the victim of a crude German ruse. Two days earlier, on the afternoon of the 19th, when Lieutenant von Bülow was killed by Belgian Army troops in Seilles, an infantry officer, with the obvious intention of implicating a civilian, gave him some of von Bülow's personal effects – his staff field map, a pair of gloves, a pack of cigarettes. The officer had had von Bülow exhumed to retrieve the articles, which he instructed the civilian to keep for two or three weeks and then send on to von Bülow's widow. The officer was apparently not disturbed that his intended victim had cared for a German soldier wounded in the attack that killed the lieutenant. The man escaped to Namur before he could be accused of von Bülow's murder.[66]

The set-up for Heurter was less complicated. He was ordered upstairs and told, by gestures, to open the window. As he approached the window, shots rang out from the street, shattering the glass. The bleeding Heurter was hustled downstairs, beaten with rifle butts and hauled off to Place des Tilleuls. (There were still cruder tricks. At 4 a.m. on the morning of the 20th, some uhlans or hussars riding through town yelled out several times, "People of Andenne come out. The French cavalry has come to help you." The few frightened souls who were deceived by this were shot.)[67] A friend translated for Heurter the one-line indictment and sentence: "He was seized with handguns, he was about to shoot, he must be made an example." Hit in the chest by the first bullet, his lung pierced, Heurter pretended to be dead while another man was shot beside him and a third bayoneted. He then lost consciousness. When Heurter revived around noon, the Place des Tilleuls was deserted.[68]

The next man to be shot in the square was Ernest Froidebise. He was charged with killing a non-commissioned officer, Sergeant Schellborn, in rue d'Horseilles. It was Schellborn's body that was on display in the square. The charge was as baseless as that against Heurter. More than a dozen German soldiers and officers and residents of the street witnessed what actually happened, and three of the latter offered sworn testimony to the post-war Commission. A soldier was battering down the door of a house with his rifle butt when the gun discharged. The unlucky sergeant, who'd been approaching the door, was shot through the temple. As the neighbors and other soldiers watched in horror, he spun around, fell, raised himself up briefly, and then collapsed. An autopsy confirmed the bullet was of German origin. Twenty-five to thirty civilians from the area were rounded up and taken down to Place des Tilleuls. Froidebise seems to have been singled out at random from this group.[69]

The third man selected was bayoneted as he tried to escape.[70]

Most of the rest of the condemned men were then conducted down to the river in small groups and executed there. A platoon under Lieutenant Bunau seems to have carried out most of the killings, first marching a column of about twenty-five civilians from Horseilles, not among those waiting in the Place des Tilleuls, straight through the square and down to the wharfs by the Meuse and shooting them. He then made successive trips down to the river to execute those condemned to death by Junge and Bronsart.[71]

Eva Comes, en route to Seilles, witnessed one group being shot. The captain escorting her warned her not to look to her left as they approached the pontoon bridge, but the young Rhinelander disobeyed.[72]

"GO BURY YOUR DEAD" After the executions, Captain Junge installed new town officials. He told Dr. Charles Ledoyen, whom he had just appointed assistant burgomaster, that he "had a great responsibility before world history. You will be showered with gold if you tell the truth, that civilians fired on German troops."[73] The brief ceremony took place amid scenes of confusion. Women were crying and pleading with the officers. Children screamed and clung to their mothers.

Some time around 10:00 a.m., the women and children were ordered out of the square. "Go bury your dead, without any ceremony," an officer commanded.[74] The women were also ordered to wash down the blood-stained cobblestones. But a few men who had been permitted their freedom (they were requisitioning supplies) interceded with the senior officers, and the actual task of burying the victims, who lay strewn throughout the city, was eventually assigned to a detail of about forty men chosen from among the hostages in the Place des Tilleuls.[75]

Those men remaining in the square were informed that they were captives, and were packed into three small houses near the damaged bridge. They would remain there from late Friday morning until Tuesday afternoon. The houses were not selected for their size or amenities. There were close to three hundred men in each house, according to one hostage. "We were lying next to each other like sardines in a can," he recalled. "The

stench was horrible; the toilets stopped working."[76] For the first twenty-four hours the prisoners received nothing to eat. Eventually, women
were permitted to bring food to their husbands, sons, and brothers. Many
women, however, had taken refuge with relatives in the countryside, fearful of being raped.[77]

There is, in fact, little direct information on rapes. In a small town like
Andenne, women who had been raped may have been even more reluctant
to discuss the experience than residents of a large city or peasant women.
The good opinion of one's friends, neighbors, and colleagues bulked
larger. Thus, though we can be fairly confident that, amid the drinking and
looting on the night of the 20th, some women of Andenne were raped, the
information is sketchy.

Léon Delvigne reported that "many girls and young women were
raped." He cites only one particular case, however, a farmer's wife in a hamlet outside town, "violated five or six times consecutively in the presence of
her husband, who was bound."[78] Abbé Thys, curé of Seilles, reported the
rape of a mother of five, pregnant with a sixth, also under the eyes of her
husband, and two young girls outraged by soldiers pointing pistols at their
chests.[79] "People speak of numerous rapes," reported Alphonse Pirsoul,
Andenne's communal secretary. "The unfortunate women who were made
victims have kept quiet about it, evidently. We'll never know the full story."[80]

The more common, and amply documented, experience of women was
shock and grief.

The gunfire was frightening and it was inconvenient to spend the night
in the cellar, but husbands and wives reassured each other and both reassured the children. The family was innocent; no one had any weapons. The
Germans were reasonable; what would they want to do? Between 4:30 and
6 a.m. the answer started coming. Some families in their cellars heard the
sound of doors being broken, the cries and pleas of men and women, and
then sporadic gunfire. Others were surprised when their homes were suddenly invaded by soldiers smashing furniture, slashing curtains and wall-
paper, and then pounding on the cellar doors with their rifle-butts, yelling,
"*Raus, 'raus.*"

In one instant someone you had known intimately for ten or twenty
years, someone you had just been talking to, whose continued existence
you took as much for granted as your own – that person, in the blink of an

eye, as the Germans say, was dead at your feet. Or he was writhing in pain, blood spurting from a ragged bullet hole or a bayonet slash.

For most women there was no time even to kneel down beside their dead or mortally wounded husband. Either their house was set ablaze or they were chased out a gunpoint and beaten with rifle-butts if they lingered.

When they returned – if the home had not been burned – they often found the house filled with soldiers drinking and singing, like the wife and daughters of Alexandre Grégoire.[81] Sometimes the woman was obliged to serve the invaders, stepping gingerly over the body of her husband with a tray of coffee cups.

"When I returned, my husband was dead," Begge Sterpin, the widow of Achille Thys, testified.

> He was in the garden, his face against the ground; he had received a blow to the back. He had been dragged from the door of the greenhouse, because that's where I found the cartridge. Soldiers had defecated around my husband and, while I was kneeling beside him, continued to do so... My husband's wallet was empty; it had contained 5,600 francs, because we had counted on leaving and the suitcases were already packed. I was forced to leave the house, because the soldiers were making fun of the body, and behaving indecently.[82]

Séraphine Demazy, the widow of 39-year-old Luc Roland, provided a no less poignant story. While they were obeying orders to leave their house, they were fired on.

> My unfortunate husband fell, crying out to me, "I'm injured." I threw myself on my knees at his side, and held his head. How long did I remain there? I don't know. A soldier, believing us dead, began searching my husband and took his wallet. He felt in my pocket and I moved. He was nonplused at first, but then ordered me to leave. 'Kill me,' I responded. He took me by the arms and started ripping my clothes. Then there were blows from a rifle butt, and I was finally forced to leave and head for Place des Tilleuls. This same soldier killed messieurs Hamoir, Marchal, and Gramtinne while I watched...
>
> Towards 10:00 the hangman in charge of the executions called out, "The women will return to their homes to bury the dead and clean the streets," and I returned home. My poor husband was begging for something to drink. I approached and saw that his stomach had been opened up, probably with a bayonet. He still had the strength to speak to me. Wounded around 5:00 in the morning, he died after 6 hours of frightful suffering.
>
> The housework and shopping remain undone. My poor children and I have done nothing but cry. The scoundrels have nicely carried out the orders of their vile chiefs.[83]

Many other wives and children didn't know the fate of their husbands and fathers until they returned, though they feared the worst. A moment after they were forced out of their home, the wife, mother, and youngest son of Camille Guillitte, a forty-six-year-old pharmacist, heard a burst of gunfire reverberate through the house. Liberated from the Place des Tilleuls at ten, they rushed back, filled with dread. "Re-entering the home," the younger son wrote, "we descended into the cellar, where we confronted a horrible scene. My brother, lying near the door, had been killed at point-blank range, my uncle had the back of his head chopped off by a hatchet blow, my father had been stabbed by a bayonet along his spine." German soldiers were still milling around the home, and the family's arrival gave them new opportunities for amusement. "Using their rifle butts, they rolled the bodies toward the door and one of the Teutons, seizing my father by the hair, hurled him at the feet of my mother, who was crazed with despair and terror at these monstrosities."[84]

⊰⊹⊱

Captain Junge had rescinded the order that the women bury all the dead of Andenne. However, they were still obliged to clean the streets. The first notice posted by the new government of the commune made this clear:

> By order of the German military authority occupying Andenne, All the men are retained as hostages.
>
> For every gunshot against the German troops, AT LEAST two hostages will be shot.
>
> The hostages will be fed by the women, who will bring what's necessary to the bridge at 6 in the evening and 8 in the morning.
>
> It is strictly forbidden for women to converse with the hostages.
>
> All the streets and public squares will be immediately cleaned BY ALL THE WOMEN IN TOWN, under penalty of arrest.[85]

The blood the Germans spilled was to be washed away by the family and friends of the victims.

PLUMS Not surprisingly, there was at least one instance where it was possible that a man was spared because of his attractiveness to homosexual soldiers or officers.

Edouard Noël, a factory worker, was among those from the Horseilles neighborhood who were marched down to the Meuse to be shot. He noticed a soldier walking deliberately close by his side, without saying a word or looking at him. Noël recognized him. It was a man to whom he had given some greengage plums the day before.

The soldier pulled him out of the ranks of the marching prisoners. When other soldiers tried to push him along, the soldier spoke with them briefly and they left him alone. According to Noël, the friendly German then conducted him to an officer who interviewed him as they stood on a slope above the Meuse. The officer first asked Noël if he had fired on German soldiers.

"No," said the factory worker, "nor has anyone else."

The officer contradicted him. A colonel had been killed. In less than forty-eight hours the Aarschot tale had spread from the Demer to the Meuse.

Having made his point, the officer told Nöel that he had a wife and children back home and asked if Noël would like to come to Germany to be a concierge for the family. Apparently the only job qualification was not having shot any Germans recently. The officer gave the startled Noël two glasses of champagne while he considered the proposition.

The officer then left abruptly. Between sips of champagne, Noël had been trying to observe what had happened to his compatriots, but a wagon blocked his view. The soldier suddenly took Noël's head in his hands and turned him around to face rue d'Hanton, away from the shooting. Nonetheless, Noël heard the fusillade that killed his friends and brother-in-law.

The soldier then accompanied him back to his home. When they entered the house, the soldier presented Noël with a safe-conduct pass. Three days later the man returned with money for Noël's child. In his testimony, the factory worker doesn't indicate if there was any further contact between the men.[86]

"IT ISN'T WAR" Maurice Montjoie, a lawyer and one of the few witnesses who felt secure enough to permit his name to be published with his testimony in the Belgian government's *Reply to the German White Book* in 1916, was fortunate in the officers assigned to lodge with him. They were a captain and lieutenant of the 28th Regiment of Pioneers, engineers who would be overseeing the construction of the pontoon bridge the following day.[87]

Montjoie described vividly the residents' terror on the night of the 20th, crouched in cellars, listening to "the whistling of rifle shots, ...the rattle of machine guns and the muffled explosions of grenades." Then something more terrifying still: "About 5 a.m. the firing ceased and we heard the sound of doors and windows being hacked and burst open. From time to time there were sharp volleys. No mistake was possible. It was the end. Civilians were being shot dead in their houses and gardens."[88]

Montjoie and the others in his house were not shot. Hands raised, they were marched to a factory not far from the center of town. An artillery column rumbled by. The soldiers pointed at them and jeered in heavily accented French, *"Vous fousillé, fousillé vous."* A more welcome German at that moment stepped out of the commander's headquarters close by. It was Captain Wabnitz, who had been billeted with Montjoie. He glanced at the captives quizzically, walked over to some other officers, conferred with them briefly, then led off Montjoie and his family. Without speaking a word, he conducted them into a public garden. Abruptly Montjoie heard behind an ominous clicking. Six soldiers were fixing bayonets. "Are we going to be shot?" the lawyer asked the captain. "No," Wabnitz said. "You're free."

As he headed back home, Montjoie observed that one of the last artillery men in the convoy, "urged on by his comrades, was aiming very carefully in the direction of Liège. I looked in that direction and saw that his target was a little girl of about twelve, who had run away and was at that moment standing still at the intersection of two roads. I shouted, 'No, no! Don't do that.' He looked at me furiously, but at last lowered his weapon."[89]

From his home, Montjoie watched the heartbreaking parade of old men, invalids, little children and their mothers trudging, along with the men, to Place des Tilleuls.

When the captain returned to Montjoie's house that evening, the lawyer pleaded with him to get some of the hostages released. Wabnitz was pessimistic. He had little authority, but he would see what he could do early the following afternoon.

Captain Wabnitz kept his word. Shortly after 12:00 on the 22nd, the lawyer and the German engineer set out to locate the hostages. They passed by 30 or 40 bodies lying by the wall of a paper mill. The corpses were unrecognizable. Most had their heads blown off. The two men stepped around more bodies and pools of blood as they proceeded. Corpses were scattered everywhere. Through the open windows and doors they saw soldiers drinking, singing, playing the piano. Fresh regiments were marching down the street, fifes trilling. "I don't like this," the captain muttered darkly. "It isn't war."[90]

OFF TO RUSSIA There was at least one other conscientious and compassionate German in Andenne on the 20th, a man willing to characterize events the following morning with greater precision than Captain Wabnitz. Dr. Uhlmann was attending civilian victims at the Institut Sainte-Begge, converted into a hospital. Uhlmann had been working most of the night when an old man was brought in who had been shot point blank while sheltering in his garden. Immediately afterwards a young woman was carried in, Berthe Demeure, who had been stabbed by a bayonet below her left breast by a soldier attempting to rape her. Uhlmann had already expressed to Georges Belin, Frère Réginald, the school's director, his indignation at the way his compatriots were waging war. This was the last straw. He strode off and returned with two officers and the chief medical officer. The enraged physician expostulated at length with the three. The chief medical officer, Dr. Gildun, was furious with his subordinate, and the officers were unsympathetic. The argument was in German, of course, but Belin understood the drift from the tone, the expressions, and gesticulations. Then at one point, one of the officers responded with the stale bromide, *"C'est la guerre." "Ce n'est pas la guerre,"* Uhlmann shot back. *"C'est l'assassination."*

While he was arguing with Gildun, a nurse asked Uhlmann to attend to some wounded soldiers who had just been brought in. The doctor refused. "I'm going to take care of this woman first," he announced. Gildun turned to the nurse. "If I were in charge in Andenne," he said, "not a single woman would remain alive."

After Gildun and the officers had left, Belin congratulated Dr. Uhlmann on his candor.

"I only did my duty, "the doctor replied bitterly, "but now I'll pay dearly. They'll send me off to Russia."

Two days later, off he went.[91]

◄◄·►►

Another witness reported a brief encounter with Uhlmann. Like everyone else in Andenne, Mélanie Génicot, with her husband Théodule Bertrand and her eighteen-year-old son Nestor, took shelter in her cellar. They were joined by neighbors, a husband and wife. A soldier appeared at the top of the stairs. He looked so menacing that the terrified Mme. Bertrand flung herself down at his feet and assured him that they were good people and would do whatever he wished. Without saying a word, the German shot the father and son and the neighbor. No one died instantly. The men were barely conscious and died within two hours, but the boy suffered grievously. He was hit in the stomach and was crying and moaning.

Though the gunfire continued, Mélanie Bertrand and her neighbor dragged the boy to the school of the Brothers of Charity after their husbands had died. Here he was attended by a German physician "who could not contain his indignation." Nestor Bertrand died the next afternoon.[92]

Before he was shipped to the Eastern Front, Uhlmann was able to arrange for the release of several hostages.[93]

FÊTE NOCTURNE The forty or so men digging mass graves were the only hostages permitted outside the houses. They worked for nearly twenty-four hours, sustained only by stale bread and water. (At one point, though, a well-disposed officer on horseback, firing his pistol, chased off a group of soldiers tormenting the prisoners, and provided soup and chocolate for some of the *"gentils civils."*) Then the men gathered the bodies. A 32-year-old worker named Jules Borsy, one of those engaged in the grisly task, counted 23 victims who had clearly been hacked to death.[94] Back in the three houses, all windows and doors had to remain shut at all times. Wedged up against each other, the men baked in the hot August sun. The stench was unbearable. On the third day, early in the morning, all the men were ordered out of the houses and made to stand on the ruined bridge. The Germans were suddenly nervous that Belgian soldiers from the Namur forts of Maizeret and Marchovelette were preparing to shell the pontoon bridge on the far side of the original bridge. This was a familiar tactic. One of the first things the Germans had done after arriving in force Thursday afternoon was to compel eight civilians to lie down on the ruined bridge as they began preparations for their pontoon bridge. If the Belgians opened fire from across the river, these civilians would be the first victims.[95]

After about an hour and a half, the older men and husbands were released, but all the single young men were marched back to the three houses.

That afternoon, small groups of captives were made to search amid the gutted buildings for bodies that had been overlooked. Some Germans had been complaining of foul odors. Then, the following day, the remaining hostages were released. A "fête nocturne" was being planned.[96]

A few evenings later, on August 29th, bonfires were lit in Place des Tilleuls, tables set up, and hot wine served. The celebration, it emerged, was called "Pardon d'Andenne." It was the town that was to be forgiven, not the Germans. A proclamation issued on the 22nd had declared that Andenne, "in the eyes of the civilized world," was "a nest of murderers and bandits." But there was hope: "It may be possible to restore the honor of this town."[97]

No Andennois would have voluntarily attended these macabre festivities, naturally. But the newly appointed officials and their families were compelled to be present, and a number of other women, including recent widows, were also obliged to come. The Germans sent a car to fetch the Dean, Abbé Cartiaux. The new burgomaster, Émile de Jaer, sitting in the back seat, explained that the authorities wanted the residents to see how German soldiers normally behaved.[98]

The civilians were forced to drink to the honor of the Kaiser and to sing *"Deutschland über Alles."* Additional toasts were proposed and there was more singing by the soldiers. Andenne's pardon was conditional, however: should the civilians fire again at the soldiers, residents were told, for each German killed many civilians would die.[99]

LIEUTENANT GOETZE Several months after the grotesque "fête," the town was visited by a young German officer who professed to be curious about what the citizens had seen and heard on August 20th and 21st. Lieutenant Goetze was conducting an investigation of the massacre. News of the fate of Andenne, Aarschot, Dinant, Tamines, Leuven, and other towns had not played well in neutral capitals, and the Imperial Foreign Office wished to publish a report explaining the actions of the German Army. It would document a sinister "Belgian People's War" waged by unscrupulous civilians, egged on by their priests.

The Germans had already conducted an inquiry, but the results had hardly been satisfactory from the Army's point of view. A reserve officer with the 83rd regiment, Lieutenant Backaus, had been responsible for the inquest, which commenced on Saturday, August 22nd. Backaus focused on the town's clerics, suspecting that a sermon by the dean had inspired Andenne's resistance. He soon abandoned this hypothesis, and then began to doubt whether there were any franc-tireurs at all. By Sunday he was willing to concede that the German troops may well have fired on each other.[100] A Lieutenant Balcke from the 28th regiment of pioneers was meanwhile conducting an inquiry in Seilles on behalf of his commander, Major Scheunemann, whom Abbé Thys found "more reasonable and more honest" than any other German he had encountered. Scheunemann himself interviewed the curé over a period of two days, and eventually abandoned what was to become the fall-back position of apologists for the Imperial Army: that Belgian soldiers disguised as civilians fired on German troops. "Tell your people that from now on no homes will be burned and no one will be killed," Scheunemann promised.[101] If Backaus and Balcke filed reports, these was suppressed by the authorities.

Goetze was more carefully briefed, and was not burdened by a background in law. He did not disguise his motives from those he interrogated. He'd been sent to Andenne, he told the physician Isidore Leroy, "to combat the underhanded campaign of the Allies against the Germans in the press of the neutral countries." He mentioned to the merchant Alexandre Wery that Germany's enemies had targeted the Netherlands in particular.[102]

The would-be witnesses soon found his questioning highly tendentious. "How do you know the burgomaster was killed by the Germans," the bulky, red-haired lieutenant asked witnesses in Dr. Leroy's presence. Dr. Camus's butchered corpse had lain on the sidewalk in front of Camille Guillitte's pharmacy for hours, and was seen, as the Germans intended, by dozens of citizens. When witnesses mentioned this, Goetze demanded to know where the individual had been at the exact moment Camus was killed. Invariably, the witnesses testified they had been in their basements. "Well," Goetze would respond smugly, "then you can't comment on the issue."[103]

Dr. Leroy would have none of this. He'd been on his way to attend a wounded man, accompanied by an officer, at about 10:00 p.m., and had

seen Camus's body surrounded by a crowd of soldiers, who were still firing
shots. No residents were in sight, naturally. Dr. Leroy, according to his
later testimony, then told the lieutenant, at great length, exactly how ridic-
ulous the charges against the civilians were. In a town of around 5000 occupied by 30,000 heavily armed soldiers, only a fool would fire on the troops,
and he had seen no evidence that anyone had been so foolish. Dr. Leroy
had had extensive contact with the population and no one, he said, showed
any inclination to take on the German Army. On the contrary, everyone
was fearful and concerned chiefly with how best to placate the soldiers.[104]

Goetze's inquiry culminated in a report signed on March 29, 1915,
and issued as part of the official German White Book purporting to document a "Belgian People's War." It is a report only a Prussian officer could
love. Goetze records triumphantly that "only" 196 persons had been shot.
Twenty-eight men whose names appeared on a list he was handed were
merely "missing." There were other pyrrhic victories: "The rumors were
also false which claimed that seven men of one family had been killed by
German bullets; this matter involved two families" – the families of two
brothers. It also emerged that only one doctor was shot, not two, and that
"not a single factory was destroyed or burned." Eleven Belgian witnesses
were named, but the testimony of nearly all was discounted because they
were in their cellars during the events. Evidence offered by the one witness who had observed the actions of German troops, Hermine Blanchaert
Froment, was dismissed as "personal grievances." A red herring – a
Flemish soldier called, appropriately, *"Le Petit Roux,"* who donned civilian clothes and fired on troops – was eagerly pursued.[105]

Goetze's report was accompanied by only three other depositions.
According to Major Friedrich von Polentz, the signal for the uprising on
August 20 was the tolling of church bells – at about 6:30. Another German
witness, Rifleman Hugo Roleff, also reported his alarm over the ringing
of the bells. There was, of course, a perfectly innocuous explanation.[106] At
that very moment, according to the imaginative witnesses, the civilians,
who had been lining the streets, passing out water to the troops, retreated
into their homes and began firing on soldiers from "cellar hatches" and
attics. As was their usual practice, they had removed tiles to facilitate the
firing. And, inevitably, "it was not only men who shot at us but also...sev-
eral of the women."[107]

Meanwhile, other enterprising Andennoises poured boiling water on troops.[108] Despite resorting to this medieval modus operandi, the civilians were well armed. In addition to "a murderous rifle fire, ... hand bombs and hand grenades were thrown at us, and machine-gun fire was also directed at us."[109] But "strange to say," conceded the Major-General von Langermann, "our losses were slight. The franc-tireurs were very poor marksmen."[110] Indeed, so inept were the guerillas that their "murderous gunfire" succeeded in wounding exactly five men and killing two, according to a statement by Dr. Gildun, the chief medical officer.[111] The German report itself provides no casualty figures, though one witness speaks of a hundred men injured by the scalding water. Unfortunately, the major testifying about this attack did not himself see any of the burned soldiers, and none provided depositions.

The Germans were always adept at finding incriminating documents after they'd occupied towns. A paper "found in the possession of the town's leader" purportedly revealed that "the assault upon us by the population had been planned in minute detail and was to take place at a pre-arranged hour." No line from the damning document was quoted in the White Book, perhaps because its existence was merely "reported to us later."[112]

Needless to say, there is no mention of any confiscated weapons. The wily civilians had even managed to conceal the machine guns they had employed so ineffectively. Perhaps they disassembled them and swallowed the parts. Nor were the Germans able to locate any of the hand grenades the ingenious guerrillas had been able to stockpile a full year and a half before these were issued to the Belgian Army. Perhaps the Andennois had purchased their machine guns from the hand grenade supplier: the entire Belgian Army had only 102 machine guns at the start of the war, and would probably have been reluctant to lend them to civilians.

Freiherr von Langermann concluded his testimony by assuring the investigators that "no cruelties whatsoever were committed by the troops under my command; in particular all inhabitants who appeared in the streets without weapons were spared; if they seemed suspicious to us, they were merely arrested."[113]

The Germans were usually able to find a few collaborators, generally fellow-Germans who had not left Belgium at the outbreak of hostilities. A certain Becker, who'd been living for less than two years in the rue d'Horseilles, was identified by several witnesses as a German spy. On the day the Germans arrived in Andenne, he conducted the commandant on a tour of the town. It was widely believed that he was implicated in the rue d'Horseilles massacre.[114] No doubt it was Becker who confided to an injured private that "the whole attack had been planned and that the clergy had issued instructions from the pulpit."[115]

RETROSPECT AND PROSPECT: The killings at Aarschot on the evening of the 19th and the following morning more than doubled the previous record in Soumagne and surrounding hamlets. The new record, however, fell within forty-eight hours. But *sic transit gloria mundi:* the triumph for the four regiments of von Bülow's Prussian Guard Reserve Corps in Andenne and Seilles was equally short-lived. Thirty-six hours later, a single regiment of the Second Army's Xth Corps executed 315 men by the Sambre in Tamines and killed 68 other residents around the same time. This impressive record endured for less than twenty-four hours. On the afternoon and evening of Sunday, August 23rd, regiments from the Third Army's XIIth Corps succeed in killing approximately 685 men, women, and children in Dinant. The universal outrage following the sacking of Leuven two days later (with a mere 248 deaths), insured that the Dinant record would stand.

Two features distinguish the Andenne killings. In the first place, they were not provoked by enemy gunfire. While there is no credible evidence in any of the towns that a single shot was fired by a civilian, in every other location troops had just faced determined opposition from Belgian or French forces, with particularly heavy losses in the case of Tamines. But there was no "Battle of Andenne" preceding the massacres; the crossing of the Meuse was unopposed. Belgian troops had retired to the vicinity of the Namur forts, and and the nearest French forces were over 12 miles away. The soldiers who raced from house to house early Friday morning, stabbing and shooting people in their cellars or butchering them in their gardens, or who carried out more systematic executions by daylight, had not come under fire recently, had not seen comrades shot or blown up.

The second difference, one of degree, not of kind, has to do with the savagery of the attacks in Andenne. The large-scale executions in Aarschot, Tamines, and Dinant were preceded by some brutal killings, but the ratio of murders by rampaging troops to executions is significantly higher in Andenne and Seilles. Of the 262 victims, only some 70 to 90 were lined up and shot. (By contrast, in Tamines approximately 315 of the 383 residents murdered by German troops during August were executed.)

It is not a case of hot-blooded versus cold-blooded murder, however. Soldiers of the Prussian Reserve Guard regiments were acting under orders. However, the orders gave greater latitude to bestiality in Andenne than elsewhere. There was more mayhem, if less murder.

There is also nearly as much evidence of premeditation as at Dinant and Leuven. It is likely orders were issued after the killing of an uhlan outside Seilles. Andenne was to made an example of.

MAJOR VON BASSEWITZ There is no chapter in this book on Huy, the largest city on the Meuse between Liège and Namur, about six miles east of Andenne, with 14,277 inhabitants in 1914. The city has no *Cimetière des Martyrs de 1914,* no tombstones inscribed *"fusillé par les allemands."* Very little happened here during the German invasion. An old man caught with an inoperable rifle was hanged on August 23rd. That night there was gunfire in the rue des Jardins, followed by the usual pillaging and burning. Two residents were killed as they sought shelter; two soldiers were injured. The burgomaster was arrested and interrogated at gunpoint.[116]

But then something unusual occurred. The commander of the troops occupying Huy, Major von Bassewitz, ordered an inquest the following morning. His subordinates took their assignment seriously, and the results were conveyed to him the same day. The major was not happy with what he learned, and promptly issued an order, which he had printed and distributed to his officers and men.

> Last night firing occurred. It is not established that the inhabitants of the town had weapons. It is also not proved that the townspeople took any part in the shooting. On the contrary, according to all appearances, the firing was initiated by soldiers who were under the influence of alcohol and in incomprehensible fear of an enemy attack. The behavior of the soldiers during the night, with a few exceptions, has made a truly shameful impression. It is highly regrettable when officers or noncommissioned officers set fire to houses without permission or the order of the commanding officer, or, in this case, the senior officer, or when they encourage troops by their attitude to burn and plunder. I am awaiting detailed information on the conduct of the troops as regards the lives and property of the inhabitants. I forbid shooting in the town without

the order of an officer.

The sorry behavior of the troops has had severe consequences, a non-commissioned officer and a soldier having been seriously wounded by German ammunition.

The Commandant Von Bassewitz Major[117]

The reprimand was effective. There were no further incidents in Huy. The sensible and forthright major, there can be little doubt, spared German as well as Belgian lives.

Diaries and letters from dead or captured German soldiers, as well as the testimony of Belgian witnesses, clearly reveal that some soldiers and officers, like Captain Wabnitz and Dr. Uhlmann, were unhappy with the way the war was being conducted in Belgium. Though they helped civilians escape execution on occasion, these ethical individuals were never the men giving orders. Major von Bassewitz was the exception. Nonetheless, his actions must be seen in perspective. The issuing of the Order of the Day required neither monumental courage nor lofty principles. Major von Bassewitz simply wished to know the facts, and when he was informed, communicated these to his subordinates, even though they did not reflect well on the German Army.

CHAPTER 5

Tamines

CROSSES "I have said that the worst of all was Tamines," wrote the American Minister to Belgium, Brand Whitlock, of the massacres of civilians during August.

> But perhaps it only seems the worst because it made such an impression on the minds of the young men of the C.R.B. [the Commission for Relief in Belgium]. They were always talking of it.
>
> "Yes, but have you seen Tamines?" they would say whenever the conversation, with a kind of fatal and persistent irrelevancy, turned on the atrocities. They knew Tamines only as they passed through it on their way to and from the Borinage, and all they had seen was the poor little cemetery there in the church yard, crowded with the new-made graves whose wooden crosses all bore the same date.
>
> Many of the young men of the C.R.B., whose experience of human kind had been as fortunate as their own natures were kind, came to Belgium with the scepticism that did so much credit to their natures, but somehow that little graveyard at Tamines was more potent as proof to them than direct evidence could have been.
>
> Tamines is a little mining town on the Sambre, down in what is known as the Borinage, the coal fields between Namur and Charleroi. The little church stands on the village-green overlooking the river, its facade all splotched where the bullets and the mitraille spattered against it. And in the graveyard beside the church there are hundreds of new-made graves, long rows of them, each with its small wooden cross and its bit of flowers. The crosses stand in serried rows, so closely that they make a very thicket, with scarcely room to walk between them. They were all new, of painted wood, alike except for the names and ages – thirteen to eighty-four. But they all bore the same date: August 22nd, 1914.[1]

THE BATTLE OF THE FRONTIERS From the Olympian perspective of the military historian, the massacres at Tamines, like those at Dinant the following day, were insignificant episodes in the first great clash of arms between German and French forces, the Battle of the Frontiers.

The cemetery beside St. Martin's Church, Tamines.

"It is a glorious and awful thought that before the week is over the greatest action the world has ever heard of will be fought," Sir Henry Wilson wrote on August 22nd.[2] Millions of soldiers and civilians shared his excitement. The great armies of the two ancient enemies were about to collide and the outcome would decide the war.

There had already been a series of engagements in Alsace and Lorraine. A French thrust in the extreme south by an auxiliary army under General Pau had captured Mulhouse on August 8th, but the general was forced to withdraw two days later. Launched on the 14th, the main French advance into the two lost provinces had proceeded methodically, if not spectacularly, for five days. Then it ran into the prepared German defenses, the machine guns and barbed wire that soldiers would come to know so well. On the 20th, the Germans counterattacked. The French were decisively routed by the German Sixth Army in Lorraine to the west of Morhange and at Sarrebourg. Its left exposed by the retreating Second Army under de Castlenau, Dubail's First Army pulled back in Alsace.

But the commander of the French Army, Joseph Joffre, did not appear much perturbed. Still wedded to the doctrine of *offense à l'outrance* – offense to the limit – and acknowledging at last that a sizable "northern group" had crossed the Meuse and was rapidly descending on France, he sought to strike a fatal blow at the fulcrum of this pivoting wing with his Third and Fourth armies. The German forces that had repulsed his thrust into Alsace had been stronger than anticipated. The more troops now flooding the central plains of Belgium, the weaker the center. The fact that his two armies were to attack through the Ardennes didn't faze Joffre. The quick-firing French 75s could be dragged through the dense woods much more easily than the heavy German guns.

What Joffre did not yet realize was that the Germans had fully integrated their reserve units into the front-line army, effectively doubling its strength. (French Intelligence at the start of the war believed they were opposed by forty-five divisions. In fact, there were eighty-three.) The forces facing Ruffy and Langle across the Ardennes actually outnumbered their two armies, some 380,000 to 361,000.[3] And further west, the numbers were far more lopsided. Three German armies of 320,00, 260,00 and 180,000 men, thirty-eight divisions, bore down on Lanrezac's quarter of a million troops and the half-sized Belgian Army and BEF. At full strength these were 117,000 and 110,000 respectively, but each had not much more than 70,000 combat-ready troops on the 23rd.

Lanrezac and his staff did not know the French Fifth Army was out-numbered exactly three to one, but they were certainly aware that they faced overwhelmingly superior forces, sliding ever westward.[4] However, they were unable to convince Joffre of this stark fact, though his own intelligence officers confirmed it. Lanrezac's frustration and fear mounted exponentially with each passing day.

The contrast has often been drawn between the two opposing com-manders. The stolid Joffre, outmanned and outgunned, placidly polishing off his five-course lunch, then napping for an hour, steering his ship straight for the rocks with magnificent sang froid, while his counterpart Helmuth von Moltke, suffering acutely, agitated, not sleeping, not eating, was franti-cally, and disastrously, altering his plans. In his anxiety, Moltke appeared to lose sight of the whole rationale for the Schlieffen Plan. Flushed by the suc-cess of the counterattacks against the invaders in Alsace and lured by the vision of a second Cannae,[5] he now permitted Prince Rupprecht to attack French positions the invulnerability of which had been the whole reason to invade Belgium in the first place, while at the same time he abandoned the sweep around Paris and the encirclement of the French armies that was the Plan's chief objective.[6]

Joffre's monumental obtuseness provides the great pathos of August. But if Lanrezac had a far keener appreciation of the strength of the forces approaching him, he did not do all he might have to parry its thrust. Indeed, the case has been made, notably by Edward Spears, that the Fifth Army's Ist Corps, under Franchet-d'Esperey, might have accomplished what Ruffey and Langle failed to do – sever the wing descending on France west of the Meuse. Most military historians, however, are skeptical. The numbers were too overwhelming.[7]

But at least the Fifth Army now occupied the angle between the Meuse and the Sambre. The revised Plan XVII had called for the army to cross the upper Ardennes in support of the offensive by the Third and Fourth Armies, which angled up through Luxembourg toward Köln.[8] Though he had con-vinced Joffre not to launch his army through the Ardennes, Lanrezac had committed himself to penetrations across the Sambre. By the 22nd, how-ever, he was having serious doubts about the advisability of any offensive.

Lanrezac's cautiousness – what the desperate Belgians regarded as his dilatoriness – had already changed King Albert's plans. When Joffre confirmed on the 18th that no Allied troops could reinforce the Belgians, massed behind the Gete, before the 24th, the King made the painful decision to abandon his excellent defensive position and begin the retreat toward Antwerp, preserving his field army.[9]

Lanrezac's reluctance to cross the Sambre was worse news for the Belgian 4th Division defending Namur, and the garrison troops within the forts, where morale began rapidly declining on the 21st, the first day of the German bombardment. ("They must see French troops marching along with colors unfurled and a band playing," the French liaison officer insisted at the Fifth Army's HQ. "There must be a band.")[10] Only direct attacks on the positions where the German and Austrian gunners were assembling their 42 cm. "morsers" and 30.5 cm. howitzers could have saved Namur; the guns were beyond the range of the fort's 21 cm. cannon.

Lanrezac's unwillingness to launch an offensive also disrupted the plans of the BEF, which, unaware of von Kluck's four corps approaching them head on, was preparing to attack across the Mons-Condé Canal on the 24th.

Lanrezac's critics charge that, having abandoned the offense, he did not prepare an adequate defense, relying on counterattacks rather than the trenches and machine guns that were to prove so effective for four years.[11] But he was given no time. Von Bülow attacked precipitously on the 22nd. One of the chief crossing points for his Xth Corps was to be Tamines.

A GERMAN SETBACK The town, with between 5,700 and 5,800 inhabitants in 1914, sits in a semi-circle formed by the Sambre as it briefly hooks northwest before turning east again to join the Meuse.[12] The main street runs north and south through the town, and bears several names.[13] It links the town's two parishes, Alloux and St. Martin. There were slate quarries as well as two large coal mines outside the town, which lies just within the eastern border of the province of Namur. Politically, Catholics had dominated local government during the 19th century. In the 1913 communal elections, however, their margin was slim. The party retained six seats to the Liberals' four and the Socialists' one.[14]

The 70th regiment of the 19th division of Lanrezac's Xth Corps had arrived from Brittany on Thursday, August 20th, to defend the town.

(Chance had pitted the Fifth Army's Xth Corps against the Xth Corps of German Second Army.)[15] Soldiers from the 7th Company of the 70th's 2nd Battalion, stationed near the Hôtel de Ville, sighted four German horsemen coming down rue de Velaine at about 6 a.m. on the 21st, and immediately opened fire. The thirty-five French had been joined by twenty uniformed Civic Guards from Charleroi, part of an artillery company, who also fired on the uhlans. There were no sharpshooters in either party: only one German was hit; the others dispersed, firing wildly at the civilians who had been watching their progress.[16]

A second, larger patrol, including motorcyclists, also fled when fired on, and also left behind one injured man, a cyclist. After these brief skirmishes, residents emerged from their homes and cheered the French troops and Civic Guards. It was their shouts of *"Vive la France"* that sealed the town's fate, some witnesses later believed.[17]

More than likely, however, it was reports by the returning uhlans that they had been fired on by civilians that set in motion the atrocities that followed. In fact, the bullet that was removed from the uhlan wounded in the first probe was of French origin. In extracting it, Dr. Scohy was able to resolve a lively dispute between French soldiers and the Civic Guard for the honor of having felled the horseman. But both the French and Belgian troops had been concealed behind a cemetery wall, while residents, oblivious to the dangers, ventured out into the streets to get a better look at the action – where they were no doubt seen by the Germans. The captain of the Guard detachment had begged the townspeople to return to their homes.[18] But the wounding of a couple of soldiers might not have precipitated the massacre had the Germans not been decisively defeated late in the afternoon as they tried to advance south of the Sambre.

After scattering the reconnaissance units, the Guards returned to Charleroi. They and the French had believed, according to Sgt. Goffin, a lawyer in private life, that the Germans would bypass the forts of Namur and Maubeuge, and turn south only after reaching Brussels. The uhlan squadrons, they assumed, were scouting for attacks on the Germans' left flank, and were not the spearheads of a frontal assault.[19] Once the numbers and intentions of the Germans had been determined, the French began withdrawing to a defensive position on the bluffs outside the village of Falisolle, less than 1,000 yards south of the river. Machine guns had been set up in at least two homes facing the bridge, but these were removed, and never fired a round. The French had decided not to defend the bridgehead, but to hit the Germans as they moved south toward Philippeville.

By 2:30 p.m. on the 21st, most of the 70th regiment had pulled out of Tamines. A single remaining company may have pretended to flee in disorder before the advancing Germans to lure them across the bridge over the Sambre. As the invaders stormed across the bridge, the French opened up with machine-gun and rifle fire from the homes and gardens lining the route de Falisolle. Then the 75s on the ridge west of Falisolle went into action. They had been dueling with the German guns at La Praile earlier in the afternoon, and now lowered their sights. The advancing troops "were literally mowed down. It was a frightful carnage," one witness reported.[20]

As in so many other places during their advance in August, the Germans took the precaution of employing human shields. A number of men had been seized at random in La Praile and elsewhere and paraded in front of the advancing columns. In other locations, the tactic proved effective in the short-run, as French and Belgian troops held their fire. Here it didn't succeed. But in the murderous fire that decimated the advancing columns, only three civilians were killed and five injured, in two incidents, so perhaps the French took some precautions.[21] The Germans retreated back into Tamines.

The commanders of the 20th Division tried again early the next morning, the 22nd, at 2 a.m. But once more their troops were checked, with heavy losses. One resident, sheltering in his cellar, counted seventeen trucks rumbling north later that morning, piled with dead soldiers. Another resident, ordered to drive only wounded soldiers back to the train station from rue de Falisolle, reported making numerous trips.[22] A breakthrough was urgent. More companies were pushed forward. Finally, at 11 a.m. the French were forced to abandon their positions. The Breton units had put up a courageous defense. At least one platoon may have been ordered to hold its position to the last man.[23]

On any map showing the advances of the Xth Corps, spearheading the assault on the French Fifth Army on a broad front east of Charleroi, only one line curls back north. It represents the units crossing the Sambre at Tamines. If a massacre of civilians had been contemplated after the brisk resistance against the reconnaissance patrols by the 7th company and the

Civic Guards, the setback the German regiments received outside Falisolle no doubt reinforced the decision. Innocent lives would pay for the dishonor and the heavy losses.[24]

DIALOGUE After establishing themselves in La Praile, north of town, and burning seven homes in the village and imprisoning fifty civilians, the Germans dispatched a woman to Tamines to fetch the burgomaster and a doctor. The burgomaster had fled, and an *échevin*, his deputy, himself a doctor, refused to parlay with the Germans. After the emissary had failed to convince Dr. Lalieu, Emile Duculot, a printer and bookseller who served as a communal councillor, set off himself, accompanied by Dr. Defosse and the president of the Red Cross, M. Ferauge, both of whom spoke German. While the doctor attended the wounded cyclist, the commanding officer queried Duculot.[25]

"'We've been fired on!' he said to me point-blank," Duculot recalled.

> I replied, "Monsieur, it's not possible! Absolutely no one could have fired. We've carefully collected all weapons, and the population has been warned to engage in no hostile actions against the belligerents. No one would even dream of it." The officer interrupted: "Someone has fired!" I again insisted, "It's highly unlikely." "I've already confiscated three revolvers," he added. He didn't show these to me, it's worth noting, and I have no doubt he would have if he'd had them. The officer then asked if it would be possible to descend into the village without danger. I told him, "It's impossible to respond to this question. You're here, but the French are there, and I have no idea if they intend to come up here, or stay where they are. As you yourself see, the route is free as far as one can see."[26]

There was an easy way to find out. Duculot was placed at the head of a detachment of twelve men and paraded into Alloux. "If anyone fires at us, you'll be shot," he was warned. But no one did.[27]

"WHERE ARE YOU FROM?" Others were less fortunate. Among those made to walk in front of the Germans as they advanced toward Falisolle were seven workers at an electric plant in Auvelais, west of Tamines. They'd all come to work on the 21st, despite the arrival of the enemy. They were arrested, held hostage for six hours, released, then promptly rearrested. This time an officer asked them where they were from. When one of the men made the mistake of admitting he was from Tamines, the officer trembled with rage and at once ordered that the men be dragged to the head of the column and precede it as it moved south. As the hostages crossed the Sambre bridge, the French opened up. The Germans dropped to the ground behind their captives. "It was a real miracle all seven of us weren't killed," one of the men recalled. Nonetheless, two of the civilians were hit, and died instantly. That Léonard Materne, the man who had admitted he was from Tamines, was not among them infuriated some of the Germans. One of them raced forward and, in a frenzy, bayoneted Materne repeatedly. For good measure, he lashed out at a second man, striking him four times. Retreating soldiers, a few minutes later, paused to stab the dead Taminois and his coworkers again and again.[28]

GRUSSEN In addition to the men killed as they were paraded in front of advancing troops, soldiers murdered two civilians who had not been quick enough to retreat to their cellars when the first troops entered town. Adelin Gilson was gunned down on his doorstep, Orlan Moreau on a street corner. By Saturday, residents remaining within their homes were no longer safe. Soldiers had been ordered to expel inhabitants from still unburned homes, and some men interpreted the assignment as a license to murder.

Between 9 and 10 a.m. Saturday morning, soldiers "yelling like madmen" banged their rifle butts on Félicien Istasse's front door. The quarry worker lived on rue de Velaine. He'd been sheltering in the basement with his family, and had taken the precaution of bringing down all his money and valuables.

As soon as the banging began, he climbed up the stairs, then flung open the door, yelling, *"Entrez!"* But no sooner had he said the word than he was hit in the head by two pistol shots. He fell on his doorstep. The soldiers immediately stole his wallet and watch, then raced into the house, which they began to ransack. Wardrobes were emptied, furniture was hurled through the windows, liquor was seized and avidly consumed. Then the Germans proceeded to the basement, pistols in hand, where the frightened family cowered. They cursed and threatened Mme. Istasse, but the sight of her two young children seemed to soften them, and they clambered back upstairs without harming the family. Various other groups of soldiers pillaged the home later in the day. For good measure, they stabbed Istasse's body before stepping over it. Civilians burying the corpse several days later counted a dozen bayonet wounds.[29]

Later that day, around 4:00 p.m., it was the woman of the household who answered the door when the Germans knocked. Thirty-six-year-old Flore Garot Evrard went upstairs with her nine-year-old son, while her husband Zacharie stayed with the couple's three-year-old girl and a neighbor, Joseph Mohimont. If the men were counting on the Germans to behave with more civility when confronting a female, they were mistaken. Flore Evrard was shot through the left breast before she even had a chance to open her mouth. The men heard a single gun shot and then soldiers running through the house. As the Germans clattered down the stairs, the two civilians hoisted themselves into a water tank. The little girl remained on a mattress. The soldiers looked around, went back upstairs, then left the house, apparently satisfied with their exploits. Eventually, the boy wandered downstairs, looking for his father. "Maman won't say anything," he complained.[30]

The children in both families were lucky. Eight-year-old Céline Huybrecht, was standing at the corner of rue de Baty St.-Barbe and rue de Velaine with a teenage girl and a young man. The three were watching a group of about twenty soldiers Friday morning as they returned with the cyclist who had been wounded during the reconnaissance patrol. The Germans suddenly opened fire on imaginary franc-tireurs, and shot the girl through the ear. Céline died instantly; the others were hit, but survived.[31]

A four-year-old girl was hit in the arm and leg as she was being carried by her uncle.[32] Several children were also among a group of fourteen residents of rue de Fleurus who were fired on as they fled westward toward Moignelée. One man was pushing his eighty-three-year-old father-in-law in a wheelbarrow, so the party was not moving very quickly and no doubt made an excellent target.[33]

Georges and Henri Skakala, 10 and 12, had an Austrian father and a German mother, but their ancestry didn't save them when the Germans poured down rue de Fleurus Friday afternoon. The family was also trying to escape into the countryside west of Tamines. The two boys and their parents were all shot. When the soldiers became aware of the nationality of the franc-tireur family, they rushed them to a military hospital, and all survived.[34]

The Germans were no respecters of age, of course. The eighty-three-year-old paralytic in the wheelbarrow, Jean-Baptiste Cobut, was killed.

Later in the day, the invaders improved on the age span of their victims. Eighty-eight-year-old Marie-Catherine Thiry was burned alive in her home on rue de Falisolle. She was confined to her bed, and her screams of terror elicited no response from the arsonists. Downstairs in the same house was the body of her grandson Georges Devillez, 17, who had been killed earlier in the day when he was placed in front of German troops attacking the French positions around Falisolle.[35]

ORPHANS Children not killed or injured, but whose fathers were taken from them, suffered a trauma that would scar them the rest of their lives. One deposition in Namur is in the handwriting of a child, Germaine Desguin:

> An order was given to collect all the men. The Germans began immediately and each house was visited. The poor fathers of the families, including mine, Henri Desguin, were torn out of the arms of their children despite their cries and tears. To compound the misery, our mother Marie Delvaux was suffering greatly. It was impossible to bear a pain so cruel. Her state worsened so badly that we were obliged, my sister Berthe and I, to transport her to the Red Cross.

The distraught mother did not survive her husband by many days: "After a short say in this village [Velaine] we were returned to Tamines with our mother on a wheelbarrow and a short time afterwards we were orphans, Berthe and I."[36]

"WE'RE TO BE PITIED" The Germans began the mass murders modestly enough – with nine men.

Around 5 p.m. on Friday, soldiers arrived at Café Hennion, an angular three-story building jutting into the Place St. Martin, Tamines' main square, overlooking the Sambre. They demanded petrol to set the neighboring buildings on fire. Mme. Hennion reluctantly obliged. She had little choice; the soldiers trained their guns on her.

Hidden in the basement were Mme. Hennion's daughter-in-law, Mme. Franz Hennion, and her two young grandchildren, one four, the other two months, and the children's other grandmother, Mme. Jaquemotte, along with the Hennion's servant, Germaine Hiernaux, and a friend of the family, Emile Lechat, director of the railway station in a neighboring town, and his wife and three children. Auguste Hennion, the cafe's proprietor, remained upstairs with his wife.

Not long afterwards, soldiers swarmed back into the house. An officer ordered that the café be converted into a field hospital for the German wounded, who were being conveyed in great numbers from across the Sambre. Mme. Hennion and her servant dragged mattresses downstairs; the civilians emerged from the cellar and were confined to the kitchen.

The Germans did not take any chances. As the first wounded arrived, Mme. Hennion, candle in hand, was escorted upstairs by three soldiers with pistols drawn. All the rooms, including the attic, were carefully searched. Wardrobes were flung open, drawers emptied. Other soldiers meanwhile took the daughter-in-law downstairs and examined the cellar rooms with similar zeal.

Auguste Hennion was then commanded to direct a party of soldiers to the home of the burgomaster. Emile Lechat offered to accompany them. The Germans were unaware that other troops had already sought him in vain.

Lechat returned alone, badly shaken. He hurried past Mme. Hennion into the kitchen. When Mme. Jacquemotte asked him what had happened to M. Hennion, he replied only, "Oh, Madame, we're to be pitied," and fell to the ground. Alarmed, Mme. Jacquemotte rushed up to him, unbuttoned his shirt and rubbed his chest. Lechat revived, but would say no more about what he had witnessed.

Auguste Hennion's body was found the next day beside the church of St. Martin. His hands were bound with wire. He was executed, presumably, because the burgomaster, M. Guiot, was not at home. The official had prudently left town a few days earlier.

The French guns now began targeting Place St. Martin, and the makeshift hospital was evacuated.[37]

In place of the wounded, German soldiers ushered nine civilians into the café. The men, who ranged in age from twenty-four to sixty-one, happened to be staying at a hotel owned by the burgomaster. They were evidently to be held hostage in lieu of the absent M. Guiot. One man was clearly culpable by German standards: George Dessoet was the nephew of the burgomaster's sister-in-law.[38]

The hostages were given no information about what they were charged with or what was to be their fate. "The hours seemed interminable," Mme

Hennion recalled. The prisoners dared not move or even speak with each other, so frightened were they of their brutal jailers. From time to time they heard shells explode and bullets strike the outer walls. Finally, a bugle sounded.

The men were then ordered out of the café, one by one. After the first man left, the soldiers were obliged to grab each of the others and push him out the door. For as soon as they crossed the doorstep, they were shot in cold blood by a man stationed outside.

> We saw them fall one on top of the other in front of the house, or on the stairs. Some fell in the doorway. Lechat succeeded in hiding himself behind his wife and children, but eventually he was spotted by the soldiers. They seized him and, despite his pleas, hurled him outside, where he was shot point-blank.[39]

Miraculously, one man survived, forty-four-year-old Joseph Ducoffre. "It was my turn," he recalled ten months later.

> One of the soldiers, already familiar with this "exercise," advanced toward me. In a decisive moment, I crouched down and, instead of letting him push me toward the fatal denouement, I leaped to the side. He pursued me, with the help of another soldier. I flailed around like a cat. During the struggle, just at the moment my two adversaries thought they had me, I used my head to butt one of them violently on the chin. I was free for a moment. The soldier I'd hit screamed with anger or pain, threw down the heavy rifle that had hindered his movements, and, helped by his comrade, pushed me toward the door. It yawned wide before me; death was waiting. There were only two or three steps to go.
>
> With a burst of energy, I attempted to hang onto the two soldiers. I felt I could drag them with me. But a violent shake sent me rolling on the doorstep. I tried to make myself as small as I could. I slid down the first step and from there down to the second, waiting for the coup de grâce. One or two seconds passed... I looked to the left, where the executioner would be standing. I saw him facing me, looking for the best place to fire. By the light of the burning buildings, our eyes met. The barrel of his gun was aimed at my chest. At this moment I flinched backward and the bullet, instead of striking my heart, slipped off to the side.
>
> I pretended to be dead. Until then, all my muscles were stretched to the limit. I let them relax, as if I were an inert object. I was hidden under a corpse. It was the slate quarry worker Thyrion. Then I lost consciousness. I have no idea how much time passed while I was in this torpor.
>
> A cavalry brigade crossed over the bridge, heading toward Falisolle. It seemed to me that dawn was breaking, but perhaps this was an illusion. The fire grew within the cabaret. My head and my shoulders rested on the body of Thyrion, who himself lay on a step, but I had one foot against the door. I felt the fire begin to intensify. My head seemed to be burning; there was a strong burning sensation in my leg. In my anguish,

I asked myself: my God, have you permitted me to escape the assassin's bullet only that I should die miserably in this fire?

Sure that I would burn alive if I remained there, I attempted, with infinite caution, to withdraw my leg first and then to work my way over to the other side of Thyrion. But my executioners were watching. A soldier approached and delivered four bayonet stabs in my back. Four times I felt the steel point penetrate, but the pain was not intolerable. I remained immobile and held my breath.

Soon I began to suffocate. Pieces of flaming wood fell from the Hennion house. In addition, my blood continued to flow out. But I no longer heard the soldiers around me, and realized that they may have left the area. Carefully I raised my eyes. By the light of the Broze house and the cinema, which were on fire, I saw, in the square, soldiers stepping over a pile of corpses. Looking the other way, to my right, I saw soldiers lying down, near the Crousse pharmacy and in the rue de la Station, some as if they were poised to shoot, but others seeming to be asleep. At first I didn't dare move, but then, little by little, I realized they were all dead.[40]

Ducoffre was able to drag himself on his hands and knees to the home of a widow, Mme. Dehant, who gave him water and brought him to a Red Cross station, where his wounds were bandaged. Anticipating a German inspection, the director burned Ducoffre's clothes and passed him off as a French soldier.

Ducoffre never fully recovered from his wounds and died in January 1917.

⊲⊶⊳

Ten men, with Hennion, were murdered. The Germans in Tamines had come under the fire of French batteries near Falisolle and from troops stationed along the road south of the bridge. There was no way any citizen of Tamines could conceivably be implicated either in the bombardment, which they themselves sheltered from, or from the deadly ambush on route de Falisolle. The Germans nonetheless held the town's burgomaster responsible. As he was absent, other men were selected entirely at random as his surrogates – they happened to be at the hotel he owned. But these men were not then used as hostages. There were no negotiations with the French, no threats to execute them if the shelling didn't cease. There were no conditions established for their release. Nor were the men deployed as human shields.

If the men were executed for having fired on the two patrols attempting to approach Tamines early Friday morning, no one was ever informed of the charge. Needless to say, not a shred of evidence connected them to the wounding of the two soldiers earlier in the day. The subsequent behavior of the civilians was hardly damning: these franc-tireurs had, improbably, all chosen to stay in one hotel, and had obligingly waited there all day for the Germans to seize them. There was no reason for the murders and the Germans made no attempt to provide one, either to the victims themselves, or subsequently.

⊷⊶

When the men had all been shot, a soldier or officer re-entered the house. He announced in pigeon-French, "You, women and children, to leave far, very far," and the Hennion and Lechat families were evicted from the café. By the light of the blazing homes from across the Place, they picked their way among the corpses.[41]

"YOU DON'T KNOW THE PRUSSIANS" Joseph Ducoffre may be forgiven the melodramatic flourishes of his tale. He provides a rare glimpse into the final thoughts of someone facing a particularly vicious form of execution. Accounts from those about to suffocate and burn in their basements are no less rare. But of those residents who barely escaped from the 242 homes that were incinerated by the Germans, at least one man, Léon Jaumain, provided a detailed account of the experience. As elsewhere, the fires were deliberately set by the Germans and not the result of the French shelling. Even at the height of the battle, incendiaries were at work. They were observed by Canon Crousse, who saw a sergeant leading a platoon equipped with torches and inflammable pellets. To fan the flames, men shot out the windows in some of the buildings they had ignited. "The majority of the homes in the south part of town were set on fire," another witness recalled.[42]

With his wife and children, Jaumain sought refuge in his father-in-law's cellar in rue de la Station. The family was joined by neighbors, the Seghins. The mood, Jaumain recalled, fluctuated between fear and hope. "After the roar of the guns and the crackling of the machine guns, there was the din of the wagons rumbling past and the plaintive cries of the wounded they carried."[43]

Soon neighboring buildings were set ablaze and Jaumain proposed leaving the cellar. His mother-in-law, born Marie-Elise Pelzer, and the neighbor, Mme. Seghin, vehemently objected. They refused to run the risk of capture by the Germans. Jaumain's mother-in-law was from Alsace and

MarieÉlise Pelzer Mombeek (left) and her husband Marcel (center). Auguste Hennion (right), proprietor of the café in Tamines where nine men were shot.

Father Adrien Docq (left) and Father Antoine Hottlet (right),
the two priests killed in Place St. Martin.

spoke German fluently. His wife pleaded with her mother to ask the soldiers to help save them, appealing to their sense of pity. "Not on your life!" the woman replied vehemently. "You don't know the Prussians."[44]

The fires roared closer. To make the situation worse, the cellar's window was blocked by a perforated metal sheet, which was secured by a lock. Though they tried to seal the cracks to the interior of the house, smoke began seeping through the fissures. It became increasingly difficult to breathe. The heat, meanwhile, grew intense.

Suddenly Jaumain's servant, seventeen-year-old Augusta Bauwin, screamed, "I'm burning...drops of fire are falling on my head."

Jaumain touched the ceiling. It wasn't hot. "That's impossible," he declared. Then he noticed that through a small gap in the ceiling, burning liquid – gasoline or oil – was trickling down. Mme. Seghin's servant also felt the drops. Then her son was hit; he fell down, writhing in pain. Suddenly Jaumain smelled the distinctive odor of carbonic acid. The petrol was splashing on a pile of coal and releasing an asphyxiating gas.

> In this situation, I understood we would all die very shortly and I prepared my family and the others with us for this awful reality. "We're all going to die," I said. "Let's quickly do our act of contrition." We exchanged touching farewells and intimate and loving embraces that I'd never experienced til then and can hardly describe. While hugging my son Marcel for the final time, I felt a terrible burning sensation on my right hand, then my right leg, where I touched the carbon that was turning into gas. Feeling the most intense pain and wanting to put an end to it, I called out to everyone to throw ourselves on our backs and take deep breaths through our mouths and be asphyxiated instantly. All the while, what cries of pain, what heart-rending pleas and agonizing tortures![45]

Death didn't come as quickly as Jaumain expected. Then abruptly, "like a madman," he leapt to his feet, and hurled himself against the metal sheet blocking the basement window, hoping to break the padlock. Finally, he begged his wife to yell for help in German. A soldier standing outside yelled back at them, "You're just fine where you are and you're going to stay there." But a second soldier who came by a few moments later was more sympathetic. He worked open the window cover with his bayonet. Jaumain handed out his three children, then escaped with his wife and one of the sons of his neighbors. He immediately returned for the others, disregarding his wife's pleas to flee. Five were already dead and Jaumain's father-in-law, Marcel Mombeek, would die the next day. Among those who were asphyxiated or burned alive was Marie-Elise Pelzer Mombeek, perhaps the only person that weekend to suffer for her excessive wariness of the Germans.

THE MASSACRE Incidents like those described took place all over eastern Belgium. What made Tamines distinctive was the event that began unfolding in the late afternoon on Saturday, the 22nd. After the French had withdrawn, German soldiers "black with powder, resembling demons," descended into the lower town.[46] Residents throughout town were rousted out of their cellars and herded northward. Many in the group, some two to three hundred, had been sheltering in the École des Soeurs, a block above the railroad tracks that divide the town. Their numbers steadily growing, the civilians were taken to a meadow outside Velaine, north of Tamines. En route, everyone was searched. Along with weapons like pocket knives and scissors, the soldiers helped themselves to any money the luckless civilians had with them. They were made to lie down flat in the field, while preparations for an execution were begun. Soldiers circled around them, rifles leveled.

Then the Germans had a better idea. The group was escorted to a large beet field along the Sambre and again compelled to lie down – this time in front of a sizable German gun emplacement. The howitzers were out of range of the French artillery, which had moved six miles south earlier in the day. No civilian was hit.

At around 5:00 p.m., everyone was ordered to stand. The crowd was now conducted south to the church of Notre Dame des Alloux. Here several hundred people had already taken refuge. Many had been instructed to go there by German soldiers; others were advised by friends and neighbors that everyone was to seek refuge there.

A second group of civilians, meanwhile, had gathered in the Institute Saint-Jean-Baptiste off rue Centrale, south of the railroad bridge. It was run by the Frères des Écoles Chrétiennes and was familiarly known as l'Institut des Frères, or les Frères. By 4:00 p.m. on the 22nd, when the establishment was converted into a Red Cross hospital, there were somewhere between 180 and 200 people sheltering there. The women, children, and elderly were escorted to the cellars, while the men were confined to the kitchen and refectory.[47]

By late afternoon, then, most of the population of Tamines, save those who managed to remain in hiding or had escaped into the countryside, was imprisoned in one of the two locations. Those in the second group, in the Institut des Frères, would survive the ordeal. Most men in the larger contingent, confined within the church of Alloux, would not be so fortunate.

At about 6:00 p.m., some of the women and children at the back of the overflowing church were taken to a school facing the church (also known, confusingly, as École des Soeurs). At a little after 7:00, all the men, well over 500, were ordered outside. There were wrenching scenes as they said goodbye to their wives, children, and mothers. The prisoners were marched southward to the Sambre along the broad street that bisects Tamines. They were roughly handled by the soldiers; there were curses, threats, and blows. As usual, priests were singled out for special abuse.

Arriving back in Place San Martin, the men were lined up in front of the Sambre. Facing them, about ten yards away, were three rows of troops, the first lying flat, the second kneeling, and last row standing. Their rifles were pointed at the chests of the civilians.[48]

Some men immediately leapt into the river. The remaining captives were briefly harangued by a French-speaking officer. Then a whistle blew and the troops opened fire. After one round, the survivors were ordered to stand up. Those who obeyed were gunned down in a second volley. This time a machine-gun was used and many of those who had escaped the first fusillade unscathed were now hit. Then soldiers raced up to the pile of bodies and began bayoneting the wounded. Some were hurled into the river. Among the troops assigned to finish off the survivors were men wearing Red Cross armbands. This was an effective trick, but many of the survivors continued to feign death. They were helped by a dark, moonless night.

One hundred eight men managed to leap into the Sambre before the firing began, or crawled in after the Germans finally departed. Sixty-eight of these men swam to safety. Eighty-four were wounded by the fusillade, but survived. Sixty-four, incredibly, were neither hit by the bullets nor bayoneted. But two hundred fifty-seven men were killed in Place St. Martin Saturday evening and another twelve died from their wounds shortly thereafter. Forty men drowned in the Sambre.

The survivors remained in the square, without any water or medical attention, until about 4:00 p.m. the following afternoon. The victims ranged in age from thirteen to eighty-four.

TO PLACE ST. MARTIN The twenty-nine-year-old vicar of Alloux, Father Louis Donnet, provided one of the most detailed accounts of the hours preceding the massacre.[49]

On Friday morning at 6:30 a.m. he saw the four or five uhlans clatter through the village toward Tamines, and then gallop back in the opposite direction after being fired on. The second group of horsemen, with cyclists, followed at 7:45.

After their retreat, a large number of terrified civilians descended on the village, with stories of German brutality.

When a third party of Germans entered Alloux, the vicar hid in a neighbor's basement, along with twenty others. The soldiers appeared especially ferocious.

Artillery fire began around 10:00 a.m., increasing the fears of those sheltering with Father Donnet. Then the Germans began burning homes up and down rue de Velaine, leading into Tamines.

However, a degree of calm had returned by evening, and the priest ventured back to his own home, which was still standing. Great numbers of troops now began passing southward. But at around 3:00 a.m. the gunfire resumed. Menacing groups of soldiers began breaking into the homes in Alloux. Expecting his own home to be invaded any moment, Donnet escaped with his sister over the garden wall and made his way to the presbytery, where the parish priest, Antoine Hottlet, lived with his sister.

The sixty-three-year-old curé had already tried reasoning with the Germans, hoping to calm them and ensure that the church would be spared. The fury of the troops had alarmed him. When Donnet and his sister arrived around 4:30 a.m., the curé rather dramatically asked his vicar if he was willing to join with him in making an offering of his life for the well-being of the parishioners and the success of the Allies defending the area. The vicar then received Holy Communion; the vow was consecrated. There were tears in both men's eyes.

But by mid-morning the situation once again seemed to improve. Though Tamines blazed to the south, soldiers were lounging in the main streets of Alloux, eating their rations. The priests brought out additional food and drink for the men. The two fathers then approached a few soldiers who appeared to be students, and questioned them. Speaking decent French, these young infantrymen claimed that French soldiers had been hidden by residents, and that civilians had fired on soldiers in Tamines. Donnet assured them that it was French troops who had done the firing, but failed to convince them.

Things rapidly deteriorated again. An officer announced that executions were imminent. Men began to be rounded up from Alloux and nearby communities, including elderly men and invalids. The two clergymen asked to join the group, which soon numbered around 200. "I discussed my fears with the curé," Father Donnet recalled.

> The poor man could hardly contain his emotions. He thought especially of his beloved parishioners. I'll never forget the impression he produced on me. I still see him now as he shuffled painfully along, dejected, carrying a valise in which he had locked up the Holy Sacrament.[50]

The group was taken north, toward Velaine, after everyone had been searched. En route, the men were cursed, spat at, and struck. Then they were conducted to a field and made to lie down flat. Soldiers surrounded them and aimed their rifles at the civilians' heads.

> We believed it was all over... There were cries of anguish from the poor people. Some cried, some prayed, some gave each other last embraces. The hand of the priest hovered over the crowd as he moved among the men, offering pardon, providing comfort and courage. What a poignant scene! What an unforgettable scene.[51]

The "execution squad" eventually dispersed, and when the priest asked other soldiers what was now to happen to the men, some were reassuring. German soldiers were far too humane to execute everyone, Donnet was told. The measures that had been taken so far were simply to remove the men from dangerous areas. They would be freed between 4 and 6 p.m. But one among them knew German, twenty-six-year-old Louis Goffin, and he was less sanguine. When panic once more swept through the crowd around 5:00 p.m., after they were herded to another field, Donnet urged Goffin to intercede with the Germans. Like Marie-Elise Pelzer, the young man refused. "These guys have absolutely no concern for us," he told the priest. "...If only you knew what I've overheard in their conversations! No. I'd prefer to be shot."[52] (Goffin was indeed executed in the Place St. Martin later that day.)

The pathos of the scene again overwhelmed Donnet. He was struck by what the desperate townspeople and brought with them. "I still see a

picture of Christ here, and there an image of the Virgin, there the portrait
of a parent, and all the other things that everyone had grabbed in the haste
of departure. For many it was the only surviving object of a home that no
longer existed."[53]

The group was now herded south to the church of Alloux. They were
stopped en route and addressed by an Austrian subject, Graf, who would
later testify that civilians had fired on German troops. Speaking on behalf
of the invaders, Graf was reassuring. This was a measure being taken for
everyone's safety; the civilians would all be released at 7:00 p.m. The group
was instructed to shout *"Vive l'Allemagne."* (Needless to say, the Austrian
didn't heed his own advice; he never set foot in the church and was not
seen again in Tamines.)[54] At this point some of the soldiers took pity on the
children, many of whom were crying hysterically. Two cows were fetched
to provide some milk. Father Hottlet removed the ciborium from his valise
and held it aloft. Everyone knelt down and prayed before it.[55]

Entering Notre Dame d'Alloux, Donnet and his parishioners were surprised to see it already filled with a great crowd. Neighbors, friends, and
relatives of the captives were massed in the choir, the sacristies, and on the
steps of the altar. Many families had been told to make their way to the
church for their own protection. Another battle was to take place and Notre
Dame d'Alloux, behind German lines, offered a secure refuge. At least one
family profusely thanked the considerate Germans who had so informed
them.[56] In other cases it was friends and neighbors who passed along the
advice to seek refuge in the church.[57] Many civilians were told that the
whole town was to be burned except for the church. One officer, however,
concluded his explanation on a distinctly ominous note: the church would
be spared "as a refuge for the women and children."[58]

At least two German soldiers, "no doubt seized by pity" tried to direct
some of the civilians toward Moignelée. But they didn't speak French, and
one family they approached shook their heads and crossed the railroad
bridge to Alloux.[59] Most of the German soldiers who circulated through
town were fully aware of what was in store for the men of Tamines. With
particular malice, some told Franz Steinier, who had remained in his
home, to run down to Place St. Martin. He arrived moments before the
fusillade. Leery of what the Germans intended, he had invited two soldiers into his living room and offered them champagne, hoping to find out

more information. The men had pointed out their home town on an atlas he brought them, wrote down their names and professions, and sung songs – but when they left abruptly, they didn't bother advising him as to what was in store for the men of Tamines.[60]

Other families were as relieved as Father Donnet to have made it to the church. The seventeen members of the Loriaux clan, including four small children, may have escaped a genuine attempt to execute them – or else the performance was even more chillingly convincing than what took place outside Velaine. All seventeen were lined up against the wall of the train station, the children crying and screaming, the grown-ups on their knees pleading for mercy, when a very young officer yelled "halt."[61]

◄‹-›►

The first concern of the priests inside the church was to try to spread everyone out as best they could and obtain some food and water. Some supplies the Germans had stolen were indeed distributed, but relatively little. Liqueurs and bon-bons were handed out to famished children by well-intentioned soldiers. But when Father Donnet began passing around some biscuits from a large box, an enraged German grabbed it from his hands, dumped the biscuits on the ground and trampled on them. Soldiers mocked the faith of their prisoners, toasting them with communion wine, ridiculing their prayers and candle-lighting. The curé was singled out. His obesity and mournful demeanor provoked much hilarity.[62]

The heat was overwhelming – both from the crush of bodies and the burning buildings nearby. Finally, some of the women with young children were taken to the school across the street.

Then, at 7:00 p.m., an officer arrived at the church, violently angry. "He advanced into the choir, bawling in German. He was a veritable fury. He threatened the curé because the man did not understand him, and pretended to shoot him..." According to one witness, he yelled that he had lost 2,000 men.[63]

There were more wrenching scenes. Spouses embraced. Young boys clung to their mothers. Many sensed they were saying goodbye for the final time. "It would be impossible to describe the despair, the sheer madness, that reigned at this moment," recalled twenty-eight-year-old Edouard Callebaut.

Put yourself in the place of fathers summarily condemned to leave their wives and children gathered around them and go to their deaths. Women with wild eyes desperately clung to soldiers, begging to be allowed to follow their husbands. Children groveled along the ground at their fathers' feet. The soldiers remained impervious, smirking and threatening us with their bayonets.[64]

Father Donnet was distributing bread in the sacristy when a young man came in and asked to be confessed. "'We're going to be shot,' he said...

It was too true. After a few minutes, the order was given to leave. Without the least hesitation, I decided to join the group. M. le curé stopped me and asked me to remain with him, telling me the Germans didn't require us, that they hadn't called the priests. I left in spite of him and tried to get him to do the same. I'd barely finished talking when a soldier led me off... I never saw M. le curé alive again.[65]

⊰⊹⊱

But many of the men, despite the anguish of parting with their families, probably left the church without any such fears. Adolphe Seron was told in halting French by a seemingly friendly soldier that the church was overcrowded and the captives were being given a chance to get some fresh air. Franz van Heuckelom was given similar information. Like millions of subsequent victims, the men speculated as to what the Germans intended them to do. Perhaps they would be compelled to dig trenches, or to bury the dead. Maybe they would be placed at the head of a battalion attacking the French, or be used to deter a French counterattack. There had to be some reasonable explanation.[66]

⊰⊹⊱

The men were herded five or six abreast down rue de l'Hôtel de Ville to Place St. Martin. The soldiers accompanying them seemed enraged. They continually yelled at them and struck them violently with their fists and rifle butts. Priests, as usual, were singled out.

"They shouted, howled, and shrieked at the priests," Father Donnet recalled.

They waved their fists, thrust their revolvers in their chests. It was the route of calvary. I was so disgusted by these scenes that, crossing the railroad bridge, I said to my neighbor, "I don't know what's going to happen to us, but there's no way to suffer more than I'm suffering at this moment."[67]

But the torments intensified. Night was falling as they left the station behind. Fresh troops surged around the men. The street narrowed. The blows rained down more furiously. The men were struck by riding whips, rifle butts, pieces of wood, iron bars, bayonets. Several men collapsed; one, a small hunchback named Justin Sevrin, did not rise again, killed by a blow or a heart attack.[68]

The two youngest Lardinois brothers, Lucien and Jules, were removed from the procession by an officer. "Children out of the ranks!" he ordered. The two boys, fifteen and thirteen, made their way back toward the church, but a soldier caught them and forced them to rejoin the group of prisoners. Fourteen-year-old Jean de Roover was luckier. An officer ordered him to join the men, but outside the church another officer, on horseback, told the boy to return to his mother. Similar dramas would be re-enacted at Dinant the following day, as interpretations of orders, or perceptions of age, clashed.[69] In the end, three thirteen-year-olds and three fourteen-year-olds would be placed before the firing squad in front of the Sambre. Three of these boys would be killed.[70]

The column narrowed once more as it passed the Hennion house, and then the men and boys were in the Place St. Martin. An artillery platoon parted to let them pass. The men were herded into two groups and placed with their backs to the river. Facing them was a company of soldiers, about thirty feet away. Troops were also deployed along the road leading to the bridge. A final victim was pushed into the ranks of the condemned. Félix Bodart, working at a Red Cross hospital in Auvelais, had been sent to Tamines by a German doctor to get medicine for the wounded. He was seized as he crossed the bridge. Bodart explained his mission, displayed his Red Cross armband and pass, but to no avail.[71]

The more optimistic among the men still believed they would be placed at the head of troops marching against the French, or subjected to another fake execution. Though his neighbor was convinced they were to be executed, Adolphe Seron could not believe the Germans would gun down so huge a group: "We were nearly seven hundred!"[72] But as the captives were led to the southern end of the Place, a number of men dove into the Sambre.

Father Donnet was mobbed by men seeking a final absolution. They grabbed his soutane, his arms, his neck. Donnet glimpsed another priest similarly besieged. It was Abbé Adrien Docq, a young teacher at the College of Virton, who was spending the vacation with his parents in Tamines. "My friends, I think things are going to get pretty hot soon," the young priest said. "I'm going to give a general absolution."[73]

Others turned desperately to the Germans. Donnet heard a chorus of shouts and pleas. *"Vive l'Allemagne!"* "Have pity on my wife and poor children. Have pity!" As the frantic men surged around him, Donnet was only dimly aware of the presence of an officer addressing the civilians.

TRIAL AND EXECUTION The officer did not speak loudly, but there were others, standing closer by, who heard his words.

"A great number of German soldiers have fallen," he announced. "Not by enemy bullets, but by those of civilians. You are cowardly, dirty Belgians. You deserve an exemplary punishment. You are all going to be shot."[74]

Some men, according to witnesses, lost their heads and cried out inarticulately. Others flung themselves down on their knees and begged for mercy. Some yelled *"Vive l'Empereur,"* as they were ordered by at least one officer present. One man, Henri Joret, convinced he had nothing to lose, yelled, *"Vive la France,"* hoping French troops were still within earshot.[75] Some of the Taminois no doubt still hoped that this would be one of the mock-executions the Germans had already revealed a taste for. Others were too paralyzed with terror or despair to react. Some realists who kept their wits about them now leapt into the Sambre. Fathers Hottlet and Docq hastily administered a general absolution. Some two hundred fifty guns were trained on the men. Then a whistle blew and the volley rang out.

Some minutes later the officer yelled, "Everyone stand up." Those who obeyed were mowed down by a second fusillade. A great many witnesses reported that at least one machine-gun was used. (One victim, Adolphe Seron, initially thought it was a camera.)[76] Then groups of soldiers rushed forward to finish off the wounded with bayonets.

They attacked "with diabolical fury, climbing on the pile of corpses and wounded, and violently striking anyone who still moved. The victims were moaning and writhing in frightful agony."[77]

GOOD GERMANS It is likely that a number of soldiers in the 1st Company of the 77th Regiment, the executioners, defied their orders and deliberately aimed high. One resident was later told by a former German soldier who had witnessed the execution that the machine gun had been seized and fired by an officer enraged at his men for shooting too high.[78] "In my vicinity," recalled the acting burgomaster, Emile Duculot, "no one was hit!...There were certainly some soldiers who fired into the air... I could clearly see the position of their rifle barrels."[79] "My immediate impression," recalled Adolphe Seron, "was that the soldiers had fired into the air, because there were no dead near me... None of my neighbors was hit."[80] "The soldiers who found themselves in front of us – at about fifteen yards away – refused to fire, fired into the air, or to the side," wrote Aurore Bruyère, who believed that an entire platoon mutinied.[81] Watching from the doorstep of St. Martin's, one of the few witnesses who was not among the condemned men, Marie-Louisa Thiry, was also convinced the soldiers fired into the air. "I heard the bullets clatter against the walls."[82] A number of other witnesses also had the impression the Germans deliberately aimed high. Still others believed, at least momentarily, that the Germans were firing blanks.[83]

We will probably never know the extent to which the resistance was organized. No doubt some friends discussed the order among themselves and resolved not to carry it out. The troops of the 77th Regiment came from Hannover, and this city, with its machine-building, rubber, and chemical plants, was an SPD stronghold that had returned four Socialists in the 1912 election. The province had a long history of resistance to Prussia and Prussianization, and there were undoubtedly anti-militarists within the ranks of every regiment of the Xth Corps. It is certainly conceivable that entire sections, with or without the consent of their sergeant, agreed among themselves not to fire on the civilians.[84]

But far more soldiers were only too willing to carry out the orders of their officers, or were driven by even greater hatred and brutality. The high survival rate probably owes more to the manner in which the execution was carried out than to the beneficence of individual Germans. There were somewhere between 530 and 545 civilians on the Place. Hastily arranged in rows seven or eight deep, they formed a dense, compact mass. There was no attempt to line up the men.[85]

One company was used, no more than about 260 men at full strength. There were probably fewer. Each soldier fired once. Even if all were trained sharpshooters, it would have been extremely difficult to kill more than half of the "franc-tireurs." The second volley, by all accounts, was far more deadly. Soldiers this time were permitted to fire at will, and a machine gun was used. Still, it would have been difficult to hit all of the many men lying beneath the dead and wounded.[86]

The killing began some time around 8:00, and the soldiers who volunteered to finish off the wounded were undoubtedly hampered by poor visibility. Louis Lardinois distinctly heard one soldier call out to an overzealous comrade, *"Genug, genug. Sie sind alle kaputt."*[87] In the end, darkness saved many of the condemned.

THE GERMAN RED CROSS After the executioners charged the pile of living and dead, stabbing, kicking, and looting, another group of Germans approached. These men wore Red Cross armbands, and relief swept over those survivors who glimpsed the insignia. Several pleaded for aid. Jules Delsauveniere, a forty-one-year-old pharmacist, very badly injured, called out, "Give me some water, please."

"Water?" a French-speaking soldier replied. "But you fired on us!"[88]

The pharmacist naturally denied this, but before he had finished speaking, he was struck by several violent blows. Others who pleaded for assistance received the same treatment.

Several of the bogus medics apparently had a sense of humor. Some men who were begging for water were told, "We'll give you something to drink." They were then picked up by the arms and legs, carried over to the Sambre, and, amid much chuckling, tossed in. About twenty of the wounded were hurled into the river.[89]

--‹--›--

It was injured and unscathed civilians, finally, who came to the aid of their fellow victims. Some time after midnight, Ernest Labarre, though gravely wounded, managed to drag himself over to the side of the Sambre. He located a bottle, filled it with water, and brought it back to some of the survivors who were begging for a drink. At dawn he was followed by several others, including Adolphe Seron and fifteen-year-old Lucien Lardinois.[90]

The men used any available receptacle for the water, including hats and boots. "We organized a regular distribution service," Labarre later recalled.[91]

SURVIVORS A high percentage of the victims survived the first fusillade and a great many were still alive after the second. Perhaps as many men were murdered by the bayonet-wielding troops and Red Cross members as were killed by bullets. Whether or not one survived often depended on one's ability to remain absolutely silent and immobile when stepped on, poked, or stabbed.

Red Cross members who approached the area in which Edouard Callebaut was lying after the fusillades promised that those who asked for mercy would be spared.

> Some among us who weren't injured let themselves be taken in by this promise and raised themselves up among the dead. Immediately, armed with their bayonets, the soldiers threw themselves on us and struck with incredible fury. They slashed exposed flesh and I could hear the soft sound of iron plunging into bodies...and the hoarse cries and agonized groans of those whom the soldiers finished off with blows from rifle butts.
>
> ... I kept asking myself by what miracle I was spared. ... the soldiers returned again and, still wielding bayonets red with blood, they went from body to body, plunging the points into faces and chests, twisting the blades again and again into the flesh, as one turns meat on a grill, skewering two bodies at a time. I found myself under the pile of dead, lying on a body, my legs spread wide, my face against the ground, the dead or wounded pressing down on each leg. How would I escape? God alone knows. I sensed the blade piercing my pants, I felt the cold steel against my skin, and I clenched my teeth, fiercely determined to not cry out and reveal that I was still alive. A moment later the point of another bayonet penetrated the heel of my shoe, and I then saw a third soldier standing over me menacingly... His blade passed by me without touching me. In this position, lying flat on my stomach on top of a body and my head crushed against the ground, the blood of other victims flowing over my face and soaking my clothes, I lost consciousness...[92]

After the Germans left, Callebaut made his way to the Sambre and drank deeply from his shoe. He brought several shoe-fulls of water back to others on the pile, then headed into the countryside. After crossing woods and climbing hills, he descended into a little valley, where he saw two inhabited homes. The residents stared at him incredulously: his clothes were torn, his hair disheveled, he was covered with blood. After he managed to tell his story, they took him in, helped him wash, gave him fresh clothes; but his nerves were shot – he was unable to eat or sleep. Late in the afternoon he was warned that the Germans were still pursuing men from Tamines, and he scampered into the woods again. All night long he heard the piteous yelping and bleating of domestic animals who had fled from burned villages nearby. "It seemed like the end of the world." After hiding in the woods and in coal mines for several days, he returned to Tamines. "Another man from Tamines who's still alive," people exclaimed after he identified himself. Even his wife didn't recognize him, the experience had so radically altered his appearance.[93]

A number of other survivors were less fortunate than Callebaut. Two of the most poignant narratives are by Emile Leroy, then thirty-six, and twenty-seven-year-old Philemon van der Waeren.

"A soldier approached, turned me on my back," Leroy recounted, "and struck me furiously with his bayonet.

> Oh! I'll never forget the features of the brutal face that bent over me. With the first blow he pierced my left arm. The second, more violent, penetrated below my left nipple and it was thanks to a notebook I had in my pocket, which was cleanly sliced through, that it did not strike my heart. I received a third cut on the right side. Fearing that my face would be stabbed next, I managed to turn over, with a superhuman effort. Exasperated, no doubt, my executioner struck me a terrible blow with his weapon. It penetrated the left side of my neck, beside the carotid artery, sliced a part of my throat, and exited beneath my chin. Having pulled out his bayonet, he administered a coup de grace, a formidable stab to the neck, then abandoned me, evidently believing he'd finished me off.
>
> By a supreme effort of will I was able to tie my handkerchief around my neck to stop the flow of blood. I'd just finished this when I suddenly heard a group of soldiers yelling like savages, charging up to the dead and wounded. Striking with all their force, they hit out at the mass of bodies. I heard blows hammer against skulls. It was then, suddenly, that I felt the boot of one of the murderers on my face. I made no movement. I invoked Providence. Minutes passed that seemed to me like a century... And at last night arrived. Ah, what a night, my God, what a night! On one hand the cries and groans of the wounded, the gasps of the dying; on the other hand, the cold that came over me. I slid under the overcoat of a dead comrade at my side. Then it was thirst that tortured me, so much so that I couldn't remain there any longer and dragged myself on my knees to the side of the Sambre, where I quenched my thirst in long draughts. I curled up and waited for daylight.[94]

⊰⊱

Philemon van der Waeren's ordeal was even more excruciating.

> At the blow of the whistle which began the fusillade, I instinctively half-turned to my left and protected my head with my right arm. I fell wounded in the right shoulder.

The bullet flattened itself against my shoulder blade after plowing through the flesh, and made a horrible wound, as big as a hand.

A second salvo succeeded the first, almost without interruption. It struck those who had not yet fallen and those unfortunates who, hearing the order "stand up," had risen.

From this mass of humanity cries, lamentations, pitiable moans rose up, along with gasps of agony. And it was then that above this sad recitative of suffering, like a satanic laugh, a volley of machine-gun fire crackled. Placed just a few yards away, the gun sprayed bullets into the mound of victims.

A new pain bit into my left side. Two ribs were broken, my left lung perforated.

I lost consciousness.

When I revived, I was suffering horribly. I was incapable of the least movement. The weight of inert bodies pressed down on my legs; I tried, however, to disengage myself. I didn't succeed at first, but with a burst of energy, managed to push off the body that immobilized my right leg. The soldiers prowling around the pile in quest of new victims to butcher perceived these movements. Two men wearing Red Cross armbands bounded up to me, carrying rifles with bayonets mounted. For a second time I thought my last moment had come. These men flung themselves on me and pierced me with their bayonets, from the back to the neck. The blood flowed over my face. Unable to stand more pain, I cried out to the brutes in Flemish "Finish me off, you cowards." One of them ran the point of his bayonet over my throat, as if searching for the carotid artery. Before he finally poked me, I instinctively seized the weapon by the blade and violently pushed it away. My gesture was so sudden that I cut my index and ring fingers to the bone.

This resistance made the soldiers beside themselves with anger, and throwing their guns on the ground, seized me by the foot and dragged me off the heap of bodies. Hearing me groan, they laughed. To prolong my agony, they dragged me around the piled up cadavers. As for me, with all the power that remained, I grabbed at everything that could offer some resistance. Turning me on my side, in order to immediately flip me over on my back, they continued to drag me, and my poor head, jolted from right to left, bounced off the ground in painful bumps, such that my clothes, sweeping the cobblestones and ashes, raised a thick dust which fell on my bloody face and mixed with the blood from the wounds in my back and throat. The cinders caked my bleeding hands, encrusted the skin of my face and my hair, and formed a thick, rough coating.

I didn't believe it possible that anyone could suffer so much. Not for a second during this punishment did I lose consciousness. I felt everything, and to these physical sufferings, the thought of my dear wife and little children added still more anguish.

When they took me back to the starting point, I believed for an instant that they were going to let me die peacefully. But no. They dragged me to the edge of the Sambre and, as if their task were accomplished, they let my legs fall heavily. Then four of the madmen took hold of me. They swung me...*ein, zwei,* like an inert mass, and hurled me into the river.

This final cruelty saved me.[95]

Van der Waeren touched the bottom, then surfaced, drinking greedily. The water staunched the flow of blood from his wounds. He remained some time in the Sambre, carried downstream to the opposite bank. Eventually, he groped his way up some stone steps and crawled to a construction site, where he spent several more agonizing hours.

Around 3:00 a.m., his moans attracted the attention of Sylvain Detry, who was hiding from the Germans in his garden with his wife and father-in-law. Detry approached cautiously.

"Are you wounded?" he asked. "Yes."

"A French soldier?"

He was a Belgian, the twenty-seven-year-old assured his rescuer, and had been shot and stabbed in the Place St. Martin.

The Detrys cared for Van der Waeren for four days. Not until the 26th did they consider it safe to move him. He was taken to the hospital established by the sisters of a convent affiliated with St. Martin's, where his wounds were at last treated. The nuns expected him to die at any moment. But he was terribly anxious about the fate of his wife and children, and the desire to see them again may have kept him alive.[96]

RINGS Others got off lightly. Fernand Micheux was among the sixty-four men who were not seriously wounded in either of the fusillades or by the troops ordered to finish off the survivors. He daubed his face with blood from the men lying around him. Then he took another precaution. Aware of soldiers reaching around him to steal objects from the dead, he suddenly became anxious that his fingers might be cut off by a souvenir hunter interested in his expensive rings. They would gleam in the beams of the flashlights some of the soldiers carried. Carefully he slipped the rings off his fingers. Soon afterwards, he was aware of a bayonet poised directly over his neck. The soldier, however, didn't strike him.[97]

There were others as well who didn't want the Germans to get their hands on their valuables, though for more mundane reasons – it was the only means of resistance remaining to them. Twenty-four-year-old Fernand Sevrin, lying uninjured among the corpses after the Red Cross had departed, muttered, "They can search me, but they won't get my money," and defiantly tossed his wallet into the Sambre.[98]

THE SAMBRE Even before soldiers began clambering onto the pile of bodies to finish off the wounded, others had begun firing on the prisoners who attempted to swim to safety. There were no lights along the river; the soldiers fired at where they heard splashes. For Joseph Legrain, it was the first time in his life he'd attempted to swim. He clung to the roots of shrubs growing along the bank after he slid into the water. Then, when the firing stopped, he let the river carry him down to the next bridge at Gripelotte.[99] Henri Joret hesitated momentarily before jumping into the river. As he muttered a quick prayer to the Virgin of Lourdes, a bullet caught him on the left side of the head. Joret managed to wriggle behind a small hill. He pretended to be dead when a soldier rushed up. But the German was only interested in using Joret's body as place to prop his foot as he fired on those in the water. Joret heard the cries of the men who were hit, and the struggles of the drowning men.[100]

François Lavis was also hit as he paused momentarily by the side of the Sambre. But Lavis was fortunate: the bullet that struck his side was deflected by his pocket watch and cigarette lighter. He was hit three more times after he lowered himself into the river, but managed to make his way twenty-five yards downstream. Lavis kept the shattered watch and twisted lighter, souvenirs of his narrow escape.[101]

Louis Lorette was shot at, too, as was about to dive into the Sambre, but the bullets whistled past his ears. He hit the water and swam to the middle of the river, where he started to sink, dragged down by his sodden clothes. With a desperate surge of energy, he resurfaced, promising the Virgin Mary to do whatever she wished if she would save him. He reached the far shore, where he and several others remained submerged for nearly three hours, fearful that the Germans were patrolling the southern bank. Lorette was able to hide in a series of abandoned homes, and had a couple of uncomfortably close encounters with soldiers, before finding refuge with an older couple, the Sohiers. Their only child was a lieutenant who had fallen at Liège. Moments after he put on the dead man's clothes, soldiers arrived and conducted the three residents to the Place St. Martin, where the men were compelled to bury the dead.[102]

AFTERMATH For the one hundred fifty or so men who had survived the gunfire and the bayonetings, but had been unable to swim or crawl away, a very tense time followed. Would there be another mass execution, this time by daylight?

Several men, including the surviving priest, Father Donnet, asked the uninjured Adolphe Seron to query the sentries. (Donnet believed that as a priest, he ran a greater risk.) But when Seron requested that he first be confessed, Donnet rose to do so, and both men were spotted by guards, according to the priest. Seron approached the soldiers, who leveled their rifles, aimed, but didn't shoot. They told Seron their commander was coming shortly. When that distinguished-looking officer arrived, he walked up to the pile of victims. Many of the survivors pleaded for mercy. "You were here last night?" the officer asked in French. When the victims assured him that they had been lying there since the shooting, he replied, "I don't believe you. Show me your wounds." The men obliged him, but the officer told them, "You fired on our soldiers. You'll all remain right here." Seron then asked permission to bring water to the wounded. "There are no wounded here," the officer declared. He turned and left. It was 6:30 in the morning.[103]

A half-hour later a German doctor arrived and permitted Seron and Franz Steinier to fetch water from a pump in the square. Abbé Donnet was allowed to walk among the piles of victims, administering absolution to the wounded. Seron was stunned by the ghastly spectacle. "There were more than four hundred bodies and wounded men sprawled in all positions, some with their skulls open letting the brain ooze out, some with their stomachs open and their entrails escaping from the wound... They were already giving off an unbearable stench. The faces were so swollen that many of my friends were unrecognizable."[104]

Seron was not the only one moved by the sight. A German non-commissioned officer arrived an hour later, and Seron noticed that as the sergeant surveyed the scene, his eyes filled with tears. The merchant immediately approached him and asked what was to happen to the survivors. "I don't know," he replied, "but I'm not going to see you shot again." The General Staff had been requested to spare the survivors, the sergeant told Seron. The decision would be made around noon. The feldwebel vowed to secretly communicate the news as soon as he heard it, showing Seron his rosary to convince the Belgian of his sincerity. It was about 8:00 a.m.[105]

An hour later, the German-speaking Franz van Heuckelom learned from a doctor that the men's fate would be decided in just two hours. Groups of soldiers were busy cleaning their rifles and polishing their bayonets nearby, showing the men their weapons and laughing menacingly. The doctor, however, gave the survivors permission to smoke while they waited.[106]

Between 9:30 and 10:00 a.m. a large group of civilians were shepherded into the square. These were the men who had been confined on Saturday in the Institut des Frères. Shortly afterward the women and children followed. No one had any idea what had transpired during the night in Place St. Martin.[107]

"I couldn't believe my eyes," Abbé Smal, curé of St. Martin, recalled.

Along the route leading to the Sambre bridge up to the wall of the Van Herck garden, the square was covered with corpses, many piled on top of each other. Later I learned that there were over 300 there! Among the victims by the side of the Sambre were a great number of men, with haggard faces, clothes filthy and torn, their faces and hands spattered with blood or coated with soot, nearly all with heads uncovered. Among them was the abbé Donnet, vicar of Alloux, all bent over, his hands supporting his knees, advancing very painfully. As for us, guarded and surrounded by soldiers, we could not approach them. We had been completely unaware of the fusillade the night before, so one can imagine our astonishment and horror to witness such a spectacle.[108]

Others had heard the gunshots, but assumed it was the response to a French raid.[109] Émile Duculot at first assumed he was looking at an enormous pile of rags, linen, and clothes heaped up along the Sambre. When he realized it was a mound of bodies, he imagined that dead German soldiers had been dragged to the Place. But Franz Steinier and Adolphe Seron were clearly standing in front of the pile and the vicar of Alloux was hobbling nearby, administering last rites. Then from the middle of the heap Léon Kaise raised his arm. These were Duculot's friends and neighbors.[110]

Shock at the horrible scene was rapidly succeeded by fear.

...the soldiers never ceased to abuse us: we had shot at them, we were all franc-tireurs. The proof was obvious: a Belgian bullet had been extracted from the body of a German soldier. We were going to pay for this crime with our lives. To these words they added the force of gestures to make us clearly understand our fate.[111]

◄◄·►►

A heartbreaking scene followed. The women and children were separated from the men and confined to the area in front of the church. Many men

attempted farewells or yelled final instructions; others were mute, overwhelmed by the prospect of their imminent death. Some tossed medallions
and crosses over the heads of their German guards, as well as other mementos, wallets, and billfolds. On the other side, there was great consternation
– tears, wailing, pleading. "Pray for us in heaven," women begged. Men
fell to their knees, clamoring for a blessing from Father Smal or one of the
other priests and a final absolution.[112]

Meanwhile, ignoring the clamor and hysteria, soldiers were setting up
tables at the opposite end of the square. Soon these were groaning under
the weight of bottles of wine, platters of ham and chicken, loaves of bread,
spice cakes, and other delicacies. Hampers filled with champagne were
carried out, along with pots of butter and baskets of fruit and eggs. The
gormandizing commenced. Each time a bottle was drained, it was hurled
at the crowd or into the pile of bodies. "When they rose from the table to
approach us," Abbé Smal wrote, "their flushed faces were hideous, and
their vile gestures and raucous howls were like a vision of hell."[113]

Soldiers displaying any humanity were sharply reprimanded. When one
infantryman passed a pancake to a wounded civilian, he was yelled at by an
officer.[114] Another sympathetic soldier who merely approached the civilians
was ordered back.[115] (Earlier in the morning, however, the friendly sergeant who had spoken with Seron gave some of the wounded drinks from
his canteen and passed around pancakes without being impeded. When
asked if they could smoke, he fetched cigars for the men. Angry soldiers
yelled and gestured at him, but he ignored them.)[116]

And then, around 11:00, the agonizing wait was over. Several superior
officers crossed the bridge on horseback and entered the square. In contrast to the drunken celebrants, they appeared calm and sober. They dismounted, examined the pile of bodies, and retired. The officers conferred
for some time, and then one among them who spoke French told the crowd
that the men would not be shot. Instead, they would be put to work burying the dead.[117]

THE SWORD OF WOTAN Throughout Belgium in August, officers conferred, and sometimes argued, over the fate of civilians. Naturally, we're
unlikely to know what was said at any such meeting. But if the losers in the
debates inevitably submitted to the decision made by their commanding

officer, they did not always do so with good grace. At Aarschot, Lieutenant Wolff, who had argued against executing the burgomaster's brother, refused to accompany his fellow officers back out to the execution site. He had given his word of honor to Emile Tielemans that the Aarschot brewer would be spared. At Tamines on Sunday morning, there was also a sore loser.

As the announcement was being made, one of the officers appeared to be enraged by the decision. His face contorted, he strode over to the church, pulled out his sword and struck several violent blows against the stone ledge over the tower door. Until well after the war, the church still bore the marks of the officer's sword.[118]

"MON DIEU, C'EST MON PERE" Shovels and picks were brought over by soldiers from a nearby farm, and the prisoners were told, "Those who want to make themselves useful and not suffer any more should come work with us and we will do you no harm."[119] The civilians grabbed the implements and, following the soldiers, went into the Van Herck garden at the east end of the square to dig a communal grave. The men worked throughout the late morning and early afternoon. They shared a single bucket of water one soldier brought out. Another soldier took a couple of baguettes, tore them up into tiny pieces, and tossed them to the men "like one would throw a bone to a dog."[120]

The completed trench was about fifteen yards by ten yards, and six feet deep. Soldiers brought over some ladders, shutters, and doors to transport the bodies. Four men were ordered into the pit to receive and arrange the corpses. The first victim carried over was Constant Dogot, the church organist. "I can still clearly visualize the face of his son as he cried out, 'My God! It's my father!' " Abbé Smal recalled.

> What a spectacle! The corpses were piled up one on another, bloody and coated with soot. Many had their clothes shredded, others bore traces of extensive bloody wounds; the heads of some were split or smashed; many of them were already unrecognizable. I was also obliged, despite my age and difficulty walking, to carry the planks bearing the cadavers.
>
> A few yards off I saw the body of Abbé Hottlet. I was not able to approach closer and had to content myself with giving him a benediction as I passed, reciting a "de profundis."[121]

When Louis Lorette attempted to retrieve the priest's eyeglasses to return to the curé's sister, he was threatened by an enraged soldier.[122]

Father Hottlet had been horribly mutilated. "His ears and one arm were cut and nearly severed from the body." Even after he had been shot, the priest continued to excite the fury of the Protestant troops.[123]

⊰⊱

Lorette, too, discovered his father among the victims. Returned to Place St. Martin after his harrowing escape, Lorette spotted the badly wounded seventy-five-year-old among the pile of victims. He quickly fetched Abbé Donnet, who administered last rites. Désiré Lorette died soon after.

Yet another son encountered his dying father on the heap of bodies. Twenty-year-old Camille Lambotte had gone through the terrifying experiences of most Taminois during the previous twenty-four hours. Seized by drunken German soldiers, Lambotte, his father, and other civilians had escaped during the fierce French barrage. They reunited in a cellar. Desperately, they hoped the French would retake the town. They kept peering through the breathing hole, but there were no red pantaloons outside – "alas, all we saw were gray uniforms."

When the Germans set fire to the building, the men survived by immersing themselves in a large cistern. After the battle subsided, the men were determined to find their wives and daughters, ignoring Lambotte's objections. They were at once seized by soldiers, marched to St. Martin, where they were made to dig trenches, then escorted to Notre Dame des Alloux. The joyful reunions with the women were short-lived.

Uninjured by the bullets, but stabbed in the cheek by a Red Cross medic, Lambotte extricated himself from the pile and began looking for anyone else who was still alive. He hadn't gone four yards when he

> fell against a wounded man whose head rested in a pool of blood.
>
> I turned him over. He was still living. He breathed with difficulty, his nose was crushed, his head hammered by rifle butts. Great God! It was my father! I questioned him; he didn't respond. I looked at him: he couldn't see me. I lifted his head, and the blood poured from his eyelids and nostrils. His jaw was dislocated, mutilated, hanging loose. My father. Yesterday did he have any inkling of the suffering he was going to endure?[124]

WAVING The burial of the victims of the massacre was a hideous task. Some bodies had been so thoroughly shredded by bullets and gouged by bayonets that they were difficult to identify. (Nine victims, in fact, were never identified.)[125] Corpses had become entangled. "It was necessary to pull them out by the arms, the legs, the trunk, however one could," Abbé Lemaire wrote.

> The boards that were used to carry the victims could be seized only at the two ends, and did not give under the weight. During the trip to the pit, this produced a sinister swinging movement, making it almost appear as if the corpse was alive, and, in combination with the hideousness of the wounds, added still more horror to the scene.[126]

But in at least one instance, the victim was not yet dead.

"While some of us were carrying the corpses along, I observed that others had stopped and called to a German doctor," a witness testified.

> They had noticed that the man whom they were conveying was still alive. The doctor examined the wounded man and made a sign that he was to be buried with the rest. The plank on which he was lying was borne on again, and I saw the wounded man raise his arm elbow-high. They called to the doctor again, but he made a gesture that he was to go into the trench with the others.[127]

It was Ferdinand Lambotte. His son Camille pleaded frantically with other Germans and at last they permitted the father to be carried to the church, along with the other wounded. He died the next day.[128]

His son enlisted in the army to avenge his father's death. Camille wrote his recollections from a trench behind the IJzer and concluded his narrative with soldierly bravado: "Power to outraged Belgium, to be able to live again and recover, with proud independence, its national neutrality. Power to England and its allies to march to Victory, and may the villainous nation pay the price for its hideous crime."[129]

GUT CHAMPAGNE Meanwhile, a few of the women and children who were held captive in the École des Soeurs during the massacre were finally released around 8:00 a.m. on Sunday. The great majority remained under guard in the school and in the church. Among those who left was the curé's sister, who returned to the presbytery across the street from Notre Dame d'Alloux.

Later that morning a large gray car pulled up. An officer and two soldiers stepped out. The officer spoke a bit of French and was able to let Elise

Hottlet know what he wanted. *"Gut Bourgogne, gut Champagne, gut fine Champagne."* Brandishing his revolver, he forced the woman to accompany him to the cellar, where he selected nearly all the wine and some other provisions, and gave her a receipt for five francs. The soldiers loaded everything into the car and sped off.[130]

The supply was evidently running low at the party in Place St. Martin. And no wonder: one witness observed the soldiers and officers swilling their champagne from large beer glasses.[131]

VIVE L'ALLEMAGNE! "When the bodies were disposed of in the communal pit," Abbé Smal testified,

> the commandant located me, along with three other priests, and told me in French, "You, parson, come say prayers and bless the dead before they're covered with earth." I went ahead then and recited the liturgy of absolution, and then we were made to walk around the pit...[132]

<-←-→->

Their work completed, a great many people believed it was now their turn to be massacred. Why trust the Germans to keep this promise after the deceptions they'd practiced on Saturday? Priests knelt down in front of the civilians, preparing to receive the first bullet. One of the priests, Canon Crousse, spotted his brother across the square and rose to embrace him. The brother was a pharmacist with the Red Cross and had been attending the German wounded. "We're going to die," the priest told him.

But a German doctor who had worked with the brother gestured for Crousse to approach him. Without waiting for the doctor to speak, the anxious priest assured him that though everyone was prepared to die for their country, all were innocent. No one had fired on German troops. Crousse melodramatically offered to sacrifice his life for those of the residents gathered behind him.

"But you're not going to be killed," the doctor told him, when he was finally able to get a word in. "Nor will the others be."[133]

Canon Crousse refused to believe the man. "We're going to share the fate of our comrades," he announced, and urged that the women and children be spared.

The doctor, now consulting his French-German dictionary, repeated that no one would be killed and that the clergyman would be required to guide his flock half a mile north of town.

The cautious canon chose not to share the good news with his fellow captives when he returned to their ranks, though they besieged him for information. "An explosion of joy," he believed, might have induced the Germans to recant their decision. He merely told everyone to be calm and confident.[134]

An officer now stepped forward and approached the crowd in front of St. Martin's church. "You're going to leave with me," he told them. "Arrange yourselves in order. Whoever doesn't understand how to follow will be shot in the street. Those who try to flee will also be shot immediately."[135]

"At this moment," Abbé Smal recalled, "the women and children, held separately from us til now, rejoined our group... There was an outburst of joy, mixed with tears."[136] But had the execution merely been postponed?

The trip north was hellish. The streets were blocked by debris. The men, women, and children had to clamber over the smouldering ruins of buildings. Facades were collapsing even as the civilians passed by; people looked up anxiously as they walked. Everyone was made to advance rapidly. The troops guarding the civilians terrorized their hostages. Soldiers screamed at their captives, and smacked them with their rifle butts.

A few soldiers, however, were moved by the spectacle. "I saw German soldiers who could not refrain from bursting into tears on seeing the despair of the women."[137] This did nothing to reassure the civilians, however.

When the procession arrived at les Alloux, it was swollen by the women and children who had been kept captive in the École des Soeurs when their husbands, fathers, and sons were marched to Place St. Martin. Among them were some men seized after the massacre. The entire group now numbered somewhere between three and four thousand.[138]

Naturally, when the women and children were led out to join the others, they searched eagerly – then, in most cases, increasingly desperately – for their loved ones. It was an extremely poignant moment. No one dared mention what had actually happened. Anxiety mounted. The evasive answers, the averted eyes, the painful silences betrayed the awful reality. (Some in the École de Soeurs had heard from an escapee who had made his way north that the men had been shot at, "with many dead.")[139]

But the threat of another mass execution still hung over the crowd, and was a powerful diversion. Gunshots in the distance caused a good deal of anxiety. At one point machine-guns were trained on the crowd and everyone was made to shout *"Vive l'Allemagne!"*[140]

By the time the middle of the procession reached Velaine, villagers with buckets of water lined the street. The captives eagerly quenched their thirst. Then, in the market place, an officer addressed the group in French. "You're free," he told them. However, they could not return to Tamines until the war was over. Anyone caught in town would be shot. Then everyone was again obliged to yell, *"Vive l'Allemagne!"*[141]

CROSSES, AGAIN During visits to Tamines in 1915, Fathers Schmitz and Nieuwland found themselves lingering before the makeshift cemetery in what had been the Van Herck garden. Abandoning the invisibility they maintain throughout the rest of their volumes, the two priests commented:

> When you enter the improvised cemetery, so hastily filled, you're seized by a sense of infinite sadness. Emotion tugs at your heart. The crosses, of different dimensions, rise up one against the other, nearly colliding, like young bushes in a thicket, and on all of them, you can read the same date, and on nearly all the same inscription: "Here lies ... died for his country, the 22nd of August 1914." "Here rests ... fell as a martyr on the Place de Tamines the 22nd of August 1914."[142]

Within a year, the second inscription was no longer to be seen. On May 20, 1916, the burgomaster, Émile Duculot, received an order from the Imperial Government in Namur requiring that the word "martyr" be replaced by a less offensive term, such as "victim," or be omitted entirely. He was advised to make the changes discreetly.[143]

⊰⟶⟶⟩⟩

When the German Army returned to Tamines in 1940, one of the first acts of the commander of the occupying forces was to dynamite the memorial to the martyrs of August 22nd.[144]

TOTALS, AGAIN The execution carried out at dusk on the 22nd was the largest mass murder of civilians committed by Germans until 1939. Two hundred fifty-seven men were gunned down or bayoneted to death in the Place St. Martin. Forty men drowned in the Sambre, many hit by the bullets of soldiers posted on the bridge. Twelve badly wounded men died in Red Cross hospitals soon after the shooting. Of the additional twenty-one who died of injuries in the days that followed, an indeterminate number, though likely a high percentage, were victims of the fusillade. Thirty-two other men, women, and children were killed by soldiers elsewhere in and around Tamines on Friday and Saturday, including the nine men murdered at the Café Hennion. Another twelve burned to death or were asphyxiated when the Germans set fire to their homes. The death toll then stood at 383.[145]

Two hundred forty-two buildings were destroyed by fire, leaving two hundred eighty-four families homeless.

It could have been even worse. Sixty-eight men were able to jump into the Sambre and swim to safety. (So many dove in at one point, that some witnesses thought they were being pushed in by the Germans.)[146] Most leapt in moments before the troops opened fire, but others were survivors of the fusillade who crawled to the river under the cover of darkness. Eighty-four men wounded by the gunfire or bayonets eventually recovered. Another sixty-four, concealing themselves under the bodies of their murdered friends, relatives, and neighbors, escaped without serious injuries.[147]

REUNIONS Most of the wounded were taken initially to the church of St. Martin in the square. Others were carried to the Couvreur farm just north of the church. They had been lying on the pavement in the square for more than eighteen hours. Unquestionably, men died who would have survived had they been given prompt treatment. The behavior of the German doctors and hospital staff was despicable, according to Dr. Defosse, who established a temporary hospital in his own home. Thirty wounded were brought there and another forty-seven to a hospital established by the Sisters of the Immaculate Conception (commonly referred to as the Sisters of St. Martin's).[148]

One of the sisters (perhaps the mother superior writing in the third person) provided a detailed account of the nuns' experiences after the mass execution.[149] Assured by a neighbor that "the Germans were civilized people who will pass through town just as the French did, without any disturbing incidents," the sisters remained in their convent. Though terrified by the sounds of the battle Friday night, they were unaware of the fusillade the following evening, until a desperate survivor seeking refuge, Philemon van der Waeren, informed them. After conferring with Dr.

Defosse and the German commandant, the sisters, who had no nursing experience, set up a hospital Tuesday evening.

The injured men were immensely relieved to be in the hands of the sisters, but they presented an appalling spectacle. "What a scene! Would it be possible to restore these human beings? Bullets had pierced their arms, legs, heads. Their chests were perforated. Blood had flowed in streams. It had congealed on their clothes, which adhered to their skin. It was very difficult removing the clothes." Conditions in the makeshift hospital were deplorable. There was no light – only two small pieces of candle. There was no bread – only a pear and some wine cut with water. The mother superior and another sister headed to a nearby bakery. It had been looted and badly damaged. Even religious statues had been attacked. The nuns were able to locate some flour, however, that had not been seized. Two famished dogs guarded the bakehouse door, snarling at the sisters. The women found some burnt bread to feed them but were unable to figure out how to turn on the electric oven. They located some charcoal briquets and wood in the yard and were able to use these to heat the oven.

When the nuns finally succeed in baking several loaves, late at night, German soldiers, attracted by the fragrance, came over and demanded some. They claimed, by sign language, that they hadn't eaten in four days. No sooner had they departed with two loaves than another group arrived and requested the rest of the batch. This time, however, an officer appeared and ordered the men to leave. Extracting a tiny cross from his flowing cape, he showed it to the sisters and told them not to worry. It was now 3 a.m.

Making their way back to the convent, the sisters encountered more German soldiers. But these men were preoccupied with looting, several had armfulls of bottles, and they didn't bother the sisters. When the nuns returned to the convent, Dr. Defosse was still busy dressing wounds by the flickering candlelight.

◂┄▸

The Germans are referred to throughout the sixteen-page account as "the barbarians." Before the arrival of the victims, one soldier entered the convent. The frightened sisters assumed he was searching for French soldiers or weapons. But as he crossed the courtyard, he stopped in front of the pump. Thinking he wanted to wash his hands, the sisters offered him some soap, but he shook his head. Instead he began drinking from the pump, using his hands. The sisters offered him a glass, but he refused this as well.

German manners only confirmed the sisters in their fear that the barbarians would desecrate the Eucharist that Abbé Hottelet had carried with him to Place St. Martin and that had been rescued by Father Donnet. "It is impossible to describe the emotion with which we received it. We all cried and yet a very sweet joy suffused our hearts." The wafers, now safe from the hands of the barbarians, were hidden in the sacristy. The first mass after the executions was celebrated by the badly injured Abbé Donnet on the 27th. Unaware that he was coming, the sisters had eaten that morning and were unable to take communion. The first to receive the Host was Dr. Defosse.

German soldiers occasionally entered the convent without any reason after the victims had been moved there. The soldiers taunted the wounded men. The sisters, terribly anxious that a soldier might decide to finish off one of their patients, refused to leave the men's bedsides whenever the barbarians arrived.

⊰⊹⊱

On the evening of the 27th, the women and children who had been expelled from Tamines were permitted to return. They raced through the courtyard and feverishly began searching the classrooms for their loved ones. Over and over the sisters had to repeat "'your husband – your son – your brother – isn't here. But perhaps if you go over to Dr. Defosse's hospital and look around, you'll find him there.'" But the usual response was, "'Sister, I've just come from there.'"

Before the 27th, some family members snuck back into town and were reunited with their wounded relatives. Sometimes this meant only an opportunity to witness their final suffering. Others didn't even get a chance to say goodbye. The wife and children of Herman Wiame arrived at nightfall on the 26th. The forty-five-year-old Auvelais resident had been repeatedly kicked in the stomach, and was suffering horribly. The sisters of St. Martin reminded Mme. Wiame that she risked being arrested and shot if she were caught in Tamines, and the family left not long after they'd arrived. When the wife and oldest son, a twelve-year-old, returned the next day, Wiame had just died. "The grief of the mother and orphan were difficult to look at," the mother superior commented.

There were happier reunions. Wearing a Red Cross insignia, the wife of department-store owner Georges Locus returned to Tamines several times in search of her husband. He had escaped the Germans and was hiding in an attic with five others. It was not until August 30th that the men became convinced that the Germans had called off the manhunt. They climbed down and began looking for their wives and children. The Locuses were reunited in Auvelais.[150]

Others among the men who had swum to safety or otherwise escaped were only gradually located by their families. For those whose husbands or sons had managed to cross French lines, the wait was longer. Around two hundred prescient residents had fled south earlier, when the Germans had first arrived.

COMMANDANTS During the weeks following the massacre, there was a dizzying succession of commandants in Tamines. They had different priorities. A Lieutenant Schluter was concerned chiefly about the franc-tireur threat. For every German injured or killed, he would execute ten civilians, he warned Émile Duculot, the new burgomaster. Duculot pointed out that all the weapons in town had been consigned to the Hôtel de Ville well before the arrival of the first Germans. Since the town had been reopened, however, a number of Flemish workers had arrived whom he didn't know personally.

Schluter was accommodating. "OK," he said. "If I need to shoot ten men, just send me ten of these Flemish."[151]

⊰⊱

Another commandant, Captain Bremer, was unusually scrupulous about pillaging. But troops were rapidly being sent south, and it's not surprising that two of the commandants were doctors in charge of the local hospital. It was one of these who appointed Duculot burgomaster and authorized him to exhume and rebury the corpses.

⊰⊱

But who was the commander responsible for the murders? The German White Book, whatever its deficiencies as an accurate record of what transpired in Belgium during August, is at least helpful in identifying the perpetrators. They testify against themselves. But while there are chapters on Aarschot, Andenne, Dinant, and Leuven, there is no section that attempts to reconstruct events in Tamines. The omission is damning. This was, after all, the single largest massacre of civilians on the Western Front during the war. What could the residents have done to warrant it?

It is not correct to say, however, that Tamines goes entirely unmentioned in the White Book. The long opening section, concerned primarily with "franc-tireur" attacks in Liège province, includes one deposition purporting to describe events in Tamines. This comes from a Lieutenant Deule of the Telephone Section of the Xth Army Corps. He claims that at 5:00 p.m. on August 22nd, he was walking through Tamines with his platoon along a street he calls "Vignées." On his right was a factory and on his left a church and a large building flying Red Cross flags. Suddenly Deule's troops were assaulted by "heavy, but badly aimed" gunfire coming from the church and the Red Cross establishment. As the soldiers took position, Lieutenant Deule observed "a great number of armed civilians" fleeing quickly into the woods behind the two buildings.

If he was in the northern parish of Tamines at 5:00 p.m. on August 22nd, there was certainly a large number of civilians in the church to his left as he led his troops southward.[152] (Red Cross flags would have been flying from the École des Soeurs next to Notre Dame des Alloux.) However, it's unlikely that, unobserved by their German guards, these civilians fired on the passing troops, fled into the woods, stashed their weapons, then snuck back into the church in time to be marched down to Place St. Martin for their execution.[153]

⤜⤛⤚⤙

The Germans apparently did make a bona-fide attempt to investigate the massacre. A magistrate with a secretary and interpreter was despatched to Tamines early in 1915. A number of residents were interviewed in the town hall. Émile Duculot was questioned for three hours.[154] The results of the inquest were never made public. One can only assume that the report was so damning that the Foreign Office felt it would not be worthwhile to try again with a less objective investigator, as was done at Andenne when the first proved too scrupulous. The compilers of the White Book were possibly troubled by the fact that the punishment was so disproportionate to the crime. The commanders of the 77th Hanoverian Reserve Infantry Regiment had killed more than three hundred men in response to the wounding of two German soldiers thirty-six hours earlier. In any event, it is to the credit either of the judge sent to Tamines or to the official who suppressed his report that no defense of the actions of the 77th Regiment was attempted.

Belgian investigators were therefore obliged to rely on the depositions of German prisoners of war in order to identify those in charge of the operation. It was Joseph Musch, a twenty-eight-year-old reserve private from Celle in the 7th Company of 77th Regiment, who first named the commanding officer responsible for the order to execute the civilians. The man was Lieutenant-Colonel von Roques. Members of the 1st Company were the actual executioners.

Von Roques's subsequent career was not distinguished. He was relieved of his command in November, in front of Ieper, according to Musch, because he was unable to provide superiors with accurate information about his regiment's gun emplacements.[155]

CHAPTER 6

Dinant: Introduction, Leffe

DINANT: INTRODUCTION Although it goes unmentioned in German records and memoirs (there is a passing reference in the German White Book)[1], a decisive French victory on August 15 may have provoked the destruction of Dinant and the massacre of its inhabitants on the 23rd. The French repelled a premature attempt on the part of the Third Army to force a passage of the Meuse. (The larger significance of von Hausen's failure is open to debate, but at least one German commentator felt it was a critical factor in the German check at the Marne two weeks later.)[2] Seven days after the German retreat from Dinant, a reconnaissance operation in the town went badly awry, and this probably sealed the city's fate, if it had not been determined earlier.

For centuries Dinant had been a vital crossing point. Three major roads descend into the steep Meuse valley from the east and one from the west. It was via the latter that Dinant had twice been conquered. In 1466 Charles the Bold sacked the city, then quite large and prosperous. (A member of the Hanseatic League, it produced bronzeware – the original dinanderie – and brass and copperware that was widely exported.) All males who fell into the hands of the Burgundians were murdered. Louis XIV repeated the achievement in 1675, with less dire consequences for the Dinantais.

Now the threat came from the east.

The French, suddenly Belgian's ally, were not long in arriving. At 6:00 p.m. on Thursday, August 6, the 1st battalion of the 148th regiment of Lanrezac's Fifth Army disembarked in Dinant after the brief train ride from its headquarters in Givet, just 42 miles to the south. Skirmishes with

Dinant before the war, from the steps leading to the Citadel.

*View of le Rocher Bayard and Dinant
from Les Rivages.*

uhlan patrols soon followed. As elsewhere throughout Belgium, the burgomaster of Dinant, M. A. Defoin, issued ordinances on the 6th requiring
residents to hand in all weapons and ammunition to the police, and forbidding any participation in the war. He even banned rallies in support of
Belgium and her allies. The regulations were posted throughout town and
published in the local paper.[3]

By the 15th, with clear indications of an impending attack, sixteen
companies of the 2nd Division of the Ist Corps, commanded by Franchet
d'Esperey, prepared to defend the Meuse crossings. Three companies of
the crack 148th Regiment, which had been earlier sent north, were recalled
to Dinant and, with a machine-gun section, guarded the Dinant bridge.
Another machine-gun section and two companies of the 33rd Regiment
defended the other bridge in the vicinity, at Bouvignes just to the north.
Two other companies of the 33rd were sent to the Citadel, towering 300
feet above the town. It had been completely rebuilt by the Dutch between
1818 and 1821, but had long been decommissioned. Apart from patrols,
these two companies were the only soldiers in Dinant proper, on the right
bank. As residents soon recognized, the French had no intention of defending the town itself – only its bridgehead. They would engage the Germans
from the heights of the left bank. Reflecting the unfortunate priorities of
the French Army before the war, the forces deployed at Dinant possessed
only one howitzer. Dinantais privy to this information may have consoled
themselves: they could survive the French bombardment in their cellars;
élan and the rapid-firing 75s would drive off the invader. On the 15th, the
French 2nd Division faced two cavalry divisions, a Guard division and
three battalions of the 5th Infantry Division, all units of the XIIth Corps
(the Ist Saxon Corps) of the Third Army.[4]

After several hours of intense fighting, the French abandoned the
Citadel with heavy losses. About half of its defenders were able to make
their way down the steps and back to the left bank, where the battalion
commander was still frantically phoning for artillery support. This arrived
soon after the retreating companies. By 5:00 p.m., the French guns, firing
from the crest above the left bank, had silenced the German artillery, and
a counter-attack from the southwest was underway. Soon French troops
were swarming across Les Rivages, the southern faubourg of Dinant.
When some soldiers imprudently dashed up the steps of the Citadel, they

discovered that the Germans had abandoned the stronghold. The German flag was promptly hauled down, and the tricolor raised. Dinantais emerged from their cellars and cheered. They joined in singing the Marseillaise with French troops. This was the extent of their participation in the German setback, but it was not forgotten nor forgiven.

Inevitably, a few civilians had been killed or wounded. Inevitably, there were war crimes. Civilians from a nearby hamlet were placed at the head of a German column marching west. They were released at the entrance to Dinant, then rearrested, beaten up, spat upon, and stabbed with bayonets. Civilians with Red Cross armbands were deliberately fired on as they prepared to carry off a wounded French soldier. One man was killed. Several French wounded appeared to have been finished off at the Citadel, and three prisoners of war were found hanged. The body of one, a corporal, had been mutilated, it was reported.[5]

⊷⊶

During the week that followed, several residents of nearby villages occupied by German troops received grim forecasts about Dinant.

A German Catholic chaplain ominously remarked to the curé of Scy that "Dinant would be remembered next Sunday." In Buissonville an officer of the 101st regiment assured a local dignitary that the Dinantais were wicked and that the city would burn. More cryptically, cavalry troops repeated to anyone who would listen in Hour on the 22nd, *"Demain, Dinant tout kaputt."* No stone would be left in place, the curé of Hulsonniaux was assured on the same day (a favorite German threat). At Lisogne, a captain informed another curé in imperfect French that *"demain Dinant tout brulé et tout tué."* Leaving a meeting with his officers, Col. Baessler assured still another curé that it would be terrible tomorrow in Dinant. After church early the next morning, he repeated his dire prediction.[6]

Yves Lamotte, a Dinant resident who was staying in Buissonville, about twelve miles east of town, dined on August 20th with officers from the Dresden-based 101st Regiment of the XIIth Corps. The conversation was distressing. Colonel Meisler, Major von Albeke and others were "not even humane or civil in the presence of my wife and daughters." The Dinantais are evil men, Lamotte was told. They had befriended the French. They'd made a trophy of the arms seized from a uhlan killed by franc-tireurs.

Dinant's prison would soon be overflowing; the day of judgement had arrived for residents. "In your own interest, Monsieur, remain here and don't return to Dinant." Later in the day a young officer with the aviation corps asked Lamotte's daughters if they were indeed from Dinant. The city will burn, the officer assured them gleefully, and the inhabitants would be hunted down and slaughtered. "My girls were very frightened, but I told them I considered it the bluster of a young man."[7]

Occasionally a warning got transmitted. M. Van Damme, the concierge of a wealthy widow, overheard some officers who were staying in her château discussing how they were going to burn a great number of houses in Dinant and kill a lot of men. He rushed off later that evening and warned some neighbors.[8]

Another resident of Dinant – a trustworthy local notable, according to Public Prosecutor Maurice Tschoffen – was staying at a nearby town behind German lines during the days preceding the attack on the city. He became acquainted with a German officer, either a major or a colonel. Sometime between the 19th and 21st (Tschoffen was told the exact date, but forgot it), the officer asked the informant if he were from Dinant. When the man answered in the affirmative, the officer warned him not to return. "It is an ill-behaved place and will be destroyed." He asked the man for information about his house. Shortly after the 23rd, the officer returned to the village and, while the Dinant man watched in amazement, the officer extracted from his luggage a small statuette. "Does this look familiar?" he asked.

"Yes indeed," the man replied, "it comes from my house."

"Then I was right," said the officer, smiling. "I saved your house. It wasn't set on fire."[9]

While it is no doubt tempting to fabricate warnings and premonitions after the fact, there are so many, from so many sources – and at least one instance of a warning being passed along – that it is difficult to discount them all.

◂┈▸

By Monday the 17th it had become clear to the Dinantais that the French were abandoning the right bank entirely. The Citadel was not re-occupied after the Germans were driven out; patrols ceased to cross the river. By

Wednesday, the Germans had gotten wind of the French withdrawal. On that day, a single cavalryman came down the southernmost road into town, route du Froidvau. He trotted the length of Dinant, heading back east on rue St. Jacques. That evening a second uhlan entered town, also along the route du Froidvau. He stopped to ask for directions to the post office, no doubt as a joke. When actually conducted there by an obliging citizen, he made a scornful gesture and rode off, heading east down rue St. Jacques, like his compatriot.[10] As a number of residents pointed out later, no one among "the fanatical population of Dinant" troubled either cavalryman. Yet a franc-tireur could hardly have asked for a better opportunity to do in one of the *sales boches*.

A third cavalryman appeared about 8:30 on the evening of the 21st. He was followed an hour later by a large group of soldiers, "yelling like demons," according to residents, smashing windows, breaking down doors and hurling incendiary bombs into the homes bordering the street. Several buildings were consumed by fire, including a large apartment complex housing workers, where the charred bodies of a mother, her child, and her two young nephews were recovered the next day.[11]

In another house, a farmer who had sought refuge in town was hit, along with his wife and young daughter. The wife received a bad stomach wound and succumbed the next day after grievous suffering.

When the Germans reached the intersection of the main street paralleling the Meuse, they headed off in both directions. They did not appear to venture closer to the river. The officers directing what they later called "a reconnaissance in force" were singularly incurious about French defenses of the bridge.

The troops heading north, towards Leffe, gunned down a gasworker on his doorstep. A butcher was killed by soldiers racing in the opposite direction, down the rue Sax. The soldiers may have been preceded, or followed, by an armored car.

Residents were baffled by the attack. From the wild whoops and reckless window-smashing, many assumed the soldiers were drunk. Officers seemed to be struggling to control their men. Orders were shouted, whistles blown, pistols discharged.

The French heard the uproar and belatedly dispatched a patrol of six soldiers across the Meuse. By the time they arrived, the Germans had vanished. Families whose homes were on fire were trying to contain the blaze and save valuables. The other residents still remained in their cellars. The patrol found about 40 unexploded incendiary bombs and hand grenades, and a number of cartridges, some packs, canteens, flashlights, and rifles with serrated-edged bayonets, along with some odder items: a large staff coated with grease that had been used as a torch and some pamphlets on the technical training of pioneers. The French soldiers also recovered several bloody caps spattered with cerebral matter.[12]

A shopkeeper who fled Dinant the next day provided the following account:

> On Friday, the 21st of August, at half-past nine in the evening, I was in the café of the Hôtel St. Jacques at the corner of the Ciney road... We heard a motor coming down from the Ciney road. At that time the right bank of the Meuse was in the possession of the Germans, and there were no Belgian or French soldiers on this side... We thought that the motor in question must be a German military motor, so we asked the proprietor to turn out the light and to shut the door, which he did at once, and we went into the building behind the hotel. Hardly had we got there that we heard a mitrailleuse put into action, and four bombs exploded in the hotel, wounding some of us. For my part, I got a wound in the left eye from a splinter. The mitrailleuse fired and the explosions went on for about half an hour, and during this time we were taking refuge in an inner courtyard of the building. We did not dare to move. When the noise stopped, we peeped out into the street, going through an empty house which had been smashed up by the mitrailleuse. It had not a single window or shutter left...
>
> Further up, about ten houses were on fire. It could be seen that the Germans had broken the windows so as to pass lighted torches into the building to keep the fires going. People who came out of their houses told us at once that there had been some people injured, and we found that a resident living in the rue St. Jacques had been struck by two bullets in the legs; that another resident had two bayonet thrusts and had been kicked out by blows from the butt end of a rifle.
>
> The wife of a farmer who was in bed with her little girl got two bullets...and her little girl had her foot torn off by bullets. (I saw the two of them carried down the Ciney road on a mattress.)
>
> Apparently, also the Germans had suffered losses, for we found four military caps absolutely full of blood. Undoubtedly some of the soldiers met their death while throwing bombs.
>
> There was no justification whatever for these barbarous acts.
>
> The population of Dinant was quite quiet and nothing which had occurred during the day gave any reason to suppose that an attack of this sort would be made. When I got back, I found a hand grenade in my shop. It had not exploded. It had been thrown in through the glass panel in the door. We picked up next morning about thirty of these grenades and put them in water.[13]

Other Belgian commentators believed that there might have been a mutiny. While this seems unlikely, there was certainly an interval when the officers struggled to restore order. Whistles were blown, pistols were fired. The bloody caps, the abandoned cases of cartridges, and reports of an armored car pursuing the troops lends additional weight to this speculation.[14]

Not surprisingly, members of the patrol appear to have believed they were under attack by civilians. The official German version of the incident vividly describes machine-gun-wielding franc-tireurs — who nonetheless fail to mow down the advancing troops as they obligingly filed past. In a captured war diary, Private Paul Förster (of the 108th Fusilier Regiment) records that "all at once something terrible and startling happened. From all the houses and all the windows people fired at once as if on an agreed signal." He fell to the ground, like the others, terrorized.

> My rifle and bayonet were snatched from me and I was delivered defenseless into the hands of the enemy. However, our comrades quickly recovered from their fright. Presently our rifles spat out fire in their turn. About twenty minutes passed, during which one might have thought the day of judgment had come... Then the sappers began their work. They threw incendiary bombs into the houses. Before long whole rows of houses were in flames. Flames broke out through the windows and lit up the night. We beat a retreat. All the houses before which we passed were also burned. We had attained our end.[15]

Förster did not actually observe any "franc-tireurs." Even when he believed that someone had brazenly snatched his rifle from him, he did not catch a glimpse of the culprit.

Not coincidentally, in the two of the six depositions in the White Book that were based on statements recorded in the regimental report the following day, no sightings of "franc-tireurs" are mentioned. Only six months later did soldiers claim otherwise. Of the affidavits submitted in February and March, a lieutenant leading an engineers battalion admitted that he never saw any francs-tireurs. However, an inventive reservist swore than he clearly saw an elderly woman fire from a house lit by a lamp burning in the street, and another soldier claimed to see a thirty-year-old woman aim at him with a revolver.[16] Unfortunately, at the time of the sortie, the city was completely dark. "The street lamps were destroyed by us," wrote the soldier who tussled with the imaginary franc-tireur. Actually, according to Belgian sources, street lights were not illuminated because the city's gas reservoirs had been emptied several days before as a precaution. There were discrepancies in the German accounts as to when the firing broke out, whether or not a "signal shot" was fired, etc.

Still another German report sheds some light on what may have happened:

> As soon as the first houses in Dinant were reached, the street-lighting was destroyed. The columns marched along closely by the two rows of houses and arrived as far as the first intersection. Here the head of the infantry column suddenly received heavy fire from the corner house on the right, which was immediately returned. Suddenly there was firing from all the houses. A violent street-fight followed. The pioneers forced open the fastened doors with hatchets and axes, threw hand-grenades into the lower rooms, and set others on fire with the torches which had meanwhile been lit.[17]

A good case can be made that the soldiers were firing on each other in the darkness, shooting at the buildings across the street, where they saw bursts of fire – coming, of course, from the muzzles of the guns of the soldiers facing them, their backs against the row of houses, firing at the invisible "franc-tireurs" in the homes opposite.[18]

The shooting may have begun when a rifle was unintentionally discharged – the "signal shot" so familiar in accounts of franc-tireur activity elsewhere. The soldiers were walking along the pavement on either side of the street with their fingers on their rifle triggers. It's equally probable that an over-anxious infantryman imagined he saw a gunman lurking behind a closed window and intentionally fired his weapon.

But it is also possible that the initial shooting was a deliberate provocation by officers to further incite their soldiers against the inhabitants, and make sure the orders to destroy the city and massacre the male residents would be enthusiastically carried out. Such activities were reported in Liège province, Andenne, Leuven, and elsewhere. A few injuries and even a death or two would have been a small price to pay for the zeal the martyred men would inspire in their avengers the following day.

Officers of the XIIth Corps took some pains to incite their men against the Belgians. Prisoners of war captured during and after the retreat to the Aisne told of stories circulated by their commanders about the nefarious Dinantais. Private Oscar Müller of the 103rd Regiment told his interrogators that "the Captain of my company informed us that as we entered Dinant an old woman posted at a window had killed the major by firing at

him with a revolver. The major belonged to one of the active regiments.
I do not know his name."[19] In the 100th Regiment, another story circulated. "We had been ordered to be on our guard, for it was said that the
1st company of the 1st battalion, which had preceded us, had been attacked
and the captain wounded by a young girl of fourteen; our captain gave us
these details."[20] The victim's rank and his assailant's age varied with each
retelling. A private in the 101st Grenadiers from Dresden reported that "a
very young girl fired a revolver at the colonel of my regiment – or, no, I am
making a mistake, it was at a major of a battalion of pioneers, whose name
I do not know, and she killed him."[21]

For obvious reasons, the tales always implicated women – old and
young – and children of both sexes. Every civilian was a potential killer;
no one deserved mercy. These civilians naturally engaged in atrocities.
Private Alfred Jäger of the 103rd regiment testified

> I heard it said that a patrol of hussars had been attacked by civilians in one of the vil-
> lages where we afterwards passed. Now, according to the story we were told, eleven
> of these hussars had been wounded, and these same civilians were said to have cut off
> their hands. The leader of the patrol in question was even supposed to have had his
> arms and legs cut off. You must understand that I did not see the atrocities I report
> with my own eyes, but they were related to us by our officers, to incite us to distrust
> the inhabitants.[22]

In at least one instance, officers with a taste for theatricals staged a rather
elaborate performance calculated to enrage the gullible. Private Alfred
Delling of the 103rd regiment recalled that "on August 22nd the lieutenant-colonel of our regiment arranged for a carriage to pass along the
front of our regiment, in which he told us there were two German Sisters
of Mercy, whose hands had been cut off by civilians. (I must admit that,
though I saw the carriage, I saw neither the two Sisters nor the mutilated
hands.)" The incident took place at Spontin. "I think I ought to add,"
Delling continued, "that in spite of this I never knew of any instance in
which a civilian of any kind fired upon us and wounded or killed one of
us." Throughout Belgium, he had earlier noted, "the population behaved
irreproachably toward us."[23]

French interrogators repeatedly asked the German soldiers about the
conduct of the Belgian population. Repeatedly, they were assured that
civilian behavior was exemplary. In their own experience, no one fired on

them. It was officers and soldiers in other companies who were the victims of the nefarious civilians.[24]

But in the end, officers did not depend merely on inciting their troops with grisly tales. Clear orders were issued to kill all civilians. A reservist of the 108th Regiment, a tramway ticket clerk in Dresden, stated under oath that "on Friday, August 21st last, in the evening, our Lieutenant Schultz, acting in place of our company commander, who was wounded, informed us that our orders were to massacre all civilians in Dinant. This was an Army Corps order."[25] Similarly, an n.c.o. in the active 108th Regiment, Johannes Peisker, a gardener, stated, "We re-entered Dinant on Sunday, August 23rd, about 10 in the morning. Orders were given to all the companies of my regiment to kill the civilians. This order was transmitted to me by Lieutenant Harich."[26]

Officers did not hesitate to add some incentives. Private Richard Eichler of the 102nd Regiment testified that "pillage was permitted in the homes of those executed for firing on us."[27]

◄‹—››

If the mysterious sortie, whatever its intentions, sealed Dinant's fate, it also saved a number of lives among those who witnessed it. Like the shopkeeper who was injured in Hotel St. Jacques, most of the residents of the quartier hastily packed up belongings and crossed the Meuse. Shopkeepers do not lightly abandon their homes and businesses. The Germans had succeeded in terrorizing the population of St. Jacques. Since the Dinant bridge was barricaded by French troops (as was the bridge further north at Bouvignes), families were shuttled across in tourist excursion boats. The French asked a member of the *Garde civique* to verify the identities of those seeking to pass through French lines.

By mid-day, however, orders were issued forbidding civilians to cross the river. But either before the order was issued, or because it was laxly enforced, much of the faubourg St. Jacques was able to flee on Saturday.[28] At least one family, however, was doomed by the French insistence on passports. When Léon Simon arrived at the Hôtel de Ville to secure one, the building was swarming with Dinantais. Simon grew tired of waiting. Besides, he'd heard that the French were blocking the Philippeville road at St. Médard.[29] Another family, the Mathieus, hotly debated among themselves whether or not to flee. Their boarder, Eugène Leclercq urged them to leave; a trusted confidante, Dr. Remy, advised them to stay. Like Simon, Émile Mathieu was finally dissuaded, en route to city hall, by reports that the French were blockading the route to Philippeville. "We passed the remainder of the day in indecision and we ended up placing ourselves in the hands of Providence and telling ourselves that nothing would happen without the permission of the good Lord." By 5:00 the next morning, the family bitterly regretted the decision.[30] Along the densely populated rue Petite and rue Sax, only thirty-three people remained. This had been the scene of the noisiest and deadliest of the German heroics, and was where most of the 15 to 20 homes that were burned down had been located.

Most of those who stayed regarded the attack as a drunken escapade. The perpetrators would no doubt be punished; the Germans, after all, valued order and discipline.

⊰⊹⊱

Meanwhile, there was more bad news for the residents of Dinant. The 73rd Regiment was ordered north and replaced by its reserve counterpart, the 273rd. Older, less experienced men would now be attempting to hold off the German assault.

Von Bülow's attack across the Sambre, which precipitated the departure of the front-line troops, also made more urgent von Hausen's presence west of the Meuse. Having failed to dislodge Lanrezac on the 15th, von Hausen now hoped to ambush the French as they retreated south from Namur. The Second Army, nearly 50% larger than his own forces at the beginning of the campaign, had been swollen by one of his cavalry divisions and an entire army corps. Still seething about the transfer of so many of his men, von Hausen was alarmed to learn that von Bülow's forces had begun crossing the Sambre on the 22nd. He was bombarded with messages from GHQ urging him to make haste and breach the Meuse.[31]

Von Hausen protested that von Bülow had attacked too soon; he needed another day to get in behind the French Fifth Army and cut off its retreat. But like von Kluck's, his own command had been subordinated to von Bülow, and now that general was further foiling his plan by ordering him to attack due west instead of sliding southwest. Von Bülow's request was reinforced by a final, peremptory order from GHQ on the 23rd: "The crossing of the Meuse by the Third Army is urgently required today."[32] The fanatical "franc-tireurs of Dinant" would provide an excellent scapegoat for the Third Army's tardiness and a convenient target for its officers' frustrations.[33]

-<-->-

Dinantais sheltering in their cellars and listening to the fierce artillery duel early on the morning of the 23rd were hoping for a repeat of the 15th. But the French 273rd, even before it recognized that it was outnumbered by about 5 to 1, had no intention of driving the invaders from Dinant. Its goal was simply to cover the left flank of the retreating Fifth Army and then join in the general withdrawal to the south.

DINANT: OVERVIEW The Germans poured into Dinant along four routes. From north to south these were route des Fonds de Leffe, which parallels route de Huy and terminates at the massive Premonstratensian Abbey close by the Meuse in the faubourg of Leffe. Just to the north of the road is Devant-Bouvignes, part of the independent commune of Bouvigne proper, most of which is on the opposite (left) bank of the Meuse. (The river flows due north at Dinant until Namur, where it is joined by the Sambre and turns east.)

Further to the south, the invaders came down route de Ciney, which becomes rue St.-Jacques as it enters town. This was the scene of the disastrous "reconnaissance in force" on the night of the 21st. Still further south, the Germans descended down the street called Montaigne de la Croix into the faubourg St.-Nicolas. The southernmost road into Dinant is route de Neufchateau, which took the invaders into the district called Les Rivages. Just north is the faubourg St. Paul and across the Meuse from the latter is the community of Neffe.

It's easiest to get a handle on the killings by proceeding district by district, beginning with Leffe in the north and moving down to Les Rivages, the southernmost quarter, then crossing the Meuse to Neffe and moving up the left bank.

Like an S.S. *Aktion* in a Polish ghetto, there were a series of roundups. Homes were invaded, the residents chased out. Like an *Aktion*, there were numerous random shootings – in homes, gardens, alleyways. But in each district there were one or more sites where the killing was carried out more systematically. The men were usually separated from the women, marched off, lined up against a wall, and shot. In central Dinant, however, husbands were executed in front of their wives and children, and in Les Rivages and Neffe, the women and children were gunned down alongside their husbands and fathers.

In Leffe, massacres took place in front of two large buildings, an abandoned paper factory and the Premonstratensian Abbey .

Further south, in the quartier St. Jacques, a good many families, as mentioned, had fled after the events of the 21st. All the remaining men who were captured were slaughtered, most against a wall running along rue des Tanneries. In the two districts combined, Leffe and St. Jacques, 312 people were murdered. In these northern faubourgs the Germans were more scrupulous than elsewhere: only nine of the victims were women and five were children under fourteen.[34]

In the heart of town, the St. Nicolas quartier, residents were taken to the home, stable, and forge of Amand and Henri Bouille. Men pushed into the forge were eventually removed to the city's prison. Those in the home and stable were escorted toward the prison, but when less than fifty yards away, they were lined up against the wall of Maurice Tschoffen's garden and summarily executed.

The wall of another garden, belonging to Edmond Bourdon, served the same purpose further south, in Les Rivages. Only here women and children joined the men. They were ostensibly being held hostage, though no one bothered to communicate the fact to the French troops on the cliffs above the left bank. These soldiers were firing on sappers constructing a bridge across the Meuse. When the French resumed shooting after a brief pause, the families were gunned down as they stood in front of the wall. Seventy-seven were killed outright, including thirty-four women and girls.

Incredibly, the killings grew still more savage. Across the river, in Neffe, several families were sheltering from the German shells in an aqueduct under a small railroad bridge. Without even troubling to order their victims out and line them up, the Germans simply fired on them as they lay packed beneath the bridge. Then the soldiers hurled in grenades. Twenty-two civilians were killed, including nine women and girls. Five of the victims were under ten.

Needless to say, in no part of the city did any civilian fire on German troops. No one was seized with guns or any other weapon. No one was interrogated. In only one instance did the Germans eventually provide the name of an alleged "franc-tireur." He was "the twelve-year-old son of the barrister Adam."[35] There was indeed a lawyer named Adam residing in Dinant. He had only one son. The lad, however, was twenty-four years old in 1914 and was out of town on August 23rd; he returned to Dinant only months later.[36]

Altogether 602 men, women, and children were killed in or near Dinant on the 23rd. An additional nine had been shot or burned to death in the city prior to that date, and from the 24th to the 28th, seventy-four more civilians were gunned down or died of their wounds. The total number of residents killed was then 685, almost 9% of the population. If a comparable percentage of New Yorkers had been killed on 9/11, the death toll would have been around 695,000.[37] At least 1,100 homes and buildings were destroyed.[38]

LEFFE: OVERVIEW The troops responsible for the massacres in Leffe belonged to the 178th Infantry Regiment. The commander of the particularly brutal 6th Company, Captain Wilke, stated that he was repeatedly encouraged by his division commander, General Edler von der Planitz, to proceed "against the fanatical franc-tireurs ruthlessly and energetically."[39]

At the end of the day, only a handful of men remained alive in Leffe and Fonds de Leffe. The latter was particularly hard hit. On the morning of the 23rd, there were 251 men in this commune. By evening, 243 were dead.[40]

Most of the men were executed in groups ranging from about ten to more than forty at one of two sites: La Papeterie at the end of Fonds de Leffe and the massive Premonstratensian Abbey in Leffe proper, a block away from the Meuse. Fonds de Leffe was comprised of the scattered châteaux, farms, and mills lining the steep ravine that descends into the Meuse valley north of Dinant. The two communities had about 1,400 inhabitants in 1914.[41] Where the ravine widens at the western end of Fonds de Leffe, a road links the main artery with route de Ciney further south. The abandoned paper factory, owned by the Ravet family, stood at this intersection. The wives and children of the men gunned down along the approaches to the factory were imprisoned in a large mill further down the road to Leffe, Moulin d'Alpre.

The other scene of repeated group executions was the Place de l'Abbaye, in front of the Servais house diagonally across from the Abbey. This abbey, founded in 1152, had been abandoned for more than a century before it was taken over in 1903 by French Premonstratensians. About twenty-two white-robed friars were in residence in August 1914.[42] Over one hundred forty men were buried in the garden behind the Servais house. The wives and children of the victims were held captive within the Abbey. Many families of men executed elsewhere in town were also taken there.

"IT'S MEN WE WANT" When German soldiers arrived at the house at which he was staying in Leffe, Victor Englebert presented the men with three pounds of butter and two large loaves of bread.

"We don't want any of this," he was told. "It's men we want."[43] There was little pity among the Saxons in Dinant, even compared to elsewhere in Belgium, where charitable acts were hardly common. When officers did intervene to save lives, it was usually to spare adolescent boys.

Eight other civilians were in the house with Englebert, which belonged to his brother-in-law, the miller François Gaudinne. Gaudinne's wife and daughter bandaged up a wounded officer while the soldiers searched for arms. As the family was pushed outside into the courtyard, the officer, glancing over at Jules Gaudinne, a slight sixteen-year-old who didn't look his age, advised Mme. Gaudinne that she had better hide him.[44] The women of the family managed to conceal Jules behind them. The other men were taken out into the street and moments later the women heard gunfire.

Jules's luck ran out at 2:00 p.m. He was seized with three other young men from a neighbor's house where the family was sheltering and taken off to be executed. His mother had little doubt what would happen to him. There was only a moment for a final embrace. "Good-bye, my son," she whispered. "If we don't see you again here, we'll see you in heaven."

"*Oui, Maman,*" the boy dutifully replied.[45]

⊰⊱

At the first massacre outside Leffe, early in the morning, another officer made a quick decision as to who was a boy and who was a man. Several times earlier in the week Germans had approached the farm where thirteen-year-old Gilbert Berthulot and his family had taken refuge. They had asked for food and drink, but had otherwise left the occupants alone.

On the 23rd they returned full of menace. A woman who didn't raise her hands quickly enough was knocked down, her son who knelt over her beaten with rifle butts. The men, including Gilbert, were ordered out, where they were joined by ten prisoners from neighboring hamlets who were bound together by twos. They were conducted to a meadow in front of a large mill, called Capelle. The men were accused of firing on soldiers. When they protested their innocence, a young lieutenant stepped forward and shot one of the villagers point-blank. The man to whom he was tied fell also, greatly amusing the soldiers who were looking on.[46]

At this point another officer walked up to Gilbert and asked his age. The boy sensed that the man was trying to save him. "Twelve," he answered. The officer told him in good French to go to the nearby village of Thynes and tell the people there that men were being killed and homes burned because soldiers had been fired on.

Gilbert was soon intercepted by other soldiers who brought him back. He was returned to a grim scene. Four of the captives lay dead. Among those still standing was Gilbert's father. They faced a row of soldiers. The officer who spoke French stopped the proceedings and ordered an old soldier to accompany the boy to Thynes. He hadn't gone far when he heard the guns go off again.

The officer was probably Captain Wuttig; the sporting lieutenant may have been thirty-one-year-old Martin Richter. He eventually testified that after a single shot came from a farm, "about fourteen male civilians were arrested." (He took care in his deposition to arm them with sundry "weapons and ammunition for hunting-rifles, pistols, etc.," as his was one of the companies charged with executing only armed "franc-tireurs".) Richter was not taken in by Gilbert's lie. "A thirteen to fifteen-year-old boy was released on account of his age; the other thirteen persons were shot."[47] More deeply affected by the execution, or possibly by another in Leffe, was a nineteen-year-old musician from Dresden, Willy Materne. "At Dinant," he told his interrogators

> I saw thirteen persons shot who had been arrested shortly before. Among them there was a youth about seventeen to eighteen years old; the others were men verging on fifty... I was about fifty yards from the place of execution, and I trembled as I watched

it. They began by tying a man to a tree; a single soldier fired at him and only wounded him; but as the man was bound, he did not fall – he merely moved his head backwards and forwards. Then all six soldiers fired on him in turn to finish him off. The other civilians who were waiting to be executed witnessed this scene, and embraced, bidding each other farewell. I repeat that I trembled, for I had never seen anything of the sort before.[48]

-<-·->-

Other arbitrary decisions were made throughout the day. Among the 68 men executed in front of the paper mill, just beyond the faubourg's eastern border,[49] were Camille Delaey and his son Charles. The latter's older brother Raymond had originally been lined up beside his father. But Charles, watching beside his cousin Mathilde, cried out, "Ah Papa, poor Papa. I want to go to heaven also." The sergeant commanding the squad obliged. Charles, who was sixteen, was shoved up against the wall next to his father. At the same time Raymond was removed and placed back among the women, because of his "mental state." He was presumably retarded, or may have been having an epileptic fit. Then Charles and the others were shot.[50]

-<-·->-

The Laffut, Pierre Poncelet, and Delvigne families from Devant-Bouvignes, just north of Leffe, weren't captured until after 10:00 p.m. They were escorted to the Abbey. The officer conducting them was apparently not sure if the killing had been terminated for the day, or if he were still obliged to shoot all captured men. After conferring with an officer seated in a car, he returned to the group of civilians and separated the men from the women. The twelve-year old Delvigne boy was taken away with his father. The women listened intently. They heard a loud fusillade. And then, miraculously, the boy reappeared, racing back in tears to his mother. He threw himself into her arms. "I've returned, Mama," he blurted out, "but Papa's dead."[51]

-<-·->-

Earlier in the day, a couple of officers also had second thoughts – but after the fact. Around 8:00 a.m., Elvira Bullens saw thirteen-year-old Alphonse Monin racing through her garden, two Germans in hot pursuit. "Help, Mama," he yelled. The Germans fired on the boy with their pistols. Alphonse fell forward on his face, yelling for his mother. When the officers turned him over and got a good look at him, they tried to stand him up. The boy slumped to the ground. Later his body was found outside the convent in Leffe, where he had been dragged.[52]

DOGS When a German patrol captured the members of the Nepper and Bultot families at their farm on a hill overlooking route Fonds de Leffe, one of the three Bultot brothers, Alexis, escaped into a field. Later in the week his sister, Thérèse Bultot Nepper, discovered the burnt remains of her other brothers in the ashes of a neighboring farm, but was unable to locate Alexis. Perhaps he'd escaped into the hills, or had been sent off to Germany

On Friday Thérèse caught sight of her brother's old fox terrier beside a hedge. When she approached, she saw Alexis's bullet-riddled body. The dog had stayed faithfully beside his dead master for the entire week.

The little fox terrier, Thérèse Nepper noted, had not been able to prevent the assassins from stealing her brother's watch.[53]

-<-·->-

At the southern end of the faubourg, off the Place de Leffe, Marie Louis Naus and her husband Charles were hiding in their cellar with some friends. They heard the Germans breaking into the cellar through the wall of the adjoining house. The soldiers were apparently trying to protect themselves from the French guns firing across the Meuse. The couple and their friends fled to the ground floor. The soldiers broke into the basement, raced up the stairs and began breaking doors and windows, and smashing furniture. Charles Naus thought it best to present himself to the Germans. He opened the big door which gave out into the courtyard and raised his hands. He was instantly shot by an officer and fell dead at the feet of his horrified wife.

As usual, the women were driven out with threats and blows. It was Friday before Marie Naus was permitted to leave the Premonstratensian monastery, where all the women were interned. When she returned to her home, there was no trace of her husband. Mme. Naus noticed, though, that her husband's old hunting dog refused to leave a certain spot in the garden. She at once asked a neighbor to dig where the dog had been patiently waiting. Two sacks were unearthed and carefully opened. They contained the cadaver of the fifty-seven-year-old mechanic, who had been cut in half.

The Naus dog, too, had not been able to protect his master's possessions. When the body was disinterred, Marie Naus discovered that her husband's boots had been removed and about 1000 francs and his papers had
been stolen.[54]

For five days, at opposite ends of Leffe, the two dogs had refused to
leave their murdered masters, even, in the case of Charles Naus, when he
had been butchered and buried.

GOODBYES Inevitably, in separating husbands from their wives and children, the Germans were obliged to use force.

Nothing in their experience had prepared children to understand
what was going on when the Germans smashed their way into their living rooms. Sometimes children tried to bargain with the soldiers. Seeing
her mother bound up with strips of linen, the young daughter of Thérèse
Dubois Monin pleaded with the Germans. "Have mercy, sir. I'll say my
prayers properly, I'll be very good, sir, but don't tie Mama's hands."[55] Her
father, though she didn't know it, was already dead.

More poignant were the last goodbyes. Throughout Dinant on the 23rd,
fathers hugged their frightened children, knowing, or suspecting, that this
was the last time they would see them.

The Charlier and Jacquet families, who lived next to the Abbey, had
had a harrowing Sunday. The families and those with them were at first
prepared to surrender to the Germans, but the violent beating on the door
and the frenzied cries of the soldiers so alarmed the residents that they
fled out the back door, across the garden, and over the wall and into the
grounds of the Abbey. However, Henri Charlier's mother-in-law and nineteen-year-old daughter were hit as they attempted to scale the wall. The
former died instantly, the later some time later. Charlier himself played
dead at the base of the wall. The Germans ran past him. He and his father-
in-law eventually fled up the mountain, but were caught by patrols. They
were conducted back through the courtyard of the Abbey. Here they were
seen by Mme. Charlier. A moment later the forty-year-old weaver spotted
her. "My wife!" he cried out. The soldiers guarding him permitted him to
stop and embrace her. His little daughter Lucienne grabbed him around the
neck and wouldn't let go. A soldier took her arms and tore her off him, and
Charlier and his father-in-law were escorted out the Abbey gate.[56]

More force was required for two-year-old Marguerite Banse. As Marie Fondaire watched in horror, the girl was brutally ripped from the arms of her father and hurled into the stream that flows through Fonds de Leffe to the Meuse. Enraged soldiers had pushed Marie and her two small children into the stream moments before. She was able to grab the floundering two-year-old before the child drowned. A German doctor assisted her up the slippery bank.

Still clutching the little girl, Marie Fondaire re-entered her house to look for her oldest daughter Pauline, who had been accompanied back into the house by an officer. Neighbors assured her that the girl had been taken off to the convent adjacent to the Abbey. In fact, Pauline Fondaire had been brutally raped and murdered by the officer. Her body was found by three residents a week later, her petticoats were raised, her face beaten to a pulp. German soldiers ordered the Belgians to burn the body.[57]

COMPENSATION Like so many workers in Leffe, twenty-eight-year-old Henri Monin was shot in front of the old paper factory, known also as la Papeterie Ravet. As happened in Lince-Sprimont and elsewhere, an officer was moved by the sight of an attractive widow in tears. He confessed to Thérèse Monin that it was he who had killed her husband. He had been forced to do so, he assured her. If he hadn't followed the order, he himself would have been shot. Before he left, he presented her with a sack of wheat and some other goods.

Earlier in the day, when Henri's mother had raced up the stairs from the cellar to plead with the Germans to spare her husband's life – Felix Monin was among the first to be seized in the Fonds de Leffe manhunt – she was at once thoroughly searched. All her money was taken. For good measure, the Germans tore into small pieces in front of her some stock share certificates worth about 1000 francs. Mme. Monin was in her fifties and did not inspire any German gallantry.[58]

"WE WON'T HARM YOU" At around 7:00 a.m. soldiers arrived at the Abbey. They broke open the gates and poured into the grounds and buildings. The invaders drove before them small groups of terror-stricken civilians, their arms raised. The priests who watched thought at first that the Germans were acting out of humanitarian motives. The inhabitants of Leffe were to be protected within the Abbey's thick walls from French shells.

The fathers were soon to be disillusioned. The units that had conducted men into the Abbey had misunderstood their orders. All males were to be killed.

At around 9:00 a.m., mass was said by the vicar, Father Joseph. (The curé of Leffe was off serving as an army chaplain with the 4th Division.) As machine-guns rattled and howitzers boomed, the prisoners prayed fervently. Though he had no idea what awaited the men kneeling before him, Father Joseph decided to administer last rites. Death threatened them all, he warned the parishioners.

Before the mass, some men who had not attended church for ages made confessions. Among them was Émile Mathieu, a fifty-one-year-old mechanic. It had been twenty-four years since Mathieu had received the sacraments, and he burst into tears of joy afterward, according to his daughter Angèle. Father and daughter embraced. He sensed it was the last time he would kiss her, Angèle guessed.[59]

At about 10:00 a.m. an officer appeared in the cloister and ordered all the men to gather in front of him. The priests, still without suspicions, urged the men to obey the summons. They located men dispersed throughout the Abbey. Some wives even encouraged their husbands to present themselves in the cloister. Mme. Lion retrieved her husband Alexis from the kitchen, where he was peeling vegetables for lunch.[60]

Other women, though, anxiously asked the Germans what was going to happen to the men. And at least one young man, eighteen-year-old Louis Servais, vividly sensed what was about to happen. He clung to his mother, sobbing. Angèle Mathieu convinced him to leave with his father and two brothers. "They're taking us outside to kill us," he told her, but eventually joined the others.[61]

Surrounded by soldiers with their bayonets fixed and brandishing a pistol in his left hand, the officer who had summoned the men asked if all were now present. When told that they were, he ordered them to raise their hands. "Don't worry," he assured the men. "We won't harm you." Forty-three men filed out. The monastery gates were slammed shut behind them.

A minute passed. It was now 10:25. Then a terrible cry was heard over the noise of the battle, and then the sound of gunfire. The forty-three men had been executed against the white wall of Maison Servais, across the

Place de l'Abbaye. Nine months later traces of blood and cerebral matter were still visible on the wall.[62]

"ECCLESIASTIC MONEY" After the shooting of the forty-three men, groups of prisoners continued to arrive at the Abbey. They were all women and children. Everyone had horrific stories. The sky was red with the fires that seemed to blaze everywhere; the acrid smoke penetrated the buildings. But it looked as if the Germans intended to spare the women and children. The priests, however, could not help but wonder what was in store for them.

Two among their number, Father Nicolas Perrea and Brother Herman-Joseph Bony, were especially anxious. Against the advice of the others, they slipped out of the Abbey along the subterranean canal that traversed the monastery grounds. (The Fonds de Leffe stream flowed into the Meuse via this aqueduct.) It was only partially filled with water, and it was possible to walk through it, hunched over. The priests presumably hoped to swim across to the left bank. They never made it. Their bodies were found some days later, one three, the other seven miles downstream. One had been shot and beaten, the other slashed by a bayonet.[63]

A few clues eventually surfaced as to what happened to them. An officer speaking little French burst into the Abbey demanding *"l'eau, l'eau!"*[64] When the fathers sought to oblige him with beer and wine, he became indignant. He was looking, it turned out, for the opening of the underground canal. When he was shown it, he ordered some soldiers to enter the opening, but they apparently didn't find the fugitives. A little later, two Belgian schoolboys were sent down for a look. The Germans were apparently convinced they could capture a couple of genuine franc-tireurs in flagrante.

The two monks probably waited until dusk to cross, and then were betrayed by their white habits. They continued to cause the Germans great excitement and were the subject, in all likelihood, of three depositions in the White Book. Around midnight, two franc-tireurs, "wearing women's clothing and wrapped in white linen" were spotted under a bridge which spanned the little canal. Soldiers discovered chairs under the bridge; the franc-tireurs had clearly intended to blow up the bridge, but, when their plot was foiled, had fired signal shots and then tried to escape. A volley in response came from a factory along the Meuse. The company that had

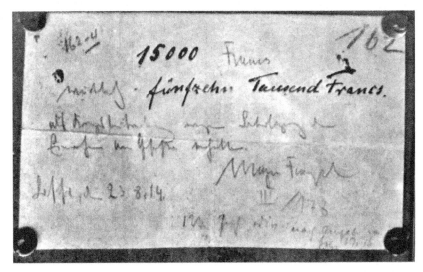

Die Einnahme. The receipt for the 15,000 franc "war contribution" paid by the women who were herded to the Premonstratensian Abbey in Leffe after their husbands, sons, and fathers had been executed.

surprised the clerics returned the fire. Marksmen then killed the two franc-tireurs as they swam across the Meuse. One drifted to the right bank. The soldiers "threw back the white cloth and saw by the face that it was a man. This man was wearing women's green stockings and a pair of low-cut black shoes such as women wear." The rifles of the crafty gunmen were not recovered.[65]

◄-◄-►-►

Apart from the two monks who attempted to flee, the lives of clerics in Dinant were otherwise spared. Saxony, though about 94% Protestant in 1914, was ruled by a Catholic king, and this may have had something of a mitigating effect on certain officers. On the other hand, fathers and brothers at the Abbey and elsewhere in Dinant, though not executed like so many of their brethren, were subjected the following days to various indignities, culminating in the forced march of thirty-three priests and monks to Marche. With whoops of *"Religionskrieg"* ringing in their ears, the clerics thought more than once that they were about to be shot.[66]

On the 23rd the Saxons wanted cash, not dead papists.

Around noon, a French-speaking officer of the 178th regiment, Major Fränzel, presented himself to the reverend fathers and requested 60,000 francs as a penalty for someone having fired on German troops from the Abbey. If the sum wasn't turned over in two hours, the entire monastery – and everyone in it – would be burned.

An hour earlier, shortly after the shooting of the forty-three men, a thirteen or fourteen-year-old dressed in the uniform of a German boy scout had suddenly appeared in the courtyard and yelled, "They're firing from the windows at our soldiers."[67] This lie may have inspired the major; it certainly succeed in inciting the soldiers who were standing within earshot.

As happened repeatedly in towns throughout Belgium, the father superior protested that it was impossible to raise such a sum in so short a time. Fränzel left the room, claiming he had to consult with his superiors, and returned moments later to announce that he would be content with 15,000 francs by 3:00 p.m. A German woman, the daughter-in-law of one of the executed men, may have interceded with the Germans.[68]

The amount was collected, though with great difficulty, and thanks to the contributions of those widows whose captors had been less thorough in their searches than their comrades. At precisely 3:00 the major returned, pistol in hand, inevitably, with menacing soldiers at his side. He carefully counted the 15,000 francs, pocketed the money, and wrote out a brief receipt. The ransom, the note indicated, was "imposed as a war contribution." No mention was made of gunshots. Fränzel expressed his regrets at having to accept "ecclesiastic money."[69]

⊰⟨⟩⟩⊱

Three monks from the Abbey almost shared the fate of the final eight civilians to be executed in Leffe, the group that included Henri Charlier, who had briefly escaped up the mountain. The three were taken arbitrarily from the regimental school just south of the Abbey, shortly after all the clergy in Dinant had been installed there on Monday. The monks were marched around Leffe, mocked and insulted, and finally conducted through the courtyard of a convent into the garden of the lawyer Hector Adam. Here two of them were undressed and subjected to more abuse from the troops. An officer, standing on the balcony of the Adam villa, accused the priests of firing on the soldiers, which they hotly denied. Brother Eugène continued to remonstrate with the officer in German, while the soldiers surrounding them yelled that the monks should be killed. Finally, as the condemned men were lined up along a stream to be shot, the officer ordered that the brothers be taken back to the Abbey.

The convent's sister superior, meanwhile, had been watching the scene in horror. She and the other nuns were forced back inside, but they heard the crackling fusillade. The next day a soldier, bragging about the number of civilians he had killed, made them come out to look at the victims. The corpses of the eight civilians were riddled with bullets. The expressions of pure terror on their faces was unforgettable, the sister recalled.[70]

"PAS DE PITIÉ POUR LES HOMMES" A number of men in Leffe were not killed in the massacres outside the Abbey or in front of the paper factory. Among these was a forty-one-year-old manufacturer, Victor Poncelet, who lived in a sprawling house behind the Abbey with his wife and seven children, ranging from ten down to twenty-two months.

Victor Poncelet, shot in front of his wife and seven children in Leffe.

Poncelet had spent much time since the 15th caring for the wounded, including some German soldiers. Like everyone else in Dinant, the family had taken refuge in their cellar when the firefight commenced early Sunday. Mid-morning they heard their windows being smashed and doors broken open, and the savage cries of the soldiers. Again, like so many others on the 23rd, the Poncelets, with their servants, fled into the garden. But the bullets whistled around them, cutting off their retreat. They re-entered the house and seconds later were surrounded by soldiers waving their rifles and hatchets and yelling like furies, according to Poncelet's widow. She herself was seized by the throat. The oldest child begged the soldiers for mercy. *"Pas de pitié pour les hommes, "* the officer in charge of the patrol replied, and, liking the phrase, kept repeating it at intervals.

The search for weapons began at once. The house was ransacked, but no gun was found. The family was taken outside, then forced back into the vestibule. Mme. Poncelet proposed getting someone to translate, as the officer's French seemed to be confined to the one phrase. The man brusquely refused. Victor Poncelet offered him anything he wished in the house. The officer again refused, or didn't understand. Desperately, Poncelet handed over his marriage certificate. "You wouldn't kill the father of these innocent children," he implored. The officer tore up the marriage certificate and again barked, *"Pas de pitié pour les hommes."* Then he grabbed the rifle of a soldier standing beside him and shot the father in cold blood as his wife and seven children looked on incredulously.

The widow and children were escorted to the Premonstratensian Abbey. Seeing the heaps of corpses across from the building, one of the children turned to her mother and said, "Mama, here's where they're going to kill us."[71]

⊷⊶⊷

Some days later, a Saxon officer of the 178th Regiment was killed during the German retreat from the Marne. In the diary that was recovered from his body, he may well have been describing Victor Poncelet's house.

> We got into the property of a well-to-do inhabitant, by a breach effected in the rear, and we occupied the house. Through a maze of rooms we reached the threshold. There was the body of the owner on the floor. Inside our men destroyed everything like vandals. Every corner was searched. Outside in the country, the sight of the villagers who had been shot defies all description.[72]

One can't be certain that the body discovered by the Saxon officer was Victor Poncelet because assassination was the modus operandi of the 178th Regiment that day: "Every house has been searched to the smallest corner, and the inhabitants dragged from their hiding-places. The men were shot; the women and children shut up in a convent, from which some shots were fired. Consequently, the convent is to be burned. It can be ransomed, however, on surrender of the guilty and payment of 15,000 francs." Thus, even this somewhat humane and intelligent officer (as subsequent entries reveal) seems to believe that the widows and orphans managed to conceal weapons from the murderous German troops invading their homes, with which, despite being placed in the Abbey's cellars under armed guards, they were then able to fire at soldiers outside the walls.

The notebook from another soldier, serving in the Regiment's 11th Battalion, explains the rationale for the massacres in Dinant's northern districts. "At Leffe, nineteen civilians shot. Women begging for mercy as we marched towards the Meuse. Ten more men have been shot. The King having directed the people to defend the country by all possible means, we have received orders to shoot the entire male population."[73]

"CE N'EST PAS DE L'ARGENT QU'IL NOUS FAUT, C'EST DU SANG." Leffe was predominantly a working-class suburb in 1914 and the chief employer was the cloth factory owned by Remy Himmer, Manufacture de Tissus. Six hundred twenty-five people worked in the vast plant which stretched along the Meuse. Himmer served as Vice-Consul of the Republic of Argentina and assumed that his position as the representative of a neutral country would enable him to protect not only his family, but his staff and workers. But betting on German observance of international law was not a good gamble in 1914.

After the events along rue St.-Jacques the night of the 21st, Himmer considered taking his family across the Meuse, but, according to his daughter, felt he couldn't abandon his workers and his factory. The family sheltered in their cellar. Hearing the Germans breaking into neighboring homes, Himmer decided it would be safer to hide in the factory. As the family approached, they saw that soldiers had already entered the reception area. However, no one spotted the Himmers as they dashed across the courtyard and descended to the lower level. Here they found a number of other families. A total of 108 people had sought refuge in the building. For the entire day they remained there, some crouching or lying beneath the massive machines, others concealed in a cellar below them. Situated as they were between the French and German lines, the booming of the howitzers and the crackling of the rifles and machineguns were particularly intense.

Late in the afternoon, with more soldiers circulating above them, Himmer felt it would be best to present themselves to the Germans rather than passively await discovery. Isabelle Himmer, the director's daughter, walked at the head of the procession with the distinguishedlooking foreman Désiré Louis, who held aloft a large white flag. Mlle. Himmer knew some German and hoped to be able to reason with the soldiers.

The Germans were initially stupefied to see so many people exiting the building. They commenced their familiar greeting: savage cries and yells and menacing gestures. Everyone was ordered to raise their hands and the men were separated from the women and children. Isabelle's young nephew André was walking hand-in-hand with his grandfather. An officer pulled him away. *"Kind mit Mama,"* he said.

Isabelle Himmer asked an officer what would happen to the men. In a reassuring tone, he replied that the men were simply being taken off so that the Germans could check their papers. This seemed reasonable enough to the daughter, who didn't think to say goodbye to her father, assuming she would see him again momentarily. But Mme. Himmer clung desperately to her husband, and had to be clubbed with a rifle butt and threatened with a pistol before she released him.

As with the earlier mass execution outside the Abbey walls, a young man also sensed what was about to happen before it dawned on most of the others. "Maman come get me. They're going to kill me," cried the adolescent son of Marie Blanchard. She was permitted to retrieve the boy, but when she pleaded for the life her husband as well, Madame Blanchard was struck with a rifle butt. "Better me than you," her husband told her. "Take good care of the children."[74]

The women were taken around the building and into the Abbey. They were shocked to see the piles of bodies around Place de l'Abbaye. The solicitous welcome they received from the fathers was anything but reassuring. Moments after she arrived at the abbey, Isabelle Himmer heard gunshots reverberate just outside the wall.

Some of the women trailing behind the Himmers had not been hustled into the Abbey in time. One of them heard Remy Himmer offer his entire fortune in exchange for his life and the lives of his workers. The officer he'd approached had coldly replied, *"Ce n'est pas de l'argent qu'il nous faut, c'est du sang."*[75]

⊰⊷⊱

Thirty workers were massacred along with the director. All together, 146 of the plant's 625 employees were killed. For good measure, the factory, valued at about four million francs, was burned to the ground some time after midnight. Tenacious franc-tireurs were still firing from the windows, according to a private in a machine-gun company of the 102nd Regiment.[76]

"WE WON'T KILL THE WOMEN; THEY MUST LIVE TO CRY AND SUFFER" What happened to the captive women? Were there rapes? Schmitz and

Nieuwland may have been nearly as reluctant to press the subject on the
women they interviewed as the women were to broach it. While eighteen-
year-old Pauline Fondaire was almost certainly raped before being murdered, any other victims among the women questioned remained mute.
In the St. Nicholas quartier, Télesphore Vigoureux, having survived the
massacre at the Tschoffen wall, encountered a mother searching for her
husband among the pile of corpses. She was accompanied by her fifteen- or
sixteen-year-old daughter. A soldier spotted the women, escorted the girl
into an abandoned house nearby, and prevented the mother from entering.
The desperate mother cried and then screamed. Another soldier eventually
came by and retrieved the girl, who was very overwrought, but said nothing to Vigoureux as to what had happened.[77]

Otherwise, we have only the testimony of prisoners of war questioned
in Bordeaux. Richard Tietze was a thirty-five-year-old sergeantmajor
in the 178th. "The women," he testified, "were separated from the men,
and sent to a convent at Leffe. I know that some of my comrades declared
that a good number of them had been violated..."[78] Kurt Schleider of the
12th Company of the 108th Regiment testified more generally that he had
"heard some of my comrades tell how they had violated women in Belgium
and killed them afterwards."[79] Willy Materne, a private in the 1st company
of the 178th, was told by other prisoners that "a few women" had been violated.[80] Max Brendel of the 101st Regiment also reported hearing his fellow
soldiers discussing rapes they had committed, though these may have taken
place after the XIIth Corps left Dinant. Otto Kuchler, a drummer in the
103rd Regiment, told interviewers at Montpelier that he'd heard stories of
"excesses against women" committed by the XIIth Corps's cavalry.[81]

There is a paucity of testimony on conditions in Abbey after the executions. Marie Naus, the wife of the man whose body had been cut in half,
was eventually able to escape to England, and provided one of the fuller
accounts, as did Angèle Mathieu, who remained in Belgium.

The women initially feared that the Germans intended to murder everyone in the Abbey. The priests did little to relieve anyone's anxiety; they
were anxious to confess everyone of age and urged the women "to prepare
for death."[82] When the ransom was demanded, many of the women were
convinced that they would be killed if it were not paid.

The women were kept in cellars, of which there were several throughout the Abbey. Marie Naus's had a vaulted stone roof and clay floor, and about sixty women and children were confined there. They remained underground from Sunday morning until Friday night, except when they received permission to go upstairs to relieve themselves, always in the presence of German soldiers. "We were given no food until Wednesday, when somebody threw into the cellar two sticks of macaroni and a carrot for each prisoner. We were not given any drink during the whole time, and did not receive any other food." Two soldiers with rifles guarded the door.

Women in other cellars were eventually allowed to dig in the monastery garden, where carrots and potatoes were growing. They ate these raw. The smell of the corpses still piled outside the walls was overwhelming. One woman received permission to venture out to view her husband's body. The Germans, she reported, had been amusing themselves by sticking ham bones they'd finished eating in the dead men's mouths.[83]

Some women and children may have been taken from the Abbey and imprisoned in houses along the Meuse. Paul Jahn, a non-commissioned officer in the 100th Regiment, told his French captors how he had personally located some food for them in neighboring houses, after his company commander forbade him from taking anything from the mess.[84]

When Marie Naus was released on Friday, she attempted to return to her house, but was unable to enter: it was full of troops. She appealed to an officer, who cleared the men out. A disheartening scene awaited her.

> When I went into my house I saw dirt everywhere. The soldiers had obeyed the calls of nature in every part of the house. All the wine in the cellar had been drunk; the furniture had been smashed, and the doors had been broken. The furniture in the first floor bedroom had been thrown out of the window into the street. Everything of value, the silver, etc. had been stolen.

She then produced for her British interrogators the top of a pepper mill. It was, she told them, "the only thing left."[85]

<+->

The captives at the Moulin d'Alprée fared no better. The interior of the mill was illuminated only by a single oil lamp. It was forbidden to go down to the cellar or up into the granary, and no one was permitted to speak. "How," asked Mathilde Delaey, "could we quiet all the little children who were dying of hunger and thirst and who cried out so wrenchingly in their suffering and fear."[86] There were threats from visiting officers. "If we cross the Meuse," said one, "your lives will be spared, but your husbands were all shot; there's not one that remains."[87] Another officer warned them, "We're going to burn the dirty Belgian women; their husbands killed our soldiers." To reinforce the threat, soldiers were ordered to place bales of hay along the homes bordering the mill.

On Monday morning an officer cut the strips of linen that bound the women; later in the day they were given some carrots and potatoes. Candy was distributed to the children. Still later, the women and children were permitted to walk outside in a neighboring meadow, under German guard. As they passed through the courtyard, they saw the soldiers slaughtering and cooking chickens and pigs. The prisoners, however, dined on rice soup.[88]

Tuesday afternoon, around 4:00, everyone was finally released. Their homes burned to the ground, many sought refuge at the Abbey.[89]

–‹·›–

As Lucie Monin watched in horror, her husband was gunned down from behind by a soldier. When she begged the German who was holding her arm to kill her and her young son too, the man replied, "We're not killing the women. They must live to cry and suffer."[90]

A CAMERA FOR FELIX The fastidious Saxon officer who had noted the vandalism he had encountered in the home of Victor Poncelet, was disturbed that the regrettable behavior continued as his troops moved south. He was not the only one to observe the wanton destructiveness of the German soldiery. "They do not behave like soldiers, but like common thieves, highwaymen, and robbers" a private in the 65th Infantry of the Landwehr wrote of his comrades. They "are a disgrace to our regiment and our army."[91] Generally, however, prisoners and diarists blamed other units for the pillaging. "The pioneers are not worth much," observed a lieutenant in a reserve infantry regiment. "As for the artillerymen, they are a gang of robbers."[92] But Baron von Hodenberg, a grenadier from the 100th Regiment of the XIIth Corps, thought the infantry most culpable, particularly the transport troops.[93] And everyone blamed the uhlans, who always foraged, and generally felt licensed to burn and murder as well. For example, Sergeant-Major Richard Tietze attributed to the uhlans the "great many fires" that his company passed. "I heard some of our cavalrymen say that corpses of Belgian civilians had been found mutilated – feet and hands cut off. From what I was told it would seem to have been the uhlans who did this." Tietze added that he had "also heard that in Belgium little children were mutilated by our soldiers. If this is true, they can only have done such things in moments of aberration."[94]

On August 17th, the Saxon officer with refined tastes wrote down the following observations:

> In the afternoon I had a look at the little château belonging to one of the King's secretaries. Our men had behaved like regular vandals. They had looted the cellar first, and then they had turned their attention to the bedrooms and thrown things about all over the place. They had even made fruitless efforts to smash the safe open. Everything was topsy-turvy – magnificent furniture, silk, and even china. That's what happens when the men are allowed to requisition for themselves. I am sure they must have taken away a heap of useless stuff simply for the pleasure of looting.[95]

Conscripted men naturally had a different perspective. "It was my colonel, Freiherr von Ompteda, who had given orders for the pillage," testified Hermann Tscharne, a private in a reserve battalion of the 103rd Regiment. "This is what happened: the troops would take possession of a town and pursue the enemy. Then, when the Reserves arrived, they pillaged the houses, taking linen, silver, jewelry, provisions, drink, etc. I saw all this. Nay, and more: when they pillaged, they piled the goods in heaps. The adjutants made a selection from these, keeping the best for the Colonel and the Major, and others for the other officers." When the interrogator asked him for additional names, Tscharne replied tartly, "How can I give you the name of any particular officer? All of them – I don't hesitate to say so – profited by the pillage they ordered."[96]

In most cases, though, reservists did not have the pick of the spoils. "The first troops who entered France," complained Paul Eichhorn, a Landwehr private in the 101st Regiment, "committed such depredations that we Reservists were strictly forbidden to sack and steal. These injunctions were superfluous, however, for there was nothing left. Everything was devastated." One of the few prisoners, along with Tscharne, to betray any bitterness toward his superiors, Eichhorn reported that "the officers sent home boxes, valises and large trunks full of valuables regularly... Such incidents took place more especially at Moronvillers, but it was above all

at Dinant and Rethel that these parcels were despatched. The officers often
had leave when they were at the front. They spent this leave in the châteaux
at the rear of the army. And it was during these holidays and their sojourn
in the châteaux that they made their little profit."[97]

But to return to the anonymous officer of the 178th regiment who had
stigmatized his troops as "vandals," he noted on August 26th that after
crossing the French frontier, officers of "the division took drastic steps to
stop the villages being burnt and the inhabitants being shot. The pretty
little village of Gue d'Hossus, however, was apparently set on fire, though
entirely innocent. A cyclist fell off his machine and his rifle went off. He
immediately said he had been shot. All the inhabitants were burnt in their
homes. I hope there will be no more such horrors." The massacre made
him recall the events of the previous Sunday. "At Leffe apparently 200 men
were shot. There must have been some innocent men among them. In the
future we shall have to hold an inquiry as to their guilt instead of shooting
them."[98]

On September 3 the officer was in Rethel, guarding French prisoners of
war. He found his attention wandering.

> The houses are charming inside. The middle class in France has magnificent furni-
> ture. We found stylish pieces everywhere and beautiful silk, but in what a state!...
> Good God!... Every bit of furniture broken, mirrors smashed. The Vandals them-
> selves could not have done more damage. This place is a disgrace to our army. The
> inhabitants who fled could not have expected, of course, that all their goods would
> have been left intact after so many troops had passed. But the column commanders
> are responsible for the greater part of the damage, as they could have prevented the
> looting and destruction. The damage amounts to millions of marks; even the safes
> have been attacked.
>
> In a solicitor's house, in which, as luck would have it, all was in excellent taste,
> including a collection of old lace and Eastern works of art, everything was smashed
> to bits.
>
> I could not resist taking a little memento myself here and there... One house was
> particularly elegant, everything in the best taste. The hall was of light oak. I found a
> splendid mackintosh under the staircase and a camera for Felix.[99]

◄◄►►

There were no doubt a few other connoisseurs among the looters in Leffe
and Dinant, but most soldiers made straight for the cellars and larders.

Private Rudolf Rossberg of the 101st Grenadiers wrote the following
journal entry:

"Dinant, August 23. We sleep on the pavement, not far from the corpses, after looting two more cafés. About one hundred fifty bottles of wine, champagne and liqueurs were the results of this operation. We were ravenous, and carried off everything, bread, butter, coffee... meat, ham, in a word, everything."[100]

Rossberg was fortunate to have arrived early in the day. By evening, drinks were available at the Leffe *son et lumière*, but no food, as Pvt. Philipp of the 178th regiment noted.

At 10:00 in the evening the first battalion of the 178th marched down the steep incline into the burning village to the north of Dinant. A terrific spectacle of ghastly beauty. At the entrance to the village lay about fifty dead civilians, shot for having fired upon our troops from ambush. In the course of the night, many others were also shot, so that we counted over 200. Women and children, lamp in hand, were forced to look at the horrible scene. We ate our rice later in the midst of the corpses, for we had nothing since morning. When we searched the houses we found plenty of wine and spirits, but no eatables. Captain Hamann was drunk.[101]

The final sentence was written in shorthand. Professor Joseph Bédier, who also reprinted this excerpt, was taken to task by German critics for misrendering *"müssten dem entzetzlichen Schauspiele zusehen."* The women were not compelled to see the corpses, argued the *Norddeutsche Allgemeine Zeitung,* but, regrettably, had inevitably to see them as they were conducted past the execution site. Bédier angrily dismissed the cavil. *"Müssen"* can indeed express compulsion and besides, morally, it is a distinction without a difference in this context. (The professor also contrasted Philipp's reticence about revealing that he saw an officer drunk with his candor about the massacre of civilians.)[102]

German soldiers who had qualms about eating or carousing in front of the dead quickly overcame them in Leffe. Some friends of the Poncelets remained concealed in the cellar when the family attempted to flee through the garden. Angèle Ravet, eventually captured and marched upstairs, glimpsed a soldier playing the piano while his comrades drank wine in the room off the vestibule where Victor Poncelet's body still lay.[103] One of the few male survivors in Leffe, Adolph Dernivois, who hid in the trunk of a tree, saw the Germans burying bodies on Tuesday to the lively accompaniment of an accordion.[104]

On Sunday, however, the Germans did not have to provide their own entertainment. The spectacle of Dinant burning was so riveting a number of diarists and p.o.w.s commented on it.

"It was a marvelous sight," wrote the aesthete who had purloined the camera for his son, "the high ground from Dinant to Leffe, overlooking the Meuse, all in flames. Every building was burning. The reflection of the fire made the waters of the Meuse run red as blood. It was almost as light as day, and helped our sappers to build a bridge."[105]

A soldier in the 4th Company of Jägers wrote "Just now, 6 o'clock in the afternoon, the crossing of the Meuse begins near Dinant... All villages, châteaux, and houses are burnt down during this night. It was a beautiful sight to see the fires all round us in the distance."[106]

For the entire month, German soldiers had the opportunity to admire burning villages. Many, no doubt, had a reaction similar to Private Hohl's: "August 24. Our company occupied some outposts outside the village. We made a resting-place with bundles of straw, and slept in the open air on the *qui vive*, because of the proximity of the enemy. Above the village the sky was dyed a dreadful red, and dancing flames bore witness to a deed of German heroism! *C'est la guerre.*"[107] "More burning," wrote Lieutenant Reisland of the 117th Regiment of the XIIth Corps on August 25th. "A village perched on a height was almost entirely in flames. When I saw it in the distance, I thought of the burning of Valhalla in the *Gotterdämmerung*. A magnificent, but heart-rending sight."[108] (The lieutenant's sentiments may help explain why officers so seldom intervened when their men were bent on arson. "Officers saw very well what happened but shut their eyes and let it happen instead of opposing it," Private Otto Pfeiffer testified.)[109]

The blazes were less inspiring when they were closer: "I was greatly struck by seeing a large number of houses in flames along the roadsides," declared the musician Willy Materne. "Sometimes they were blazing on either side of the road, and the heat was so intense that we had to hurry past to avoid suffocating."[110]

CHAPTER 7

Dinant: St. Jacques, St. Nicolas

ST. JACQUES: INTRODUCTION The authors of the crimes in the quartier St. Jacques were soldiers of the 46th Brigade of the 23rd Division, in particular the 182nd and 108th Infantry Regiments.

The officers and soldiers who executed civilians in Leffe and in the districts south of St. Jacques attempted to explain and justify their actions in the German White Book. But the principal massacre in the quartier St. Jacques, the shooting of thirty men against a wall in the rue des Tanneries, goes unmentioned by its perpetrators in that bulky volume. The identity of the killers would therefore have been difficult to determine had it not been for their lack of thoroughness. Unlike the men captured and lined up by the efficient 178th Regiment, some victims in St. Jacques survived the shooting and clearly saw the number 108 on the helmets of their would-be executioners.

"I'M GOING TO HELP THOSE PEOPLE OVER THERE" Seeing all of the neighborhood in flames, members of the Disy family left their own cellar for the greater security, they thought, of the brasserie Nicaise across the street. A number of their neighbors had the same idea. The Germans came knocking only around 5:00 p.m. The civilians faced the dilemma that confronted all Dinantais who had remained concealed until late in the day: should they open the door, stay hidden, or attempt to flee? Much depended, naturally, on what those hidden had seen or heard during the day. In the brasserie cellar there was a hot debate, conducted in whispers, when the furious pounding began. Some urged that no one budge. However, the proprietor,

Jules Monin, thought it would only exasperate the Germans if the door remained locked. They would break in regardless, and he still hoped to save the brasserie.

Within moments he was negotiating for his life. The Germans poured in and immediately pulled out the women and children and drove them up rue St. Jacques toward the Abbey. An officer then informed the men in bad French that they were all going to be shot. Monin offered the Germans a large sum of money, but he was pushed back with others, and the men forced down a side street to the rue des Tanneries. There they were lined up against the wall of the Laurent house, their backs to the Meuse.

Prosper Junius, a fifty-one-year-old professor at the Collège Communal, had taken refuge with his wife and child in the home of the lawyer M. Barré. There was easy access to the garden and the family reckoned they would be able to escape without great difficulty if the Germans set the house ablaze. The garden door opened onto rue des Tanneries, and hearing a ruckus in the street, Professor Junius ventured out to see what was going on. Horrified to observe the thirty men lined up, facing a platoon of soldiers with their guns leveled, he raced back to his wife and told her, "I'm going to help those people over there." He spoke German fluently and no doubt felt confident he could clear up whatever misunderstanding had led the soldiers to line up the civilians and prepare to shoot them.

Junius approached the officer in charge and began to explain that these men were well disposed toward the Germans, and did not even have the means of harming them if they had wished to. The officer turned away without responding. Junius persisted, pleading the case of the condemned men. Such rank insubordination on the part of a civilian – addressing an officer without receiving permission – was intolerable. The officer ordered his soldiers to seize the professor and thrust him into the row of victims. Desperately, Junius now addressed the soldiers facing him, but he was cut off by a shrill blast from the officer's whistle and the platoon fired on the men. Everyone fell. A second fusillade hit those who'd escaped the first.

Several men still remained alive, however. They listened in disbelief as the platoon broke into a victory song. The soldiers then marched off, leaving behind a few men to finish off those still alive.

For whatever reasons, these men were less than thorough. When they headed off to join their comrades, three of the victims were still alive.

Prosper Junius, would-be translator, executed in rue des Tanneries.

Felix Longville, Police Commissioner, gunned down in front of his home in the St. Jacques district.

The Wasseiges. The banker Xavier Wasseige (left) and his two sons Pierre (center) and Jacques (right) were executed at the Tschoffen wall.

Alexandre Disy was the luckiest: he had been only slightly grazed by the bullets. He and one of the other survivors then hid under the quai de Meuse where it extended out over the river. They were in water up to their waists. Thus began a harrowing four days in which Disy hid, sometimes alone, usually with others, in various places, winding up crouched in a w.c. behind a house near rue St. Jacques. At one point he was fired on as he made his way up to a circular tower below the Citadel. Later, soldiers with police dogs were spotted along rue St. Jacques and those hiding with him were certain they would be detected. Finally, on Thursday, he was told that everyone was now free to circulate throughout Dinant unmolested. The manhunt was over.[1]

SHOOT FIRST Some troops didn't bother separating the men from the women and were quite happy to shoot all and sundry on the spot.

When the Lion family heard the distinctive sound of hatchets whacking their front door, the parents made their way up from the cellar to open it. They were more than a little apprehensive. Earlier in the day Charles Lion, a forty-year-old tailor, and his son Maurice had ventured out the front door to take a look at what they thought would be a similar battle to that of the 15th, where civilians were not molested. The men were spotted by soldiers, who aimed their rifles at them. Father and son scurried back downstairs. Now, without any preliminaries, the soldiers, as soon as they had forced the door, began screaming like furies and firing their weapons. Charles was hit in the chest, staggered backward, clutched his cutting table, then fell dead. His mother rushed over to her son, and was herself hit in the neck. Charles's wife, shot through the shoulder, cried out in pain, but was able to slip back downstairs. Joseph Lion had seated himself in an armchair to watch his son's colloquy with the Germans. He was killed instantly. As for Maurice, though bullets whistled past his ears, he was not hit.

Their mission accomplished, the soldiers took off. Maurice strained to listen for some sign of life in the room, not daring to move. Eventually he heard muffled groaning. It was his mother, in great pain, in the basement. Maurice was able to drag her upstairs and mother and son hid in their terraced garden, cut out of the side of the mountain behind rue St. Jacques. They had an excellent view of the inferno raging below. Soon after they arrived, they saw soldiers busily pillaging their own home. In the afternoon it, too, was set on fire. When Maurice raced inside to rescue some of his father's ledgers, he found that both Charles's and Joseph's pockets had been turned inside-out and his grandmother's skirts torn off.[2]

GOOD HUMOR There are occasional glimpses of the attitude of the Germans as they went about their work. They were not always screaming like maniacs, and smashing and shooting at random. Sometimes they appeared to be having a good time.

Hearing the Germans attempting to manipulate the mechanical shutter that sealed the front door, Felix Longville told his wife and daughter that he would open it and offer the soldiers something to eat and drink. Longville was Dinant's superintendent of police. Most of his officers had been mobilized and he had been unable to make it to the Hôtel de Ville, as the bullets were flying thick and fast in that part of town, but he must have sensed what the Germans were up to. Before he opened the door, he turned to his wife and daughters and said somberly, "I'm going to have to say goodbye. If I've ever caused you pain, I never intended to."[3]

"*Messieurs*, I'm unarmed," Longville told the soldiers at the door. "What can I do for you?"

The Germans were delighted to see Longville. "A man! A man!" they cried gleefully. Taking him by the shoulders, they dragged him outside. His daughter Jeanne wanted to follow, but she was pushed back inside the house with her mother and sister. "You're not going to kill him?" she yelled at one of the soldiers.

"But of course," he replied in French, laughing.

Jeanne glimpsed her father trying to reason with the soldiers who surrounded him, but one of them hit him from behind with the butt of his rifle and pushed him up against the side of the house. The police superintendent turned to face the soldiers.

Jeanne Longville fell on her knees and pleaded with the Germans to spare her father. They just looked at her and laughed.

She heard her mother beg a soldier to permit her to leave the house; Jeanne moved toward her, hoping to prevent her from witnessing the horrible scene. She had barely reached her mother when she heard a single shot and the sound of a body falling to the ground. Then she was pushed back inside again.

The soldiers searched the house to make sure there were no other men around, then left the grieving women. Jeanne rushed out, hoping against hope that her father might still be alive. But he'd been struck through the head; his entire left eye was gone. Blood and cerebral matter spattered the wall behind him. So her mother wouldn't have to view the frightful wound, Jeanne and her sister wrapped their father's head in towels and dragged him to the basement, where they placed him on a mattress.

The women hid in their garden and watched as the Germans set fire to their house. As Mme. Longville and her daughters attempted to battle the blaze as best they could, another group of soldiers came along and hurled more incendiary bombs into the building. Again the mother and daughters hid in their garden and watched the entire quarter burn.

In the midst of the savage howls of the marauding troops, Jeanne recalled, they occasionally heard the shrill blast of an officer's whistle. Then everything was silent briefly, as if under a magic spell.[4]

THE BOVYS The 178th murdered more civilians than any other regiment. It's no wonder; they were more disciplined killers. They took greater pains to separate the men from the women and, once he was placed against a wall in front of the execution squads, no man survived. Soldiers of the 108th and 182nd killed more wantonly and capriciously. There were far fewer men on hand to murder, and far more cafés and brasseries to loot than in Leffe.

It was the sight of drunken soldiers crashing around the Café Rondelet that frightened the large Bovy family into fleeing up the mountain. This was a mistake. They were quickly spotted by other soldiers. Family members stopped and put their hands up. The Germans fired at them nonetheless. They seemed to be particularly incensed at the one person who didn't fully comply with their order. Marie Defays Bovy was holding her four-year-old grandson Marcel and so was only able to raise one hand. At least three shots were fired at her. The first broke the arm of Marcel, the second hit his grandmother's wrist, the third went through her head. Two of Marie Bovy's daughters, Adèle and Éloïse, were also killed. Four family members were able to hide behind rocks from the intoxicated Germans. Two-year-old René Bovy, Éloise's son, was picked up by the Germans, who presented him to two women en route to the Abbey in Leffe. René was completely drenched with blood, and the women were surprised to see that he was unwounded. It was the blood of his dead mother.

Marcel's fate was less happy. His Aunt Albine had seen him hit only through the arm. But the next day, when the bodies of the family members were interred, Marcel's was among them. Early Monday morning, Alexandre Disy, one of those who survived the massacre in the rue des Tanneries, stumbled across the bodies of the family, lying side by side on a terrace behind the Bovys' garden, Marcel's among them. Later in the day Arthur Bietlot was compelled by the Germans to bury the victims of rue St. Jacques. He swore the boy's body was literally in pieces.[5]

THE "PRETEND DOCTOR" One final incident in central Dinant is of interest primarily because it intersects revealingly with testimony in the German White Book.

In the bustling neighborhood bordering the rue Sax, only two families remained after the events of the night of the 21st. The Couillards invited the Simons to stay with them the following day. Auguste Couillard, a seventy-one-year-old cabinet-maker, was very ill during the night. At 5:30 a.m. his son went out to fetch help and returned around seven with Dr. Eudore Remy. A quarter of an hour later the thirty-nine-year-old doctor tried to leave, either to get medicine or because he'd satisfied himself that the patient had recovered. He was ordered back in the house by German soldiers, though he pointed to his Red Cross brassard.

Soon after, the French bombardment intensified. On the advice of Dr. Remy, everyone descended into the cellar, except for Amand Couillard, who placed mattresses behind those windows that hadn't been broken. (This practice infuriated the Germans, who testified frequently about the way the franc-tireurs had barricaded their strongholds.)

At 9:00 a.m. came the hatchet blows on the door and the frightful uproar that accompanied German visits that morning. Dr. Remy spoke a little German, and offered to open the door and find out what the Germans wanted. He returned moments later, visibly shaken, and followed by an officer who ordered everyone out, with hands raised. The street, testified one witness, was "black with Germans." Many were busy pillaging the stores along rue Sax. The family members were thoroughly searched and everything confiscated and tossed on the ground. The men were bound together. Dr. Remy was released soon after. The last glimpse the others had of him was about twenty minutes later, when they were marched off toward rue St. Jacques. Remy was standing next to the pharmacy Paquet, looking totally devastated.

Later in the day a woman reported seeing the body of a man in a great black coat and straw hat. He was wearing a Red Cross armband.[6]

Dr. Remy figures in two German depositions. A corporal swore that he saw a man's arm thrust out of a second floor window above a pharmacy. On the arm was a Red Cross band, and in the man's hand was a pistol, which was fired at the soldiers. Corporal Saring then broke open the door with a pickaxe and out came several people, last of all the man with the armband, who was taken to the regimental commander, Colonel Francke. Saring then rushed off toward a church, where he was convinced civilians were firing from the tower.[7]

After Saring had told his tale to Colonel Francke, the suspect, "without being asked," explained in barely intelligible German that he was a doctor and had not fired on soldiers. Presumably in order to prove the former claim, the colonel ordered him to bandage one of the German wounded (who, Francke had already convinced himself, "could only have been hit from the houses or straight through them from houses along the river"). When the "pretend doctor" said he had no bandages, which Francke thought suspicious, the colonel ordered him to fetch some from the pharmacy behind him, accompanied by a corporal and another soldier. Some time later the corporal, whom Francke doesn't identify, reported that the man had tried to escape and he had therefore been taken out in front of the pharmacy and shot.[8]

The man with a Red Cross armband firing from the window of a building Dr. Remy hadn't entered is, of course, an invention. The execution of the unlucky doctor says as much about the paranoia of the colonel as it does of the mendacity of the corporal. The former, who became a major-general within six months, found it entirely plausible that in a street swarming with Germans, from a house filled with women and children, a lonely franc-tireur would have extended his entire arm to fire on German troops with a pistol – and then, when apprehended, would fail to use his gun, trusting that his armband, which he had neglected to remove while shooting, would deceive the much put-upon Germans.

ST. NICOLAS: INTRODUCTION The St. Nicolas quarter lies at the southern end of Dinant. Just as dawn broke on the 23rd, troops of the 100th Guard Regiment descended into this district down rue Montagne de la Croix. The regiment was commanded by Lieutenant Colonel von Kielmannsegg. In his deposition in the German White Book, the Lieutenant Colonel cites the orders he issued on the 23rd: "Sections of the town were assigned to the companies to be searched and cleansed, with the injunction to take those inhabitants to jail who did not offer any resistance. Arms would immediately be used against those who resisted... No infringements of the orders I gave were reported to me."[9] Unlike in Leffe, a number of men survived in the quartier St. Nicolas, but it was hardly because von Kielmannsegg's orders were adhered to, if they were indeed worded as he later claimed.

In this district, as elsewhere, residents were ousted from their homes. It was done in a somewhat more orderly and less violent manner than further north. Individuals and families in St. Nicolas were less likely to be shot in cold blood during the procedure than elsewhere in Dinant. The savagery would commence in the afternoon.

The northern part of the St. Nicolas district came under the direct fire of the French machine-guns deployed around the bridge and the 75s situated on the heights of the left bank. Until late in the day, the Germans didn't occupy this area, situated between rue de Palais de Justice in the south and Place Notre Dame directly across from the bridge. They did not even make use of civilians to move through this zone, as they did further south, where some 125 civilians served as a screen for soldiers. The French ceased fire promptly on that occasion, but not before one young woman was fatally wounded.

Those men and women used as screens, along with several hundred others from quartier St. Nicholas itself, were imprisoned in three buildings off rue St. Roch belonging to Amand Bouille, a prosperous blacksmith – a large house, with a café occupying the ground floor, a stable, and a forge. The particular building one was assigned to was a matter of chance, though some German units were inclined to put older and infirm captives in the home. Early in the day, it was possible to change locations.

There were preliminary executions of four and then fourteen men outside the Bouille house. Then, around 2:00 p.m., those confined to the forge were conducted down rue Léopold and rue du Faubourg St. Nicolas to the large prison on Place d'Armes. Here they were fired upon, mistakenly, by soldiers patrolling the heights above the prison. Later in the day, about 6:00 p.m., the men in the stable and home were taken along the same route, their wives, mothers, and children accompanying the procession. Then, about forty yards short of the prison, the men were lined up against the wall of a garden belonging to Maurice Tschoffen and shot. Of the 137 men selected to be executed, thirty survived. After this senseless massacre, the Germans then freed the women and children. The men who had been conducted to the prison earlier in the day, along with others captured elsewhere in Dinant, were sent to Kassel. Transported by cattle-cars, the 412 prisoners remained in Germany until November 18th.

"AND I THOUGHT THE GERMANS WERE DECENT PEOPLE!" The 100th Regiment had explicitly been changed with "cleansing" the district. According to observers, they advanced along the roads in two single-file columns, each hugging the edge of the road next to the rows of houses, eyes trained on the houses opposite.

The experience of Maurice Tschoffen, Dinant's Public Prosecutor, though in some respects not typical, reveals the haphazard modus operandi of the troops.

The artillery duel began at dawn and, like everyone else in town, the Tschoffens sheltered in their cellar. At about 6:30 a.m., the family heard German soldiers at their door. There was a violent ringing of the bell and shots were fired at the windows. When Tschoffen opened the front door, he was greeted by a dozen rifles pointed at his chest. One soldier signaled him to hold up his hands. Tschoffen obliged. Everyone was ordered out of the house and family members were each searched. Tschoffen was asked if there were any weapons in the house or any wounded French soldiers. Satisfied with the negative answers, the platoon moved on, leaving the family at liberty, though forbidden to re-enter their home.

The Public Prosecutor had been given the key to the house of a neighbor who had fled the city, and the family took refuge there. However, they were driven out once again, by the same methods. Out in the street once more, Tschoffen encountered his neighbor, Judge Herbecq, and the judge's wife and eight children.

The families watched the Germans move down the street, the soldiers keeping close to the walls of the houses on either side, staring at the windows opposite, each man with his finger on the trigger of his rifle. If a resident was slow in responding to the summons, the door was smashed in with hatchets and rifle-butts. After the residents were searched, they were taken away. Tschoffen was not sure why he and the Judge had been treated differently. He guessed it was because they both spoke a bit of German. In fact, as Herbecq later testified, his wife spoke the language fluently and the couple managed to shame an officer into letting them remain at home. In addition, the Tschoffens and Herbecqs, two of the leading families of Dinant, were anything but deferential, and their imperiousness may have impressed some of the officers and men. The judge had already disputed the charges recited like a school lesson by the corporal who had rung his doorbell. Herbecq assured the soldier that no civilians had fired on German troops, and pointed out with some asperity that the French were defending the opposite bank. Mme. Herbecq refused to leave the house when ordered. A lieutenant colonel overheard the conversation and came walking up. "You're German!" he exclaimed.

"No," the woman replied, "I'm Belgian."

"You're going to have to leave then," the officer told her, "because we have orders to burn the entire town."

"And I thought the Germans were decent people!" the judge's wife snapped.

At that moment the judge observed a neighbor, M. Franquinet, about to be executed and impulsively raced out into the street, shouting the words he'd just heard his wife say, *"Brave Leute!"* He heard the officer's whistle shrill behind him and the soldiers lowered their rifles. The officer then wrote out a note for the Herbecqs, which began "These people are friendly" and was signed "Von Zenker, Lieutenant Colonel, I.R. 100."

It was at this point that the Herbecqs invited the Tschoffens back in with them. Both families, however, were evicted by the next group of soldiers to come along. The agitated officer in charge of the section barely glanced at the note. *"Das bedeutet nichts,"* he told Herbecq. *"Alle heraus."*[10]

More effective was the measure taken by a simple soldier. Émile Lelièvre, after being removed from his home with his sister, was permitted to return because, he believed, the lone soldier who accompanied them had taken a strong liking to Lelièvre's mother. She apparently reminded him of his own. The family was able to remain at home the entire day, distributing cookies, beer, and juice to the passing Germans. When anyone tried to enter the house, Lelievre merely pointed to the message the original soldier had written on the window forbidding anyone from disturbing the family. Everyone dutifully obeyed the injunction of the homesick soldier.[11]

A few others were spared as well during the early morning operations. Because his wife was pregnant, M. Henquin was allowed by a well-disposed officer to stay by her side. Before he took his leave, the officer remarked cryptically, "By the evening, many will no longer be alive."[12]

⊰⊱

The Tschoffens and the Herbecqs were taken to Amand Bouille's stables. They asked various soldiers guarding them what was to become of them and they received conflicting replies. Some assured them they had been brought there for their own safety. Others told them they would all be shot. A thirteen-year-old girl had fired on a major, went one story, and now they would all pay. *C'est la guerre.*

At one point the captives in the stable observed some men being marched by. Then, above "the noises of the battle, volleys were distinctly audible. We looked at one another. The Germans had just shot those poor men."[13]

The idea that they might all be executed, unthinkable as it had seemed moments earlier, was suddenly plausible.

FRANC-TIREURS By 7:00 a.m. on Sunday morning, all of the *quartier* echoed with cries of *"Heraus! Heraus!"* In at least three instances, families that were slow to make their way upstairs were fired at, though there were no serious injuries.[14]

Some eye-witnesses saw terrified young children, clutched tightly by parents who raised their free hand, themselves lift up both hands to show the Germans that they, too, had no guns.

The families living at the base of Montagne de la Croix, before being transferred to the Bouille buildings, were assembled by the Germans outside the Waeyen's house, down the block from the more opulent Herbecq and Tschoffen dwellings, with their extensive grounds.

Here, two revealing incidents occurred.

Mme. Frankinet, whose husband had faced execution earlier, before the timely intervention of Judge Herbecq, watched as a soldier grabbed her brother-in-law by the sleeve. When the man, M. Grigniet, wriggled free, the soldier seized the man behind Grigniet, a thirty-eight-year-old quarry worker named Joseph Pécasse. As Mme Frankinet watched, the soldier shoved a pistol into Pécasse's pocket and then pulled it out with a great show of indignation. Pécasse protested heatedly, but his hands were bound. Four other witnesses observed the crude ruse.

Before the victim could be led off to be shot, another malicious soldier also attempted to implicate civilians. As M. Grigniet watched, the soldier headed up Montagne de la Croix, then hid himself behind a parapet. From the spot where the soldier disappeared came a singe gunshot in the general direction of the civilians and soldiers guarding them.

The soldiers fired back at the shooter, provoking a hail of bullets from troops guarding the heights above rue du Faubourg St. Nicolas and from others descending into town. Four civilians were hit. Two died not long after, including fourteen-year-old Marie Altenhoven.[15]

"I HAVE MEN TO PROTECT" Running and sliding, a platoon descended down the steep gully "Trou de Loup" which led off rue de Montagne de la Croix onto rue St Nicolas behind the prison. The men were heading south to link up with troops advancing into Les Rivages along rue de Froidvau.

However, south of the Defoy carriage factory, there were no houses lining the Meuse for a distance of about 300 yards, until the beginning of the faubourg St. Paul, in neighboring Les Rivages. In crossing this sector, the Germans would be directly exposed to French fire.

The platoon had cleaned out all the families from the quarter who lived south of the prison. They proceeded to form the approximately 125 people into a column which they forced to advance southward with them, toward Les Rivages, the soldiers walking on either side of the civilians. When they reached the exposed area, an officer adjusted the formation. He ordered the line of soldiers walking beside the river to join the troops on the far side of the Dinantais, where they would be shielded from the French guns. When she saw what was happening, a woman yelled, "But they're going to put us in front of them!"

"I have men to protect," an officer responded brusquely.[16]

Civilians who hesitated were forced ahead at gunpoint. They had just advanced beyond the carriage factory when those in the lead were hit by French gunfire. Twenty-two-year-old Madeleine Marsigny cried out. She had been struck in the head. Three others went down. Everyone frantically waved hats and handkerchiefs and the French stopped firing. Madeleine Marsigny's parents were permitted to carry her to a German first-aid station set up in rue Courte St. Roch. The army doctor there, however, refused to care for her, claiming that the soldiers who had been injured by Belgian franc-tireurs required all his attention. The parents carried their daughter, who was in great agony, to the prison.

The behavior of German doctors varied widely, as one might expect.

The first two platoons coming down rue Montagne de la Croix descended without incident. Behind them came a doctor distributing chocolate to residents.

Joseph Firmin, in turn, asked the friendly doctor if he needed anything. *"Oh! Non, merci!"* he replied. When Firmin asked if there was any danger, the doctor simply told him to remain inside his house.

No sooner had the doctor descended down the hill than a third patrol approached, behaving quite differently than its predecessors. According to Léonie Firmin Defrance, Joseph's daughter, the men were yelling like savages, howling and whooping. At their head was a frenetic officer, sword in one hand, pistol in the other. Still standing innocently in their doorway, Defrance's brother Joseph Jr. received a slash on the arm. Then the officer shot her father through the ear. Defrance's husband dashed into the garden and concealed himself behind a bush. He remained there until Tuesday and survived the carnage.

The doctor, meanwhile, had observed the troops behind him and came racing back, yelling, *"Halt!"* He was ignored by the soldiers.

Running across the doctor a little later, at the bottom of the hill, Alexis Firmin told him that the men had killed his father. "They're cowards," he replied bitterly.[17]

BAD ODORS It's not clear why the Germans chose the Bouille buildings to hold residents of the quartier. But by 10:00 a.m. most families from St. Nicolas had been conducted to the stable or the house. It seemed to some residents that the sick and old were being selected for the house. A few soldiers appeared to believe this building was reserved for women. Then, quite by chance, the forge was opened up.

Soon after the Herbecq family had entered the stable, Mme. Herbecq began complaining to her husband about the foul odor. Judge Herbecq approached one of the guards, a schoolteacher from Dresden. The man was exceptionally obliging. "Would you like to go into the house?" he asked.

Herbecq declined. The house was reserved for the ill, he explained, and his wife suffered not from an illness but from an indisposition, something quite different. Might it not be possible to go into the forge?

The soldier promptly retrieved a hatchet from one of his comrades and broke the lock on the forge door.

If he had other motives in transferring his family, Herbecq didn't disclose them. Perhaps he felt the house was already overcrowded, or perhaps the company interned there left something to be desired. The forge certainly did not provide any more of a refuge from French shrapnel than did the stable. In any event he, the Tschoffens, and several other families trooped over to the forge. Later in the day they would appreciate Mme. Herbecq's indisposition. The move saved the lives of most of the men among them.[18]

◄◄►►

Residents of the quarter continued to be ejected from their homes and conducted to the buildings. A soldier stationed at the bottom of rue du Pont-en-Ile then directed them to go either to the left – into the house – or to the right – to the forge and stables. But it didn't seem to matter to the Germans, at least early in the day, which of the latter two buildings anyone entered.[19]

The executions that followed were thus wholly arbitrary: those in the stables were no more guilty of any franc-tireur activities than those in the forge. And in the house were people who had been ousted from their homes shortly after dawn, as soon as the Germans entered the district. No one, of course, had fired on German troops. Kielmannsegg had ordered that anyone caught using arms would be shot immediately, and everyone else imprisoned – orders that were obeyed, Kielmannsegg swore. By the Germans' own reckoning, all the people crammed into the three buildings during the morning were innocent.

KADDISH Needless to say, the captives were extremely anxious about what the Germans planned to do with them. Most had had no breakfast. There were episodes of fainting and hysteria. The bombardment itself was profoundly stressful. The crashing of the French shells, the roar of the German guns, created a hellish din. Mothers, themselves distraught over what was happening, had a great deal of trouble explaining the situation to their children. Why had they been chased out of their homes by soldiers shouting threats and curses in a strange language and waving menacing looking weapons? Why had these bad men smashed their windows? Why were homes burning around them and no one putting out the fires?

As they had walked with their frightened children down to their cellars when the shelling began at dawn, parents all over Dinant had reassured them that it would be just like a week earlier – board games, books, lessons, and prayers, to the accompaniment of loud booms and rattatat-tats outside. Though the parents may have suspected that the outcome of the battle would not be so happy, nearly everyone imagined it would rumble on above them. As long as their home wasn't hit directly by a French shell, they would remain downstairs, uncomfortable but unharmed.

At first the soldiers who were queried by the parents in the Bouille forge were reassuring. A German-speaking woman was told that soldiers would be checking everyone's house for arms. When the search was concluded, the families would be permitted to return home.[20]

The Dresden schoolteacher told residents that they were being held captive for their own security. Though the buildings offered little shelter from French shells – German guards in the stables had expressed anxieties on this score – the civilians were being protected from overexcited German troops. When the brigade had crossed the Meuse, everyone would be released. This explanation had some plausibility: most of the captives had already witnessed German overexcitement and had little desire to be exposed to more.

In an action not inconsistent with this pretext, occupants of the forge were escorted to the Dinant prison in Place d'Armes around 2:00 in the afternoon.

Why were those in the forge released? German depositions provide no clue. The sparing of the lives of the men in this building was wholly arbitrary. Officers of the 100th Regiment, like their counterparts throughout

Dinant, never made the least attempt to establish anyone's guilt, let alone consign the innocent to a specific building.

One intriguing, though unconfirmable, explanation was provided by Léon Sasserath, one of the town's *échevins* and a future burgomaster. A soldier from Leipzig approached his wife, he testified, and asked if her husband were Jewish. When she said he was, the soldier asked Sasserath himself.

"I'm of Jewish origin," he replied guardedly.

The soldier then asked Sasserath to prove this by reciting a prayer.

Sasserath, appropriately enough, chose the prayer for the dead.

This satisfied the soldier, who then told him that Jews would not be killed.

"Is there a danger of this?" Sasserath asked incredulously.

"Yes," the soldier assured him. "You're all going to be shot."

"Save me!" Sasserath gasped.

"I shall be delighted to," the soldier replied chivalrously.

Taking Sasserath's children by the hand, he led the family toward the prison.

"Follow me!" Sasserath called to the others in the forge, and the families crowded out the door and accompanied him and his family to prison.[21]

It is certainly possible that a Jewish soldier in the German Army might make some effort to save a co-religionist. However, it is hard to believe that one soldier could deliver from death an entire building full of condemned civilians on his own initiative, even if we believe that Sasserath chose to jeopardize his family's survival by summonsing everyone else. While a particularly gutsy individual might have taken a family under his protection, the evacuation of the forge almost certainly would have required an order from the officer commanding the troops in rue St. Roch.

What additional testimony does confirm is that Sasserath told the anxious men and women in the forge that he had been authorized to assure them that they had nothing to fear. They were to be escorted to the prison and no one was to be harmed. Sasserath was then taken into the stable and the Bouille house itself, where, accompanied by an officer, he repeated the good news.[22] No doubt Sasserath himself believed what he had been told by the Germans. Though as an *échevin* he would have been a logical choice to placate the anxious civilians, it remains possible that Sasserath was nominated for this task by the friendly soldier. The fact that his family was permitted to return home from the forge suggests that he had a protector there.[23]

Sasserath's original story is further complicated by the fact that it appears as if the Germans intended to execute most of the men conducted to the prison. (Of course, if his rescuer knew this, he may have been confident that he could prevent Sasserath from being among those selected to be shot.) Nonetheless, Sasserath's version, as Schmitz and Nieuwland point out, is precise and categoric, and not altogether flattering to himself. It is possible that after delivering his cheering message, he then learned of the actual German plans from the Jewish or philosemitic soldier, and gratefully accepted the man's offer to save him.

In any event, when Sasserath and the others in the forge were led off to prison, his reassurances seemed to have been vindicated. Those in the stables who saw the families leaving the forge attempted to follow, but they were prevented from doing so. "Later, later," a soldier called out.[24]

"VOUS ETES LIBRES!" The situation was still harrowing for those who left the forge. There were very few soldiers guarding them, but the streets were filled with Germans. The captives hurried past blocks of burning homes. In one of the buildings still standing, the house of a judicial colleague, Maurice Tschoffen glimpsed officers sitting in the dining room, surrounded by open bottles of wine, examining the judge's papers. Corpses lay sprawled in front of the burning buildings. The French guns were still firing and everyone made a mad dash across Place d'Armes, including the German guards, for the security of the prison. "We were frantic to enter the prison yard," Maurice Tschoffen recalled.[25]

A sergeant searched the new arrivals. Just as Tschoffen himself was about to be searched – for the third time that day – shots rang out from the heights of Herbuchenne, overlooking the prison. Most of the civilians scampered through the hail of bullets to the central building; others sheltered behind the high wall beside the entrance. The German guards yelled repeatedly at their comrades, but the firing didn't stop until one soldier opened a skylight in the attic and waved a white sheet. Because of the height of the eastern wall of the prison and the small size of the courtyard, most of the bullets were fired too high, raking the upper half of the far wall. "But for that," said

Tschoffen, "there would have been a frightful slaughter among the prisoners, crowded together in a compact mass, among whom were a large number of women and children." As it was, two civilians were killed instantly, nineteen-year-old Joseph Lebrun and eighty-five-year-old Euphrosine Stevaux. Eight others were hit by German bullets, six of them women.[26]

When the shooting began above the prison, some of the hostages from the forge had already been confined to their cells. Still others in the southernmost neighborhoods of Dinant had been taken directly to the prison, bypassing the Bouille buildings. At least one hundred fifty may have been imprisoned already by the time the St. Nicholas contingent arrived.[27]

Victor Thonon had managed to keep his daughters with him when his family had been brought over from the forge, but he had been separated from his wife. Anxiously peering out into the courtyard after the shooting ceased, Thonon noticed the body of a young man in one corner. It was covered with something familiar. Thonon looked again. It was his wife's mantle.

Thonon's oldest daughter was permitted to check up on her mother, and after half an hour, her father was also taken across the courtyard to see his wife. She was lying on the floor of a small room, wounded in four places. They spoke only briefly. Marie Thonon urged her husband to return to the children, and he did. Victor Thonon never saw his wife again. She died the next day while he was en route to Kassel.[28]

Meanwhile, order had been restored after the barrage of "friendly fire." Soldiers shed their packs and guns, and began amusing themselves with cards, writing, and drawing. A sergeant forbade conversation between the civilians and their jailers. But officers scurried about busily, seldom, recalled Maurice Tschoffen, without making threats.

> Towards six o'clock, the threats became definite. We were to be shot. Abbé Jouve, curé of St. Paul's, gave us all absolution. The men were separated in a harsh manner from the women, and placed in a row in the yard. They were opening the door when suddenly an extremely well-sustained fire began quite close to the prison. Soldiers in the prison square re-entered in a great fright, and began to fire in the air or at the square through the broken panels of the door. One officer went to the governor's office and fired through the window at a surgeon who was bandaging the wounded... In the momentary confusion, everyone took the opportunity of slipping over to his own family. All thought that the French had come back. Unfortunately, the firing which had given rise to that thought ceased immediately, and we then realized that an execution en masse had taken place.[29]

A civilian was killed and another civilian and a soldier were injured by the gunfire of the panicked Germans within the prison yard, who were whispering excitedly *"Die Franzosen! Die Franzosen!"* after the loud fusillade. *"Vive la France!"* shouted some of the imprisoned civilians, convinced as well that Belgium's allies had again crossed the Meuse. "Shut up," Maurice Tschoffen hissed. "It's the Germans who are out there." As a few soldiers within the prison yard began taking aim at the celebrating civilians, several of the men prudently called out *"Vive l'Empereur."* Father Jouve, who had been sheltering in a prison office, ventured out to the concierge's box. He desperately looked around the deserted Place d'Armes for the *pantalons rouges* of the French Army. When he returned a second time, he saw a platoon in field grey, Germans, rifles on their shoulders, crossing the square.[30]

Victor Thonon remembered it being around 5:00 p.m. when the Germans began assembling all the young and middle-aged men in the center of the courtyard. About forty civilians were selected, and they were formed into four rows. Twenty soldiers stood facing them. The fifty-five-year-old Thonon had been permitted to remain with his family. But before anything further was done with the men, there came the furious gunfire outside the prison wall.[31]

Why the execution of the other civilians should have prevented the shooting of the men within the prison is something of a mystery. The Germans, after all, had had no trouble four days earlier despatching three separate groups of hostages on the Leuven Road outside Aarschot. The timing of the execution at the garden wall and the aborted execution in the prison could have been a coincidence, but it's likely that an order had been issued that all able-bodied men were to be killed by 6:00 p.m. However, there may have been some dispute among the officers in charge of the civilians within the prison, and that those uncomfortable with the order, including, perhaps, the officer who had given his word to Sasserath that civilians would not be harmed, were able to prevail on the commander. Someone higher up may have had second thoughts: there were rumors of a car pulling up outside the gates and an officer scampering out.[32] In any event, the men were brought out into the courtyard a third time. But now an officer announced, *"Vous êtes libres!"*[33]

◄--►

The German idea of freedom proved somewhat different than what the civilians had anticipated.

At a little before 8:00 p.m., a machine gun on the prison roof opened fire. The noise panicked the women and children confined within the buildings. Then the doors were flung open and the families driven out. Were they now widows? the women wondered.

"It had become absolutely dark," recalled Thérèse Drion.

> We were reunited with the men in the courtyard, then together we were led out to the street and conducted toward Rocher Bayard [the enormous rock spire that stands at the southern end of town.] The spectacle was unforgettable: the Citadel illuminated by the burning roof of the church, blood-stained mattresses on the sidewalk outside the prison, the brutality of the soldiers who surrounded us, illuminating us with their torches, the wounded, the elderly and infirm, somehow supported by others. The profound anxiety we had about what would happen to us – along with the fact that no one had had any food – was utterly draining. We were like human rags. To the right and left homes were burning. The sky was a fiery red.[34]

Just beyond Rocher Bayard, the able-bodied men were again separated from the women and children. The latter continued on to Anseremme, while the men were forced back to Dinant. Heading south, the procession had detoured to view the damage German shells had done to Neffe, on the left bank. Now, going north, the column was repeatedly halted so that soldiers could enter the homes they passed and set them ablaze. It took an hour, Tschoffen recalled, to traverse the half mile that separated Rocher Bayard from Montagne de la Croix.

> During one of these halts we were ordered in French to hand over our money. Then we were searched by soldiers, who watched us while others went round with cloth bags collecting the money which had been taken from us. One prisoner asked an officer for a receipt. He was threatened with a revolver. I had 800 or 900 francs in coin, some of which was gold. When we separated, I had given my wife and my son all the notes I had. The silver was put into one of the bags, but I saw the soldier who searched me surreptitiously put the case which contained the gold into his own pocket... They took everything they could find on us. Even savings bank books were eagerly sought after.
>
> When this fine deed was done, they made us continue. Alongside the prison wall several bodies of civilians were lying. A little further on, in front of my house, there was a heap of bodies.
>
> The soldiers made the prisoners carry their packs. They took us to Herbuchenne by way of Montagne de la Croix. We had to step over bodies of people who had been shot. On the top of Herbuchenne there are a number of scattered farms and houses.

Everything we saw was burning. Dinant, in the valley, was like a furnace... In the distance, toward Onhaye, the sky was red.[35]

What were the Germans going to do with them? They would be shot at dawn, claimed some of the soldiers. Others told them they were to be taken to Germany and imprisoned. This time the reassurances were warranted. The men were driven into cattle cars the next day and shipped east to Kassel.

◄◄••►►

The goodbyes exchanged near the Rocher Bayard were nearly as poignant as those earlier in the day near the Tschoffen wall. No one had any assurance that the men were out of danger.

The residents of the neighborhood south of St. Nicolas, in the quartier St. Paul (part of the semi-autonomous commune of Les Rivages) had been rounded up only late in the day, and were taken directly to the prison. Among them were Emile and Elisa Demaret Michat and their three-year-old daughter Andrée. Crossing Place d'Albau on their way to the prison, the civilians were fired on. A bullet struck Emile on the left side, then passed through his daughter as it exited, killing her instantly. When the prisoners were escorted up the Meuse after being "freed," the heartbroken mother carried the body of her daughter in her apron, while supporting at the same time her badly wounded husband.

After the couple had bid each other goodbye and been forced apart, she watched Emile being beaten for not keeping up with the other men. Elisa approached several soldiers who had been assigned to guard the women and children, and begged them to permit her to accompany her husband. To stir their sympathy, she showed them the dead child.

According to Elisa Michat's testimony, this didn't have the effect she had intended. The soldiers scuffled with her, grabbed Andrée's body and undressed it. They spat on it and three men began to urinate on it. While it is possible the distraught mother subsequently embellished the story, so barbaric does the behavior of the soldiers seem, her ending is unexceptional. She was beaten with rifle butts and forced to rejoin the women who were being herded toward Anseremme.

Only on Tuesday was Elisa Michat at last able to bury her daughter.[36]

"PAPA, FORGIVE ME IF I'VE CAUSED YOU PAIN" Not long before the captives were taken from the forge to the prison, things began to get nasty for those still imprisoned in the two other Bouille buildings. Earlier, for no apparent reason, a young warehouse worker, Eugène Février, had his daughter ripped from his arms and hurled to the ground while he, his wife and their three young children were being conducted to the buildings. Now he was placed on a chair in the courtyard in front of the house, alongside two other men. On the pavement beside them was Lambert Thirifays, the somewhat unbalanced thirty-three-year-old son of the Judge of the Children's Court. He had recently lost the power of speech, owing to a mysterious partial paralysis. With his wild glances and disheveled appearance, Thirifays was a source of much amusement for the troops. The Germans paraded him back and forth in the rue Grande, knocking him about, spitting in his face, and jabbing him with bayonets. As he lay on the sidewalk, trembling and foaming at the mouth, Henrietta Jaumot tried to bring him water. She was forbidden, but managed to slip out the door and give him some anyway. "Say goodbye to Papa and my sister," he whispered. When Jaumot attempted to give water to the other men, she was dragged away.[37]

As the torture continued, the young man became unhinged. He recovered his ability to speak out loud, but only to piteously cry out "Papa, Papa!" A doctor who had been given permission to retrieve his son-in-law from the Bouille house tried to intercede with the soldiers, but they pushed him aside, and continued to kick and spit at Thirifays.[38]

With the help of the German-speaking Mme. Müller, Eugène Février's wife received permission to go out and see him for two minutes only. As a precaution, she was accompanied by a soldier who held a pistol against her head.

What in world had he done to get placed out there? she asked her husband.

In response Février just shrugged his shoulders.

When Marie Février gave her husband a piece of couque – the hard Dinant cookie – his hands were icy. "Take courage," she told him. "You're only a prisoner."

But Février had no illusions. "My God, girl, never leave the children. This is it." The soldier then forced her back inside.[39]

Shortly afterward Février, Edmond Manteau, and Henri Vaugin were shot in the middle of the street. Thirifays was murdered where he lay on the pavement.

⊰⊹⊱

The gratuitous cruelty toward Thirifays had a dispiriting effect on the several hundred civilians packed into the buildings. "All who tried to intervene to ask for pity had guns pointed at them," recalled Anna Leblanc Vilain, the wife of a music professor who would be assassinated at the Tschoffen wall.

> At this point, the people imprisoned with us in the house lay down on the floor to avoid the awful spectacle. When someone stood up timidly and attempted to see what was happening, through windows steamed up by the breath of the eighty people crammed into the room, gunshots immediately burst out, shattering the windows. You could see the terror on every face. There was no spirit of revolt. Stupor and fear crushed us. The most courageous men were paralyzed by the consciousness of their weakness and the gravity of the danger. It seemed as if a great millstone pulverized one and all. It was not even possible to think. When a soldier occasionally entered the building, we held up our children and asked for mercy and pity – we who had committed no crime. And the criminals pushed the children away. There was no trace of pity.[40]

Others confirmed the profound impact the treatment of Thirifays had on the captives. "Seeing this barbaric torture inflicted on him, I didn't know what to think," Télesphore Vigoureux wrote afterwards.

> I believed he must have committed some extraordinary act to have provoked the Germans. But I knew him fairly well: he was perfectly harmless. I simply couldn't believe him capable of any hostile, or even disrespectful, act toward the Germans. I felt an instinctive revulsion against the cruelties this guileless man was being subjected to... Soon after, it occurred to me, with some anguish, that there had indeed been no provocation on his part – the behavior of the Germans had turned vicious toward all of us. In the street, soldiers with hideous faces shouted incomprehensible threats, made enraged signs and murderous gestures – acting out beheadings, hangings, and, more realistically, shouldering a gun, aiming and firing. The cries and howls swelled into a frightful din that seemed to surround us and overwhelm us. We whispered among ourselves about the ominous things that had already taken place, and terrible apprehensions filled our hearts.[41]

Whatever the causes of the gratuitous cruelty, it was clearly inflamed by drink. Numerous witnesses, arriving in the early afternoon at the forge or stables, remarked on the constant drinking that was going on among the officers and troops.[42] These men had been assigned to guard – and execute

– the franc-tireurs. They were not marching anywhere that day. Until the first week in September, this in itself was always cause for celebration.

A large table had been pulled out from Mme. Hubin's café across the square, along with several dozen bottles and glasses. Both officers and men helped themselves. The informality of the arrangements suggests that at least some of the officers thought the alcohol might lubricate the grim work the men would soon be called on to perform.

One drunken soldier tried to set the stable on fire, and was prevented from doing so only with some difficulty by a non-commissioned officer.[43]

As happened elsewhere, the soldiers were further provoked by an injured officer. As he was carried past the stable on a stretcher, the Saxon shook his fist at the men and women at the window. "You've spilled my blood," he yelled. "I'll spill yours!"[44]

Shortly afterward an officer entered the stables, revolver in hand, and accused the civilians, who had already been searched once or twice and were under armed guard, of having fired again on German troops.

But, it was the forge, not the stable, from which the selection was made. The former building had been once again filled with prisoners from among those crammed into the stable and from recent arrivals. The same enraged officer now burst into the forge. "You've killed our soldiers," he screamed at the civilians in French, "and now you're going to be shot, men, women, and children."[45] This time he brought soldiers with him, but it was only men they seized. Fourteen of the men, generally the younger, more vigorous looking, were taken out into the street, driven forward by blows from rifle-butts and fists.

However, some older men were also chosen, and there were tense moments for those who were passed over. At one point the eyes of the officer locked on Prosper Massart. As the German approached, Massart embraced his wife and tried to come up with a parting reflection for his son. But an elderly man, M. Smets, interceded, and the officer, muttering that Massart's turn would come, selected another victim.[46]

The youngest of those chosen, seventeen-year-old Camille Lemineur, was for some reason singled out for particularly brutal treatment. He was violently seized by the chin, his jaw was twisted, and his arms were pulled behind him, crossed, and elevated with a kind of hook. The boy cried out to his horrified father, "Papa, forgive me if I've caused you pain."

"Courage, Camille!" the father responded. "Courage Camille!" And he kept yelling it until the seventeen-year-old was shot by four soldiers. An officer, for good measure, fired a pistol through the boy's ear.[47]

The rest of the men were then lined up against a building across the street from the stable. The soldiers toyed with them for about half an hour. They were made to hold their hands up for some time. When anyone attempted to lower them, one or more soldiers would take aim. Tiring of this game, the soldiers made their prisoners cry "long live Germany!" and then shot them.[48]

At the last minute a woman had been thrust among them. She was Mélanie Laverge, the thirty-eight-year-old wife of police officer Robert Anciaux. He had been shot as he attempted to escape with others from his house by the Meuse. Anciaux was mortally wounded, but not yet dead. His distraught wife took off for the Sisters of Charity on rue d'Enfer where she obviously hoped to get help. She was running across rue Pont-en-Isle just as the Germans were preparing to execute the civilians. Soldiers ran down the street, grabbed the "franc-tireur," ripped her blouse, forced her to raise her hands, and placed her in front of the condemned men. The soldiers were lined up in three rows, the first row kneeling, and fired when the commander shouted the order.

One man survived the shooting, Victor Coupienne. He pretended to be dead, naturally, though in great pain. He listened as the executioners yelled "hurrah" three times in unison. Shortly before the captives from the house and stable trooped past en route to the Tschoffen wall, he lost consciousness. After the mass execution Coupienne was brought by Adèle Jaumot to the Sisters of Charity, where Mélanie Anciaux had been headed.[49]

Another survivor was not so lucky. After the execution, one of the soldiers, sitting on the pavement with his comrades, drinking champagne and joking, saw the man move. He got up, made a comment that caused great laughter, then ambled over to his victim. He watched the man for a long time, then shot him in the head and rejoined the party.[50]

FIRE All the civilians in the stable were nearly annihilated before they were taken out to the Tschoffen wall. Several of those confined there saw soldiers tossing straw at the base of buildings lining the aptly named rue d'Enfer, which angles into rue Pont-en-Isle. The soldiers then seized a man from the forge, Alfred Brihaye, a twenty-five-year-old waiter, and shoved him into the house across the street. Then they set the house ablaze. As the civilians watched in horror, Brihaye broke open a window pane to escape, only to be confronted by the muzzles of ten rifles leveled at him. He retreated back into the inferno. Brihaye's body was later recovered unburnt from an annex to the building which escaped the fire. He had been shot in the back, and his corpse mutilated.[51]

Meanwhile, the execution of the fourteen men was proceeding in the rue Pont-en-Isle. Just after the fusillade rang out, soldiers slammed the stable door and pocketed the key. They then warned those inside to stay away from the single window in the building or they would be shot.

Panic swept through the crowd within the stable. The wife of Louis Drion, who spoke some German, climbed up on a chair – the window was about five feet high – and begged the soldiers to open the door. The key had been lost, she was told. After determining that she would not be shot if she broke the pane and climbed out, Mme. Drion proceeded to do this, cutting herself in the process. Others followed. "If you want to save yourself," a soldier yelled, "jump out the window." Then Léon Lebrun was able to force open the door with an iron bar and the desperate civilians poured out.[52] There were more than two hundred, and, milling around in the rue de St. Roch, the smoke from the fires stinging their eyes, they felt enormously relieved to have escaped a potential inferno. Now, surely, they would be permitted to return to their homes. The Germans had terrorized them enough. But the Germans, of course, had other plans.

GOODBYES Residents imprisoned in the house and those who'd been transferred to the forge after the departure of the first group were now brought out to join those who had escaped the stable. The captives, now well over four hundred, were herded into Place de Roch and then up to rue Léopold. At Place Benjamin Devigne, the broad street becomes rue du Faubourg St. Nicolas. Between the Place Devigne and Place d'Armes in front of the jail, the boulevard passes the extensive grounds of the Herbecq and Tschoffen villas. Here the procession was halted. Some of those at its head were pushed into the prison. The men among them would survive the fusillade, save for one, Camille Fisette, who dashed back out to be with his wife, from whom he'd become separated. Léon Sasserath urged him to remain behind the prison gates.[53]

En route, the Belgians were insulted and threatened by a number of soldiers. Once again, it was a wounded officer being transported to a Red Cross station, this time on a mattress, who made the most vivid impression. Literally foaming at the mouth, the enraged officer spat on those closest to him. *"Sales chiens de Belges,"* he kept yelling, waving his fist.[54]

◄‹··›►

In front of the Herbecq house the Germans separated the men from the women and children. "Women to the left, men to the right," officers shouted.[55] Some women – and no doubt some of the men – clung to the hope that the men were being sent off to help construct a bridge. This seemed like a reasonable supposition. When they entered rue Léopold, the civilians saw enormous wagons descending the Montagne de la Croix, each pulled by four horses and carrying piles of small iron boats and other material to be used for the construction of a pontoon bridge. Léon Sasserath, in the presence of an officer, had promised that the civilians would not be harmed, and at least one soldier assured an anxious wife that this was precisely what the Germans were intending to do. One woman gave her son some money. Another urged her husband to try to work beside M. Drion, who knew some German.[56]

Putting the men to work seemed eminently sensible. The French wouldn't fire on civilians and the soldiers could be assigned other duties in preparation for the Meuse crossing. Besides, no one had done anything wrong. What purpose could be served by killing them?

Many of the prisoners, however, feared the worst. They had filed past the bodies of the eighteen men and one woman who had been executed in front of the Bouille buildings. They were repeatedly threatened and reviled as they trudged along. Then the procession was halted in front of the Tschoffen garden wall.

"It is impossible to describe the harrowing scene," write Schmitz and Nieuwland, who collected over 2,000 pages of testimony on Dinant. "The depositions we are looking at are very restrained, but how much emotion the laconic phrases reveal!"[57]

◄‹··›►

Every goodbye was heartbreaking.

"I'll do my best to save myself," Albert Renard, a twenty-seven-year-old carriage driver, promised his sister Adeline as he was shoved toward the wall. Before Adeline took his young daughter from his arms, Albert told the girl, "This may be the last time I'll hug you."[58]

Another sister tried to comfort her younger brother, Auguste Lenel, a twenty-one-year-old hairdresser. "Don't worry, m'boy. You'll be building the pontoon bridge. But even so, have you made your act of contrition?" When Auguste assured her he had, Blanche Lenel-Lemineur turned to her agnostic brother-in-law, the pharmacist Louis Paquet, and urged him to do likewise. "Relax," he told her. "I've already done it three times."

"Stay as close to the wall as you can," Blanche yelled at her brother as they were separated. Hearing her, a malevolent soldier grabbed the young man and thrust him into the front row.[59]

"Think of me. Say a prayer for me once in a while," Jules Gillet told his wife. When she tried to return the twenty francs he'd just given her, along with her papers, he said, "It's pointless. I won't be needing it anymore." The couple was forced apart by blows from a rifle butt.[60]

Joseph Firmin, the man killed on his doorstep by enraged soldiers moments after a friendly exchange with a German doctor, had three teenage sons. Now they were about to die. The Firmins were Jewish, but Sasserath's rescuer was not in the vicinity. The oldest boy, Alexis, assured his mother that he and his brothers would meet their father in heaven. He asked his brothers not to leave his side. They awaited the bullets with their arms draped around each other. Their mother watched them fall under the hail of bullets. The next morning, around 6:00 a.m., when she returned to the heap of corpses, she found her sons still locked in the same embrace.[61]

Sometimes there were no parting words. Fernand Panier, a thirty-eight-year-old pharmacist, had married late. He was devoted to his two young sons, ages five and three. He did not leave his family for an instant, clutching in his arms the youngest, Max. The boy understood what was going on, and raised his hands and pleaded with the soldiers not to do his father any harm, while Fernand kept kissing him. His brother, in tears, clutched his mother's hand and tried to reason with the Germans.

As the soldiers began separating the couples, Fernand attempted to hand Max over to his wife, but the boy clung to him with all his strength. At that moment, Fernand attempted to say something, but the words died

on his lips. Then he murmured under his breath, *"Au revoir."* As he tried
to give his wife some papers and memorabilia, a soldier tore him violently
away and pushed him up against the wall.[62]

◄-◄--►►

In Belgium as a whole, it is something of a toss-up as to whether officers or
ordinary soldiers were more savage. On some occasions, as we've seen, officers made efforts to restrain their men; on other occasions, soldiers spared
civilians they had been ordered to murder. While it's a little problematic to
speak of humane acts in the midst of a horrendous massacre, at the Tschoffen wall both an energetic officer and a few soldiers saved several lives.

Marie Biname, governess to the family of the banker Xavier Wasseige,
recalled the father's last words to her and her charges. Looking pale and
resigned, he urged them to renew again their pledge to sacrifice their lives
to God. But the extent of the literal sacrifice required of the family was not
yet clear. The two oldest boys, Pierre, 20, and Jacques, 19, both students,
had been required to go with their father. Their younger brothers André
and Etienne, 17 and 15, were permitted to remain with the governess.

"You'll pray for us, won't you?" Pierre asked Marie Biname just before
he and his brother were taken away. Jacques remained silent.

But then a soldier seized the two younger boys and thrust them into
the group of men. An officer promptly removed them. When he left, the
soldier again placed them among the condemned men. The officer, when
he returned, again pulled them out of line. The slapstick routine was re-enacted one more time. It's not clear why the officer did not simply order the
soldier to desist, unless he didn't wish to call attention to his charitableness.
In the end, though, he took his turn last and the boys were permitted to
remain with their governess.[63] (The family had become separated. Elise
Wasseige had ducked into the forge with her two youngest children, Simon
and Marie-Thérèse, while her husband and the others had been forced to
enter the stable. The mother, with the boy and girl, was taken to the prison,
and didn't learn of the fate of the rest of the family until some days later.)[64]

The same anonymous officer apparently rescued several other civilians.
"Cheveaux blancs, allez," he told Léon Lebrun, sending him back to the
women and children. Moments later, two soldiers forced him back to the
wall, but the persistent, if unassertive, officer removed him again.[65] The

man may well have been the young officer who then placed beyond the extreme end of the line several other older men, including Eugène Pierre.[66] Sending men back among the women and children seemed to guarantee that they would be dragged back to the wall.

An officer, possibly the same man who had rescued the others, entered into a brief discussion with a retired Belgian officer about the culpability of civilians. Colonel Roulin vigorously denied that he or anyone else had fired on German troops. "I have a clear conscience... I know the laws of war," he maintained. The officer asked Roulin if he were afraid. "No," the colonel assured him, "but I think it's rather undignified for an officer to die this way. And also, I'm the father of a family." This was apparently the right response. Roulin was sent away from the wall. (The colonel believed that his savior was actually the officer in charge of the operation, and was carrying out the executions reluctantly, under orders. "He had, certainly, some humane feelings.")[67]

Overhearing the conversation, Paul Thirionnet pointed out that he, too, also had small children. Though this was true of a great many of the men facing execution, the officer excused him.[68]

It may have been this same officer who permitted François Gilles to leave when Gilles told him that he had been wounded by French bullets while retrieving the body of a German soldier, and showed him his injured arm.[69]

Finally, an officer spared Dr. Albin Laurent, under unusual circumstances. Laurent's wife, who had just given birth on the 20th, was borne aloft on a blanket or bedspread by several obliging German soldiers.

They passed down rue du Faubourg St. Nicolas not a moment too soon. Mme. Laurent spotted her husband after the civilians had already been arrayed in rows, and stood facing the execution squad. "That's my husband," she called out to an officer. "Let him come with me." It was her great luck to have selected the right officer.

"*Portez votre femme,*" he told Laurent.[70]

<-+->

A few soldiers also did what little they could to reduce the death toll: they aimed high. One corporal actually signaled his intentions to the man facing him, Télesphore Vigoureux, who survived the execution.[71] Colonel Roulin, who watched from behind the soldiers, also noted that several appeared to fire over the heads of their intended victims. He later saw the traces of bullets in the stones lining the top of the wall and against the side of Louis Drion's house fifty yards beyond the wall. One witness, Julie Louis, heard an officer upbraiding some soldiers for such poor shooting.[72]

These men were hardly typical. Most soldiers participated with great enthusiasm. When officers discovered that the original platoon selected to execute the civilians was too small, more men were counted off: *"Noch zwölf. Noch sechs."* Those chosen rushed forward eagerly, as if to a celebration, according to one witness. After the killings, soldiers amused themselves for some time by kicking and spitting on the corpses. Others hurled empty bottles at them.[73]

⊰⊱

One hundred thirty-seven men were arranged in four rows along the wall. In some places they were six deep. The 125 or so soldiers facing them were lined up in three rows, the men in front kneeling.[74]

Altogether forty-five men who were escorted to the wall from the Bouille buildings managed to escape facing the firing squad. Either they were not chosen by the Germans on account of their age, or they were able to hide among the women, or were subsequently removed by the compassionate officer or officers. Age alone did not determine who was spared, however. Among those executed, seven men were over sixty and eleven under twenty, two of whom were fifteen.[75]

When the troops raised their rifles, heart-rending cries rang out: "Mercy! Mercy! Pity our wives and children!" "No mercy, no pity," responded an officer.[76]

⊰⊱

A superior officer with a flushed face and moustache, possibly Lieutenant Colonel von Kielmannsegg himself, advanced on a horse and briefly harangued the men in poor French. "You're franc-tireurs. You fired on our brave soldiers. You're going to be punished as an example."[77] A chorus of final shouts came from the men: "That's wrong! We're not franc-tireurs. We didn't fire! Pity! Mercy! Long live Germany."[78]

A whistle blew and the soldiers fired. Anguished cries from the men, screams and yells from the women and children watching.

Louis Raemaekers, *The Massacre of the Innocents.*

Everyone ranged along the wall fell. There was a second salvo. Where the men had been standing six deep, there was a pile of corpses a yard high. Officers and soldiers walked back and forth in front of the wall, finishing off the wounded. An exception was made for those who begged to be finished off. "No, Belgian pig, you won't be finished off," one wounded man heard a soldier reply.[79] There was another burst of gunfire fifteen minutes later.

Most of the women and children had been pushed by soldiers up rue Léopold, but a great number still remained close enough to the wall to see their husbands, fathers, sons, or brothers gunned down.

They then received a brief order in pigeon-French, either "Now, women, return to your burning town" or "Women and children, return in the fire."[80]

WOMEN AND CHILDREN Some women were in shock, some overwhelmed by grief. But the urgent need to find shelter in the burning city and to avoid the dangers that still threatened them and their children temporarily overshadowed the anguish.

Some sought refuge in one of the small convents in town or in the cellars of some of the larger homes that were still standing. One had to be careful. Soldiers aiming from the top steps of a basement where Mathilde Guillaume Simon took shelter with her child fired down on her, then locked up the house in which she was sheltering. As fire roared through the adjacent homes, Simon was able to force the door.[81]

After her husband was executed, Pauline Sorée Hubert headed toward the Meuse with her two small children. As she crossed Place St. Roch, a German soldier threw himself on her, but another soldier, more chivalrous, pulled him off and knocked him down. The rescuer may have fired at the would-be abductor.[82] The nightmare continued: the family was caught in the glare of a spotlight and fired on. At one point Pauline Hubert's son turned to her and yelled, "Mommy, your skirt is on fire." She had been walking too close to a burning house. She finally dragged her exhausted children into a garden, but loud noises nearby frightened her and she fled again. As she passed by the pile of corpses outside the Bouille buildings, a voice called out, "Pauline, save me!" It was Victor Coupienne. But Pauline Hubert was so unnerved by the evening's events that she ran off with her children in terror.[83]

Like so many others, Marie Biname, in charge of the four surviving Wasseige children in her custody, attempted to flee the city, along with the Jassogne family. But the grottoes of Monfat, where the group sought refuge, were already overcrowded. Somewhere between fifty and one hundred forty people had packed into the small caves.[84] The group, along with some others, then scaled the wall of a small monastery, entered the garden, and climbed up the terraces carved out of the mountainside. But a German patrol spotted them as they reached the uppermost terrace, and opened fire. Two were killed, and several badly wounded.

The soldiers took the survivors to a farm behind the Citadel, where the farmer and his three sons had been murdered earlier in the day. Here they slept in a field. During the night, one of the wounded, twenty-seven-year-old Théodorine Jassogne, died in great agony in the arms of her mother.

The next morning, the soldiers methodically counted the party. There were twenty-one civilians left. The soldiers then dug twenty-one graves. By signs and gestures, the men guarding the Dinantais made it clear that the graves were intended for them. The work was completed. An excruciating five minutes passed. Then another. After half an hour, the Germans, much amused, began dragging over the bodies of their comrades who had been killed on the heights the day before.

The civilians were then ordered to return to town. The streets, however, were choked with German troops. Fires still smouldered in the charred remains of the buildings lining rue St. Jacques and rue St. Pierre. The Warsseige children and their governess and the Jassognes were able to make their way eastward along the former street, towards Ciney.[85]

THE WOLF'S HOLE Dr. Laurent's family had an even more harrowing time. His miraculous rescue in front of the wall is worth recounting from the perspective of his wife, Madeleine Le Boulengé.

The Germans did not break into their riverfront home until around 3:00 in the afternoon. Mme. Laurent imagined that the sight of little children would calm the Germans, and asked her husband to carry upstairs with him Émile, age two. The maid followed with one-year-old Suzanne. Mme. Laurent remained on a mattress in the cellar with her new-born baby boy. She heard violent blows and ferocious cries from the soldiers upstairs, then the cellar was invaded by men brandishing pistols and shining their flashlights everywhere. They didn't respond to the questions she asked in German. In tears, she begged the soldiers to bring her family back down to her.

A few minutes later the two children were returned to the cellar. Twenty minutes went by – it seemed like centuries, she recalled – and Dr. Laurent came down the stairs. An officer had toured the house with him, had seen the instruments, books, and diplomas that established his bona fides as a doctor. The family would be left alone, it appeared.

But not long afterward an enraged soldier ran down the cellar steps yelling *"Man heraus."* Albin followed him back up, hoping to locate the sympathetic officer.

For hours, the desperate Madeleine pleaded with soldiers passing her house to permit her to rejoin her husband. If they bothered to respond, they repeated the all-purpose explanation *"c'est la guerre"* or *"civils ont tué nos soldats."*

Finally, after three hours, some well-disposed soldiers agreed to help her. They carried her and her infant on a bedspread. The two other children were entrusted to the maid, who was to find a refuge for them.[86]

Fires raged everywhere. The men first deposited Mme. Laurent in Place St. Roch and then, after making inquiries, took her down rue Léopold. She had arrived just in time.

> Near the Tschoffen house, I suddenly saw a compact mass of people holding their hands up. There were about fifteen or twenty in front and many rows behind. Oh, the livid faces, the wild eyes, the contorted mouths. I was staggered, my breath jerky, my temples buzzing. Where was my husband? I wanted desperately to see him, to save him. I instinctively knew he was there. Luckily, he was in the front row. I suddenly spotted him and cried out, "Albin." He looked at me. I was startled. What a change in three hours. It was indeed him, but he had aged ten years.
>
> I pleaded with a passing officer. "It's my husband," I stammered. I pointed to him. "Let him come with me. I beg you." The officer relented, and when Albin raced toward me for a last goodby, he ordered: "Carry your wife."[87]

The family's troubles were far from over.

Madeleine Laurent was taken, with her husband at her side, to a square behind the prison, where she was deposited on a mattress among wounded Germans. These men yelled and swore at them "like demons."

Suddenly a fusillade rang out very nearby, barely concealing a hundred voices crying out in terror. Albin, who was kneeling next to me, turned his head and glanced rapidly in the direction of the Tschoffen house. Then pale, still stunned by what he had just seen, he leaned toward me and muttered in a voice filled with powerless rage, "Pigs. They've killed them all."

Some minutes later, the execution squad passed very close to us, its task accomplished. I could read in the looks of these assassins a pervasive blood-lust.

The officer stopped in front of us and eyed Albin for a long time. What a moment! I felt that Albin's life lay in the hands of this bandit. I gasped. Finally, after some moments which seemed to me immeasurably long, the officer abruptly ordered us to leave. One soldier, more humane than the others, helped my husband carry me. A hundred yards further we stopped opposite the Dumont-Bourdon house. Here we saw soldiers finishing off their own wounded with rifle and pistol shots.[88]

We were petrified by this picture of incredible barbarity, when suddenly a voice cried out *"Die Franzosen!"* Immediately the Germans, seized by fear, ranged themselves along the wall and fired their arms at random. The one who was helping transport me left us precipitously, telling Albin, "Carry your wife into this house," indicating M. Dumont's. My poor husband, exhausted, struggled to maneuver the mattress. He had managed to pull me as far as the doorway when a fleeing soldier passed by. The man stopped abruptly and aimed at Albin, who called out that he was a doctor. The soldier took off again.[89]

◄‹·›►

The couple, with their three-day-old baby, entered the house. So stressful had the preceding minutes been that they realized they hadn't given a thought to their other two children. Albin, as he awaited execution, had seen them being led by the nanny down rue Léopold toward the prison, moments before their mother arrived.[90] Now they wondered where Émile and Suzanne had subsequently been taken and fervently hoped that they were all right. Ironically, at this moment the couple ran into two other parents who had taken refuge in the house with their son. It was the Marsignys, grief-stricken and in tears. They knew exactly where their missing daughter was, and in what condition they had left her. During the panic that had followed the massacre at the Tschoffen wall, the Marsignys had been forced at gunpoint to abandon Madeleine as she lay in great agony behind the prison.[91] Their tragic story touched the Laurents; they forgot their own anxieties as they consoled the desperate parents. Soon enough, though, Albin and Madeleine were forced to consider the precariousness of their own situation.

Albin felt that the house was not sufficiently safe, and suggested a hiding place which, while certainly less comfortable, seemed much more secure. This was a sewer, vulgarly known as Trou du Loup. It was deep, narrow, and filthy, but the outlet, beside the Meuse, was virtually undetectable unless you knew about it. We decided to go there.

With a thousand precautions, we threaded our way along the Meuse and, without being seen, slipped into the sewer. To get well into it, we had to crawl on our hands and knees. How was I able to make this effort? Simply because, in such perilous situations, one's nerves tighten to their limit.

After a few minutes, Albin judged that it was impossible for me to remain on the wet sewer floor and returned to the Dumont house to retrieve a mattress.

There followed three days and three nights of privations, suffering, and anguish that I don't know how to describe. All we had for nourishment from Sunday evening to Wednesday was water from the Meuse that my husband passed through an old felt hat belonging to M. Marsigny, and some blades of grass torn from around the mouth of the sewer. That's all!

During the day we stayed about twenty yards deep into the sewer; at night we came closer to the opening to breathe a little fresh air. We didn't dare speak. The hours succeeded each other interminably.[92]

At one point a soldier loitering around the mouth of the sewer peered in for some time, but didn't spot the couple in the darkness.

Tuesday night, the baby, who had so far kept very quiet, began to cry for long intervals. I wanted to calm him by letting him nurse, but, exhausted by the anguish and privations of the past days, I couldn't satisfy him. This was perhaps the most painful moment. What could be done? The crying of the infant would undoubtedly betray us. After two hours I decided to bury him under the bedclothes to conceal the noise. Albin and I addressed a fervent prayer to heaven. Would the Virgin of Lourdes, in whom we had such confidence, abandon us and let our poor infant die of hunger? While still praying, my husband cut open a vein in his arm to provide the infant with something to drink. I tore the penknife from his hands. We continued to pray.

Soon the exhausted infant was asleep. When he woke up, I was finally able to suckle him: he was saved.[93]

On Wednesday at dawn, the couple was encouraged to hear people across the river speaking the local dialect. Cautiously, they entered the nearest house, hoping to find something to eat. But there were a great number of soldiers milling around the street with intimidating expressions, and so the Laurents thought it would be prudent to return to the Trou du Loup.

Finally, on Thursday, Madeleine saw someone approach the opening. "Monsieur Laurent, are you there?" he asked in perfect French. It was an Oblat Father, accompanied by a Sister of Charity.

The danger had passed, the Laurents were assured. Their house had been burned down, but they were invited to stay with the Sisters. There they learned that their two children had been taken to nearby Dréhance and were safe and sound. The saga was over. Dr. Laurent obtained permission to see the children, and began caring for the wounded.

ESCAPEES Thirty men who were placed against the Tschoffen garden wall survived the fusillades and the shots of the officers and men finishing off the wounded.[94] Five of these men were subsequently killed by the Germans. The rest lived to tell what it was like to look up the barrels of an execution squad.

Some of the survivors had been placed at either end of the line, where there were not enough soldiers to do the job properly. Others were the beneficiaries of those humane soldiers who aimed high. The remainder were simply lucky.

Louis Drion had been placed near the Wasseiges. The father, Xavier, was only slightly injured in the first fusillade. As other troops marched by, he whispered, "Don't move" But he was overheard. Moments later an officer walked up and shot him in the head. Jacques, the younger son, had been killed instantly, but Pierre survived for a time, though grievously wounded. After the soldiers left, he asked for assistance "with sweetness and resignation." He requested Drion to please turn him over on his side, to move his arm, etc. "Thanks so much," he said once. "When I'm up above, I'll pray for you." Only once did he say, "I'm suffering!" At that moment Drion glanced at his watch. It was 6:45. A single sentinel stood by the Place d'Armes, about twenty-five feet away. Drion continued to play dead.[95]

Some time afterward, he observed a man extricate himself from the pile of corpses, crawl across the street, and disappear into the Frankinet house. Another man followed. Drion decided to risk it, but he headed in the opposite direction. With three others, he entered Maurice Tschoffen's garden, climbed a wall into the Herbecq estate, and then scaled a second wall onto his own grounds. Here he met up with his brother, a physician. The men concealed themselves in a hidden cellar under a tannery on the Drion property, where they remained until Thursday.

◄◄▸►

Like the first two men to get up from the heap of dead and dying, most of the survivors entered the Frankinet house directly across from the execution site. The lower panel of the front door had been broken by the Germans. The back of the house gave directly onto the mountain. However, patrols combed the paths; anyone caught was shot. Louis Godart, one of three men who walked away from the wall unscathed, hid in the Fonds des Pélerins woods with another escapee. But while crossing a pasture in search of something to eat, the men were spotted by two soldiers, who opened fire. Godart's companion, Charles Guillaume, was killed instantly. Godart fled into a neighboring wood and managed to elude his pursuers, though their bullets whistled past him. He made his way to the château d'Hordenne, where he was given a warm welcome and refuge by the aptly-named Baron de Bonhomme.[96]

Godard was exceptionally lucky. Many of the escapees were recaptured by the Germans and suffered further torments. Prosper Massart, a high-ranking customs official, enjoyed a special distinction: he was singled out for a trial of sorts. Captured by a patrol on Wednesday, the sixty-year-old civil servant was beaten and taken to a farm on the Château d'Herbuchenne, on the plain above Dinant. Here he was accused of being a franc-tireur, his wounded hand and torn and dirty clothes being sufficient to convict him. His wounds were untreated, he was chained to a threshing machine, kicked repeatedly, and given no food except a bit of rancid lard and some milk.

The next evening Massart was taken into a room where about fifteen officers were drinking and smoking. He would be pardoned, he was promised, if he would acknowledge his participation in "franc-tireur" activities and denounce his accomplices. Massart categorically refused. "Tomorrow at 6:00 a.m. you'll be shot," an officer then announced, after a mock consultation with his colleagues. Massart's two companions received the same sentence.

At 6:00 the next morning, the men were placed in the midst of three or four hundred soldiers. But instead of being executed, he and the others were marched back to town. Massart's wounds were so painful – he'd been struck by bullets on both sides, as well as his hand – that he could shuffle along only with the help of a fellow-prisoner. Then, in front of the new pontoon bridge at Rocher Bayard, an officer announced that the men were free.[97]

⊰⟶⊱

Télesphore Vigoureux's experience was no less exceptional: on Monday morning, he encountered a sympathetic soldier. The forty-five-year-old barber had recently begun producing post-cards of a Dinant that now no longer existed.

Wounded by five bullets in the legs and thighs, suffering horribly, Vigoureux and another victim, Louis Lamberty, tried to slit their wrists on glass fragments strewn on the pavement, but without success. The men had just viewed the handiwork of the Germans by daylight: "a horrible carnage...bodies pell-mell, heaped one on another, perforated and ripped by bullets, rigid and pale." The men then called out to a sentinel standing forty yards away and begged him to finish them off. The soldier aimed but didn't fire. Instead, he bandaged up the men's wounds and summoned a companion, who helped carry Vigoureux into the Frankinet house. When the Germans returned for Lamberty, they found he was dead. Eventually Vigoureux was transferred to a hospital.[98]

More typical was the experience of Paul van Heden. On Monday, when he asked an officer for help – he'd been hit in the upper and lower back and right arm, and had broken his left arm in a fall – he was told, *"Non. Pas de pitié."* A soldier reiterated the message: when Van Heden's eyes filled with tears as he was led past the charred remains of his home, believing that his family had been burned alive, the German struck him on his wounds.[99]

⤙⤖

Finally, at least one man was rescued by a daring woman, Nelly Laurent. After nightfall, observing that the pile of bodies was unguarded, she approached from Place d'Armes looking for survivors. Léon Gillet and François Grigniet were both alive, and had been unable to move from the front of the wall. Grigniet, however, was near death, and Laurent and her servant had to abandon him after hoisting him onto a ladder and carrying him a few feet. But they managed to transport Gillet to the Sisters of Charity, where he eventually recovered.[100]

BURIALS Marie Février, the woman permitted to leave the stable and speak briefly with her condemned husband in Place St. Roch, in front of the Bouille buildings, didn't discover his fate until a day later. Though driven out of the stable to the Tschoffen wall with the others, she had not seen his body. That night, after the mass execution, Février slept outdoors with her three small children. Very early the next morning, German troops, smashing doors and windows, yelling furiously, drove everyone in the vicinity to the Place de la Meuse. It was only here that Février learned her husband had been killed the day before. And now it looked as if the surviving women and children were also to be massacred: several machine guns faced the civilians across the square. An Oblat Father offered a general absolution. But then soldiers began stuffing candy into the pockets of children and everyone was conducted north to the Abbey of Leffe.

At the Abbey, Février located the commandant and asked for permission to return to Dinant to recover her husband's body. This officer spoke fluent French and was surprisingly civil. "Madame, given the present situation, I can't grant you the favor."

Marie Février was furious. "But you shot my innocent husband! It's not enough that you kill him; now you're denying me his body. Whether you permit me or not, I'm still going to go."

"I beg you to speak to me in a different tone."

"And what tone was used when you killed my husband?"

The commandant turned to leave, but Février grabbed him by his sleeve. "If you have even a little bit of heart," she told him, "if you're married and the father of a family, you wouldn't reply to me like that." The man was apparently moved by her plea. He couldn't give her a written pass, he told her, perhaps knowing something of their efficacy, but he offered to provide two soldiers to accompany her to Place St. Roch.

Février proceed south with her aunt, her three children, and the two Germans. They were stopped by an officer in Place de la Meuse, who assured her that all the bodies had been collected. Nonetheless, Février proceeded with her escort down to rue d'Enfer, where her husband had been shot. The first thing she saw as she turned into the street was Eugène's body. Another officer approached her. "What are you doing?" he asked.

The soldiers explained. Marie Février asked for permission to remove her husband's money and his watch – a memento for the children. The officer refused to allow her to do this. It was forbidden to search the dead. But moments later, after she had paid a civilian six francs to take her husband's body to a cemetery, the officer intervened. He struck the civilian, grabbed the money, and returned it to Février. It was one thing to inflict suffering, but to profit from it was quite a different matter.

The soldiers had meanwhile located a small cart and hoisted the body onto it. Eugène Février was wrapped in a red shroud provided by the Sisters of Charity in the rue d'Enfer. The group set off for Leffe. When they passed Marie Février's house, she asked that they stop so she could find something for the children to eat and get them some clothes. A soldier accompanied her inside. As she began searching through the ruins of her home, the soldier told her in halting French, "You cry... Don't be angry at soldiers. We didn't want war... The Emperor..." He stopped and made a quick gesture with one hand across his throat.

◄←·►►

After a harrowing week, Marie Février and her children were able to return to their burned out home on Friday.

On September 28th she went with her aunt to the Leffe cemetery to reclaim her husband's body and transfer it to the cemetery in Dinant. The two women were so exhausted, Fevrier confessed, that on the return trip they sat down on the seat in the hearse instead of walking behind it.[101]

◄←·►►

Anna Leblanc Vilain, the widow of the young music professor executed at the Tschoffen wall, recalled the days that followed the killings. The shallow mass graves the Germans dug added much to the wretchedness of the survivors.

> I remember very well the first expedition [into town], many days after we were set free. I was trying to cross the debris (because that's all there was of the streets) and I really had to make an effort to orient myself as I walked through the ruins. All of a sudden I found myself in the Grand' Place. At this moment an indescribable emotion gripped me, the sobs welled up in my throat, and in front of this appalling scene, I began to cry.
>
> How many Dinantais like me found themselves crying over their beloved town, instead of over their own fate? How many times will strangers who've come here out of curiosity tell us, with unexpected eloquence, how sorry they are to witness this unforgettable horror.
>
> Next to the ruins there was a morgue. From August 23rd, the men who were shot in Leffe remained unburied. The seven hundred fifty Dinantais massacred on the 23rd, the Germans felled by French bullets, the carcasses of horses and other animals, all lay in the streets and under the debris. Many residents were buried in their homes. Often the Germans, after having shot people, threw the bodies into the cellars

Dinant after August 23rd. Place de l'Hôtel de Ville. The Citadel is in the background.

Dinant after August 23rd. Rue Petite.

of neighboring homes. Thus a foul odor began spreading immediately and continued growing for six long weeks. Nothing can express the horror of this new torture, the torment that was inflicted on us by this vile smell penetrating everywhere... The haunting odor of putrefying remains was everywhere, day and night; it was impossible to escape from the disgusting torture.

Dr. Cousot, with other doctors, was eventually able to end this woeful situation. He personally presided over all the exhumations and collected the evidence necessary to identify the bodies. He returned any keepsakes and mementos to the families. The grim task lasted more than three weeks. Despite his work, even long after the burials, people returning to Dinant still encountered the awful pestilence which for so long was such an unspeakable physical and psychological torment for all of us.[102]

GRIEF Anna Vilain was also one of the few of the thousands of bereaved who attempted to express their sense of loss in writing.

"If I had turned back I might have seen the murder of my husband. But for a very long time I needed to hope, despite everything." Vilain wrote of the "long days and still longer nights passed in anguish," of "brief moments of hope" alternating with "cruel uncertainty."

It was necessary for someone to bring me his wedding ring after the exhumation before I finally was convinced, before I knew that he was dead – and with him all hope for future happiness for me. During ten years, he gave me such happiness as no one can know. He was infinitely good, with an exquisite simplicity. In his kindness there was the tenderness of a husband blended with a kind of paternal affection. I remained for a long time his "girl" and it was not until after seven years of marriage that he had another child to love – the poor little girl who is now orphaned, penniless, homeless, and who will never know what she has lost.[103]

CHAPTER 8

Dinant: Les Rivages, Neffe

LES RIVAGES: OVERVIEW Les Rivages in 1914 consisted of two streets running parallel to the river. Homes faced the water across quai de la Meuse and lined both sides of rue des Rivages a block east. Because of its exposed position, the Germans didn't reach the Meuse at Les Rivages until mid-afternoon on Sunday, the 23rd. The first man to arrive that day was an engineer, Karl Ermisch, the captain of a company of the 12th Pioneer Battalion, who came by himself to locate the most advantageous site for a pontoon bridge. Only after he had been reconnoitering the area for an hour did the rest of his company arrive. No francs-tireurs troubled the lone German. "In Les Rivages, all was peaceful," Ermisch recalled.[1]

Soldiers in the company nonetheless rounded up all the civilians in the immediate vicinity. A more thorough cleansing was carried out not long after by a detachment under the command of a Colonel Meister.[2] Not surprisingly, when Major Karl von Zeschau, a staff officer, arrived around 6:00 p.m., all the houses appeared closed up and there were no residents in sight. Nevertheless, the major dispatched a patrol to once again search the homes. They were indeed quite empty, the sergeant in charge of the patrol reported.[3]

For a quarter of an hour von Zeschau watched the German artillery bombard the left bank. He then took off to report to the Corps Headquarters. When he returned at 8:00 p.m., he was surprised to find a heap of corpses by the bridgehead. He was told that after his departure, "firing had come from the seemingly empty houses."[4]

Needless to say, the unarmed hostages under German guard beside the Meuse did not suddenly escape their captors, rush back to their homes, locate hidden weapons, and begin firing on German troops. When the pontoon bridge had nearly reached the middle of the river, French rearguard troops opened fire on the exposed pioneers. The gunfire then slackened.

Edmond Bourdon, the commune's deputy registrar, whom the Germans took to be the burgomaster, was sent across the river to warn the "franctireurs" to cease firing. He was given half an hour; if he did not return in that time, everyone would be shot.

Bourdon naturally found no franc-tireurs. The residents remaining in Neffe, across the river, were sheltering as best they could from the German barrages. He returned, not without being shot at by the Germans, and reported that there were only French troops firing from the heights.

A short time later, there was more rifle fire from the French. Bourdon and eighty-nine others were shoved up against his garden wall and shot. Thirteen escaped with injuries. Of the seventy-seven massacred, thirty-four were women and girls, and sixteen were children under fifteen years of age. The youngest were Gilda Marchot and Claire Struvay, both two years old, two babies a little over a year and a half, Gilda Genon and Maurice Bétemps, sixteen-month-old Félix Balleux, one-year-old Nelly Pollet, and, finally, Mariette Fivet, three weeks old.[5]

Major von Schlick, the commander who issued the order to slaughter the civilians, was pleased with the performance of his troops: "I have always since admired the calmness our men maintained in the presence of such brutes, and the way they abstained from all cruelty."[6]

THE BOURDON WALL Six families were completely annihilated. Five others had but one survivor. One of the latter was the Bourdon family, in which fifteen-year-old Félix was the only member to escape.

On Friday, the 21st, some German soldiers entered the garden of the Bourdon house and four adjacent houses facing the Meuse, and began digging trenches behind the walls of the homes. They also made loopholes in the walls to fire across the river. Early the next morning they installed a machine-gun in a window of one of the homes. The occupants thought it prudent to leave.[7]

The soldiers did not otherwise disturb the inhabitants. They dug and drilled without the least regard for any franc-tireurs who might be lurking in the vicinity. (The activities of the troops apparently escaped the notice

Jeanne (center) and Henri Bourdon (left) were among those shot against their father's garden wall in Les Rivages. Their brother Félix (right) survived.

of the French on the opposite shore, or else they had been ordered to wait until a crossing was attempted before opening fire.)

Saturday was calm, as was the following morning and early afternoon. Then at 3:30 p.m. the Bourdons, sheltering in the kitchen, heard a formidable noise. Troops were pouring down route Froidvau. Soldiers broke into the house and demanded to know if there were any weapons. Though assured that all weapons had been deposited in the Hôtel de Ville, they conducted a thorough search and, of course, turned up nothing. Some soldiers took the opportunity to begin pillaging. All the men from Les Rivages were lined up across the street, but an officer signaled Félix and his seventeen-year-old brother Henri to cross back to the other side. A more systematic "requisitioning" of the houses began, and Félix was compelled to help out. The soldiers were drinking while they looted and as the fifteen-year-old loaded the wagons with sugar, chocolate, wine, and coffee, he was repeatedly struck by rifle butts. One of the soldiers was more sympathetic. He whispered to the boy in pigeon-French, "Save yourself. Leave town. Dinant all burned."[8]

After helping the Germans, Félix returned to the kitchen. He watched as the men were led off. French machine-guns had begun firing, and he assumed the civilians were going to be used to protect German troops.

The soldiers soon found more work for Félix. He was dispatched to his uncle's house, where he was ordered to help break open a safe. And then all the women, children, and old men who were still indoors were compelled to go back to the street in front of the Bourdon house. An aunt who had concealed herself in a wardrobe was beaten and shoved downstairs, but otherwise no one was hit.

Out in the street, Félix spotted his father, very agitated and limping badly. He had been hit in the leg by German soldiers shooting from the quai as he rowed back across the Meuse. (Bourdon is described in the German White Book as "stiff-jointed" and "lame," without any indication as to how he came by these disabilities.)[9] The Deputy Registrar had been ordered to cross over to Neffe to warn the civilians there not to fire on German troops. It was a hopeless assignment. Bourdon had had thirty minutes to cross the river, convince imaginary franc-tireurs to cease firing, then return to Les Rivages within the allotted time or see his entire family killed. As he limped off to find the officer who had dispatched him, he appeared to Félix to be totally devastated.

Arriving at the far shore, Bourdon had headed straight for the home of the curé of Neffe, M. Fries.

Toward 4:30 I heard footsteps in the garden and saw M. Edmond Bourdon of Les Rivages arrive at the presbytery. His face was contorted with terror and his whole body trembled. He wanted to speak, but no words came to his lips. Finally, after several moments, he was able to tell me, "M. le Curé, excuse me, I've been sent by the Germans to come here to tell you not to fire on them. They made me cross the river in a small boat half-filled with water, and I almost capsized several times. They fired on me while I was in the boat. Look at my pocket – there's a bullet hole through it. At Les Rivages, they've seized the women and children. I'm a hostage, but it's hopeless for me. I have to return to them because I'm holding in my hands the lives of my family. Tell me where I ought to go in Neffe to talk to people who are firing."

This speech, the emotion and grief of the old man, made an impression I'll never forget.

I replied to him, "M. Bourdon, let the Germans know that no civilian is firing on them from here. We're all in our cellars. Tell them it's the French alone who are firing from the heights. Don't cross in front of the presbytery. You'll be exposed to German bullets. Go to the village by passing through the garden behind my house."

I took him to the wall and placed a ladder against it. On the other side, before he disappeared – I could only see his head – the unfortunate man said to me, "M. le Curé, give me a last benediction." Then I saw him uncover and bend his head down in profound meditation.

I replied, "My dear friend, repent your transgressions – that's the absolution I give you," and I recited the sacrament.

"Thank you, M. le Curé," he said. "Adieu." I never saw him again.

He went to the homes of M. Fabry and M. Mathieu, who both urged him to stay here and not cross back to the other shore. "I can't," he replied, "I hold too many lives in my hands."[10]

Mme. Fabry vividly recalled Bourdon's visit. "M. Bourdon asked that we not fire, all the while convinced that it was not civilians who were shooting. The poor man was beside himself. 'I have only half an hour,' he said. 'The lives of so many people depend on me.' I rubbed him with vinegar and gave him something to drink."[11]

Not all the Germans believed it was franc-tireurs who were shooting at them from across the Meuse. Just before Edmond Bourdon returned to his family, an officer on horseback approached the civilians. Speaking decent French, he told them, "If the French fire again, you will all be shot. You'll go first over the bridge, and if there's a rifle shot, you're all dead." Naturally, everyone was extremely upset at this announcement. Félix's thirteen-year-old sister Jeanne fainted.[12]

As the civilians were ordered to advance toward the Meuse – Félix was more convinced than ever that they were about to be used to protect the troops constructing the bridge – two boatloads of families from Neffe arrived at the near shore.

At this moment, gunfire erupted at the group of civilians. Félix and his sister threw themselves on the ground. Henri, slower to react, was hit and cried out in pain. Several witnesses saw German troops firing from Rocher Bayard. A Luxembourger, Nicholas Tock, saw soldiers open fire from the house next door. It's possible additional shots came from French soldiers. Crossing in one of the small boats, a Neffe resident heard guns go off behind her.[13]

Immediately after the shooting, the civilians were forced across the street by blows from rifle butts. There was a great deal of scuffling and shouting. Sensing what was about to happen, people panicked. One woman, whom Félix didn't know, went mad and hurled herself on him, badly biting his lip.

As the soldiers facing them raised their guns to fire, Félix again threw himself on the ground. Time slowed. He heard bullets whistle around him and felt bodies fall heavily on top of him, "first one, then two, then three."

I heard screams, cries and groans. Above the tumult I could distinguish the voices of small children. All this time the soldiers were singing.

My brother, lying on his back up against the wall near me, had been hurt much more seriously than the first time. I heard him call out for quite a long while, "Mamma, Pappa, Jeanne." A soldier approached and fired a shot point blank. Emile Dury pleaded for water and begged the soldiers to finish him off. He died shortly after.

Sometime after the first salvo, there was another round of fire and, once again, I was not hit. After this I heard fewer cries, save from time to time a small child calling its mother.[14]

An officer with a lantern went around finishing off anyone who moved. Finally, around midnight, some of the survivors, communicating with each other in whispers, resolved to get up from the pile of corpses. An officer signaled them to approach. The survivors were minutely searched once again. Their money was confiscated and they were bound together in pairs. The men were commanded to lie down flat on the ground. Then an ambulance drove back and forth, inches away, as if the driver intended to crush their legs. After they grew bored with this prank, the soldiers ordered the men to rise. Because they were tied together, and most were seriously injured, this wasn't easy, and the soldiers were much amused by their difficulties.

The captives were once more ordered to lie down, this time alongside the Meuse. Here, while three or four soldiers stood guard, passing troops threw the remains of their meals and spat at the survivors. When one man raised his mangled arm to elicit the pity of the soldiers guarding them, they struck it with their rifle butts.

The next morning the Germans found a better use for the survivors; they would help bury their murdered relatives. Soldiers had already dug a large pit in the garden of Alexandre Bourdon's house. The corpses were carried over one by one. Then the captives were made to thoroughly search the victims' pockets. Everything they extracted was piled at the feet of the soldiers, who took what they liked and discarded the rest. Félix Bourdon and another prisoner were ordered into the pit to line up the bodies that were handed down to them.

When I saw Mama's body, I felt weak and supported myself against the wall, but a blow from a rifle butt forced me to resume the sorrowful work. I couldn't establish where my mother had been hit by the bullets. I saw my father, my brother Henri, and my sister Jeanne. Papa's head had been nearly taken off by the bullets, my brother's back was torn open, and my sister's brain was exposed...

Hubert Kinique also saw the bodies of his father, mother, sister, and two brothers.

We remained there for some time, true human debris, hardly aware of what was going on around us. Up to that time we had been given nothing to eat or drink. Finally, we received a bucket of water drawn from the Meuse.[15]

A French-speaking officer harangued the survivors. France, he told them, would soon be ignominiously defeated. Belgium had chosen its ally unwisely. All Belgians deserved to die for opposing the passage of the German Army. However, owing to the mercy of the Kaiser, their lives would be spared and they would merely be imprisoned in Germany.

The survivors were unimpressed with this act of beneficence. When the officer commanded them to shout *"Vive l'Allemagne,"* the men refused. The civilians were then taken down the route de Froidvau in the company of about fifty French prisoners. On a farm at Herbuchenne, the French were given something to eat; the "franc-tireurs" received nothing. Nonetheless, when they resumed their march eastwards, the soldiers made them carry their packs.[16]

-<-+->-

Camille Fivet also survived the fusillade

> Hardly had we arrived in front of the Bourdon wall when they fired on us; I fell. Alexandre Bourdon was on top of me. At around 9:00, I wanted to get up. Immediately, there was gunfire in my direction, but as I was under Bourdon, it was he who was hit.
>
> I was able to take note of what was going on around me. I heard a baby crying and asking for something to drink. It was little Gilda Marchot, aged two. A German approached her, stuck the end of his rifle in the child's mouth and fired.
>
> Disgusted, I turned to the other side and saw a soldier carrying something on the end of his bayonet. I recognized the body of my little niece, Mariette Fivet, three weeks old. After playing with the child's body, the soldier disposed of it by putting his foot on her stomach and removing his bayonet.
>
> ...The next day I buried the body of my brother, my sister-in-law, and little Mariette, twenty-two days old. I clearly saw that the baby's linen wrap was completely torn at the stomach and filled with blood.[17]

"THEY'RE NOT GOING TO KILL US, MAMA?" Forty-three of those killed at the Bourdon wall had been brought across the Meuse only moments earlier from the left bank community of Neffe.

Civilians on this side of the river had some reason to be more confident than their neighbors in Dinant and Leffe. The French were holding the left bank, their machine guns covered the waterfront, their artillery batteries commanded the heights on both sides of the route de Phillippeville. They had decisively defeated the Germans a week earlier. Surely they would again repel the enemy's attempt to seize the Meuse crossings.

The family of nineteen-year-old Félicie Bétemps, sheltering with three other families in the Bétemps' basement, were thus alarmed when the French 75s slowly ceased responding to the enemy guns between 3 and 4 p.m. Panicked, they consulted their neighbor, M. Morelle, who advised them to remain where they were. To flee would be to risk exposure to German shells and French gunfire. The families returned to their basement and were joined by another group whose home had been hit. The Germans came knocking shortly afterwards; as customary, they broke down the door, yelling furiously. The Bétempses had been slow to respond.

Everyone in the neighborhood was expelled from their homes and herded together, *Hände hoch*, facing the pontoon bridge the Germans were constructing. "We hadn't the least idea of the reason for these tactics, but the sight of the homes on fire on both sides of the river and the brutality of our guards was hardly reassuring."[18]

The civilians were divided into two groups, on no clear basis, one of about forty-five and the other a dozen. The former were to be taken to the right bank. About twenty to twenty-five were counted off and driven into a large boat. While they crossed the Meuse, Félicie Bétemps watched as one of the civilians asked a soldier what the Germans intended to do with them. In response, the soldier took out a cartridge and placed it against his temple. "From that moment on I understood. The others, happily, had not noticed the gesture."

> Debarking on the other shore, we found ourselves surrounded by a compact crowd of German soldiers who stared at us and made fun of us. The sight of women with children, babies, even, didn't inspire the least pity. We were compelled to advance through the midst of this crowd of soldiers. We joined a group of residents from Les Rivages in front of the Bourdon house.
>
> At this moment, a large officer began to harangue us. "You're all franc-tireurs, and you've all fired on our soldiers. If the French fire again even one more time, all, without exception, men, women, and children, you will all die."
>
> We were then led in the direction of Rocher Bayard, nearly opposite the place where we'd debarked. We remained there around ten minutes. I can't confirm that anyone fired at this moment, I was so devastated, but I recall that on the order of the same officer who addressed us, soldiers lined us up against the wall of the Bourdon garden. It was at this moment that the little boat arrived filled with the second group of prisoners from Neffe, around twenty people... These new arrivals were brutally shoved to our sides, so that we now formed a considerable line. The mothers carried their babies, who cried, while the older children clutched their skirts, and tearfully asked them, "They're not going to kill us, Mamma?" As for me, I held my mother

by the arm and my brother, who carried little Maurice, was on Mamma's other side, with his wife.

Facing us was a row of 20 or 25 soldiers, rifles pointing at us, ready to fire. The same officer, revolver in his hand, ordered us to kneel, then, stepping to one side, he cried out, "Fire!"

I hadn't immediately kneeled, and I was thrown back by the bodies of my brother and sister-in-law, which fell against me. Both, and their baby also, were instantly killed by the shots. Also weighing on me were the bodies of Julie Deskeuve and Joseph Marchot, who had been on my left.

I wasn't injured, but it was impossible to make the least movement. I heard several more gunshots and could feel the blood flow abundantly over my face. I could barely succeed in lifting a head which rested on my shoulder. I saw it was my brother. "Auguste, Auguste," I cried. Alas, I got no response; he was dead. With my right hand, I still held my mother's hand. I called to her then, crying "Mamma, Mamma." Silence. I squeezed her hand very hard, as hard as I could. Not the least response. She, too, was dead! It was only then the reality of the situation hit me.

A horrible silence seemed to spread around me. The cries and groans died out; there was only, from time to time, a final convulsion from one of the victims.

Someone near me still moved. He pressed tightly against me and kept flinging his arm against my side. It was Emile Dury. He was suffering greatly and cried out to be finished off. I believe that a soldier did administer a coup de grâce, because he stopped moving.

While all this was going on, night had fallen. What should I do? Remain silent in the middle of the dead, or reveal my presence by calling out. The first alternative was safer, but the weight of the corpses was such that I wondered how long I could remain in this position. It was impossible for me to move by myself. But to ask the Germans to help was to risk being finished off by them. In this terrible dilemma, I began to pray. I begged little Sister Theresa of Jesus to help me.

I suddenly heard a noise. It was the soldiers looting the corpses. I kept constantly hearing the word "mark." Having finally decided to ask for help, I took advantage of the presence of a soldier close by... He turned, bent down toward me, raised me by the neck, then let me fall back again. He left. About five minutes later he returned, accompanied by the officer who had ordered the fusillade. When I saw his face, I began to tremble. He shined his flashlight at me. "Can you get up?" he asked me.

"It's impossible, Monsieur," I replied. "Kneel," he ordered.

I told him, "I can't. Someone first has to pull off the bodies that are lying on top of me."

Then a soldier approached, seized me violently by my two arms, and, with a great shake, pulled me from the pile of corpses.

At that moment I sensed that my legs were broken, my right leg in two places below the knee. The soldier had pulled me out so violently that my stockings and shoes were torn off and remained in the heap of bodies.

Two soldiers brought me over to the house of Alexandre Bourdon, the merchant, and deposited me on the floor. On entering the house, I noticed that the time was exactly 10:10.

My condition at this moment can't be described. From head to foot I was covered with blood, which soaked my clothes, and the remains of intestines clung to my garments. I was not capable of moving, and the house in which I had been deposited was full of soldiers. I asked one of them for some water to drink, because I was literally dying of thirst. He brought over a glass of water and gave it to me. I couldn't raise my arms, and he told me, "Open your mouth." He emptied the glass so violently down my throat that I nearly choked, and then he flung the rest of the water in my face.[19]

Félicie Bétemps' suffering was far from over. Her injuries finally received some attention when other prisoners arrived and tended to her. The following morning the homes next to the house to which she had been taken were set on fire. Everyone fled from the Bourdon house without thinking to take her out. The house indeed caught fire, flames swept up the stairway, and for a moment she thought she might be burned alive. But two soldiers passing by heard her calls for help and carried her out on a sofa, depositing her in the middle of the street. Some time later, she was taken to another house. This also caught fire, and once again she had to be removed. Only on Wednesday was she taken to a first-aid station across the river. Two more weeks passed before she was hospitalized in Dinant.

◄◄►►

At one point the following morning civilians from other parts of Les Rivages were escorted past the mound of corpses in front of the Bourdon wall. Miraculously, at least one of the victims appeared to be still alive. "Papa, papa," cried out the children of Octave Warzée, a forty-seven-year-old foreman. They were being cared for by their aunt, Julie Servais. Warzée seemed to be uninjured, but the Germans forbade anyone to stop and help. The next day, when she was able to return, Servais found her brother-in-law dead.[20]

THE "WITCHES' CAULDRON" Even the most ardent apologists for Germany in Britain and the U.S. were embarrassed about the massacre at the Bourdon wall. "In certain instances," E. N. Bennett conceded guardedly, "e.g., the shooting of the hostages at Les Rivages, the invaders acted in a manner condemned by the general consensus of civilized opinion."[21]

The Germans themselves appear to have had no such doubts. According to Major von Schlick, commander of the 1st Battalion of Grenadier

Regiment 101 and the officer responsible for the killings, his soldiers exercised remarkable restraint.

> I for my part can only testify that the inhabitants – men of all ages, women, girls – fired frantically on us after a signal and that the measures we took were only an act of self-defense. The situation in which the troops found themselves, especially in the place where the bridge was being thrown up, was, in a true sense, a witches' cauldron. It would have been hard to imagine a worse situation than that precipitated by this raging army of men and women. Despite the awful impression of this fighting, I continue to admire the calmness of our men in the presence of such beasts, and how far they remained from any thought of cruelty, even though the worst cruelty was inflicted on them.[22]

"The guilt of every single person was dispassionately considered by the officers present," insisted a first lieutenant, Freiherr Heinrich von Rochow.[23]

"FRANC-TIREURS" There were other murders in and around Les Rivages and at Herbuchenne on the heights above. In the section of town called la Dinantaise, one witness saw a rare spectacle: German regret. As soldiers chased after some civilians seeking refuge, one man's rifle went off inadvertently as he stumbled. A thirteen-year-old boy was struck and killed. The soldier seemed to be plunged into despair by what he had done.[24]

But moments later, ensconced in a house that the residents had just been driven out of, other soldiers fired into the large group of civilians that had witnessed the accidental killing.

Elsewhere in the area, soldiers also amused themselves by playing franc-tireur.

From her farmhouse at Herbuchenne, Victoire Simone Alardo had distributed bread to German troops on previous days. On Sunday she rose early to bake fresh loaves. Soldiers arrived at 6:00 a.m. The bread wasn't ready, but the soldiers asked for milk, and carried off nine bucketfulls.

Meanwhile, some soldiers entered the house, went up to the attic, fired off a few shots, then raced downstairs crying, *"Man hat geschossen!"* The family was immediately seized and conducted into the courtyard, hands raised.

Mme. Alardo asked the Germans what they wanted, since, she said, she and her family had done nothing but help them.

Soldiers replied, "The French have fired on us from the farm, they've cut off the arms of our soldiers, and a farmer burned a soldier after scooping out his eyes." For these crimes, the Alardo males, Martin and his three sons, were led off and shot.[25]

NEFFE: OVERVIEW Maurice Tschoffen called the murder of the civilians at the Bourdon wall "truly the most odious crime" committed in Dinant on the 23rd.[26] "No language in the world," wrote Monsignor Heylen, Bishop of Namur, "contains an expression adequate to stigmatize such horrible deeds."[27] Yet the Germans very nearly exceeded themselves across the river at Neffe. Here soldiers of the 11th Company of the 101st Regiment went on a killing spree to rival that of the 178th in Leffe. Firing on anyone they found, including women and children, they killed twenty-one civilians at various homes before coming upon fifty-five men, women, and children huddled together in a shallow aqueduct beneath a railroad bridge. This was too good an opportunity to pass up. Without warning, soldiers crouched at the entrance and fired into the families lying side-by-side. They then raced around to the other side and hurled grenades at the prone civilians. Twenty-three were killed, twelve wounded. Among the dead were nine women and girls and five children under ten years of age.[28]

The franc-tireur pretext wears especially thin on the left bank. Here the French artillery and infantry fired on the Germans all day, until early evening. The 75s were hauled off by late afternoon, but rearguard detachments protected the river front for some hours after. The French would never have permitted Belgian amateurs to operate side-by-side with them, and, needless to say, there's no evidence any civilian attempted to do so.

"OFFIZIER" As the artillery fire intensified during the morning, sixteen Neffe residents took shelter in the cellar of the Even-Matagne house. Though fronting the river, it seemed to offer great security than its neighbors.

Around 6:00 p.m. the civilians heard loud noises in the street, then a violent pounding on the door that opened onto the courtyard from a small street behind the house. Léon Even couldn't locate the key to this back door, and crossed the house to open up the front door. Most of the others left the cellar with him and walked out into the courtyard. Moments later the door was smashed in and the Neffe civilians faced a group of German soldiers.

"Instinctively," recalled Mme. Burniaux, "we raised our hands. The first Germans didn't seem to want to do us any harm, when suddenly an officer burst into the courtyard, gesturing like a man possessed, and commanded the soldiers to raise their rifles immediately."[29]

The soldiers fired and everyone in the courtyard went down. Five were killed instantly. They included a handsome young couple, Rachel and Joseph Guerry, Guerry's mother Marie, Clothilde Even, and Ernest Burniaux. Only three appeared to have escaped unscathed: the two-year-old son of Léon Even, Mme. Burniaux, and her oldest son Robert, age nine.

> That crime accomplished, the soldiers departed by the garden, disgusted, it seemed to me, at having been made to carry out such a task. I had fallen under the body of the widow Even, Léon's mother, and I heard Robert say to me, "Mamma, I haven't been killed."
>
> "Be quiet," I said. "Don't speak."
>
> The Even child kept sobbing "Momma's been killed." He was wrong, happily. She was only injured, struck on the ear and in the back....
>
> I raised myself up, to the great astonishment of the soldiers, who believed we were all dead. I threw myself on my husband, who gave no sign of life. My little Robert meanwhile hurled himself at the feet of our executioners and begged them, his hands clasped. "You won't kill Momma, will you, Messieurs?"
>
> By gestures the soldiers made me understand that the officer who ordered the massacre ought not to see us alive when he returned, and took us with them. I wanted to look for my little Franz, but, not knowing where he was, I resigned myself to leaving without him. I found out a little later that he'd remained in the cellar.
>
> As the soldiers conducted me along the Meuse, they carried a package I'd taken with me, and held Robert by the hand. But suddenly they returned the package and released the child's hand. One whispered to me, *"Offizier."*[30]

⤛⤜⤛⤜

It was probably the same officer, more than likely Major Arnd von Zeschau (not the staff officer of the same last name), who found sixteen-year-old Jeanne Lempereur crouching behind a bush in her garden. Despite her cries of "don't shoot," he fired point-blank and killed her.[31]

"HOW COULD I NOT GO MAD?" "I had a beautiful family" recalled Adèle Houbion Charlier,

> comprised of six children, my husband and I, making eight people; and in addition my old father Pierre Houbion, eighty-five years old, lived with us. We were very happy. My husband Saturnin Charlier (age 40) was employed in the business firm of M. Legros in Dinant, the oldest of my children, Maurice (age 16), worked at the train

station, Anna (15) was learning needlework and the four others were still in school: Claire (12), Georges and Georgette, twins (9), and finally little Gustave(4).

On the morning of August 23rd, with the first noise of the bombardment, we descended into the cellar and spent the whole day there, until around 3:00, when a shell blew up the front of our house. Then, with my husband, my six children and my old father, we all took refuge under the railroad aqueduct. My old father, on account of his great age, couldn't lower himself enough to enter the aqueduct and so remained just outside, and my husband and oldest son kept him company. They were constantly exposed to the shells and shrapnel that fell all around us.[32]

Adèle Charlier begged her husband to allow the family to take shelter together in the Florins' house opposite the aqueduct, and he finally consented. The Florin family consisted of a widow, Mme. Monin-Florin, her two sons Raoul and Louis, the latter's wife Charlotte Laloux, and the couple's four-year-old son. Nicolas Monin and his three children Aline, Jeanne, and Georges had joined his sister's family earlier in the day. With the arrival of the Charliers, seventeen people were crowded into the Florins's cellar.

Two explosions rocked the house. Then a neighboring home caught fire and the families feared it would spread the Florins'.

We had to leave very quickly and find a new refuge. I suggested that we return to our basement, as the enemy no longer seemed to be aiming at the house. But while the others left, I went back downstairs to find something I'd left behind. On returning to the street and not seeing anyone, I assumed they had followed my advice and taken refuge in our cellar. I found it empty. Then I began to cry and to call out, and at that moment my old father arrived, accompanied by Mme. Florin. They reassured me that the others had found a safe shelter, and the three of us descended again into my basement. I learned later...that her family and mine had once more gone to take cover in the aqueduct.[33]

If one was worried about German shells and not about Germans, this was not a bad choice. Though the space underneath was small, the vault was very solidly constructed. The arch at its apex was some 15 inches thick, and nearly 40 inches thick at the sides.

After about ten minutes, which seemed to us like centuries, we heard a frightful uproar: cries, gunfire, exploding bombs...then the silence of death. Concerned about the fate of our families, we clambered upstairs, along with my old father. On the doorstep a German seized me, pushed me brutally into the middle of the street, and asked me if I had any money.

I looked around hoping to see my family, when I spotted my little Georges lying on the ground, injured. He had just been pulled out of the aqueduct by Jules Vandurme. I raced over to him and asked what had happened.

"The soldiers fired," he told me. I took him in my arms and sat down on the little wall near our house.

But what did I see then? Raoul Florin and Constant Pollet, as ordered by the soldiers, were busy pulling from the aqueduct the injured survivors, and in what state, Oh! My God![34]

As Adèle Charlier watched in horror, the two men pulled out various victims, still living but horribly mutilated. A fifteen-year-old boy, Edouard Pollet, died as soon as he was lowered to the ground by his father. Others moaned and writhed in pain. Especially heart-breaking were all the injured children, some with ghastly wounds.

Kept away from the aqueduct by soldiers, Adèle Charlier could only wait until other family members emerged themselves or were carried out. Suddenly she saw her daughter Claire with her youngest son Gustave.

"My God, Momma," Claire cried. "You weren't killed?"

Her mother assured her that she was alive, and asked about the others. Where were they?

"Below, in the aqueduct. We followed father."

Claire then turned to some soldiers standing nearby and asked them to kill her. Stunned, her mother asked why she was talking like this.

"Anna and Georgette are dead," the girl sobbed.

The shock was so overpowering that I couldn't speak, I couldn't utter a cry. I was annihilated.

When I had recovered a bit, seeing a neighbor, Adolphine Bultot, I asked her if she had seen my husband and my other son.

"My God," she replied, "they've been killed."

What a blow. The barbarians had killed four of my family. How would I not go mad?

Not content with having killed our family members, the Germans forced us to abandon their remains and, what's more, prevented us from tending to those who still lived and who were suffering atrocious tortures caused by their horrible wounds. It didn't matter; we had to leave. The order was given to leave the corpses in the aqueduct. Those not able to move, though still alive, were abandoned in their sorry state.[35]

The survivors were taken to the Meuse, where they were officially arrested and placed among a large group of other civilians and some French soldiers. The men were then separated from their families and taken across

The Charlier children pose in front of the aqueduct in Neffe where three of them would be killed.

Among the other victims in Neffe were Charlotte Laloux Florin (a), Marie Thérèse Delieux Meurat (b) and the latter's two children Eva (c) and Emile (d).

the river, where they would board cattle cars for Germany.

Even the badly wounded were obliged to make this journey, unless the injuries made it impossible to walk.

The women and children spent the night in the open, on the grass by the riverside. Three children shot at the aqueduct died during the night.

The following evening, Adèle Charlier was finally permitted to take her injured son home. When she arrived with Georges in her arms she found the corpses of her husband and oldest son Maurice lying on the floor of the kitchen. Between them, on his knees, was her father. He was praying fervently.

The old man, half-deranged, had been released by the Germans after they had briefly and unproductively tortured him. He had prevailed on a couple of neighbors to help carry the two bodies back to his house.

When Georges Charlier saw the scene in the kitchen, he began wailing inconsolably. He refused to stay in the house. His mother carried him to the convent of the Clarisse Sisters, where he was permitted to remain.

Returning to her house through her garden, Adèle Charlier saw the body of Renée Dufrenne Bultot submerged in the manure pit. The day before, Mme. Bultot had been carried out of the aqueduct more dead than alive. Her chest was covered with blood, her left arm was dangling; it was nearly detached at the shoulder. She had attempted to rise, staggered a few steps, and had fallen. Renée Bultot had seen her husband and two children killed, along with several other close relatives. She had either fallen into the pit by accident and drowned, or had thrown herself in.[36]

MOTHERS Cleaning up after the Germans was never fun, but Raoul Florin's task had been particularly onerous. He saw some excruciating sights during his evening's work. Hoping desperately to find more civilians still alive, he pulled on the arm of Thérèse Delieux Meurat. Her three small children, Émile, Eva, and Victor, were lying on her chest, face down. To his horror, the arm came off and the children were flung to the ground. All three were dead.[37]

Florin and Pollet gently lifted out another mother, Léonie Bultot Bourguignon. She had been nursing her sixteen-month-old baby when the Germans arrived. Mme. Bourguinon had been struck through the breasts. The baby died within thirty minutes, the mother after several agonizing hours. Raoul Florin had observed Léonie Bourguinon hold her baby up for a moment so the Germans could see him, and beg them not to shoot. They could not have missed seeing her: she was lying at the very entrance of the aqueduct, only two or three yards from the soldiers when they opened fire.[38]

Edmond Gustin also helped bring out the wounded – the Germans insisted that the dead be left where they lay. He had lost all of his in-laws: Léonie Bourguinon was his wife's sister, and Bourguinon's twenty-nine-year-old husband Jean-Baptiste was killed along with his wife and baby. Gustin's wife's brother Norbert Bultot and his two sons were also among the dead. Bultot's wife Renée would die or kill herself soon after.

Unlike the executions elsewhere in Dinant, the deaths in Neffe were particularly ghastly and protracted, and no one described the injuries more graphically than Gustin. A bullet had plowed into Léonie Bourguinon's chest, ripping it open. She was also hit in the back of the neck. "Leave me alone," she whispered, as her brother-in-law lifted her up. Her nursing baby was hit in the stomach and suffered atrociously for half an hour. Gustin's other sister-in-law, Renée Bultot, had also been hit in the breast and was horribly mutilated. A bullet or grenade fragment had nearly severed her left arm. Her husband Norbert, hit in the stomach, staggered out clutching his intestines, which spilled from the wound. The couple's nine-year-old son had both legs torn off by a grenade. He also died in agony beside the Meuse.

Gustin's own two children were also among those so badly wounded they died within hours. Like mothers elsewhere in eastern Belgium, Mme. Gustin's grief and anger were temporarily eclipsed by the urgent desire to bury her children. The Germans were threatening to throw the bodies into the Meuse. The anguished mother prevailed. She and her husband were permitted to bury twenty-year-old Maguerite and ten-year-old Edmond in the garden of Achille Delinoy.[39]

-<-+->-

When Raoul Florin had at last removed all of the injured from beneath the railroad bridge, he asked an officer for permission to look for his mother.

"Where is she?" the man asked.

"Probably in our cellar," Florin told him. Permission was granted and Florin started to enter his house. The officer shouted an order and soldiers pushed past Florin and began firing through the basement window. Convinced his mother had been killed, Florin fell to his knees and began praying. Luckily, though, Mme. Florin had taken refuge with Adèle Charlier across the street, and her son was not compensated for his labors as the Germans had intended.[40]

⤙⤚

The family of Léopold Dauphin was not so fortunate. Like the Charliers, the husband and wife had disagreed over the best refuge. When the nearby Even house was set on fire after the killings in the courtyard, Mme. Dauphin argued that the family should flee at once. Her husband thought the cellar more secure.

Mme. Dauphin refused to go with her husband and children, and hid by herself in the garden. From there she saw two soldiers who had spotted the family race into the cellar, which had an outside entrance. "What are you going to do with us?" she heard her daughter ask. The answer was a brief burst of rifle fire. In a matter of seconds, the Germans had killed her husband and two children, her mother-in-law, her brother-in-law, and a boarder. She was no longer a wife and mother.[41]

"CIVIL SUSPECT" The Florin family had hidden with the Charliers. During the late afternoon, it seemed as if the Germans were targeting their riverside neighborhood, though no French troops had been in the vicinity for some time. An explosion shattered the front of the house, and shell fragments went flying into the basement. Louis Florin was struck in the arm. After another direct hit at around 5:00 p.m., the families decided to shelter under the railway bridge which faced the front of the house.

It was a tight squeeze. A great number of others were already gathered here. The fifty-five civilians were lying in an area of about 25 square yards, with a maximum height of 34 inches at the center of the arch, tapering to 13 inches by the walls. People were lying on top of each other.[42]

> We had hardly been there a few minutes when we saw five or six German soldiers advancing toward us along the little street leading up from the Meuse. When they were four or five yards or more from the aqueduct, they began to fire on us, all their

bullets claiming victims in the compact mass of civilians piled one upon another. The cries of horror of those not hit by the shots drowned out the moans of the wounded and the groans and gasps of the dying. Not content with this first fusillade, the soldiers climbed onto the railroad line and started throwing hand grenades through the other opening. They also dropped some grenades into the middle of the group through holes in the vault.[The bridge was under repair at the time.]

My left foot was nearly torn off by one of the grenades and when the pain made me cry out, my wife asked if I were wounded. When I said yes, she embraced me, and, at the same moment, a bullet struck her. She fell on me, instantly dead. She held our son in her arms; he was unhit, luckily.[43]

Florin was eventually carried out by his brother and Constant Pollet. Because he was unable to walk, he was placed on a mattress on the railroad embankment, along with the critically wounded Maurice Charlier, Jean-Baptiste Bourguinon, and Aline Monin. Young Charlier died during the night in excruciating pain, and Bourguinon succumbed early the next morning. Around midnight the four were given a little water by an officer; that was the only care they received.

The other survivors, meanwhile, had been forced to march off. Florin's mother had been entrusted with her little grandson.

As he lay in great pain, Florin watched the homes blaze around him. Soon a steady procession of infantrymen marched past, followed by artillery batteries. At one point Florin had to slide over a few inches to avoid being crushed by the heavy wheels of the guns.

Jeanne Monin, who had received permission to take her sister to the Clarisse convent, arrived with two soldiers, who carried off Aline. But when another resident, Edmond Toussaint, attempted to cart Florin to the Sisters in a wheelbarrow, the two men were almost executed by irate German soldiers in front of the convent.

It was not until Saturday evening that Florin received medical attention, apart from some morphine given him by a sympathetic corporal. Each time the doctor entered Florin's ward, he ignored the patient, while attending to others. When Florin asked to be examined, the doctor invariably replied, *"Morgen."* Each day he received the same response. At the base of the pallet Florin was lying on, he eventually discovered, was a small notice on which was written "civil suspect" and a sentence in German.

Finally, on Saturday, Albin Laurent arranged for Florin's transfer to a hospital in Dinant, where he was finally seen by another Belgian physician.

The next day his leg was amputated. Tetanus had set in. Florin had four bad hemorrhages and thought many times that he was about to die. He remained hospitalized for eight months.[44]

THE FINAL VICTIM When M. Carlier, a cautious rentier, headed for France at the outbreak of war, he entrusted his dog to thirty-three-year-old Norbert Bultot, a wagon-driver like his brother-in-law Jean-Baptiste Bourguinon. The dog adopted the family. After Bultot and his two young sons were killed, the dog stood guard over the bodies remaining under the bridge, refusing to leave. The Germans consulted briefly, then shot the dog.[45]

THE GERMAN VERSION According to the summary report of the section on Dinant in the White Book, this is what happened in Neffe. Approaching the culvert, the company commander (Major Arnd von Zeschau) saw a dead civilian with a carbine lying in front of the entrance. From the top of the embankment, another officer shouted down that he had been shot at from the culvert. "Come out, nothing will be done to you," yelled von Zeschau in French to the civilians concealed within. When there was no response and no one emerged, the major ordered four or five of his men crouched at the entrance to fire. He then took off. "The detachment left behind for clearing-out and securing the culvert brought out about thirty-five to forty civilians, men, half-grown boys, women and children, and with them about eight to ten rifles, not hunting rifles, but apparently military weapons."[46]

"WE DON'T TAKE PRIESTS PRISONER" In Neffe, as in Leffe and elsewhere in Dinant, Saxon brutality did not extend to priests.

Father Fries, the curé of Neffe who met briefly with Edmond Bourdon on the latter's ill-fated mission to persuade the "franc-tireurs" to stop firing, administered the last rites to some of the aqueduct victims – on the fly.

Seeing that the Germans were setting fire to all the homes in the suburb, Father Fries thought it would be prudent to flee into the neighboring woods with his sister, his niece, and his two nephews.

Everyone had heard the gunfire and the anguished cries coming from the aqueduct, but they imagined French and German soldiers had been engaged against each other.

A patrol captured Father Fries's group in the woods, and they were forced to descend back down to Neffe, the commanding officer, as usual, menacing the civilians with his pistol. The priest's niece spoke fluent German, and was able to calm the officer and his men somewhat. As they were escorted toward the Meuse, the family members passed the railroad bridge and aqueduct. Father Fries was astonished to see a pile of corpses under the vault. As he approached, hands were raised and voices called out to him. He slipped out of the group and began giving absolutions and trying to comfort the wounded. He was ordered back into the group, and they continued down to the river. Here he administered last rites to several mortally wounded civilians and French prisoners.

Father Fries and the other men were separated from the women, put into boats, and rowed across. No one as yet knew about the Bourdon wall massacre. As the men disembarked at Les Rivages, a major speaking good French told the priest to step aside.

"What do you think of the day's events, M. le Curé?" the man asked.

There followed a fruitless discussion, the priest assuring the major, at first cautiously, then more emphatically, that no civilians had fired on the Germans, the major repeating that they had indeed, though without furnishing evidence.

The officer eventually terminated the debate. "M. le Curé, I'm going to have you taken back to your presbytery. We don't take priests prisoner."

He consulted with a superior officer and returned with a lieutenant, who told the curé that he would accompany him with two soldiers. Father Fries's sister and niece would be permitted to return home with him.

The lieutenant stayed the night and more than once prevented soldiers from ransacking the house and mistreating its occupants.[47]

"ICH BIN GUT" The soldier who was upset over having inadvertently killed a thirteen-year-old was not the only conscience-stricken German in southern Dinant. Émile Dony, head of the post office, was also treated to a glimpse of remorse. First he had to spend a day as harrowing as that of any uninjured survivor in Neffe.

Whether in Leffe, St. Nicolas, or elsewhere in Dinant, the great dilemma of those who had successfully hidden was to determine when it was safe to emerge. Some decided prematurely that the danger was past, and paid with their lives. Others were caught when the Germans increased their patrols and the desperately hungry refugees grew incautious.

Dony had no illusions about the Germans. There was a window in the cellar he and his family sheltered in that permitted them to look across to the right bank. They saw the civilians being led across the open area south of St. Nicolas to protect German troops; they saw great walls of flames in Dinant.

After a particularly intense bombardment, there was a lull, and then an enormous uproar close by – gunshots, cries, ferocious yells. Unlike Father Fries, Dony had little doubt about what was transpiring. Not long afterward they heard their own windows shattered and the door smashed in and the echo of boots through the floor above them.

The anguish of the families was acute. At one point Dony was advised to surrender to the Germans, but resisted. To be discovered was to die, he was convinced. Then the Germans left without venturing downstairs. The danger had passed.

Mme. Dony made a brief sortie outside. What she reported further inflamed everyone's anxieties: all Dinant was burning, everyone was being killed.

Though they had with them a bed-ridden invalid, Dony decided to flee to the woods with his family. Two soldiers passed close by as the civilians laboriously advanced up a ravine behind Neffe. But night had fallen and the family members were able to conceal themselves. They stumbled on in the darkness, brambles and branches ripping their clothes and cutting them. Occasionally they passed other civilians who were hiding. Finally, at the far end of the woods, they took shelter within a bushy thicket. There was a near-encounter with another German soldier, who advanced cautiously, gun leveled, as if hunting.

Then once again the Germans appeared to have tracked the refugees down. Surrounded in the darkness, Dony attempted a few words in German. But the soldiers turned out to be neighbors from Neffe, the Lempereur family, whose daughter had been killed in their garden. They had similarly assumed the Donys were Germans, until they heard the postmaster garble the language.

Convinced by other civilians that the manhunt was over, Dony and his wife cautiously returned to town Monday morning, leaving the children with others. They were not reassured to see the dead bodies, now a ghastly violet, of Maurice Charlier and the others by the culvert. The village was deserted except for old M. Houbion, whose mind was gone. He didn't respond to their questions. But Edmond Toussaint, now wearing a Red Cross armband, warned the Donys to flee again. "Save yourselves. They're killing everyone."[48]

Nonetheless, later in the day, exhausted by their ordeal, the couple surrendered. *"Komm! Schnell!"* they were ordered.

The first officer they encountered who spoke French breezily told them, "We're going to shoot everyone. But first we're going to show you how we destroy your homes — they spoil the landscape."[49] The friendly sadist, an artillery commander, then ordered his gunners to fire on homes along the right bank. Albin Laurent's house was hit, as was an orphanage that had only recently been evacuated.

Dony was then recruited to bury the dead at the Bourdon wall. As he started to lift one victim, Marcelline Meurisse, the woman groaned and raised her hand. The conscripted workers pointed out to the Germans that she was still alive. Soldiers nonetheless forced the men to fling her into the pit with the others.

This gratuitous cruelty, on top of the massacre, was apparently too much for one of the guards. *"Ich bin gut,"* he told Dony earnestly, and kept repeating the sentence to the men burying the victims. *"Ich bin gut."* Furtively, he tried to do what he could to help the civilians.[50]

By night, the Germans had assembled about three hundred prisoners, mostly women and children. "Lie down," the guards commanded, "and no talking." The flickering flame of a large candle placed on a chair threw a sinister light on the scene: everyone packed together on the grass by the Meuse, with haggard, tear-streaked faces, heads bowed in grief. Children were crying continually throughout the night. No food was distributed until 11:00 p.m., when some of the civilians received a bit of soup.[51]

Dinant still burned. Troops continued to pour across the pontoon bridge, whooping and yelling.

"RELIGIONSKRIEG" Sporadic killings continued in all sections of Dinant over the next few days. The death toll continued to climb. Between August 24 and August 28 no less than fifty-eight men and women were gunned down. But among them were no priests or nuns.

The ecclesiatics nonetheless had some uneasy moments. They were repeatedly reviled and abused. Plenty of soldiers and officers were keen on doing them in. "It's those pigs of curés who got you in trouble," Dr. Cassart was assured by a lieutenant who accompanied him back from a meeting with some staff officers on Monday. (A small delegation of leading citizens had gone to the Corps Headquarters in Leffe to appeal for an end to the violence.)[52]

Like the 416 men who were interned at Kassel, Dinant's priests were gathered together and escorted east. However, the procession halted in Marche. Here, after more denunciations and threats, the clerics were released.

⊰⊹⊱

Having taken refuge in a small monastery near the collegiate church after Mass on Sunday, the Dean of Dinant, Abbé Schiltz, was unaware of the extent of the killings until Monday. Only during the early afternoon on that day were he and his companions forcibly evicted. The priests among the group of twenty were singled out for abuse. Amid the cries of "dirty pig" and other insults, the Dean heard soldiers shout out *"Religionskrieg"* – religious war – at least thirty times.[53]

One of the guards finally reprimanded his companions. When the Dean asked this man what the Germans intended to do with them, he was told the clerics would be locked up for their own security. But at this moment three drunken officers sauntered up and took charge of the prisoners. They were arranged in rows, placed on a flight of stairs leading down to the river, and told to turn and face the Meuse. They were then shot at. Everyone fell down. But the soldiers had been instructed to fire over the prisoner's heads, and the bullets whistled by harmlessly. The soldiers laughed until they cried. The officers, no less amused, pretended that franc-tireurs had fired on the men.

The priests and civilians were then escorted to the École Régimentaire, where the women and children were sent off to the Abbey in Leffe. New captives swelled the ranks of the men who remained. Again the civilians were arrayed in rows, the Dean in front, and faced a line of soldiers with rifles raised. As they waited, hearts racing, sweat darkening their shirts, a soldier snuck up and whispered in the Dean's ear that he needn't worry; the men wouldn't be shot.[54]

After this ordeal the captives were led off – they numbered thirty-nine – and were locked in a cell intended for six. Three days later, on Thursday the 27th, the Dean was released.

◄◄-►►

The rest of the priests in Dinant experienced a longer and no less trying captivity.

Most of the city's clerics resided in the Abbey in Leffe. This was invaded around 10:00 a.m. on Sunday. The doors were smashed in, furniture and beds ripped by bayonets, bookcases overturned. There was "an infernal uproar...the noise of hatchet blows, wardrobes broken, glass shattered, punctuated by the strident orders of officers and the savage cries of soldiers," recalled the Prior, Father Adrien Borrelly.[55] The priests and monks were told by the officer in charge, pistol in hand, inevitably, that the Abbey was a refuge for franc-tireurs and that if any arms were discovered, all the priests would be shot. The soldiers rampaging throughout the Abbey turned up the following: a small pistol, corroded with rust, in a night table; a sixteenth-century Swiss halberd in the sacristy; and, in an attic, a lamp constructed out of an old artillery shell from the Franco-Prussian War.

These dangerous items were triumphantly displayed. The priests thought their final hour had come. They administered last rites to each other, while the officers consulted. They were then led outside, but instead of being lined up in front of the 120 corpses that already lay on the ground in front of the Abbey, the priests were led off to the École Régimentaire. They were threatened and insulted en route, naturally. Officers took part.

After they were locked up, a superior officer berated the priests. Eyes blazing, his pipe clenched in his teeth, he growled, "You miserable servants of God, you're hypocrites who fool the people. You've preached war here and in France. You're responsible for all the dead strewn on the streets. You're going to be shot for your crimes. All the civilians are victims of your lies; they suffer on your account. You're the cause of the harm that's come to them..."[56] Protests by the priests were silenced.

The fathers were held for several days, fed on soup and dirty water. When the women were released from the Abbey on Wednesday, a number brought food for the priests, their first decent meal since Sunday. On the same day they were told by M. Van Rijckevorsel, the Dutch vice-consul who had been negotiating with the Germans, that they probably wouldn't be shot, but kept hostage until the troops passed through. (Van Rijckevorsel remained in Dinant during the German occupation and secretly recorded the testimony of dozens of eyewitnesses.) The following day, Thursday, the civilian prisoners at the École Regimentaire, of whom there were now more than seventy, were released, along with the Dean. The ranks of the priests had been thinned: on Monday, two of their number were led off – to be executed, everyone feared. (The pair were menaced repeatedly, spat on and beaten, but survived, thanks to the intervention of a couple of officers. They rejoined their fellow priests not far from Marche.)[57]

On Friday, the *Appel*, the roll call, was sounded early – at 5:00 a.m.. The fathers were lined up two-by-two and led out into the courtyard. As they waited in the cold, soaked by a fine drizzle, they were again sure the end was near. The day before, a superior officer had gone through the litany of accusations against the clergy, and revealed that the Germans were going to seize the opportunity the invasion afforded to wage a religious war – *ein Religionskrieg* – in Belgium.[58]

A little more than two hours later, an announcement was made at last: you won't be shot, but you'll be sent to Germany and imprisoned there. Five of the older or infirm priests were exempted, and the remaining thirty-three led out of the courtyard of the school, past the smoking ruins lining rue St. Jacques and east toward Ciney.

The priests were the object of curiosity to some of the troops they passed – at one point officers snapped pictures – but at Achêne, where the road was blocked by soldiers and wagons, the priests were subjected to renewed vilifications. They were spat upon, pummeled with fists, struck with riding whips and batons, and had water hurled at them. One soldier performed some blasphemous imitations of Catholic rites. Egged on by the impromptu performance, other soldiers shouted various obscenities at the fathers. When peasants attempted to bring food to the "dirty papists," they were held off by bayonets. The other prisoners were allowed to accept the food.[59]

Two times en route the priests heard a lone gunshot from a village they were passing, and then watched as soldiers eagerly invaded the hamlet, chased out the inhabitants and looted their homes. "For all of us it was clear as day that the so-called franc-tireurs were none other than the Germans themselves."[60]

At Marche, the priests were informed that they would not be sent to Germany after all. They were to be lodged in a Carmelite convent. Eventually an inquest was held. The officer in charge expressed his annoyance at the lack of any formal legal proceedings against the priests on the part of the officers in Dinant. A few days later, the men were released.

On December 29th, the priests were officially exonerated by the Military Governor of Namur, General von Longchamps.[61]

KASSEL: "THE MILITARY AUTHORITIES IN BERLIN ARE NOW CONVINCED THAT NO ONE FIRED IN DINANT"

The 416 men from all over Dinant who had been fortunate enough to be taken prisoner on Sunday were herded up to the Herbuchenne plateau above the Citadel. There they slept on a bit of straw. Before they were commanded to be silent, they had quizzed their guards as to what would be done with them. They received conflicting answers. Some were told they would be shot at dawn, some that they would be taken to Koblenz. More frequently they were told they would be sent to Marche, some twenty miles to the east, where the headquarters of the Third Army was located. There the generals would decide their fate.[62]

Maurice Tschoffen heard a worker complaining to some friends about how hungry he was. "And yet," he said, "I've never had so expensive a supper as last night"

"So what did you eat, then?" he was asked.

"Three 100-franc notes," he replied, smiling. "I swallowed them when the Germans searched us. They won't get their hands on them."[63]

No one was shot at dawn. Some of the prisoners, under armed guard, fetched water from a nearby farm, no doubt the Alardos', where they saw the bodies of the men. Nothing seemed to be planned for the morning. The officer in charge grew bored. "The captain...saw a fine stallion in a paddock. He called it, and when it got near him, he wantonly shot it dead with his revolver. Shortly afterwards (I did not see it myself, but several eye-witnesses told me of it) he killed a mare and a foal in the same way."[64]

Under the supervision of the captain, the men were searched yet again. What money a few of the men had managed to conceal was confiscated. The cautious officers flourished their pistols during this procedure.

Finally, in the afternoon, they set off toward Ciney. The procession passed burned and gutted hamlets. The soldiers they passed were more menacing than those they'd encountered the previous day.

> Everywhere we were abused and threatened. They made signs that we were going to be shot, to have our heads cut off, to be hanged. Filth was thrown at our heads. They spat in our faces. We kept our heads up, though; it was not we who were degraded. An officer superintending the westward march kept striking with a horse-whip everyone who passed within reach. Other officers in motor-cars – or a number of them – yelled at us or flourished revolvers in our direction. This happened wherever we met any troops, until we entrained.[65]

The second night, near Camaux, one of the prisoners went insane.

> About midnight there arose piercing, heartrending cries of "Help! Help!" We heard the soldiers say, "Don't shoot. He's mad." Then the sound of heavy blows and the falling of a body. The cries became fainter and at last ceased.
>
> Next morning a body was lying about twenty yards away from the camp, with one hand feebly moving. It was one of the prisoners – a poor fellow of limited intelligence. His father, who was with us, was forbidden to go near him. Nothing was done for him, and we departed, leaving him on the ground.[66]

The next day, after four boys under fourteen were released, the march east was resumed, only with a new formation. Formerly, columns of soldiers walked on either side of the civilians. Now the troops were placed between two rows, four men wide, of Dinantais. Later the men learned that there were rumors of a French detachment in the vicinity, trapped behind German lines.

After nine hours, they reached Marche. The streets were crowded and everyone hoped to be spotted by an acquaintance who would report back to anxious relatives in Dinant. The prisoners were housed in a room that was supposed to accommodate one hundred soldiers. Once more they were searched, for the people of Marche had been permitted to bring the prisoners shoes (many had been taken off in slippers or sabots), hats, caps, sandwiches, and coffee. The Germans devoured the food, throwing to the prisoners, some time later, a few crusts of bread.

The next morning the men were taken to the railway station in Melreux. Here a train of cattle-cars was waiting. The men were hustled on board with kicks and punches. They were locked in. The dung had only just been removed. No straw was provided. After a two-hour delay, the train took off.

> Every time the train stopped, the soldiers guarding the stations insulted us. When we reached Germany it was still worse. If the platform at which the train stopped was not on the side where the door was open, that was at once shut and the other opened... We were treated like beasts in a menagerie. Officers and soldiers – and they were everywhere – gave the lead to the civilians. The women and children kept on insulting us and making threatening gestures.
>
> Our escort was welcomed as if they had done something heroic.
>
> At some station or other we saw a woman cheering from her window. She unfastened her dress, showed her breasts, and made as if to offer them to the soldiers.[67]

At 3:00 a.m., after a journey of twenty-three hours, the train pulled into Kassel. As they were marched off to the prison, the men were astonished to see jeering crowds lining the street, despite the hour. Women and children were among them.

The men were locked up, three or four to each cell. No father was permitted to be with his son. After two days, the men were allowed to shower and made to fill out identification forms.

> The prison authorities were astounded at the criminals who had been brought to them! The majority were artisans and tradespeople. There were also the burgomaster of Dinant, a deputy-burgomaster, professors..., the postmaster, the inspector of forests, ... lawyers, three assistant judges, two judges, the public prosecutor and one of his deputies.[68]

If the Germans truly believed in the myth of an organized attack by francs-tireurs in Dinant, they had in their hands the chief culprits; the plan could hardly have been executed without the knowledge and complicity of the town's leading citizens. In fact, the identities of the prisoners seems to have precipitated new inquiries. After eight days of imprisonment, the civilians were assembled in a courtyard and informed that they had been found not guilty. There had been no trial, of course, nor any inquest at which they had been invited to testify. But despite the verdict, the men would continue to be detained, they were told, "for reasons of public safety."[69]

Now the men were permitted to write home. However, they had to wait over a week before they were provided with writing materials, and then, in the end, fewer than a dozen letters ever reached Dinant.

Like generations of political prisoners after them, the civilians were surprised to discover how much better the common criminals were treated than were they, and how much more humane the criminals were than their jailers. Criminals could open their frosted windows to glimpse the courtyard and countryside; this was forbidden to civilians. Criminals had a chair and a bed. The Belgians were made to sleep on straw. This was soon pulverized to dust, but was not renewed for two months. Various excuses were offered. Criminals were given exercise every day except Sunday. Until mid-October, civilians were taken out only once a week, for about an hour. They were not permitted to walk in pairs. Criminals received lard, herring, and meat. The civilians received a pound of bread each day. In addition, they had "a pint of some tepid fluid that may have been coffee" in the morning, three-quarters of a quart of greasy turnip or cabbage soup at noon and another pint of soup at night. Three times in three months they were treated to potatoes. At the beginning of their sojourn, some of the German prisoners threw bread into the courtyard of the civilians, but the authorities stopped this practice.

The Dinant prisoners, Tschoffen recalled, were always hungry. At the end of October, those with German relatives were permitted to receive money from them. With this they purchased bread, sausage, and medicines.

The medical care was deplorable. One prisoner, a young man, had a slight bullet wound on the forearm. It had begun to fester on the march, but he was refused medical attention for several days after the men had arrived at Kassel. Finally, the entire arm was amputated, but so tardily and so badly that he died two days later. "The infirmary, according to those who went there, was a marvel of uncleanliness."[70] Neither the young man's father nor his brothers were permitted to see him while he was still alive or after he died.

Boredom weighed heavily on the men, competing with their anxieties about family members still in Dinant. Eventually the prisoners were given something to do. Tailors and shoemakers were permitted to practice their trade. Others were assigned to do gardening, paving, washing, meal preparation, and other activities.

Dominoes and cards were improvised, and even chessmen, from small breadcrumbs.

Then, abruptly, the civilians were released.

One fine day they told us that we were about to leave. Our return was carried out in four parties. The first left on November 18th. The others followed at intervals of a few days.

It would be unjust not to mention the courage with which all bore their captivity. "Let them keep us as long as they want, provided they are driven out and we shall be masters in our own house when we return," one of the prisoners, a young worker, told me. He thus expressed a feeling which I know was held by all: Liberty for us, yes, but for our country first.[71]

Before he was shipped back to Dinant, Maurice Tschoffen was told by the prison governor, "The military authorities at Berlin are now convinced that no one fired at Dinant."[72]

THE SQUARE AT PHILIPPEVILLE While the men of Dinant who had been captured by the Germans were marched east to Kassel, the women and children and old men trekked westward to Philippeville. They were joined en route by refugees from other towns and villages along the Meuse between Namur and Givet. Also converging on Philippeville were those fleeing from the towns lining the Sambre from Charleroi to Namur, and from the farms and hamlets in both regions.

Philippeville was then serving as the headquarters of the General Staff of the Fifth Army, and the depressing spectacle was witnessed by its officers, including General Lanrezac, who stood all morning grimly watching the columns shuffle past. Among the witnesses was Lieutenant Edward Spears, the British Liaison Officer with the Fifth Army. "A grey mob," he recalled,

grey because the black clothes most of them wore were covered with dust, was filing endlessly by; they occupied the whole width of the road, pouring past like a crowd returning from a race meeting, but in absolute silence, the only sound being that of very tired feet dragging on the *pavés*. Each individual in that slowly-moving mass looked the embodiment of a personal tragedy; men and women with set staring faces, carrying heavy bundles, moving on they knew not where, formed a background of grim despair to this or that group or individual whose more vivid suffering seemed to illuminate that drab flow of desolation.

I can still see a couple of young girls, sisters perhaps, helping each other, hardly able to drag themselves along, the blood from their torn feet oozing through their low silk shoes; a very sick woman, who looked as if she were dying, balanced somehow on a perambulator; a paralytic old man in a wheelbarrow, pushed by his sturdy daughter; a very old, very respectable couple, who for years had probably done no more than walk arm in arm round a small garden, now, still arm in arm, were helping each other in utter bewilderment of mind and exhaustion of body down the long meaningless road. I remember too a small boy playing the man and encouraging his mother, and an exhausted woman sinking under the weight of her two babies.

Boys pull a wagon through a damaged village or town in Namur province.

And none might stop: the gendarmes pounced on any who tarried and shoved them forward. If they halted they would hopelessly block the communications they were already so seriously encumbering.... Here and there [was] a huge cart drawn by oxen, packed with children. Some of these carts must have contained the entire infant population of a village thrown in pell mell. Were their parents trudging behind, or had they fallen by the way? The column must go endlessly on, whoever might drop out or get left behind, on and on and on, a wretched, racked, miserable mass of humanity, whose motive power was fear, and whose urge was a sound, the dull rumble of guns, ominously near, growling ceaselessly to the north.

Whenever there came a particular sharp burst of artillery fire rending the air like a sudden thunder clap, the whole miserable column trembled and staggered forward, all but the oxen moving faster for a moment, then relapsing into the former slow drag.

The morning typifies war as it really is. It destroyed once and for all such illusions as any of us may still have cherished concerning what is after all only a dreary massacre, a stupefying alternation of boredom, fatigue and fear.

When those who were at Philippeville that day meet and fall to talking of old times, they always end by saying – "Do you remember the square at Philippeville?" and there is a silence, for no words are needed and none are adequate to describe that dreadful scene.[73]

CHAPTER 9
Leuven: Preliminaries

SAINT THOMAS HOSPITAL Hervé de Gruben, a student at the Higher Institute of Philosophy (Institute St. Thomas), left Leuven on July 22nd, just before the three-week examination period ended. He was looking forward to a restful vacation in the country.

> Scarcely had I settled there when, in the newspapers of the 25th, I read Austria's ultimatum to Serbia. Then one grave item of news succeeded another, causing general anxiety.
>
> Some private business brought me back to Leuven on the 30th. I was eager to know what the masters I had left there thought of the situation and what was their forecast of the future. I rang the bell at the Institute... The examinations were over, the students had gone. In the lecture hall, where the examiners had sat, the big table was still covered with its green cloth. Presently I encountered the President of the Institute, Monseigneur Deploige, and his friend and colleague Canon Thiéry. Both were at work in a classroom, clearing away the furniture, which they were removing to the attics.
>
> Surprised to see them so busily employed in this unusual way, I asked what they were doing.
>
> "We are going to arrange an ambulance for the wounded," was the reply, as they continued to carry away the benches.
>
> "Then you think we shall have war?"
>
> "You see that we do."
>
> I then recalled an incident that had taken place two months before. In May or June, a German spy had been discovered in Brussels who had made a list of motor petrol depots and had procured the addresses of the generals of the Belgian Army. "Information of this sort," Mgr. Deploige had said at a students' club to which I belonged, "is collected by the enemy on the eve of war," and they showed us on a map where the German invasion would take place. We had been incredulous.[1]

While at Lourdes in June, the two priests had asked the nurses and aides accompanying the pilgrimage if they would be willing to serve at the Institute St. Thomas during the next war. They had agreed.

...I returned to the country in the evening, pensive and still a little skeptical. On the following Sunday, August 2nd, I read in the papers that the German Minister at Brussels had just declared to the correspondent of *Le Soir:* "Perhaps you may see your neighbor's house in flames, but the fire will spare your dwelling."

Forty-eight hours later Belgium was invaded by the German Army.[2]

A few days later de Gruben returned to Leuven to offer his services as a stretcher-bearer to the newly renamed St. Thomas Hospital. De Gruben was amazed at the transformation.

The house was humming like a hive. Nurses and stretcher-bearers were coming in to be registered, to get their identification cards and their Red Cross armbands... The experimental psychology lab had been turned into a model operating room; the apparatus for sterilization was installed in the small room adjoining this; radiology had found a place in the large classroom; the chem lab was converted into a pharmacy. In the reading-room were pile bales of cotton, bundles of gauze, stacks of sheets, pillowcases and shirts; the nurses were already at work making bandages.[3]

The doctors did not entirely forget that they were professors of medicine: "notices written in chalk on a blackboard invited nurses and stretcher-bearers to attend daily lectures."

The town itself had altered no less radically.

The walls were covered with official notices relating to mobilization, requisitions and the engagement of volunteers; one of them, reminding the inhabitants that the defense of the country was entrusted exclusively to the Army, enjoined civilians who possessed arms to bring them at once to the Stadhuis. Long trains of motorcars, laden with provisions, were rushing through on their way to Liège. Troops marched past, loudly cheered by the population; the police kept guard on the Grote Markt, where the Headquarters Staff was established, and now and then, in an automobile, we observed the tall figure of the King.[4]

Léon van der Essen, a Leuven history professor, was among the thousands who watched the arrival of the 2nd Division as it passed through town on its way east. Van der Essen was serving in the *Guarde civique,* and was on duty at an ammunition depot.

With the first streaks of light we heard the rhythmic tramp of feet on the Mechelen road; soon singing became audible and came nearer: we could recognize the melody and the words of "The Lion of Flanders." Then, in the grey morning light, the head of the column appeared on the sunken road which enters the city under the slopes of Keizersberg. In spite of the fatigue of the march, the soldiers appeared joyful and proud, covered with dust and dripping with perspiration, but in perfect order, without stragglers. Soon the street was lined with spectators, mostly peasants and workmen's wives. The general enthusiasm was shown by the cheering, the echoes of which grew fainter as the troops penetrated further into the city. Never before had Leuven worn such an air of rejoicing, with all the houses gay with flags and the streets full of enthusiastic townsfolk preparing a warm welcome for the soldiers. From everywhere they were brought dainties, cigars, tobacco, and beer; they were overwhelmed with attentions and flattery. Never before had there been seen such touching unanimity. Factory girls left their work to bring the soldiers their simple lunches, university professors kept open house and handed round armfuls of bottled beer. The torrent of hospitality was such that the commandant...was forced to take repressive measures in the interest of the health of his men.[5]

The division continued on to Tienen, on the Gete. The festive atmosphere remained, as de Gruben observed.

The national flag was flying on every house. Animated groups were talking eagerly in front of the railway station, on the pavement and on the boulevards; men who had not known each other the day before seemed to have become close friends; the tri-colored cockade was in every buttonhole. The subject of conversation was always the same: the War; Germany's insolent ultimatum; the proud reply of the Belgian Government; the invasion; the siege of Liège; the first encounters.

Two questions recurred perpetually: "Where are the Allies?" "When will the great battle take place?" And the newspapers invariably answered: "The Allies are where they should be. The great battle is imminent."[6]

The volunteers staffing St. Thomas Hospital avidly followed the progress of the war. But along with news of military operations came other, disquieting rumors.

There were reports that at Visé and in the outskirts of Liège there had been massacres of civilians, and that churches and private houses had been burnt. Most of us refused to believe these horrors. Among the staff there were many who had studied in Germany. "War is not waged in this fashion in the 20th century," they said. "Germany is too civilized to be capable of such atrocities; you will see presently how well her army will behave."[7]

For several days it appeared as if the great battle everyone anticipated, the battle that would decide the war, might be waged close to Leuven. Then, abruptly, around noon on the 18th, the news whipped through town that the General Staff had taken off for Antwerp. The Army was retreating to its stronghold. All the Belgian wounded in the hospital were to be conveyed to the train station.

By late afternoon only two men remained, a Belgian soldier in the final stages of consumption and a Pomeranian uhlan with a perforated lung. "He had arrived two evenings before, in a state of terror. The German officers had told him that the Belgians killed their prisoners and wounded. After forty-eight hours of compassionate care, he was beginning to take heart."[8]

The mood in Leuven altered dramatically. "The flags disappeared, the shops were closed. A terrible agitation spread through the town. Then suddenly, at three o'clock, there was a stampede towards the station when it became known that the last trains for Brussels were leaving, and that afterwards the railway bridge was to be blown up. Some took luggage with them; others had no time to pack anything."[9]

The evening of the 18th, after the staff had thoroughly cleaned the empty hospital, they heard strange noises in the street,

> not the measured tramp, now familiar to our ears, of marching troops, but the confused noise of a disorderly crowd, in which the shouts of men, the moans of women, the crying of children and the grinding of wheels on the pavement were mingled.
>
> Hundreds of villagers were pouring in from the direction of Tienen. They were fleeing wildly; old men staggering along, mothers dragging their children by the hand, young girls carrying household wares tied up in sheets over their shoulders. Sick persons half-dressed had been brought along in wheelbarrows. Some dozen babies were crying in a hand-cart. In the midst of the flood, swept along by the living tide, were soldiers, covered with dust, their heads bowed, and their kepis in their hands.
>
> A family – father, mother, and five children – halted at our gate. "Come in," we cried. "Come and rest."
>
> "No, no. We have lost our youngest. He's only two. Someone put him on a cart. Pray God we may find him!"
>
> "But tell us what's happened!"
>
> "Look!"
>
> The peasant pointed in the direction of Tienen. The sky was red. Houses and farms were ablaze.[10]

At around 10:00 p.m. on the 18th, a Belgian sergeant warned the staff that the army's rearguard was now engaged at nearby Roosbeek and Boutersem and that the hospital should expect the arrival of the wounded shortly. Those on duty an hour later would never forget the first new patient.

> A cart pulled up in front of the hospital. A young army doctor, a former student at Leuven, was standing in it. A nurse, a young French woman attached to the Belgian ambulance service, was with him.
>
> "A wounded man," she said. "He is horribly mutilated."
>
> In the dim light we distinguished a human form in a blue overcoat lying on the straw at the bottom of the cart. A stream of blood was trickling to the pavement.

It was for everybody a moment of indescribable emotion. Mgr. Deploige and M. Thiéry clambered into the cart. A few moments later they returned, walking slowly, and deposited their ghastly burden in the operating room, which was brilliantly lighted by arc-lamps. The wounded man was a splendidly built Fleming. His right arm had been torn off at the shoulder, his left forearm shattered; both eyes were hanging out of their sockets on his swollen and blackened face. The unhappy man was conscious. Canon Thiéry confessed and absolved him. At the conclusion of the rite, the soldier murmured "Long live Belgium!" The operating surgeon, Professor Schockaert, suppressed his tears as he set to work. Death came to the rescue of the poor mutilated creature...

In the pocket of his tunic we found a letter from his mother, stained with blood: "Do your duty, my son," she had written. "Defend your country bravely. We are all praying for you here. God keep Belgium."[11]

The next morning, the 19th, retreating Belgian soldiers filled the streets. They were mostly in good spirits. One assured De Gruben that they would soon return.

At 1:00 p.m., Belgian guns covering the retreat began firing from just outside the city gates. Half an hour later the artillerymen came galloping through town. "They're here," one of the gunners yelled.[12]

It was a chilling feeling. Leuven was to be occupied, cut off from the rest of the country. There would be annoying regulations, endless requisitions. The trains, streetcars, telegraph and telephone systems would be commandeered by the Germans. There would be no Belgian newspapers, no letters. Life would assuredly be difficult. But despite the terrorized villagers who streamed through town, most residents didn't imagine anything worse than repression and shortages.

⊰⊱

Not all the Belgian rearguard retreated. Another young Leuvener, René Chambry, watched with horror and admiration as three Belgian soldiers loping westward passed the intersection of the Tiensesteenweg and Geldenaaksevest. Two continued toward the center of town, but the third stopped, knelt down, calmly raised his rifle and resumed firing at the advancing Germans. He was quickly killed.

A lone uhlan ventured as far as the first houses in Blijde-Inkomststraat. He waited a moment, then turned and shouted to his squadron, *"Alles ist frei!"*[13]

⊰⊱

A Dutch doctor and professor of medicine at the Catholic University of Leuven, Adriaan Noyons, returned home from the St. Thomas Hospital just before 1:00 p.m. on the 19th. (The Higher Institute of Philosophy was part of the Leo XIII Seminary, and the hospital was sometimes referred to as Hospital Leo XIII.) Noyons lived on the outskirts of town, beyond the Tiensepoort. From his house, he could see clearly the fighting retreat of the Belgian cavalry on the hills above Boven-Lo. He observed individual horsemen fall. Then a stray bullet whizzed past him. The war had come to his front porch. As Dr. Noyons made his way back into town with his wife, the gunfire increased. A servant of a neighbor, Meneer Schallaert, was hit and killed – the first victim in Leuven.[14]

OCCUPATION Around three o'clock on the 19th, two German officers clambered up the steps of the Stadhuis, where the town council was in session, apprehensively awaiting their arrival. An usher directed them to the council chamber. A staff officer, Captain Kriegsheim, announced that the German Army had entered Leuven. He asked the council members if there were any remaining Belgian troops in town, and was assured that they had all left. The civilians had nothing to fear, then, Kriegsheim said. There would be no extraordinary war levy, only those requisitions required by "military necessity." However, the Captain continued, any hostile acts would provoke immediate reprisals – "as we 've done in neighboring villages." The burgomaster, Léon Colins, hastened to assure the emissaries that the civilians would be peaceful. All weapons had been turned in two weeks earlier. Besides, this was a university town, over five hundred years old. It was one of the most important intellectual centers in Europe. In consequence, it had been declared an open city, and he trusted its status would be respected by its occupiers.[15]

Without making any further promises, the officers asked that one member of the council accompany them as they verified that the Dijle bridges were still intact. Alderman Van der Kelen volunteered. He returned an hour later badly shaken. He'd been conducted to the hill overlooking Kessel-Lo. The countryside around him presented a horrifying spectacle: bodies of dead peasants lay on the ground, entire villages were in flames. This was to be the fate, he was warned, of any town where the population proved hostile.[16]

After the threats, the next order of business was the requisitioning of supplies and the billeting of troops. Burgomaster Colins offered the Germans the use of the town's military barracks and the communal schools. These were rejected. The soldiers would be billeted on the local residents. As for the "military necessities," over 100,000 francs worth of food were demanded within forty-eight hours, including 40,000 kilos of meat and fifty-one casks of wine. The alternative to provisioning the troops was a fine of 200,000 francs a day.[17]

The fifty-one casks proved to be a drop in the bucket, needless to say. Throughout the day individual officers made further requisitions and soldiers casually helped themselves to bottles from the cellars of empty homes.

"Ten thousand bottles here, thirty casks there, were requisitioned. Their demands in the matter of wine were continual: they must have been afflicted with an insatiable thirst," a lawyer observed a month later.

> This unquenchable thirst of the German soldier will be an unforgettable characteristic of this campaign. The troops smashed the doors of many unoccupied houses and pillaged the cellars. The private residences in Leopoldstraat and in Volksplaats, in the wealthy quarter, were devastated, and this under the eyes of the General Staff.[18]

In several cases the soldiers did not content themselves with the wine and champagne. A number of empty residences were thoroughly looted. Particularly scandalous was the ransacking of the home and laboratory of Dr. Arthur van Gehuchten, a world-renowned professor of neurology. This was the first shock for a self-proclaimed "friend of German *Kultur*," Professor of Philosophy Laurent Noël.

> I thought it was impossible that we should experience any harm from German soldiers. We might have to pay, and to give *Einquartierung;* but matters would be conducted in an orderly fashion, because everything in Germany goes by rule. And also, I believed in the theories of international law, that non-combatants had to be respected.

But troops arriving in the evening

> plundered a number of houses. To be precise, the house of Professor Van Gehuchten, a very prominent neurologist known and esteemed in every German university...was entered. His papers were actually torn to shreds and his scientific instruments broken to pieces, an act of sheer wantonness. ...Similar things happened at other houses. Pictures were slashed with bayonets and furniture destroyed. Acts which would have disgraced a beast were performed.[19]

The pillaging of Van Gehuchten's residence, another witness recalled, "aroused intense indignation. It was brought to the notice of the German General, who seemed very much annoyed by it, but ordered no measure of protection."[20] A number of others commented on this outrage.[21]

On the 19th, Professor Albert Carnoy also left town. A young servant, Maria Cammaerts, agreed to house-sit. When she showed up the following day, she found that

> the German soldiers had taken possession of the place and they refused to let me enter. The Germans had five motorcars outside the premises and I saw them removing from my master's house wine, blankets, books, etc., and placing them in the vans. They stripped the whole place of anything of value, including furniture. The whole place was in disorder and I saw the soldiers smashing glass and crockery articles and the windows.[22]

The troops also broke into the communal museum, smashed the display cases, and made off with gold coins and other objects of value. Soldiers would later attempt to use the money as payment in cafés and stores. But other soldiers and officers were already issuing receipts bearing the words "payable by the town of Leuven" or "payable by the German government." On the following day, too, all the cash left behind in the private banks in Leuven was confiscated: 500 francs at the Bank of the Dijle, 16,000 at the People's Bank.[23] Soon after, all the German currency well-intentioned soldiers had used the first day to pay for their meals was also seized by officers, in exchange for more pieces of paper. When one shopkeeper questioned the worth of these notes, the officer replied coolly, "He who loses pays."[24] Another officer simply pulled out his pistol, pointed it at the café owner, and growled, "Here's your receipt."[25]

◄◄--►►

German forces had arrived from three directions, but the great mass of troops marched along Stationsstraat, down Brusselsestraat and out the Brussels gate, passing the length of the town.[26] The Germans intended to overawe the population by a massive show of force, as they would do in Brussels two days later. The parade, which commenced about 2:30 p.m., was almost reassuring.

> First came the cyclists... Following the scouts tramped the infantry in compact masses, marching in time to the shrill cry of fifes and the grave rumble of drums. The faces

of these men were young, hard and heavy; their blue eyes gleamed in proud certainty of victory. Now and again, at a hoarse word of command, all mouths opened to chant the *Wacht am Rhein*. The hussars came next, riding spirited chargers; haughty and elegant, they looked about them with an air of detachment, glancing scornfully at the inhabitants who had ventured out on the thresholds of their houses. Then there was another interminable procession of infantry in spiked helmets, and, after these, came the field guns and a long string of ammunition wagons, ambulances and field kitchens. Finally, more infantry battalions, more batteries of artillery and squadrons of uhlans and dragoons. By the side of the marching columns, cyclists unrolled telephone wires and fastened them to the street lamps and electric posts. At the head of the battalions and squadrons rode officers, holding in their hands maps of the district in leather cases...[27]

The procession continued for several hours. Then the homes were occupied. Sergeants chalked on every door the number of men to be lodged there. Transport troops camped on the streets; officers were generally billeted with professors and the town's other *haute-bourgeoisie*.

René Chambry's family lived on Léopoldstraat, in an upper-class neighborhood.

Upon the stroke of 8 o'clock, a violent ring at the bell resounded. As our future guests found that we were slow to open the door, blows of a rifle butt immediately began to shake it. An officer, who was raging on the doorstep, shouted out to us, "Quarters for fifty men!" He had no billeting ticket, but all discussion was useless; we were obliged to submit. Fifty soldiers, as though our house were a barrack! My father convinced the officer of the impossibility of our receiving fifty men, and we offered to take twenty-five, including four non-commissioned officers. The officer agreed, and, revolver in hand, he came into the house and inspected every bedroom minutely. *"Wenn es nicht gut geht, alles kaputt."* That was how he finished the business.

Our house is very large, without being a barrack, as I was saying. But the officer was not content that the men should sleep in the annex at the back; they must be lodged in the five available bedrooms. Luckily the non-commissioned officers were agreeable people. "Go to bed in peace," they said to us; "a sentry will keep guard at the door on the street, which must remain open." None of the twenty-five men spoke French.

We gave them what was necessary for washing. Throughout the night we kept them supplied with coffee, bread, and meat. The soldiers constantly repeated, *"Die Belgieren sind unsere Kameraden, aber die Franzosen nicht."* and they added, "We are going on straight to Paris."

So we had no cause of complaint. One of the soldiers, however, had been to loot the cellar of a neighbor; he returned with several bottles of wine. For in the town the doors of several houses, deserted by their owners, had been burst in, the cellars emptied, and, by way of thanks, there was to be found the next day filth in every corner.[28]

Not far off, on Stationsstraat, Julien Sterckx was obliged to accommodate no less than forty soldiers. He also had no complaints; at least within his home "the troops behaved decently."[29]

For most residents, this was the only night they were obliged to host their conquerors. Many soldiers and officers were polite, and even sympathetic. Major Förster himself, the Commandant of Leuven until the 22nd, was always courteous, though the same could not be said of his subordinates.[30]

A general who lodged in Stationsstraat with the wealthy businessman and philanthropist Pierre David-Fischbach and his son Léon enjoyed the old merchant's warm hospitality. On his departure, he issued his hosts a certificate testifying to the fact that he had been well treated. They might show it to any German officer who came to their door, he assured them, and their persons and property would be respected.[31] The retired Belgian Colonel Neuchâtel received a similar testimonial.[32]

Officers even occasionally confided in their hosts. Julien Sterckx was told by an officer – whose name and regiment he never learned – that en route to Leuven "he had seen things done by German soldiers which had made his heart bleed. He said, 'I saw a poor woman with two little children in her arms and watching her own house burning. I am a father myself, and I cannot bear this. It is not war; it is butchery.'" The officer also mentioned events at nearby Aarschot.[33] Another officer, taking his leave early the next morning from the convent of the Sisters of St. Mary at Wesemael, muttered something about Aarschot as well. There were tears in his eyes.[34]

Early the next day, most of the forces moved on.

At 5:00 a.m., Hervé de Gruben heard bugles and the shouts of the *feldwebeln*. Then came *"Helm ab!"* – helmet off. It was time for a prayer. When this had been chanted, the men roared, *"Hoch dem Kaiser!"* and the field kitchens began to pass along the ranks with coffee. Soon officers barked out marching orders and the massive army rolled off toward Brussels.

When we went out, toward noon, Leuven was like a stable. Streets, pavements, public squares and trampled flower-beds had disappeared under a layer of manure. In the station buildings the furniture had been smashed and the railway tickets thrown about on the floor. In Leopoldstraat the house of Professor Van Gehuchten, who was spending his holiday at the seaside, had been broken into. The furniture was strewn about on the floor, empty bottles were lying in the hall. The same sight was to be seen in other houses whose owners were absent. The shelves of the provision shops were empty; meat, bread and preserves had all been carried off by the invading flood.[35]

Remaining behind was the 3rd Battalion of the 53rd Regiment, Landsturm Battalion Neuss. And plastered on the walls throughout town was an ominous proclamation in barbaric French which warned sternly against "franc-tireur" activities, claiming *"acts of the most gruesome cruelty"* had already taken place "in great numbers."[36] An 8:00 p.m. curfew was imposed on the town and citizens were required to hand in their weapons and to keep all doors open and widows lit up at night.

> The German flag, the symbol of occupation, floated over the Town Hall. The *Etappen-Kommandant*, Major von Manteuffel, a little fat man with a round head and furtive eyes, was installed in the session-room of the Communal Council. The great hall on the ground floor, where the guard slept, was full of mattresses and trusses of straw; in a corner there was a pile of foils with the buttons on, and pocket-pistols. Shot-guns and revolvers had been handed over to the Belgian authorities a fortnight ago; when the Germans repeated the order to hand over all weapons, our citizens hastened to give them all that was left – ornamental arms.[37]

The threatening notice had been printed in Germany; the typeface was not one used in Belgium. It had made frequent appearances since the 4th. There was no Flemish translation, though Lodewijk Grondijs, the Dutch professor who had witnessed the devastation at Aarschot, picked up one with the text in Russian.[38] It referred to "mayors," but there were none in Belgium. Would lives be jeopardized because of "cruelties" invented in Berlin before the war?

The answer came the next day, with the taking of two hostages, the *échevains* Van der Kelen and Schmit. The burgomaster was permitted to go home. The stress had exacerbated a chronic heart condition and he was confined to his bed. The two hostages were replaced the following day by Mgr. Ladeuze, Rector of the University, the senior parish priest, Father Ceulemans, the Dean of St. Pieter's, Judge De Bruyn, and Meneer Van den Eynde, a senator and member of the Brabant Provincial Council. Also serving as hostage during the next two days were another judge, another senator, and the Vice-Rector of the University, Mgr. Coenraets. Town and gown, layman and cleric, were impartially represented.[39]

The hostages were confined to the Stadhuis, where, as De Gruben observed, a number of troops were billeted on the ground floor. The

General Staff had chosen more comfortable quarters in the Palace of Justice. Within the Stadhuis, the ante-chamber of the Council Hall was strewn with straw, but the sentries stationed there smoked incessantly, despite repeated warnings from the hostages. Otherwise, however, neither lives nor property appeared to be in imminent jeopardy after the first twenty-four hours.

Meals came to the hostages irregularly – food brought by the townspeople often wound up in the guards' mess – but otherwise conditions were tolerable. The conduct of the senior officers toward the university and town officials was outwardly correct, and no one believed that any among the cowed residents of Leuven would offend the Germans in the least, though there was some concern about nine common criminals of German nationality who had been "liberated" by soldiers the first day. However, at the request of the Public Prosecutor, Major von Manteuffel ordered that they be recaptured and confined to the barracks. Six were caught.[40]

Things changed dramatically on Monday, the 24th.

"YOU MEAN A PRUSSIAN OFFICER HAS NO RIGHTS HERE IN BELGIUM?" At about 9:00 in the evening, two cars pulled up in front of the house of Marinus Rutgers, the director of the Dutch-owned utility company responsible for the town's water supply.[41] Rutgers, himself a Dutch citizen and his country's consul in Leuven, was hustled into the first car; in the second was Léon Colins, the burgomaster. They were driven to the train station. Here a captain and lieutenant in charge of railway transport questioned them about diverting water to the station for the locomotives; the Germans were having trouble operating the pumps. (The station's water supply was independent of that of the town's.) The burgomaster had tried to explain to the soldiers who had been sent to fetch him that he had nothing to do with this matter, but orders were orders.

Seated around a table with Colins, Rutgers and the two officers discussed how best to connect the city's water system with the station's. Suddenly a colonel burst in. In a booming voice he demanded to know why two German officers were sitting with two "bourgeois." The two officers leapt to their feet. They began to explain who their guests were and what they were doing there.

As soon as the colonel learned that he had before him the town's burgomaster, he demanded, in a loud and threatening voice, that he be immediately supplied with meat, bread, and mattresses for the two hundred men under his command who had just detrained. He wanted straw and hay for the horses as well. "While I attempted to interpret for the burgomaster, the two officers took the opportunity to slip out, and we were left alone in the presence of the worst brute I've ever encountered in my life," Rutgers recalled.[42]

Four soldiers were assigned to guard the hapless Colins. If the supplies weren't delivered in their entirety within an hour, the officer bellowed, the burgomaster would be shot. In order to save some time, Rutgers asked politely if he couldn't be taken to police headquarters in one of the many cars parked outside the station; the police would then be able to help round up the food and mattresses. Rutgers could take a Belgian car if he wanted to, the colonel shouted, but he would never permit him to sit in a German car. (All Belgian automobiles had been confiscated by the Germans, of course.)

So Rutgers set off on foot for the police station, about a two-thirds of a mile away. Out of breath, the thirty-three-year-old director explained his mission to the eight policemen on duty. They all rushed back to the train station and began furiously ringing doorbells and calling out to the residents that meat, bread, and mattresses were urgently needed or their burgomaster would be killed. Mattresses were dragged downstairs. Servants brought out parcels of meat. There was not much bread left; it was after 10:00 p.m. One police officer headed for the town's slaughterhouse. Rutgers himself ran off to the home of the director of Public Works to secure some straw and hay.

Then he spotted an angry Emile Schmit, the *échevin* in charge of public education, who was hustling to the station from the Stadhuis, where he'd been informed of the situation. Schmit, a lawyer, spoke perfect German, and de Rutgers accompanied him back to the station, providing additional details. The *échevin* ignored the fulminating colonel and addressed his adjutant. The town was under the orders of the commandant, and all requisitions had to come through him. The colonel had no right to impose ad hoc requisitions.[43]

"*Sie meinen, ein preussischen Offizier hat hier in Belgien keine Rechte?*" the colonel yelled furiously. (You mean a Prussian officer has no rights here in Belgium?)[44]

Schmit tried to reason with the man. At this late hour, he would have much better luck if he requested the supplies directly from the commandant, who had access to abundant stores. The colonel was not interested in such utilitarian considerations. If everything he'd demanded wasn't provided within an hour, he vowed, he would carry out his threat to execute Colins.[45] Soldiers with fixed bayonets then hustled Schmit and de Rutgers from the station.

But the first of the provisions, a cart filled with meat, was already arriving, and Rutgers followed it back in. Then he glimpsed a young lieutenant from von Manteuffel's staff entering the station ahead of the cart. Rutgers missed the man's laconic message, but witnessed the response.

> The colonel immediately pitched into him. For at least ten minutes he spat at him the most wide-ranging insults and the most energetic curses, with a torrent of words and a choice of expressions that would make the most foul-mouthed porter jealous. Standing at attention, his right hand on his kepi, the young lieutenant took all the abuse that rained down on him heroically, without uttering a word of protest. It was beautiful. When the colonel had finally unburdened himself, he consented to set the burgomaster free and to give up his booty.[46]

The next day Rutgers was advised that the Germans had figured out how to operate the station pumps and so it wouldn't be necessary to tamper with the city's water supply system after all.

⊰⊱

The late-night requisitioning created as much of a scandal as the pillaging and looting the first night. Most of the residents in the streets around the station had been in their nightclothes, preparing for bed, or were already asleep.

The loquacious Baron Alfred Orban de Xivry gave up three mattresses from his house and two from his daughter's next door. No sooner had they been hauled off than eleven officers showed up requesting lodging at the two homes. The Baron apologized for the uncomfortable beds he was obliged to offer.[47] Also offering an apology was Major Walter von Manteuffel, the new Commandant. A German apology was something of a rarity in August 1914, and Colins was duly appreciative. Von Manteuffel even promised that he would not take any more hostages after the 25th.[48]

⊰⊱

The events of Monday night were disturbing, but they were also reassuring. Von Manteuffel had, in the end, asserted his authority; the rogue colonel had been obliged to back down. Perhaps the dispatching of his youngest staff officer to the station had been a deliberate rebuke. But it may have merely reflected the major's own dread of confrontations. If the chubby *Schreibtischoffizier*, polite, though evasive, did not himself seem to pose a threat to Leuveners, Schmit and his colleagues couldn't help but wonder if the major would be able to control undisciplined troops in larger numbers and over-rule officers more importunate and higher-ranking than the combustible colonel.

PORTENTS Very little news came into Leuven. What did arrive was not reassuring. The fires in the villages to the east, Kessel-Lo and Korbeek-Lo, had been visible throughout the city. More detailed reports of what had happened to the residents began circulating. Some stories were exaggerated, but the reality was sufficiently grim. As might be expected, residents were especially riveted by reports of rapes.

On August 20th, a couple and their sixteen-year-old daughter, the Lamproyes, were arrested in their own home in Korbeek-Lo. According to the girl's uncle, she was then taken to the nearby château of Mr. Frantzer. While the parents were held off at gunpoint, ten soldiers forced the girl to drink wine, then led her off to a lawn behind the château, where five or six of the men raped her. The girl resisted, and was stabbed several times with a bayonet. The parish priest, Pastoor Rosiers, was able to bring her to a Leuven hospital the next day. He protested vigorously to German authorities.[49] This may have been the young woman examined on the 20th by Dr. Tits in the Leo XIII Hospital, and then transferred to the St. Pieter Hospital. But this young woman, stabbed and repeatedly violated beside the Tiensesteenweg, may well have been another victim.[50]

An additional rape – of a visibly pregnant woman – was reported the day before in Korbeek-Lo. There was still another at Kessel-Lo two days later, according to another witness: the old father, defending his married daughter, was shot and killed in the presence of neighbors.[51] A sixteen-year-old girl died from bayonet wounds at Leuven's main hospital after having been raped in Herent.[52] There were undoubtedly other rapes in the farms and hamlets east of Leuven.[53]

◄◄·►►

Shock and outrage over the reports of rapes hardly led to a spirit of vengeance. The people of Leuven, *échevain* Emile Schmit recalled,

> already impressed by rumors of the cruelties at Visé, Mouland, etc., were terrorized
> by the stories of burnings and executions recounted by the inhabitants of the neigh-
> boring villages. They were all the more concerned after detailed news arrived from
> Aarschot, confirming scenes of massacre and burning that nothing appeared to justify.
> The attitude of the residents was really one of profound fear.[54]

The terrorized population did everything it could to placate the invader.
The sole representative of Belgian nobility in Leuven, Baron Orban de
Xivry was somewhat pained by the submissiveness of his fellow citizens.[55]
Numerous other witnesses recounted the fear and depression that gripped
the residents. "The people of Leuven were preoccupied with not getting
into trouble with the occupying forces," observed the Dutch physican
Adriaan Noyons.[56] "The population of Leuven, not considered heroic at
the best of times, was depressed and intimidated by the imposing numbers
of troops which passed through the town," reported the representative of
Cardinal Pifft of Vienna.[57] "The bourgeoisie was very anxious," a professor who fled to England recalled, "and hoped that nobody would give a
pretext for the use of force."[58]

Unfortunately, many Leuven residents had already witnessed German
paranoia at first hand. On the evening of August 19th, the first day of occupation, a small crackling explosion went off near the home of a friend of the
Chambrys, where twenty-eight soldiers were billeted. A sergeant grabbed
the homeowner, "shouting out like one possessed: '*Man hat geschossen!*
Man hat geschossen!'" If he found the culprit, the man would be hanged
and the city would burn the next day. Family members tried to reassure the
German. There were no arms left in the city. Besides, the noise sounded
nothing like a gunshot. Finally one relative, after anxiously searching in
front of the house, located the source of the noise – a firecracker, called a
"kalotje," that some children had been playing with. The sergeant nonetheless took the precaution of confiscating the dangerous *Spielzeug*.[59] When
a short above an electric trolley in Tervuren produced a loud bang and a
shower of sparks, the tram was stopped and all riders were searched. The
men were told they would be sent to Germany.[60] There are numerous other
accounts of German paranoia in and around Leuven.[61]

◄◄--►►

But did residents have any precise information as to what lay in store? There were some ominous signals. On Monday the 24th, Alfred Nerincx, the professor of law who served as chief administrator of the St. Thomas Hospital and would soon become the town's burgomaster, was given a surprising order to evacuate all German wounded, whatever their condition. No reason was given for this order, and the protests of the Belgian doctors were over-ruled. All military and civilian hospitals throughout town received the same order.[62]

The next day, around 1:30 in the afternoon, Emile van Hauw, a fifty-four-year-old merchant whose house was next to the swank Café Royal on the Grote Markt, was summoned over to the café's terrace, where champagne-drinking officers were studying a map that a young lieutenant had just brought them. The town's main arteries had been heavily penciled in. The young officer wished to confirm that the university's principal buildings were mostly along Naamsestraat. Van Hauw pointed out the locations of some of them on the map, and these were duly circled. Before he was dismissed, Van Hauw was subjected to a tirade by the commanding officer, who told him that Belgians would soon be made to pay for their opposition to Germany.[63]

Several direct warnings were later reported. On the 24th, a friend living in Stationsstraat warned the Chambrys that "'we are going to have here some new troops, composed of men of bad character. Some of them even had not completed the terms of imprisonment to which they had been condemned.'"[64] Disturbing rumors proliferated the following day. Mevrouw Rooman, the wife of a notary, was advised by an officer late in the afternoon to leave town. Terrible things were about to happen. She told several people about the distressing warning.[65]

Dr. Ide, Professor of Medicine at the University, making a house call in Tiensesteenweg, was interrupted at 5:00 p.m. by the patient's daughter-in-law, Mevrouw Albert Michotte, who lived next door. She was very disturbed by the parting words of the German officer who had been billeted with her: "Madame, I thank you for your kind welcome and I hope you will be spared, for it's going to begin now." Dr. Ide told the Belgian Commission of Inquiry that he never would have believed the story had he not himself heard the words repeated before the violence began.[66]

An hour later, shortly after 6:00 p.m., a police agent told seventeen-year-old Franz Dieudonné that "there's going to be a massacre here this evening," and suggested he leave Stationsplein right away.[67]

Interesting also are the reactions of various Germans when the alarm was sounded at about 7:30 p.m. throughout town. An officer in the home of Albert Michotte's brother Paul, also a professor, muttered *"Arme Leute!"* as he left. (Poor people!) Another academic, Professor Frateur, reported an officer weeping when the order to form ranks was given. An officer dining in a café in Stationsstraat was summonsed out of the room at 7:30 p.m. He returned "in a state of great emotion." The man happened to be a business acquaintance of the owner's brother, who was staying there at the time, and the two men had renewed their friendship. When the mayhem commenced, the officer sent his orderly back to the café to see what had happened to the family. They had been seized and hauled off to the station, where the officer took them under his protection and eventually liberated them.[68]

Finally, in the presbytery at Blauwput, just beyond the railroad tracks east of town, four Rhinelanders were lodged with the curé, Pastoor Eugen Vander Heyden. At 8:00, when the sound of gunfire erupted from the vicinity of the station, the men grabbed their weapons and crept out along the road into town. The last of the four to leave turned to Father Vander Heyden and said softly, *"Pauvre ville! Pauvre habitants!"*[69]

⊰⊹⊱

In the villages and towns around Leuven a number of individuals heard other alarming warnings, of varying precision, as to what awaited the university town.

In Tongeren on the 19th, General von Bertram told his interpreter, a professor at the city's Atheneum, that German troops had been fired on by civilians in Leuven and that the city would be devastated.[70]

On the same day, the curé of Dongelberg, Abbé Roland, was assured by a major that the Germans intended to destroy Leuven, after troops there had been assaulted by francs-tireurs. *"Löwen muss ganz kaputt."* The officer had received details by telephone; fighting between civilians and soldiers had taken place along Naamsestraat. Two other residents of the town also heard the same news. Several officers, in the company of the pastor, climbed up to the attic of a hilltop house in order to see the spectacle of Leuven in flames. Naturally, they were disappointed.[71]

A priest living near Leuven reported that he had been told on the 22nd, after his own village had been burned, that "Leuven will not remain standing much longer either." The soldiers would tell him nothing further. Anxious about family members living in town, he sent a messenger to Leuven the following day. "All is quiet," the priest was told.[72] At 2:00 in the afternoon on the 23rd, Mevrouw Jean Lenaerts, her servants, and Dr. Taverniers left Leuven for Sint-Joris-Winge, where they lived. At Linden they encountered a column of troops heading west. One of the officers asked them where they were coming from.

When told it was Leuven, he asked whether it was burning. "Absolutely not," Mevrouw Lenaerts assured him. "Then why are you fleeing?"

The travelers protested that they weren't fleeing, but merely returning to their homes after a visit. The officers shook their heads in disbelief.[73]

Back in Sint-Joris-Winge, Mevrouw Lenaerts overheard a conversation early in the day of the 25th between the staff officer lodging with her and a superior officer. The latter mentioned that Leuven had been shelled.

When Mevrouw Lenaerts expressed doubt about the information, the officer insisted that he was correct. *"Si, si, Louvain a été bombardé."*[74]

Also during the day of the 25th, Pastoor De Clerck, the chaplain at Gussenhoven, was stopped by soldiers while en route from Tienen to Leuven. They spoke with great anger about the city and its "Priest-University," whose students had fired on German soldiers. Not long afterwards, at Boutersem, a detachment of soldiers was preparing to resume their march westward. According to the chaplain, the officer in charge of the company yelled at his men, "We're going to Leuven. It's a three-hour march. When we get there, you can pillage the town for three hours and then set it on fire."[75]

The same day, a German officer insisted that an insane asylum in Brussels, the St. Joseph Institute, be evacuated because it was being used as a refuge for franc-tireurs. When the chaplain, Pastoor Van der Meulen, expressed his skepticism as to the existence of franc-tireurs, the officer exclaimed, "How can you not believe in franc-tireurs! In Leuven there are more than four hundred in Stationsstraat and at their head are two priests. Go look this evening. At around 8:00 you'll see Leuven burn." Three hours later the priest could just make out a red light glimmering in the distance. It was Leuven burning.[76]

Again on the 25th, around 1:30 p.m., Dr. Caluwaerts and Judge Janssens visited the German commandant in Tienen, Freiherr von Veitheim, to obtain authorization to return to Zoutleeuw. They were not well-received. The commandant accused them of being Russians traveling with forged documents. In Leuven, he told them, Russian students had fired on German troops. As a result, the town would be burned. The newly-minted pretext for the massacre in Liège was taking on a life of its own.[77]

⊰⊹⊱

As in the case of the warnings received by individuals near Dinant prior to the massacres there, the stories are difficult to evaluate. At the very least, rumors about "franc-tireur" activity in Leuven were being circulated far and wide in eastern Brabant. But it's hard to believe, in the first place, that all of the reports of predictions, warnings, or expressions of pity were fabricated out of whole cloth. The accounts are too numerous and too detailed; in several instances there were multiple witnesses. Many are recorded in sworn depositions by reputable individuals. As to the quality of the information the Germans imparted, this must obviously remain a matter of speculation. Undoubtedly, some of the rumors of an impending attack had no basis in fact. Others, however, may have reflected some acquaintance, albeit at second or third hand, with the plans of the General Staff of the First Army.

CHAPTER 10

Leuven: Fire and Sword

INTRODUCTION Until the night of the 25th, one of the most distressing things about the German occupation was the dearth of news. Leuven residents had no idea that the "First Sortie" had commenced the afternoon of the 24th until they heard guns booming in the distance the following morning. The Battle of the Frontiers had been raging for over forty-eight hours and the Belgian Army, which only learned of it the morning of the 24th, hoped to contribute to this first great contest between the invaders and the Allies by crashing into the German rear, lightly defended by two Landwehr corps, and thus compel the diversion of men and materiel from the Sambre. But perhaps they could do more. With any luck, they might retake the northern Brabant towns over-run by the Germans five days earlier.

On the 25th, the artillery fire grew louder to the northwest as the morning progressed. Plumes of smoke drifted skyward beyond Herent. There was much activity at the train station. Fresh troops were arriving continuously. Residents who had seen little of the Germans since Thursday morning, the 20th, learned that they would again be billeting soldiers. By evening no less than nineteen different detachments were in town, ranging in size from a company (about 260 men) to a full regiment (around 3,220 men). Hospitals were told to expect large numbers of wounded shortly.[1]

Between 7 and 7:30 p.m. soldiers in many parts of town were put on an alert. They left the residences where, in some cases, they had only recently arrived, and poured into the streets. Officers and men anxiously anticipated the arrival of the Belgians or the French. Ranks formed, but the columns did not move north.[2] In the city's center and in Stationsplein, however, the troops that had occupied Leuven since the 23rd continued to lounge in cafés and restaurants, oblivious to any threat.

Then, at 8:00, signal rockets went off behind the station and isolated gunshots were heard in various parts of town, followed by an intense fusillade in which machine-guns took part. Belgians headed for their cellars full of hope, anticipating the liberation of Leuven. Some prudent Germans took shelter as well.[3] Other residents, however, thought a mutiny was in progress, and were less sanguine.[4]

In several parts of the city, riderless horses galloped down the main streets. Disorder among German soldiers was particularly evident in the large Stationsplein, where transport troops were camped and infantry units continued to arrive at the station, and where, shortly before 8:00, a company of Landsturm Battalion Neuss returned to the square from a skirmish northeast of Leuven.[5]

In Volksplaats, where cavalry troops had massed, there was also much confusion. Troops along Tiensestraat, Tiensevest, and Blijde-Inkomststraat in the east, and along Tiensesteenweg, beyond the city gates, on Brusselsestraat in the west, and around the Grote Markt in central Leuven also went on rampages, firing indiscriminately.

After the fusillades subsided, some twenty minutes to an hour later, those buildings from which the Germans imagined or pretended that franc-tireurs had been firing were set ablaze. Entire neighborhoods were then burned systematically, including the Oude Markt, with the University Library. Arsonists also set fire to St. Pieter's, the collegiate church. Some residents were shot before their homes were ignited, or when they attempted to flee the flames. Others burned to death or were asphyxiated in their cellars. Many families were marched to the square in front of the train station. Here and along Tiensestraat a number of the men were executed. Others were driven north and were repeatedly told that they, too, were going to be shot. The captives in Stationsplein, along with residents who had been able to remain at home, were expelled from Leuven on the morning of the 27th, on the pretext that the town was to be bombarded.

The Germans massacred 248 civilians in and around Leuven and destroyed 2,130 homes and other buildings.[6]

OPENING SHOTS Naturally, nearly everyone who eventually wrote or testified about the sack of Leuven recalled the opening shots.

Isolated gunfire was reported in neighborhoods all over town around 8:00 p.m., but much of the initial firing seems to have come from the vicinity of the station, and may have been preceded by a signal rocket or rockets. These appear in a number of German accounts.

Lieutenant Colonel Max Schweder, commander of 2nd Mobile Landsturm Battalion Neuss, reported seeing a single flash above Stationsplein, though his second in command, and a number of other soldiers observed nothing.[7]

Other soldiers claimed to see more dramatic displays. Sergeant major Arnold Schmiele saw "coming in a southwesterly direction a swarm of small blueish balls of light that silently descended on us."[8] A private, Hubert Kueppers, reported a single green rocket go up from above the Hôtel Marie-Thérèse in the station square. The rocket exploded over the monument in the station square, releasing "a number of bright, multicolored little balls." These, too, went out before hitting the ground.[9] "Hardly had the green rocket and the small balls become extinguished when, from the opposite side of town, and also coming toward the station, a red rocket became visible. After a moment, it also went out, and immediately afterwards a number of luminous little balls, blue, red, and green, fell down from the rocket and were extinguished before touching the ground."[10]

There were at least a couple of other sightings of green rockets, though without the spectacular after-effects.[11] A non-commissioned officer stationed in a guard house eight hundred yards in front of the station saw the red rocket, but not the green, and no multi-colored balls.[12] Like his commander, a corporal saw simply "a blaze of light" above the station, as did a second corporal and a non-commissioned officer, who saw the rocket ascend from a bush to the right of the station. A rifleman stationed in the square saw two rockets, both apparently launched within the Stationsplein. Neither was colored nor released colored balls.[13]

Only four Belgians reported seeing rockets; residents were confined to their homes by the curfew. Three of these devices were fired later in the evening, and two appear to have been incendiary rockets.[14] But Professor Van Hecke of the Faculty of Science at the University reported seeing

signal flares shortly before eight. He is the only witness claiming to have
seen anyone actually firing a rocket.

> A military automobile, coming from Tiensesteenweg, stopped for a moment. The
> driver spoke to one of the German soldiers and the car went on again at full speed
> along the Tiensevest. It passed another, which had come from the station, halted half-
> way up Tiensevest, and left off some luminous signals, and disappeared. Suddenly a
> fusillade burst out around us from the direction of Tiensevest. My wife had her skirt
> pierced by a bullet. We rushed down a side street – Pleinstraat – where we found
> shelter in a cellar.[15]

The Belgian Army possessed no signal rockets whatsoever in 1914; the
German Army, however, was amply supplied with *Leuchtraketen* or *Leucht-
kugeln*, and with a special pistol to discharge flares.[16] The area in front of
the station, where the rockets were reportedly launched, was swarming
with German troops. All the hotels and homes in the vicinity were occupied by German officers and the ground-floor cafés by soldiers.[17] There
was an 8:00 p.m. curfew in effect; anyone out on the streets who was not
wearing a German uniform was liable to executed. Any signal rocket set off
just prior to the first shots was likely to be of German origin.

There may have been other signals. One of the few Belgians in
Stationsplein that evening who managed to survive the experience, café
owner Franz Vranken, distinctly heard a whistle shrill at 8:00 p.m. This was
immediately followed by a burst of gunfire.[18] (Whistles also figure in the
account of Father Pieter De Strycker, Vice-Rector of the American College.
A soldier arrived at the College during a fusillade that commenced around
8:00. He requested that a doctor come at once to attend a wounded officer
at the clinic of the Franciscan Sisters across the street. While De Strycker
crossed the street with the soldier to have a look (no physician being present at the College), the firing abruptly ceased. It resumed as soon as they'd
crossed the street. The same thing happened when De Strycker returned. It
both cases a whistle-blow had been the signal.)[19] There was additional testimony that the firing was not always spontaneous. In Kessel-Lo, just east of
Tiensepoort, a bugle call preceded the first shots, according to one resident.[20]

＊＜-＞＊

If they differ as to the fireworks display around Stationsplein, German
accounts agree that firing immediately erupted in the station square, and

seemed to be directed from the hotels facing the station toward the troops that had recently arrived in the square. A train pulling into the station was also hit.[21] Some soldiers identified the first shots as coming from the Hôtel de l'Industrie, on the right of the semi-circular plaza in front of the station.[22] Lieutenant Otto von Sandt, commander of the company, claimed to see firing from the window of the very room that he occupied in the hotel.[23] Other soldiers pinpointed the Marie-Thérèse on the opposite side[24], all four hotels[25], or all "houses" in the square.[26] The "murderous fire,"[27] however, resulted in virtually no casualties.

Lieutenant-Colonel Schweder, the battalion commander, reported only six wounded, five men and a non-commissioned officer.[28] "That so few were wounded can be explained by the fact that the inhabitants fired too high," Lieutenant von Sandt explained.[29] Non-commissioned officer Friedrich Hullermeier concurred: "I noticed that the inhabitants fired much too high. This was our good fortune..."[30] At one point, Schweder crossed Stationsplein with ten men. Though under a "continual hail of bullets" for over five hundred yards, no one was hit.[31]

If there were few injuries, the gunfire nonetheless caused great panic among the troops in the square.[32] Soldiers within Stationsplein opened fire on the entire arc of buildings facing the station, shooting at random without having received any order. Whatever gunfire the men heard initially – and, significantly, von Sandt admitted in later, unpublished testimony that it was only isolated shots initially and that he couldn't tell where these shots came from[33] – the first company of Landsturm Battalion Neuss responded with a furious barrage.

Troops of this battalion, it will be recalled, were responsible, three days later, for firing indiscriminately on the civilians who had been forced to walk to Leuven from Aarschot, mostly women and children. The unprovoked attack upset at least two officers who witnessed it, and they later filed damning depositions.

The battalion certainly did not enjoy a good reputation among the officers of other detachments in town. "Unfortunately, I must state that the discipline of this troop was not good," Major von Manteuffel, the commandant of Leuven, admitted.[34] Captain Förffer, in charge of the railway station, was less restrained.

> I don't have particularly fond recollections of the conduct of the men of the Landsturm Neuss battalion, including its commander, Lieutenant Colonel Schweder. Discipline was not observed and I repeatedly saw certain soldiers of the battalion drunk. From the beginning, I had a number of suspicions regarding them, and I believe they could well have been responsible for the fusillade.[35]

Other German witnesses testified to the habitual drunkenness of the troops.[36] Non-commissioned officers were assigned to police the restaurants around the station to try to reduce the incidence of drunkenness. One n.c.o. assigned to this duty on the evening of the 25th heard gunshots coming from within the restaurant where he was attempting to keep soldiers under surveillance, but, he added, "as to who fired, I couldn't say."[37] A Belgian witness also observed soldiers of the Landsturm battalion drinking in the hotel cafés shortly before the first shots rang out.[38]

⤛⤜

The soldiers who buzzed the doorbell at the home of Professor Léon Verhelst shortly before 8:00 p.m. were not drunk, though the professor had seen plenty of intoxicated soldiers earlier that day. They told him they needed to go to the third floor. Though they offered no good reason – simply repeating *"Wir müssen auf"* – the professor didn't impede them. He remained with his servants on the ground floor. Verhelst's wife was working in the St. Thomas Hospital and no one else was in the house. He heard the soldiers open the door to a room giving access to a window overlooking Léopoldstraat. "Hardly had the two soldiers climbed upstairs than I heard repeated rifle shots fired from above toward the street." Soldiers in the street returned the fire. The two soldiers rushed downstairs and out into the street. Verhelst followed. He was immediately seized by Germans outside and accused of having fired on them. The two shooters were right beside him, but they remained silent. Verhelst was lucky; had they claimed that they had seen him fire, he would have been executed on the spot. As it was, three shots were fired at him as he stood there, but he wasn't hit. He retreated to his cellar and was not pursued.[39]

Germans fired from another home around 8:00 p.m., with more dire consequences for the owner. Joseph van Steenberghe, a thirty-six-year-old engineer, lived with his wife and five children beyond the city gates on Tiensesteenweg. Four officers were billeted with the family. The parents and officers were dining when they heard the distant sound of gunfire; the children were in bed. The officers reassured the couple, then ran upstairs to get their weapons. Van Steenberghe escorted his wife and the servants to the basement door, then went upstairs to get the children.

His wife glimpsed him starting up the steps to the second floor, then stepping aside for an officer, armed and helmeted, who clattered past. That was the last Madeleine van Steenberghe saw of her husband.

She descended into the cellar with the servants. Five minutes later the house was raked by gunfire and Mevrouw Van Steenberghe heard the cries of her children from the ground floor hallway. She rushed upstairs to take the children to the basement. To her surprise, her husband wasn't with them. They said they hadn't see their father; it was the Germans who had gotten them out of bed and sent them downstairs. Also missing was the youngest. Gunfire sounded again outside, and the maid raced upstairs to retrieve the four-year-old while Madeleine van Steenberghe led her other children back to the cellar. After the maid returned with the child, the cellar door opened again. It was not her husband, as Mevrouw Van Steenberghe expected, but one of the officers. Anxious now, she climbed back up to the ground floor, which was swarming with Germans. An officer thrust a revolver in her face and told her someone had fired from the house. Madeleine van Steenberghe protested heatedly, and a search was undertaken. Though no weapons were discovered, she was nonetheless advised to leave the home. In the street, she was surrounded by angry soldiers and officers who swore to her that someone had fired from the house. The family was arrested and held in a nearby field, where they watched their home being pillaged and then burned. Mevrouw Van Steenberghe was again obliged to defend herself before some kind of tribunal the next day. An enormous revolver was produced that she had never seen before in her life.

Waiting in the basement on the 25th, she herself had heard no shots coming from the house – not even the shot that killed her husband somewhere upstairs. His charred body was found in the ruins of the home when the family returned two days later. He may well have been murdered by his guests when he surprised them as they were firing out of a second floor window.[40]

Gunshots were reported elsewhere in town at the same time. At precisely 8:00 p.m., Dr. Louis Maldague, a professor of pathology, heard a single shot coming from the Tivoli bridge on the Tiensesteenweg. Only

afterward did he hear other shots coming from the station and then close
by, on Tiensevest. The first shot heard by a Red Cross nurse came from the
garden of the Kind-Jezus hospital on Blijde-Inkomststraat, where she had
seen a German soldier moments before. This was followed by an intense
fusillade. Cyrille van Impe (Broeder Rudolf) also heard what he believed
was a pistol shot in the same area, right around 8:00, and observed troops
in Blijde-Inkomststraat firing on each other shortly afterward. Officers
invaded the Kind-Jezus hospital and threatened to execute two doctors.
They were saved only through the intervention of some wounded German
soldiers who had been permitted to remain there.[41]

A resident living close to Volksplaats, Felix van Aerschot, testified
that the initial shots came from within the leafy square, where the cavalry had assembled. They went off at exactly 8:00. Then a succession of
squadrons charged down Léopoldstraat toward the station, firing as they
rode. Moments later a sustained fusillade commenced within the exclusive
square, as soldiers raked the homes with gunfire.[42] (Another resident, however, Felix Giele, living on Stationsstraat, believed the cavalry troops in the
Volksplaats were responding to gunfire coming from the station, though,
significantly, he thought the firing commenced at about 8:15. He watched
a car heading to the station squeal to a stop directly in front of his house.
The driver put the car in reverse, as the passengers fired down the street
toward the station.)[43] Meanwhile on Brusselsestraat, about two-thirds of a
mile west of the station, a resident observed two parties of German soldiers
firing on each other, again at about 8:00 p.m. According to the witness, the
following day a German private, Hermann Otto, told him that Bavarians
and Poles had been shooting at each other in the street.[44]

On the days that followed, German soldiers were observed on a number of occasions firing from concealed positions with the clear intention of implicating civilians. On the 26th, at 2:00 in the afternoon, Mgr.
Paulin Ladeuze, Rector of the University, observed two Germans kneeling behind trees in the garden of the Arenberg Institute and firing toward
Schapenstraat. Mgr. Ladeuze watched from a second floor window as
the men continued shooting for at least twenty minutes.[45] That morning
Professor Laurent Noël also observed a soldier walking alone down a side-
street "shooting peacefully in the air."[46] Not long after, Abbé Tuyls, the
prison chaplain, saw a soldier enter his own home moments after he left to

walk to the prison. The man fired a shot from the entry hall, then rushed outside and pointed to the startled priest. *"Haben-sie das gehört? Er hat ges-chossen!"* the soldier yelled to his comrades. Abbé Tuyls was immediately seized, hit and insulted, and dragged off to the station.[47]

⊰⋯⊱

Were the initial shots fired in the Stationsplein intended to implicate civilians? We will likely never know, of course. It is possible, naturally, that the sack of Leuven was precipitated by a friendly-fire incident. Disorderly troops entering Stationsplein along Diestsevest may have been mistaken by drunken comrades for Belgian soldiers who had crossed the Dijle and were attacking the town. But this does not explain the simultaneous gunfire in other parts of town, nor the curious pyrotechnics in the vicinity of the station preceding the firing.

Moreover, Lieutenant von Sandt testified that his troops returned to Leuven in close formation.[48] The company, he also swore, was standing around beside its baggage for at least five minutes before anyone opened fire.[49] Von Sandt watched as other troops, disembarking from the station, proceeded up Stationsstraat toward the Stadhuis. The men of Battalion Neuss were thus not greeted by gunfire as soon as they arrived back in town. Nor is it clear why von Sandt's men should have inspired panic. As the lieutenant correctly noted, his soldiers were not being pursued by Belgian forces, and there is no reason they would have raced back into town pell-mell.

It is important to be perfectly clear about the position of the Belgian Army on the evening of the 25th. The main thrust of the First Sortie, made by the 6th Division, was toward Hofstade and Elewijt, with the 1st and 5th Divisions operating on its right. The objective of the 2nd Division, providing support on the left flank of the main attack, was Boortmeerbeek, a good eight miles from Leuven. They never made it. The 2nd Division failed to debouch on the west bank of the Leuven-Mechelen canal, across from Boortmeerbeek, and was forced to withdraw by evening. Some small patrols, and possibly a company or two, may have penetrated as far as Buken, and even Herent, during the afternoon, before they were pulled back, and one company crossed the canal above Tildonk the following day. A brigade, circling above the main concentration of forces on the 25th, briefly occupied Haacht, to the east of Boortmeerbeek, but was driven out by a counterattack. In the end, the Belgian Army in the First Sortie had come closer to capturing Brussels than Leuven. When German troops throughout town were put on the alert between 7:00 and 7:30 p.m., there was no threat from Belgian forces; the nearest units of any size were about nine and a quarter miles to the northwest.[50]

Dr. Maldague, heading back from work after 7:00 p.m., was puzzled to see the streets swarming with German troops; when he arrived home he went straight up to his attic to see if he could detect any sign of a battle outside town. Earlier in the day, like many other residents, he had heard the distant booms of cannons, but the noise had diminished toward evening, and he saw no evidence now of fighting on the outskirts of Leuven.[51]

-<-+->-

Von Sandt's testimony, if accurate, reduces the likelihood that drunken soldiers fired on his men, mistaking them for Belgians. And above the cafés where the soldiers lounged, only officers were billeted. Few could have been in their rooms at 8:00 p.m.; troops had been mobilized throughout town. While it's possible that some of these hypothetical officers who remained behind may have been drinking, it is hardly likely that they would have been panicked by von Sandt's men milling about below them. On the other hand, the deserted hotels would have made an ideal site for an agent provocateur. No Belgian family need have been inconvenienced, and the officer could have fired from the comfort of his armchair.

Once they were shot at, the reaction of company von Sandt of Battalion Neuss was predictable. The troops had just returned from observing an encounter between German forces and a Belgian patrol, albeit desultory, in an area north of Herent. Lieutenant Colonel Schweder had received no order to withdraw. He merely "felt the company was more necessary there [at the Leuven train station] than outside the town" – where some intermittent firing was still going on a little less than a mile from the company's position.[52] When the company returned to town, its officers apparently believed, according to von Sandt, that "there were no other troops in Leuven on this day except a section of railway engineers, of about 60 men," though the lieutenant contradicts this testimony moments later by noting all the troops that passed by en route to the Stadhuis.[53] Von Sandt's commander went further: "On the 25th there were only about 100 men of the von Sandt Company, because about 100 men were assigned for guard and sentry duty. As far as I know, no other troops were present in Leuven on Tuesday, August 25th, except this company."[54] These are astonishing claims. In fact, there may have been well over 17,000 German soldiers in Leuven if all the fighting units whose presence is documented in the German White Book were at full strength – even excluding troops of the 27th Brigade, ordered back into town by General von Boehn, but who had probably not arrived before the violence commenced. Most estimates are in the neighborhood of 10,000.[55] The White Book, as mentioned, indicates that nineteen different detachments were in town, as well as four groups of sick and wounded soldiers – who had been permitted to retain their weapons, despite the pleas of the Red Cross director. Naturally, if the men of von Sandt's company were the only German soldiers in town, anyone firing on them was, ipso facto, a franc-tireur.[56]

But whatever role men of Battalion Neuss may have played in exacerbating, if not precipitating, the gunfire in Stationsplein, the evidence of premeditation for the sack of Leuven is compelling. There were the numerous warnings and predictions issued by officers and men, however dubious a few of them may have been. There was the abundant evidence of signals, of German origin, from both German and Belgian sources; Professor Van Hecke's testimony is particularly interesting. (The signal, moreover, was repeated. An additional rocket was fired into the Oude Markt at 9:30 p.m. after troops had been marched into the square, precipitating the destruction of the University Library.) There was much testimony as well about firing in other parts of town at 8:00 p.m., not apparently in response to the fusillade in front of the station, and, specifically, the evidence of German officers intentionally shooting from windows at this time, also in other parts of town. But whatever the motivation of those who took potshots at von Sandt's men in Stationsplein, the response of his company virtually insured that firing would spread rapidly to other neighborhoods in the vicinity of the station.

⊰⟶⟶

And it did not take many shots to get things going. Most Belgian witnesses reported hearing one or a few gunshots, and then an intense fusillade. A

man living close to Stationsplein heard a rifle shot just before 8:00, followed by two others. Seconds later a barrage of gunfire shattered the calm.
From his garden, the man distinctly saw German soldiers firing on another
group of German soldiers some 200 to 300 yards away.

> At 8 o'clock it begins to be dark, but I am perfectly certain it was Germans fighting
> Germans. The firing on both sides passed right in front of my house and from the
> other side of the railway. I was lying flat on the balcony and watched it all. They
> fought hard for about an hour. The officers whistled and shouted out orders; there
> was terrible confusion until each side found out they were fighting each other and
> then the firing ceased.[57]

Half an hour later, the man heard a machine-gun firing from the far side of
the railroad tracks.

Nearly everyone describing the initial shooting heard the distinctive
tac-tac of the machine guns within twenty-minutes to a half an hour of the
opening gunfire. Sometimes more than one were deployed. The Germans
were always incensed to hear the noise – it inevitably proved that the franc-
tireurs were exceptionally well-armed and well-organized. "Personally," a
major reported, "I had the definite impression that we were being fired on
with machine-guns from the Hotel Marie-Thérèse; the bullets were raining
down on us. On the following morning we were able to ascertain that we
had been fired upon with machine-guns, because at the station entrance one
could clearly see the lines made by the bullets."[58] The fact that no Belgian
machine-gun was ever captured in Leuven troubled the accusers no more
than did the amazing ineffectiveness of these deadly weapons in the hands
of the city's franc-tireurs, who had brazenly set them up in hotels occupied
entirely by Germans.

-<--»-

Though much of their focus was on Stationsplein, German witnesses, like
Belgian civilians, also reported firing in several parts of town at 8:00 p.m.,
or shortly thereafter: in Volksplaats,[59] along Tiensestraat,[60] and in the city
center[61].

Major Walter von Manteuffel, the German commander in Leuven, was
dining at the Hôtel Métropole on Decosterstraat in central Leuven, and
was summonsed back to the Grote Markt. In his surprisingly brief and cir-
cumspect deposition, he reported gunfire in the vicinity of the Oude Markt

and Stadhuis around 8:00, as did his staff officers, in their no less laconic and guarded depositions.[62] No one observed a franc-tireur. One staff officer, Lieutenant Paul Telemann, was dining with two surgeons in the Café Royal in the Grote Markt. When the firing broke out, the patrons – all officers or n.c.o.s – retreated "into a back room so as not to be hit from the street. As the greater number of us were without arms *and as we didn't want to be subjected to the fire of our own men,* we decided to remain there temporarily."[63] (The published version of the White Book prudently omitted the italicized phrase.) As for the German victims in central Leuven, "I believe there were three," von Manteuffel recalled vaguely, "wounded chiefly in the legs." This was the toll from "a tremendous fusillade" in the square in front of the Stadhuis, which was "filled with artillery – one battery – with infantry columns, motorcars and gas tanks."[64]

The German White Book is surprisingly imprecise about the total number of German casualties. Individual witnesses are repeatedly evasive, reporting "several soldiers of our company are said to have been badly wounded," "I saw several with gun-shot wounds," "we had some wounded," and similar declarations.[65] General von Boehn, the commander of the IXth Reserve Army Corps is more specific: German casualties totaled 5 officers, 2 "officials," 23 men and 95 horses.[66] But these figures include killed, wounded, and missing, and subtotals for each category are not listed. The wounded officers are all named, so presumably no officers were killed. The Summary Report of the Military Inquiry Office merely repeats these numbers and provides no additional totals.[67] Obviously, German losses were so disproportionate to the death and destruction wrought by the troops that it was thought best to suppress the figures. It speaks volumes that Major von Manteuffel concludes his deposition with the following observation: "I wish to add that in front of the Stadhuis a horse was killed by a shot in the head."[68]

⊷⊷

In their accounts of the location, duration, and intensity of the firing – if not as to its origin – German and Belgian testimony is often not at odds and sometimes dovetails. To take but one instance, a private, Stanislaus Dadaczynski, lying in an infantry barracks in Tiensestraat, reported, damningly, that he suddenly "heard shots directed upon our barracks from the hospital opposite. Shots also came from the houses near the hospital. I can say with certainty that shots were also fired from the hospital."[69] German soldiers guarding the St. Thomas hospital down the street fired indiscriminately from within the hospital, to the consternation of its director and staff. It is quite possible that their colleagues at the Military Hospital did so as well.[70]

Sometimes individual German depositions dovetail as well, though not always in ways anticipated by the compilers of the White Book. Believing that his men had come under fire from the hotels directly opposite the station, von Sandt "sought cover with my company inside the doors of a few houses" – presumably on either side of the station, as they would not have run directly toward the gunfire.[71] As a train pulled into the station, carrying Reserve Infantry Regiment 75 of the 3rd Battalion, occupants of the cars found themselves fired at. "The enemy could not be seen because it was already quite dark," Sergeant-Major Hilmer testified. "We only saw the flashes of the shots and assumed that they came from the houses at each side of the railway" – precisely where von Sandt and his men had taken cover and were blazing away at the "franc-tireurs."[72]

◄◄─►►

Clearly, some soldiers did not approve of the promiscuous gunfire. When Professor Gustave Verriest cautiously approached a patrol on the morning of the 26th, the n.c.o. in charge attempted to reassure him. "We're Jägers and are trained not to fire one cartridge needlessly. We have yet to fire a shot."[73]

Long before the 25th, there was abundant evidence, even in the heart of Brussels, that the Jägers' philosophy was not universally shared. While he was in the capital, before leaving for Leuven, the Dutch physics teacher Lodewijk Grondijs had passed by a German soldier bound by his hands to a transport wagon in the main square in St. Joost-ten-Node.

Humiliated before the conquered Belgians, he "alternately shrieked with rage and silently shed hot tears." His crime, Grondijs was told by a non-commissioned officer, was to have caused a panic in the garrison by firing his rifle. Later, in Leuven, on one of his many visits to the Stadhuis, Grondijs saw in the courtyard a soldier bound to a wagon wheel for the same reason. "This man made no complaint; his punishment was not public."[74]

The barber who shaved Grondijs in Leuven every day pointed out to him one morning holes in the ceiling where two soldiers had fired to amuse themselves while they waited. The bullets pierced the bed of a child on the floor above, he told Grondijs, but no one was injured.[75]

◄◄►►

While some Germans went into homes and other buildings and impersonated franc-tireurs, other soldiers were more inventive. The man who had watched German troops fighting each other along Stationsstraat also observed soldiers driving what he believed was a Belgian Red Cross wagon down the street. The men released the horses, frightened them into a gallop, then shot three of them. "Two fell quite close to my house. They then took a Belgian artillery helmet and put it on the ground, so as to prepare a mise en scene to pretend that the Belgians had been fighting in the street."[76] Professor Nerincx also observed what he considered a suspicious tableau. Beside the carcass of a dead horse in Maria-Theresiastraat lay the grey-blue tunic of a non-commissioned officer. It looked as if it had been carefully placed there. Others commented on this display[77]

Horses figured in a number of other accounts. Following the first bursts of gunfire in northern Leuven at 8:15, Gustave Verriest saw two horses galloping down Mechelsestraat toward the center of town. In the darkness, he couldn't determine if they had riders.[78]

Charles de la Vallée-Poussin, a professor living on Stationsstraat, saw a troop of saddled but riderless horses galloping by his house at about ten or fifteen minutes past 8:00.[79] They, too, were headed toward the Grote Markt, away from the station. They may have been the Red Cross horses that were gunned down moments later, though the earlier witness didn't report them being saddled.

At nearly the same time Mevrouw Léon Dupriez observed riderless horses charging down Brusselsestraat, in the city's northwest district, also heading in the direction of the Grote Markt.[80]

There were thus at least three sets of riderless horses – if no cavalrymen were astride those racing down Mechelsestraat – coming from different directions toward the Grote Markt, a singular coincidence. This was in addition to the repeated cavalry charges down Léopoldstraat and the abortive dash of the Red Cross horses near Stationsplein, if these were not the horses spotted by de la Vallée-Poussin.

German soldiers also reported seeing riderless horses at various times, though mostly on Tiensestraat or in the vicinity of the station, where horses of the transport troops bolted.[81]

◄-◄--►-►

Shortly after the woman living in Stationsstraat heard machine-gun fire coming simultaneously from the station and from the vicinity of the Stad-huis, she observed groups of soldiers roaming down Stationstraat, shoot-ing out windows and cutting down the tram wires. The soldiers appeared to her to be drunk. She observed some groups firing on each other.[82] A café-owner in the same *quartier*, Sylvain van Hulst, also saw soldiers who appeared to be drunk, and seemed to be firing random shots, as did others elsewhere in town.[83]

Lodewijk Grondijs, whose Dutch passport enabled him to circulate through town at night, frequently encountered drunken soldiers, as did Professor Bruylants, who also ventured out very early Wednesday morn-ing, and Father Valeer Claes, who set off to fetch a gravely ill woman from a house threatened by fire.[84]

It was over the next several days, though, when looting began in ear-nest, that civilians repeatedly observed intoxicated soldiers.

◄-◄--►-►

Everyone commented on the fires. The spectacle of entire neighborhoods in flames was unforgettable. But a number of witnesses were also privi-leged to see the fires being ignited.

At least two Leuveners saw what appear to have been incendiary rock-ets. An attorney living in the center of the city saw some small rockets exploding over the center of the town around 11:30 p.m.[85] Law professor and future burgomaster Alfred Nerincx also observed rockets from his attic window. They rose low over buildings in the vicinity of the Grote Markt that were not yet ablaze, then, bursting into balls of fire, they crashed onto rooftops in the center of the city.[86]

The woman who observed the drunken soldiers trashing Stationsstraat also had an opportunity to witness the activities of an arsonist brigade.

> They had a broad belt and in front of it were the words "God is with us" in German...
> Some of these belts were afterwards found in the street, worn by soldiers who had

been killed or wounded. On these belts were all the materials for putting houses on fire, namely, a hatchet, a syringe, a small shovel, and also a revolver. The light caused by the fire was very great.[87]

As he was conducted down Stationsstraat the next morning, another resident watched soldiers shatter windows along the street. "Then they threw a white powder in and also on windows and shutters. They then threw in straw bottle covers which blazed as if they were soaked in paraffin. They lit them and threw them in. The powder made the house burn in no time. They carried it in a box, and pitched it in with shovels."[88] Lodewijk Grondijs made a more complete inventory of the paraphernalia used by the arsonists.[89]

Wholesale burning was also carried out along Tiensevest and Tiensesteenweg, just beyond the city gates. Maria Cammaerts, Professor Carnoy's young servant, watched from her cottage as "the Germans began systematically burning houses in and near Tiensesteenweg…

> I noticed my master's house burning fiercely at 10 that night. It was entirely destroyed. In one house in this neighborhood three women and two men were burned or suffocated in their cellar. This was in a hamlet called the Mol, about 300 yards from my master's house. The houses were burnt by means of hand-bombs, some egg-shaped and some square. They broke shutters and windows and threw these bombs into the houses; they exploded and set the houses on fire.[90]

Dr. Adriaan Noyons had the dismaying experience of entering his own home on Tiensesteenweg just as it was being set alight, though without the benefit of chemical explosives, fortunately.[91]

◄◄─►►

The fires that were watched with the greatest anxiety were those in the city's center. Here were the magnificent Stadhuis and the college church of St. Pieter, the city's two architectural gems. Just to their south, in the Oude Markt, a long, rectangular square, the University's celebrated library was housed in the buildings of University Hall on the eastern side. Accounts of the burning of these buildings weave their way into many of the narratives that follow.

◄◄─►►

At least one German soldier was appalled by what he saw the first night. Overcome with emotion, he told his host, Mr. Dumoulin, "This is horrible.

The soldiers are drunk. They're shooting at each other without compassion or pity. They're firing on anything that moves. This is tragic. It's horrible. Everything's burning."[92]

"I EXPECT THE FRENCH ARE HERE" Among those residents whose homes were not threatened the first night was the Chambry family on Leopoldstraat.

"On Tuesday the 25th of August, about nightfall," René Chambry recalled,

> fresh troops made their entry at Stationsstraat, with fifes and drums at their head, according to their custom. A big detachment turned into Léopoldstraat. Having piled their arms, the soldiers went to demand lodging and food. A non-commissioned officer and sixteen men presented themselves at our house. We offered them the same hospitality as we had given to their brothers-in-arms who had left us six days ago.
>
> Their leader was particularly civil. He spoke good French, which he'd learned in Brussels. Towards 7:00 my father and brother were giving them their supper, when a whistle blew.
>
> "The alarm," said the men. They rose hurriedly and fastened their belts. One of them, who seemed very much disinclined to leave a well-supplied table, put very little zeal into his preparations, obviously hoping to get left behind.
>
> The non-commissioned officer, in taking his leave, said to us, "We must be off in a hurry; the alarm has sounded. I expect the French are here." On the doorstep he turned around and called out to my father, "Good-bye. Doubtless we shall never see each other again."[93]

The family watched through the window of their cellar as the troops fell into rank and waited. One soldier did take the opportunity to sneak off, but not to finish his own supper; he asked Chambry for some milk for a stray dog he'd picked up en route from Tienen.

Other soldiers whose dinner was interrupted were less polite. Jules de Becker, Rector of the American College of Leuven, heard a bugle sound around 7:00 and saw an officer going house to house telling soldiers to prepare to leave. "I shall never forget," he recalled

> the diabolical expression on the faces of the angry soldiers who had to leave their quarters and set out, on an empty stomach, towards Keizersberg and the road to Mechelen. We went to the students' recreation room to watch them go by. They bellowed their *"Wacht Am Rhein"* and the savage looks they gave us foreboded evil.[94]

After cleaning up, the Chambrys resumed their meal. It was again interrupted.

At 8 o'clock exactly a violent fusillade broke out. I learned later that shots were fired in several streets at the same time.

The soldiers encamped in Léopoldstraat took flight at once, as fast as their legs could carry them. From our cellar we saw them running until they must have been out of breath.

Unfortunately, the fusillade continued. It was a mad tumult. In the Blijde-Inkomststraat, from the Tiensepoort to Maria-Theresiastraat, the firing rattled incessantly. The bullets aimed at the houses flattened themselves against the walls, or went through the shutters and the doors. Some people who were quietly taking their meals fell wounded. One woman, who had just been confined, and whom her husband was carrying into the cellar, thinking it was a bombardment by the Allies, was killed outright.

As for us, we were literally paralyzed. We supposed, after what the soldiers had said, that the French had succeeded in forcing their way into the city and that fighting was going on in the streets. All at once we heard a prolonged whistle followed by a continuous rumbling sound, of which we could not divine the cause. My brother and I left the underground kitchen where we had taken refuge, and went up to the first floor.

The blaze from the fires lit up our rooms. At the window one could easily have read a newspaper; the block of houses forming the corner of Stationsstraat and of Justus-Lipsiusplein was in flames. We hurried up to the higher floors. In every quarter as we looked out, flames were rising high, and columns of smoke were mounting to the sky, already purple-red.[95]

"A MIRACLE" Gustave Verriest was caught outside when the firing began, but, luckily, was in the company of a German officer. Oberarzt Porst, unlike the cognac-swilling "gay blade" whom Verriest was also lodging, had seemed to the young engineering professor an amiable and sensible man. He'd invited the doctor to dine with him at his sister's and brother-in-law's, the Dupriezs. The men were returning when the firing broke out.

The subsequent behavior of the well-intentioned German doctor is revealing. After escorting Verriest home, Porst said that he needed to go briefly to the St. Martin's barracks. It was 10:30 p.m. before he returned, during which time there had been more firing quite close by. The doctor was accompanied by a dozen soldiers who pointed their rifles at the professor. Porst brusquely announced that he had come for his luggage. Upstairs, in private, he told Verriest that the front door of the barracks had been fired on by civilians in the buildings opposite. Though he was the highest ranking officer in the barracks at the moment, he was unable to prevent soldiers from burning down these two buildings and others along Rijschoolstraat. He expressed some chagrin at the failure of the soldiers to obey his commands.

This did not especially augur well. Verriest asked if Porst wouldn't mind accompanying him back to his sister's house in the more remote and secure St. Jacob district at the western end of town. The doctor agreed. On the way over, they stopped back at the barracks so Porst could report to a superior officer. The detour nearly cost Verriest his life. As they entered, soldiers aimed their rifles at him, screaming *"Erschiessen! Erschiessen!"* Shoot, shoot. The doctor nimbly stepped in front of him before anyone squeezed his trigger, and calmed the troops. "I had the distinct impression that if he left me for a moment I was lost," Verriest recalled.

A major arrived and promptly had Verriest searched. Porst then reported to him that civilians had opened fire from the top of two houses, which he pointed out.

"Were any soldiers wounded?" asked the major.

"No," Dr. Porst conceded. "It really is a miracle that in such a violent fusillade no soldiers were wounded."[96]

The professor noted that Porst did not himself claim to have seen the inept marksmen in action. The next morning, when Verriest saw one of the dead "franc-tireurs," who lay where he had been shot, the man had clearly not been fleeing from the buildings from which the errant shots had purportedly come; he had actually been approaching the barracks, and from another direction altogether.

"YOU FIRED! DIE!" A few of those accused of being francs-tireurs – and anyone venturing outside ran that risk – were able to convince their captors that they were innocent.

The doctors of the St. Thomas Hospital in Tiensestraat had every reason to expect that they would have nothing to fear if fighting erupted in the streets. In addition to the protection provided by the large Red Cross flag that flew above the clinic, and by their arm-bands, the hospital was guarded by a detachment of twenty-four soldiers under two sergeants. Hervé de Gruben recounted what happened.

> At 8 o'clock in the evening, fifteen of us had assembled in the dining-room of the house occupied by Mgr. Deploige and Canon Thiéry. Suddenly, at ten minutes past the hour, a shot was fired quite close to the house. We had scarcely taken note of it when other reports followed. In less than a minute, rifle shots and machine-gun fire mingled in a terrific din. Accompanying the crack of the firearms, we heard the dull thud of galloping hoofs in Tiensestraat.

The Allies are entering the town, everyone thought. The troops are fighting in the streets.

In about twenty minutes the firing ceased. Mgr. Deploige and Dr. Tits, the chief surgeon of the hospital, went out. They had advanced but a few steps when three soldiers on guard at the hospital rushed at them with their bayonets fixed, yelling: "You fired! Die!" Mgr. Deploige spoke to them energetically in German, and Dr. Tits, unbuttoning his coat, offered his chest to their weapons. One of the two sergeants had witnessed the scene; he ran over and pushed away the rifles.

"We heard firing under the window," said Mgr Deploige. "Were your men shooting?"

"They have to defend themselves," the sergeant replied. "They were being fired at on every side."

"If there is firing in the streets, let the soldiers come out. They must not fire from here. The hospital is protected by the Red Cross flag. The Allies will respect it."

"This has nothing to do with the Allies. The shots came from a window. Civilians are firing on us."

"That's absurd. I know my neighbors. They no more fired than we did ourselves."

We heard this conversation as we stood inside. It had not come to an end when the firing began again a few paces from the house. We could clearly distinguish the report of a machine-gun."

"There!" said Dr. Tits to the sergeant. "You don't suppose those are civilians firing?"[97]

The sergeant acknowledged that it was unlikely civilians were operating machine-guns.

Monseigneur Deploige and Dr. Tits returned to the hospital, convinced that German troops in town had panicked in the face of a Belgian offensive.

THE BOOT The Dupriez family had a much narrower escape than the doctors and staff at the St. Thomas Hospital. They lived at the far end of Brusselsestraat in the St. Jacob district, across town from the Stationsplein. Léon Dupriez, Professor Verriest's brother-in-law, was a distinguished professor of law at the University. He was member of the Royal Academy of Belgium and sat on the Colonial Council. Such credentials meant nothing on the night of the 25th. Being able to protest vigorously in German, however, proved to be of some use.

On Tuesday, August 25th, at about a quarter past eight, our children, aged 13 ½, 10, 9, and 6, were preparing to go to bed, when I heard shots which seemed to be coming near. I at once decided to make the whole family go down into the cellar for the night; I went at once to the cellar myself, to make beds for the children there. Meanwhile Mrs. Dupriez saw a troop of a dozen horses, saddled but riderless, galloping madly at breakneck speed past the front of the house. They were coming from the top of Brusselsestraat and heading towards the middle of town. We passed the night of the 25th – 26th in the cellar, hearing firing from time to time, but ignorant of all that was happening in the center of town. On Wednesday morning I learned from neighbors only about the burning of the Halles and Church of St. Pieter. In the St. Jacob district the conflagration in Stationstraat and the neighboring streets was not yet known. Toward 7:35 a.m., while Mrs. Dupriez was in the garden with the children, I went to the second story of the house to fetch some clothing and heard the measured tread of a detachment of Germans passing the house. This detachment, as I leaned shortly after, must have numbered between seventy-five and a hundred men. Suddenly a shot rang out, followed immediately by tremendous shouts, and a volley of shots directed at my house; at least one bullet penetrated a window of the room I was about to enter. I hastened below to fetch the children and take them into the cellar.

When I reached the porch, I met my wife, who had already taken the children downstairs. At the same moment, we heard violent blows from the butt-end of a rifle on the outer door and loud shouts. What were we to do? "Let's open it right away," I said. "It's our only chance of safety."

I hastened to open, but my wife preceded me, saying, "No, not you. I speak German better than you, and besides they are not likely to fire at a woman as quickly as at a man."

We opened the door together, but Mrs. Dupriez was in front of me in the aperture. Scarcely was the door open eight inches when my wife had six rifles pointed at her chest and a revolver under her nose.

"*Um Gottes Willen, schiessen Sie doch nicht,*" she cried out to them. "*Wir haben nichts getan.*"

But in two seconds the door was violently pushed open. A little sergeant rushed forward, yelling, "*Hände hoch!*" He searched me and furiously threw on the floor everything he found in my pockets – wallet, coin purse, keys, etc. Then he pulled me into the street and here, for four or five minutes, I was continuously assaulted by soldiers, white with passion, who held the barrel of their rifles twelve to fifteen inches away and kept shouting that I had fired on them. Meanwhile, others covered Mrs. Dupriez with their rifles.

The couple remained calm, explaining in German that they had not fired. They had no weapons and the windows were all shut. Dupriez had an uncomfortable moment: one of the soldiers aiming at him began fingering the trigger. When the professor slowly pushed the barrel aside, the soldier whipped off his bayonet and whacked him on the left shoulder. The bruise was still visible several months later.

Then I saw that the two soldiers who until now had their guns leveled at Mrs. Dupriez left her to rejoin the main body of the detachment. But a tall sergeant – the same who had brandished the revolver at the moment we were opening the door and who seemed to be leading the whole attack – rushed towards the two soldiers, and called out to them some words I didn't understand, persistently pointing to his boot. The two soldiers returned towards Mrs. Dupriez.

Dupriez noticed that his children had come up from the cellar. They assembled on the porch, "eyes wide with terror." But they had the presence of mind not to shout or cry, but to plead with the soldiers in German.

> All of a sudden the little sergeant cried in a terrible voice, *"Alle heraus!"*
>
> Then Mrs. Dupriez and I, each taking two children by the hand and followed by two servants, escaped as fast as we could, thinking they were going to shoot us in the back. After running like this for a hundred yards, we saw ahead of us, coming towards us, a second German detachment. We rushed into the middle of the street, so that our aggressors could no longer fire on us without at the same time hitting the approaching troops.

No one fired. The section that had been called off to execute the "franctireurs" rejoined the platoon waiting down the street.

> We only escaped death thanks to a certain hesitation on the part of the soldiers, a hesitation no doubt due in the first place to the fact that we opened the door immediately, then to our calmness and presence of mind, and finally, and especially, to the perfect knowledge of German, which they noticed even in the children. We think that they wondered whether by chance they had not attacked a German family
>
> We were attacked by two sergeants and six or seven soldiers. The bulk of the detachment halted a hundred meters from our house, near Judge Maes's front door, and looked on passively at the whole scene. It may be asked why the officers in command of the detachment did not intervene, either to punish us if they thought us guilty, or to protect us in the opposite case.
>
> Who fired the first shot which was the signal for the attack?
>
> It was the tall sergeant with the revolver. I didn't see him. But three weeks afterward, I met in Brussels a resident of Leuven who told me, "I know who fired the bullet that nearly caused you to be shot. I watched the detachment pass your house, from a distance. I saw a tall sergeant fire into the air, then run shouting and showing his boot to the soldiers."
>
> Was this not obviously the same tall sergeant whom I also saw showing his boot to the men to summon them back to Mrs. Dupriez? I had been the only one to notice this detail, and as I hadn't attached any importance to it up til now, I hadn't mentioned it to anyone.[98]

"LOUD SHOUTING ALWAYS MAKES AN IMPRESSION ON GERMANS" Dr. Adriaan Noyons, standing beside Hervé de Gruben, witnessed the same confrontation between his colleagues and the soldiers assigned to the hospital. Unlike Léon Dupriez, Noyons, a Dutch citizen and Professor of Anatomy and Physiology, was convinced that a truculent tone was more effective with the Germans than dispassionate analysis: "it was only by shouting louder and more shrilly than the Germans that they [Mgr. Deploige, Canon Thiéry, and Dr. Tits] managed to make the non-commissioned officer understand that no member of the staff had, or could have, *geschossen*."[99]

Thwarted on Tiensestraat, the soldiers raced around the seminary grounds searching for the imaginary franc-tireurs. Suddenly, one soldier cried out in pain. When his comrades and the hospital attendants rushed over to him, he yelled that he had been shot by a franc-tireur. He was brought to the operating room and examined by Dr. Noyons. The diagnosis: a simple contusion of the foot. The man then confessed that he had simply fallen off the top of a garden wall.

Early the next morning, the first civilian patients arrived. Noyons was operating on an engineer, Meneer André, who had been hit in the upper thigh by a hand-grenade as he was distributing drinks to German soldiers in Blijde-Inkomststraat, when someone announced that his own servant had been brought in.

> She had been dangerously wounded by three bullets, one in the arm, another in the back, grazing the ribs, and the third in the buttock. I attended to her myself, and thus learned that she had been wounded in my house, at the moment when, hearing the front door being broken in, she and another servant had tried to escape over a garden wall. I had taken the precaution of draping over my house the Red Cross flag and I had attached to my front door a notice which bore my name, my doctor's degree, and my address at the Leo XIII Hospital.

A fellow servant who accompanied the wounded girl reported to Noyons that she had seen his house set on fire. She was mistaken, though only by an hour or so, but Noyons was determined to investigate for himself. After completing the two operations, he asked a couple of the soldiers guarding the hospital to accompany him to the Stadhuis. Here he protested to Major von Manteuffel that he was a neutral, a Dutch citizen, and demanded an escort back to his house. The major complied. On the way back, the doctor and his two-man guard passed troops leading a man of about forty and a fourteen-year-old boy, both tied to the tail of a horse by ropes tightly bound around their wrists. *"Die werden erschossen,"* one of the soldiers accompanying him remarked. (They're going to be shot.) Everywhere doors were being broken in and shots fired, but the soldiers accompanying Noyons didn't seem in the least troubled. Tiensevest looked like a battle-field; wreckage was strewn everywhere.

> As I drew near my house, I at once saw smoke coming out. Some soldiers were busy bringing straw from my neighbor Kleyntjens. When they saw us, they came rushing towards me, yelling, *"Da haben Sie den Franctireur der geschossen hat!"*(You've got the franc-tireur there who shot!) I began at once to vociferate louder than they, in German, ordering them to extinguish the fire they had lit in my house. Loud shouting always makes an impression on Germans. These men immediately calmed down, said they would put out the fire and did, indeed, set to work to extinguish the blaze which flamed high in the middle of the drawing room, burning furniture broken into pieces and heaped up together with torn books and albums. About three square yards of floor was already charred. In the drawing room, a great Japanese porcelain vase was in fragments. They had opened every gas-jet in the house. In the dining room they had slashed the pictures and engravings with bayonets or smashed them with rifle butts, they had broken porcelain and statuettes, broken open the panels of the sideboard and dresser and entirely destroyed the flatware, cups and saucers, etc. within these two pieces of furniture.
>
> However, the incendiaries did their best to retard the spread of the fire; I worked with them and they gave me advice on the best way of proceeding. At one point I wanted to open a window opposite the railroad tracks. The soldiers warned me that it would be dangerous to appear at a side window; soldiers on the tracks or in the imme-diate vicinity would likely shoot at any civilian they saw at a window.
>
> In front of the house of the architect Lenertz, I saw his corpse; the skull had been smashed in on the left side. I saw the dead bodies of several civilians on the other side of Tiensevest and at Tiensepoort, as well as the dead bodies of horses and the corpses of some German soldiers.[100]

Yelling at the Germans paid off again. Later in the week Noyons encoun-tered a convoy of wagons along Tiensestraat. One of them stopped in front of Professor Schockaert's house and a soldier began shouting that someone had fired from it and that it must be burned down. Noyons strode up to the soldiers and angrily shouted back that no one had fired from the house. The convoy continued on its way.[101]

"LONG INQUIRIES IN THE DARK NIGHT" A sound sleeper, Lodewijk Grondijs, the Dutch physics teacher turned journalist, missed the opening hours of the sack of Leuven. He was awakened at 4:00 a.m. by his host, Professor Scharpé, a specialist in German and Flemish literature. There had been shooting in the streets for hours, fires were raging over much of the town, dead bodies had been reported lying in the streets. However, the area around Schapenstraat, where Scharpé lived, had so far been spared, and the professor begged Grondijs, armed with his Dutch passport, to go downtown and offer shelter to some good friends who lived in the center of Leuven. On the way, he was stopped by a group of intoxicated soldiers. But as before, Grondijs's imperious manner impressed the soldiers, who conducted him to their lieutenant. The officer confirmed that there was no curfew, and set him free. Grondijs requested a "laissez passer" so he wouldn't be stopped every five minutes, but this the lieutenant was unwilling to provide.

The friends of Scharpé, the Persoons, declined the professor's offer. Their home was adjacent to the Stadhuis, and Grondijs noticed as he approached the building that the Germans were pumping water on the roof. At first surprised that the troops would be making efforts to spare a building, Grondijs recalled that the commander's headquarters were in the Stadhuis and that a great many soldiers were billeted there. As he left the Persoons to head back to Schapenstraat, Grondijs paused before the hellish scene. Flames roared like thunder, burning timber cracked and popped, walls collapsed with a crash. (Like Bart Mokveld at Visé, Grondijs noted that the roofs were consumed first, and the houses still standing blazed like torches.) The sinister scene summoned up a fierce, cold anger.

> At such moment, when chaos appears to reign, and when one sees the most precious and rarest objects, the heritage of centuries, trodden under foot, life itself seems to lose all value. Now I can understand easily how those who are placed against a wall to be shot are able to maintain a contemptuous silence, or to utter lofty words of rebuke. Some soldiers tried to stop me again; angrily I flung one of them my passport... "Can't you read that, blockhead!" And when they threatened me with their rifles: "Take me at once to the guard; I won't bandy words with you." I looked them straight in the face. After a few threats they let me continue on my way.[102]

Further along a soldier pulled him into a shop to show him the body of the store's owner. The man was clad in his nightclothes and had a small, black hole in his forehead.

"Was it you who killed this man?" Grondijs asked quietly.

"No," the soldier replied, "but I was with those who killed him. We'll teach those *Schweinhunde* to fire on German soldiers!"

"How do you know that this was the man who fired on you?"

The soldier responded with a question of his own: "How do you expect us to be making long inquiries in the dark night?"

"In this short answer," Grondijs concluded, "the whole logic of reprisals by the military against civilians is summed up."[103]

⊰⊹⊱

As he was approaching the Scharpé house, Grondijs noticed that the low tower of the church of St. Pieter, the collegiate church, was ablaze. Built in the mid- and late- 15th century, with seven exquisite chapels, outstanding iron work by Quinten Matsijs and celebrated paintings by Dirk Bouts, St. Pieter, along with the Late Gothic Stadhuis, was the city's chief architectural attraction. But the buildings surrounding the church, Grondijs clearly saw, were still intact. The fire must have been set deliberately.

As he watched the fire, outrage again welling up in him, he was approached by several frightened-looking residents, who motioned to him to enter their house. They shut the door and excitedly told him that a number of young women from that district had been marched off in the direction of Brusselsepoort by German soldiers. He was directed to the house of an elderly widow, whose daughter had been among those taken. The woman herself had been marched, with hands raised, toward the gate, but had been ordered home. Grondijs walked directly to Brusselsepoort, but found no trace of the abducted women. He made several inquiries in Brusselsestraat and his information was confirmed: several small groups of women had been escorted westward down the street. Behind him, the collegiate church tower collapsed and tiny flames licked up from the roof. Dead bodies lay in small piles along the street. Undaunted, Grondijs strode back to the Stadhuis and located the commandant.

"Are you aware," he asked von Manteuffel, "that during the night a large number of women were taken by soldiers outside the town?"

The major said that this was the first he'd heard of this.

"Do you think it is in conformity with the honor of your army that defenseless women should be subjected to such treatment?"

"Do you think it is in conformity with the honor of the Belgian army to make civilians fire on soldiers from their houses?" the commandant asked in turn.

Grondijs failed to see the logic of the response, and refused to be drawn into a futile discussion of the "franc-tireur" question. Brusquely telling von Manteuffel that he simply wished to bring the matter to the major's attention, he took his leave.[104]

Having done what he could for the women, Grondijs was now engaged
by Dr. Scharpé in an effort to save the Schapenstraat district, which had
thus far escaped damage. The professor had organized something like a
neighborhood watch. Sentries were posted in pairs every hundred yards
to be able to vouch for the good conduct of the residents, should soldiers
enter the quarter. When panicked crowds from a poorer neighborhood surrounded the Scharpé house, they were persuaded to return to their homes.
Scharpé himself went to the Stadhuis and obtained Major von Manteuffel's
promise that no patrols would be sent into the neighborhood. Nonetheless,
the ad hoc Schapenstraat committee took no chances. Grondijs, accompanied by three young women and a locksmith, knocked on all the homes in
the street where doors were closed. A number of residents had fled Leuven,
sometimes leaving a lighted candle in their drawing room. But if a patrol
should encounter a locked door, the home would almost certainly be pillaged and burned, and adjacent homes jeopardized. Grondijs was occasionally disturbed by evidence of Belgian carelessness. In the home of the
widow of a French officer, he located her husband's revolver. He buried the
weapon in the garden.[105]

⦗←→⦘

Late in the morning of August 26, Grondijs went to the Premonstratensian
Abbey of Park, just outside town, with a letter of introduction to its widely
respected Abbot, Father Nols. The Dutch professor had only gone a few
hundred meters from the Scharpé house when an odd sound caused him
to whirl around. Behind him, a German soldier was taking aim. Grondijs
waved frantically. The soldier approached and searched him. He had called
out to the Dutch journalist, the man claimed, but the wind had carried
away his words.[106]

The monastery was teeming with refugees who had watched the fire
in University Hall throughout the night. At 2:00 a.m., they told Grondijs,
there was a sudden surge of flames. Sparks shot up in an immense column.
The 13th century manuscripts and the incunabula were burning.

⦗←→⦘

Leuven burned again on the night of August 26th, but the Schapenstraat
district was once more spared. More houses along Stationsstraat were

alight. Grondijs observed soldiers in sharp relief against the flames, feeding the fire with the incendiary devices they carried with them. Grondijs had noted earlier the extensive equipment the special units carried: grenades, petrol sprinklers, nickel cans of benzine, and cakes of cotton nitrate.[107] Belgian soldiers in Dendermonde seized a number of incendiary tablets, and the government had them analyzed. The discs were made of gelatinised nitro-cellulose and coated with lead. They had a hole in the center to enable them to be strung together and ignited.[108] Above the flaming houses, the underside of the clouds "seemed to burn like an immense brazier."[109] But again the Schapenstraat district was spared, although civilians continued to be shot not far away.

When Grondijs arrived at the Stadhuis the following morning, the 27th, more intoxicated soldiers were milling around, bearing enormous bundles of clothes, boxes of cigars, and bottles of wine. Leuveners were obliged to raise their hands in the air as they walked by. The sight of some of the city's leading dignitaries so humiliated moved Grondijs even more than did the fires themselves, he claimed. When Grondijs met up with the usually affable and unruffled Dr. Scharpé, the professor was pale and anxious. Leuven is doomed, he told his friend. He had just received word that the city was to be bombarded.

A day earlier, on the steps of the Stadhuis, Grondijs had overheard a tall, elegant lieutenant addressing his men. "'Hitherto,'" he told them, "'we have only burned villages – Tongeren, for instance – and well done, too! It has been razed to the ground. Now we are beginning on the towns. Leuven will be the first to be destroyed.'"[110]

DR. BERGHAUSEN AND MR. DAVID-FISCHBACH On August 13, Léon David-Fischbach presented the St. Thomas Hospital with a magnificent new car, a 40 h.p. Dion-Bouton. The forty-two-year-old banker was devoted to his ailing father, Pierre-Hubert David-Fischbach, and slept in the same room with the old man in their magnificent home on Stationsstraat, where it intersects with Justus-Lipsiusstraat, Koning Léopoldstraat, and Melsensstraat. The senior David-Fischbach was known throughout town as a generous philanthropist and an amiable old gentlemen. When he turned over the car to the hospital, Léon David-Fischbach told Mgr. Deploige, "The Belgian Army hasn't requisitioned it and I don't want it to fall into the hands of the

Germans. I give it to you; it will be useful for the transport of the wounded and re-supplying your hospital." His eighty-two-year-old father had already donated 10,000 francs to the Red Cross.[111]

◄◄►►

Dr. Georg Berghausen, the chief medical officer of Landsturm Infantry Battalion Neuss, soon became well known in Leuven. Dr. Noyons quickly formed an unfavorable impression of the ebullient physician. "He often came to the hospital. He neglected all his medical duties. Though he was a staff surgeon, he never performed operations."[112]

Berghausen, it turned out, had a thousand and one other things to attend to. One of his most notorious acts was to liberate all the German prisoners in Leuven. He ordered them sent back to Germany on the condition that they enlist in the army. After repeated protests by city officials, Berghausen was over-ruled by von Manteuffel. The major's successor, Colonel Lubbert, was indignant when he learned about the doctor's action: "How could this charlatan have arbitrarily substituted his own authority for that of the Belgian king? And what made him believe that the German Army recruits in prisons?"[113]

Others were initially impressed with Berghausen. Touring the Kind-Jezus Hospital in Blijde-Inkomststraat with the Oberarzt, Baron Orban de Xivry was struck by how compassionate Berghausen seemed with the Belgian wounded. "In the realm of charity," the German doctor declared grandly, "there are no enemies."[114] Passing the baron on the street in his staff car, en route to the hospital, Berghausen had ostentatiously insisted that Orban take a seat in the vehicle, forgetting that he was originally to have picked up the baron at home some time earlier. At the hospital, Orban noted, the *Oberarzt* appeared to be a favorite of the nurses, who greeted him warmly.[115]

The manic Berghausen weaves his way into the narratives of a number of prominent Leuveners. Dr. Georges Guelton, professor of law, was initially impressed with the officious staff doctor, who presented him with a laissez-passer to return home on the 28th. A few days later, after soldiers had been ordered to cease burning the town, a neighbor's home was set on fire. Guelton ran across Berghausen shortly afterward, and protested vigorously. The doctor had been loudly trumpeting the new communiqué and had reassured everyone that order was to be restored in Leuven. Unfortunately, Berghausen coolly explained, a German soldier had been discovered in the basement of that particular house with his eyes gouged out. In the face of Guelton's indignant protests, the *Oberarzt* changed his story. German soldiers, he now claimed, had set the house on fire by mistake.[116]

Brand Whitlock, head of the U.S. Legation, provided a damning profile of the chief physician merely by citing Berghausen's own account of his activities – for, as Whitlock notes, "there is this terrible and fatal quality in all writing, which should no doubt adjure us all to silence – namely, that, no matter how imperfect a picture the writer gives of everything else, he always draws a perfect portrait of himself."

> "I arrived at Leuven," says our doctor, "on the twenty-fourth of August, in the afternoon, and went to the hotel. In order favorably to impress the landlord and his waiters I turned out of my pocket the sum of fifty francs, destined to the purchase of food."
>
> There you have him, at his entrance on the stage. Arriving at the hotel with a flourish, striking an attitude, twirling his moustache, impressing the natives.
>
> No sooner arrived in Leuven than he goes to the penitentiary in order to set at liberty all prisoners of German nationality – not prisoners of war, but Germans condemned long before the war for felonies.
>
> Again, on the twenty-first of September, we find him in the heat of the fray. He went out to battle, and at the head of several hussars captures a mitrailleuse from the Belgians, and was given the Iron Cross – of the second class.
>
> Next we see him bending to kiss the hands of Belgian nurses at the hospital, expatiating to them on the solidarity that binds all workers of the Red Cross together. Later on in September, according to a newspaper in Köln, he is at a religious ceremony in Leuven, mounting to the pulpit beside the Dominican father and translating into German, for the benefit of the German soldiers present, the sermon which the monk had just delivered in French to his own people. Thus it is not surprising to find him in the midst of the affray there in the Stationsplein on that night...[117]

⤛⤜⟶

When sustained firing broke out around the Stadhuis, several residents were meeting with Major von Manteuffel, who had just been summoned back from dinner.[118] The day's hostages, Mgr. Coenraets, vice-rector of the University, and Judge Maes were already in the building. Three representatives from a Red Cross hospital established in the Dominican monastery on Justius-Lipsiusstraat – Joseph Parijs (Father Hyacinth), its director, Dr. Joseph Meulemans, and the hospital's pharmacist Amedée de Koninck

– had come to get authorization to circulate through town after the curfew, in order to retrieve the wounded expected imminently. Also on hand was Eugène Nijs, whose car had just been requisitioned. Von Manteuffel was at his desk, putting his papers in order, when a volley rang out. An intense barrage followed, and when this died down, soldiers within the Stadhuis began firing out the windows. Only one soldier appeared to have been injured in the firing. He had a superficial wound in his thigh, and was hardly bleeding.[119]

While the shooting continued, the six hostages, who been seated on benches, were ordered to stand at the illuminated window and face outwards. They fully expected to be targeted by the troops in the square.

Not long after, Emile Schmit arrived; he had been sent for by von Manteuffel. Schmit had already heard the clatter of machine guns and, scrambling to his upper floor, had seen fire raging on one side of Volksplaats, a hundred yards away. On the short drive over, he saw the streets were swarming with soldiers. There were numerous fires and occasional gunshots. The Grote Markt was filled with troops, "like a teeming anthill"; a number were firing into the homes lining the square.[120] *"Nos soldats sont un peu nerveux ce soir,"* an officer had confessed to Schmit's wife.[121]

The Germans seem to have regarded Schmit as de facto burgomaster, in lieu of the incapacitated Léon Colins. Schmit was told by von Manteuffel that franc-tireurs had attacked the German Army and were continuing to fire. Reprisals were already taking place. Schmit was then presented to an irate general who had just arrived in town. General von Boehn told the *échevain* that the entire town was guilty in this attack on the German Army and would be made to pay. Hostages were to immediately circulate through the town, announcing that if another shot were fired, the entire town would be razed, a war ransom of 20,000,000 francs would be paid, and the hostages would be hanged.[122] Schmit had been selected to be one of the hostages who would tour the streets. Major von Manteuffel would accompany the group[123]

Joseph Parijs was on hand when General von Boehn arrived. Not long before 8:00 p.m., when he had entered the Grote Markt, the priest had been struck by how tranquil the square seemed, and how few soldiers were present. Von Boehn, toward whom everyone seemed deferential and addressed as "your Excellency," was in a state of singular excitement. Haughty and brutal, he had us searched. Nothing was found. What had he expected to find? Then he declared in German (which he had another officer translate into French) that if anyone fired again we would be hanged. We tried to explain to him our rights as members of the Red Cross; we were wearing armbands issued by the German authorities, but he prevented us from getting a word in.[124]

Perhaps Parijs didn't conceal his disdain; he was ordered to substitute for Judge Maes on the tour of Leuven. Schmit also protested that the arbitrary arresting of civilians was illegal, but he also was ignored.[125] When gunfire erupted nearby about half an hour later, von Manteuffel ordered the three men, Coenraets, Parijs, and Schmit, into the streets, repeating the general's dire threat: "If anyone fires again, the town will be burned, it will pay twenty million francs war indemnity, and the hostages will be hanged!" Von Manteuffel followed with an escort of twenty soldiers and a drummer.

"The Grote Markt was black with German soldiers," Parijs recalled,

and we could hardly cross through their ranks. Mgr. Coenraets was very exhausted and overwhelmed; it was I who made the proclamation in the two languages. [Some witnesses had recalled Coenraets speaking in French and Parijs in Flemish.] It was like crying out in the middle of a desert because, apart from the German soldiers, not a soul was around to listen to us.

Our procession headed down Stationsstraat. Near Van der Kelenstraat, a gunshot rang out, fired by whom or from where I had no idea. The soldiers fled, leaving us in the middle of the street. They ran in all directions, trying to determine where the shot had come from, but they were unable to discover the shooter.[126]

A short time later four or five more shots rang out. This time the soldiers seemed to be less excited, and made no effort to discover the source of the gunfire. They simply claimed that the shooting had come from this or that house, chosen at random, and broke open the windows. When the procession arrived at the home of Baron Orban de Xivry, von Manteuffel invited the head of the Leuven Red Cross to join them. (The commandant undoubtedly had no intention of executing the hostages at this point.) Orban volunteered to assist the Dominican Father, delivering the announcement in French, while Parijs continued to recite it in Flemish. (Before setting off, Orban and his son-in-law offered water to the parched Parijs and several officers. One of them unintentionally made off with the empty glass, brandishing it aloft, "having confused it, no doubt, with his revolver.")[127]

A "singularly excited looking" officer bounded up to the group in front of the Baron's house. It was Dr. Berghausen. Schmit had just been trying to convince von Manteuffel that the franc-tireurs existed only in the Germans' imagination. The major's response was not especially cogent: General von Boehn had just missed being hit and a number of soldiers had been wounded. The group just then heard some distant gunshots from the vicinity of the station. Berghausen rounded on Schmit. These were clearly of Belgian origin, he claimed; he could distinguish between the sound of German and Belgian firearms. Schmit remained skeptical.

"I'm going to show you a corpse of one of our soldiers!" Berghausen promised, illogically.[128]

The hostages and their entourage arrived at the intersection of Justus-Lipsiusstraat and Stationsstraat and Léopoldstraat. At the center of the plaza where the streets converge is a statue of the Brabant scholar for whom the first street was named, Joost Lips. At its base, Parijs recalled,

> was the corpse of a German soldier, next to which were several soldiers and an officer, who I later learned was Dr. Berghausen. He was in a state of extreme over-excitement. He briskly took me aside, and began claiming that the priests and monks were the cause of this death, because they had aroused the population.[129]

The doctor ordered Parijs to carry off the corpse, but von Manteuffel intervened and over-ruled him.

Berghausen then jumped onto the sloping pediment of the statue. He announced, first in French, for the benefit of the hostages, that the soldier had been killed by shots fired from that house, and he pointed to the David-Fischbach mansion. "The life of a German soldier," he declaimed, "is worth more than that of the entire population of Leuven!" Then he made the same accusation and the same declaration in German. "My dear Landsturm," he continued. "You know how to avenge the death of a comrade. It's from there that someone shot this soldier," and he again pointed at the David-Fischbach house.[130]

Berghausen's inflamatory speech had the impact he intended. The enraged soldiers stormed the house. Baron Orban, who happened to be David-Fischbach's cousin, hastily pointed out to an officer than only an autopsy could determine whether the dead hussar had been killed by a Belgian bullet. "It seemed infinitely more probable that the man was hit by one of the numerous German bullets whistling by since 8:00."[131] The officer was not impressed; by way of response, he whipped out a pistol and thrust it against the baron's temple. Another, saner officer restrained his colleague and pulled him away.

A soldier hurled an incendiary grenade through a second floor window.

Orban tried again. M. David-Fischbach, he assured several officers, was an entirely harmless old man. Within l'hôtel DavidFischbach were paintings and art objects of extremely great value. The officers were not moved by either consideration.[132]

The hostages were led off toward the station. They had only time to glimpse an old servant, Pieter van der Mosten, dash out of the building briefly, and seeing the menacing soldiers approach, run back inside to warn his masters, instead of fleeing. His charred body would be discovered the next day.

Dr. Berghausen himself broke open the front door of the house. When the David-Fischbachs came downstairs, the Oberarzt questioned them about the dead soldier. "Old David-Fischbach," Berghausen testified, "declared that he knew nothing about it." Nonetheless, Berghausen hauled the father and son out into the street. "At this moment," according to the physician, "a tumult arose in the street because the soldiers standing near the monument, and I myself, were shot at from some houses further down on the same side of the street. During this time I lost sight of David-Fischbach, his son, and their servant in the darkness." Proceeding down the street, Berghausen and the other Germans were subjected to "a murderous fire." As usual, the inept "franc-tireurs" missed their targets: "That we – or some of us – weren't killed, I can only explain by the fact that the officers and soldiers were advancing down the same side of the street from where the shooting was coming from and also that a profound darkness reigned."[133]

Dr. Berghausen rejoined the group of civilians and their escort as it proceeded down Stationsstraat. When the party halted one more time for Parijs and Orban de Xivry to make their announcement, the irrepressible *Oberarzt*, standing beside Schmit, pointed at a window on the upper floor of the Hôtel d'Industrie, on his left. "Our soldiers were fired on from here as well," he told the acting burgomaster. Schmit looked up to where Berghausen was pointing. He saw two helmeted German soldiers in the window.

The doctor spotted them at the same time. "I meant to say that someone fired from the hotel opposite at our poor wounded men who were billeted in that hotel."[134] (*"Oder daneben"* – "or nearby" – was a favorite German response when civilians disputed the claim that firing could have come from a certain home.)

When the hostages were paraded back up Stationsstraat, they saw the bodies of the two David-Fischbachs. The father had apparently been shot, the son stabbed, shot, and then battered by rifle butts.[135]

"I assume," Berghausen innocently observes, "that the comrades of the soldier who had been shot, having seen that it was from Fischbach's house that their comrade had been shot, had immediately carried out this punishment on the occupant of the house."[136] So forthcoming about other adventures, Berghausen modestly makes no mention of his latenight theatrics preceding the murders.

Berghausen nonetheless devotes the bulk of his deposition to the incident – no doubt reflecting the outrage the murders evoked throughout town – on a night when there was no dearth of outrages in Leuven.

◄◄––►►

There was a sequel. On September 2nd, Berghausen came by the St. Thomas Hospital to request a favor. Could he borrow the Dion-Bouton, the David-Fischbachs' luxury sports car, for an hour and a half? He had to visit some wounded soldiers in Aarschot and Diest, he claimed, and would return it as soon as he had finished. After some discussion, the staff agreed to lend him the vehicle. "We never saw it again," Noyons recalled.[137] Questioned the next day, the Oberartz claimed that his chief had appropriated the car. But von Manteuffel, Berghausen was told, had earlier decreed that the car would not be requisitioned. A week later Berghausen returned with a worthless old jalopy to replace the superb new car. Encouraged by another medical officer, Dr. Ohren, no admirer of his colleague, the hospital staff filed a claim with the *Kommandantur*. No written answer was ever received, but Dr. Ohren eventually explained the decision. Léon David-Fischbach, he had been told,

> had been executed on the evening of the 25th of August, and they had found on his body a will dated the day before, in which he had left his motor to the Hospital of Saint Thomas.

This will, they went on to say, was worthless because having been condemned to death by the military authorities, all of Léon David's goods were de jure forfeit to the German Empire...

Hervé de Gruben was not impressed. "Dr. Ohren always seemed to us a perfectly honest man, but he was no lawyer, and this theory of confiscation did not seem to him extraordinary."[138]

A neighboring house had collapsed on top of the murdered father and son, and their bodies were not recovered until twelve days later. Needless to say, no will was found on the mutilated body of Léon David-Fischbach, who had been clad in pajamas. There had been no inquest, no judgement, no sentence. The man had been lynched, and the organizer of the lynching had simply confiscated a particularly choice bit of the spoils. [139]

"I'M THE ONLY ONE IN COMMAND HERE!" As they continued back to the Stadhuis, Orban de Xivry informed von Manteuffel, over the roar of the fires and the shouts of the soldiers, that the murdered old gentleman, Pierre-Hubert David-Fischbach, had been the uncle of the Baroness von Mirbach, whose husband was a chamberlain in the entourage of the German Empress.

The commandant saw the murder in a new light. *"Das is traurig,"* he conceded, *"aber Krieg."* (That's sad, but that's war.)[140]

Whatever provocations may have been staged by German authorities, it is most unlikely the plans had been disclosed to von Manteuffel. Deferential, not very bright, the pudgy major was outranked by a number of officers in town, and barely respected by his own men – an excellent front for more sinister types in the *Kriegsministerium*. The hapless von Manteuffel was having a very trying night.

As the group turned back from the station toward the Stadhuis, soldiers busy breaking shop windows on Stationsstraat rushed up to the two priests. Shouting, waving their fists in Parijs's and Coenraets's faces, they accused the *"hässliche Pfaffen"* – "ugly priests" – of organizing the attack on their comrades.[141] Several times von Manteuffel intervened to disperse the furious soldiers. Further along, a few yards beyond the bodies of the David-Fischbachs, a family in their nightclothes had been lined up against the wall of a house. It was the café owner Franz Vranken, with his mother, wife, son, daughter-in-law and the couple's thirteen-month-old baby.

Their accusers had claimed that the family had fired on them. When Vranken vigorously denied this, the soldiers said, "Yes you have – we saw you!"

"But come into the house," Vranken pleaded. "The upper floors are completely closed up."

"Well then, you fired from the roof."

The soldiers brought them up Stationsstraat to serve as shields while they attacked the nests of franc-tireurs further up the street. The escort was about to fire on German soldiers emerging from the David-Fischbach house when an officer cried out, "Stop! Those are our people!" When the luckless father and son were dragged outside, one soldier propped his rifle on the shoulder of Mevrouw Vranken to steady his aim while he shot Léon David-Fischbach.

Vranken had the strong impression that Berghausen was directing the entire operation. The family was watching when the doctor first discovered the body of the dead soldier below the statue, and then announced that the man had been shot from the David-Fischbach house.[142]

And now several menacing-looking soldiers were facing the Vrankens, rifles in their hands. It appeared to Schmit that the family was about to be shot. Von Manteuffel reached the same conclusion. He rushed up to the ad hoc execution squad and dispersed it. "I'm the only one in command here!" Schmit heard him yell, in response to a remark by one of the soldiers.[143] The terrified family was escorted back to the Stadhuis with the hostages.

"I'm no longer the master of my men," von Manteuffel bitterly confided to the de facto burgomaster.[144] He placed himself directly in front of the hostages, to reduce the risk that someone would fire on them. Parijs some time before had observed the cold fury of von Manteuffel, as frenzied soldiers surged around the small group. The Dominican stayed close beside the commandant, who, though he'd lost control of his troops, at least retained his sang-froid. To Baron Orban de Xivry, however, von Manteuffel seemed rattled. And with good reason. Orban had witnessed the iron discipline of the German Army. The simple word of an officer was instantly obeyed. But here was von Manteuffel, on the way down to the station, yelling at his own escort "Who's in charge here?" as the men, inflamed by Berghausen's rhetoric, rampaged through the square around the statue of Justus Lipsius. Beneath a calm exterior, the commandant was clearly mortified.[145]

⤙⤚

From the room where he was confined after the harrowing tour of the town, Schmit noticed at one point that "the sky was filled with sheets of paper burning at the edges. The wind carried a few in through the open window. The printing was still readable on some of the old texts. It was all that remained of the treasures of the University Library."[146]

Earlier in the evening, shortly after they'd returned from the station, Major von Manteuffel entered to the hostages' room. Schmit asked the commandant a simple question: they had just gone a mile and a quarter through an area supposedly infested with franc-tireurs. No shots had been fired at soldiers from any building. The searches of numerous houses had turned up not a single gun. Clearly, Schmit said, "it was not a question of franc-tireurs, but of the misapprehensions of soldiers."[147]

Von Manteuffel did not dispute the analysis. He merely replied that "his Excellency" – meaning General von Boehn – had given him orders and he was obliged to carry them out.

The major returned to the room around 11:00, complaining that civilians were continuing to fire on his soldiers. "They're firing on each other," Schmit assured him, and proposed that autopsies be conducted on the dead German soldiers, in the presence of a Belgian physician, to determine the origin of the fatal bullets. Von Manteuffel hesitated, but then accepted the proposal. The major took his leave, and Schmit wrote out brief notices to some of the town's doctors inviting them to participate in the inquest. But when von Manteuffel returned an hour later, he retracted his consent, claiming that a cache of German bullets had just been found in a large building near the church. Extracting a German bullet from the body of a dead soldier would thus not be conclusive proof that the man had been shot by a comrade. "But it would be most interesting for the Germans to find Belgian bullets in the bodies of their soldiers," Schmit persisted. The commandant changed the subject.[148]

When Schmit had earlier implored him to spare the town, von Manteuffel had simply shaken his head. On Wednesday, however, the Major repeatedly wavered. "At one moment he would say the entire town was going to be razed and bombarded; at other times he would tell me that the reprisals would cease."[149] Schmit, who had the opportunity to observe von Manteuffel closely over a period of several days, wrote that the major "gave me the impression of having little will, of being a weak character dominated by his entourage."[150]

◄◄-►►

Von Manteuffel's difficulties with the troops under his command did not end after the burnings and killings of the first twenty-four hours, nor after the expulsion of the 40,000 Leuveners. Homes were still plundered and fires continued to be set after he had decreed that the "reprisals" were at an end. Von Manteuffel tried posting signs on homes that remained standing. An early version read: "It is forbidden to burn this house." This was quickly replaced by a more specific injunction: "It is forbidden to visit or burn this house." But homes were still invaded and burned, so von Manteuffel tried a different formula: "This house is under the protection of the garrison." The new injunction was no more effective; soldiers knew who the commander of the garrison was. Von Manteuffel next opted for a simple declaration: "This house must not be entered."[151]

Then, on August 30, soldiers again tried to set Dr. Noyons' home ablaze, but were again thwarted. The doctor protested indignantly to von Manteuffel. The beleaguered commandant personally drove over to Noyons' house and posted on the doctor's front door a notice that read: "Any man caught in this house will be shot!"[152] This drastic threat may have saved the home of the Dutch physician, but on September 2nd three more houses were set alight on Maria-Theresiastraat and another on Léopoldstraat. The newly appointed town council threatened to resign. A mortified von Manteuffel assured them that he would take the sternest measures against soldiers looting or setting fires. Residents did not learn what orders were subsequently issued, but the arson finally ceased.[153]

◄◄-►►

On the same day that Dr. Noyons had protested the second attempt to burn his house, von Manteuffel had another Dutch visitor, the journalist Bart Mokveld.

I had expected to meet a terrible creature, but must admit that he was as kind as possible. As soon as he had learned from my papers that I was a journalist from the Netherlands, he jumped up and appeared to regard me as if I were the personification of the Kaiser himself. He already probably felt the pangs of remorse, and now wanted to try to justify himself as far as possible in the eyes of the public.[154]

Von Manteuffel offered Mokveld what was to be the new German line on the "uprising" in Leuven. World opinion would never countenance the notion that professors and shopkeepers had recklessly fired on German troops from their own homes, von Manteuffel had apparently been made to understand. Rather, "Belgian soldiers in civilian dress had stayed behind in Leuven, waiting to attack the German army from behind at the first favorable opportunity."[155] This came with the retreat of the Germans during the First Sortie from Antwerp.

> He did not seem to mind much the destruction of University Hall, with its world-famous wealth of books; anyway, he spoke about it in an unconcerned tone. But he seemed to attach great importance to the safety of the Stadhuis. He said that when the buildings adjoining the Stadhuis began to burn, he had them blown up in order to keep the fire away from the beautiful monument.[156]

The major assured Mokveld that he would be perfectly safe spending the night in the gutted Oude Markt at the home of an old man who had remained behind with his grandson. But in the middle of the night the Dutch journalist was arrested by German soldiers, accused of spying and, of all things, arson. He was searched, threatened, and cursed at, and spent the night on an open platform at the station, where sentries kicked him as they passed. (Mokveld's flippant attitude with authorities probably didn't help. Asked why he had in his possession a German map of Belgium marked "For Military Use Only," the journalist coolly explained that he "had bought the thing in Aachen for one mark, where it could be had in many shops, and that the words 'For Military Use Only' merely revealed the shrewd German commercial instinct, which knows that people always like to possess things which are not meant for them.")[157]

At 7:00 a.m., Mokveld was ushered into von Manteuffel's office. The major had transferred his headquarters to the station.

> He jumped up immediately and came toward me with a charming smile. I pointed to my escort and explained that I was a prisoner.

He flushed red with anger and asked the sergeant what it all meant. The latter told the story and I filled in some details.

He showed the most profound indignation, and offered his apologies with lively gestures. He said that my papers proved quite clearly that I was a Dutch journalist. He declined to allow any further examination, and gave the peremptory order that everything that had been taken away from me should be returned at once. When I had put everything in my pockets, he asked: "Have they given you back everything?"

"Yes, sir," I replied, "except my pocket-knife."

"Where is the knife?" von Manteuffel asked the sergeant who had fetched my belongings.

"But it's a weapon, Major."

"Return that knife at once!"[158]

The sergeant reluctantly obeyed the Commandant of Leuven.

⹻

Lodewijk Grondijs also witnessed the atmosphere of incipient insubordination within the *Kommandantur*. He and his friend Dr. Scharpé had come to the Stadhuis on the 26th to inform von Manteuffel of the measures they'd instituted to police the district, and to urge that he not send any patrols there. The major agreed. (During the meeting, he kept repeating fretfully, "Why did they fire on us? You see the result. Just look – now the Cathedral has been burned.")

When Grondijs and Scharpé emerged from von Manteuffel's office, they were told by an angry lieutenant, "The commandant was much too kind with you two."[159]

LIBRARY AND CHURCH Nothing about the German invasion outraged world opinion half as much as the burning of the Leuven University Library. In the major British newspapers during August and September, there are only a couple of reports, always second or third-hand, of children whose hand had been cut off. But a stream of articles, editorials, and pamphlets described in detail, and condemned with passion and eloquence, the destruction of the venerable library in University Hall on the Oude Markt. The library had been burned intentionally; it was not consumed by fires raging out of control in nearby buildings. At a time when books were more valued than today, this act represented the sine qua non of barbarism. For the duration of the war, the Germans would be compared to Huns, Vandals, and the Mongol hordes. And, as usual, the Germans made matters worse for themselves, in neutral and Allied countries, if not in Germany itself, by refusing to acknowledge the guilt of those responsible. The crime was denied, the value of the library's collection disparaged, and the Belgian librarians blamed for the catastrophe.

The destruction of the building that housed the library's collection was nearly as great a loss as the incineration of the books themselves. Work was begun on the Cloth Hall, the *Halle aux draps*, in 1317 and the original building was completed in 1345.[160] Regarded as the finest specimen of civic architecture in Brabant from that century, the building contained two large halls. One underwent complete renovation, but the other, though restored, preserved the original molded arches resting on pillars ornamented by fruit and foliage. Brackets supporting the oak beams of the ceiling were decorated with magnificent carvings, unique in Belgium, of burlesque scenes and bizarre creatures.

Part of the building had been used as a library since 1432, but in 1676 the university purchased it from the town and four years later added a Baroque second story. An additional two-story building was constructed adjacent to the hall in 1723, in the English High Gothic style of four centuries earlier. It was exquisitely decorated – the oak wainscoting was particularly admirable – and contained life-sized statues of renowned scholars and philosophers. Within the vast book gallery of the old library, scholars associated with Leuven were memorialized. Among the many irreplaceable paintings destroyed on the 25th were portraits of Pope Adrian VI, formerly a professor at the university, Justus Lipsius (Joost Lips), Erasmus, who spent several years in Leuven, and Vesalius.

The Library was home to about a thousand manuscripts dating back to the 12th century, the most famous of which, written partly on parchment and partly on paper, was by Thomas à Kempis, sermons on the life of St. Lidwina. There were several lavishly illustrated books of hours. The collection also included manuscript notes of the university's most revered professors, spanning four centuries.

The Leuven Library was perhaps most famous for its incunabula and postincunabula, printed books from the 15th and early 16th centuries. In 1473, John of Westphalia established a press in the town and his first work appeared the following year, twenty years after Gutenberg's Bible. He and his followers printed over 120 works. John was succeeded by others, including the celebrated Dirk (Thierry) Martens, who, with the assistance of some of the greatest Renaissance Humanists, edited and published numerous texts in Latin, Greek, and then Hebrew. The library owned some 800 incunabula – they were in the process of being recatalogued when the blaze incinerated them. The collection, needless to say, was priceless and irreplaceable.

Of special interest among the library's 230,000 other volumes were those relating to the Reformation and Jansenism. Leuven theologians issued a torrent of books and pamphlets refuting Luther and the other Reformers. Cornelius Jansenius was a professor at Leuven, and his quarrel with the Jesuits riveted educated Europeans in the second half of the 17th century. The library had well over 3,500 volumes on the controversy. It also had an invaluable collection of treatises on medicine and mathematics, including a magnificent velum copy of Vesalius's *De Humani Corporis Fabrica*.

The Library was also home to an extensive collection of medals, coins, maps, and some outstanding examples of Flemish bookbinding from the 16th century. It contained as well all kinds of memorabilia associated with the university, including the original papal bull that established it.

The Library's large hall on the ground floor had been broken into early on the 25th by about fifteen cavalrymen, who used it as a stable for their horses, the same use the Germans made of the reading room in the library at the University of Liège. At about 7:30 p.m., the soldiers requested that the concierge turn on the lights in the hall; they couldn't find the switch. It was located upstairs, and when the concierge went up to flick it on, everything was in order.

When the firing broke out, the soldiers claimed someone was shooting at them from the house opposite. This house was unoccupied. Sometime later there was a second burst of gunfire, much closer now, and more agitation. Abruptly, the soldiers mounted their horses and took off, calling out to the concierge that the French had arrived. It was about 10:00 p.m., the man believed.

The concierge went back upstairs and turned out the light. He went up a second time to remove some valuables he had hidden. (The report of the Belgian Commission of Inquiry does not indicate what he removed.) Everything was still intact; no one was in the building. Suddenly the concierge heard the roar of flames close by. Moments later he was overcome by smoke, and staggered out of the building. The library had been ignited on all sides.[161]

Thanks largely to the Germans, there is only one eyewitness who left an account of what transpired in the Oude Markt. Ten residents of the square were killed. Seven were asphyxiated in their cellars and three were shot, including two Josephite monks from Trinity College at the southern end of the square. [162] Brother Allard Forger and Brother Sebastien Stratman, a German subject, were waiting in the porter's lodge to meet with some officers. When panicked firing raked the square, the first of two German victims fell nearby, a sentry posted in front of the College. The two clerics were seized by soldiers and hustled to the train station. Smacked by rifle butts and prodded by bayonets, they were subjected to further torture in front of the station before being shot.[163]

All was quiet in the square when the firing broke out elsewhere in town. Then, according to Father Florent Jules Devijver, beginning around 9:30 p.m., hundreds of troops and horses arrived, hauling artillery and munitions wagons. A little before 11:00, Devijver observed what looked like a ball of fire, a grenade, he guessed, hurtling down Kortestraat at the north end of the square, the street that links the Grote Markt and Oude Markt. "It explodes over the Markt. I see men crashing down and a horse, too. Soldiers fire in all directions. Soon some of the troops line up in front of the College, while others break doors and windows of houses some distance from the College (there are a dozen homes on each side before you arrive at the College)."[164] Devijver had no doubt why the fires never reached Trinity. The arsonists started at the north end of the square, and much time was lost looting the homes on behalf of the officers whose trunks he observed in the Oude Markt.

Some time after 11:00 p.m. soldiers began setting ablaze the first homes that had been pillaged. When they reached the University Hall, Devijver, alarmed, rushed over to an officer who seemed to be commanding activities in the square. When he told the German it was the University Library his men were setting on fire, the man replied, *"Es ist Befehl."* It's an order.[165] Other residents also observed the soldiers placing inflammatory material along the building's facade, but dared not intervene.[166]

The glare of the burning homes woke up a professor of physics and mathematics at Trinity College. He climbed to the roof of the college for a

Main Hall of the University Library before and after August 25th.

The Salle des Pas perdus on the ground floor of the University Library.

better look. "Houses blazed up and collapsed one after another," he wrote. At 1:45 a.m. "the first fires darted through the roof of the Library." By 2:15 "the Library was entirely consumed."[167]

There had been one final chance to save the building. Father Devijver had noticed that the Germans had brought some firefighting equipment into the north end of the square. Hoses were played on some homes in Krakenstraat. The Josephite Father approached an officer and urged him to use the fire engine to extinguish the blaze in the Library. The man brusquely refused. When Devijver persisted, he received the same response as he had earlier: *"Ich habe Befehle."*[168]

Afterward, those searching the rubble for anything salvageable discovered a number of incendiary tablets.[169] Petrol may have been used as well. According to Professor Van der Essen, the windows overlooking the Oude Markt were smashed and "an inflammable liquid" introduced. Van der Essen himself inadvertently saved one of the few manuscripts or volumes to survive the blaze. He had checked out Ms. 906, containing official correspondence of the university between 1583 and 1637, and it remained unharmed at his home.[170]

Could more have been done by the Belgians themselves to save the library? The German penchant for blaming the victim extended to the *Kaiserreich*'s librarians. In an article in the *Zentralblatt für Bibliothekwesen*, the case was made that had the Leuven librarians been present in the building to point out to the soldiers the value of the collection, it would have been spared. Leuveners were outraged by the supposition. The concierge was lucky to escape with his life. Any civilian approaching the arsonists from within les Halles and remonstrating with them would likely have been shot or have perished in the flames. Of the civilians asphyxiated in their cellars in the Oude Markt, a family of three, the Symonses, lived in the building next to the library. When the family tried to escape, soldiers forced them back into the inferno, ignoring their frantic pleas.[171] And someone had indeed ventured into the square to point out to officers that it was the University Library their troops were burning. He was twice informed that this is what had been ordered.

Even some residents assumed that the library had been destroyed following an outbreak of shooting between drunken soldiers sitting in cafés around the Oude Markt.[172] Rather, a good-sized rocket or artillery shell had been fired into the square from Kortestraat, shortly after several hundred men had been ordered there. For what reason had these troops been issued commands to assemble in the square at 9:30?

And, needless to say, after the first day of occupation, there was no reason for Belgian anxieties about the library. Apart from the appearance of the volatile colonel in the train station, there had been no untoward incidents. The commandant, if not particularly intelligent or assertive, was not a brute; some of his staff officers were university-educated men. There was no reason to expect that the renowned building would be in jeopardy.

-‹-›-

A church is harder to burn than a library. The Germans expended correspondingly greater efforts on this task.

Groups of soldiers entered St. Pieter's late at night on the 25th. They piled chairs, curtains, and painting frames around the altars or in the center of the chapels along the nave, and in the choir. The wood was saturated with inflammable liquids, including liquor from a pillaged shop on Naamsestraat, and set alight. Five altars were destroyed. The thick door of the sacristy was smashed open with axes, a large wardrobe broken into, and the church's safe extracted. But soldiers were unable to burglarize this before they were overcome by smoke and retreated. Sometime later, several soldiers climbed onto the rafters and set fire to the solid oak beams. But the burning rafters failed to ignite the massive vault, and other soldiers, carrying torces, eventually clambered onto the slate roof. At 3:30 a.m, the professor of physics and mathematics at Trinity College, watching from the roof of his college, saw a single soldier up in the belfry of the church. Using a torch, he was attempting to set fire to the louver boards of the roof, but was having no luck. An hour and a half later, police across the street observed several men moving slowly along the balustrade, blazing torches in their hands. But it was only shortly afterwards, when a magnificent 16ᵗʰ-century wood door at the church's northwest entrance had just gone up in flames and the rush of air fanned the smouldering rafters, that tongues of fire shot through the roof and the objective was accomplished. By 7:15 a.m. the entire roof was on fire. The campanile holding the carillon began burning and the massive bells crashed through the roof to the transept below. Even as the flames consumed the tower and the roof began to

A view of the Stadhuis and St. Pieter's looking east from Brusselsestraat.

Religionskrieg! *The altar in the chapel of Our Lady of Consolation, St. Pieter's.*

collapse, the homes surrounding the church were still intact.[173]

Canon Thiéry had observed the preparations underway to burn the church's interior, and protested vigorously to Lieutenant Telemann. Finally, around dawn, about 4:30 a.m., Lieutenant Ibach was despatched to inform the hostages that anyone wishing to save precious objects from the church was free to do so. Soldiers conducted the hostages to the church, and the civilians quickly set about pulling out paintings, small statues, monstrances, crucifixes and other valuable objects. The soldiers, meanwhile, "remained prudently by the door."[174] Nor were any reinforcements assigned to assist the men when they returned breathlessly to the Stadhuis and reported that they needed help with the larger paintings. "A shrug of the shoulders was the only response we received."[175]

Dirk Bouts's famous *The Last Supper* was among the pieces left behind. A homely, devout Jesus, with an elongated Flemish face sits surrounded by his smaller disciples around a sparsely laid table. Jesus's delicate right hand is raised, the index finger pointing upward. In his left hand, he holds a white host above a goblet of wine. The disciples listen attentively. But across the table, his bulky back to the viewer, an unkempt Judas averts his eyes from his teacher. Judas's left hand rests defiantly on his hip, a bright red cloak slides off his shoulder. Two servants, peeking through a window behind Christ, look straight across at Judas with some concern. The painting was preserved only because the fire in the chapel in which it hung did not reach it. Lieutenant Telemann had it removed on the 27th.[176]

One of the objects saved from the church was a particularly striking altarpiece. A gold cross rises from a large silver globe. Encircling the globe is a chillingly realistic snake. In the snake's mouth is a smaller globe. The serpent's fierce expression is hard to decipher. Is he choking on the miniature globe? Is he recoiling from the cross? In either case, his scaly, muscular body is still wound tightly around the sphere.

◄--►

Moments after the hostages had returned with the rescued paintings and sculptures, they were informed that they were all going to be executed. Soldiers led off to the station Meulemans, De Koninck, Coenraets, Maes, Parijs, and Nijs. (Schmit was to remain behind and Orban had been released.) A French-speaking officer in charge of the detachment leaned down from his horse and shouted at Mgr. Coenraets, "We're Protestants and we're going to show you how we shoot dirty Jesuits like you."[177]

A WHITE FLAG The Valkenaers family, two brothers with extensive farms between Tildonk and Wespelaar, less than four miles north of Leuven, could neither speak (nor shout) German, like the Dupriez family or Dr. Noyons, nor did they benefit from the fortuitous intervention of Major von Manteuffel, like the Vrankens.

Units of the Belgian army were still moving south on the morning of the 26th. A company occupied various buildings on the farm of the older brother, Isidoor. From these positions, troops fired on a German platoon sheltering in a wood near the railroad line. Then the Belgians were ordered to retreat.

"At least a hundred men," the Belgian Commission of Inquiry concluded,

> had fired on the Germans. They could not, therefore, have reasonably supposed that it was the residents who had fired.
>
> An hour later, a detachment of fifty German soldiers, commanded by an officer who was short and fat, with red hair, and wore glasses, burst into Isidoor's farm.
>
> The farmer and two young men, his nephews, the sons of Frans-Edward, were immediately seized in spite of the supplications of Louise, his eldest daughter, who clung to her father, begging the soldiers to spare his life. They repulsed her brutally and the three men were shot immediately...
>
> The two nephews (Frans-Jozef and Julien) died at once; Isidoor survived. He had a horrible wound under his right collar-bone.

The farmer eventually managed to drag himself over to a large rock. He lay behind it until the following day, when he was discovered by neighbors. Nearly dead from loss of blood, he was transported to a clinic in Brussels.

> The terrified family had fled into the garden, and formed a melancholy party of eleven persons: the farmer Isidore's wife, with eight of her children; then her sister-in-law, the wife of Frans-Edward and mother of the two young men who had just been killed, and her young son, age thirteen.
>
> This group consisted solely of women and children.
>
> The carnage continued after strange preparations had been made. The Germans placed in the hands of Louise Valkenaers a kind of pennant made from a vine-stake to which they tied a white cloth. Then they opened fire from different directions.
>
> Seven victims fell, five of them mortally wounded: Louise, age eighteen and a half, who died a few hours later, without having received any kind of aid; Melanie,

age sixteen and a half; Jeanne, age six and a half; Victorine, age two and a half; and
Jozef-Karel, age thirteen. The first four were the daughters of Isidoor, the last was the
son of François-Edouard.

At the moment of execution, Mme. Isidoor Valckenaers was carrying in her arms
little Victorine, who, seized with terror, pressed her face against her mother's and put
her arms around her neck. A bullet fractured the little girl's arm and injured her face,
tearing the mother's upper lip at the same time, and piercing her left eye.

Her sister-in-law was holding Jozef-Karel by the hand. The bullet which shattered the head of the boy splashed blood and brains over the mother's clothing.

The wound which caused the death of little Jeanne was frightful; it was in the
upper part of the thigh and was 8 inches long and 2 3/4 inches deep.

The seventh victim was the twelve-year-old son of Isidoor. He was hit in
the dorsal region and survived, along with his father, his mother, and his
aunt. His uncle, three cousins, and four sisters had been killed.

After the second massacre, which took place around 8:30 a.m., the
Germans burned the two farms and everything in them, including the livestock and the harvested grain. They did not concern themselves in the least
with helping the wounded.

> The killings took place without any provocation. The Germans could not logically
> accuse the Valkenaers family of firing on them, and even if they persisted in believ-
> ing that the thousands of shots fired at them came from the occupants of the two
> farms – in which, however, not a single weapon was found – what excuse had they for
> assassinating the women, girls and children, constituting the second group? And what
> explanation other than that of a refinement of cruelty can be given for the improvised
> flag which the eldest of the girls had to wave while she and her family were gunned
> down![178]

◄‹·›►

The account by Ferdinand Passelecq was based on interviews with survivors and the seven certificates of death filed at the Tildonk communal office
on November 11th. The injuries were also laconically recounted by an
English-born nun in an Ursuline convent at Tildonk, the Reverend Mother
Marie Georgine, who nursed the wounded family members. "The horrors
of Wespelaar defy description," she concluded.[179]

◄‹·›►

There is no attempt to justify the massacre of the Valkenaers in the White
Book, nor was it discussed in the German press. But not long after the killings, a local hotelier, Jules Schadts, had a chance to hear a rare condemnation

of the behavior of German troops by a German officer. Schadts ushered Captain von Stunzner, of General von Beseler's staff, into the ruins of the finest home in Tildonk. It belonged to the wealthy widow of Léon Vincart, who had traveled extensively and had collected souvenirs and objets d'art from all over the world. Everything was smashed and desecrated. *"Ce sont de vrais vandales,"* muttered the captain. But von Stunzner was a realist. When Schadts asked him how the Germans intended to indemnify their victims, he replied, "If we win, we'll pay you. If we lose, you won't get anything."[180]

"SHOOT THEM FIRST" It's unlikely that anything the Valkenaers could have said or done would have saved them. But a quick-witted Leuven resident, Mevrouw Rooman, the notary's wife who had received advanced warning of the city's destruction, may have saved her husband's life and her own through her resourcefulness.

The Germans broke into the Rooman home on Volksplaats, accused the couple of being franc-tireurs, and told them they would be shot. The wife asked them to wait a moment. She fetched her children and pushed them forward. "Shoot them first," she said coldly.

The Germans hesitated, then decided not to execute anyone after all. But the family was ordered to stand outside in the square and watch as their home was destroyed.

As they stood there, overcome with shock and grief, a soldier knelt down next to one of the children. "Take a good look at the fireworks show," he said.[181]

⤙⤚

A number of people whose homes were invaded on the first night were not so lucky.

Several witnesses passed the body of the architect Vincent Lenertz on Tiensevest. The fifty-year-old Lenertz served as chief draftsman at the University, and was well known in town.

As soon as he opened his front door, the architect was hauled out and beaten to death with rifle butts. When his anxious wife ventured up from the cellar moments later to check on him, she was confronted by an unrecognizable corpse on the doorstep. Her brother identified the body.

Lenertz had not even had time to tell his murderers that he was not a Belgian citizen, but a Luxembourger.[182]

-‹-›-

Others never made it outside. Storming down Blijde-Inkomststraat from Tiensevest, soldiers smashed open the front door of the Verleysen house with rifle-butts and began firing from within the house. Troops on the street riddled the windows of the upper floors with bullets. Others had broken into the garden and directed a withering barrage at the rear of the house. Marie-Pauline Verleysen, twenty-eight, had just given birth to a boy two days earlier. She also had a four-year-old daughter. The girl was downstairs with the nursemaid when the gunfire erupted.

Paul Verleysen wrapped his wife in a blanket and began carrying her downstairs. But bullets were flying everywhere, piercing the walls, shattering windows. Still carrying his wife, Verleysen knelt down on the stairs.

> Sensing something warm running over his hand, Mr. Verleysen lit a match. His wife had been killed in his arms. A piece of skull had been shot off and her brain protruded. A bullet had also entered her throat, and blood was flowing out in waves. Mr. Verleysen himself was wounded in the face. And the fusillade still continued.[183]

The anguished husband left his wife's body on the landing when the firing subsided and went looking for his daughter. Unable to locate her, he assumed the nurse had taken her and the baby. He crept back upstairs, and let himself out onto the roof. When he clambered back down, he found the new-born boy still alive in his cradle. The little girl, who had managed to conceal herself in the w.c. during the firing, was crouched beside the body of her mother, and was covered with blood. The girl was talking to her mother softly, reassuring the dead woman. When Verleysen tried to lead her away, she burst into tears. At that moment, soldiers invaded the house and caught the father. Kicking and battering him with rifle butts, they forced him outside and took him off to the train station. It is superfluous to add that no one in the house was firing on the Germans in the street. Verleysen had hosted two officers and six men, who had left the house half an hour before the firing commenced.[184]

CHIVALRY The story of the Mahy family is, up to a point, depressingly familiar.

Hearing some commotion among soldiers standing outside their home on the Tiensesteenweg at around 6:00 p.m., the parents descended to the cellar with their ten children. At exactly 8:00, they distinctly heard the order to fire, followed by an intense barrage against the side of the house. Then their front door was broken in and the home invaded. An officer and two soldiers clattered down to the basement. "You fired," the officer informed the cheese merchant. He at once ordered one of the soldiers to place the unlucky man against the wall and shoot him. Jean Mahy begged for mercy, but the soldier did as he was told, as the family watched in horror. But Mahy was not killed outright, and the officer himself finished off him with his pistol.

Then it was the turn of the oldest son, age eighteen. He was also placed against the wall and shot. The next oldest, a fifteen-year-old, was selected. When he had been shot, the only boys remaining were young children. The officer's eyes alighted on the oldest girl. He ordered the soldier to execute her. But here the man apparently drew the line. He flatly refused to carry out the command.

The officer hesitated, then contented himself with ordering the family to leave the cellar. When Mrs. Mahy bent down to embrace her dead husband, the man struck her with his fist.

Outside in the street, while gunfire rang out around them, the family saw the second son being carried out by soldiers. He had been stripped, and cried out "Mamman, Mamman," when he spotted his mother. They never saw him again.

The oldest son was also not fatally wounded. He managed to conceal himself for a day, but was then captured and sent to Germany. The rest of the family suffered the same fate. One can only wonder what happened to the soldier who disobeyed his order, after aiming so badly – and what happened to the brutal officer himself.[185]

"YOU TOO, YOU FIRED!" By Wednesday afternoon over two hundred residents had sought refuge in the St. Thomas Hospital. The staff heard dozens of harrowing stories. Everyone had one, of course, and succeeding days would provide a great many more.

One was told by two brothers, both professors, who arrived at the hospital around noon, Paul and Albert Michotte. It was the latter's wife to whom the German officer billeted with the family had addressed the ominous parting words that she immediately repeated to Dr. Ide, "I hope you will be spared, for it's going to begin now."[186]

The brothers lived near their parents – Albert was next door – on the Tiensesteenweg, beyond the city gates. Their ninety-year-old father had himself been a distinguished professor of art history, and was now dying.[187]

Because of Professor Michotte's grave condition, and his international reputation, von Manteuffel had consented to give the professor's wife a written order expressly forbidding German soldiers from entering the house. This proved to be as effective as von Manteuffel's other efforts to control troops within the city.

The two brothers had had a traumatic night. All the houses around them had been set on fire; the villa in which they were sheltering was repeatedly hit by bursts of gunfire. In the morning they were hauled out and driven along Tiensevest to the station. They were insulted and clubbed with rifle butts en route, and, inevitably, threatened with execution if anyone fired on the troops – who busily set fire to all the houses still standing on the street. In the station, the brothers were hauled before an ad hoc tribunal and threatened with execution. But after three hours, they were released. "While they were away," De Gruben reported, "another drama was in progress in their parents' house."[188]

Despite von Manteuffel's order, soldiers marching into Leuven

> excited by the spectacle of the fires that were raging along Tiensesteenweg, yelled, "You, too, you fired!" It was in vain that Madame Michotte assured them that she lived alone with her husband and had no weapons. Their rage was not even assuaged by the sight of the dying man. They took the mattress by the four corners and carried it out on the road.
>
> When the two Michottes were released, they found their paternal home in flames before their parents' eyes. It was then that they came to ask us for shelter.
>
> An hour later the whole family was installed at St. Thomas. The old man died there the next day in the cellar, where we had taken him in case of bombardment. He was buried in the garden.[189]

◄←→►

As with the looting of Professor Van Gehuchten's house, the kidnaping of the burgomaster, and the murder of the David-Fischbachs, Leuveners, focusing their indignation on the outrages suffered by others, repeated the story of ninety-year-old Professor Michotte, in great pain, barely conscious, unable to rise from his bed, accused all the same of being a franc-tireur and dragged into the street. Perhaps, some said, Michotte had been fortunate. Less charitable troops might not have left him his mattress, or might have tortured and shot him.[190]

CONTEMPT No doubt some ordinary German soldiers and perhaps a few officers were disgusted by what they witnessed in and around Leuven. However, most of these men kept their thoughts to themselves. Gaston Klein, a *Landsturmer* motorcyclist from Halle, must be permitted to speak for them.

Klein was killed or captured in early September. The following diary entry is dated August 29th. "After Roosbeek we began to have an idea of the war: houses burnt, walls pierced by bullets, the face of a tower carried away by shells, etc.; a few isolated crosses marked the graves of victims." Leuven was "a true military ants' nest. The battalion of the Halle Landsturm arrived, dragging with it all kinds of things, especially bottles of wine." Many soldiers, he noted, were already drunk. The city "presented such a picture of devastation that it would be impossible to imagine anything worse. Streets were blocked by burning and falling houses; only a few remained standing. One had to walk over broken glass and pieces of burning wood. The tram and telephone wires were dragging in the streets and obstructing the way." Klein's battalion was ordered to break into houses "to carry off the wine and anything else, under the name of 'requisition.'

> They assembled, a disorderly mob, everybody going off as he pleased. Officers went in front to set a good example. There were numerous drunken men in the barracks at night; that was enough. That day inspired me with a contempt which it is beyond me to describe.[191]

◄-◄-►-►

It was not, however, beyond the capacities of Sergeant Schulz of the 46th Reserve Regiment of Infantry, Vth Corps, Fifth Army, to describe the emotions inspired by similar German behavior in northern France. He made the following diary entry on October 15th, near Verdun:

This way of making war is purely barbarous. I am amazed that we can complain about the conduct of the Russians when our behavior in France is far worse; at every opportunity, on any pretext, we pillage and burn. But God is just and sees everything. His mills grind slowly, but they grind terribly small.[192]

"THE DAY COMETH WHEN THE SON OF MAN SHALL JUDGE EVERY MAN ACCORDING TO HIS WORKS" When it became clear that the Germans were indiscriminately setting fire to the town, the volunteer staff of the St. Thomas Hospital was stunned. "While the wounded were sleeping peacefully upstairs, undisturbed by the terrific spectacle of the lurid sky, we downstairs were counting the hours of this interminable night," Hervé de Gruben recalled.

I was in a room with two or three nurses and the doctors; all the lights were out and the wide window-panes were aglow with the reflections of the fire. The silence was only broken by a sigh, the clink of a rosary, the crackling fusillade which erupted again several times during the night...

Toward one o'clock in the morning, Mgr. Deploige came in and told us, "The University Hall is on fire." We hastened with him to a window in the attic. Thousands of flakes of fire leaped from a burning mass and whirled around, scattering to the four winds of heaven the ashes of books, incunabula and unique manuscripts in the University Library.

A few hours later there was a fresh alarm. Flames were issuing from the belfry of the Church of St. Pieter and spreading to the roof. We were overcome.

St. Pieter was the foremost sanctuary of the city, and so closely linked with its history that for centuries it had furnished a nickname to the natives of Leuven, who are familiarly known throughout Brabant as "the men of St. Pieter."

University Hall, the venerable home of the Faculties, without which one can no more conceive of the University than one can imagine the town without its Church of St. Pieter! University Hall, whose austere image is to thousands of Belgians bound up with the most moving memories of their student days!

Why was the frenzy of destruction immediately directed against the shrine of the Catholic University and the center of religious life?

-<-+->-

At 5 o'clock in the morning, Mgr. Deploige said mass at an altar set up in the ward reserved for the severely wounded. There were some who said to themselves that this was perhaps the last at which they would be present.

On August 26th the Catholic Church commemorates the martyred Pope St. Zephirin. The Epistle and Gospel of the day suggested appropriate meditations. In the Epistle, St. Paul blesses God, the Father of mercies, who comforts us in all our afflictions and enables us in our turn to comfort those in tribulation. In the Gospel, Our Savior says, "What shall it profit a man if he gain the whole world and lose his soul?" "The day cometh when the Son of Man shall judge every man according to his works..."

At the moment of consecration, the cannon thundering at the gates of the town accompanied the thin tinkle of the bell with its formidable bass...

–‹–›–

Outside, day was breaking. The sky was yellow, heavy and lowering. The acrid smell of smoke poisoned the atmosphere. A rain of charred parchment and paper was falling slowly on the town.

Once more we asked the sergeant of the guard: "But what really caused the fusillade yesterday and the burning of the town?"

"A conspiracy. Civilians attacked the Stadhuis and killed thirty of our men in the Grote Markt."

This explanation, repeated like a lesson that had been learned by heart, was too absurd to permit discussion. We could only shrug our shoulders.[193]

BOMBARDMENT Wednesday night in the St. Thomas Hospital, the 26th, patients, refugees, and staff

hunkered down as best they could. Cellars and hallways were invaded. When there was a shortage of seats, our guests lay on the ground.

The night, like the preceding one, and like those which followed, was one of horror. The fury of the incendiaries had free play. The echo of their savage cries, mingling in sinister chorus with the howling of dogs, reached us through the din of falling roofs and crumbling walls. Many of our guests wondered whether the next day they would not find a heap of smoking ruins on the site of their dwellings. Every fifteen minutes one or another would go up to the attic or the roof, scanning the horizon and noting the progress of the fires. It was not always easy at night to situate the centers of arson, and, according to temperaments, this uncertainty either kept hope alive or increased the anguish of those who knew their homes to be in danger.[194]

–‹–›–

Early Thursday morning, August 27th, after changing his mind several times over the previous twenty-four hours, Major von Manteuffel told Emile Schmit that the killing and burning was over. With an armed escort, the acting burgomaster was sent out to fetch the day's hostages.

But on his return to the Stadhuis, Schmit was informed that hostages would no longer be necessary. At 1:00 p.m. the town was to be shelled by German artillery. The entire population, some 40,000 people, was to be evacuated by noon.[195]

–‹–›–

On Thursday morning, August 27th, while we were busy feeding those who had arrived without provisions, a terrible rumor began to gain ground – the town, it was said, was about to be bombarded. By whom? Why? In the anguish of the moment, very few thought of asking these questions.

Two of our doctors, Professors Debaisieux and Noyons, hurried to the Stadhuis, without bothering to take off their white hospital scrubs. [196]

Alfred Nerincx accompanied the two doctors. He and Noyons had prepared a map on which all of the establishments protected under the Hague Convention – asylums, hospitals, cultural and scientific institutions – were circled in red. At the Stadhuis, the Belgians were informed that von Manteuffel was at the station. Not trusting the soldiers who had told them this, Noyons and Debaisieux went into the Town Hall to search for the major, while Nerincx headed over to the station.

The law professor was disturbed to see that a number of trenches had been dug in the vicinity of the terminal. Already a crowd had begun to gather in Stationsplein; they'd been told trains would be taking them to Tienen shortly.

Within the station, Nerincx spotted two officers. They were seated by the entrance, incongruously writing on the back of post-cards with pictures of a Leuven that no longer existed. The law professor took in another detail: though one was a doctor and one an infantry officer, they both wore Red Cross armbands. An extraordinary number of officers were wearing these, Nerincx noticed, as he looked around the station.

I told these officers that I wanted to talk with the officer who was going to be in charge of the bombardment.

"Talk away!"

After having listened to me and looked over the map of the town which indicated the locations of the establishments to be spared, they asked if we had any German wounded.

"You know perfectly well that the Germans evacuated all their wounded on Monday," I replied. "But we still have injured Belgian soldiers, injured and sick civilians, and women and children refugees."

They snickered unpleasantly. "If there are no Germans there, then we don't really care."

I replied that in that case the doctors, priests, and professors directing the hospital would share the fate of the wounded and remain there. [197]

Noyons had been right; von Manteuffel was still at the Stadhuis. When the two doctors located him, he was conferring with Abbé De Strycker,

Vice-Rector of the American College. De Strycker had come on a similar mission, arguing that the College, the property of a neutral nation, must be spared. The commandant said that he could not permit anyone to remain at the College, but offered the Vice-Rector a safe-conduct pass. This, naturally, proved to be of no value.[198]

When the priest left, the major confirmed that the entire town was, indeed, going to be bombarded. Noyons told von Manteuffel that it was impossible to evacuate the hospital. There were over 150 wounded who could not be transported. The hospital was doubly protected under the Geneva Convention, Noyons argued: it was an officially recognized Red Cross establishment and was located in an open city.

The hapless von Manteuffel took Noyons over to the officer in charge of the bombardment. "He told me," Noyons recalled, "that 'we're going to bomb and destroy Mechelsestraat, Brusselsetraat, and Naamsestraat.'" The train station, however, would definitely be spared. "'Above all, we need to keep the route to Herent open.'"

"But why is a bombardment necessary in that case?" Noyons asked, exasperated.

Receiving no response, the Dutch surgeon told the officer that "on the streets you've said you're going to destroy, there are hospitals, rest homes, scientific institutions..." Noyons took the officer outside and pointed out some of the establishments that the Germans were required to protect.[199]

Back inside, Manteuffel would make no promises, but he granted permission for the medical personnel and staff to remain with the patients.

The refugees, however, would have to leave. He dispatched an officer and six men to kick them out.

At the hospital, a desperate Noyons located another map of Leuven and circled with a red pencil for the officer all of the other institutions under the protection of the Red Cross.

But the whole exercise was an elaborate charade. There was no bombardment. As at Visé, as at Aarschot, the threat was simply a means of clearing out the population in order to facilitate a more thorough and systematic pillaging of the town. Noyons disgustedly described the threat as "one enormous hoax."[200]

‹‹-‹--›-››

Leuveners learned about the impending bombardment in different ways and at different times on the 27th. Whatever time they were notified, most residents were told to rush to the station; the bombing was to start imminently.

At the Jesuit College in Minderbroedersstraat, the fathers were informed at 8:00 a.m. that the town was to be evacuated within one hour.[201] Around 9:00 a.m. a group of mounted officers shouted to Professor Verriest that the town was going to be bombarded in ten minutes.[202] The Chambry family on Léopoldstraat was given the message around mid-morning by soldiers going from house to house, pounding on doors with their rifle butts.[203] Lodewijk Grondijs watched as a tipsy detachment of soldiers, staggering and arguing, was given instructions by a haughty-looking officer who rode up on horseback. Enlightened, the soldiers raced over to Grondijs and his friend and tried to hustle them off to the train station. "Quick!" they yelled. "Be off." The shelling was to begin at noon.[204]

Drummers were employed in various parts of town to get the word out. One man encountered them on Diestevest.[205] Professor Nerincx, who had been informed about the bombing at 8:00 a.m., ran across them about an hour later at the corner of Maria-Theresiastraat and Tiensestraat. Leading the small procession was the ubiquitous Dr. Berghausen.

The Oberartz, whom Nerincx had not yet met, confirmed that the town would indeed be bombarded at noon.

"Why?" asked Nerincx.

"Because earlier this morning a German major had his throat slit by a Leuven barber," replied Berghausen, with a straight face.

"What major?" asked the outraged Nerincx. "What barber? On what street?"

"None of your business," snapped Berghausen.

The pretext was so grotesque and the response so peremptory that Nerincx only asked in what direction the population ought to head to avoid encountering military operations.

Berghausen told him that everyone should go to the station, as the town was being bombarded from this position. The entire population would be evacuated in trains.[206]

DEUTSCHLAND ÜBER ALLES Virtually the only people remaining in Leuven were the patients and staff of the St. Thomas Hospital, and the families of the latter.

"When our last refugees had left us on Thursday morning," Hervé de Gruben recalled,

we suddenly felt a strange sense of isolation at St. Thomas. All our neighbors had fled; even the guards had been removed. The only sound that reached us from outside was the sinister crackling of the fire, fiercely pursuing its work of destruction. The sky remained obstinately yellow and the daylight sickly. You could see in faces already ravaged by lack of sleep the terror inspired by the imminent bombardment. Under the perpetual rain of burnt paper, stretcher-bearers ran from one place to another, carrying mattresses and planks on their shoulders. These were for blocking the low windows of the basements where the wounded had been laboriously carried, so as to be safe from bombs...

The night was even more dismal than the two preceding ones. The wounded spent it in the cellars, lying on the ground on mattresses laid closely beside each other. Dim candles stuck into bottles shed a feeble light in these damp, dark, dormitories. At intervals we heard in the distance the echo of drunken voices. The plunderers were yelling the *Wacht am Rhein* in the street.[207]

◄◄─►►

The pillagers did not have to bother breaking open the doors, for they had ordered the expelled inhabitants to leave them open. Once in the house, it was easy enough to shatter the panels of wardrobes with the butt of a rifle and to force open the drawers of writing tables with the point of a bayonet. Safes were harder to force, but a burglar's tools could do the work. The contents of the cupboards were strewn on the ground and everyone could choose. Silver plate, linen, works of art, children's toys, scientific instruments, pictures, all were worth taking. What the thieves could not carry off they tore, broke, and defiled. Then they passed into the kitchen, and went down into the cellar. Finally, hands and stomach full, they bore the booty taken from the enemy in triumph to the station. How many people would be made happy in Germany with these presents![208]

The goods were carefully packed at the train station and sent back to Germany, where sales were held "of objects from Belgium, on behalf of officers," as De Gruben saw advertised in a Köln paper in October.[209]

De Gruben described the community of about a hundred people, the staff and their relatives, that sheltered in St. Thomas.

It was not a family, for several of its members had been strangers to each other the day before. Neither was it a convent, for some were Catholics, others unbelievers, and, further, there were some dozen babies, who were not yet of an age to take vows, even the vow of obedience.

It was necessary to organize the life of the community, to lodge and feed it.

With good temper, common-sense, and energy all things are possible.

The premises were very spacious; each person soon had his corner, and at least a mattress for the night. The beds were reserved for the wounded, whom we had brought back to their wards. We then decided that there should be a common table. All gathered round it, morning, noon, and evening, in fraternal proximity. After supper we repeated the rosary, the Litanies of the Virgin, and the Pace Domine in the refectory itself.

But everything had begun to fail us at the same time: water, light, and bread. The water supply had broken down; the heat had burst the conduits in the burnt streets, and the pressure had become insufficient. There was no more gas, no more electric light; the staff of the two utilities had been expelled, and the current destroyed in various places. Finally, the stock of bread we had bought on the 19th was exhausted, and there was not a baker left in town.

A party of stretcher-bearers was sent off each morning to go and draw water in the neighboring houses that possessed cisterns.

With the water they also brought us back candles to light the refectory and the wards. A few days later we found some petroleum lamps in an ironmonger's shop, and a student of philosophy was promoted to the office of lamp-trimmer.

At the first meals we had been content with rice. But presently a law student took it upon himself to procure some bread for us. He got over the wall of a neighboring bakery, lit the oven, kneaded the flour without yeast or leaven, and let it cook for several hours. The next morning he served us up in triumph some flat discs, a kind of brown petrifaction which we broke with a hammer before dipping it in our coffee.[210]

⊰⊹⊱

On September 1st, the ad hoc "Committee of Notables" – the new civilian government of Leuven – met officially for the first time. It had been formed at the St. Thomas Hospital on Sunday, the 30th, and was made up chiefly of the doctors and staff there. Relations had been established with von Manteuffel the following day, and placards were printed and distributed.[211] Tuesday, when the new municipal council assembled in the Stadhuis, was the first day members of the community at St. Thomas felt it safe to venture out.

The few witnesses who, like ourselves, wandered about Leuven in these early days after the sack, will never forget the cataclysmic vision. It was almost impossible to pass along some streets, so obstructed were they by ruins. Fallen facades and balconies, street lights overturned, twisted iron beams, gaping safes were heaped in wild disorder across the whole width of the street. Every now and then gusts of wind would raise clouds of hot and blinding dust from the heaps of ashes. A sickening smell of burnt and decaying matter pursued one obstinately, and too often one stumbled over the body of a man who had been shot, or the carcase of a horse. Here and there some individual, bewildered by the catastrophe, would be seen searching among the ruins for the site of his home, which had been obliterated. Others turned over the ashes in the vain hope of recovering some treasured object, abandoned in the distracted flight on the day of the expulsion. Near the Stadhuis, German soldiers shouted *Hoch dem Kaiser* and *Deutschland über Alles* as they got drunk on champagne to the sounds of a violin.[212]

⊰⟨⋅⟩⊱

Our first visit on September 1st was to the Church of St. Pieter. We could see from outside that the steeple and the roof were completely destroyed. Inside, a desolating spectacle greeted us. The ruins of the fallen vault and the melted bells were strewn across the floor. In each of the lateral chapels of the great central nave, a regular pyre had been lit, and all their contents, furniture, and pictures had been destroyed. In the middle of the choir another pile of chairs had been heaped up and ignited, and had ruined the high altar and damaged the tabernacle. The two famous pictures by Bouts, *The Last Supper, The Martyrdom of St. Erasmus,* had hung in one of the apsidal chapels. If the fire had gone as far as that, these masterpieces, too, would have been destroyed, for they were not, in fact, removed from the church until after the fire. I know this from Lieutenant Telemann himself, adjutant to Major von Manteuffel, who had them taken on the 27th to the Stadhuis. The massive oaken door of the sacristy had been forced and the furniture within broken.

Climbing over the heaps of debris, we next made our way to the University Hall. Here the ruin was complete. Nothing was left of the immense building but a few fragments of walls. In the great hall on the ground floor, the columns, which had supported the now shattered vault, scarcely rose above the heaps of smouldering ashes, of what had been the Library of the Catholic University. Not a single book or manuscript had been saved.[213]

⊰⟨⋅⟩⊱

Also roaming around the deserted town was the Dutch journalist Bart Mokveld. Eventually he made his way to the St. Thomas Hospital, where he was befriended by Dr. Noyons and his wife. Mokveld dined at the hospital on potatoes, a few vegetables, and "a finely calculated piece of meat."[214] (He was deeply impressed with the work of his host, Professor Nerincx, and Father Claes. "After the war it will undoubtedly be the duty of the people of Leuven to twine a magnificent wreath around the three names Noyons-Nerincx-Claes.")[215]

Approaching Leuven the day before, Mokveld had smelt the fires, mingling with the odor of decaying carcasses, several miles outside town,

> The town was on fire, and ruddy smoke hovered over it. Deserted like a wilderness, not a soul moved in the streets. The first street I entered was Stationsstraat. Large, imposing mansions used to stand here, but the devouring fire consumed even the last traces of former greatness.

All houses were on fire, and every now and then walls fell down with a roar of thunder, shrouding the greater part of the street in a thick cloud of suffocating smoke and dust. Sometimes I had to run to escape from the filthy debris...

Farther on in the Stationsstraat lay nine rotting carcasses of horses, the intestines oozing from the bodies, and a greasy substance coated their skin. The stench was unbearable and made breathing nearly impossible. I jumped on my bicycle and escaped as quickly as possible...

The sun was already setting, and became still redder, making even more abominable and more infernal the glare of the burning town. Nobody stirred in this abode of death.

I roamed about aimlessly in a scorching heat. Where? I didn't know myself. I wasn't familiar with Leuven and met nobody whom I might ask anything. I passed streets that were only ruins. The walls had collapsed against each other and filled the roadway with rubbish, so that sometimes I couldn't see whether I was walking on or beside a former home.

Bicycling was of course out of the question. I shouldered my bike and stepped across the glowing cinders, which singed my soles. One spot could still be recognized as a street corner. Suddenly, three soldiers were aiming at me with their rifles.

I explained who I was and was allowed to approach. They were drunk, and with glassy eyes talked about franc-tireurs, the friendship the Germans felt for the Dutch, and so on. One of them entered the still-burning corner house and returned with three bottles of wine and a bottle of champagne. Corks were drawn and one of the bottles handed to me. First I said that I never drank wine, then that the doctor had forbidden it. It was no use. The fellow who held the bottle in front of me got nasty, shouting, "If you don't drink with us you are not our friend!" He began to beat the ground with his rifle butt. I had to drink.

Suddenly several shots sounded in the neighborhood. The three took their rifles and looked around, somewhat scared. They assured me that they would protect me. If there had been occasion for it, it would have been against their own comrades, for a troop of soldiers came sailing along, wheeling their rifles around and shooting at the burning houses as they walked, without rhyme or reason. These were drunk also.[216]

It was at 10:00 that evening that Mokveld was arrested, accused of arson. He spent the night on a platform in the station, and witnessed the Germans bringing leafy branches to the hot rubble of Leuven.

It was a fantastic night. Trains arrived out of the foggy darkness, their whistles screeching from miles off. When they steamed into the station, a storm of noise arose. All these trains brought British prisoners of war, captured by the Germans at St. Quentin. Hundreds of German soldiers escorted the trains, which were all covered over with green branches, and looked like a copse-wood sliding along. As soon as they rumbled into the station, the escorts chanted their patriotic songs, and *Deutschland über Alles* vibrated through the fog.[217]

CHAPTER 11

Leuven: Exodus

INTRODUCTION For most of Leuven's residents, the suffering inflicted on them after they were expelled from the city exceeded what they had endured during the first forty-eight hours of the sack. Much depended on where one went. Most families were directed to the station, where hundreds of individuals had been taken by force before the 27th. But others received no instructions except to leave town at once. The great majority of those who did proceed to the station were quickly made the captives of German forces and were treated with appalling brutality. At various times they were joined by large bodies of prisoners from neighboring villages and towns, sometimes the men only. There were the usual diversions: sham battles with the French, fake executions, beatings, occasional shootings and stabbings, and, as always, an endless stream of insults and threats. But before pleasure came business. The "franc-tireurs" were repeatedly searched. What valuables and money they had managed to bring with them were at once taken. The worst tortures were hunger, thirst, and exhaustion. The hostages were seldom given food or water, and were sometimes deliberately deprived of sleep. Many refugees slept in fields and pastures, others in barns and livestock enclosures. Still others were packed into churches, and occasionally barracks and schools. The sheer ordeal of trekking miles in the rain, inadequately dressed in slippers and chemises, quickly took its toll, particularly among the elderly and infirm. Ultimately some four to five thousand were shoved into filthy cattle-cars and shipped east, to be exhibited at Köln or interned at Munsterlager. (The prison-camp was near Munster in Hannover, not the better-known Münster in Westphalia.) The physical deprivations, on top of the psychological abuse – most refugees were repeatedly told that their execution was imminent, a highly credible threat – drove a number of men and women insane. The shock caused by the violation of all conventions regarding hygiene and modesty undoubtedly contributed to breakdowns as well.

Tens of thousands of innocent people, perhaps over 60,000, were on the move in central Brabant, or en route to Germany, on the 27th, 28th, and 29th.

><-->-<

The best choice was to remain in Leuven. Ironically, most of those who stayed – the physicians and staff of St. Thomas Hospital – did so not out of concern for their own safety, but to continue to care for the wounded and sick. However, other civilians, particularly from among the two hundred or so refugees who had sought shelter in the Leo XIII Seminary, decided either that the Germans were bluffing or that they could survive the barrage in basements and other buildings. The much-respected director of the hospital, Mgr. Simon Deploige, urged residents to remain. Among those who stayed was a professor of civil engineering, A. C. G. van Hecke, and some friends. They improvised a bomb shelter in a covered manure pit in the professor's garden near the Tiensepoort. They drained the pit and placed the children in it. The adults sheltered in a stable at the base of the garden. After an anxious twenty-four hours – during which they heard artillery pieces wheeled out to Tiensevest, unlimbered, and then removed – the families escaped to Brussels.[1]

><-->-<

Of the Leuveners who left, the most fortunate were those who headed south along the Naamsesteenweg or the Geldenaaksebaan to Heverlee, where the Duke of Arenberg, a German subject, owned extensive property. The Germans had orders to respect his holdings. Refugees in Heverlee were generally unmolested, and were among the first able to return to their looted and gutted homes.

If you were not a priest, the road southwest, to Tervuren and on to Brussels, was the next best choice. (The Brusselsesteenweg, the direct route to the capital, was blocked by troops.) Most of those who headed due southeast, to Tienen, also had reason to consider themselves lucky. As in the provinces of Liège and Namur earlier in the month, the further one was from the fighting, the better the prospects. Where German forces were not anxious about Belgian troop movements, the surveillance was looser, the "retributions" less frequent, and freedom came sooner.

The fate of those who were driven northwest – for no one chose voluntarily to flee in the direction of the fighting – was considerably more dire. The deprivations were more severe, the threats more specific, the captivity longer. Some prisoners were used as human shields.

Those shipped east by rail had a still more trying experience. Many among them had already been marched toward Mechelen before being herded into the cattle-cars. Some two thousand were sent to Köln and exhibited to angry mobs there, after a horrendous journey. For many, the calvary continued long after their return to Belgium. They were again driven toward the Belgian lines, where they were finally released. The civilians were given little or nothing to eat or drink on the trip to Köln, and were obliged to urinate and defecate in the fetid cattle-cars.

The ordeal was considerably longer for those sent on to Munsterlager. Like their compatriots from Visé, Aarschot, Dinant, and elsewhere, they suffered from inadequate food, poor medical care, and draconian regulations. Just as they had the opportunity to preview transport by cattle cars, so these individuals had the chance to preview something of the treatment meted out to political prisoners in the twentieth century.

◄┄►

Generalizations about the fate of the refugees are inevitably risky. There was a wide range of experiences everywhere. Much was up to the whim of individual officers. But in addition to the geographical distinctions listed above, women and children were usually treated differently. Among those crowded together in Stationplein, men were placed at the head of columns moving toward the Antwerp forts; the women and children were driven east or released. But among those sent to Köln or Munster, often no distinctions were made en route. "No milk for prisoners of war," a woman was told by a Red Cross nurse in Hannover when she begged for some milk for her one-year-old.[2]

Priests invariably fared worse. In some places this meant being spat, hit, and insulted. In other places it meant a bullet in the back of the head.

The scenarios are complicated as well by the fact that numerous individuals were compelled to go first in one direction, then in another.

TERVUREN: "WE WALKED MECHANICALLY" For most civilians, the trip to Tervuren was anti-climactic.

Gustave Verriest, the young professor who, when the firing began on Tuesday, was returning from his sister's with the *Oberartz* he had befriended, headed toward Tervuren Thursday morning, shortly after 9:00. He joined a large mass of refugees trudging in that direction.

Verriest encountered relatively few German soldiers. When the civilians did meet a detachment, they were required to raise their hands. At one point an officer passing by in a car leveled his pistol at the column of refugees. When a young man near Verriest held up only one hand – he was holding a valise with the other – the officer threatened him. The man hastily dropped his suitcase and raised both hands. The electric tram service from Tervuren to Brussels was still operating, and Verriest was in the capital by 3:00 in the afternoon.[3]

⊰⊹⊱

Though they didn't suffer physically, the anguish of the refugees was acute nonetheless – something too easy to overlook in the grim accounts that follow. Franz Dieudonné, a young student with literary ambitions, tried to capture the mood. Dieudonné's father, a physician, had been on his way to the civic hospital on Brusselsestraat when he was told the entire town was to be bombarded. Incredulous, he asked two different officers. Each confirmed the news.

Dr. Dieudonné nonetheless hoped to be able to remain with his family at the hospital, like the staff at St. Thomas. But when they arrived, soldiers massed in front of the gate prevented them from entering. Other soldiers were circling the wards, expelling everyone, ignoring the arguments and pleas of the doctors and nurses.

> There remained only one option, to leave the town, to go far away. We seized a stretcher for my grandmother and left, but the weight was too much... We found an abandoned cart in Tervuursestraat, grabbed it, and hoisted her off of the stretcher. On to Brussels.

We walked mechanically, overwhelmed by successive emotions, literally dazed. The officers we passed sneered... among the soldiers, some took pity.

And however far one could see on the interminable route, there was a long procession, an unreal exodus of the suffering, chased from their homes, robbed of everything, ruined, many separated from their families, their eyes wild. And behind us Leuven burned... Leuven was going to disappear.[4]

TERVUREN: "KEIN WORT MEHR" On the outskirts of Tervuren, beside the Colonial Museum, officers established a checkpoint. Lay civilians were permitted to pass through, but all priests were detained. They were held in a large pasture. The numbers grew. There are several accounts of what followed. One of the most detailed is from the professor of mathematics and physics at Leuven who had watched the burning of the library and collegiate church from the roof of Trinity College two nights earlier.

Amid insults and threats, I was searched from head to foot. The soldier engaged in this task suddenly cried delightedly "cartridges" and pulled out of the pocket of my cloak – a half pound packet of chocolate. He handed it over to an officer, who examined it and turned it over suspiciously. I couldn't help laughing. I tore open the parcel with my fore-finger and revealed the supposed cartridges. The officer gave me back the packet. They took nothing from me. From my companions they took razors, pocket-knives, and notebooks, and from one of them twenty francs.

During the examination we were exposed to every sort of insult. Here are specimens of a few of these insults, which I refrain from translating: *"Lauerer,"* *"Halunken,"* *"Hässliche Pfaffen,"* *"Schweine,"* *"Man wird Sie kastrieren Schweine."* [sneak, scoundrels, ugly priests, pigs, we 'll castrate you pigs.] This last pleasantry especially was repeated with every sort of variation. I was made to walk through the mud amid cries of *"Durch die Scheisse die Schweine!"* [Pigs through the shit!]

This will suffice to show the filth to which we were subjected. I dare say it would be possible to find in every army dregs capable of such conduct, but the incredible thing is that this took place before three officers who did not interfere. One of them even accused us loudly of being responsible for the shooting and of having incited the people to fire on the soldiers. One of these three – a junior officer – seemed sickened at the scene. He looked at me as though he wished to apologize, but did not dare say anything.

I was taken into a field with a fence around it where I found about a hundred ecclesiastics drawn up in a quarter-circle on the grass under a guard of soldiers with rifles ready. I was tired out after two sleepless nights and I lay down on the grass and fell asleep.

When I woke up there were about a hundred forty ecclesiastics inside the fence. Among them were the Rector of the University, Vice-Rectors, the President of the American College, an American Monsignor wearing the purple band on his cassock. There were also two nuns.

An officer took to one side twenty-six ecclesiastics, of whom I was one, and lined us up against the fence as if we were going to be shot. The priests gave absolution. We waited seven or eight minutes. An officer came and told us that we had been taken as hostages and that we should have to follow the column until the end of the campaign.

This group of twenty-six was then led outside the fence and taken across a field toward a neighboring wood. A non-commissioned officer walked beside me; we passed close to a soldier who said a few words to him that I did not catch. The non-commissioned officer muttered back, *"Es wird einer geschossen."* [One of them is going to be shot.]

Two hundred yards from the wood we were drawn up in two rows with our backs to the wood. At this moment Monsignor Willemson, an American, and the President of the American Seminary, Monsignor De Becker, stepped out of the line, handed their identification papers to an officer, and began to explain. They were not listed to. *"Nein, nein,"* roared the officer, and, turning on his heel, walked away.

We then saw, brought between two soldiers with fixed bayonets and accompanied by two officers, Father Eugène Dupierreux. He held in his clasped hands his crucifix and rosary. We understood. Four yards from us the group halted. An officer asked us which of us understood German. Father Schill, a native of Luxembourg, steeped forward.[5]

Père Schill offered his own account. Like his confrères, he had been meticulously searched. A soldier had ripped open his cassock and then attempted to slip a cartridge into his pocket. Another priest observed the trick and instantly reported it to an officer, who, Schill assumed, disciplined the soldier. Moments later there was a reversal of roles: "A kindhearted and honest soldier" who had allowed some of the priests to wander off was violently abused by an officer. "He rushed up to the soldier, pistol in hand, yelling "'What did I tell you? If anyone moves, he'll be shot. Is this the way you obey my orders?' The soldier was indignant and without saying a word looked the officer straight in the eyes. I was standing close by and witnessed the whole scene."[6]

When the officer demanded an interpreter, I was called upon. But what did I see? The Father had a large cross marked in chalk on his back. He held a crucifix in his hand and looked at it intently. The soldier presented the paper to me and the officer said, "Listen, you will first read this paper in French and then translate it into German. If you omit or add a single word, you will be shot along with him." My heart was beating violently. The poor Father was already condemned. What was I to do? If I refused to read the paper there would be two victims. If I read it, the Father would be shot on the spot! The substance of the notes was as follows: "The Germans have invaded Belgium with fire and sword; this horde of barbarians has laid waste to the whole country. When Omar destroyed the library at Alexandria, no one thought that such an act of vandalism could be repeated. It has been repeated at Leuven; the library has been destroyed. Such is the *Germanische Kultur* of which they boasted so loudly!"

As I was reading these words, the officer stopped me: *"Genug, ab!"* (That's enough!) And when someone tried to pacify him, *"Kein Wort mehr."* (Not another word.)[7]

Mgr. Jules de Becker, the Rector of the American College, testified later that he recalled the words perfectly. "Decidedly, I have no love for the Germans. In my youth I learned that there were centuries in which the barbarians burned unfortified towns, pillaged the homes, and assassinated the innocents of the town. The Germans have done the identical thing. I was told that once Omar burned the library of Alexandria. The Germans have done the same thing in Leuven. These people may be proud of their *Kultur...*"[8] The observation, as another witness pointed out, "was written on a half-sheet of notepaper, inadvertently placed in his pocket along with other papers in the haste of departure."[9]

> When the paper had been read and translated, there was silence for a moment. Father Dupierreux asked to be allowed to receive absolution. "Absolution! What's that?" was the brutal reply. He answered "To see a priest." They assented. A priest advanced. Father Dupierreux knelt down, and the priest heard his confession and gave him absolution. When the Father arose, his confessor grasped him by the hand, and after a few words had been exchanged, Father Dupierreux advanced alone in the direction of the wood. He was pale but quite calm.
>
> At this time we all had our backs to the wood. In order to force us to witness the execution, the order was given for us to turn around and soldiers were placed behind us with the order, "If anyone moves, shoot him."[10]

"The officer gave the command, *"'Vorwärts vor die Front!,'"* Schill recalled.

> Without a moment's hesitation, the Father walked forward, his eyes fixed on the crucifix. At about fifteen yards from us, the Father stopped at the officer's command. Then four soldiers were summoned and placed themselves between us and the victim. The command rang out: *"Legt an! Feuer!"* We heard only one report. The Father fell on his back; his limbs gave one last shudder. Then the spectators were told to turn away; among them was the twin brother of the victim. The officer bent over the body and discharged his revolver into the ear; the bullet came out of the eye.[11]

It is worth reflecting for a moment on the execution of Father Dupierreux. The young Jesuit was not accused of firing on the Germans or encouraging anyone else to. He was not accused of making any public remarks about the Germans that might incite opposition to the invasion. Rather he was guilty of a thought crime. He had written on a scrap of paper unflattering observations about the burning of the University Library, though he did not call for retribution. One would like to imagine that the Germans recognized that the comparison with the burning of the library at Alexandria was apposite, and that it stung. In reality, however, Father Dupierreux was murdered in order to terrorize the priests who had been selected to accompany the troops, and to terrorize, by extension, the entire Belgian clergy – the imaginary leaders of an imaginary franc-tireur campaign. It is impossible to conceive of an officer in any other European army in 1914 ordering the execution of a clergyman for an unflattering opinion written on a piece of paper in his pocket. (It is equally impossible to imagine the head of any other European government scornfully referring to a treaty as a scrap of paper.) Indeed, it's probably safe to say that for over a century in Europe, even in Czarist Russia, no one had been executed simply on account of an opinion scribbled on a slip of paper and shown to no one. Things were about to change.

⤙⤚

Following the shooting of Father Dupierreux, according to Mgr. De Becker,

> an officer in a loud voice gave orders concerning us. "Each of you will climb into one of the wagons heading toward Halle. Your mission will be to precede the troops who are going to occupy Flanders. Two hours before the arrival of our troops, you will announce our arrival. You will speak to the curé, to the burgomaster and the authorities in each village. You will tell them that if a single shot is fired, you'll all be put to death. Each house from the poorest to the richest will be burned. And now, climb into your respective wagons."
>
> Nearby were eighty wagons filled with provisions for the troops and horses. Each of us was made to climb into a cart. The one into which I climbed was loaded with sacks to a great height and covered with a canvas cloth. At the center of the front part was a small depression filled with water from the rains of the previous night. I tried for a while to empty the water. The convoy got underway.
>
> When we entered Brussels, I recognized in the terrified crowd that watched us pass down rue de la Loi, M. Alfred de Ridder, director-in-chief at the Ministry of Foreign Affairs. I cried out to him, "For the love of heaven, go find M. Brand Whitlock and tell him what the Germans have done to the priests, and particularly to the Rector of the American College."
>
> "I'll go at once," he replied, and I saw him disappear down a side street.[12]

Brand Whitlock was one of Woodrow Wilson's more inspired appointments. Ironically, the former four-term mayor of Toledo, who had gained a national reputation as a reformer, was chosen largely at the behest of influential friends, and for reasons that would appall most Midwestern progressives. (Luckily, Whitlock was not one on whom irony was lost.) The position of U.S. Minister to Belgium was regarded as a well-paying sinecure, and Whitlock wanted more time to write – though he had managed to complete a major novel, *The Turn of the Balance,* while serving as mayor. The lanky, affable Whitlock, well along on the trajectory that would carry him from a Methodist parsonage in Urbana, Ohio, to a château on the French Riviera, would do much to help keep Belgium from starving in 1915 and would record his wartime experience with acuity and wit.

On the 26th, Whitlock, who had remained in Brussels despite German efforts to persuade him to follow the Belgian government to Antwerp, had had a memorable visit with the new Military Governor of Brussels, Baron von Lüttwitz. (When Whitlock had presented his credentials to Lüttwitz a day earlier and had asked for news – then the most valuable commodity in Brussels – the general had responded, *"Nôtre Dieu nous a été très gracieux,"* and proceeded to rattle off a string of German victories.) Now the head of the U.S. Legation – Belgium did not rate an embassy – had come with his Spanish counterpart, the Marquis de Villalobar, to discuss the provisioning of Brussels and other matters. The general put them off, albeit graciously. When they rose to go, he told them, "A dreadful thing has occurred at Leuven.

> The general in command there was talking with the Burgomaster when the son of the Burgomaster shot the general, and the population began firing on the German troops."
>
> We did not at once grasp the whole significance of the remark.
>
> "And now, of course," he went on, "we have to destroy the city. The orders are given and not one stone will be left on another. I'm afraid that that beautiful Town Hall, which we saw as we came through there the other day, is now no more."[13]

Lodewijk Grondijs, the Dordrecht physics teacher, also heard two different staff officers in Brussels tell the story of the treacherous burgomaster of Leuven. One assured him that the culprit was the mayor's brother, the other, his son. When Grondijs asked each officer if the fact was official, he was solemnly assured that it was. Without the resources at the disposal of the German General Staff, it nonetheless did not take very long for Grondijs to establish that the elderly burgomaster of Leuven had no brother and that his only son had died ten years earlier.[14]

Now, in the early evening on the 27th, while he was having dinner, Whitlock received the news from the breathless de Ridder. He immediately phoned his Spanish colleague Villalobar, who had also just been informed about the priests. Stopping to pick up the Marquis en route, the American Minister sped off to von Lüttwitz's headquarters.

> It was seven o'clock. There was a heavy guard at the Ministries and the sentinels were ugly; one of them impudently mounted on the footboard of the car. At the Foreign Office we were told that we could not see the General. We insisted on sending in our cards, and sat there waiting... The windows were open and the Marquis and I stood there looking out into the little Place before the Palais de la Nation. There were groups of grey soldiers on the steps of the Palace, and their arms stacked on the pavement. Two ugly machine-guns were mounted to sweep the Park.
>
> "They vomit death!" said Villalobar, as though speaking to himself. We turned away from the window.
>
> Finally Major Hans von Herwaerts, who had once been Military Attaché at the German Embassy at Washington, and was then on the staff of General von Lüttwitz, wearing a great pair of tortoise-shell reading glasses, came out to receive us. To him I made my protests about the treatment of the priests and the professors of the American College, and indeed such treatment of priests in general, and Villalobar made similar representations on behalf of the Spanish priests. Major von Herwaerts understood, and rushed into the room where behind the closed door was General von Lüttwitz.[15]

The general immediately recognized the enormity of the blunder.

> He came out and assured us that the release of the priests would be immediately ordered... Then we all went with the General into his – or into Davignon's – room.
>
> He was serious, and instantly instructed Major von Herwaerts to give orders liberating the priests; told him to give them by telegraph, by telephone, and in addition to send out mounted orderlies to meet the columns on the road and to liberate the priests at once.[16]

◄◄─►►

The following morning, De Becker came by the American Legation to thank Whitlock. *"Vous m'avez sauvé la vie,"* he assured the Minister.

"He sat there at my table," Whitlock recalled, "a striking figure – the delicate face, dignified and sad, the silver hair, the long black soutane and the scarlet sash, in his white hands a well-worn breviary...

> Monseigneur described the experience. He told it calmly, logically, connectedly, his trained mind unfolding the events in orderly sequence: the sound of firing from Herent, the sudden uprising of the German soldiers, the murder, the lust, the looting,

the fires, the pillage, the evacuation and the destruction of the city...

The home of his father had been burned, and the home of his brother; his friends and his colleagues had been murdered before his eyes, and their bodies thrown into a cistern; long lines of his townspeople, confined in the railway-station, had been taken out and shot down; the church of St. Pieter's was destroyed, the Stadhuis – the finest example of late Gothic extant – was doomed, and the Halles of the University had been consumed. And he had told it all calmly. But there in the Halles was the library; its hundreds of thousands of volumes, its rare and ancient manuscripts, its unique collection of incunabula – all had been burned deliberately, to the last scrap. Monseigneur had reached this point in his recital; he had begun to pronounce the word "bibliothèque" – he had said, "la biblio...," and he stopped suddenly, and bit his quivering lip. "La bib..." he went on – and then, spreading his arms on the table before him, he bowed his head upon them and wept aloud.[17]

TERVUREN: "I RENOUNCED LIFE ITSELF" Lodewijk Grondijs had repeatedly noted the animus toward priests displayed by soldiers and officers alike.[18] He was to get fresh evidence on the 27th.

He left Leuven with the Rector of the University, Monseigneur Ladeuze, and a professor of History, Canon Cauchie. The three men set off for Tervuren with the Rector's old servant, who carried a loaf of bread, an enormous ham, and a fat little dog. Some of their fellow refugees, Grondijs noted, were in dressing gowns, others, the old and sick and, nearby, one pregnant woman, were trundled along in carts and wheelbarrows, or carried aloft on mattresses. Along the way, passing German troops insulted and threatened the refugees. Priests in particular were targeted. Soldiers shouted, "Down with Catholicism! Death to priests! All priests should be shot!"[19]

Incongruously, Grondijs took note for the first time since his arrival in Belgium of the beauty of the fields on either side of the road, undulating carpets of unharvested wheat and rye. He entered into an animated discussion with Professor Cauchie on the relative merits of the contributions of the ancient world and of Christianity. The conversation moved on to St. Thomas Aquinas and then the doctrines of the Jansenists.[20] At a village outside Tervuren, the servant took leave of the men. Still clutching the bread, ham, and dog, she begged a blessing from the Rector and a final caress for her dog.

When the priests were hauled off to the fenced meadow beside the Colonial Museum, Grondijs was indignant. As usual, he had no hesitation in remonstrating with German soldiers. A corporal in charge of the guard assured the Dutch professor that "'the priests incited the people to fire on us,'" but Grondijs was convinced that the imprisonment of the priests had not been authorized and that the first officer he could corner would set them free.

He was soon disabused of this notion. The tall, bearded major he contacted in Tervuren was polite and responsive, and agreed to accompany Grondijs to the meadow, though he informed the Dutchman that "two of the foremost strategists of Germany" had been assassinated at Aarschot and Liège. Grondijs asked innocently if his two priests were implicated. The major agreed they weren't, but assured Grondijs that priests throughout Belgium "had excited the people from the pulpit." Again Grondijs tried to focus on specifics. Were his two friends accused of preaching inflammatory sermons? In fact, they never preached at all; they were scholars and administrators.[21]

When they arrived at the meadow, the major was told by the corporal that incriminating papers had been found on one priest, who had then been executed. The major refused to countermand the order. Grondijs was permitted to convey the bad news to his two friends. While he spoke with them, he was repeatedly interrupted by soldiers yelling the by-now familiar accusations. The priests smiled and shook their heads, but this only elicited sarcastic retorts.

The best option now seemed to be to hasten to Brussels as quickly as possible and enlist the aid of the Rector of the Free University of Brussels to liberate his Leuven colleagues. But once he arrived in the capital, Grondijs decided he'd probably have better luck himself. He headed over to the Town Hall, and, with a sure eye for identifying scholarly types, approached a lieutenant who, it turned out, had a Ph.D. in law. Dr. Lincke was confident the commandant would liberate Ladeuze and Cauchie. While the lieutenant was reassuring Grondijs, some fellow reserve officers approached with news of Leuven. Entire quarters were being systematically burned. Forgetting themselves momentarily, the officers denounced the arson indignantly. It was thoroughly disgraceful. But when Grondijs heartily concurred, Dr. Lincke hastened to point out to him "that one must be an officer to be able to understand the necessity of such measures..."[22]

Lincke had correctly anticipated the response of the Governor General's staff at the Ministry of Foreign Affairs. Lüttwitz, with whom Grondijs, like

Whitlock, was impressed – he was "a fine man, with the distinguished air of a consummate diplomatist" – [23] listened sympathetically as the Dutchman explained that the two internationally recognized scholars had had no contact with the public, and could have done nothing to inflame popular passions.

A racing car was put at Grondijs's disposal, with a delighted staff officer and chauffeur. Zipping along at sixty miles an hour, they were soon in Tervuren, and able to locate the missing priests at the Town Hall. Officers in charge of them were furious – one tried to provoke a duel with the Dutch professor – but *Befehl ist Befehl,* and the two priests were released into Grondijs's custody. The others, he was told, would be set at liberty in Brussels.

Over dinner in a small café, the priests recounted their ordeal. There were some light moments, at least in retrospect. For some reason, Mgr. Ladeuze's servant had thrust some silverware into the Rector's valise. The Germans, after the prolonged deliberations of a "war council," confiscated the forks; they qualified as *"waffen."* The spoons were returned. After the search, the Rector told the commanding officer who he was and that one of his purposes in going to Brussels was to secure the protection of the goods and property of the German Duke of Arenberg in Leuven, as well as what remained of the university. "I don't know the Duke of Arenberg and I don't know the Rector of the University," the officer snapped. If they had to relieve themselves, the captive priests were required to inform Father Schill, who would then ask for permission. If granted, no less than three soldiers accompanied the priest.[24]

Despite the comic absurdities of their imprisonment, the fathers took the repeated threats very seriously. "If one of you says a word to his neighbor, you'll all be shot. If anyone leaves the group, you'll all be shot. In whatever village in Belgium the column is passing through, if there's the least act, or even any ridicule, directed against German soldiers, you'll all be shot." And the litany continued. The priests were permitted two minutes to confess each other.[25]

Mgr. Ladeuze and Professor Cauchie were not among those assigned to the carts. They were taken to a barn for the night and ordered to lie on the ground. If you move an inch or utter a single word, they were warned, you'll be shot. "At twenty I renounced the pleasures of life; at thirty I renounced its riches," Cauchie concluded, "and yesterday evening I renounced life itself."[26]

But during the meal everyone's spirits revived. At one point a beam of sunlight lit up the crimson wine in the three glasses. It seemed a happy omen: a reminder of life's small delights, never again to be taken for granted – sunshine, fine burgundy, the sparkle of crystal – and, for the priests, a summons to renew their vocation with greater piety and fervor.

TIENEN: A PIGSTY A group of priests fleeing east, toward Tienen, may have had as close a call as their colleagues outside Tervuren. At Lovenjoel, beyond Korbeek-Lo, they encountered a German artillery battalion, and were at once arrested and taken to a farm. There, in the presence of at least one of the clerics, Cyrille van Impe (Brother Rudolph), the fifteen officers debated what should be done with the ecclesiastics. "With the exception of one man, all wished them to be shot. One alone demanded what authority they could find for such an action." There was none; the priests were spared. The other officers, however, argued strenuously that, if, indeed, there had been no order to murder the priests and friars, there was certainly no reason to release them. They were responsible, after all, for the franc-tireur attack in Leuven. If their pettifogging colleague was going to deprive them of the opportunity to shoot the priests, they would content themselves with humiliating the *Schwarze Teufeln*.[27]

The fathers were herded into a small, filthy barn or stable. Then three of the clerics, including Brother Rudolf, were forced to undress completely, and were pushed into a pig sty, from which the pig had just been driven out. Everyone else was searched and everything of value seized, including, in one case, 6,340 francs and in another, around 4,000. The priests' breviaries were hurled onto a dung heap. Soon other priests who had been seized on Tiensesteenweg were pushed into the stable, until there were twelve.

Several times the captives were assured by soldiers that they would be executed shortly. When a soldier came in, counted the men, then yelled to his comrades, "Twelve! Twelve ropes!" Canon Lemaire was convinced. "My friend, they're going to hang us," he told his colleague, Professor Laurent Noël.

Protests of innocence and references to guarantees by officers in Leuven were dismissed with *"Kein wort mehr!"* Everyone made last confessions.[28]

Canon Noël, who had been among the most recent arrivals, asked if he might not give his traveling bag to his mother, who was waiting in the road. A trooper went out to fetch her. She returned with a senior officer, perhaps the dissident at the war council. Mrs. Noël reiterated the assurances of officers in Leuven that the priests would have free passage to Tienen. Standing in the doorway of the stable, the officer repeated the familiar accusation: the priests had incited the population to shoot at soldiers.

"I told him," Noël recalled,

> that I was a professor at the University, and in my whole life had never said a word to anyone of the Leuven "population." Also, I said I knew personally a number of professors in German universities, and I gave him the names of some of them with whom I was friendly. I told him that these gentlemen would perhaps be somewhat astonished when they should hear of my death. "Nevertheless," I said, "do as you like."
>
> The officer seemed to reflect a moment, and then suddenly said, *"Alle frei."*
>
> There was still a moment of difficulty, because the soldiers apparently did not wish to understand this order, but at length we were allowed to go.[29]

The officer was obliged to accompany the priests back to the Tienen road. He repeatedly had to admonish soldiers threatening the clerics.[30]

TIENEN: "JEDER NACH TIENEN" The Tiensesteenweg was even more congested than the Tervuursesteenweg. At least six to eight thousand residents trudged southeast, and possibly as many as twenty thousand.[31] The column stretched for miles. The sights the refugees passed were anguishing – village after village east of Leuven had been destroyed. Soldiers lining the route repeatedly menaced and harassed the refugees. At several points the way was barred.

Professor Van Hecke, who wound up spending the next two nights in Leuven, had originally set off for Tienen with family and friends. The group was halted by cavalry troops outside the Tiensepoort, grew frustrated, and returned.[32]

The column of refugees was again detained outside Tienen for several hours. However, a persistent merchant armed with a German passport was able to gain entry and secure lodging for his family and friends, after lengthy negotiations. Everyone else was admitted in the evening. The inhabitants made heroic efforts to house and feed the refugees. Nearly all private homes as well as schools and churches were opened up to the Leuveners.[33]

By Saturday there were serious shortages of flour, and the merchant with the German passport was permitted to resupply the city from a large mill in Wijgmaal that was still operating. En route, he and his escort passed through Stationsplein in Leuven, which had been transformed into a vast depository of goods in transit to Germany. Soldiers had set up tables in the devastated square amid the crates and cartons, and ate and drank oblivious to the nauseating odor of the unburied corpses.[34]

⊰⊱

Abbé Noël described the experience of those driven east.

> We make our way along the ruined avenues, past houses where a few weeks ago, at the start of vacation, our friends received us, houses that are now heaps of smoking debris. We see the dead bodies of men and horses. One of the bodies, dressed in civilian clothes, is wearing the boots of a German soldier. What is the meaning of this detail? Strewn around the street are bags and coats. The blue cloak of an officer has been draped over the cadaver of a horse. Soldiers line the road, their rifles leveled at us. Sometimes we are ordered to hold up our arms, in spite of the parcels we are carrying. As far as the eye can see, fugitives straggle along the Tienen road. Among them are cripples and invalids, conveyed in wheelbarrows, or dragging themselves along painfully, clinging to the arm of a friend. Refined women of the upper classes have not even been allowed time to put on a walking dress, a hat, or a pair of boots. Of the numerous villages that used to fringe the whole length of the road, nothing remains. And the whole day we can get neither a piece of bread nor a drop of milk.[35]

René Chambry's family, stunned by the order to evacuate, his "aged parents broken with emotion and grief," first sought refuge at the St. Thomas Hospital.[36] Evicted, they headed to the Stationsplein.

> Those who saw the square will tell you that it was a scene of desolation. All the buildings were in ruins, and still smoking. We saw in the station thousands of people hemmed in like cattle. There were people of every age and station, from plain workmen to the richest citizens... From afar, we clearly saw the soldiers taking aim at these poor people, unarmed, inoffensive, and trembling with fear.
>
> We looked on astounded, incapable of making a decision, blankly staring round.
>
> What road ought we to take after we had arrived at the junction of Tiensevest and Stationsplein? We were hesitating, when a soldier near us made a cautious sign, one sign only, and that almost imperceptible. With his finger he pointed out to us the road to follow; it was the Tiensevest. I looked for a moment at that man, our preserver; not a muscle of his face moved, but his eyes, his poor eyes, were of unutterable sadness. His signal was our preservation. A little movement – hardly that – and yet it was going to save a whole family![37]

Had they proceeded to the station, the Chambrys would have been separated, the men either marched toward the Antwerp forts at the head of German columns or sent east in cattle-cars to Köln or Munster, including, no
doubt, René's seventy-year-old father. (Professor Van Hecke had received
the same advice to avoid the station, after bribing a German soldier.)[38]

Young Chambry noted that among the soldiers lining the road out of
town, though the great majority jeered and mocked the refugees, or threatened them with leveled rifles, there were a few who seemed profoundly
unhappy with the assignment.

After passing burning buildings and swollen and reeking corpses in
pools of blood, the family arrived at the Tiensepoort.

> We ought to have borne to the left, but the crowding was so great that we could only
> mark time where we were. Nothing but heads was to be seen, a sea of heads. Oh, the
> poor wan faces, the sick pushed in little carts, the mothers, who drew round them their
> large brood of children, and even a paralytic, who was being pushed along as well as
> was possible in an armchair!
>
> On both sides of the road the Germans made a continuous barrier. One would
> have wished to hurl oneself upon them, to bite and claw them, the ferocious ruffians,
> who executed those hateful orders! One would have to go back far into the night of
> time to find the like of them.
>
> At that moment the wind was blowing violently, and a remorseless rain scourged
> us. Then the miserable herd, trembling, blanched, sick, and enduring a thousand suf-
> ferings, nerved itself with infinite pain to march towards Tienen, which seemed to us
> like the oasis of a dream, where we should be able at last to breathe freely, far from
> the crowd, which was pressing upon us, suffocating us, and sometimes literally lifting
> us along like a wave, our feet not touching the ground! We progressed with difficulty,
> and had to stop every ten yards.
>
> Sometimes a German asked us if we had any arms! The question would have been
> truly grotesque at a time less grievous. Those who walked too slowly were driven on
> by blows of the butt-ends of rifles. On the other hand, some soldiers, sickened at the
> brutality of their leaders, offered drink to the women and children. They were the
> powerless witnesses of that grievous exodus. They looked on with an expression of
> distress that I cannot forget. But that was a minority, only a very few of them... The
> others exhibited a savage joy, as if they drew the most cruel pleasure from seeing
> driven from their homes old women and old men, little children, and the sick! Oh,
> what a torturing and poignant spectacle! Never to be forgotten!
>
> Against the sides of the main road some cannon were pointed, as if the soldiers
> still feared that this herd could make a fight, with nails and teeth, against those burly
> ruffians, armed from head to foot. Indeed a brave show, and well calculated to pro-
> voke the indignation of those fugitives, if indeed they had been still capable of an
> outbreak of energy and revolt! But no! Those poor wretches, who had lost all, their

relations and their goods, prostrated by the repeated shocks of that sudden catastrophe, were no longer capable of raising their heads...

All of a sudden we heard three discharges of cannon, which seemed to have been fired from the drilling-ground, to make us believe that the bombardment of the city was beginning. A sinister jest, gunpowder exploded against the sparrows!

We had scarcely passed by the Villa des Conifères, belonging to M. A. Carnoy, when, from a deserted farm, some soldiers hailed us: *"Kommen Sie mal hier: Gastfreiheit, Gastfreiheit!"* (Come here, then: good fare for you, good fare!) Some unfortunate people, trusting the invitation, entered without suspicion. But only the men were able to get back, thrown out, in fact, without a word. The troopers kept the women... That is how they understand hospitality.

The murderous trick made us mend our pace, and all the more because the soldiers were shouting out: *"Nach Tienen. Jeder nach Tienen!"*

For the second time chance smiled upon us. We did not go any farther. A crossroad appeared. Some good peasants helped us to escape from the crowd. We were saved![39]

-<-->-

Many Leuveners went to Tienen not "voluntarily" – not on the basis of tips from sympathetic German soldiers – but because they were compelled to. Among these were the women and children seized during the first twenty-four hours of the sack. Their husbands, fathers, or sons had been either killed or driven toward Mechelen. The women spent one or two harrowing nights camped in the square, with little or no food or water. When the town was to be shelled, they were driven eastward. There are comparatively few detailed accounts of the sufferings this particular group of civilians endured.

One victim and witness was Mevrouw Sterckx, the wife of a man of independent means.

Early in the morning of the 27th, the women were told they were free. Then the Germans changed their minds: the prisoners were to be sent to Aachen. But this order was promptly canceled. Everyone was to walk to Tienen, obviously a more cost-effective option. "There were thousands of prisoners," Sterckx recalled. "I could not see the beginning of the prisoners, nor the end of them..."[40]

Like so many of the other civilians, Sterckx was riveted by the dead bodies along Tiensevest.

I saw the corpses of three young men, and then a little further on, the dead body of another young man, all dressed as civilians, all with their faces downwards. They must have been shot as they were walking along the road, and they lay just as they had fallen. I also saw the bodies of a man and a child of about seven years old. The child appeared to have been shot through the head, as was the father. These people both had little packages, showing that they were traveling on the road when they were shot. Their hands were not tied. This was some distance from town.[41]

The Germans went out of their way to torment their captives.

> I asked if I might have a drink of water. The soldiers were drinking at streams on the way, but they refused to give any of the prisoners a drop of water. At the house of a farmer who also kept an inn, I asked for some milk. This man was serving out milk to some of the poor old women when the Germans came. Pushing the women away, they drank the milk themselves. I had just lifted the glass of milk to my lips when it was taken from me.[42]

As the refugees approached Tienen, there were fewer and fewer sentries posted beside the road. Like the Chambrys, Mevrouw Sterckx seized the opportunity to slip away, crossing a field to a farm house, where she was invited to spend the night. When she returned to Leuven, the bodies of the father and son were still lying beside the road.

MECHELEN: STUPEFYING BARBARITIES Julien Sterckx, the husband of the woman who was made to walk to Tienen after having been freed briefly, was not of a particularly heroic predisposition. When, on the night of the 25th, he heard the cries and moans of a young woman next door, and then her plea "Oh, come and save me," he yelled back, "I cannot save myself. Go and hide."[43]

Around 1:00 p.m. on the 26th, he was arrested at his front door by an officer who shoved a pistol against his throat. No pretext was offered. "I had only my slippers on and no hat or waistcoat."[44] But he was seized by two soldiers, hauled out into the street, and his hands were bound. "When I implored my torturers to allow me to go into my house again to fetch some shoes and some of my belongings, I was struck a violent blow with a rifle butt and fell to the ground."[45] Any complaints or even a groan of pain elicited fresh abuse. The cord cut deeply into Sterckx's wrists. He was tossed onto a wagon and was struck several more times with rifle butts, including "a terrific blow in my private parts," which caused him to faint.[46]

He revived with the jolting of the wagon when the convoy began to move. Turning back quickly, Sterckx glimpsed his wife waving at him from across Stationsplein.

When they reached the Mechelensesteenweg, beyond the canal, he was brought down from the wagon and the cord was cut. His hands and arms were numb for three days and the wound took months to heal.[47]

Just outside town, Sterckx joined a group of about five hundred men. They were searched and everything of value was confiscated, though an officer returned a pocket watch when he saw it had initials engraved on the back that didn't correspond to his own. The men were compelled to tramp through fields and meadows until midnight. The villages of Herent, Tildonk, and Kampenhout blazed in the distance. The captives didn't sleep much when the column halted. A driving rain thoroughly drenched everyone. In any case, the men were roused around 4:00 a.m. and given a piece of bread, and the pointless march resumed. They arrived at Rotselaar by mid-afternoon and at around 4:00 p.m. they were ordered into the church, already teeming with over 1500 hostages – men, women, and children ranging from one month to over eighty years old. These wretched people had been provided with nothing to eat or drink, but now buckets of water were brought in. However, the hostages had to use their hands and the water soon became filthy.[48]

Not all of the villagers had made it to church, however. An elderly couple, the man seventy, his wife seventy-three, did not obey an order quickly enough after they'd been expelled from their home. According to witnesses, the man was thrown to the ground and an officer on horseback attempted to trample him. The horse was too humane, however; it refused to step on the man. The German was obliged to dismount and shoot the villager.[49]

Like their compatriots in Aarschot and Leuven, the Rotselaar residents had been told the village was to be bombarded. Instead, of course, the homes were looted and then burned. Sterckx observed one of the incendiary devices – a pear-shaped grenade with aluminum at one end.[50] As usual, special abuse was reserved for the priests. They were spat at and cursed. Everyone was finally ordered out of the church and driven through the still-burning village toward Leuven. When the column of refugees was halted outside Rotselaar, an old priest reproached the commander. *"Herr Offizier,* what you are doing now is a cowardly act. My people have done you no harm. But if you want a victim, kill me. I have received my soul from God and I give up my soul to God's keeping."[51] The old man, who may have been the vicar of Herent, Father Huypens, was not rewarded with a martyr's death. Handfuls of mud were hurled at him by enraged soldiers, and he was led off.

When they got to Leuven, the refugees were crowded into Stationsplein and, some hours later, shipped off in cattle-cars to Köln. Their ordeal was only beginning.

◄◄─►─►

The more fortunate among those seized during the first twenty-four hours were not shipped to Germany. Among these was a group of about seventy-five to eighty men that included René Staes, an engineer, Felix van Aerschot, a businessman, Alexandre Rémy, a teacher, and a priest from Paraguay, Father Manuel Gamarra.

Like all residents in the vicinity of the railway station, Staes spent a terrifying night on the 25th, fleeing with his mother and servants from one cellar to another and winding up, with thirty others, sheltering in a stable. As sparks flew in from neighboring buildings, the refugees wrapped themselves in woolen sheets soaked in water. At around midnight they heard a knock on the door and a woman's voice calling out for help. Just as Staes opened it, a shot rang out and the woman fell dead at his feet.[52]

When things appeared to have quieted down at 9:00 a.m., Staes ventured out. He encountered a German soldier carrying off, incongruously, a silver pyx – the container for the consecrated Eucharist wafer – and several boxes of cigars. The soldier told him that everyone was to go to the station. Unwisely, he and his family followed his advice and were made prisoners as soon as they arrived at the Stationsplein. Various orders were barked out and the captives were marched from one location to another within the square. They were searched and robbed. An officer confiscated 7,805 francs from Staes's manservant, Maurice Ghémar, for which he was issued a receipt for 7,700 francs, signed "von Frishow, Commanding the 90th Regiment of Infantry." The missing 105 francs represented, presumably, a service charge. The men were then divided between different bodies of troops and marched off at the head of the columns toward Herent.[53]

The Belgian sortie had ground to a halt between two and three miles south of Mechelen, on a line running roughly from Eppegem to Werchter.[54] Now, to assist in driving back the four Belgian divisions and recovering the four villages these troops had liberated, the Germans placed the unlucky Leuveners at the head of the columns advancing northwest. But the Belgian forces had begun retreating rapidly by late morning and the Germans had the opportunity to regale themselves with a favorite pastime, fake executions.

The Mechelsesteenweg was lined with demolished homes and farms. Many were still on fire. The heat was so intense in Herent that everyone had to scamper through the village to avoid being singed, or overcome by smoke. The captives glimpsed a number of charred bodies. Outside of town, the troops and captives rested in a field.[55]

"We were terribly ill-treated along the way," the South American priest, Father Gamarra, recalled. He and a Spanish priest, Father Catala, head of a college on Stationsstraat and Vice-Consul of Spain, and three Spanish students, had tried unsuccessfully to impress on the officers that they were the citizens of neutral countries.

> We were made to run, to halt, and to walk in step, while we were struck with sabers, butts of rifles and lances. We were kicked and spat on – and heavens, what insults! I was supporting an ailing old man who was dragging himself along on my arm in order to escape death, for he would have been bayoneted or shot if he had stopped. We all gazed at one another from time to time, stupefied by such barbarities.[56]

Late in the afternoon, the column halted again, this time in a meadow outside Kampenhout. Gamarra had felt forebodings for some time. Earlier, when he and the Spaniards had thrust forward their passports, he believed that death "was imminent, for the Germans, both men and officers, were no longer human beings, but wild beasts. God alone could save us by a miracle." Now the seventy-five or so men were informed that they were going to be shot. Father Gamarra again offered his passport to an officer. "Eyes blazing, the man shouted that it was I who should be shot first 'because I had concealed in my church rifles, machine-guns, and other weapons.'"[57]

The men's hands were then tied behind their backs with their own handkerchiefs. They were commanded to walk behind a German flag between two rows of soldiers – the men who were to be their executioners. Then they were made to lie face down in a shallow trench. Soldiers positioned themselves on both sides of the trench, guns leveled at the victims. A minute passed. Five minutes. There was still no order to shoot. After more time had elapsed – somewhere between ten and thirty minutes – the captives were ordered to stand up, the bonds were removed and the badly shaken men were marched into Kampenhout. Here they were locked in the church with all the male inhabitants of the village.[58]

At about 4:30 a.m., an officer entered. He told the Leuven men that they could make their last confessions if they wished, for they were all going to be shot in half an hour. One of the priests was ordered up to the altar, and received confessions. At around 5:00 a.m., the names of all the men were taken down. Then, abruptly, they were told they were free and were to return directly to Leuven. René Staes, the only one who spoke German, was presented with a safe-conduct pass. Gamarra, Catala, and the Spanish students were permitted to make their way to Brussels, where they arrived, after more difficulties, at noon on the 27th.[59]

The travails of the other Leuveners were not yet over, however. Bands of soldiers insulted and threatened them en route, as they trooped south. One man was whacked with a butcher's knife, another with a shovel.[60] The civilians were once again arrested. "They're incorrigible! They've all been shooting!" an officer shouted.[61] Within a few miles of the city, the men encountered a German brigade moving north. Leuven was to be razed, the men were told. Everyone would have to head back in the other direction. There was more abuse. The civilians were again berated, threatened, spat upon, and beaten.

As they headed back north, the captives were joined by a group of about two hundred villagers from Herent and elsewhere. En route, one of the women gave birth. The hostages were released at the last German outpost before Mechelen and made their way into town, arriving about noon. Four hours later the bombardment of the city commenced. By evening, much of central Mechelen was in rubble.[62]

STATIONSPLEIN: "HERE IS SOMETHING YOU WILL UNDERSTAND" More fortunate than those who were eventually conducted to Mechelen were the civilians who were simply released after being detained in the Stationsplein, without being herded north. Even for these residents, however, their captivity was an agonizing ordeal, especially for the priests among the group.

A man living close to the station had extensive and well protected cellars. Thirty-three friends and neighbors sheltered with him and his wife and daughter. The next morning they watched, fascinated, from the back of the basement while soldiers, in groups of about fifteen, pillaged the neighborhood. "I could see German soldiers in the bedroom of a lady who was taking refuge with us. The Germans picked up the little toilet ornaments and silver things and put them in their pockets and threw others down or out of the window. I could see the Germans examining the value of them before taking them or throwing them away."[63]

When soldiers entered the house next door, everyone fled into the garden. The witness, his wife, and daughter then scaled several garden walls.

When we were crossing a particularly high wall, my wife was on top of the wall and I was helping her to get down when a party of fifteen Germans came up with rifles and revolvers. They pointed their weapons at us, telling us to stop. I told them not to shoot my wife, but to shoot me instead. They didn't fire. They told us to come down, which we did. My wife did not follow as quickly as they wished. One of them made a lunge at her with his bayonet. I seized the blade of the bayonet and stopped the lunge. The German soldier then tried to stab me in the face with his bayonet, but I ducked and he hit my hat and I only got a scratch on the scalp. I then seized the rifle with my two hands and appealed to a non-commissioned officer who was standing near by, asking him if the Germans had orders to kill us. This man gave some order to the soldiers, and they fell back.

We were ordered to put our hands up. They kept hitting us with the butt ends of their rifles, the women and children as well as the men. There were thirty-six of us in the garden. They struck us on the elbows because they said our arms were not raised high enough. I was carrying some parcels containing among other things jewelry, and they made me drop the packages. They knocked them out of my hands three times, and on the third occasion I was not able to pick them up again. I had bruises all over from their maltreatment, and so had my wife.

We were driven in this way through a burning house to the Stationsplein. There were a number of prisoners already there. In front of the station entrance there were the corpses of three civilians killed by rifle fire. The women and children were separated. The women were put on one side and the men on the other. One of the German soldiers pushed my wife with the butt end of his rifle, so that she was compelled to walk on the three corpses. Her shoes were full of blood. The men were drawn up in the square in front of the Diestsevest. The women and children were confined behind barbed wire in the station yard.

Two or three German officers, one of whom was very big, and another thin and very young, came and told us many times that we were going to be shot. They came not only to the group of men, but to the women and children also. Other prisoners were continually being brought in from all parts of the town and were brutally ill-treated. One young woman, while passing by the three corpses, had a fit of hysterics, whereupon the German soldiers struck her most brutally with the butt ends of their rifles. I saw one prisoner with a bayonet wound behind his ear. A boy of fifteen had a bayonet wound in his throat in front. A German soldier (the one who had tried to bayonet my wife) came up to me and spoke in German. I said I did not understand, whereupon he said, "Here is something you will understand," and struck me several blows with his fists in my face and elsewhere.[64]

One officer at this point told the soldiers to use a little less violence.

The five to six hundred men were then told they would serve as screens for the troops moving against the Belgian Army. Then it was decided to give the civilians a taste of the combat they might not have the opportunity to experience.

> Certain orders were given. The bulk of the German troops began to retreat, and those who were immediately around us posted themselves behind lamp posts, in the doorways of the houses, and behind the posts of the electric tramways, as skirmishers. They actually fired, but not in our direction. This was all arranged to frighten us. An officer came out of the station and fired his revolver twice into one of the corpses for pure amusement.[65]

Soon tiring of this, the Germans then informed the men that they were all going to be shot. "I asked for permission to kiss my wife goodbye, but this was refused." The men were counted off and assigned to different groups. Some were then taken off in carts. The witness heard gunfire, but did not know what it signified. While he was waiting, "some German soldiers came up to me snickering, and said that all the women were going to be raped. That is, they spoke and I didn't understand what they meant. When they saw that I did not understand, they explained themselves by gestures."[66]

More time elapsed. No preparations for an execution seemed underway. Then the remaining captives were told they would not be shot after all, but would be sent to Germany, where they would be imprisoned. Some time later, the men were told they would be released. No explanation was offered. The women and children were freed at the same time, and the family was able to return home together. "The streets were full of empty wine bottles. We saw many bodies of men, women, and children in the street, all of them lying face downwards. None of them had any arms beside them, only packages. These had been ransacked."[67] The following day, the family joined the exodus to Tervuren.

At one point during the afternoon, the man asked a French-speaking officer why the soldiers under him were committing such horrible acts in Leuven. The officer replied that he was simply following orders and would himself be shot if he failed to do so. The man's wife had been told something similar by a sympathetic-looking n.c.o. when she was waiting with

her daughter behind the barricade. "He was executing his orders," the sergeant said, "but he was executing them with great unwillingness."[68]

◄-‹-›-►

Also released from Stationsplein before the expulsion was Hubertine van
Kempen, the wife of a major.

Around 8:00 a.m. on the 26th, she went voluntarily to the station,
naively hoping to be able to leave town by train. She wound up spending fifteen hours in captivity, both in the square and on Tiensevest. She
observed some twenty to twenty-five executions, mostly along the latter
street. Soldiers standing on the roof of a warehouse fired on victims placed
on the sidewalk opposite.[69]

Before she was released, Van Kempen, along with about fifty other
women, was ordered into a cattle-car. But then the women were removed.
Perhaps the Germans were only trying to determine how many people
could be crammed into a single car. Around 11:00 p.m., Van Kempen was
released, without having received any food all day. The next morning she
joined the refugees heading east toward Tienen.

◄-‹-›-►

Numerous people saw and smelled the corpses in Stationsplein and strewn
along Tiensevest, but there's little surviving testimony of eyewitnesses to
the killings. Most Leuveners were still sheltering in their cellars and gardens when the executions were carried out. Those in Stationsplein were
positioned with their backs to the square and commanded not to look.
However, a young woman, the niece of Felix van Aerschot, claimed to have
seen several men shot. Taken to the station with her grandmother, uncle,
aunt, and baby cousin, and a servant, she was told the family would be sent
by train to Liège. According to the woman's testimony, the van Aerschots
watched the Germans select every fifth man from a group of captives they
had gathered in the square. These men were taken aside and shot. If the
fifth man was considered too old, the sixth was chosen.[70] Van Aerschot
himself does not mention witnessing the executions, and it's possible the
family was told about the procedure by others, or that the killings resumed
after he was taken away. Van Aerschot did see ten to fifteen bodies in the
square. Six were lying side-by-side in a small public garden.[71] The eventual

autopsies revealed that each had been shot in the back of the head at very close range.[72] "Look at the corpses of the civilians who shot our soldiers," an enthusiastic German yelled at van Aerschot's niece, punching her on the shoulder and kicking her to make sure he had her undivided attention.[73]

Marie Willemsen Detige, wife of the manager of the Leuven train station, was one of those who did witness an execution in process in the Stationsplein. As she watched from the station waiting room, four men were marched out, among them Edgar de Becker, General Director of the Ministry of Agriculture and a cousin of the Rector of the American College. The men were murdered moments later. Mevrouw Devyver, defying the command not to turn around, also saw a civilian led to the Van de Weyer statue in the center of the Place, ordered to kneel, and then to lie on his stomach. She looked away and heard a gunshot a moment later.[74]

Father Pieter de Strycker, Vice-Rector of the American College, also watched as a civilian was murdered, a fellow priest, Hippolyte van Bladel, the curé of Herent. The two Josephite fathers were shot in front of the station some time during the night of the 25th. A fourth priest would have been killed in Stationsplein had he arrived. Pastoor Engelbert Lombaerts of Boven-Lo, a village less than a mile and a half due east of the station, had for some reason excited the fury of the Germans. Earlier he had provided troops with wine, food, and information. A grateful officer had placed a placard on his gate ordering troops not to harm the house or its occupant. But while Lombaerts was eating lunch on the 26th, a sergeant burst in and told him, "You must come with me." When the priest asked to be permitted to fetch his hat, he was told, "You won't be needing a hat anymore." He was lashed to the wheel of a canon, and the artillery column set off for Leuven. However, in Blauwput, just east of the railroad tracks, a soldier took pity on the priest and finished him off with a blow to the back of the head with his rifle butt.[75]

Following the expulsion order, Father De Strycker had left the Stadhuis armed with his pass from Major von Manteuffel. This meant nothing to the soldiers who seized him on the 27th and hustled him down to the station. He joined a group of about 250 civilians. The captives were herded into cattle cars. But like the fifty women with Hubertine van Kempen, they were forced out again. Escorted back to the front of the station, they were ordered to stand at attention. "If you move, if you try to untie yourself, or if you sit down, you'll be shot," an offer told them. They remained standing all night. Toward morning, the civilians watched as soldiers dragged the pastor of Herent to the Van de Weyer monument and shot him. Then they themselves were lined up as if they were to be shot in turn. Soldiers trundled over little hand-carts and told them these were "to carry the corpses." Convinced everyone was about to be executed, De Strycker recited a collective absolution: *"Ego vos absolvo a peccatis..."*

While the anxious civilians were waiting, a shot rang out, followed by an intense barrage. "We're surrounded by franc-tireurs," an officer cried out. But when three wounded German soldiers were helped into the square, the Vice-Rector heard a sergeant mutter, "The idiots have shot each other again."

Finally, at 7:00 a.m., De Strycker was untied and escorted into the station's waiting room, where he spent the day listening to the curses and threats of soldiers. In the evening an officer brought him a little food, but told him ominously, "This is the last time you'll receive something to eat."

Early Saturday morning, however, he was released. A German Franciscan who lived in Leuven had intervened with the authorities. It may also have occurred to the Germans that there might be unpleasant consequences if they were to execute an American citizen, even if he was a priest.[76]

How many people were shot in the Stationsplein will remain a mystery. A university student who left Leuven at 8:00 a.m. on the 26th said he counted about fifty corpses lying on the lawn and flower beds around the statue of Van de Weyer. Others, like Father Gamarra, reported seeing about twenty.[77] The bodies of twenty-seven civilians were eventually exhumed from the square.[78]

⊰•⊱

There was a second American in the Stationsplein on the 27th. Richard Harding Davis, novelist, adventurer, and now reporter for *The New York Tribune,* was the first correspondent to arrive in Leuven after the events of the 25th. To those who knew him, this was not surprising. In his eagerness to get to the front, the enterprising Davis had already nearly gotten himself executed as a British spy. (With typical bravado, he had proposed to his executioners that he be permitted to write a note to Brand Whitlock; if the U.S. Minister didn't come to fetch him within a specified time, they could shoot him. He was permitted to return to Brussels, where Whitlock secured his release the next day.)[79] Davis was only in Leuven for two hours on Thursday evening, and was kept locked in a railway carriage the entire time. But his impressions were vivid, and what he saw shocked and appalled him, though he'd covered wars on two continents.

> When by troop train we reached Leuven, the entire heart of the city was destroyed and fire had reached the Tiensevest, which faces the railroad station. The night was windless, and the sparks rose in steady, leisurely pillars, falling back into the furnace from which they sprang. In their work, the soldiers were moving from the heart of the city to the outskirts, street by street, from house to house...
>
> In other wars I have watched men on one hilltop, without haste, without heat, fire at men on another hill, and in consequence on both sides good men were wasted. But in those fights there were no women and children, and the shells struck only vacant stretches of veldt or uninhabited mountainsides.
>
> At Leuven it was war upon the defenseless, war upon churches, colleges, shops of milliners and lacemakers; war brought to the bedside and fireside; against women harvesting in the fields, against children in wooden shoes at play in the streets.
>
> At Leuven that night the Germans were like men after an orgy.
>
> There were fifty English prisoners, erect and soldierly. In the ocean of gray, the little patch of khaki looked pitifully lonely, but they regarded the men who had outnumbered, but not defeated, them with calm and uncurious eyes. In one way I was glad to see them there. Later they will bear witness as to how the enemy makes a wilderness and calls it war. It was a most weird pleasure.
>
> On the high ground rose the broken spires of the Church of St. Pieter and the Stadhuis, and descending like steps were row beneath row of houses, those on the Geldenaaksebaan. Some of these were already cold, but others sent up steady, straight columns of flame. In others, at the third and fourth stories, the window curtains still hung, flowers still filled the window boxes, while on the first floor the torch had just passed and the flames were still leaping. Fire had destroyed the electric plant, but at times the flames made the station so light that you could see the secondhand of your watch, and again all was darkness, lit only by candles.
>
> You could tell when an officer passed by the electric torch he carried strapped to his chest. In the darkness, the gray uniforms filled the station with an army of ghosts. You distinguished men only when pipes hanging from their teeth glowed red or their bayonets flashed.
>
> Outside the station in the public square the people of Leuven passed in an unending procession, women bareheaded, weeping, men carrying the children asleep on their shoulders, all hemmed in by the shadowy army of gray wolves. Once they were halted, and among them marched a line of men. They well knew their fellow townsmen. These were on their way to be shot. And better to point the moral, an officer halted both processions and, climbing into a cart, explained why the men were going to die. He warned others not to bring down upon themselves a like vengeance.
>
> As those being led to spend the night in the fields looked across to those marked

for death, they saw old friends, neighbors of long standing, men of their own household. The officer bellowing at them from the cart was illuminated by the headlights of an automobile. He looked like an actor held in a spotlight on a darkened stage. It was all like a scene upon the stage, so unreal, so inhuman, you felt that it could not be true, that the curtain of fire, purring and crackling and sending up hot sparks... was only a painted backdrop; that the reports of rifles from the dark rooms came from blank cartridges, and that these trembling shopkeepers and peasants ringed in by bayonets would not in a few minutes really die, but that they themselves and their homes would be restored to their wives and children. You felt it was only a nightmare, cruel and uncivilized. And then you remembered that the German Emperor has told us what it is. It is his Holy War.[80]

LIÈGE: MEN OF THE WORLD For a few of those sent east by train, the journey ended in Liège. It was a miserable trip nonetheless, and some of the victims had already experienced as much misfortune and heartbreak as any survivor of the sack of Leuven.

For Marie Detige, the pounding on the door came at 6:00 a.m. on the 26th. The family lived on the Tiensesteenweg, just beyond the city gates. Detige's husband, assuring her that they had nothing to fear, answered the knock promptly. She saw a soldier fire wildly at him and miss, and then seize him and hurl him outside.

"My wife and child!" Detige heard her husband yell in Flemish. "They'll be coming," a voice responded in German. She never saw her husband again.[81]

The distraught woman raced upstairs, the soldier who had fired at her husband in hot pursuit. She ran into the room where her little son was sleeping, threw herself on her knees in front of the German and begged him to spare the child.

"I'm not going to do anything to him. I've got three of my own at home," he told her, and then nonchalantly asked for some matches. She didn't have any, but he located his own, smashed the window with his rifle to create a draft, and then set fire first to the curtains and then to the child's bed. Detige grabbed her son and raced downstairs. The soldier didn't impede her.

After standing in the street for a few minutes, dazed, surrounded by burning buildings, she joined a group of women fleeing toward the station. Detige witnessed a nightmarish scene en route:

I saw unimaginable things: on both sides of the street were rows of Germans firing like madmen, yelling, without aiming, holding the rifle butt against their hips, discharging their guns in all directions, and continually reloading. It's no doubt because of this way of shooting that there were so many victims from among their own ranks. Lying on the ground were dead civilians, horses, and German soldiers. I stared at the corpses of the civilians, trembling that I would recognize that of my husband.[82]

In Stationsstraat, the women were arrested by soldiers looking to amuse themselves. The captives were commanded to lie on their stomachs. Bullets were suddenly whistling over their heads. The women around Detige screamed with terror.

"Get up, don't cry, we won't do anything to you. That was for the French," the Germans reassured them. The women looked around. There were no French soldiers. The prank was so entertaining, it was worth repeating. Now within Stationsplein, by the station gates, the women were commanded to fling themselves against a wall. "There are the French!" cried the soldiers, and again fired over the heads of their captives.[83]

The Germans repeated the jest four or five more times before its pleasure waned. An officer finally ordered the women released. But after leaving her son with the family's cleaning women, who lived nearby – and being fired on by cavalry troops while she was attempting to do so – Detige was re-arrested and returned to the station. Here she watched the troops lug into the square some of the goods they had pillaged:

blankets, clothes, hats, and all sorts of eatables, etc., etc. They had so many objects of all kinds that they even threw some to the prisoners, obliging them to accept these. The captives didn't dare refuse, but tossed the objects behind them. The Germans even lugged over a phonograph. They put a record on it and began to dance in front of us.[84]

Some time after 4:00 p.m., Detige was ordered onto a train bound for Liège. The trip was ghastly. The journey of thirty-eight miles took nearly twenty-four hours. The cars were filthy and the captives were given nothing to eat or drink. And, naturally, Marie Detige was consumed with anxiety about what had happened to her husband.

However the train – with normal third and fourth-class cars – did stop in Liège, and the hostages were freed.

One phase of the nightmare was over.

-<--->-

Other Leuven residents on the first trains rolling east disembarked in Liège as well, but it took some cunning and good luck.

Baron Alfred Orban de Xivry had an odder morning than most residents on the 26th – he spent much of it with Dr. Georg Berghausen. The mercurial *Oberartz*, when he and von Manteuffel had liberated Orban on the way back to the Stadhuis, had ordered a sentinel to guard the Baron's house and that of his daughter and son-in-law, the Countess and Count Ruffo di Calabria. Berghausen returned around 5:00 a.m. and announced he was going to establish a field-hospital in the Baron's home and that of his daughter to insure their safety. The burly staff doctor said he would bring over a couple of wounded shortly. The one hundred or so civilians who had gathered in Orban's garden, including Felix van Aerschot and his family, were immensely relieved.[85]

Berghausen may have regretted inciting the soldiers to kill the David-Fischbachs earlier in the evening – Orban suspected this. Possibly he was animated by some warm feelings he had for the Baron in their earlier dealings – this was Van Aerschot's niece's impression. But the Oberartz clearly enjoyed high drama, and a magnanimous gesture would do as nicely as a summons to murder. It was no doubt gratifying for the middle-class Rhinelander to save an aristocrat and his family, and the fact that this particular one was happened to be a gentleman did not detract from Berghausen's pleasure. The *Landsturm* physician was also not obtuse: the cold-blooded murder of the President of the Leuven Red Cross would probably not sit well with neutrals.

Hastily, Orban's family and friends improvised a hospital, pulling mattresses downstairs and unfurling a Red Cross flag. But Berghausen returned without any wounded men. He had bad news: the entire town was to be bombarded. Everyone had fifteen minutes to pack. When Orban insisted on staying, Berghausen arrested him.[86]

The civilians were divided into two groups. The men in the larger one shared the fate of van Aerschot; the women were eventually released from the station or sent on to Tienen.[87] Orban and his family, along with all foreign nationals, were conducted directly to the station, after the troops at Berghausen's disposal had finished looting a cigar shop. While they waited, the doctor congratulated the Dutch citizens in the group on their country's having permitted German troops to cross their territory, unlike the obdurate Belgians.[88]

There were problems inside the station. An indignant cavalry officer who outranked Berghausen demanded to know what authority the doctor had to send Orban to Germany. When the irritated *Oberarzt* listed the Baron's credentials, and then proved them to the officer's satisfaction with documents, the man turned on Orban. Did he know King Albert? Yes, indeed, the baron replied. He had had the honor of meeting him, and greatly admired his sovereign. This observation enraged the officer. Orban faced him down. Crossing his arms over his chest and looking fixedly into the man's eyes, the baron told him that he could not discuss the conduct of his sovereign when he was alone, unarmed, confronting an enemy officer surrounded by numerous troops. However, if the officer would be so kind as to give his name, Orban would be happy to resume the discussion after the war, in the calm and dignified manner befitting *hommes du monde*.

This worked like a charm. "You and your family can go," the officer said, "and tell your king that you owe your life to the Freiherr von...."[89] But Orban didn't quite catch the name, and wasted a good deal of time after the war trying to locate it in the *Freiherrlichen Taschenbuch*.

The baron and his family were placed in a third-class carriage, his servants in cattle-cars. The train departed. At one stop, non-commissioned officers tried to force some of the party off the train. They were franctireurs and deserved to be shot. An officer intervened. However, there were no Germans in the corridors when the train pulled into Liège. Lightly injured soldiers swarmed alongside the carriages, calling out for seats. Orban obliged them, disembarking with his party. Their Red Cross armbands made their generosity plausible. The baron and his entourage found refuge with friends, and returned to Leuven a few days later.

<-->

Octave-François Beauduin, a monk at the Benedictine Abbey on Keizerberg, after checking with his Father Superior, also coolly stepped off a train – in Tienen, in his case. Beauduin simply asked the officer in charge of the Liège-bound train he was traveling on if he might descend in Tienen. He had family there, he explained. Surprisingly, the officer granted permission.

The other Benedictines continued on to Munsterlager. Beauduin offered no hint as to why the monks happened to be traveling in a third-class car, or why the officer proved so obliging.[90]

MUNSTERLAGER: "YOU CAN BOAST IN BELGIUM OF HOW WELL YOU'VE BEEN TREATED HERE" Of those shipped off to Germany, two groups left before the general exodus on the 27th: members of the Leuven Civic Guards and those who found themselves at the Stadhuis on the night of the 25th – the designated hostages and the others who had come to confer with von Manteuffel.

The Civic Guard was summonsed around 1:00 p.m. on the 26th. Soldiers and military police circled through town, accompanied by drummers, announcing that all Guards were to assemble at the St. Martin Barracks at 2:00. They also announced, at least in some quarters, that no one was to leave the city; there was to be no further destruction of Leuven. Some Guards, indeed, were given to understand that they would be helping to extinguish the fires. Others were told they would be burying the dead.[91]

Guard members debated whether to obey the German summons. René Chambry's older brother was a member, and tried consulting a friend. But gunfire broke out once again and he had to retrace his steps. After thinking it over, the brother decided that it seemed reasonable that the Germans would require the Guard to bury the many victims of the previous night, and he felt honor-bound to assist his fellow Guardsmen. Other members of the Civic Guard were informed that anyone not obeying orders would be severely punished.[92]

Those members who had responded to the summons were marched by the Germans from the barracks to the Stadhuis, where they were joined by some late-arriving comrades. Here the group was divided up. Some men were taken to the station where, after long delays, they boarded baggage cars that had been provided with seats and were en route by 6:30 p.m. The trip east was far more civilized than subsequent convoys. The cars were not overcrowded, and the men in some received a little food and water. Though the guards pretended to be enraged when the train pulled into stations, yelling, "Murderers from Leuven! No pardon!," between stops they were quite friendly.[93]

Other Guard members, however, numbering about 150, were taken toward the Antwerp forts. Horses were unharnessed in Herent, and the men were compelled to push and pull guns and wagons for three hours. Two of those who fell were killed. The expedition would not be complete without fake executions. The Guardsmen were compelled to kneel in front of about two thousand troops, who bawled threats and insults. A Jesuit father gave a final absolution. But after a quarter of an hour, the men were ordered to stand and resume pushing the carts.[94]

The following day the Guardsmen dug trenches and were placed beside the guns bombarding Fort Walem. The point of this last exercise was lost on the men, as they were not visible to the Belgians in the fort. Nonetheless, the Belgian guns did not respond to the shelling. The men spent one night in the village church in Kampenhout and another in the cavalry riding school back in Leuven.

Several thousand hostages were crammed into the riding school. (Estimates range from two to seven thousand.) During the night, the glass roof exploded from the heat of the burning buildings nearby. One woman went insane and two children died. Another was born. Some of the refugees received biscuits, but a great number got nothing. "We witnessed terrible scenes there," said a Guardsman.[95]

The next morning, an officer announced, "You are all free to leave, because Antwerp has surrendered. Namur has fallen with 25,000 soldiers. German warships have successfully bombarded the English ports. King Albert will dine in Berlin at midday and we shall have supper tonight in Paris."[96]

But as on other occasions, the German idea of freedom was not that of other European nationals. The refugees were divided into groups and conducted on guided tours of the devastated villages northwest of Leuven. They were made to pause before the more grisly sights. "Passing through Buken," one former captive recalled, "the soldiers pointed at the dead and completely nude body of a woman, charred by fire and lying in front of the ruins of her house. Everywhere on the way the soldiers showed us with particular pleasure the dead bodies of civilians, which had lain there unburied for three days."[97]

After being shown the Germans' handiwork, the civilians were divided into groups by age and sex. Women and children were freed, then the old men, then men forty to sixty. The younger men were finally abandoned by their escort beyond Kampenhout, and eventually reached Belgian lines around 11:00 p.m on the 29th, after being fired on by the Fort Walem sentries.[98]

—‹‹··››—

The other Civic Guards, about ninety-five in number, reached Munster a little before midnight on the 28th. One member, a doctor of law in Leuven, provided a detailed overview of the civilians' captivity. But first came the journey east.

En route, soldiers in at least one carriage, disobeying orders, distributed to the prisoners some of the bread and butter they received from Red Cross women in various stations. But in Hamburg, the law professor witnessed the refusal of a volunteer to provide milk for the sick child of Geneviève Kleyntjens. "One of the soldiers in charge of the van was so disgusted by this that he went to the canteen at the station to ask for some milk for himself, which he gave to Mevrouw Kleyntjens."[99]

The train ride, though long and arduous, was otherwise uneventful, except when the professor was struck by a soldier in a passing train as he stood in the doorway of the carriage. However, other civilians sent on to Munster later the same day had a more harrowing trip. A young man, Gustave Hermans, was ordered into the cattle-cars with his wife and baby. When the train stopped in Aachen, the men were separated from the women, and then every fourth man was ordered to one side. The men were told they were going to be shot. An officer, however, intervened. The men were innocent, he maintained, and ought not to be shot. They were permitted to rejoin their families. While waiting on the platform, Hermans asked some soldiers for a little water for his child. This was refused. He was spat on and robbed. The prisoners were spat on again by Aachen residents when they were escorted to a compound with a machine gun in the middle. Here they were kept for a day and a night, and forbidden to lie down, according to Hermans.[100]

> During the whole time we were being taken from Leuven to Munsterlager, we had nothing to eat or drink. We could not sit down in our car and had to stand the whole time. There were some benches in the other cars, but not in ours. My wife was suckling our child, but her milk came to an end. My wife was crying nearly all the time.

The baby was dreadfully ill and nearly died. When we got to Munsterlager, the men and women were separated, the children being placed with the women. I did not see my wife again until the 6th of December.[101]

Dr. Louis Maldague, a professor of medicine, was appalled by the fury of the crowds of Germans lining the station platforms. His journey took sixty-two hours. He was in a cattle-car, but a few benches had been placed inside, and the prisoners did receive bread and water and even, on the third day, a little soup.

"When our train arrived at the station at Aachen, we were immediately welcomed by shouts of hatred and curses. On the platforms, a mob brandished canes, umbrellas, and anything they could find to hit the prisoners."[102] Two soldiers guarding the car yelled to the German civilians that the Belgians were hostages, not francs-tireurs, all of whom had been killed, but the crowd became so menacing at one point that the train was moved beyond the platforms. Most soldiers, however, encouraged the demonstrators. "Our guards were particularly eager to announce that there was a priest among the prisoners," Abbé Tuyls recalled. He was invariably subjected to insults and death threats.[103]

The trip was also a nightmare for the small group of hostages who had been in the Stadhuis when firing commenced at 8:00 p.m. on the 25th. Crosssing the Grote Markt after rescuing paintings and other objects from St. Pieter's, they were promptly marched off to Stationsplein, where "an indescribable tumult" raged. The men were mobbed by soldiers shouting hysterically and then searched. This was bad news for Amadée de Koninck, the pharmacist. He had in his pocket a small box of bicarbonate of sodium tablets and a flask of horse-chestnut extract. The Germans were delighted; these were obviously poisons. Luckily, de Koninck spoke German, and was able to save himself from being lynched on the spot. He was pushed into the cattle-cars with the others.[104]

After crossing the border, the guards regaled the German civilians who swarmed onto the platforms with tales of the pharmacist they had on board who had been caught in the act of poisoning the German wounded. For good measure, they informed the credulous crowd that he had gouged out the eyes of other patients.

Suffering terribly from hunger and thirst, and tormented by the guards who made a great show of downing the beer they received at each stop, de Koninck managed to hurl himself from the train at one point. He was badly beaten, tied up, and suspended from the ceiling of the car for three hours, but survived the ordeal, like the two priests in the same car who were treated to a very convincing mock execution at one of the stops.[105]

<-+->

The reception the prisoners received at Munsterlager was predictable. On his arrival, Pastoor Huypens, vicar of Herent, was shoved into a stable with a few dozen others. To amuse themselves, or acting under orders, soldiers whooped loudly, banged pots, and then fired into the stable. Several Belgians were killed or wounded. One man went insane, and others appeared on the verge. The next day, the men were relieved of money, watches, and valuables. An officer hurled the vicar's house key as far as he could throw it, telling the priest, "You won't have any need of this." The men were left out in the sun the rest of the day without food or water. When the priest had been conducted to a shed for the night, a soldier struck him in the face with his bayonet. Huypens' glasses partially deflected the blow; he would have been killed or blinded, without them, he reckoned. His eye was badly injured. The bandage he eventually received only inspired more mistreatment; the wounded priest was unmistakably a franc-tireur.[106]

One Civic Guard member, the law professor, was lodged in Stallbaracke 1A with over three hundred other men.

All classes of society, all professions and all ages, from eleven or twelve up to eighty, were represented.

Stallbaracke 1A was a wooden shed covered only with tarred cardboard, serving in ordinary times for the housing of cavalry, both men and horses. On the floor there was straw in the two rooms where the men slept and in the stables. It was on this straw that we slept. It had already been used by Belgian soldiers for a fortnight when we arrived. It was still being used when I left on October 30th.

As regards blankets, we had about one for every two persons. They were used blankets; none had been disinfected or washed. Many were thin and threadbare. Later, a few additional blankets were occasionally distributed, so that by the end of October there was almost one apiece. This was quite insufficient, and most of my companions complained bitterly of cold, especially on bright nights.

Fire and light were unknown luxuries.

For food we received one loaf for three people every other day. It seemed that these loaves were supposed to weigh six pounds, but those accustomed to judging weights concluded that they weighed less.

At 6:00 a.m. we were given a soup ladle of coffee, and at 11:00 a.m. a ladle of soup. This was generally made of meat or bacon (sometimes of doubtful quality), of potatoes and also cabbage or peas, turnip-tops, or rice, etc. About 5:00 in the evening we got a ladle-full of coffee, tea, or cocoa. Sometimes (on an average of once in five or six days), we were given a piece of cheese, sausage or bacon, but in this case nothing to drink. The food was quite insufficient for the great majority.[107]

The fare varied in the different barracks. For the first week, Father Huypens was given only bread and water, though when he was moved to the p.o.w. barracks with other priests, things improved. Gustave Hermans received "water, rice, and stale bread served out to us once a day at noon. The water was given to us in a glass and we got about a liter; it had some sugar in it. It was a good portion of rice and the bread was about seven ounces. It was black bread made out of rye. We never had any coffee or tea or butter or anything but the water, rice, and bread."[108] In Abbé Tuyls' barracks, "the food was so bad that, despite the hunger that devoured them, the poor people threw the contents of their bowls into the latrine."[109] The latrine itself consisted of a trench in front of the barracks, above which was fixed a long pole on which the men sat to defecate, *"in conspectu omnium,"* as Abbé Tuyls wrote.

Eventually, those in the lawyer's barracks were able to purchase bread at the canteen. The Guardsmen and the other civilians with them had luckily not had their money confiscated. Most prisoners, like those with Alphonse Verlooy, Leuven's postmaster, were thoroughly searched and everything of value seized.[110]

Everyone's health suffered. No linen, towels, or fresh clothes were issued. For six weeks, the prisoners in Hermans' barracks were denied water to wash with. Those imprisoned with the lawyer had some access to water, but were issued no soap until mid-October, though this could be purchased in the canteen.[111]

Dr. Maldague had an opportunity to observe in action the camp doctor, a man named Mayer. He continually insulted the prisoners, calling them pigs and bandits, and arbitrarily refused to treat some who were brought to him. The sick lay sprawled outside the infirmary, in all weather. Maldague did what he could for the prisoners who were ill, including some who had become incoherent, but without any medicines at his disposal, he was continually frustrated. There were cases of tuberculosis, scurvy, and syphilis. When the doctor attempted to have a woman with syphilitic sores in her mouth placed in isolation, he was told that there was no room in the quarantine station.[112]

◄◄-►►

Dr. Maldague was particularly affected by the deplorable condition of the women and children. There were around a hundred, and for two weeks the doctor was denied permission to visit them. When he did, he "found all the poor women reduced to a most lamentable condition... Most of the women and children had become sick, and I had nothing with which to treat them."[113] Even the soldiers accompanying him were appalled, telling Maldague they couldn't bear to look.

Having to live side-by-side with "women of the people" was almost as distressing for *"les dames de la bonne société"* as the physical privations, which were considerable. Housed in a barn, they slept on hay, and covered themselves with dirty sacks. For plates, they had tin basins, shared among five. Their soup was prepared in bathtubs and brought over in buckets. A board over a barrel served as a toilet; there was no privacy.[114]

Geneviève Nagant Kleyntjes summarized the deplorable conditions.

> Arriving in Munster Friday night, we were conducted to the prison camp between two rows of soldiers, where we were placed in a barn. [Kleyntjes had a three-year-old and a five-year-old in addition to the baby.] We found there one hundred five women and children, reduced to a most frightening state of physical and moral distress. We remained there until Tuesday evening, lying on straw, receiving only a stingy portion of bread and some awful soup at midday and at night. During these four days and four nights, the barn was filled with scenes of desolation and terror. Children became sick and their tears and cries increased the anxiety of the other children and the suffering of all. The old women, and there was one of eighty-two, were dying of exhaustion and misery. One of them went insane, and during the night crept up to her neighbors and cried that she was looking for her house. We had nothing, and could do nothing, to console ourselves, or relieve one another's misery. [115]

After four days, those who were not sick were permitted to move into a large house, though they still had to sleep on straw.

The women and children were sent back to Belgium on September 27th. A priest from Munster, Friedrich Unverferhrt, who had visited the wretched women several times, urged them not to say anything about what they had endured when they returned to Belgium. Was he telling them not to be truthful? Kleyntjes asked him. It would be best to say nothing, the priest replied uneasily, but if you must speak about what you've suffered, say that it all happened as the result of an error.[116]

⊰⊱

For many, the monotony and isolation were as agonizing as the physical deprivations. The prisoners were given no work, and most had nothing to read. There was no organized recreation. Singing was forbidden in some barracks, as was smoking. The Leuven captives amused themselves by conversing with one another and by constructing primitive utensils and other objects. Later, in October, permission was occasionally given to hold public lectures. There were also frequent recitations of the rosary and other liturgies, additional spiritual exercises, and sermons. But only twice were the prisoners allowed to celebrate mass.[117]

Most prisoners were never permitted reading material. However, in some barracks a few books were distributed, which were promptly read aloud, and in at least one case, texts were actually assigned to inmates. Early in September, prison authorities decided that there might be some imposters among the ranks of the priests. Why anyone who was not a priest would wish to impersonate one in August 1914 was not explained. In any case, an arrogant young German priest examined his Belgian colleagues on various doctrinal and theological points. When asked why he was doing this, he replied airily, *"C'est la guerre."* Satisfied at last that the men he had interviewed were indeed all priests, he offered them a parting gift: German grammar books. "Since you're now Germans," he told them, "I thought you could usefully pass your time learning the national language."[118]

Most prisoners were entirely cut off from the outside world. It was only in November that they were permitted to write home. The letter had to repeat a prescribed text, however; otherwise it would not be sent: "I'm at Munster. I'm holding up very well and am very well treated. I have everything I want here, and hope to return to you in good health."[119]

⊰⊱

However miserable their existence, the prisoners could console themselves that at least their lives were not in jeopardy, after the shootings – and at least one execution – on the first day.[120] This changed one night in early September. A sergeant whom he had gotten to know warned Louis Maldague that a detachment of camp guards was going to be sent to the front the next day, and were in an ugly mood. If the prisoners heard knocks on the door, or gunfire, they ought to lie down flat on the floor and not move. Maldague and Jules Kleyntjes set out to warn as many of the prisoners as they could. The doctor calculated that at least 4,000 men eventually received the word. But the camp was vast, and many were given no warning.

That evening around 10:00, soldiers did indeed invade the camp, racing around the barracks, yelling furiously and banging on doors and walls. No one moved. Ten minutes later the men heard gunfire from another part of camp. They were told the next day that five men had been killed in a barracks building occupied by prisoners from Wesemaal, Rotselaar and Haacht. Maldague saw several body bags. The Germans announced the next day that a revolt had broken out among the prisoners, and several had tried to escape. There was more gunfire the following night. Alphonse Verlooy saw seven bodies loaded onto a cart.[121] Louis Maldague was also informed by some Belgian p.o.w.s that they saw seven corpses lined up outside one stone building where civilian prisoners were housed.[122]

Male prisoners were released at different times, ranging from mid-October to late January. As there had been no reason for their imprisonment in the first place, so there was no logic to the order of their departure, though generally the youngest and oldest captives were permitted to leave before the others, along with the priests.[123] The professor of law was sent back to Leuven on October 30. He returned in comparative comfort – 3rd class carriages and ample food were provided. *"Prahlen Sie nun in Belgien wie gut Sie hier behandelt worden sind,"* a cheery officer told the professor at one point. ("You can now boast in Belgium of how well you've been treated here.")[124]

KÖLN: JOY WHEEL It remains something of a mystery as to why some two thousand Leuven residents were shipped to Köln, held there overnight, with the usual threats and simulated executions, and then returned to Belgium for further abuse. The German authorities took care to organize crowds in the Rhenish cathedral city and in the towns en route. People turned out everywhere to jeer and harass the Leuveners.[125]

It is conceivable that authorities sent the hostages east simply to stir up hatred against the Belgians, a dash of tonic for the home front. The spectacle of these ragged, disreputable-looking individuals appears to have further inflamed German civilians against the "franc-tireurs." But the trip was primarily punitive. The number of German Socialists and Catholics questioning the Army's practices in Belgium was minuscule, after all. The government may originally have intended to imprison the Leuven residents sent to Köln, but was thwarted by the more pressing need to provide facilities for the 100,000 or so Russians captured at Tannenberg. On the other hand, the prisoners were told repeatedly that they would be shot, by officers as well as soldiers, and it's possible that some of those ordering them east intended and expected this outcome.

◄--►

As noted, civilians from Leuven being conveyed to Munsterlager – and Dinantais to Kassel – were frequently put on display. Alphonse Verlooy, the Leuven postmaster, vividly recounted his experience en route to Munster.

> After crossing the German border, we stopped in all stations, and each time we were exhibited like beasts to the crowd of Germans who were invited to come see us. They hurried forward with a hostile curiosity. The priests in particular were the objects of great curiosity and animosity. We had to believe that our route had been announced in advance, because of the masses of the curious not only in the stations, but beside the railroad bridges, and even along the embankments lining the tracks. We were the franc-tireurs, and no doubt the displays of furious hostility we witnessed were entirely sincere. We looked the part. Most of my companions had been seized at work in the fields, and were dressed in their oldest clothes. As for myself, I'd had to leave so hastily I had no time to attend to my appearance; I was wearing an old gray cap and around my neck was a red handkerchief with white spots. And so one night, when we were stopped in a large station, I sensed the light of a lantern on my face as I was pretending to sleep in a corner of the car. I heard in German: "He's obviously a criminal. He ought to be shot immediately."[126]

Priests were the prize exhibits en route to Köln. "As for me," wrote Abbé Wouters, the parish priest of Rotselaar, "I was placed in front of the open door, in a good position to receive all the insults, especially as I was a priest... The arrival of our train had no doubt been announced in Germany, for at all the stations there was a mob to insult us. Naturally, I was always the principal target."[127]

◄--►

There is a good deal of testimony on the horrendous trip to Köln.

"We were kept in the station all night in the rain without shelter or food," a bricklayer from Leuven recalled.

> In the morning we were put into cattle cars – 80 were put into a wagon that would hold only 30, and we were knee-deep in dung. We left Leuven on a Friday morning and arrived at Köln on the Monday afternoon following. We had nothing to eat or drink during this time and were never allowed out of the wagons to obey the calls of nature.[128]

Other witnesses commented on the appalling quantity of excrement already in the cattle-cars when the civilians were pushed inside.[129]

The men in another car, despite its wretched state, had made it a point of honor not to relieve themselves inside the car. But unlike those in other carriages, they were able to share a single wine bottle of water. When the train arrived in Köln, "we went down on our knees and begged the soldiers to allow us to get off."[130]

The men in the bricklayer's car were forced to lie on top of each other, making what room they could for the sick and injured. The Germans had confiscated everything – "money, papers, jewelry, umbrellas, and overcoats" – so there was a little more room than there might otherwise have been.

> When we reached Köln, a crowd came around the cars jeering at us, and as we marched out they prodded us with umbrellas and pelted us and shouted "Shoot them dead!" and drew their fingers across their throats.[131]
>
> We still had nothing to eat or drink.
>
> During this journey, one man in the second car went mad, two in the same car tried to commit suicide, and about twenty of the men urinated blood. I was told this after we reached Köln by other Belgians in that wagon and I saw some of these men and spoke with them. They were ill and haggard.
>
> In my car, one man tore out the lining of his coat and chewed it up and, removing his shoe, used it as a vessel to drink his own urine. Only one of us attempted to prevent him from doing this, without success....
>
> When we marched off the train, some limped and some were bent down, and all were filthy and terribly exhausted.
>
> We were taken to an "Exhibition" and placed in ranks facing officers and soldiers; the soldiers leveled rifles at us. After some time, one of the officers said, "We will put off the shooting until tomorrow." Then we were made to sleep on planks on the ground. There was no covering overhead, and it was raining.[132]

The "Exhibition" was an amusement park called "Luna Park." Here some slept on the ground without the comfort of planks. Other captives were placed in sheds or other buildings in the park, after being paraded through town. Still others were made to sleep, bizarrely, on a "joy wheel," something like a Ferris wheel on its side, and in the hall that housed the ride. One man noticed the word "Hachenrad" written on the contraption.[133]

Julien Sterckx was one of those packed into this building.

> In a few moments the benches were occupied; we thought we deserved a little rest. The soldiers thought otherwise. They picked some person at random and compelled him to kneel down in the middle of the wheel. We were threatened with shooting. Men stood up with wild eyes, and deafening cries rang out; I saw several of my compatriots who had gone mad. Others implored the soldiers for a piece of bread or a glass of water; others asked for their belongings, so that they might go home to their families. We remained at Luna Park until noon of the next day.[134]

The following day, some of the men were again threatened with execution. One man was among a group of hostages placed in rows of three and made to face a line of soldiers with rifles aimed at their chests. Then "a German soldier arrived on horseback and brought a despatch to the officer in command. I then heard the officer say in German, 'It is the Kaiser's will.'" The men were then led back to the joy-wheel.[135] This was probably one more version of the mock-execution game played with such abandon during these days, though it's not clear why the Kaiser's beneficence wasn't announced in French or Flemish.

The bricklayer whose shooting "was put off until tomorrow" was told, the next day, by "one of the Belgians who spoke German, that the officer in charge had received a communication from the American Ambassador that we were not soldiers and must be set free."[136]

While this second-hand story was obviously false, it contained a kernel of truth: it is possible that sensitivity to American opinion had a mitigating effect on the fate of the hostages. By the week of the 30th, it undoubtedly was the Kaiser's will that public-relations disasters like the massacres in Aarschot and Dinant and the burning of Leuven should not be repeated.

Everyone was now fed, though the men got only one loaf of bread for every ten individuals, and it was blue with mold. But the captives had not eaten for two and a half days, and so the bread was eagerly devoured, and the filthy water that accompanied it was guzzled down.

The Leuven residents were then herded back to the trains. Though they now had third and fourth class carriages, the return trip was as hellish as the journey to Köln. (Some civilians continued to be held in Köln. These men were eventually released in Limburg province by Bavarian troops.)[137]

The places were taken by storm; the soldiers made the people who were coming up occupy the still vacant places, and in a few seconds, the train was overflowing with travelers. The over-heated compartments, the pervading odors, the state of dirt we were all in, will suggest an idea of the situation... The sufferings we had gone through since our arrest, since our painful pilgrimage from Rotselaar to Leuven, our transport from Leuven to Köln, were all trifles compared with what we experienced on our return to Belgium. The refuse, the unspeakable filth, the foul air we had to breathe, added to the hunger and thirst and terror, will explain how it was that in this hell many of the travelers either killed themselves or went raving mad.[138]

In one instance, eighteen people were crushed into a compartment intended for eight. In another compartment, twenty-five were packed in during the forty-eight hour ride. People were standing, sitting in each others' laps, lying scrunched under the seats or wedged up on the luggage racks.[139]

When the train stopped just over the Belgian border, around 3:30 a.m., one man left the carriage to relieve himself. As several passengers watched from ten yards away, three German soldiers approached him.

One of them caught hold of him and threw him on the ground and he was bayoneted by one or another of them in his left side. The man cried out. Then the German soldier withdrew his bayonet and showed his comrades how far the blade had gone in. He then wiped the blood off the bayonet by drawing it through his hand... A few minutes after the German soldier had wiped his bayonet, he put his hand in his pocket and took out some bread, which he ate. After this incident, we were allowed to get out of the train three times in forty-eight hours to relieve ourselves.[140]

More imaginative soldiers came up with other diversions. "During the night," a Bulgarian student reported,

the train pulled up occasionally, always outside the stations. The guard, walking beside the tracks, called out in German, "Shut the windows." But when we shut them, the soldier who was keeping guard over us inside ordered, "Open the windows." Then an officer passed along the carriages, asking, "Who disobeyed the order?" The soldier pointed out a prisoner near the window, and the officer ordered him to get out. When the prisoners thus pointed out in every carriage were standing on the railway tracks, a picket of soldier surrounded them, and the officer gave the order to shoot them. This scene was enacted two or three times a night during our three day's journey.[141]

In Verviers, the townspeople tried to get food to the hapless Leuveners, but an officer observed what was going on and ordered the doors and windows shut. Soldiers confiscated what the prisoners had been given. There were long delays just outside of Liège, from about 7:00 p.m. Saturday until 11:00 a.m. Sunday.[142]

"We arrived in the station at Liège at noon and left again at 3:00 p.m.," Professor Van Steenbeeck of the Academy of Music recalled. "It was here that one person threw himself under the train."[143] The incident left a vivid impression on several passengers. "The train had run over his stomach and I saw the contractions of his mouth as he was taken out." "'See whether it is a German or a prisoner,'" an officer ordered.[144]

"About 8:00 p.m.," wrote Van Steenbeeck, "we reached Korbeek-Lo.

> The lights were out; here and there in the stations there was a little light. This produced a phantasmagorical effect in our carriages. Here and there a shot rang out... Then again a bugle sounded... Then came the shouts of sentries... and here and there madmen. What barbarity!
>
> We reached Brussels about midnight. This journey had thus lasted fifty-two hours, and that after being shut up for ten hours in a shed![145]

Back in the Leuven station, passengers in some of the cars were told by officers that they were now going to be shot. The preparations were convincing. "The panic among us was so great at this moment," the Bulgarian student recalled,

> that Father Eugène Schaffner, a French Alsatian, the Superior of the Fathers of Zion at Leuven, entrusted to me, as a foreigner belonging to a neutral country, an envelope on which he had scribbled in pencil a few words, begging me, if I escaped, to hand it to his brother, Father Henri Schaffner, Superior-General of the Fathers of Zion in Paris...: "My heart is God's, my life for God. Farewell, dear Henri. Sunday, August 31st, half-past three in the morning."[146]

But no one was executed, and the train proceeded to Brussels. "On our arrival in Brussels," wrote Professor Van Steenbeeck,

> we asked for food, but could obtain nothing. And we had to remain in the carriages in an unspeakably filthy atmosphere. Again a considerable number of people went mad during the night. In the morning (Monday, the 31st) I awoke early and I wept... An officer asked me if I were ill. I said, "No," but I told him that I was weeping from pain, from sorrow, from hunger, because of my family, and because I was innocent.
>
> Then, suddenly, during the morning, a distribution of white bread was made, but we learned that it had been given by the town of Brussels, and provided by the Burgomaster, M. Max. What joy! But could it satisfy such famished people?[147]

Everyone on board recalled the arrival of Adolphe Max and his party.

> We were let out of the train. M. Max and the people with him were crying when they saw the condition we poor fellows were in. M. Max send for food and drink, and

people brought to us bread, wine, and coffee. We could not wait. We snatched it and tore it to pieces. Then they brought us cigarettes and tobacco.[148]

The Germans, however, would not give up their prisoners. The men were ordered back onto the train and taken to Schaarbeek. From here they were made to walk to Vilvoorde. They went by a circuitous route: they were on the road for over eight hours. "We were marched to Vilvoorde in rows of six," a mechanic testified. "I was in the last row. We were made to run quickly, and the soldiers struck us on the back with their rifles and on the arms with the bayonets."[149] En route, "one man sprang into the water, a canal," the bricklayer recalled. "He was mad then. The German soldiers threw empty bottles at this man in the water – bottles they had picked up from the houses they had passed and had drunk along the way."[150]

The captives were dispersed in various ways. "We're sick of you," one group of men was told by their guards, who then released them. But for good measure, these soldiers fired a few parting shots at the retreating prisoners. One man was hit in the arm. (Professor Van Steenbeeck turned down a couple of proposals from soldiers that he escape, no doubt wisely.) The refugees who were fired on eventually encountered Belgian sentries on the far side of the Willebroek canal. The bridge the men hoped to cross had been mined, the soldiers told them. They would need to spend the night in the woods. The next morning Belgian soldiers guided the civilians across by another route.[151]

Other contingents from the Köln group found themselves repeatedly re-arrested. It was a distressingly familiar routine for those of the civilians who had been driven north before being sent east in the cattle-cars. More prisoners went mad, one badly injuring the young man ordered to hold him. One group of men was eventually issued passports, around midnight, that said "Direct to Mechelen." If challenged by German sentries, they were told to say, *"Pass. Halt. Flüchtlinge. Fugitifs."* Other officers also freed Leuveners recaptured by patrols and ordered them toward Mechelen, sometimes on pain of death. That city, however, had been re-occupied by Belgian troops, and some refugees were turned away. "Our painful calvary continued," Van Steenbeeck wrote. "We wandered from village to village until we arrived at the outskirts of Antwerp, where we were rescued by the *Comité de Secours.*"[152]

CHAPTER 12

Leuven: Aftermath

"A COMMENDABLE JOB" Armed with bleaching powder and carbolic acid, and wearing a surgeon's apron and rubber gloves, Frans Claes (Father Valerius), Professor of Social and Political Science, began the daunting task of locating and transporting to the cemetery the bodies of those massacred on the 25th and 26th. He and his assistants began with corpses still lying in the streets and in homes, and then moved on to disinter and identify the remains of those who had been buried in shallow graves, or tossed into fields or basements. In one case sixteen bodies had been thrown beneath a building under construction[1]. Claes, a Capuchin friar, was the director of *Oeuvres Sociales,* the Church's social service organization in Leuven, and had made several forays out of the St. Thomas hospital to retrieve the wounded during the height of the violence. But nothing had prepared him for the grisly scenes he and his second in command, the architect Lucien Speder, were to witness.[2]

They commenced work early in the afternoon on Sunday, August 30th. The next morning they were called to Blijde-Inkomststraat. The street was littered with spent cartridge shells, the windows and doors smashed, the outer walls riddled with bullets. In front of number 113, the men smelled "the characteristic odor of a cadaver.

> Pushing open the main door, the initial glimpse of the corridor convinced us that something terrible had taken place in this residence; traces of bullets in the walls and ceiling, the broken windows, the paving stones covered with debris and, at the foot of the stairs, a pool of blood already turning putrid. The steps of the stairs were covered with blood; there were also splinters of skull and spatterings of cerebral matter swarming with worms. The walls and ceilings were stained with large red and

"You're doing a very commendable job here."
Lucien Speder and Father Claes bury the dead.

black splotches. All of a sudden I saw a woman's body lying across the landing, a foot wedged between the pillars of the bannister. The woman was dressed only in a chemise and the arms, extended in front, were submerged in a sea of blood, which also covered the woman's back. And – horror! – the corpse had no head. It was the body of Mevrouw Verleysen, a young mother, who had just given birth to her third child.

My companions, who rejoined me at this moment, contemplated the horrible spectacle with an indignation equal to mine. We climbed up the stairs to look for the child and see if there were other victims of German savagery upstairs. We went up to the second floor. Everything was in great disarray. They'd pillaged the rooms. All the chests and wardrobes were open, the drawers and a heap of objects spilled out on the floor. There were bullet holes in the walls, the ceiling, the furniture, the windows.[3]

But the men discovered no more bodies. When they descended to the ground floor, they saw a large strong box that had been broken into. "Papers were scattered all over, but no object of any value had been left behind; there were empty jewel cases on the armchair, other chairs, and the table. The bandits who had been at work here knew their trade well."[4] The men went back upstairs to remove the body.

It was an arduous task. As we attempted to lift the body, we slipped in the blood and it coated our hands and clothes. Pieces of brain were scattered everywhere, along with skull splinters. There were some on the victim's chest and on the windowsill on the landing. Above the shoulders, only a stump remained, a braid of black hair still curled over it.

The head had not been severed with a sharp instrument. We saw around the corpse the fragments of many bullets and some small whole bullets flattened and buckled. The brutes had undoubtedly blasted off the victim's head by discharging their revolvers at point-blank range.[5]

Claes and his team went on to remove from homes, gardens, streets and alleyways the bodies of civilians, and soldiers, who died during the sack of the city, as well as Belgian and German soldiers who were killed in combat in nearby villages during the Second Sortie. The work continued intermittently until the end of April, 1915.

"Initially," Claes wrote, "the work went relatively well.

Extracting the cadavers was not extraordinarily difficult, but soon, as we went deeper, the work became painful, because of the heaviness of the bodies, the lack of space in the narrow pits, and also the overwhelming heat, the formidable number of flies that harassed us, the smell of decay... At certain moments we were overcome with vertigo, and we had to clamber out of the hellish pits and breathe air less poisoned...[6]

The Amsterdam reporter Bart Mokveld was hardly squeamish, but nausea quickly got the better of his curiosity. "I witnessed Father Claes's labors for a moment only, for the smell was unbearable even at a somewhat considerable distance."[7]

There were other observers. On September 8th, as Claes and his colleagues were working in a pit on Tiensevest, they noticed that they were being watched by two German officers standing about twelve yards off. One was Major von Manteuffel. The commandant called out to Claes in German, "You're doing a very commendable job here."[8]

Claes himself does not record any response he may have made, but in the stories that quickly circulated throughout town, he was supposed to have replied, "Thanks Monsieur le Commandant, but it would have been better if you'd spared us the necessity."[9]

"WE WENT CRAZY IN LEUVEN" "'Is it not a pity to be obliged to destroy such a beautiful town?'" a Leuven businessman was asked several times during the weeks that followed the sack, "even by soldiers to whom I had made no mention of the destruction of Leuven." Invariably, they would add, "'It was the fault of the inhabitants, who fired on our soldiers.'"[10]

"It was a lesson they had been taught," the businessman concluded. *"Man hat geschossen"* had been the password to pillage, burn, and murder, except where the occasional scrupulous officer intervened, and now this was the formula to express regret. *"Es ist sehr traurig, solch eine schöne Stadt zerstören zu müssen, aber…"*

A few soldiers, however, were not quite so quick to absolve the German Army. On September 1st, Father Claes had the opportunity to conduct the commandant of Tongres through the ruins of Leuven. "It's horrible. It's horrible," he kept repeating, without attempting to justify the devastation.[11]

A German colleague of Claes's had the same reaction. Dr. Sonneschein, head of the Popular Catholic Association of Gladbach, questioned Claes closely about what he'd seen. "This is terrible! This is horrible!" he exclaimed intermittently. The soldiers must have been in the grip of a pathological fear of civilians, Sonneschein concluded.[12]

On another occasion, on January 17, 1915, three German officials, along with some members of the civilian government, gathered to witness the exhumation of corpses interred in Van de Weyer Square in front of the station. Among them was the new commandant, Colonel Lubbert. (Major von Manteuffel had been succeeded by Colonel von Thiel in September, who in turn was replaced by Lubbert on December 12th.)[13] "In just one pit," Claes recalled,

> there were eighteen bodies, thrown in pell-mell, in such disorder that the most painful part of our work was to disentangle the interlocked arms and legs. There were smashed-in skulls, shattered arms and legs. At a certain moment, Colonel Lubbert could not contain his indignation at this hideous spectacle and cried out, "Have we worked for forty years at civilizing our people in order to arrive at this result?"[14]

"I'm thankful I wasn't in Leuven during that tragic time," the colonel's aide-de-camp, Lieutenant Tilemann, added sententiously.[15] The Belgian witnesses were overcome with emotion. Dr. Maldague, back from Munsterlager and serving now as the team's pathologist, had been among the group of captives from which the Germans had selected individuals to be killed. He broke down during the exhumations.

Some of the victims still had personal belongings in their pockets, and these, and the engraved rings some wore, made the process of identifying them easier, for many of the civilians were unrecognizable. A number had been shot point-blank by rifles as they knelt or lay down in the square, and then bayoneted. The personal articles also provided, naturally, poignant little glimpses into the lives of the victims. Fernand Humbeek was visiting from Brussels. He had with him an identity card from the Touring Club de Belgique, a ticket from the 1910 International Exposition of Brussels, and a moustache brush. Edouard van Ertryck, a twenty-five-year-old cigar manufacturer living on Stationsstraat, wore a signet ring with his initials on his right ring-finger and a wedding ring on his left. Inside was engraved "Marthe et Edouard 2 Sept. 1913." In addition to wallets and keys, he had carried in one pocket a child's vest. Was he a new father, or was his wife expecting? Killed alongside him was his own father, François. The skulls of both men were shattered. Curiously, another victim also had a child's shirt in his pocket. This was Charles Meunhemer, married, according to his wedding band, on 5 October 1909. The lanky twenty-nine-year-old was a German subject, born in Adelsheim and never naturalized. Dr. Maldague believed he had been shot by a pistol. What were his final moments like? Did he have a chance to speak with the officer who killed him?[16]

Professor Alfred Nerincx, the burgomaster, accompanied the three

Germans as they walked from the Stadhuis to the station. It was Nerincx who had originally requested the disinterment. Passing the statue of Justus Lipsius, Colonel Lubbert confided to Nerincx that "we've now discovered the culprit in the assassination of old M. David. It was ordered by the famous Dr. Berghausen, who finished him off with a revolver shot. But we still don't know if he was acting on the order of a superior."[17]

Further down the street, after the colonel had left the burgomaster's side, Dr. von Sandt, the chief civil administrator of the General Government, expostulated with the commandant. Lubbert had been telling him the pressing reasons for authorizing the exhumation. "Yes, but what will become of the impression?" von Sandt asked, sotto voce. Nerincx was not quite out of earshot, and spoke German fluently. "The impression," the burgomaster understood from the context, was that franc-tireurs had attacked the Germans. "No one's believed that for a long time," the commandant replied contemptuously.[18]

⋖—⋗

One morning in November, Colonel von Thiel announced to Professor Nerincx that all the chimes in the surviving clock towers in Leuven were to sound. Some very distinguished visitors had arrived.

Early in the afternoon, Dr. Theobald von Bethmann Hollweg, Chancellor of the German Empire, was ushered into the burgomaster's office. After introductions, Bethmann Hollweg pointed to an officer in the Grote Markt below. With two or three other officers, he was taking in the ruins, and quite approvingly, to all appearances. This was Prince August-Wilhelm, fourth son of the Emperor, traveling incognito. He did not wish his identity to be known by any other local authorities. This was fine with Nerincx.

When the Chancellor suggested a guided tour for his party, the burgomaster was happy to oblige. They visited the interior of St. Pieter's and the ruins of the Library, and Nerincx carefully explained how the arson was methodically carried out, and described some of the murder and mayhem of the 25th and 26th.

> The Chancellor excused the barbarity of the German troops, reminding me that terrible things always happened in wartime and that soldiers were not angels. He appeared, however, to be struck by what he'd seen, because he felt obliged to say, by

way of excuse, that what had happened was unfortunate, and that the time had not yet arrived in which full light could be shed on the events. But he gave his assurance that when the pressure of fighting had diminished, the hour would come when justice would be rendered us.[19]

⋘⋙

There was, of course, an official German inquiry. Most, but not all, of its findings were published in the German White Book. Conducting one phase of the investigation, during November, was a military judge, Dr. Stempel of the Strassbourg Court of Appeals, "about sixty years old, with a wrinkled face and severe, rather forbidding, gaze," Father Claes recalled. As he waited outside Stempel's office, the priest heard Canon Thiéry adamantly refuse to sign a statement. "No, I'm not going to sign this because it's not what I said!"[20]

"Stempel's bad faith was scandalous," Dr. Adriaan Noyons concluded. The Dutch professor of medicine had no sooner finished describing what he had witnessed the Germans doing in his home, when Stempel turned to his secretary and dictated in German, not realizing that Noyons spoke the language fluently, "The Germans soldiers behaved very well in Leuven, in Professor Noyons' house as they did elsewhere." Once again Noyons found himself shouting at Germans. He heatedly denied the judge's verdict, and a lengthy discussion followed.[21]

When his turn came after Thiéry's, Claes was asked for details about the priests who had been killed. The Capuchin father described the corpses of the five priests he had disinterred, including their injuries and mutilations. Then he began to relate what he had observed at the Verleysen house. Stempel quickly cut him off. "No, no, that's enough. I've already heard so many terrible things."

"But since you're conducting an inquiry, you certainly ought to wish to know the full truth."

"Monsieur, I'm only charged with questioning you about ecclesiastics," the judge replied. The interview was at an end.[22]

Joseph Parijs, Brother Hyacinth, also had a memorable interview with Dr. Stempel. "We know that civilians fired on soldiers," the judge told him, and handed him a deposition from Dr. Berghausen. Parijs assured Stempel that he was prepared to testify under oath that the *Oberarzt's* claims were false. One week later, the Dominican Father-Superior found himself face to face with Berghausen himself. When it was clear that even Stempel was convinced by Parijs' testimony, the irrepressible doctor abruptly switched tack, claiming it was not Parijs but another Dominican who had accompanied him on the night of the 25th. This desperate lie backfired, naturally. Stempel summonsed first one, then a second Dominican, before he refused to listen to Berghausen any further. If Stempel expressed reservations about the *Oberartz* credibility, they were ignored by the editors of the White Book, who published his mendacious deposition.[23]

◄-┼-►►

Stempel was succeeded in January by a Dr. Bemme. Professor Noyons was once more called upon to testify, and this time was listened to more attentively. When he'd finished speaking, Dr. Bemme was quiet for a moment. Then he told the physician, *"Wir sind verrückt gewesen in Löwen."* We went crazy in Leuven.[24]

If Dr. Bemme submitted any reports or depositions, those who compiled *Die völkerrechtswidrige Führung des belgischen Volkskriegs* did not see fit to include them.

REINBRECHT With complete impunity, soldiers repeatedly defied Major von Manteuffel's orders to cease burning Leuven. What would happen to an officer who disobeyed explicit orders to burn buildings?

Octave-François Beauduin (Dom Lambert), the Benedictine monk who was able to disembark in Tienen from a train bound for Munster, discovered the answer on August 31st. If the officer were persistent enough, the buildings might be spared.

On the way back to Leuven, Beauduin watched as train after train rumbled past, laden with booty. Buildings were still on fire when the monk walked down Stationsstraat, then north to Keizersberg, which rises over four hundred feet above the city. It was 10:00 p.m. on the 30th when he at last arrived. Beauduin was immediately arrested by four soldiers, taken into the dining hall, undressed, searched and then interrogated for two hours. At last satisfied with the results of the questioning, the officer in charge introduced himself. "My father, you see before you the abbey's benefactor," he said. He was First Lieutenant Reinbrecht, and after he had told his story, the grateful Beauduin, suspecting that the preservation of the abbey may have been a unique event in the German invasion, pressed the officer to write down an account of the affair, and to leave behind copies of the memoranda he'd sent von Manteuffel. After some hesitation, Reinbrecht agreed. If he should die, the lieutenant said, Beauduin could do what he wished with the material. Reinbrecht's report runs a little under one thousand words. He refers to himself in the third person.[25]

At noon on the 29th, immediately after his company arrived at the station, an adjutant for his regiment, the 53rd Landwehr, informed Reinbrecht and his field lieutenants that his company had been assigned the task of setting on fire the abbey on Keizersberg. Gunshots were reported to have been fired from the abbey on German troops. The orders were quite detailed: the monastery was to be searched for arms, any monk found with a weapon was to be executed; the monks were to be escorted out and after a half-hour search, the monastery was to be burned. A detachment of pioneers and an interpreter were assigned to the company. If the main door was shut, the pioneers would break it open.[26]

Reinbrecht carefully repeated the order and then asked the adjutant what must have been a startling question: "Even if we don't find any weapons, do we still set the monastery on fire?" *"Auf jeden fall,"* the adjutant assured him. In any case. Not content with this answer, Reinbrecht walked over to the commander of the regiment and posed the same question. Major Planke confirmed his subordinate's understanding of the order.

The monks had abandoned the monastery before the Germans arrived. Instead of searching the premises for one half hour, the lieutenant's troops spent four and a half hours carefully going through the monastery buildings. Another company could have pillaged and burned half a dozen monasteries during this time. Nothing suspicious was found. (Reinbrecht dismissed a note one soldier claimed to have found beside some bottles on the second floor: "Don't touch. Poison intended for the sick.")

Then, in his report, still referring to himself in the third person, Reinbrecht recorded a remarkable moment in the German occupation of Leuven. "He decided to preserve at least the most precious treasures of the Benedictine monastery, because he was of the opinion that it would be barbarous to destroy them."[27] The *Oberleutnant* wrote up a detailed inventory of the items, and had them taken outside and loaded onto a wagon.

Having finished, Reinbrecht came back in, sat down, and thought some more. "First Lieutenant Reinbrecht told himself that it was impossible that the commandant of the army intended him to set fire to so marvelous a monastery, and one that appeared to be entirely organized to care for the next person to be brought in. Moreover, this was a Benedictine monastery, and he knew the good work this order had done in Germany."[28]

Reinbrecht then wrote a memorandum to von Manteuffel.

> After 4 ½ hours of a minute search of the vast monastery of Keizersberg, I can tell you that the monastery was apparently evacuated by the occupants in great haste when we approached. Fresh food was laid out; some of the beds were still warm. Nothing resembling any sort of weapon was found... The most precious of the sacred objects have been taken out on my orders and provisionally entrusted to Brother Van Bergen, who accompanied me here and who has been given a receipt. All has been prepared to set the fire.
>
> I have a very strong impression that the monastery was devoted solely to the care of whoever entered. It was organized for the treatment of the wounded. Based on what I've said, I respectfully ask if the convent still ought to be burned.[29]

While the orderly who delivered the note waited, von Manteuffel scribbled underneath the message *"Nicht Abbrennen!"* Do not burn down.

But Reinbrecht was still not satisfied after he received the new order. The front door had been smashed open. If his company left, the monastery would be thoroughly vandalized within a short time. The *Oberleutnant* wrote a second note to von Manteuffel explaining this.

> I ask to whom I ought to turn over the monastery of Keizersberg. The pioneers have blown open the main door. All the other doors were broken open, according to orders received. The windows that could not be opened were broken, in preparation for the burning of the monastery. The most precious treasures of the church – the gold and precious stones – have been placed in a small wagon in the courtyard, after an inventory. Brother V. Bergen hesitates to keep the objects, because he wishes to leave tomorrow. What will happen then? Other inventoried objects are equally valuable: in the large library, in the museum. In all the immense buildings there is no one beside the 3rd Company of the 53rd Regiment.
>
> Where should 3/53 go?[30]

Manteuffel was again obliging. He ordered that the company remain on the premises until it was relieved. The monastery and its contents were preserved.

Beauduin felt free to turn over to the Belgian Commission of Inquiry the documents that had been entrusted to him, for Reinbrecht, unlike von

Sandt, Schweder, Berghausen, von Manteuffel, and von Boehn, did not survive the war. He was killed outside Soissons.[31]

Reinbrecht – whose name suggests in translation a "clean break" – appears to have stumbled into Leuven from another time and place. Though he wears the field-grey of a German infantry officer, he questions his orders three times, albeit with great discretion. He believes that a body of Catholic monks is doing good work in Leuven, as it has done in Germany. He believes it would be an act of barbarism to destroy valuable works of art. The contents of libraries and museums ought to preserved as well.

Reinbrecht also appears to question the propriety of punishing an institution if no member is guilty of any wrongdoing. He seems to believe, further, that more evidence of guilt ought to be required for the destruction of a building than the word of a single anonymous soldier.

Still more remarkable, he appears to have infected his troops with some of these unorthodox ideas. There is no looting, no wanton destruction. Paintings, draperies, and furniture are not slashed by bayonets; excrement is not deposited on mattresses. Instead, valuables are carefully collected, listed, and described with the intention of preserving them for their owners.

◄-◄-►-►

Von Manteuffel soon had reason to be grateful to the eccentric first lieutenant. "I received a telegram from the Kaiser telling me to spare the abbey," he told Beauduin. "I was able to respond that I had already given the order."[32]

Reinbrecht may not have reciprocated von Manteuffel's warm feelings. When the lieutenant and the Benedictine monk were walking through town a few days later, Reinbrecht pointed to a partially burned building and told Beauduin that his company had been fired on from its windows by men in German uniforms. "I informed the headquarters, but I was told that they were Belgian civilians disguised as German soldiers."[33] Always discreet, Reinbrecht did not elaborate on what he thought of officers who had such a low opinion of his intelligence.

A USELESS DISCUSSION During his long and difficult labors, Father Valerius Claes had discussions with a number of German soldiers and officers.

He recorded the following conversation with an officer just as he left the Stadhuis.

> Gesturing at St. Pieter's directly across the Grote Markt, the officer asked, "Who set that on fire?"
>
> "German soldiers, the same who burned the entire town."
>
> "Are you absolutely sure it was German soldiers?"
>
> "Monsieur, you don't mean to tell me that the people of Leuven burned their own church."
>
> "And why would the soldiers do this?"
>
> "How would I know? Why did they kill? Why did they commit arson? Your leaders will surely know better than I."
>
> "But all the same, they couldn't have done this without a reason."
>
> "Again, Monsieur, I don't know the reasons, but I know that this town (and with a sweeping gesture I indicated the Grote Markt, Brusselsestraat, Stationsstraat, and Tiensestraat), which had done nothing to your soldiers, was burned over four days and that more than one hundred innocent people were killed."
>
> "But we're not barbarians."
>
> "That's possible, Monsieur, but how do you describe this work?" (I pointed again to the ruins that surrounded us.)
>
> At this point the German officer made a signal to the soldiers who were standing around us and walked off, saying in a skeptical tone, "Bah! It's useless to discuss this subject. Adieu."[34]

"WE ARE SO HELPLESS" Hugh Gibson, Brand Whitlock's young secretary in the two-member U.S. legation, set off to visit Leuven on the 28th.[35]

"There is bad news from Leuven," Gibson wrote in his journal on August 27th, although "no two reports are alike." That evening, "the wife of the Minister of Fine Arts came in with the news that her mother, a woman of eighty-four, had been driven from her home at the point of the bayonet and forced to walk with a stream of refugees all the way to Tervuren, a distance of about twelve miles, before she could be put on a tram to her daughter's house."[36]

The next day Gibson decided to set out for Leuven with an American friend, Blount. They were joined by the Swedish and Mexican chargés d'affaires, Pousette and Bulle.

> The road was black with frightened civilians carrying away small bundles from the ruins of their homes. Ahead was a great column of dull gray smoke which completely hid the city. We could hear the muffled sound of firing ahead. Down the little street which led to the town, we could see dozens of white flags which had been hung out of the windows in a childish hope of averting trouble.

We talked with the soldiers for some time in an effort to get some idea of what had really happened in the town. They seemed convinced that civilians had precipitated the whole business by firing upon the staff of a general who was parleying with the Burgomaster in the square before the Stadhuis. They saw nothing themselves, and believe what they are told. Different members of the detachment had different stories to tell, including one that civilians had a machine gun installed on top of the Cathedral [the collegiate church], and fired into the German troops, inflicting much damage. One of the men told us that his company had lost twenty-five men in the initial flurry. They were a depressed and nervous-looking crew, bitter against the civil population and cursing their ways with great earnestness. They were at some pains to impress upon us that all Belgians were *Schwein*, and that the people of Leuven were the lowest known form of the animal.

After talking the situation over with the officer in command, we decided to try getting around the town to the station by way of the ring of outer boulevards. We got through in good shape, being stopped a few times by soldiers and by little groups of frightened civilians who were cowering in the shelter of doorways listening to the noise of fighting in the town, the steady crackle of machine guns, and the occasional explosions.

They were pathetic in their confidence that the United States was coming to save them. In some way word has traveled all over Belgium that we have entered the war on the side of Belgium, and they all seem to believe it. Nearly every group we talked to asked hopefully when our troops were coming... A little boy of about eight, in a group that stopped us, asked me whether we were English, and when I told him what we were, he began jumping up and down, clapping his hands, and shouting: *Les Américains sont arrivés! Les Américains sont arrivés!*

...About half way around the ring of boulevards we came to burning houses. The outer side of the boulevard was thirty yards or so from the houses, so the motor was safe, but it was pretty hot and the cinders were so thick that we had to put on our goggles. A lot of the houses were still burning, but most of them were nothing but blackened walls with smouldering timbers inside. Many of the front doors had been battered open to start the fires or to rout out the people who were in hiding.

We came to a German ammunition wagon, half upset against a tree, where it had been hurled when the horses had turned to run away... Nearby were the two horses, dead and swollen until their legs stood out straight. Then we began to see more ghastly sights – poor civilians lying where they had been shot down as they ran – men and women – one old patriarch lying on his back in the sun, his great white beard nearly hiding his swollen face. All sorts of wreckage scattered over the street, hats and wooden shoes, German helmets, swords and saddles, bottles, and all sorts of bundles which had been dropped and abandoned when the trouble began. For three-quarters of a mile the boulevard looked as though it had been swept by a cyclone. The Tiensepoort had evidently been the scene of particularly bloody business. The telegraph and trolley wires were down; dead men and horses all over the square; the houses still burning. The broad road we had traveled when we went to Tienen was covered with wreckage and dead bodies.[37]

The view down Stationstraat.

Some drunken soldiers – "in the sodden stage, when the effect begins to wear off " – allowed the men to proceed, after berating the Belgians. They told the diplomats that the entire city was going to be destroyed systematically.

We thought at the time that they were exaggerating what was being done, but were enlightened before we had gone much farther.

We continued down the boulevard for a quarter of a mile or so till we came to the station. Sentries came out and looked through our passes again. We parked the motor with a number of German military cars in the square and set off on foot down Stationsstraat, which we had admired so much when we had driven down its length just ten days before.

The houses on both sides were either partially destroyed or smouldering. Soldiers were systematically removing what was to be found in the way of valuables, food, and wine and then setting fire to the furniture and hangings. It was all most business-like. The houses are substantial stone buildings, and fire will not spread from one to another. Therefore the procedure was to batter down the door of each house, clean out what was to be saved, then pile furniture and hangings in the middle of the room, set them afire, and move on to the next house.

It was pretty hot, but we made our way down the street, showing our passes every hundred feet or so to soldiers installed in comfortable arm-chairs, which they had dragged into the gutter from the looted houses, till we came to a little crossing about half way to the Stadhuis. Here we were stopped by a small detachment of soldiers, who told us that we could go no farther; that they were clearing civilians out of some houses a little farther down the street, and they there was likely to be firing at any time. The officer in command spoke to us civilly and told us to stick close to him so that we could know just what we ought to do at any time. He was in charge of the destruction of this part of the town and had things moving along smartly.[38]

The officer, it emerged, spoke English fluently, and when he discovered that he knew Bulle's father and uncle, he became still friendlier.

From where we stood we could see down the street through the smoke, as far as the Stadhuis. It was still standing, but the Cathedral across the street was badly damaged and smoke was rising in clouds from its roof. The business houses beyond were not to be seen; the smoke was too dense to tell how many of them were gone.

Machine guns were at work near by, and occasionally there was a loud explosion when the destructive work was helped with dynamite.

A number of the men about us were drunk and evidently had been in that state for some time. Our officer complained that they had had very little to eat for several days, but added glumly that there was plenty to drink.

A cart, heaped high with loot, driven by a fat Landsturmer and pulled by a tiny donkey, came creaking past us. One of our party pulled his kodak from his pocket and inquired of our guardian in English: "May I take a picture?"

His intent evidently escaped the German, who answered cordially: "Certainly; go ahead. You will find some beautiful things over there on the corner in the house they are getting ready to burn."[39]

The diplomats did not correct the officer's misapprehension. Soon he began sharing with them his feelings about the natives.

He was rabid against the Belgians and had an endless series of stories of atrocities they had committed – though he admitted that he had none of them at first hand. He took it as gospel, however, that they had fired upon the German troops in Leuven and laid themselves open to reprisals. To his thinking there is nothing bad enough for them, and his chief satisfaction seemed to consist in repeating to us over and over that he was going to the limit. Orders had been issued to raze the town – "till not one stone was left on another," as he said.

Just to see what would happen, I inquired about the provision of the Hague Conventions prescribing that no collective penalty can be imposed for lawless acts on individuals. He dismissed that to his own satisfaction by remarking that "All Belgians are dogs, and all would do these things unless they are taught what will happen to them."

Convincing logic!

With a hard glint in his eye he told us the purpose of his work; he came back to it over and over, but the burden of what he had to say was something like this: "We shall make this place a desert. We shall wipe it out so that it will be hard to find where Leuven used to stand. For generations people will come here to see what we have done, and it will teach them to respect Germany and to think twice before they resist her. Not one stone on another, I tell you — *kein Stein auf einander!*"

I agreed with him when he remarked that people would come here for generations to see what Germany had done — but he did not seem to follow my line of thought.[40]

Not long after, a single rifle shot went off. Soldiers rushed into one of the houses, fired a few shots, then emerged "wiping the perspiration from their faces."

'Snipers!' said our guide, shaking his fist at the house. 'We have gone through that sort of thing for three days and it is enough to drive us mad; fighting is easy in comparison, for then you know what you are doing.' And then almost tearfully: 'Here we are so helpless!'[41]

An extended charade followed. Other shots rang out and the officer urged the diplomats to head back to the station. They didn't need much urging. Bulle, leading the retreat, got into an altercation with a sentry further down the street. "Our officer waded into the soldier in a way that would have caused a mutiny in any other army, and the soldier, very drunk and sullen, retreated, muttering, to his armchair on the curb."[42]

Officers ushered the men into armchairs of their own in what Gibson imagined was a freight yard, but was likely a part of Stationsplein littered with pillaged goods. A bottle of wine was sent for.

We settled down and listened to the stories of the past few days. It was a story of clearing out civilians from a large part of the town; a systematic routing out of men from cellars and garrets, wholesale shootings, the generous use of machine guns, and the free application of the torch — the whole story enough to make one see red. And for our guidance it was impressed on us that this would make people respect Germany and think twice about resisting her.

Suddenly several shots rang out apparently from some ruins across the street and the whole place was instantly in an uproar. The lines of civilians were driven helter-skelter to cover — where, I don't know. The stands of arms in the freight yard were snatched up, and in less time than it takes to tell it, several hundred men were scattered behind any sort of shelter that offered, ready for the fray.[43]

Here Gibson's story intersects with that of the captives from Aarschot, who had been driven down to Leuven that day after being imprisoned in the town's church. When the firing broke out, the four young tourists dashed for cover, and missed what happened to the unfortunate men, women, and children. As mentioned, Gibson was more than half-convinced that a band of desperate Leuveners had holed up in some of the ruined buildings, determined "to sell their lives as dearly as they could."[44] He was so disconcerted by the gunfire that he failed to wonder why the hundreds of German troops, armed with machine guns and mortars, were unable to capture the desperados.

Repeatedly, the officer provided updates for the frightened diplomats, who were lying prone on the train tracks behind the station, amid some tethered artillery horses, a decidedly "undignified position." The officer helpfully pointed out where the "attacking force" lay concealed. He assured them later that reinforcements had been sent for, and speculated on the diplomats' chances of getting out of Leuven that evening. He returned yet again to warn them that "it looked as though an attempt would be made to take the station by storm, and that there might be a brisk fight."[45]

Finally the diplomats were permitted to leave, after being required to obtain the consent of von Manteuffel, "a pleasant-faced little man."[46] After passing Tiensepoort, the men began to see civilians again.

> In harmony with the policy of terrorizing the population, the Germans have trained them to throw up their hands as soon as any one comes in sight, in order to prove that they are unarmed and defenseless. And the way they do it, the abject fear that is evident, shows that failure to comply with the rule is not lightly punished.
>
> Our worst experience of this was when, in coming around a corner, we came upon a little girl of about seven, carrying a canary in a cage. As soon as she saw us, she threw up her hands and cried out something we did not understand. Thinking that she wanted to stop us with a warning of some sort, we put on the brakes and drew up beside her. Then she burst out crying with fear, and we saw that she was in terror of her life. We called out to reassure her, but she turned and ran like a hunted animal.
>
> It was hard to see the fear of others – townspeople, peasants, priests, and feeble old nuns who dropped their bundles and threw up their hands, their eyes starting with fear. The whole thing was a nightmare.[47]

◄‹·›►

As noted earlier, Brand Whitlock refused to permit Gibson and Blount to testify that they had seen franc-tireurs firing on soldiers, though German officials repeatedly begged him to do so.[48] What Gibson did eventually testify to was the fact that the Germans had clearly intended to destroy the entire town following the expulsion of the residents.

While we were there it was frankly stated that the town was being wiped out; that its destruction was being carried out under definite orders. When the German Government realized the horror and loathing with which the civilized world learned of the fate of Leuven, the orders were canceled and the story sent out that the German forces had tried to prevent the destruction, had fought the fire, and by good fortune had been able to save the Stadhuis. Never has a government lied more brazenly. When we arrived, the destruction of the town was being carried on in an orderly and systematic way that showed careful preparation. The only thing that saved the Stadhuis was the fact that the German troops had not progressed that far with their work when the orders were countermanded from Berlin.[49]

STRAWBERRIES AND WINE Several weeks later Whitlock himself visited Leuven. The beauty of the countryside made him almost imagine that there was no war going on – except for "the ruins of houses by the roadside...or some lovely and abandoned château at the end of its long avenue, its white facade blackened and spattered by bullets."[50]

Even Leuven itself was not entirely a scene of desolation.

The narrow twisting streets...had ruins on every side, as though an earthquake had shaken down the houses and fire had consumed them all; within they were burnt black, in some places the walls about to fall. But at the American College, with its old wall and its linden-trees, the old garden with its terraces where strawberries were still ripening in the late September sun, there was a peace almost classic, untouched by the fury that had swept away so much of the town.

A strange silence indeed filled the whole city; amid the ruins that cumbered the streets, the people stood about, idle and curious, with sad, solemn faces, and as our motor passed they uncovered in mute salute of the flag that had somehow come to express for them what had been expressed by their own, which they might no longer fly.

The Stadhuis was intact, and workmen mounted on a scaffolding were cleaning the stains from its Gothic facade. Across the street the ruins of the cathedral stood, the lofty nave and transept blackened and charred and filled with rubbish, and the sunlight pouring through the great windows from which the stained glass was broken, and through the wide aperture in the roof through which the great bell had fallen when the tower gave way. The doors had been battered in, the marks of the axes were there on lock and panel, and within on every door, even in the coffers where the treasures of the old pile had been kept, the marks of like blows were visible; and every one of the side chapels had been deliberately burned out, for the thick walls between them, still standing, had resisted the flames. And though nearly a month had passed, the sack of the city was still going steadily on, though in a more orderly and organized manner, for soldiers were bearing forth from the houses great baskets of wine.[51]

"NOT FAIR" Not all American citizens who found themselves in Leuven in August or September were as eloquent as Whitlock or as witty as Gibson.

Mr. W. H. Workman of Wellsville, Ohio, Continental Sales Manager for the British car manufacturer Willys-Overland, headed east from Brussels on the 26th. His destination was the Netherlands, but it was impossible to pass through the rings of barbed wire encircling Antwerp. The route he chose had its risks: a German officer assured him that he was "going to his death," and offered to buy the suit he was wearing for ten pounds, before it was riddled by German bullets.

In Leuven, Workman passed several dead civilians sprawled in the streets, including an old man who had been cut open. Then the route was blocked by a group of about a hundred civilians marching between soldiers. Workman approached one of the officers, who told him all the hostages were to be executed, because four German soldiers had been murdered. "That's not fair," the American blurted out indignantly. The officer explained that it was "revenge," but as the salesman did not seem to appreciate the German perspective, he was promptly arrested. A superior officer came by after awhile and liberated Workman.[52]

HOME What did the residents themselves find when they returned to Leuven? For obvious reasons, there are comparatively few accounts. Most memoirs and testimony focus on the events of the 25th and 26th and the subsequent expulsion. The return home was invariably a depressing anti-climax. Hubertine van Kempen's experience was no doubt typical:

> After some days I returned to my home at Leuven. I found my house completely ransacked, the beds dirtied, nothing left at all. The dregs of the Leuven populace helped in the looting, moreover. It was the same in all the houses. A German officer forced me to take him and his men to the cellar and show him what wine I had left.
>
> The town was still burning. All along the streets were numbers of unburied corpses.[53]

Gustave Verriest, the young professor who fled to Tervuren, returned to Leuven on September 3rd.

> I found my parents' house plundered. A great deal of furniture was smashed, and the contents of cupboards and drawers were strewn about the rooms. On all sides were bottles of wine... In my sister's house the mirrors on the ground floor were smashed. On the back of the mirrors the marks of the butt end of a rifle could be plainly seen.[54]

Often the Germans were still on the premises. The encounters were seldom pleasant. Felix van Aerschot's niece returned to her home three times.

As my house was still standing, I went to see it. I had to go with a soldier, and had to have a passport. When I got there, four soldiers came out of the cellar. One of them held a revolver to my head, but the soldier who accompanied me presented my passport, and I was allowed to go in. I went to the house a second time, and saw twenty soldiers in the house. Everything in the place had been ransacked, and it looked like a pigsty. I went to the house a third time, and the soldier who accompanied me tried to kiss me, but I resisted, and he pushed me down the stairs, and afterwards got hold of me and kissed me.[55]

A friend of René Chambry, another upper-middle-class young man who was serving as a hospital attendant, permitted Chambry to reprint his diary for this period.

29th August – My father at some risk went back to Leuven. On the way, he was forced to drink toasts with drunken soldiers. Everyone is compelled to help in burying the dead. Children nine to twelve years old first drench them with benzine.

Nothing startling on the 30th August.

On the 31st, at 11 in the morning, my father found his house intact, but occupied by seven officers and their five orderlies. The officers invited him to take a glass of his own wine, for the cellar had been looted, just as in all places where the Germans passed through. My father told the senior officer – he was a *"hauptmann"* of the name of S. – what he thought about the abominable sacking of that peaceful city. Captain S. – he will be able to give evidence concerning it if he is still alive – returned to my father the watch which one of the orderlies had stolen. At 4 o'clock the officer returned the keys of the wine cellar, but, during his absence, the orderlies, arrant knaves, broke the glass of a little window, and stole 250 bottles, which they distributed among their comrades all around the neighborhood. The *hauptmann* S. was furious when he heard of that new robbery. He made them get a padlock for his chest, because, he said, his own soldiers continually stole things from it. Inside the house everything is upside down: beds taken down and moved from one room to another, bicycles and the record player thrown into the attic. ...The floor, which is very old, has been broken in several places. The ground is strewn with flowers and silver plate not belonging to our house, the writing-room filled with buckets and basins, in which they had cooled the bottles of champagne. The dining-room is turned into a smoking-lounge. There also they had their music, if one may judge by the collection of accordions, mandolins, and ocarinas that are there. There was straw everywhere. In short, the place was like a barn. To crown everything, my father was not allowed to sleep in his own house. It was necessary to get express permission from the *Kommandantur*, and after endless discussions he was conducted to his apartments between two soldiers with leveled bayonets.

When the Germans at last left our home, it was necessary to cleanse and disinfect everything. The lowest stable was cleaner than our bedrooms, where scraps from the gormandizing and pieces of meat lay rotting in every corner amidst half-smoked cigars, candle-ends, broken plates, and hay brought from I don't know where.[56]

CHAPTER 13

Explanations

A MASS PSYCHOSIS? If there were no franc-tireurs, the German White
Book at least demonstrates that many soldiers believed there were. How
did they come to acquire this conviction?

Drawing on the work of Ferdinand van Langenhove, John Horne and
Alan Kramer argue, as will be recalled, that German officers and soldiers
were suffering alike from a psychological disorder – a "franc-tireur myth
complex," a species of paranoia. The invaders were certain that they were
being repeatedly fired on by civilians, while their comrades – though
always in other units – were being poisoned and mutilated by the treacherous Belgians.

"The complex," Horne and Kramer conclude, "was generated essentially from below during the first phase of the invasion, by soldiers in the
field..."[1]

There are several problems with this thesis.

1. The fear of franc-tireurs, according to Horne and Kramer, was based
on the experience of the German Army during the Franco-Prussian War.
How did ordinary soldiers acquire this fear? No soldier who invaded Belgium
in 1914 had also participated in the invasion of France forty-four years earlier.
Only some senior commanders who had been young officers in 1870 would
have been able to recall directly the abhorrence of the franc-tireurs then
current. Only officers would have read the condemnations of franc-tireurs
in Hartmann's respected textbook on military theory. Only officers might
have noted that the handbooks for infantry and cavalry officers established
that the German Army need not honor the Hague covenants legitimizing a

levée en masse and forbidding punishment of innocent civilians. Some book-
ish soldiers may have carried *Thus Spake Zarathustra* in their packs; few
dragged along the memoirs of von Moltke, von Goltz, and other generals, in
which disparaging references were made to franc-tireurs. Civilian guerillas
did appear in a novel published not long before the war, but, as Horne and
Kramer concede, there was a much larger body of anti-militarist popular literature.[2] There was also a compelling counter-myth, of more distinguished
pedigree, celebrating the role of civilians in the struggle against Napoleon
after Jena – that of *das Volk in Waffen,* the People in Arms.[3] The evidence
suggests, then, that the fear and loathing of franc-tireurs was communicated
by officers, however responsive ordinary soldiers and the general public were
to the tales of civilian outrages after the war's outbreak. The assumption that
many such stories originated with officers is confirmed by the sworn testimony of prisoners of war from the Saxon XIIth Corps, which devastated
Dinant. It was invariably officers who recounted stories to their men about
franc-tireur barbarities. It was commanders, too, who issued dire warnings
to their troops about civilians when their units crossed into Belgium, forbade
the drinking of water from wells, etc. The sequence is thus likely to have been
the opposite of that suggested by Horne and Kramer: if ordinary soldiers
soon began inventing and circulating rumors of atrocities by Belgian civilians, it was under the inspiration of officers.

  2. Problematic as well is the use the two Irish historians make of the
work of Georges Lefebvre on the Great Fear in France in 1789 to reinforce
the case they adopt from van Langenhove. German officers and recruits
in the early 20th century had little in common with French peasants in the
late 18th century. British travelers in France like Arthur Young and Samuel
Romilly were struck by the poverty, backwardness, and superstitiousness of
the peasantry at the time of the Revolution. The crop failure in 1788, after
successive poor harvests, reduced farm workers and cottiers to near famine
conditions, and did nothing to make them more civilized and humane.

  German officers and recruits in 1914 were neither starving nor illit-
erate. For decades, Germany's education system had been admired and
imitated throughout the civilized world. A generation after serious scholars began flocking to its universities, educational reformers started visiting primary and secondary schools and issuing largely glowing reports.
Bismarck's social welfare system was the object of equal adulation, and the

Wirtschaftswunder that propelled the Empire to the forefront of industrial-ized nations was no less celebrated.[4] Horne and Kramer's use of Lefebvre begs the question as to why German officers acted like French peasants of a century and a quarter earlier. Why should they have been as credulous and brutal as impoverished and uneducated share-croppers?

3. A comparison of the behavior of German soldiers with their American and British counterparts thirty years later would seem to be more *a propos* than with that of French peasants in the late 18th century. Allied troops entering Germany in 1945 had excellent reason to fear gue-rilla warfare conducted by die-hard Nazis, cooperating with packs of S.S. "Werewolves." Government radio repeatedly called for an army of civilian snipers to resist the invaders, and Allied authorities had no illusions about both the depth of popular support the National Socialist regime still enjoyed and the enormity of the crimes it was capable of. But the Anglo-American commanders of the Allied Armies crossing the Rhine never held civilians responsible for the resistance offered by pockets of S.S. troops or retreat-ing Wehrmacht forces – let alone for episodes of friendly fire. There were no summary executions, no seizure of hostages, no use of human shields. *A Guide to Occupation of German Communities by Small Units*, issued by 9th Army Headquarters on 12 December 1944, was concerned mostly with restricting fraternization with German civilians.[5]

Though they were experienced, combat-hardened troops, unlike the German invaders of 1914, Allied forces entering Germany had every rea-son to be wary of civilians. But they were constrained by the belief that charges against anyone accused of a crime had to be satisfactorily proved. Evidence had to be obtained and evaluated. This was based on the princi-ple that only an individual who had actually committed a crime could be punished; there was no such thing as collective guilt, let alone the belief, repeated ad nauseam by German officers and soldiers, that the innocent must pay along with the guilty.[6]

There was some looting by Allied soldiers and requisitions by offi-cers—homes of National Socialist officials were targeted—and Germans living near liberated concentration camps were sometimes forced to walk past the piles of corpses or help bury the victims. But civilians were never subjected to the forced marches, fake executions, gratuitous stabbings and beatings, and the other abuses so fully documented by Belgian witnesses.

It is not only the mass executions for imaginary crimes that need to be explained, but the frequency with which other "punishments" were administered, and their cruelty.

4. Paranoia was not restricted to the supposed franc-tireurs. Mabel St. Clair Stobart, hailed as the Florence Nightingale of the Balkan Wars, accepted an invitation from the Belgian Red Cross to establish a hospital in Brussels. Before her nurses even arrived, the German Army occupied the capital. Personally issued passports by Governor General von Goltz to the Dutch frontier via Venlo, with additional papers from the U.S. Legation, Stobart and her companions were arrested in Hasselt on the grounds that her passport had not been signed by the Governor General himself. "You are spies," they were told. The evidence: a map and a Kodak camera in Stobart's bag. There followed six excruciating days in which they were neither given food, permitted to sleep in a bed, nor change their clothes. When they pleaded with a major who was holding them at one point to at least look at their papers, they were told "You are English, and whether you are right or wrong, this is a war of annihilation." The one sympathetic officer they encountered, married to an Englishwoman, warned them that their situation was very serious. Stobart was eventually freed by a judicial officer in Aachen, after further harrowing adventures.[7]

Spy-fever was rampant in all the warring nations, but it is difficult to imagine a distinguished Red Cross nurse with full documentation subjected to this ordeal in other Western European countries. Nor is there a case of any journalist – especially one with an international reputation like R. H. Davis – condemned to death without any pretext. German subjects were also menaced.[8]

In fact, most educated Germans shared beliefs that can only be called paranoid. George McClellan, Princeton professor turned German propagandist, returned from his Potemkin Village tour of Belgium and the Fatherland to report that "every German believes that when the German Army entered Belgium, that country had already surrendered her neutrality."[9] It was an article of faith that Edward VII had orchestrated the encirclement of Germany, and that the war was caused by English treachery. Envious of Germany's commercial prowess, perfidious Albion had incited France and Russia to attack the *Kaiserreich* so it could humble its trade rival. The demonization of Grey was particularly pathological.[10]

5. Paranoia in any case cannot explain the purely vindictive mass-killings in Liège province after the defeat in front of the forts, nor the massacre in Place St. Martin, Tamines, and other crimes where the local population could in no way be implicated in the loss of German lives. In Les Rivages, captives were explicitly told they would be killed if the French fired again on German soldiers.

TERRORISM?[11] If Belgian civilians were not the victims of a spontaneous outbreak of mass hysteria on the part of the invaders, is it possible they were killed as a result of intentionally staged "franc-tireur attacks"?

There is a great deal of credible evidence that individual soldiers fired weapons to simulate guerilla sniping as a pretext to loot – and perhaps to rape and murder. Fraggings and self-inflicted wounds were also attributed to franc-tireur gunfire. But did officers intentionally discharge weapons in order to provoke reprisals that would terrorize the civilian population in other towns and villages, helping to insure a speedy passage for German troops and a peaceful occupation of Belgian territory?

It is highly unlikely that we will find out from German sources whether franc-tireur gunfire was ever simulated by order of military authorities as a pretext to execute civilians. Orders to agent provocateurs would undoubtedly have been communicated verbally. No officer who valued his life – or, still more important, his reputation – would have confessed, either during or after the war, to having staged a franc-tireur attack. Indeed, it is almost inconceivable that any officer would even have contemplated such a betrayal. Nonetheless, the satisfaction expressed in Germany at the time with the outcome of the razing of Leuven, Andenne, and the other towns – not to mention the conspicuous absence of any public expressions of guilt or remorse – makes the suspicion plausible. The sentiments of the officer supervising the burning of homes on Stationstraat were undoubtedly widespread. As, the novelist Walter Bloem wrote in the *Kölnische Zeitung* on 10 February 1915:

> The burning of Battice, Herve, Leuven, and Dinant was a series of warnings. The unavoidable burnings and the bloodshed of the beginning of the war have saved the great Belgian cities from the temptation to fall upon the scanty garrisons with which we were able to occupy them. Is there in the world a single man who imagines that the Belgian capital would have borne with us, who today go to and fro in Brussels as in

our own country, if that capital had not trembled, and did not still tremble, in terror of our vengeance?[12]

In lieu of German evidence, we are obliged to rely on Belgian testimony a) that specific warnings were issued to civilians prior to an incident, b) that suspicious actions were observed immediately before the first shots that signaled a "franc-tireur" attack, and c) that the opening shots were in fact fired by German officers or soldiers.

a) One has to be somewhat leery of reports of warnings, for at least a couple of reasons: 1) It is gratifying to claim advanced knowledge of an event; people are always trying to predict the future, and it is tempting to pretend one knew something before anyone else did. 2) Angry soldiers no doubt made vague threats on numerous occasions. The fact that events proved some of them correct in a few instances could be the result of coincidence and not reflect their foreknowledge.

Nonetheless, nearly everywhere there were mass executions after the 14th, these were preceded by warnings, according to credible Belgian testimony. Even in Aarschot, where there is the least evidence of premeditation, two families were warned late in the morning of the 19th to leave the town, which would be "pulverized."[13]

In Andenne, there are numerous reports of warnings prior to the violence, apart from the impassioned cry of an officer to the corpse of the lieutenant killed in a skirmish with a Belgian patrol: "Comrade, you will be revenged."[14] A doctor was told by an officer on the 20th that no man would be left alive in Andenne by that afternoon, though the doctor himself would be spared. Six additional witnesses reported that they received warnings from imprudent or sympathetic officers or soldiers on the 19th and 20th. A seventh, the director of École St. Begge, where one of the regiments in town made its headquarters, though he was not told specifically of Andenne's fate, received a dramatic hint as to what was impending. Presenting him with a note declaring that he and his fellow monks had behaved admirably toward the Germans, a captain was overcome with emotion. "You could have good use of it," he told the astonished cleric.[15]

At least one resident in the city of Liège was informed of an attack on civilians prior to its taking place on the 20th, and multiple warnings preceded the massacres in Dinant three days later. No less than seven witnesses from neighboring towns reported being tipped off, as were two

Dinant residents who happened to be out of town, in separate incidents. Both were specifically advised not to return to Dinant.[16]

Three residents of neighboring communities received hints of Tamines' fate ahead of time. A Captain Schmitzen told Joachim Janmart in Velaine on Friday the 21st that all of Tamines would be burned. Two inhabitants of Moignelée, including the curé, received the same message in halting French. The second individual was strongly urged not to return to Tamines, where he was from.[17]

Four inhabitants of Leuven received direct warnings that terrible things were about to take place. One of them was so upset that she repeated the words of the officer to the doctor who was attending her father-in-law next door.[18] At least eleven Belgians living in or traveling through nearby towns and villages were told by German officers prior to the 25th that Leuven would be destroyed. The witnesses included four clergymen, two doctors, and a judge.[19]

◄-◄-►-►

b) In some locations, witnesses reported signs of suspicious behavior shortly before incidents that precipitated the killings. In Andenne and Liège, several individuals observed bizarre actions by troops just prior to the outbreaks of violence, including the antics of the men housed in the Emulation Building and the preparations that seemed to be going on among various detachments in Andenne. The activities in Leuven, remarked upon by a number of witnesses, were consistent with fears of an impending attack on the city by Belgian troops.[20] However, as noted, there was no military reason for the mobilization of troops during the dinner hour. Granted that communications are less that perfect in wartime, there is still no reasonable explanation for the sounding of the alarm. At the same time as soldiers were pushing back from the dinner table and grabbing their weapons and gear, the bored Company von Sandt of Battalion Neuss, after observing some desultory gunfire nearly a mile away, was trooping back to town, its presence not required. Further north, where the main body of Belgian forces was concentrated, the situation was even more clear-cut by late afternoon. Soldiers attempting to cross the Mechelen-Leuven Canal had been driven back, and the troops that had briefly occupied Haacht had been ousted. What makes the order especially suspicious is a second order about two and a half hours later, when hundreds of troops were sent into the Oude Markt. The square had been even more tranquil than the front northwest of Leuven. On both occasions, once soldiers had been assembled outside, rockets were fired either overhead or at the troops. Was this purely coincidental?

◄◄─►►

c) Even more compelling is the direct evidence. On numerous occasions, Belgians witnessed German officers and soldiers firing shots that appeared to be either the signal for an *Aktion* or else simply provoked spontaneously a fusillade against nearby homes – and the sequence of events that invariably followed.

There was no shortage of such witnesses in Liège province, though in most of the massacres between the 5th and 7th, the Germans did not even bother providing themselves with this pretext. In Francorchamps on the 8th, café owner Henri Depouhon testified that he observed a non-commissioned officer fire three times into the air with his rifle. These shots were heard by other witnesses as well, and were followed by a fusillade against the nearby homes.[21] In Blégny on the 15th, a nun at the Blégny Institute observed four maladroit agents provocateurs open fire outside the building. Ten days earlier, an officer had attempted a similar ruse.[22] On the 6th, at Soumagne, a Belgian man and his German-born maid also witnessed an officer, this time in a car, discharge his pistol. As at Blégny, this was immediately followed by indignant soldiers screaming about franc-tireurs.[23] The task of any soldier trying to provoke troops by firing was greatly simplified in most towns by the curfew the Germans imposed on residents – usually 8:00 p.m. Thus, while no resident of Visé witnessed the shots heard around 11:00 p.m. that preceded the brief fusillade that became the pretext to burn the entire town, the Dean, when the shots rang out, observed the utter nonchalance of the officers with whom he was staying. The civilians are firing on our troops, he was told matter-of-factly.[24]

On some occasions, particularly in Liège province, the shots that resulted in the execution of civilians were fired by soldiers attempting to murder unpopular commanders. Lincé provides a particularly vivid example.[25] A fragging may have precipitated the Aarschot massacres. One witness testified that a soldier racing from a café was fired on by his comrades; another resident believed two groups of soldiers sitting in different cafés exchanged shots with each other. But a third witness testified that six or seven soldiers deliberately fired at the burgomaster's house, where the commandant was standing exposed on a balcony, overlooking the marketplace.[26]

In Seilles, several witnesses heard gunfire from homes and cafés where intoxicated Germans were ensconced.[27] Across the river in Andenne, one witness observed officers firing over roofs on both sides of the street and laughing as gunfire hit the opposite sides of the buildings in reply.[28]

In Liège, on the same day, a resident reported seeing a soldier fire a rifle out of a building on Place Cockerill, which triggered the first fusillade.[29]

The first shots fired in Leuven, according to a number of German witnesses and one Belgian civilian, were from signal rockets that only the Germans then possessed. Professor van Hecke actually observed men discharging flares from a car on Tiensevest.[30] If any Belgian witnessed the first exchange of shots in the Stationsplein, he did not survive the butchery that followed. Other civilians, however, observed Germans firing at each other nearby.[31] More important, several witnessed officers or soldiers intentionally fire their guns elsewhere in town to simulate a franc-tireur attack, punctually at 8:00 p.m., in one case. Among them were Professors Verhelst and Dupriez, both of whom were nearly executed in consequence, Mgr. Ladeuze, Rector of the University, Professor Noël, and two other priests.[32] Particularly damning is the report of another rocket or artillery shell fired into the Oude Markt after hundreds of troops had been ordered there, though the men firing the weapon from Kortestraat were not visible to the witness.[33]

⤙⤜⤛

A second key question can be answered from German sources. When the Germans believed their troops had come under fire from civilians, men were executed en masse without trial. There was no attempt to distinguish the guilty from the innocent. How high up the chain of command was the decision made to impose collective punishment on specific towns?

The commander of the Second Army, General Karl von Bülow, provided a succinct answer. The day after the killings in Andenne, he had a proclamation posted in Liège in which he acknowledged responsibility for the shootings: "It was with my consent that the General had the whole place burned down and about 100 people shot."[34] While we can't know what von Bülow was told by Major General von Langermann und Erlencamp, commanding the 83rd infantry regiment in Andenne, it is hardly likely the major general invented tales of tribunals or courts martial preceding the executions.

There is no reason to suspect that Generals von Kluck and von Hausen exercised less oversight over the actions of their corps commanders than did their colleague. Without being able to follow a paper trail revealing responsibility for the decisions in other locations, it is not unreasonable to assume that Army commanders approved of the mass executions in Liège and Namur provinces, and probably at least brigade commanders in Brabant.

It was no secret that the General Staff of the German Army gave a green light to officers to deal ruthlessly with civilians. The so-called German War Book, *Kriegsbrauch im Landkriege,* issued to all officers prior to the war, explicitly sanctioned total war. "A war conducted with energy cannot be directed merely against the combatants of the Enemy State and the positions they occupy, but it will and must in like manner seek to destroy the total intellectual [geistig] and material resources of the latter. Humanitarian claims such as the protection of men and their goods can only be taken into consideration in so far as the nature and object of the war permit."[35] The reader was warned against "excessive humanitarian notions." Military history "will teach him that certain severities are indispensable to war, nay more, that the only true humanity very often lies in a ruthless application of them."[36] In the chapter specifically dealing with non-combatants, officers were admonished that "to protect oneself against attack and injuries from the inhabitants and to employ ruthlessly the necessary means of defence and intimidation is obviously not only a right but indeed a duty of the staff of the army." Advice and edicts from Napoleon and the Duke of Wellington were cited. "Both men resort to terrorism as soon as a popular rising takes place."[37] Hostile activities by an occupied population were regarded as "war rebellion" and "war treason," one of four categories of crimes subject to martial law and courts-martial.[38] However, there were no guidelines in the War Book for conducting these trials, except for a single injunction: "Courts-martial must base any sentence on the fundamental laws of justice, after they have first impartially examined, however summarily, the facts and have allowed the accused a free defence."[39] Significantly, in a discussion of cases where civilians called upon to guide troops failed to conduct them by the most direct route, officers, while encouraged to put the guilty civilian to death, were warned that "in this case a court-martial must precede the infliction of the penalty," implying that this was not presumed to be the case otherwise.[40]

The handbook echoes the sentiments of the revered von Clausewitz[41] and the principles espoused by one of the leading legal texts, von Holtzendorff's *Handbuch des Völkerrechts.* The latter, after acknowledging the natural right to defend one's country from invasion, makes the case for recognizing the combatant status of fighters raised in a *levée en masse* – but then ominously adds, "unless the terrorism so often necessary in war does not demand the contrary."[42] Germany's most influential military theorist, General Julius von Hartmann, concurred: "Where there is a popular uprising, terrorism becomes a necessary military principle."[43]

If, in the end, it cannot be proven that the German General Staff, or the commanders of the Armies invading Belgium, ordered the razing of towns and villages and the murder of civilians as a means of deterring guerilla warfare in the rest of Belgium, irrespective of events in that location – i.e., that towns were purposely selected in advance to be made an example of – it is indisputable that the High Command of the Imperial Army authorized collective retribution for alleged franc-tireur activity. The mere allegation was always sufficient: no investigation was required as to the culpability of any of the victims, or even as to whether any such activity had actually taken place. Whether they were preemptive or not, the mass murders of innocent civilians were acts of terrorism.

-<-->-

The belief in collective responsibility was continually reaffirmed. When Bertha Tielemans, the wife of the burgomaster of Aarschot, pointed out to the captain who had just seized her husband that he knew the burgomaster had not fired – Jozef Tielemans had been in the company of several soldiers when the shooting broke out – the officer replied, "No matter, madam, he is responsible."[44] Earlier that morning, when Louis Michiels, the train station guard, assured his captors that neither he nor his wife had fired a shot, this did not trouble the commanding officer. "The good will pay with the bad," he told Michiels.[45] "The innocent must pay with the guilty," Captain

Junge informed Eva Comes in the Place des Tilleuls at Andenne.[46] "The innocent will suffer with the guilty," an officer repeated in Wavre. *"Il a fallu punir les innocents avec les coupables,"* Professor Bruylants was told on Tiensestraat in Leuven.[47]

But not everyone was on the same page. The Saxon officer of the 178th Regiment who compared his rampaging troops to Vandals reflected later that of the two hundred men he believed were shot in Leffe, "there must have been some innocent men among them. In the future we shall have to hold an inquiry as to their guilt instead of shooting them."[48]

There were other, more significant, exceptions. Just as the few S.S. guards who treated concentration camp prisoners with ordinary decency came to be regarded as saints, so Belgians hailed as small miracles those instances when German officers insisted on conducting genuine inquiries into allegations against civilians. The sense of justice, or merely the intellectual curiosity, of Major von Bassewitz in Huy, Lieutenant Welcke in Wandre, and Lieutenant Reinbrecht in Leuven were extraordinary in August 1914. Empiricism was in short supply among the invaders.

More numerous were those officers or soldiers who expressed their discomfort, disgust, or even outrage to Belgian witnesses about what was transpiring. They, too, had reservations about the doctrine of collective guilt. Many, no doubt, were Catholic. At least one officer, Dr. Uhlmann in Andenne, remonstrated in public with his superiors. These exceptional individuals were not, however, in a position to do much to ameliorate the suffering of civilians, except to aim high, to pull young men or old men from the ranks of the condemned, or to allow prisoners to escape.

TERRORISM: LOCAL AND REGIONAL DIFFERENCES The pretext for the persecution of civilians varied according to region. In the Flemish towns, the executions were most likely precipitated by a breakdown of discipline, with German troops firing on each other for a sustained period, some fifteen minutes in Aarschot and as long as an hour in Leuven – leaving aside the critical question as to whether the chaos was intentionally provoked. A good many murders in the two Brabant towns, as well as in the villages within the bloody Aarschot-Mechelen-Vilvoorde-Leuven quadrangle, were ad hoc affairs. However, once discipline was restored, many of the killings at Leuven and most at Aarschot were carried out under orders, though in the latter case these orders may on two occasions have emanated from no higher authority than the captain who supervised the killings.

In the French-speaking half of Belgium, there is clearer evidence of advanced planning. In each of the three Walloon cities where the worst massacres took place, the killing of civilians was preceded by small incidents in which the Germans sustained slight casualties. In Andenne these were encounters with Belgian patrols from the 4th Division; in Tamines, it was an ambush by a Breton platoon and uniformed *Gardes civiques*. In an analogous incident in Dinant – the abortive "reconnaissance in force" on the 21st – no enemy troops were encountered. The Germans fired on each other. In Dinant, however, there had been a major assault on the town a week earlier, on the 15th. The inability of the four German divisions to capture the city was a significant setback for the Third Army. Defeat at the hands of the Allies, albeit temporary, links Dinant and Tamines, as well the martyred villages in Liège province that lie just east of Forts Fléron and Barchon. Clearly, civilians were killed to avenge German losses – but also to divert attention from German failures. At Tamines and Dinant, the Xth Corps of the Second Army and the XIIth Corps of the Third Army, respectively, breached the Sambre and the Meuse behind schedule, the only two such failures during the Battle of the Frontiers. Commanders would have been quick to seize on the excuse that civilian sharpshooters had disrupted the German crossings. During the abortive attack on the 15th, some troops of the Third Army's XIIth Corps may have been deceived by the acoustics in the steep canyon in which Dinant sits, and by the velocity of the projectiles fired by the French Lebels, and imagined that they were being shot at from nearby homes, though no "franc-tireurs" were seized during the operation. On the 23rd, however, soldiers had simply received orders to kill all males in town. But in Tamines, no one could pretend that the fierce gunfire coming from the hill in front of Falisolle, including machine guns and 75 mm field guns – which hit the German troops after they'd crossed the Sambre – could have emanated from residents of the town behind them. There was good reason for the Germans not to include a chapter on Tamines in the White Book.

The Foreign Office would have been shrewder to have omitted the chapter on Andenne as well. Unlike in Dinant and Tamines, no enemy forces had been engaged by the three regiments of the Second Army that wreaked havoc on the city. Apart from the two casualties, which took place well out of town, the bridge had been blown and a tunnel mined by Belgian Army sappers; that was the sum of the provocations. However, unlike in Tamines and Dinant, there is evidence that undisciplined, intoxicated troops were firing at each other, at least in Seilles, as occurred in the Flemish towns. Nonetheless, there is much credible testimony that the initial gunfire was prearranged, that Andenne was to be made an example. The disorder in Seilles, in short, may well have been provoked.

Andenne is thus linked to Leuven. The execution of residents and the burning of the towns was likely preceded by deliberate firing to incite the troops to attack civilians. In both cases there were abundant warnings and much suspicious behavior indicating the outbreaks were not spontaneous.

Aarschot remains something of a mystery. On the one hand, the Germans had encountered stiff resistance to their advance by Belgian forces, not French troops. Moreover, some of the retreating Belgian soldiers may have fired from buildings on the outskirts of town, and even from the church tower. Some no doubt removed their uniforms after the battle and fled west. There was a stronger prima facie case for suspecting franctireurs here than anywhere else. Yet there is far less evidence of premeditation in Aarschot than elsewhere. No resident reported soldiers or officers raging against civilians or vowing vengeance on the town. Whoever fired the initial shots that triggered the riot in the Grote Markt, he was not likely to have been acting under orders. (This goes without saying if the first shot was that which killed Colonel Stenger.)

⊰⟷⊱

Clearly, greater violence was directed at French-speaking Belgium. It should be recalled that the upper classes in Leuven were then entirely francophone. The towns that appear to have been targeted in advance were in Wallonia. But this has much to do with the path the German armies took through Belgium. By the time they reached the two Flanders and the province of Antwerp, the German government, concerned about how the killings were playing in neutral countries and also convinced that *Schrecklichkeit* had already served its purpose, likely countermandered earlier standing orders.

Though Germany was soon to make great efforts to woo the Flemish, fraternal feelings on the part of officers for the western-most representatives of *Deutschtum* probably did not play much of a role.

Nor is it likely that the religious differences between the two halves of Belgium were of much weight. The fact that a higher percentage of Dutch-speakers were practicing Catholics would not have especially endeared them to officers convinced that "the Belgian people's war" had been preached from the pulpit, and that priests directed the assaults on their troops.

‹‹-›-›

It is as difficult to rank the culpability of the German regiments in the different locations as it is to answer the question as to whether officers or soldiers were more murderous.[49]

Andenne may have witnessed the most savage behavior of any town. Troops had been ordered to kill all men with their bayonets in the early morning of the 21st, and though the order was apparently rescinded after objections, many soldiers felt they had a license to murder all men in the homes they raided, and that brutality was welcome, if no longer required. More traditional mass executions followed later in the day.

But the execution in Place St. Martin at Tamines, the largest single massacre in Belgium, probably qualifies as the most cold-blooded. More time elapsed between the precipitating incident and the mass killing than elsewhere and that incident was more trivial than any other that was blamed on franc-tireurs in the towns experiencing the worst depredations. There was no breakdown of discipline in Tamines on account of friendly fire or enemy fire that might be attributed to civilians.

Dinant is a close second in this respect. Here, too, every male resident was to be shot, and they were executed by disciplined troops acting under orders. The lucky victims in the jail were probably the beneficiaries of the confusion caused by the execution at the Tschoffen wall, though some officers may have had a change of heart. If such was the case, their charity was more than offset by the extemporaneous massacre in Les Rivages and the indiscriminate killings in Neffe. Not only was Dinant the site of the only mass execution to be witnessed by the families of the victims, but it was one of the few places where women and children were lined up and gunned down by German troops. For sheer cruelty, the men of the Saxon XIIth Corps should probably be awarded the palm.

It is worth recalling that German terrorism was not confined to the towns
and villages covered in the last ten chapters. A little over 1,700 civilians
were killed in Aarschot, Andenne (with Seilles), Tamines, Dinant, and
Leuven. Another 420 were massacred in the city of Liège and those villages near the forts that were covered in Chapter 2. That means nearly
two-thirds of the Belgian victims of the German invasion perished in other
locations. Civilians were mowed down in northern France as well; close
to 900 were shot. And between December 16, 1914, when four German
battle cruisers shelled Scarborough, Whitby, and Harltepool, killing forty
civilians, and August 9, 1918, when the Krupp long-range Paris gun fired
for the final time, hundreds of noncombatants in England and unoccupied
France were blown up or killed by collapsing buildings.

The U.S. was also hit. Nine-eleven was not the first terrorist attack on
American soil. Eighty-five years earlier, on July 30, 1916, German agents
set off powerful explosives that rocked Black Tom Island in New Jersey,
which served as a munitions depot. About 2,000 tons of war materiel were
destroyed and seven people killed. The blast illuminated the Manhattan
skyline and shook buildings and shattered windows throughout the city.
The perpetrators, tracked down in South America, were never tried, so
it's impossible to say whether those responsible in Berlin intended only to
destroy this major depot, or to intimidate munitions and transport workers
throughout the country.[50]

KULTUR? Why did the Germans engage in terrorism in 1914 and after?
In attributing the killing of Belgian civilians to a mass psychosis, Horne
and Kramer do not ignore German culture. They note in particular the
way in which anxieties about "internal enemies" of the Reich were projected onto the Belgian population by officers steeped in Pan-Germanism
and influenced by Social Darwinism. Like antisemites who felt menaced,
simultaneously, by Jewish capitalists and Jewish communists, these officers saw both the Catholicism of the Flemish countryside and the socialism
of the Walloon towns as fomenting a spirit of reckless resistance to the
invasion, just as they were subverting the Kaiserreich at home. But this
brief, suggestive discussion quickly moves on to a consideration of the attitude of Alsatians during August 1914, and is not alluded to in the book's

conclusion. Here, again, it appears that early modern *mentalités*, along with a traditional Prussian aversion to the idea of civilians waging war, are of far more relevance for understanding what caused the massacres than what German professors were teaching, and schoolteachers and journalists repeating, in the two decades before 1914.

I am convinced that an approach emphasizing to a greater extent German intellectual and cultural history – *Geistesgeschichte* is probably a better word – would provide a more comprehensive and persuasive explanation for the behavior of the Army during the invasion. This, however, is the provenance of historians of Germany. It is beyond the scope of this book and the competencies of its author.

Readers curious about the etiology of German behavior in Belgium, however, could do worse than consult the books and articles of foreigners who resided in Germany before the war, individuals like Valentine Chirol,[51] Ford Maddox Hueffer, Thomas F. A. Smith, Anne Topham, Elizabeth von Arnim, Austin Harrison, Elmer Roberts, the anonymous author of *The German Army from Within* and Ambassadors James Gerard, Eugène Beyens, and Jules Cambon, as well as German expatriates like Richard Grelling, Otfried Nippold, Wilhelm Mühlon, Hermann Hesse and the anonymous author of *Why Germany Will Be Defeated*. Memoirs and reminiscences published during and after the war ought perhaps not to be so steeply discounted as they appear to be.[52] Sometimes it takes an astute foreigner, one fluent and well-connected, to register what is anomalous in a culture. Militarism, nationalism, and materialism affected the daily conduct of ordinary Germans, and the aperçus of a foreigner walking in a park or sitting in a café can be telling.

Also in bad odor are the dozens of books and pamphlets dissecting the German national character that appeared in Allied countries between about 1900 and the mid-1950s. Most deserve to be forgotten, but several – even with unpromising titles like *The German Mind, The Mind of Germany, The Soul of Germany, The War Against the West, From Luther to Hitler* – are sometimes instructive. The most damning pages in several of these books consist of extended quotations from eminent Germans. Other writers from Allied and neutral countries simply compiled anthologies of choice observations, largely from professors and Lutheran pastors, glorifying *Volk* and Fatherland, extolling war and the State, and expressing contempt for other peoples. By no means did these come exclusively from spokesmen for the *Alldeutscher Verband* and the *Flottenverein*. The most thorough collection of excerpts, by Sorbonne professor Charles Andler, runs to four plump volumes.[53]

The question of influence is always a vexing one, but extracts from speeches and sermons by German clergymen collected by the Danish theologian J. P. Bang suggest that even anti-Christian writers like Nietzsche and Haeckel had shaped their outlook.[54] And there is simply no gainsaying Treitschke's influence[55] or that Bernhardi's views were not representative. Nor was the best-selling author Houston Stewart Chamberlain an invention of Allied propagandists, as hyperbolic as were his claims and as convenient as it was that he should have been idolized by both the Kaiser and the Führer.[56]

What I propose to do in the next few pages is merely to sketch briefly and in broad strokes the case made by British and American observers familiar with Germany in 1914 that something more troubling and profound was responsible for the August massacres than a collective delusion that the German Army was under attack by civilians. They were made uneasy by militarism, by nationalism, and by materialism.

◄◄➤➤

Why was it so easy for anthologists to find material? The novelist Ford Maddox Hueffer, half-German, who spoke the language fluently and had spent much time in southern Germany, was willing to swear that he had never in his life "heard an Englishman say that war, academically regarded, could be beneficial either to the British State or to the private individual. I have never in my life heard an Englishman advocate war with any European nation." On the other hand, he claimed, "I have never met a German – with one exception, that of Professor Walther Schücking of Marburg – who did not, if the subject of war came up in general conversation, allege it as his opinion that war had very great advantages as a panacea for human and national diseases. A great many Germans also have in my hearing advocated the thorough beating down and humbling of the French nation and the complete extirpation of the British Navy."[57] He found that the State was a preoccupation not only of German historians, but of scholars eminent in a number of other fields, and that all regarded war as essential to the development of the State. Hueffer had no trouble compiling a collection of a hundred "militarist utterances" from respectable German sources, including Kant and Humboldt.[58] On the other hand, despite greater intimacy with the literature, he was unable to collect any passages expressing militarist sentiments from writers of similar stature in England. "Neither Darwin nor Huxley, neither Spencer nor Mill, neither Lord Acton nor Professor Gardiner, neither Pater nor D. G. Rossetti, have yielded me any passages whatever which would go to prove that the basis of the State was the waging of war, or that war in itself is a sublime occupation without which nations suffer intellectual and material decay."[59] (Hueffer's statement was intended to refute the pacificist canard that German militarists had their counterparts in England. Carlyle is the exception that proves the rule.)

In the most sophisticated publication of the anti-war Committee for Democratic Control, Goldsworthy Lowes Dickinson conceded that "there was certainly a bellicose minority" in Germany. This minority included, however, soldiers, "high officials," members of the Conservative parties, armament manufacturers, and journalists. "To these must be added the 'intellectual flower of the universities and schools'... The professors at the universities, taken en bloc, were one of the most violent elements in the nation."[60] Not only are the lists fairly encompassing, but they include, clearly, the most influential individuals in the country, Dickinson's protests that they were really "a very small minority" notwithstanding. Unfortunately, the representatives of "'the mass of the workmen, artisans and peasants who are peace-loving by instinct,'" exercised little power in the Reichstag over diplomatic and military policy. And as professors, clerics, and journalists, the "militarists" wielded influence over young Germans enormously disproportionate to their numbers.

By the final decade of the nineteenth century, war had received the imprimatur of science. It was essential for the development of the species. The contrast between Social Darwinism in Britain and Germany is instructive. For Herbert Spencer, its most influential popularizer in the U.K., the lesson was to maximize individual freedom. This would enable wealth-producing individuals to benefit society, while the absence of welfare provisions would spur ordinary individuals to greater productivity. (The gradual growth of freedom – the emergence of "industrial" from "military" societies – corresponded to the movement from simplicity to complexity in nature.) While survival of the fittest was applied in England to individuals, Ernst Haeckel, the distinguished University of Jena zoologist who was the leading Social Darwinist in Germany, applied it to nations and races. The fate of the latter was "determined by the same 'eternal laws of iron' as the history of the whole organic world."[61] If phylogeny recapitulated ontology, history recapitulated phylogeny, and it was driven by conflict. Big battalions were indispensable in the competition for the means of subsistence in which all nations engaged.

The scientific rationale for war echoed and reechoed in the decade before 1914. "Unless we choose to shut our eyes to the necessity of evolution, we must recognize the necessity of war. We must accept war, which will last as long as development and existence; we must accept eternal war."[62] "War is a biological necessity of the first importance, a regulative element in the life of mankind which cannot be dispensed with... The weak nation is to have the same right to live as the powerful and vigorous nation[?] The whole idea represents a presumptuous encroachment on the natural laws of development."[63]

◄-◄--►-►

Militarism, however, meant much more than bombastic statements about the virtues of war in shaping national character, or its political expedience or biological necessity.

The American Ambassador to Germany, James Gerard, one day took his brother-in-law to the Jockey Club in Berlin. Between races, the pair went down to look at a horse. When they returned, a Prussian officer and his wife had taken their seats. The couple refused to leave and the terrified ushers were unwilling to ask them to. Only after an exasperated Gerard showed the head usher his passport identifying him as an ambassador did the Americans get their seats back. Time and again Gerard observed officers cutting to the front of lines. No one ever challenged them.[64]

Why not? The future British diplomat, Robert Vansittart, while studying in Berlin, accidentally bumped into an officer as he left a theater. He jauntily wished the man a good evening. The German friend who was with him fled in terror. Vansittart was baffled. Then it occurred to him: not only was the officer entitled to cut down Vansittart with his sword for the young Englishman's impudence, but he was likely to take a swipe at the friend as well.[65] An officer was obliged to defend the *Kaiserrock*, the king's uniform.

An insult to his person was an insult to the Kaiser, and the military code of honor demanded that the offender be punished in order for the dishonor to be expunged. Humane officers crossed the street when approaching a drunk, so they would not be obliged to kill him if he became too friendly. Prudent civilians, even when sober, were known to step into the street when an officer approached. Humane officers were few and far between.

Not many officers, however, looked forward to slashing civilians. It was a duty and privilege, however, to slash a fellow officer if circumstances demanded it. (When challenged to a duel during a tennis match, Vansittart coolly pointed out to his opponent that he was not *Ehrenhaftig* – worthy of dueling – and if the man insisted on challenging him, he would box his ears. The officer would then have to kill him or commit suicide.)[66] (In English, incidentally, there are five words with the prefix "honor" and another four expressions where the first word is honor, i.e., honor code. In German, there are at least forty-five words with the prefix "*Ehren*.") Honorableness, *Ehrenhaftigkeit* defined the caste. You were expected to defend your honor aggressively and repeatedly. Bismarck reportedly had over a dozen *Schmisse*, dueling scars. (The weekly dueling matches, *Bestimmungsmensuren*, between members of rival student Corps or *Burschenschaften*, the source of most dueling scars, were not the result of individual challenges. Nonetheless, they contributed to the brutality and arrogance for which Corpsmen were notorious, and had no counterpart at other European universities.) The quality prized above all others in Corpsman and officer was *Schneidigkeit* – literally sharpness, but meaning a penchant for aggressive self-assertion. After it had virtually disappeared from the rest of Europe by the middle of the 19th century, dueling enjoyed a great revival in Germany in the decades before the war. And unlike elsewhere on the continent, it was frequently fatal. Middle-class men were as zealous duelists as aristocrats. A young officer looking for a pretext to challenge a fellow officer to a duel had only to accuse the other of staring at him (*fixieren*).

Dueling was ostensibly illegal, as was killing civilians. But an officer convicted of either crime could expect to serve at most a few months in a comfortable fortress. The alternative was grim: if he failed to respond to a challenge, a Court of Honor would expel him from the Army.

The distinction between officer and non-officer overshadowed class, religious, and regional divisions in Germany, significant as these were. There can be little doubt that the fierce pride, the hypersensitivity to slights against one's honor, and the contempt for civilians contributed much to the savagery of the invasion in August 1914. It is hardly surprising that officers quick to be offended by a stare ordered the shooting of peasants gaping at passing troops.

⊰⟨⟶⟩⊱

After 1871, when the King of Prussia became the Emperor of Germany, insults to his uniform were insults to the German nation. Its leaders were advised by no less a figure than Treitschke to adopt the insolence and swagger of the Corpsman: "That State which will not be untrue to itself must possess an acute sense of honor. It is no shrinking violet. Its strength should be shown in the light of open day, and it dare not allow that strength to be questioned even indirectly. If its flag be insulted, it must ask satisfaction; if that satisfaction be not forthcoming, it must declare war, however trifling the occasion may be."[67] It follows that there was no obligation to observe treaties: "the limitations which States lay upon themselves are merely voluntary; all treaties are concluded with a mental reservation – *rebus sic stantibus* – so long as circumstances remain unchanged. No State exists, no State ever will exist, which is willing to observe the terms of any peace for ever; no State can pledge itself to the unlimited observance of treaties, for that would limit its sovereign power."[68] Besides, war is fundamentally "just and moral" and "is the direct outcome of the very nature of the State."[69]

⊰⟨⟶⟩⊱

It may have been unsporting for critics of Germany to always capitalize the "S" in the word State – all German nouns are capitalized – but the reverence for that entity in the Fatherland alternatively amused[70] and alarmed Anglo-Saxons conditioned to view the government with some skepticism. Möser, Schelling, Müller, Novalis, Schlegel, Arndt and, especially, Fichte, among others, frequently ex-seminarians, provided a bouquet of idolatrous sentiments for the better-read anthologists. Few could resist quoting the notorious passage from Hegel's *Philosophy of Right:* "The State is the course of God through the world." But as with militarism, worship of the State was not merely a matter of orotund declamations. It affected the behavior of ordinary Germans. Many observers commented on what James Gerard dubbed "the Rat System," the obsessive pursuit of honors dispensed by the government, and the extravagant displays of *Ehrenzeichen*, signs of deference to authority.[71]

⊰⊷⊱

The ways in which German nationalism deviated from its counterpart in other countries was the subject of keen interest to foreign observers during and after both World Wars. Those writing from the late 1930s through the '50s and beyond tended to focus on *völkish* thought. Instead of Treitschke, Bernhardi and the other usual suspects, writers like Jahn, de Lagarde, Langbein, Lienhard, Wagner, and his prolific disciple Chamberlain were in the cross hairs.[72] (Chamberlain fascinated the earlier generation of critics as well.) Writers also scrutinized antisemites like Stoecker and Marr, Treitschke doing double duty with Chamberlain here as well. Hitler's racism and hatred of Jews had a long and distinguished genealogy.

What troubled writers shortly before and during the First World War, however, was the way nationalism, as it had developed in the first and final decades of the nineteenth century, was responsible for "Germany's Swelled Head," as one jeremiad was entitled.[73] Other nationalists pressed for statehood or autonomy for their ethnic group without making the extravagant claims for its merits that were commonplace in the Fatherland.

For those who pored over the literature from the '90s through the war, the most characteristic utterance was the couplet by Emmanuel Geibel quoted repeatedly by German writers: *"Und es mag am deutschen Wesen/ Einmal noch die Welt genesen!"* (And the world may once again be healed by German ways.) J. P. Bang, Professor of Theology at the University of Copenhagen, after reading through hundreds of pages written by his German colleagues, concluded that they believed to a man that

> Germany is not only the strongest nation in the world, but is also the nation which, without comparison, stands highest in every respect. The Germans are the chosen people, the crown of creation. All moral virtues are, in the German, nothing but his natural, inborn qualities. All that is noble, good, and beautiful can therefore be described as German. It follows that the German people as such cannot possibly do wrong; it will always be preserved from wrong-doing by its inmost nature. That is why, for example, German men of science can stand forth and unhesitatingly, without any argument, demand that it shall be acknowledged that the German army... cannot

commit any crimes – it is simply inconceivable.[74]

Some of the longest and most lurid chapters in the anthologies were entitled *"Deutschland Über Alles,"* "German Humility," "A Chosen Race,"
"The Mission of Germany."

The peril for Belgian civilians was that these convictions deadened conscience. Crimes were not crimes when they were committed in behalf of a
nation whose victory meant the salvation of the world. The other side of
self-adulation was contempt for others.[75]

What was particularly disturbing for British, French, and Belgian critics
was the way in which vanity crossed over into sacrilege. If nationalism had
become idolatry, this was a direct consequence of the rejection of Christianity
in the Fatherland, many contemporaries believed. German writers gave such
critics much ammunition. Heine's prophesy was widely quoted:

> Christianity – and this is its finest merit – subdued to a certain extent that brutal
> Germanic lust for battle, but could not destroy it, and if some day that restraining
> talisman, the Cross, falls to pieces, then the savagery of the old warriors will explode
> again, the mad berserker rage about which the Nordic poets have told us so much.
> This talisman is decaying and the day will come when it will sorrily disintegrate. The
> old stone gods will then arise from the forgotten ruins and wipe the dust of centuries
> from their eyes, and Thor will at last leap up with his giant hammer and smash the
> Gothic cathedrals.[76]

The hammer blows, however, came from Hegel's wayward disciples. The
betrayal was poetic justice. Kant little imagined that the *Critique of Pure
Reason* would spawn a generation of Idealists. The subsequent conversion
of Idealism to materialism was hardly surprising, according to George
Santayana, who sniffed the corrosive egoism inherent in the conception
of an Absolute subjectively apprehended.[77] But well before the divinity
of Jesus and the idea of a transcendent Being were called into question,
Schleiermacher – hailed as the nation's greatest theologian since Luther –
had already hinted that the essence of Christianity was a warm and fuzzy
feeling, without ethical content or scriptural sanction.[78]

"While pursuing a course of studies at one of the German Universities
some years ago," wrote a Prussian-born professor who had become a naturalized British subject,

> I found to my amazement that, outside of the definitely Catholic element, there was
> not a single professor or student in the University who believed in the existence of

God or in man's survival of physical death. And if there really existed any such person, I am confident that he would not have had the moral courage to admit it, seeing that such notions were universally regarded as antiquated and as wholly unscientific and out of date.[79]

Within a decade of Marx's death, the people no longer consumed the "opiate" the upper classes had forsworn many years earlier.

> ...Modern Protestant Germany is today materialistic to the backbone. The scientific conclusions which at one time were the possession of the University Professor and the savant have, in the course of years, filtered down to the man in the street, and in so persuasive and irresistible a form have they been presented, in many instances by men of world-wide renown, that they have been instrumental in effacing from the most loyal heart the last remnant of belief in a personal God, in the spirituality of the human soul, and a future life.[80]

"Social Democracy fights against every religion and every faith," declared Karl Liebknecht. August Bebel had already announced that "Social Democracy is not only an enemy of dogmatic faith, but we strive on principle to destroy the need for religion in mankind."[81] Among all classes, the clergy were despised civil servants. The churches were empty; their renovations were funded by the proceeds of the state lottery.

> I have often, in order to gather true and accurate impressions, looked into some of the Protestant churches in Germany during divine service, and I have marveled how men of education and self-respect can have the courage to enter a pulpit and address such microscopic congregations, and how they can for such services accept a substantial annual income and a pension for themselves and their families... And it is, of course, a well-known thing in Germany that the Protestant clergy themselves are becoming increasingly conscious of the incongruity and untenableness of their position.[82]

This awareness may have increased the clergy's propensity to jingoism. Few things irritated intellectuals in other countries more than repeated references to *"unser Deutsche Gott"* – as if He were a tribal deity. Ordinary soldiers responded similarly when they came across the notorious belt buckle inscribed *"Gott mit Uns."*[83] Anthologists like Bang had no trouble collecting sacrilegious quotations from published sermon collections: "We are beginning slowly, humbly, and yet with deep gladness to divine God's intentions," wrote the Reverend Walter Lehmann. "It has a proud ring, my friends, but we are conscious that it is also in all humbleness that we say: the German soul is God's soul; it shall and will rule over mankind – in the same way as God is wont to rule: without outward force, without compulsion, with an inward, invisible strength, with purity, truth, righteousness, love."[84] Others were more concise: "The German people are the elect of God, and its enemies are the enemies of the Lord." "It must please God to see Himself mirrored in the German soul."[85] In another book, still another pastor revised the Lord's Prayer so that it addressed a god of war.[86] Werner Sombart and H. S. Chamberlain could always be counted on: "Now we understand why the other nations pursue us with their hatred: they do not understand us, but they are sensible of our enormous spiritual superiority. So the Jews were hated in antiquity, because they were the representatives of God on earth." "...[W]e may say, without extravagance or the least trace of self-exaltation: Germany is chosen. Germany is chosen, for her own good and that of other nations, to undertake their guidance. Providence has placed the appointed people, at the appointed moment, ready for the appointed task."[87]

Others, like Heine, had much earlier given "the German God" his true name – Thor. A great project of the Romantics (though the movement also inspired conversions to Catholicism) was the recovery of pre-Christian German culture. The Grimms, von Arnim, Brentano and others sought to unearth the folk tales, songs, and maxims that the Church had not succeed in eradicating. (The popularity of that unedifying saga of treachery, lust, and greed, the *Nibelungenlied*, dates from the first decade of the eighteenth century.) In *Deutsche Mythologie* (1835), published twenty years after his *Kind und Hausmärchen*, Jacob Grimm had represented the Church as an oppressive colonial power, intent on obliterating the customs and beliefs of a conquered people.[88] The religion the Saxons practiced before being forcibly converted by Charlemagne was a benign pantheism that bore much resemblance to liberal Protestantism, except for the occasional sacrifice of an unlucky girl or boy. Wotan and Hertha represented the power of the weather and the fecundity of the earth, and the elves, sprites, and genii who still peopled the forest were mostly delightful creatures.[89] But Romantic paganism was too pastelcolored for most tastes. The poem quoted alongside Geibel's couplet, Arndt's "The German Fatherland,"[90] and, of course, Lissauer's "Hymn of Hate" was Felix Dahn's "Thor's Hammerthrow":

> Thor stood at the midnight end of the world,
> His battle-mace flew from his hand:

'So far as my clangorous hammer I've hurled
Mine are the sea and the land!'
And onward hurtled the mighty sledge
O'er the wide, wide earth, to fall
At last on the Southland's furthest edge
In token that His was all.
Since then 'tis the joyous German right
With the hammer, lands to win.
We inherit world-wide might
As the Hammer-God's kith and kin.

Thor was the god of *Weltmacht*.

The complaints of European intellectuals about German materialism and paganism no doubt strike the twenty-first century reader as incredibly quaint. But perhaps they should not be dismissed out of hand. Christianity, after its revival in the late eighteenth and early nineteenth centuries, constrained nations as it did individuals. It taught charity and empathy. That the contempt of German officers and soldiers for religion was a proximate cause of the August massacres is not an entirely farfetched proposition. The deaths of Belgian civilians and the desecration of their churches may have been linked.[91]

Epilogue

DEJA-VU At 3 a.m. on May 17, 1940, a monk in the Benedictine abbey of Keizersberg high above Leuven was startled to observe flames flickering from the roof of the University Library, rebuilt in the late 1920s. An hour later, a Minorite friar in town stepped outside and saw small pieces of burned paper flying up in the air. Like Emile Schmit, Lodewijk Grondijs, and hundreds of others in Leuven on August 26, 1914, he immediately suspected what was happening. Not long afterward a woman rushed up to the Minorite cloister to confirm that, indeed, the library was once again on fire.[1]

With the fall of Eben Emael and the destruction of the Belgian air force on May 10th, the reoccupation of Leuven by the Germans was nearly inevitable. Not surprisingly, this time most residents fled. Only four to five hundred of Leuven's 38,000 inhabitants remained on the 16th, but there were enough witnesses to reconstruct what is likely to have happened.

The Germans were at the outskirts of Leuven within a week. Batteries were set up in Kessel-Lo and Lovenjoel on May 16. A farmer outside the latter town was asked to accompany an officer to a bluff overlooking Leuven. "What is that tower?" the officer asked. The farmer replied that it was the library. Some time later he observed two guns shelling the tower. A large column of smoke soon arose from the building, obscuring the view.[2] A surveyor living in Roosbeek, eight miles east of Leuven, stated that on May 15th a German artillery unit parked a vehicle in his garden that appeared to regulate the fire of the company's guns. Over dinner, one of the officers mentioned to him that *Furore Teutonico* was inscribed on the library railing. The surveyor told him this was not the case, the Rector had vetoed the controversial epigraph, but the officer insisted that he was correct. Firing began the next day.[3]

A Belgian commission concluded that it was in fact the unflattering inscription intended for the balustrade that provoked the Germans. Whether or not this is true, the commission produced abundant evidence

*Déjà vu. May 1940: a German soldier stands in front of the monument
to the martyrs of 1914 in Martelarenplein (formerly Stationsplein).*

that it was artillery shells that damaged the building and, for a second time, destroyed its contents.[4] A dozen shells were discovered by the University's Rector when he inspected the damage; several unexploded shells were located much later.[5] The library may also have been bombed. A lawyer living in Kessel-Lo observed more than forty planes flying low over the city at 3:30 a.m. on the 17th. He saw bombs fall on the library, directly behind the tower, he testified.[6] A woman on her way back from Paris to Leuven, anxious about her home in town, was told by a Luftwaffe officer at Le Bourget not to worry. Only the suburbs and library had been bombed, he assured her.[7]

As in 1914, the Germans provided their own account of the event. It was intentionally started by British soldiers in the early hours of the 17th, they claimed. They reported finding evidence of benzine in twelve places. In the cellar, two trunks of benzine were ignited by grenades.

The star witness for the Germans was a Belgian soldier, Louis Leclercq. He heard four muffled explosions, probably mines, German newspapers reported, and then saw British soldiers leaving the arcade in front of the library and sheltering against the wall of a nearby building. But Leclercq later testified that he had said nothing of the sort. He did encounter British soldiers, who told him to put on his gas mask. He then heard an explosion, and saw the library illuminated briefly. But no soldiers were near the building or came from it. Several more explosions followed. Leclercq stated that he was interrogated for four days in Brussels and required to sign a statement he was not permitted to read.[8] The university librarian was also questioned. The "benzine," he pointed out to the Germans, was simply melted gum-resin and varnish. His testimony was not reported in the *Völkischer Beobachter*.[9]

One act of vandalism the Germans did take responsibility for. Half of a large plaque in Leuven's Stadthuis was removed. It had listed the names of the civilians killed in 1914. The other half, with the names of soldiers, was left intact.[10] The names of civilians were also eliminated from the memorial in Martelarenplein (Martyrs Square, formerly Van der Weyer or Station Square).

⊰⊶⊱

In Dinant, the destruction of monuments was more thorough. Shortly after their arrival in the town, German troops dynamited the massive monument in the Place d'Armes which had incorporated the *Furore Teutonico* inscription from Leuven. Other memorials at the Tschoffen and Bourdon walls and in the rue des Tanneries were removed.

The Germans withdrew from Dinant in September 1944. But on Christmas Eve, they nearly made it back for a third time. Hitler's last throw of the dice in the west was a counteroffensive by over 200,000 troops and 600 tanks. The Germans would drive to Antwerp, splitting the British and American armies. The latter would be demoralized, the former evacuated. Both nations would be ready to conclude peace, enabling all German forces to swing east and repel the Russians. But before the Wehrmacht reached the Schelde, it would have to cross the Meuse. The most advantageous crossing would be at Namur, and Hasso von Manteuffel's Fifth Panzer Army was assigned that objective. However, when the panzers failed to take Marche-en-Famenne, von Manteuffel's forces headed for Dinant.

This time it was the British who rushed to the town. They came in greater numbers and, obviously, with vastly superior firepower than the French thirty years earlier. And just behind the units of the 29th Armoured Brigade that were assigned to hold the Dinant and Bouvines bridges were squadrons of rocket-firing Typhoons.

The Allies didn't wait for the Germans to attack. Before dawn on December 24, British and American guns opened up on the 2nd Panzer Division, the spearhead of the Ardennes offensive. While the 3rd Royal Tank Regiment hit the nose of the Bulge at Foy-Notre-Dame, just over three miles east of Dinant, the American 2nd Armored Division of VIIth Corps swept down on the Germans at Celles. The Panzers had outrun their support, their right flank was exposed, and they were annihilated. The skies cleared on Christmas morning, and the feared "Jabos," the fighter bombers, took out the super-sized Panzers and the Tigers rushing up to support the trapped division. The German advance was over.[11]

The invasion would not have been complete without the massacre of civilians. More than one hundred thirty were killed in and around Stavelot, thirty-two at Bande. This was the work of the notorious S.S. division that also executed eighty-six American p.o.w.s at Malmédy, after killing at least sixty-nine other American prisoners.[12]

≺‹·›≻

On Christmas Day, the war had nearly returned to Dinant. The following Valentine's Day, it arrived with fury at Dresden, home of the Saxon XIIth Corps that had devastated Dinant thirty years earlier. British squadrons hit the city twice on the evening of the 13th and in the early morning hours of the 14th; waves of American B17s followed the Lancasters after dawn. The attack was carried out at the request of the Soviet Union; Stalin claimed the city was being used as a staging area for troops moving east. Between 25,000 and 40,000 civilians were killed in the firestorms that engulfed Dresden.[13]

The bombing of *Elbflorenz* (Florence on the Elbe) is controversial to this day. The city of porcelain shepherdesses, magnificent baroque churches and theaters, renowned museums and clinics, was also home to over 125 factories producing war materiel and a rail network and communications center that might have been used to help deploy troops east for a Bulge-style counterattack. Whether or not this justifies the scale of the raid is not at issue here, however.

Instead, one can't help but wonder if those residents of Dresden who were veterans of the companies that had destroyed Dinant recalled the earlier fires. "It was a beautiful sight to see the fires all around us in the distance," one soldier had written. "Above the village, the sky was dyed a dreadful red, and dancing flames bore witness to a deed of German heroism. *C'est la guerre!*" wrote another. "I thought of the burning of Valhalla in the *Gotterdämmerung*. A magnificent, but heart-rending sight," still another reported.[14]

Vengeance does not appear to have played a part in the planning of the attack on Dresden, but if any individual airmen were moved by the spirit of retribution, it was surely not Dinant that was being avenged.[15] Yet the two events were linked. "The dice of God are always loaded," wrote Ralph Waldo Emerson, the 19th century American author perhaps most admired in Germany. "Every secret is told, every crime is punished, every virtue rewarded, every wrong redressed, in silence and certainty. What we call retribution is the universal necessity by which the whole appears wherever a part appears."[16]

Unpunished, unacknowledged as a crime, it was inevitable that the killings in Dinant would be repeated. This time there were consequences.

-<-->-

God's dice were iron. As many as 600,000 German civilians may have died in Allied bombings during World War II. Several hundred thousand more were killed by Soviet troops, most as they fled westward. Some fifteen million ethnic Germans were expelled from Poland, Czechoslovakia, Yugoslavia, Rumania, and Hungary after the war. The operations were carried out with great brutality, and more than a million may have perished.[17]

◂—‣▸

"History repeats itself," proclaimed Karl Marx, surely the most popular 19th century German writer in America, "the first time as tragedy, the second time as farce."[18] As far as the first half of the 20th century goes, Marx was wrong in this, as in much else. The first World War was the greatest tragedy to befall Europe since the Black Plague. The second was a far greater tragedy. It was so in terms of the scope of the killing and destruction, but also because, like the downfall of the hero in a Sophoclean drama, it was caused, in part, by an excess of virtue. Compassion and forgiveness eventually blinded the victors of the Great War, and undercut their will to resist mortal dangers. The *Times* of London ran a column nearly every day throughout the war called "Through German Eyes" that excerpted German news stories and leaders. (It is impossible to imagine the *Berlin Lokalanzeiger* running an analogous column.) Eventually, the views that it recorded moved from that column to the editorial page. The adage that history is invariably written by the winners is manifestly untrue.

REVISING REVISIONISM This book was conceived as a simple narrative history, not an argument. It has attempted to show what happened to some individuals and families in the path of the German Army when it invaded Belgium in 1914. But I have also documented, in the first edition, the way in which the accounts of eyewitnesses were dismissed, discredited, or ignored by historians and popularizers alike for the rest of the century and beyond, particularly in Britain and the U.S. It is to revisionism that I would now like to return briefly. Beliefs about the origin, conduct, and conclusion of the war that date mostly from the 1920s are still passionately defended, despite the fact that they have been abandoned by most professional historians who are specialists in the three areas.

Revisionism is always gratifying. Participants and spectators were manipulated; we see the marionette strings and the hovering hand. In the case of World War I, the sordid tale told in the 1920s (and revived with gusto in the 1960s) of senseless slaughter, greed, vindictiveness and eventual retribution is nearly irresistible. It has the additional appeal of representing the upper classes as imbecilic, gratuitously martyring their long-suffering social inferiors and then lying about their crimes.

1. To begin with the conclusions of the preceding chapters, the German Army did not systematically cut off the hands of Belgian children and the breasts of Belgian women. Precious few such accusations, however, appeared in the leading British and American newspapers during the first two months of the war, or in the reports of the Belgian Commission of Inquiry. What the Army did repeatedly was to loot and burn towns and villages, and to seize and abuse hostages, shipping nearly two thousand to concentration camps in Germany. Hundreds of hostages served as screens to protect German troops. Thousands were herded pointlessly around Brabant, and repeatedly threatened with death, before being released or shipped east. These were among the fortunate ones. Nearly 6,000 civilians were murdered, a great many during an eight-day killing spree between August 19 and August 26. The victims were primarily men shot in a series of ad hoc executions. Other civilians were massacred in their homes or perished in the fires the Germans set; still others were gunned down as they attempted to flee.

The victims were accused of being franc-tireurs. There is virtually no credible evidence to support this charge. The Germans conducted no inquiries before the mass executions. As officers stated explicitly several times, they had no interest in determining the guilt of their victims. These men were being punished for the actions of others – the French Army in Dinant and Tamines (as well as a uniformed *Garde civique* platoon in the latter town), the Belgian Army in Andenne and in the villages east of Liège, and "friendly fire" in Aarschot and Leuven. In the latter town, as in Andenne, Visé, Blégny, Battice and other places in Liège province, there is compelling evidence that such gunfire was deliberate. In some instances in Liège, soldiers discharged their weapons as a pretext to loot; in Leuven and Andenne, officers are likely to have fired weapons as a pretext to devastate the towns.

The resistance of the Belgian Army had not been counted on, and was infuriating. In the first place, it delayed the critical river crossings. In the second place, it required the presence of large bodies of troops in Belgium to defend the Army's rear from attacks, and from threats posed by patrols or civilians to German communication lines. It is most unlikely that orders to or confessions from agents provocateurs will ever turn up. But persuasive circumstantial evidence suggests that army commanders resorted to mass murder in order to demoralize the Belgian government and to terrorize Belgian civilians so as to facilitate speedy passage through the country and to reduce the number of troops required to hold it.

There were few scruples to be overcome. Military doctrine dismissive of individual rights reflected deeply held convictions about the status of civilians. Beliefs about Germany's nature and destiny did nothing to temper the savagery of the Army's response to the Belgian government's decision to resist the invasion, and, especially, to its army's successes and those of the French, however brief. Anti-Catholic sentiments and post-Christian morals also contributed to the abuse of civilians.

2. Nations do not "slither into war" (in Lloyd George's unfortunate phrase). Wars are willed by individuals, and take place when those with the power to launch them have concluded that the potential advantages outweigh the risks, including the risk of a bad conscience. From 1912 on, the German military pressed for a preemptive strike against France and Russia. The fear was not so much that the two countries would attack Germany, but that they would be capable of resisting a German attack within five years. It was essential that the war be fought over an issue involving Austria, so that the Franz-Josef's forces would engage the Russians on the eastern front. Happily, a Balkan casus belli was easy to come by and would be remote from British concerns. The pretext, however, could not be so trivial as to raise eyebrows in Rome and London, and outrage in working-class Berlin – i.e., Serbia's efforts to obtain a port on the Adriatic. The role of the civilian government was to insure the neutrality of the British, the acquiescence, if not the support, of the Italians, and the support, if not the enthusiasm, of the German working classes. As the Foreign Office could not negotiate the former, owing to the Kaiser's unwillingness to abandon his naval ambitions, or even to scale back the rate of ship-building, British

neutrality as well as socialist approval had to be achieved simply by representing Russia as the aggressor.

For their part, the Chancellor and leading Foreign Office officials did not necessarily wish for war, even the limited continental war envisioned by the military. They would have been more than content with a rupture of the Entente – i.e., the estrangement of France and Russia over the former's failure to support the Czar. This required, however, the threat of war. As in 1905 and 1909, the government did not hesitate to issue the threat. As in those crises, though unlike in 1911, it was reconciled to proceeding with a European war if France and Russia failed to back down.[19] Civilian officials had been warned repeatedly about the two countries becoming formidable adversaries in five years, and had been reassured that the German War Plan would succeed brilliantly. The generals had been right the last three times. Who were they, these civilian officials, all reserve officers, to deny Germany yet another lightning triumph, especially one that promised so many economic and political benefits? Among the former were the seizure of French and Belgian colonies, the mines of Briey, and the imposition of trade and currency policies on much of Europe favorable to Germany. Chief among the latter was the opportunity to reverse the gains of the SPD, which, in the elections of 1912, had become for the first time the largest party in the Reichstag. The prestige of a quick and decisive victory would be a boon to the conservative parties. The war itself would unite the country; if it didn't, repressive measures not permissible in peacetime could be resorted to. The military benefits were obvious: the seizure of the French forts, the reduction of France to military impotence, and the securing of naval bases along the Channel and of the Belgian rail network to transport troops to the coast.

The truism that the war was precipitated by the European alliance system is not supported by the evidence. On the contrary, it was precisely because there was no military alliance between Britain and France that Germany took the calculated risk of launching the invasion of Belgium. Once Austria cashed its blank cheque in July, the British Foreign Office, Russian Foreign Minister Serge Sazonov, and French Ambassador to London Jules Cambon were probably correct to argue that war could only be averted if Britain were to announce that it would stand by Russia and

France should the Germans insist that Austria had the right to invade and occupy Serbia – that is, that the minor differences between the Austrian ultimatum and the Serbian reply could not be negotiated.[20] The mere hint that Britain might intervene instantly brought some pressure from the Chancellor on Vienna on the night of July 30. But this was not applied in earnest, and the Viennese, insofar as they considered British feelings, were more impressed by Grey's backpedaling. After initially appealing for negotiations, he had swiftly reconciled himself to an Austrian invasion and occupation of northern Serbia. Appeasement (albeit of an altogether different magnitude) was no more effective in 1914 than it would prove to be in 1938, when another "quarrel in a far-away country between people of whom we know nothing" broke out. Britain, too, was rehearsing.[21]

3. The fact that the war was horrendous does not mean that it was meaningless. The fact that it dragged on for over four years does not mean that the Allied generals learned nothing.[22]

For most of four centuries, since the advent of gunpowder, developments in weaponry and transportation had favored the offense. By 1914 these favored the defense. Moreover, the fighting in September 1914 had converted the entire Western Front to one long trench, with no flanks to attack. The line could be punctured, and was repeatedly, but was always resealed.

However, with Germany occupying nearly all of Belgium and one-fifth of France, and enjoying spectacular successes in the east, it was not an option for the Allies to retire to the trenches and await the results of the naval blockade or the development of new weaponry to break the stalemate – though patience, in retrospect, would have saved millions of lives. With the failure of Gallipoli in spring of 1915, "Westerners" in Britain (i.e., the General Staff of the British Expeditionary Force) gained critical leverage – the French and Belgians, of course, opposed deployments elsewhere. Campaigns in other theaters were not allocated the manpower or munitions to enable them to menace the Central Powers. Nor is it likely they could have. Though the Royal Navy's control of the seas made possible the opening of an additional front in southeastern Europe (i.e., a campaign by the Army of the Orient in Salonika) this would likely have been no more successful than the Gallipoli campaign of 1915—though, like all counterfactuals, the assumption is debatable.

The chief problem of the war, then, for the Allies, was developing effective artillery attacks and new weaponry that would permit the infantry to dislodge the enemy. This problem was solved during the course of the war, as demonstrated in its final three months. It necessitated tactical and technological innovations more impressive than those achieved in any other war. More attention has been paid to the latter, naturally – the use of aircraft first as artillery spotters, then to interdict the movement of reserves and supplies to the front – and tanks, hardened mobile artillery which, while they took out the machine guns, had the additional virtue of cutting the barbed wire and diverting enemy fire.

But improvements in tactics were also crucial. These were made possible by enormous increases in the production of ammunition after 1915 – and in its quality after 1916 – and improvements in mapping, camouflaging, and communications. The tactics involved hurricane barrages, creeping barrages, effective ratios of high-explosive to shrapnel shells, and massed machine-gun firing. More important still were strategic changes, above all the acceptance – far too long in coming – of the "bite and hold" approach, whereby troops would not attempt to push on once they had seized enemy trenches (pursuing the chimerical breakthrough), but await the arrival of the guns and the staging of a second "set-piece" operation, while artillery cut off counterattacks. What was achieved by the end of 1917, above all, were carefully coordinated attacks by all arms, commencing with elite "storm troopers" infiltrating enemy positions and concluding with "moppers" resupplying troops in the captured trenches. The celebrated Blitzkriegs of 1939 and 1940 were largely anticipated by Allied tactics (as well as German, of course) from the final two years of the war. Conventional wisdom holds that generals fail because they insist on fighting the last war. The Germans succeeded during the first two years of World War II because this is precisely what they did. The Allies forgot how they won, as they forgot why they fought.

Not all commanders were equally quick to employ the novel methods and resources, naturally, though Haig himself, myths to the contrary notwithstanding, was a great believer in tanks, to the point of using them prematurely. By 1916, generals like Maxse, Monash, Birdwell, Byng, Rawlinson, and Plumer began implementing what they'd learned. But the

first day of the Somme and the last days of Passchendaele have obliterated the memory of the 1917 battles in between, like Arras (notably Vimy
Ridge), Messines Ridge, Menin Road Ridge, Polygon Road, Cambrai –
successes by any measure, or the retaking of the Verdun forts, which also
involved innovative tactics.[23]

A second powerful myth concerns the attitude of British troops. The
demoralization and cynicism experienced by some officers and men in the
'20s has been routinely projected back into the trenches. It is worth distinguishing between disillusionment and despair. Conditions were horrible,
of course, nothing like what most men had anticipated when they enlisted,
but a great many memoirists convincingly reported bonds of loyalty to
comrades tighter than any they'd previously experienced, and a respect
for the judgement and courage of junior officers, who suffered the highest
casualty rates of any modern war. A number described in surprisingly
positive language how the intense experience of combat made post-war
existence pallid. While not minimizing the misery and terror of trench
life, they did not regard themselves as victims. Every army mutinied or
collapsed in the final two years of the war except for three: the British
and Dominion, the Belgian, and the American. The Belgians did not
participate in any of the Allied offenses before September 1918, and the
Americans only joined the war in April 1917. Some credit must be given
to British morale.

Officers and men knew why they were there. The war was not fought
for the idealistic reasons proclaimed by Woodrow Wilson and the American
press, but to liberate Belgian and French territory seized by the German
Army, and to prevent further losses. The French mutineers in 1917 made
clear they had no intention of abandoning their positions; they were protesting suicidal offenses and the deplorable conditions in the trenches. For their
part, British troops may not have known the details of Germany's pre-war
naval program or the intensity of the invective against England both before
and after the war's outbreak, but they knew their nation was menaced by
Germany, and they did not forget what had happened during the invasion of
Belgium. Perhaps some German infantrymen, like Paul Baumer, the narrator of *All Quiet on the Western Front*, may have puzzled over how they were
defending the Fatherland from the Cossack hordes by standing in a trench
behind the Aisne. But for those facing them, it would be a mistake to assume

that, notwithstanding an ungrudging respect for the courage and resource-fulness of the enemy, they had no clue as to why they were there.[24]

4. Students who know nothing else about the war will assure you that the Versailles Treaty was "vindictive," a draconian victor's peace that hypo-critically betrayed the high ideals the Allies professed to be fighting for. It made a rematch inevitable; it was a gift to Hitler. Nemesis follows hubris, always a popular scenario. The Treaty (or, rather, the way it was enforced) was indeed unfair – to the Belgians and French. They were never ade-quately compensated for the damages inflicted by the German Army, in a war Germany began, nor were they offered effective protection against the third German strike westward, which came two decades years later, just as perceptive observers had predicted in 1919.[25]

According to the most comprehensive survey of the damages inflicted by Germany on western Europe (conducted by the U.S. Army Corps of Engineers), Germany ought to have been liable for 160 milliard gold marks to Belgium and France alone. ("Milliard" means, in the U.S., "billion," but the latter term has a different meaning in the U.K. Totals will be given in dollars as well: 160 milliard gold marks equals approximately $40 bil-lion or 8 milliard pounds, the exchange rate being roughly 4 marks to the dollar and 5 dollars to the pound.) This figure exceeded other estimates of damages, which varied widely.[26] The total for Belgium, as determined by the government, was approximately 9 milliard gold marks ($2.22 bil-lion), plus 2.15 milliard ($537.5 million) in indemnities German authori-ties had charged towns and villages.[27] Estimates for damages to the occu-pied French departments ranged upward from 64 milliard gold marks ($16 billion).[28] The destruction in both countries was not an unintended consequence of the fighting. It was the result of a deliberate policy of the Kaiser's government. As with the evacuation to the Hindenburg Line in northern France in 1917, even before the Army began to withdraw from Belgium and France, property was systematically destroyed. Factories were stripped and dynamited, orchards uprooted and, in France, where the destruction was more methodical, mines flooded. The total owed by the Central Powers was eventually set at 132 milliard gold marks ($33 billion), 28 milliard ($7 billion) less than the Army Corps of Engineers' estimate for Western Europe alone. The figure represented a compromise, proposed by Belgium, between higher French and lower British figures.[29]

Of the 132 milliard gold marks owed by all the defeated Powers, however, the Germans were in reality only expected to pay 50 milliard ($12.5
billion). The remaining 82 milliard ($20.5 billion) was consigned to "C"
bonds, the issuing of which was contingent on successful repayment of
series "A" and "B." The subterfuge was adopted in part to deceive voters in
the Allied countries. The debt was so structured in order to enable the Allies
to forgive 62% of what the Germans were assessed, when this was politically possible. (Article 231 of the Treaty, the focus of so much outrage, was
similarly intended to placate public opinion. Germany's responsibility for
making good the damages it had inflicted was stipulated, but not the right
of the Allies to full restitution. As the "act of aggression" against Belgium
mentioned in the so-called "war guilt clause" had been openly acknowledged by the German Chancellor on August 4, 1914 – it was a "wrong"
that "we will try to make good" – the phrase seemed unexceptionable. The
following article, 232, expressly acknowledged that Germany's resources
did not permit it to fully recompense its victims.) Given the way the debt
was funded, the Germans had a strong additional disincentive, if one was
needed, to repay the first two series in full and on time.[30]

In the end, Germany actually paid only about 21.5 milliard gold marks
($5.375 billion), a little more than the down payment assessed in 1919
on the total reparations bill, and representing about 28% of the damages
inflicted on Belgian and France (13%, according to the U.S. estimate). (The
Reparations Commission's figure for total payments was 22.891 milliard
gold marks.) The tenacity with which Germany evaded its obligations
remains impressive.[31] After paying the equivalent of 1.5 millard gold marks
in 1921 ($375 million), of the 2 milliard required, apart from a sum equal to
26% of the value of its exports, which was not paid, Germany requested a
moratorium and suspended payments. When it reneged on its agreements
to deliver timber and coal in 1923, the Ruhr invasion and hyperinflation followed. Payments resumed under the Dawes Plan in April 1924 at a significantly lower rate.[32] The Young Plan in 1929 reduced the total owed to 37
milliard gold marks ($9.25 billion). With the onset of the Great Depression,
a one-year moratorium on reparations and debts was declared. All additional reparation payments, though not Allied debts, were then effectively
canceled by the Lausanne Convention of 1932. By 1935, Germany had
defaulted on its Dawes and Young bonds.[33] In short, assessed 132 milliard

gold marks ($33 billion), Germany was only expected to pay 50 milliard ($12.5 billion), of which it actually paid 21.5 milliard ($5.375 billion). Of this total, Belgium received not much more than 2 milliard ($500 million), about 18% of its damages and fines.[34]

To make its payments of 21.5 milliard marks, Germany borrowed around 23.5 milliard, mostly from the U.S., and received an additional 5 milliard in purchases of discounted mark notes by sanguine foreign investors. Including other investments, the country received about 30 milliard of foreign capital by 1931.[35] German taxpayers were thus not burdened with the direct cost of reparations (though they certainly suffered from the machinations of the government to evade its internal debts and to subsidize passive resistance to the Belgian and French occupation of the Ruhr).[36] "The flow of capital from the United States and certain European countries to Weimar Germany in the 1920s gave rise to one of the greatest proportional transfers of real wealth in modern history," Stephen Schuker has written. "Had the sorely tried Berlin government drawn up a master plan in 1919 to make the victorious powers subsidize consumption and leisure time in the Reich over the next thirteen years, it could scarcely have hoped for more dazzling success..."[37]

Meanwhile, the German national economy was humming along. Even with territorial losses, by 1927 net national product exceeded its highest pre-war level in constant prices. The final three years of the decade, it averaged 81.3 milliard marks.[38] Visitors were impressed by the signs of affluence in the major cities. When Germany began rearming in earnest after 1933, the Nazi government averaged over 13.5 milliard gold marks per year in military expenditure, nearly seven times the 2 milliard gold marks Keynes had regarded as the maximum Germany could be expected to pay toward reparations, and more than double the approximately 6 milliard per annum Germany would theoretically have been required to pay by the Commission. Payments would have been 5.37% of Gross Domestic Product in 1921 and would have averaged 7.21% of GDP for the years 1925–29, a little more than half the percentage of the net national product devoted to rearming the following decade.[39]

‹‹‒·‒››

The reparations issue is enormously complex and justice cannot be done to it in a few pages, let alone a few paragraphs. It is futile to attempt to determine exactly what Germany could have paid. The political will to require the costs that Germans would have to have borne was never there. But the following conclusions are beyond dispute: the "war guilt clause" was a statement of fact acknowledged by the German government, the Weimar Republic paid only a small fraction of the amount assessed, about 16%, and it did so by accepting loans and credits, largely from America, that it never repaid. And Belgium, in the end, received compensation for no more than a quarter of the damages inflicted by Germany. The victims of German aggression were victimized again, while the aggressor was able to fund lavishly its preparations for the next war.

<--->

The Versailles Treaty cannot be judged without considering at least briefly the treaties a victorious Germany concluded with France in 1871, Romania and Russia in 1918, and Poland in 1939.

France, in addition to losing Alsace and most of Lorraine, with their iron deposits, coal mines, foundries, and mills, was charged an indemnity of 5 billion gold francs. German territory had not been invaded; no damages were sustained. The indemnity was intended so that the new Empire would profit from the war; the sum was nearly double the Prussian war costs. France, in addition, would be deterred from rearming for ten to fifteen years. (In fact, the indemnity was paid off in two years by the Third Republic, without protests and evasions.)[40]

The Treaty of Bucharest required Romania to surrender southern Dobruja to Bulgaria, the Carpathian mountain passes to Austria-Hungary, and to lease its oil wells to Germany for ninety years on favorable terms. By the Treaty of Brest Litovsk, signed in March 1918, Russia was stripped of a quarter of its territory in Europe. The new quasi-independent nations of Eastern Europe, Poland, Ukraine, Bylerus, and the Baltic states, were to become political and economic satellites of Germany, with German-appointed rulers. In addition to losing 90% of its coal mines, 50% of its industry, and 30% of its population, the new Soviet state was compelled (by a supplementary treaty) to pay six milliard gold marks in reparations, a figure bearing no relation to the losses suffered in East Prussia in August 1914.[41]

As for what would have been assessed France and Britain had Germany been the victor in 1918, German officers stated repeatedly that the Kaiserreich, following its inevitable triumph, expected to be fully reimbursed by the Allies for its war costs. Bethmann Hollweg's September program outlined the bare minimum in territorial changes that Germany would have imposed on its vanquished enemies. These included the cession to Germany by Belgium of Liège and Verviers, a part of the province of Luxembourg, and, possibly, a corridor extending from Liège to Antwerp. If Belgium were permitted to continue to exist as an independent nation, it "must be reduced to a vassal state, must allow us to occupy any militarily important posts, must place her coast at our disposal in military respects, and must become economically a German province." The Grand Duchy of Luxembourg would become a German federal state. In France, Germany would be ceded a coastal strip from Dunkirk to Boulogne, Belfort, the western slopes of the Vosges, and the ore-fields of Briey. A war indemnity would be levied sufficiently high to prevent France from re-arming for fifteen to twenty years. The terms of the treaty would make France entirely dependent economically on Germany. The Netherlands "must be left independent in externals, but be made internally dependent on us." A "central European economic association" (to include Belgium, France, the Netherlands, Denmark, Austria-Hungary, Poland, and possibly Italy, Sweden and Norway) would "stabilize Germany's economic dominance over Mitteleuropa."[42]

By contrast, the territorial losses imposed on Germany, though not negligible, were modest. Blood and iron had welded together thirty-eight of the thirty-nine independent principalities and free cities of the German Confederation between 1862 and 1871, but Germany, though it lost its colonies, was not dismembered in 1919. No autonomous state was created in the Rhineland. Alsace and Lorraine were restored to France. Eupen and Malmédy were transferred to Belgium, about 400 square miles and 64,000 people. Denmark, after a plebiscite, was awarded northern Schleswig, with fewer than a quarter million inhabitants. Danzig was lost to the League of Nations, the 260 square mile "corridor" to Poland, and Memel to Lithuania. But plebiscites enabled Germany to retain southern Schleswig, Allenstein, Marienwerder, part of Upper Silesia, and, eventually, the Saar. The three million former subjects of the Kaiser who became citizens of Poland were overwhelmingly Polish. The German speakers remaining outside the new boundaries were primarily some twelve million Austrians and Bohemians who had previously been Hapsburg subjects. Concerns about the security of Germany's neighbors trumped a commitment to national self-determination. And it seemed unfair as well as imprudent to permit Germany to emerge from the war with more territory and a larger population than in 1914.[43]

Twenty years after Versailles, the Germans again had an opportunity to dictate a peace treaty. No independent rump Poland was permitted. Germany annexed almost 92,000 square miles, with a population of 10.1 million, 8.9 million of whom were Poles. Over one and a half million of these residents were immediately driven into exile. The unincorporated "General Government," with 16 million inhabitants, was controlled directly by Berlin. There were executions of political and cultural elites, mass killings of civilians, confiscation of food, levies of forced labor, etc., followed by the internment in ghettos and then the massacre of the country's Jews.[44]

In the end, the problem with the Versailles Treaty was not its "draconian" terms, but, rather, the fact that it was so feebly enforced. It was indifferently enforced because it was never believed in. Keynes's skewed views were shared not only by a number of other young diplomats, but by some senior British officials as well. Whatever his motives,[45] the groundswell created by Keynes's critique was irresistible. It was considered both humane and sophisticated to denigrate the Treaty, a fatally attractive combination.[46]

⋙⋘

Appeasement commenced before the loss of nerve in the 1920s.[47] The failure to enforce Articles 227–230 and to bring to justice those guilty of crimes against Belgian civilians was anticipated by the failure to defeat Germany, or, rather, to impress on the German people that the Kaiser's armies had been defeated. In 1918, as in 1944, a massive German offensive late in the war surprised the Allies; they fell back with heavy losses. But when it had been repelled and the German Army, after retreating for three months, was on the point of collapse, there was an armistice, not an unconditional surrender – despite the strenuous objections of the American commander.[48] No Allied or American soldier marched through Berlin.

The returning German troops were greeted by President Ebert as heroes: "I salute you, who return unvanquished from the field of battle."[49] And so was born the compelling *Dolchstoss* myth – the stab in the back, the identical charge made against Britain in 1914.

Because Germany was not defeated, the authors of the massacres in Belgium and the beliefs that inspired them were not discredited. The derisory sentences handed down by German courts in the 1920s – to enemies of the Republic as well as to war criminals – followed. The route from Leipzig to Dresden is not quite so direct as it is on a map of Saxony, but the judgments at the first led inexorably, if circuitously, to the tragedy at the second. This time the civilian victims were German.

Afterword

1. INTRODUCTION

Even in a book of over 800 pages, as was the first edition, scores of pages and hundreds of draft pages get shredded. Readers no doubt have reason to be grateful for most of the cuts. However, as I was reading the second set of galleys, I had a spasm of editor's remorse at having cut discussions of two related propositions.

The first, amply illustrated throughout Chapters 2 to 12, was the role of anti-Catholicism in the persecution of Belgian civilians. It was not merely "materialism" that was responsible for the desecration of churches in Aarschot, Leuven, and elsewhere in Belgium. Clearly, the animus toward the Church that had precipitated, and was exacerbated by, the *Kulturkampf* survived the end of that campaign, and resurfaced in the heat of the invasion. An entire chapter had been excised that included a discussion of anti-Catholicism. It was entitled *"Die Schwartze Teufelen,"* literally the black devils, a derogatory reference to priests. The chapter surveyed the *Kulturkampf,* but it also looked back to the near-genocide of the Hereros in Southwest Africa in 1904, hence the title, and related it, as well as the suppression of the Boxer Rebellion in 1900 and the Zabern Affair of 1913, to the August war crimes. In taking up other precursors of German behavior in 1914, the chapter also obviously had more to say about "militarism" than was included in the final section of Chapter 13 (which had itself been reduced to less than half its original length).

If the first edition failed to include the backward glances I had drafted, it also neglected to include observations I had written on subsequent events, for I had originally discussed, albeit briefly, the way in which August 1914 was in fact a rehearsal—and the ways in which it was not. I was less troubled by this omission. I figured readers familiar with the Holocaust, for example, might recall, when reading about the activities of the German "Red Cross" in Tamines, the fact that the Zyklon B canisters were transported to the gas chambers at Auschwitz in white trucks emblazoned with a red cross. (The "infirmary" at Treblinka also operated beneath an enormous Red Cross flag. Here the old and sick were "cured with one pill"–shot in the back of the head–so as not to impede the flow of arrivals into the gas chamber.) Similarly, descriptions of the forced marches around Brabant during the week of August 23rd would, I hoped, remind readers of the far more lethal but equally pointless treks of concentration camp survivors after the closing of the camps during the late fall and winter of 1944–45. And I trusted that the spectacle of cattle-cars rumbling eastward packed with innocent *Staatsfeinden* would also resonate, and that parallels between massacres in Belgian towns and villages in August 1914 and in Polish towns and villages after September 1939 would not be lost on readers. Still, in retrospect, I regretted omitting a discussion of the ways in which the events of August anticipated the subsequent behavior of Germans in uniform. But as I observe later, the events of August 1914 were far less a rehearsal for the Holocaust than for the treatment of Polish civilians in the early fall of 1939, and of other Eastern Europeans subsequently. Under *Wehrmacht* rule, which lasted only until October 25, 1939, 531 Polish towns and villages were intentionally burned and 16,376 civilians killed in 714 mass executions.[1] The Aarschots, Tamines, and Dinants of western Poland are remembered today only by the families of the victims.

In what follows, I would like to try to redress both omissions together— to look forward to the persecution of civilians in Eastern Europe after September 1st 1939 (and German Jews after 1933) and back to the persecution of German Catholics that began in 1871, and of Chinese and Southwest Africans at the beginning of the 20th century—persecutions, obviously, of very different magnitudes. Specifically, I would like to consider how the August massacres were prefigured by, and, in turn, anticipated, other campaigns by focusing on the roles of fear and greed as incitements to murder.

Fear and greed are obviously not incompatible. Historians are always suspicious of monocausal explanations and any day trader knows that both can be equally importunate at one and the same time.

Students watching nearly any documentary on Nazi Germany are treated to scenes from *Das Ewige Jude* (The Eternal Jew), Fritz Hippler's

1940 film, that juxtapose images of rats scampering out of a sewer with Polish Jews. The Jews were parasites threatening the health of the Aryan nation, a favorite motif in Nazi propaganda, but never so vividly illustrated. The leading Nazis believed their propaganda, and may have convinced millions of others, that "International Jewry," unlike benign parasites, was actually intent on exterminating the German people and it was essential that Jews be eliminated first if Germans were to survive the war. The Second World War was a war against the Jews: *Auschwitzdienst ist Frontdienst*, SS guards were told, and Hitler and his subordinates made no secret of the German objective.[2]

No less memorable, and no less inevitable in the documentaries, are scenes shot by Russian cameramen shortly after the liberation of Majdanek, showing piles of shoes, children's clothing, and human hair that the Germans had been unable to ship west before abandoning the camp. In one arresting bit of footage, a soldier holds up a little girl's vest. Before the Jews were gassed, they were robbed. The robbery began with the businesses, bank accounts, and investments they were obliged to liquidate, the buildings, property, and valuables they were forced to sell, or that were simply seized, the cash, jewelry, and food taken from the arriving convoys, and, finally, the gold extracted from the teeth of the corpses before they were incinerated, and that was shipped to Germany along with the hair and clothing. There was also the value of the labor extracted from the ghetto workshops and from the factories and mines ringing Auschwitz and other camps.[3]

-<-->-

2. FEAR

It should be clear that I am not now reverting to Horne and Kramer's thesis, which I criticized in Chapter 13. I suggested there that, while there was much paranoia about franc-tireurs, the killing of Belgian civilians was not a recapitulation of the Great Fear in France of 1789. The operations in the summer of 1914 were supported by a set of attitudes—an impatience, arrogance, and ruthlessness—that grew out of the kind of nationalism that had emerged in Germany by the end of the 1890s, complemented by "militarism" and intensified by "materialism." Militarism meant a belief in the inevitability and desirability of war and the conviction that it must be waged with lightning speed and annihilating brutality. It also meant contempt for civilians and a hypersensitivity to slights against one's honor on the part of officers and, on the part of soldiers, a willingness to do what other European nationals would have found unconscionable, merely because it was ordered. For what has to be explained, in the end, is not only the shooting of civilians and the burning of their homes by enraged troops immediately after gunshots were heard, but executions carried out many hours, and sometimes days, after the incidents they were supposedly avenging.

"Materialism," meanwhile, ratcheted up the commitment to the German nation and *Volk*. There is a large and impressive body of literature describing how nationalism became a surrogate religion in the French Revolution and then in the 19th century independence movements, before reaching a hideous apotheosis in Germany in the 1930s.[4] In August 1914, these attachments overrode commitments to European legal norms (not to mention conventions of chivalry and charity) that would have moderated the treatment of Belgian civilians, even in wartime.

What I neglected to unpack from German nationalism, however, though it was made obvious in the narrative, was a lingering anti-Catholicism that resurfaced during the invasion, and became a pretext to pillage and murder.[5]

Bismarck called off the *Kulturkampf* in 1879, recognizing that socialism posed a more dire threat to German unity than its trans-national rival, Catholicism, and that the successive May Laws and other legislation had only resulted in a larger and stronger Center Party and in the revival of Polish nationalism.[6] Persecution had been counterproductive, as is frequently the case in Western Europe. Indeed, the Center Party, Bismarck eventually decided, might make a better ally than the Liberals against socialism. However, the hatred of the Church that was revealed, and much exacerbated, by the *Kulturkampf* persisted.[7] It is impossible to disentangle animosity toward Belgians from anti-Catholicism, though this was something leading German Catholics wished to do (in absolving the clergy but not denying that franc-tireurs had committed atrocities or questioning the army's reprisals). Their Catholicism had very much to do with the wickedness of the civilian population, in German eyes, particularly with their deceitfulness and lack of self-control. There had been, of course, no hostility to Belgians qua Belgians on the part of any segment of German society prior to August 1914.[8] But clearly a substratum of anti-Catholicism persisted after the 1870s and flared up during the invasion.

It is not far-fetched to compare it to anti-Semitism.

"*Ohne Juda, ohne Rom/Wird erbaut Germanias Dom,*" chanted Pan-Germanic students in Vienna during the Los von Rom movement in the first decade of the 20th century. (Without Judea, without Rome, Germania's cathedral will be built.)[9]

Jews and Catholics threatened the German *Volk*—with whom the Austrian Pan-Germans wished to unite politically—in different ways, but by similar means.

Jews, in the formula that united antisemites in all European countries after 1873, were dangerous because they were the bearers of capitalism—an economic process that uprooted and despoiled peasants, marginalized small shopkeepers, and concentrated great wealth in a few corrupt hands. But they also posed a threat as agitators for radical political change, seeking to usurp the positions of traditional elites (including the bankers, merchants, and industrialists responsible for the social and economic dislocations the antisemites deplored) in the name of the workers, an identification that naturally intensified after 1917.

Catholicism, however, was menacing precisely because it was anti-modern. It undermined the loyalty of believers to the German state, guardian of the German people, on the one hand, while, on the other, it subverted the critical intellect that was essential for freedom and autonomy, themselves essential for social and economic progress.

But what united Jews and Catholics was their modus operandi. The destructive work of both was carried out surreptitiously, behind the scenes—invisible to innocent Michael—much like the activities of the franc-tireurs.

"Here we are so helpless," sighed Henry Lorensten, the officer supervising the burning of homes along Stationsstraat in Leuven. "Fighting is easy in comparison." The franc-tireurs were infuriating precisely because they did not give battle in the open, but cut down German soldiers and officers from the shadows. Their tenacity was diabolical. Even after the residents of Les Rivages had been expelled from their homes and the houses searched three times, the elusive franc-tireurs continued firing from the residences. The commune, according to the German commander, was a "witches' cauldron."

"International Jewry" and the Jesuits, the shock corps of the Church, also operated clandestinely. In the satiric "Battle Song of the Jesuits," published in *Kladderdatsch* in June 1872, members of the order sang "We are elusive like the air/Quietly floating through the night,/Like vapors rising from a bog/Or shrub or poisoned goblet./When you think you've grabbed us,/We have already disappeared,/Slipping away into a hidden lair;/You can sooner fumigate pests,/Than us, the Jesuits."[10] The solution for pestilence was *Säuberung*—cleansing—a word that recurs in German testimony about actions against franc-tireurs—for instance, the assault on the families sheltering under the railroad bridge in Neffe—as against Jesuits and Jews. The cleansing had been more thorough, if less lethal, in 1872, when foreign-born Jesuits were expelled from Germany, German Jesuits forcibly dispersed, and the order banned. In the cleansing after 1941, the Jews, of course, were literally fumigated.[11]

It did not take long for some Catholic intellectuals in Germany to grow suspicious of the reports of franc-tireur atrocities. The charges of Catholic treachery and deceit that circulated widely in the German press in August were too reminiscent of accusations made during the *Kulturkampf*, even before chilling information began surfacing about the destruction of churches, amid cries of *Religionskrieg*, and the execution of priests. Even military authorities were concerned about the level of popular anti-Catholicism.

Similarly, by June of 1872, a year after the war against the Church had commenced,[12] two leading Liberals began to have second thoughts. What was disturbing for Edward Lasker and Ludwig Bamberger was that the anti-Jesuit legislation targeted not criminal activity by individuals, but a specific group. "What if there had been a law against the *Nationalverein*?" fretted one of the party's Nestors, the Saxon historian Karl Biedermann, in a letter to Lasker.[13] But Lasker and Bamberger were Jews, and it was not only a hypothetical attack on the Party that troubled them. "We are acting in self-defense and cannot restrain ourselves with liberal phrases about citizens' rights," Bismarck declared angrily, when questioned about the Jesuit Law.[14] Could not the same rationale be used to target Jews?

Lasker's fears were echoed, in turn, by the leadership of the Center Party two decades after the *Kulturkampf*. "We...have not forgotten what happened to us," wrote its chairman, Ernst Lieber, at the height of the antisemitic campaigns of the '90s. "Even if more elevated considerations and more fundamental motives did not restrain us, we cannot offer to forge the weapon to be used against the Jews today..."[15]

In the end, though, it was more than a common modus operandi that united Jews and Catholics, in the minds of German nationalists. Though antithetical in other respects, they were both, at bottom, "materialists," like the hypocritical English. The God all three worshiped was the Law, not the Spirit. It sufficed to follow the rules laid down in the Talmud or in Catholic liturgy and canon law, or in the British Constitution and the laws of supply and demand. And in the end, what Jews, the Catholic Church, and the English sought was wealth and power, not redemption. And all three menaced Germany; they profited from her weakness and disunion, which they cunningly exacerbated. The themes echoed and re-echoed in the work of nationalist writers in the fifty years before 1914.[16]

Notable among the torrent of anti-Catholic literature appearing in 1872 was a satirical booklet by the popular cartoonist (and inventor of the comic strip) Wilhelm Busch, *Pater Filuzius*, which chronicled the adventures of a wily Jesuit as he tried to convince an elderly spinster to leave her fortune to him. Unlike priests, who were generally depicted in anti-Catholic publications as lazy gluttons, short and fat, Jesuits, in Busch's cartoons and elsewhere, were tall and thin, and much more threatening.[17] Busch's cartoons notoriously included vivid antisemitic caricatures: "The Hebrew, sly and craven,/Round of shoulder, nose, and knee,/Slinks to the Exchange unshaven/And intent on usury."[18] *Die fromme Helene*, from which the verse comes, is also a repository of anti-Catholic stereotypes. The message: when dealing with Jew or Jesuit, hang onto your wallet.

On the eve of the *Kulturkampf*, Richard Wagner decided to republish under his own name his anonymous pamphlet of nineteen years earlier, "On Jewry in Music (1850)." Emancipation had been a mistake. "For all our writing and speaking of Jewish emancipation, we always felt instinctively repelled by any real, active contact with Jews."[19] There were a couple of reasons for this repugnance, apart from their foreign looks and manners: the language and culture of the Jews was derivative; it was not rooted in a *Volkgeist*, and so they could not make truly original contributions to European culture. Worse, without this spiritual sheet anchor, Jews sought only money and power, and their power menaced Germany: "I hold the Jewish race to be the born enemy of pure humanity and everything noble in it. It is certain it is running us Germans to the ground."[20] Wagner is credited with coining the word "Judaization" (*Verjüdung*).[21]

Wagner abhorred Catholicism as well. It was a "huge perversion" perpetrated by "the Semite-Latin Church."[22] Munich was a "vile place" to which he refused to return, he explained to King Ludwig, because its people were misled by Jews and Jesuits.[23] But it was still preferable to Vienna: it was because of the Jesuit influence in Austria that Wagner favored an alliance between Bavaria and Prussia, despite his loathing of Bismarck.[24]

It was left to Wagner's son-in-law and fervent admirer, Houston Stewart Chamberlain, to flesh out, amply, Wagner's prejudices. Chamberlain famously inaugurated the racial antisemitism that was taken over virtually in tact by Alfred Rosenberg, the Nazi Party ideologue. (The extent to which "racial" antisemitism differed from the antisemitism that went back to antiquity should not be overstated, though the latter usually held that individual Jews could be redeemed.) Precisely because of their own racial consciousness, according to Chamberlain, Jews posed a threat to Europe. They were intent on destroying idealistic Indo-European culture and enslaving the continent's inhabitants. Catholicism was anathema precisely because it retained Semitic influences. Like the Jews, the Papacy was bent on dominating the world; the history of Germany was largely the struggle to free itself from the clutches of Rome.[25] Thus, in popular culture and high culture alike—from the newsstands of Berlin to the drawing room of Wahnfried in Bayreuth—Jews and Catholics, Jesuits in particular, were reviled, sometimes in tandem.

From the 1760s Jesuits were repeatedly expelled from most European countries and it would be easy to push too far the analogies between the persecution of Jesuits, Jews, and franc-tireurs—and, for that matter, Freemasons, in which the Jesuits distinguished themselves, as some certainly did in campaigns against the Jews. (The antisemitism of *Civilità Cattolica*, the Jesuit organ, was notorious after 1880; some French and Belgian Jesuits, however, demurred.)[26] But a nation founded on the triumph of a *Volk* was bound to have a more vivid and lively perception of the Other against whom it defined itself than did nations whose most celebrated founding events were declarations of rights—particularly when German culture owed so much to an individual, Luther, who harbored such animated hatreds of Catholics and Jews, combined with so exalted a notion of what was owed the State.[27] One cannot in the end avoid viewing

what happened to *Staatsfeinde* in 1914 in the light of what had happened to
them in the 1870s and what would happen to them in the 1940s.

◄-◄-►-►

3. GREED

For at least a century and a quarter before the outbreak of the Great
War, nationalist writers repeatedly claimed that the German people, thanks
to their distinctive *Volkgeist*, were more spiritual than the materialists and
egoists across the Rhine, the Channel, and the Atlantic. They were heroes,
not shopkeepers, idealists, not utilitarians or pragmatists. Duty and honor
beckoned, not profit. This was hardly the view of most Belgians in August
1914.

Returning through Leuven to secure supplies for the refugees in
Tienen, a merchant was surprised to see the Stationsplein crammed with
merchandise to be shipped east. An American diplomat standing in the
square thought he was in a supply depot. He had earlier watched soldiers
moving slowly down Stationstraat, removing everything of value from
each home before it was burned. A Dominican friar approaching Leuven
by train watched car after car rumble eastward, laden with goods.

The looting in other towns was hardly less thorough. On August 15,
a resident of Visé recalled, "two officers inspected my house, and finding
there were things worth taking, they wrote and signed a paper directing the
house to be spared and pinned it to the door. When the valuables had been
removed, the place was burned down. I took the paper off the door and
preserved it." Marie Naus, of Leffe, also came away with a souvenir—the
top of a pepper mill, which she showed to the British solicitor interviewing her. Everything else in her house had been stolen or destroyed, she
told him. Over and over, Belgian witnesses offer similar testimony. Their
homes were thoroughly looted, and what was not carried off was smashed
or burned.

Candid German diarists and p.o.w.s repeatedly confirmed this. "This is
what happened," explained a private in the 103rd Regiment of the Saxon
XIIth Corps that destroyed Dinant. "The troops would take possession
of a town and pursue the enemy. Then, when the Reserves arrived, they
pillaged the houses, taking linen, silver, jewelry, provisions, drink, etc. I
saw all this. Nay, and more: when they pillaged, they piled the goods in

heaps. The adjutants made a selection from these, keeping the best for the colonel and the major, and others for the other officers." Booty not wanted by individual officers was sold.

Repeatedly, civilians also report that when they were expelled from their homes, they were relieved of their wallets and purses. Even after the most horrendous of the mass executions, the shooting of men, women, and children against the Bourdon wall in Les Rivages, the Germans did not fail to confiscate money from the few survivors of the massacre. Then the victims were thoroughly searched the next morning, and everything of value taken. At the northern end of Dinant, officers did considerably better: the widows of the men they'd just shot were compelled to hand over 15,000 francs at the Abbey in Leffe.

Apart from confiscating the goods and money of individuals, the Germans compelled communal and provincial governments to subsidize the invasion. Arriving in towns, officers frequently assessed steep war taxes in addition to the requisitions they ordered. It was his protest against the confiscation of all the communal funds that led to the execution of the burgomaster of Andenne. Most of his counterparts were more obliging. Brussels was required to pay 50 million francs as a "war contribution," Brabant another 450 million.[28] This was on top of the 40 million francs per month the Belgians were required to pay to subsidize the occupation. The amount was raised to 60 million in 1916.[29] Additional fines were routinely imposed as punishments. When Cardinal Mercier was cheered by crowds as he crossed Brussels in his car on the second anniversary of Belgium's Independence Day under occupation, the city was fined a million marks.[30] In another incident, when a crowd attacked two men working for the German Secret Service and the police failed to intervene promptly, Brussels was fined 5 million marks.[31] In all, the assessments totaled $537.5 million, according to the Belgian government, over $11 billion today.[32]

This was all petty thievery compared to the larceny that took place in 1917 and 1918. Germany had already established very profitable monopolies for the production and distribution of all domestic commodities, from coal to butter. In March of 1917, in order to maximize its production of war materiel and also to eliminate potential Belgian competition in the future, Germany set about systematically dismantling most Belgian factories. Machinery was transferred to the *Kaiserreich*, along with iron roofs and copper pipes. All raw materials and semi-finished products had already been seized.[33] As usual, everything not requisitioned was destroyed. In their retreat in 1918, the Germans tore up rail lines for iron, confiscated locomotives and rolling stock, and destroyed 350 railway bridges. (The Army had intended to flood the mines, as they did in France. However, Hoover intervened with Wilson, and most were spared.) As a result of the depredations, production of coke, iron, steel, lead, and zinc were at one-fifth to one-twentieth of pre-war levels in 1918, and total industrial production at about 15%. When the Treaty of Versailles was signed, three-quarters of the workforce was unemployed. Also indiscriminately seized during the retreat were livestock and poultry. Herds didn't recover 1913 levels until 1930. Belgian forests were decimated; Eupen was requested partly for its timber. Works of art in private collections were also stolen throughout the country, in addition to those destroyed at Leuven and that disappeared from the University of Liège; the country's premier collection of manuscripts and incunabula had of course gone up in smoke.[34]

-<--->-

Apart from the massacres and looting of August, the most notorious rehearsal was the drafting of forced labor that began in October 1916. Once again, it takes some effort to appreciate the outrage this practice evoked at the time. Even the Governor-General of Belgium was profoundly unhappy with the idea, and resisted the plan for several months. Thirty years later some 12 to 15 million slave laborers would be toiling away in Greater Germany. This time no German authorities would object and other, more spectacular Nazi crimes would divert attention from the drafting of workers.

From the beginning of 1916, military and industrial leaders had urged the government to ship unemployed Belgian workers back to the Reich. The additional labor would help meet production quotas in the arms factories and free up men to serve on the front at a time when the Army's needs were particularly acute. But when the War Ministry proposed sending 400,000 Belgians to German factories, General von Bissing vetoed the plan. The effect on Belgian morale would be devastating, he argued, particularly as he was about to grant autonomy both to Flanders and to Wallonia, the first step in their eventual incorporation into the *Kaiserreich*.[35] Von Bissing stepped up efforts to recruit volunteers, but only some 21,000 unemployed men signed up to work in Germany. In October pressure was renewed, and this time von Bissing, told by the Chancellor that the requisitions were essential to Germany's survival, relented.[36]

The deportation of captured Belgians in August 1914 had been an ad hoc affair. The operation in the fall of 1916 was better organized.[37] Lists of unemployed were requested, but as the communal governments refused to provide these, men were seized at random and herded into schools and empty factories. (In northern France, women had been taken from their homes at gunpoint and compelled to work in the fields in the south, but this had excited so much indignation in Allied and neutral countries that von Bissing wisely refrained from drafting women in Belgium.) Here their papers were inspected, they were interrogated briefly, and then sent either to the left, to freedom, or to the right, to work for the Germans. No soldiers were posted at the entrance of the collection centers, to deceive the workers, but troops often lined the route out to the trains, some soldiers acting "like real brutes," one witness recalled.[38] As in August 1914, the first deportees often rode in open cattle cars; later groups had boxcars and sometimes overcrowded coaches. Conditions in the prison camps were deplorable, by design. The Germans were trying to induce their captives to sign contracts. About 58,500 men were sent to Germany; 62,155 worked in labor battalions behind the front, or constructing the Hindenburg Line.[39] A press campaign was naturally launched in Germany against the "work-shy" Belgians, wallowing in luxury and self-pity, but public opinion in Allied and neutral countries was appalled. Bethmann-Hollweg, who had anticipated the outrage, prevailed on the Kaiser to halt the deportations in March, 1917.[40] In the military zone, however, comprising East and most of West Flanders, the Kaiser's order was ignored, and men continued to be seized and compelled to work behind the trenches until the German retreat.

◄◄·►►

The profits extracted from Belgium increased exponentially in the next war, both for individuals and the state. Götz Aly's controversial 2005 book *Hilters Volkstaat* (translated as *Hitler's Beneficiaries* in 2007) makes the case that the Nazis were indeed national socialists, confiscating wealth not from the country's bourgeoisie, like democratic socialists, but from the nations the regime had conquered, and dutifully redistributing it to working-class

Volkdeutsch. This explains German support for Hitler until well into the war: the masses were bought off—directly, by goods German soldiers were permitted to buy and ship home at nominal cost, but also by the low, progressive tax rates the state was able to maintain throughout the war, thanks to what it expropriated from Jews and from what it extorted from the occupied countries. Aly is certainly not the first to describe the regime's egalitarianism, but no one has emphasized it to this extent, and with such a wealth of evidence. (His inversion of the traditional, discredited materialist take on the Third Reich—that Hitler was the tool of "big capitalists"—has been popular in the *Bundesrepublik*, critics allege, because it reduces the charge against the German people from murder to robbery. They did not hate the Jews and despise non-Aryans; they merely coveted their wealth and were indifferent to their fate.) Aly's figures have been questioned by a number of economic historians, along with his downplaying of ideology.[41]

As for Belgium, though soldiers were initially ordered to treat civilians correctly in 1940, the country was exploited far more ruthlessly than under von Bissing. Occupation costs were demanded of the state, according to an official, "that it can just barely, with the greatest sacrifice, raise."[42] Additional "accommodation services" were also assessed. These were double the government's average monthly tax revenues. In all, the Germans demanded 18 billion francs per year from a government whose entire budget had been 11 billion in 1938; the income funded the construction of airfields and defenses along the Atlantic coast.[43] Belgium's gold, forty-one tons, was also confiscated by the occupiers, and used to purchase valuable resources from neutrals.[44]

As for forced labor, not only did the Third Reich enlist more than double the number of Belgian workers as its predecessor (at least 250,000; much higher in some estimates), but it seized, in addition to the exorbitant wage taxes it collected, that portion of their income that the workers sent back home. The amounts were then paid to their families out of occupation costs. Belgian tax-payers subsidized the country's forced laborers.[45]

Once the occupiers confronted an actual resistance, they proved as ruthless as their predecessors. More than 17,000 Belgians working for the resistance were killed, including 12,000 in concentration camps. The total civilian death toll was around 33,000, excluding those killed in Allied bombing raids in 1944 and the nearly 27,000 Jews murdered at Auschwitz.[46]

Finally, the second time around the Germans could not resist stealing from Leuven Bouts' *The Last Supper*. After failing to burn it in 1914, they had left it in Belgian hands. The Versailles Treaty had ordered the return of its two panels, but the entire triptych was removed to Bavaria in 1942 for "safe-keeping."[47] The other Belgian work that the Germans most coveted was the renowned Gent altarpiece *The Adoration of the Mystic Lamb* by the Van Eyck brothers, six panels of which had been in Germany until 1920. The remaining six had been hidden from the Germans in 1914. In 1940, the Belgians spirited off the entire altarpiece to the Pau caves in southern France (the Vatican had been the intended destination), but the Vichy government turned it over to the Germans two years later.[48]

-<-->-

4. REHEARSING THE REHEARSAL

The behavior of the German Army in August 1914 did not represent a radical departure in its practices. The Army's response to revolts in China and Southwest Africa (and to disturbances in Alsace) anticipated the killing and looting in Belgium. The difference was that the repression now took place in Europe, and was not preceded by a rebellion.

While the Boxer Rebellion was directed against all foreigners, Germany played a distinctive role both in precipitating the conflict and in exacting retribution at its conclusion. The Germans, in the metaphor that gained wide currency, had arrived late to the table, but with a ravenous appetite. Using as a pretext the murder of two missionaries at Juye, the Kaiser's government seized Jiaozhou (Chiao-chou) Bay in Shantung province in 1897, precipitating territorial demands from other Powers.[49] Ironically, thanks to its governor, the province itself was comparatively calm in the spring and summer of 1900, at the height of the uprising. But further north missionaries and large numbers of Chinese converts were tortured and killed, and, beginning on June 10, the European and Japanese Ministers and their staffs, along with newly arrived guard contingents, were besieged in the Legation quarter of Beijing, just south of the Forbidden City. The attitude of the government toward the Boxers had been ambivalent.[50] But after the leveling of the Taku forts and the dispatching of a multinational force to rescue the Westerners trapped in Beijing and in Tianjin, the Chinese government began openly siding with the Boxers. It was Imperial soldiers who killed the German Minister, Baron Klemens von Ketteler, when he ventured out of the compound. Although a total of about 78 foreigners were killed during the siege, Klemens was the only Minister to die, and the German government was determined to avenge his murder.[51] "When you come upon the enemy, smite him," the Kaiser exhorted troops departing from Bremerhaven in July.

> Pardon will not be given. Prisoners will not be taken… Once, a thousand years ago, the Huns under their King Attila made a name for themselves, one still potent in legend and tradition. May you in this way make the name German remembered in China for a thousand years, so that no Chinaman will ever again dare to even squint at a German.[52]

While the Emperor's troops were still en route, the siege was lifted. (There were only about 900 German soldiers in the 20,000-man force that liberated the diplomats.) The newly arrived regiments set out at once to fulfill the Kaiser's expectations. The expedition was diverted south to, in Wilhelm's words, "busy itself with the complete cleansing and subjugation of Jiaozhou and its hinterland."[53]

"The violence of the German troops," one historian concluded, "made the Chinese people detest and fear them more than any other foreign force," besting the accomplishments of the large Russian and Japanese contingents.[54] The total number of Chinese deaths cannot even be estimated, but the U.S. commander guessed that for every Boxer killed in the punitive expeditions the Germans launched, "fifteen harmless coolies…including not a few women and children, have been slain."[55]

⤜⟶⤛

The other colonizing Powers were certainly capable of brutal responses to uprisings by subject peoples (China, though callously exploited, was not itself colonized, of course), but the German campaign against the Hereros in the summer and fall of 1904 was qualitatively different from those conducted by other European governments in the 19th century.

As with the Boxer Rebellion, the comparison with events a decade later, in this case, cannot be pushed too far. Racial antipathy obviously affected the response, and there had been a real uprising. About 158 German settlers and soldiers were killed during the revolt, most of whom lived on the 267 isolated farms in the north of the colony. Though the Herero warriors largely refrained from murdering women and children, and missionaries as well, they did mutilate corpses, leaving the Germans to assume the victims had been tortured.[56] What distinguished the German campaign was the infamous *Vernichtungsbefel*, the extermination order, issued by the commanding general, Lothar von Trotha on 2 October 1904. German Southwest Africa was to be made Herero-frei: "The Herero people must leave the land... Within the German border every male Herero, armed or unarmed, with or without cattle, will be shot to death. I will no longer receive women and children, but will drive them back to their people or have them shot at."[57]

There are some misconceptions about the proclamation. General von Trotha was probably acting on his own initiative. He had not received a specific order to clear out the colony, only to defeat the uprising "by all means," a standard instruction.[58] In the Reichstag, August Bebel speculated that a secret order had indeed been given, similar to the notorious injunction from the Kaiser to troops departing for China, but "which one did not want to express publicly a second time."[59] Also, the order was issued long after the policy had already been adopted. Instead of a inflicting a decisive military defeat, followed by negotiations, as the governor, Colonel Theodor Leutwein, an old African hand, had intended, once the Hereros had retreated en masse to Waterberg, a high plateau due north of the capital, Windhuk, von Trotha, who was summonsed to the colony in June, 1904, planned to surround and annihilate the tribes.[60] In fact, the warriors broke out to the southeast, toward the Omaheke Desert. Contrary to many summaries of the campaign, it does not seem to have been the original intention of the Germans to permit this escape, though it proved convenient. German forces pursued the retreating tribes further into the desert, preventing access to wells, shooting those who approached, or poisoning the water. The Hereros had numbered between approximately 60 and 80,000 before the uprising; in 1911 there were a little over 15,000. More natives died in internment camps (over 7,500) than were killed in battle, but the great majority starved to death or were hunted down as they attempted to surrender or approached water holes.[61]

What distinguishes the episode, and what is relevant for events a decade later, is the emphasis on "punishment" and the latitude with which that imperative was interpreted.[62]

-<-->-

At one point during the Zabern Affair—a comic opera with a sobering denouement—which occurred between October, 1913, and January 1914, Karl von Wedel, Governor of Alsace-Lorraine, protested to Chancellor Bethmann Hollweg that civilians in Zabern "have a right not to be treated like Hereros."[63] Within six months of his statement, Wedel, a Major General and a Conservative, was obliged to resign, like Leutwein. The lesson was the same: whatever your rank, however extensive your experience with the "natives," you were subordinate to the local army commander, and, for the army, necessity knew no law. Regulations and customs could be freely abrogated to achieve military objectives. In the case of Zabern, this was the right of officers not to be laughed at.

No one died in Zabern. However, residents who happened to be on the streets on November 26, 1913, were charged by soldiers with fixed bayonets and twenty-six were imprisoned overnight in a damp coal cellar, without any sanitary facilities. Among those arrested was a judge.[64] The detention was illegal; martial law had not been declared. (The commander of the local garrison, Colonel Adolf von Reuter, had been unhappy when residents arrested two days earlier had been released as soon as they were turned over to the police.) In a second incident, in a village outside town, a shoemaker with a club foot, pinioned by soldiers, was struck with a sword by an officer, and badly injured. He was accused of lèse-majesté, having laughed at the officer, though he protested his innocence.

The perpetrator of the second incident and instigator of the first was a boyish-looking twenty-year-old second lieutenant, Günther Freiherr von Forstner. In a lecture to recruits on October 28, he had told the men that "if you knife a *Wackes* [a disparaging term for Alsatians] you won't get two months... You'll get ten marks." The jeering and the informal demonstrations that took place in town when von Forstner and other officers appeared convinced Colonel von Reuter that an uprising was imminent. (Most military men shared the views of the Kaiser: Alsatians were treacherous, disloyal, unruly—the *Reichsland* "could almost be Bohemia or Bosnia"—and regretted the liberal constitution of two years earlier, which the All Highest threatened to "smash to bits.") As public pressure mounted, von Forstner received a slap on the wrist—he was confined to his rooms for six days—but ten soldiers were arrested, charged with leaking the lieutenant's remarks to the press, and the offices of the *Zaberner Anzeiger* were ransacked. When von Forstner made further inflammatory remarks to recruits (telling them they could "shit on the French flag" for all he cared), Wedel asked the commander of the XVth Corps, General Berthold von Deimling, who had served alongside von Trotha in Southwest Africa, to post the lieutenant elsewhere. He told the Kaiser, "In my view, the prestige of the army will not suffer but will gain if an injustice which really happened is not covered up but is punished."[65] This was hardly the opinion of most military men, including Deimling, who instead urged Reuter to be more *schneidig*. The bayonet charges and arrests of civilians followed.

On the very day Wedel compared the Zaberners to the Hereros and Forstner struck the shoemaker, December 2nd, the Crown Prince sent telegrams of support to both Deimling and Reuter: "Bravo!" "Beat'em up!" Immediately, there were political repercussions. Questions were asked in the Reichstag. When Bethmann Hollweg, who privately sympathized with Wedel, made a characteristically evasive response, members of the Center and the National Liberal parties, as well as the Socialists and Progressives, were visibly angered. (Conceding that "the limits of the law were not observed," he argued that nonetheless "the Kaiser's uniform must be respected in all circumstances.") The War Minister, von Falkenhayn, poured oil on the flames. In a defiant speech, he staunchly defended the army and displayed his contempt for what he regarded as a parliamentary "mob." An uproar followed, and the government suffered a crushing no-confidence vote, 293 to 54, with 4 abstentions. In any other Western European country, the government would have fallen. But under the constitution of the Second Reich, the Chancellor served at the pleasure of the Kaiser, and Wilhelm was pleased with Bethmann Hollweg's performance.

There were court-martials in January, but Reuter and the lieutenant ordering the bayonet charge were acquitted under an 1820 Cabinet order permitting a commander to act "if civilian authorities waited too long." Reuter was promptly awarded the Order of the Red Eagle by the Kaiser. Forstner, who had been found guilty of illegal use of his weapon, had his sentence overturned a few days later, on the grounds that the shoemaker had a penknife in his pocket, and the lieutenant had acted in self-defense. And the "Zabern Coalition" collapsed. When the SPD tried to withhold funds from the government ten days after the no confidence vote, all non-Socialists deserted the cause.

There were angry editorials and sarcastic poems, but the message was unmistakable. Also prefiguring events in Belgium was the willingness of the army command to dissemble. By "*Wackes*," it was claimed, von Forstner was referring only to unruly characters, not to all Alsatians, and by "French flag," the lieutenant meant the flag of the Foreign Legion.[66]

◄◄—►—►►

5. STROLLING DOWN THE SONDERWEG

Things were different in Germany, British intellectuals were convinced by the end of the war, as many fewer had been before 1914. From the 4th of August, German operations scandalized public opinion in London. Most of the handful of British writers who were not outraged by the invasion of neutral Belgium were appalled by the treatment of Belgian civilians. And the burning of the Leuven library and the shelling of Rheims cathedral shocked educated Europeans to a degree difficult to appreciate a hundred years later. Twenty-first century readers are apt to discount British indignation at submarine attacks. But this practice seemed to contemporaries a flagrant violation of the rules of naval warfare that had been honored from time immemorial. The German government itself recognized that the sinking of unarmed ships with civilian passengers—without warning, without permitting lifeboats to be launched—was barbaric (or at least was anathema to the Americans), and ceased doing so for a year and a half, until exigencies overcame scruples.[67] But even readers jaded by subsequent atrocities are surprised to learn that the u-boats were permitted to sink hospital ships within certain zones after 1917, though they were not supposed to turn their guns on the survivors in lifeboats, as one crew did.[68] Poison gas had been banned by the Hague Conventions of 1899 and 1907. Again, one has to make an effort to appreciate the horror this practice evoked. Flamethrowers were perceived as yet another nefarious German innovation. What is perhaps most difficult to grasp for people born in the second half of the 20th century is the shock and dismay at aerial bombardment, another practice pioneered by the Germans. When Antwerp was bombed by an airship on August 25th, 1914, with twelve dead and more than forty injured, the first such attack in history, the outrage in Allied and neutral countries was nearly as great as that occasioned by the bombing of Rotterdam twenty-five-and-a-half years later. The shelling of Scarborough, Whitby, and Hartlepool in December 1914, with forty civilians killed, was another first.[69] What kind of mind-set could countenance these violations of international law and the conventions of European warfare, British and American intellectuals asked. The search for a special German path to modernity did not begin in the 1940s.

⤛⤜

Regarding the threats posed by Jesuit and Jew, things were indeed different in Britain. The country, too, of course had a Catholic Question and a Jewish Question. When certain disabilities were removed from Catholics in 1778 to induce them to enlist in the Army and fight the Americans,[70] anti-Catholic rioting broke out in London. By the time the army was ordered to fire on the mob four days later (when the Bank of England and the homes of the Prime Minister and Archbishop of Canterbury were threatened), much of London had been burned and nearly 300 people were dead. The inevitable next step, Catholic Emancipation—permitting Catholics to sit in Parliament—was finally granted in 1829, after the King and Lords were given an ultimatum by Wellington, the Tory P.M., who was finally convinced of its necessity. (Protestant dissenters had been admitted to the House only two years earlier.) The agitation was spearheaded by Daniel O'Connell's Catholic Association, providing a model for political pressure groups forever after. In 1850, Rome re-established in Britain the diocesan hierarchy and titles eliminated by Henry VIII. Still smarting from the Tractarian schism and the defection of Newman and other leading lights to the Church, and irritated by Cardinal Wiseman's tactless wording of the announcement, Anglicans and dissenters took umbrage. Russell, the prime minister, not above capitalizing on popular prejudices, introduced and passed a bill to prohibit the Church from taking titles already in use by the Anglican Church. But the Anglican Church was disestablished in Ireland in 1869 and Catholics permitted to hold fellowships at Oxford and Cambridge two years later. Though some satisfaction was expressed in London at the *Kulturkampf* (while it was considered thoroughly un-English), Britain and Germany were moving in opposite directions by 1872. Jesuits, of course, had never been banned: one of the great English poems of the final quarter of the 19th century, by a Jesuit priest, celebrated the martyrdom of German nuns who drowned when their ship sank off Kent.[71]

As for the Jewish Question, Jews, readmitted to England de facto, though not de jure, during the Protectorate, suffered under the same disabilities as Catholics until the 19th century. (The famous "Jew Bill" of 1753, granting citizenship to foreign-born Jews, was repealed the following year, after orchestrated protests.) Jews were admitted to Oxford in 1854—they could already matriculate at Cambridge—and were permitted to take degrees at both in 1856. In 1858 they were able to sit in Parliament. The mass immigration of Russian Jews after 1881 (some 140,000 to 150,000 entered Britain by 1914)[72] aroused antisemitism, particularly in East End neighborhoods near where the immigrants settled. But there was no antisemitic party or movement. While individual publicists held forth on the Jews (most notably Chesterton and Belloc), "even in the most extreme of ultra-nationalist right-wing circles—let alone among mainstream Tories—there is simply no evidence of antisemitism in the continental sense," in which Jews were viewed as irredeemably alien and destructive, W. D. Rubinstein has concluded.[73] (Mosely's BUF turned antisemitic in 1933. But unlike its predecessor, the New Party, it never contested a General Election—perhaps because the New Party had polled only .2% of the total vote in 1931—and never captured a council seat. There were a few acolytes of Hitler in Britain—Beamish, Lease, Ramsay—but they were marginal figures, spurned even by Mosley.)[74] The Russian Revolution undoubtedly raised levels of antisemitism on the British Right, as the Boer War had on the British Left. English editions of *The Protocols* began circulating in 1919, but were seldom taken seriously even in the most reactionary circles. Two years later, the *Times* correspondent in Constantinople exposed the book as a forgery. While antisemitism persisted, and was exacerbated by the Depression, and, more recently and markedly, by British immigration policy, antipathy to Jews has so far had no political traction, and there is no chapter on antisemitism in Britain in the mostly widely used anthology on the subject.[75]

The German government's persecution of Catholics that took place in the 19th century and Jews in the 20th century would have been unthinkable in Britain.

-<--→-

There is of course something futile about the hoary *Sonderwegfrage*; it would hardly be such a popular subject otherwise. Was there a unique German path to modernity? Of course there was. But there were also unique English, French, Spanish, Swiss, Swedish, Dutch, and Belgian paths, though naturally if you half-shut your eyes, or consider the development of what were to become the European states at sufficient remove (say from Beijing, Delhi, Cuzco, or Timbuktu), you see similarities. Why should we be surprised if the values of people conquered and subjected to a strong central administration in the 11th century, and to another in the 16th, and conscious of itself as a nation by the 14th, a people living behind a formidable moat, the Channel, enabling warriors to become gentlemen by the 16th century, a people that had circumscribed the rights of its ruler—who, in any case, did not imagine himself the successor of Augustus and Charlemagne—in the 13th century, with additional checks in the 17th and 18th centuries (when preoccupied or malleable foreigners had been selected king, following the first trial and execution of a monarch in history), a people who had seen serfdom disappear by 1500, over three centuries before it was abolished in Central and Eastern Europe, who had resisted the re-imposition of Roman over Common Law as well as absolutism, uniquely retaining its medieval Parliament, and who were attracted to a form of Protestantism insisting on the right to rebel against an ungodly ruler (and which encouraged collective decision-making as well as exalting conscience), and who, finally, as a result of these and other factors, forged ahead of the pack in commerce and banking, developing the laws and habits facilitating both, and acquired a vast colonial empire and industrialized before anyone else—why should we expect that the outlook of such a people would be similar to those of the subjects of a nation where none of this had happened—and where unification, when it finally took place in the 19th century, was achieved by the conquests of Prussia, the absolutist, militarized state par excellence?

The light opera made its debut in Britain just as Germany was premiering the heavy opera.[76] Its mildly satiric songs ridiculed a First Lord of the Admiralty whose office was a reward for polishing handles and never thinking for himself, and who went below "whenever the breezes blow," a major general who knew "no more of tactics than a novice in a nunnery," though au courant on many other subjects, and another general who led his regiment from behind ("he found it less exciting"). These songs were wildly popular with the middle and upper classes. Can we imagine audiences from the same strata in Berlin applauding ditties mocking field marshals? Can we imagine a German Chancellor who was a converted Jew? Conversely, can we imagine a parson in Surrey telling his congregation that it must please God to see Himself mirrored in the English soul or praising "our English God"? Can we imagine a British officer informing his troops that the life of a single soldier was worth more than the entire population of Heidelberg?[77] Can we imagine a Prime Minister assuring the House that necessity knows no law? Can we imagine him authorizing a "Jew count" in 1916, and then suppressing the disappointing results?

⊰⊹⊱

6. OTHER REHEARSALS

Germany was not the only country rehearsing in 1914. As mentioned in the Epilogue, Grey made a desperate bid to appease Austria. Refraining from publicly condemning the ultimatum, he urged Vienna, through Germany, to, first, delay the deadline for the Serbian reply, and then, when the Ballhausplatz refused, to negotiate the trivial differences between the Austrian demands and Belgrade's response, which had accepted nine of the ten demands and offered to submit the tenth to international arbitration. Again, no public expression of regret was issued when Vienna rejected this request. Implicitly accepting the Empire's right to resolve the dispute by force, Grey then pleaded with the Ballhausplatz to content itself with the occupation of Belgrade. While the Liberal Cabinet would have countenanced no concrete action to pressure Austria and its ally, sharp protests and realistic prognostications delivered in private might have had a sobering effect on both Franz-Joseph's and the Kaiser's governments. The thickly veiled warning that Grey finally issued on July 30 alarmed Bethmann Hollweg and resulted in his first and only attempt to reign in Berchtold and the war party, though its sincerity is open to question. While one can only speculate as to what would have happened had Grey privately cautioned the German Chancellor at the outset of the crisis that Britain would very likely wind up fighting beside its Entente partners if an Austrian invasion of Serbia was followed by a German invasion of France, there can be no doubt that appeasement failed in 1914 no less spectacularly than in 1938, however less egregious it may have been.

The Church was also rehearsing. The issue of the role of the Vatican in the Holocaust is certainly one of the most contentious questions in the history of the 20th century.[78] While there can be no doubt that the Holy See protected some Jews after the German occupation of Italy, as did many hundreds of priests and nuns throughout Europe, Pope Pius XII not only issued no condemnation of the extermination of the Jews, but failed to refer to it explicitly in any papal communication during the war. The Pope's fear of Bolshevism exceeded his unhappiness with Nazi racial policies, and he hoped to broker an alliance between Britain and Germany to defend Western Civilization from the Soviet barbarians.[79]

Belgian Catholics, including the leadership of the Church, were hardly less disappointed in Pope Benedict XV than were Jews, and many Catholics, in Pius XII. Like Eugenio Pacelli twenty-five years later, Giacomo Della Chiesa—with whom he shared an atypical background for a 20th century pope, urban and aristocratic—hoped to negotiate a peaceful resolution of the conflict, and feared Russia above all combatants, though for very different reasons than his successor. An Allied victory would further extend the influence of the Orthodox Church into Europe; Constantinople would be resurrected as Rome's rival. The Vatican openly sympathized with the Austro-Hungarian Empire, Europe's only avowedly Catholic regime, and long perceived as a bulwark against Russia. German influence was also strong at the Vatican, owing in part to the thirty-year Triple Alliance, while the Entente was scarcely represented. The staunch anti-clericism of recent Radical ministries in Paris further alienated the papacy from the nation which, from the days of Clovis, had been its defender against German emperors and then Italian revolutionaries.[80]

The failure of the Pope to denounce the massacres and destruction during the invasion baffled and frustrated the Belgian Church. Forty-five members of the clergy had been murdered and several churches looted and gutted.[81] The Vatican had already been well informed of the massacres by its chargé d'affaires when Cardinal Désiré-Joseph Mercier, on his return from Rome, began reporting German crimes to the new Pope.[82] When Mercier did not hear back, he pointedly requested "a word of consolation" to the Belgians.[83] In response to the continued silence, the Cardinal issued his famous pastoral letter just before Christmas, "Patriotism and Endurance."

In January 1915, Benedict finally condemned the German invasion, but only as a violation of the country's neutrality and a breach of international law. No mention was made of the executions and arson. Frustrated by the Vatican's policy of *imparzialità*, Mercier and Cardinal Thomas Heylen, the Bishop of Namur, who had zealously publicized German crimes in his dioceses, called for a joint German-Belgian Catholic Commission to investigate the issue. This was, of course, torpedoed by the German bishops, headed by Cardinal Hartmann, though they naturally wished to exculpate priests.[84] Faced with the Vatican's continued intransigence, Alfred Baudrillart, rector of the Catholic Institute in Paris, concluded bitterly, and prophetically, "There was a time when the Holy See took the trouble to see which side was in the right and had the courage to say it. By assuaging everyone, the Holy See will concede the role of moral arbiter at the end of the war to the President of the Protestant United States."[85]

-<-->-

7. A REHEARSAL IS NOT A PERFORMANCE

Clearly, there are limits to the way in which war crimes in Belgium in 1914 were a rehearsal for later exploits. World War I was not a racial war nor a war for *Lebensraum*. It was launched and prosecuted by generals, not by a brutal and paranoid megalomaniac with an apocalyptic agenda. (The Kaiser, it's fair to say, was manipulated into declaring war—by the government's withholding from him the Serbian response to the Austrian ultimatum and withholding from the Ballhausplatz his own proposal for a halt in Belgrade. He was informed of strategic decisions, but did not initiate them, and was increasingly marginalized after 1916. Conversely, the War Minister, the Foreign Minister, and the Commander-in-Chief of the Army were appalled when they learned of Hitler's war plans on November 5th, 1937. But the Führer got rid of them, and neither they nor the Army protested.) Anti-Catholicism was hardly a core belief of the military leadership in 1914. The War Ministry had no wish to jeopardize the *Bergfrieden* by alienating German Catholics, nearly a third of the population. Even among anti-Catholic zealots, the idea of subordinating military objectives to an ideological crusade would have been unthinkable. The Second Reich was also far more sensitive to public opinion in neutral counties than the Third; foreign policy was in the hands of professional diplomats.

The differences in the treatment of civilians in the two World Wars are no less striking. On the morning of August 21, 1914, it may be recalled, an incongruous debate took place in the Place de Tilleuls in Andenne. Eva Comes, a twenty-five-year-old Rhinelander, took on Captain Junge, the Prussian directing the killing in the square. It is difficult to imagine a young German woman a generation later arguing heatedly with an SS officer on behalf of group of Poles—not to mention Jews—about to be executed. It is harder still to imagine a repetition of the denouement, with the captain chivalrously pretending to call off the mass execution, promising to kill only two instead of fifty men. Both the officer and the woman would have been aware that appealing to his sense of fair play was not only futile but dangerous: he easily could have had her shot as well, an option that certainly would not have occurred to Captain Junge in 1914. An Eva Comes who turned up in Poland in 1939 or in Russia in 1941 would have been told for years that the civilians about to be executed were not only *Untermenschen* unworthy of compassion, but a menace to Germany. And of course the indoctrination, in the case of Jews, would have drawn on centuries of prejudice.

⊰⊹⊱

In the end, the events of August 1914 in Belgium anticipate the treatment of civilians in Poland, Czechoslovakia, Russia and other Central and Eastern European countries, rather than that of Jews.[86] Something had allegedly happened before each of the mass executions that the Wehrmacht carried out so promiscuously in the East,[87] as was the case with Belgian civilians a quarter century earlier. The attack or act of sabotage that became the pretext may not, in fact, have occurred, or it may have been the work of enemy soldiers or, in Eastern Europe, partisans—or *agents provocateurs*. In any case, there was never any serious attempt to link the civilian victims to the alleged crime. The point was to use terror to deter future resistance. With the case of Jews, however, there was seldom a precipitating incident.[88] No lesson was being administered. They were killed because they were members of a "race" that was intent on exterminating Germans, their murderers believed.

⊰⊹⊱

In Belgium, though fewer than 8% of the Jews residing in the country in 1940 were citizens (about 4,341 of about 55,670), 46% survived the war. The contrast with the Netherlands is striking: 80% of Jews perished in a country where 83% were Dutch citizens, and the community dated back to the 17th century.[89] This partly has to do with the fact that Belgium was administered by the military and the Netherlands by a *Zivilverwaltung* dominated by committed Nazis under Seyss-Inquart. Also, owing to their high degree of assimilation, Dutch Jews may have been more complacent than their co-religionists to the south. But the survival of nearly twice the percentage of Jews in Belgian has something to do as well with the country's experience during the First World War. As a result of the August massacres and the occupation, Belgians were more wary of Germans, more skeptical about German promises, and, were familiar with the strategies and tactics of resistance.[90] The victims of 1914, in short, were not forgotten; their martyrdom insured there would be fewer Holocaust victims than would otherwise have been the case the next time the Germans invaded. It is not coincidental that the only instance in which a train bound for a death camp was stopped and captive Jews liberated was in Belgium, between Boortmeerbeek and Haacht.[91]

◄◄─►►

The Report of the British Committee on Alleged German Outrages (RBC)

On September 15, 1914, Ronald McNeill rose in the House of Commons and asked if the Government had any plans to investigate charges of atrocities against the Germany Army. Replying for the Government, the Prime Minister said that he had already instructed the Home Secretary and the Attorney General to "take the steps necessary to ascertain the truth."[1] The popular novelist H. Rider Haggard had recently called for a Royal Commission to take evidence of instances of atrocities, and the proposal had attracted much support.[2] The Belgian *Commission d'Enquête* had released its first report on August 28th, and two more had already followed.

MacNeill may have been primed; the dilatory Asquith had just authorized a British inquiry. Reginald McKenna, Home Secretary, passed the request along to George A. Aitken, Assistant Secretary. Attorney General Sir John Simon asked Sir Charles Matthews, Director of Public Prosecutions, to oversee the investigation, and he, in turn, enlisted Guy Stephenson, Assistant Director. Stephenson recruited three interpreters, two sisters, a Mme. Rue and a Miss Patton, and Max Peteers, all of whom were fluent in both French and Dutch.[3] A circular was drawn up by the Home Office and issued to police departments and newspapers urging that Belgian refugees who had witnessed German war crimes identify themselves to authorities.

On September 21st, McKenna and Simon issued a joint directive, probably drafted by Aitken, that lay down the ground rules for the investigation. "Anonymous and vague stories," it warned, only raise indignation, but what is needed in justice both to those who make these allegations and to those who are accused, is that every statement should so far as possible be tested and verified with the same care and calmness with which statements of prospective witnesses are collected by public authorities in this country.

Assertions should be discredited altogether unless they are supported by details of time, place, and circumstance, and unless those who give first-hand information are prepared thus to have recorded in writing the truth of their allegations. The good English rule against hearsay is the most valuable check against possible exaggeration.[4]

The Ministers urged that the actual words of the witnesses be used and that the statement be read back to him or her and then signed. The names of the witness and examiner were to be included. McKenna and Simon proposed that a "small committee," under the auspices of the Home Office, review the statements and, presumably, draw conclusions.

A rough division of labor between the Home Office and Attorney General's Office was agreed upon. The Chief Clerk of the Office of Public Prosecutions in the latter, William Lewis, interviewed witnesses at the depots in London to which refugees were initially taken. The three translators circulated among the Belgians, identifying those who claimed to have witnessed war crimes. Statements were taken in shorthand from those who had, read back to the witness, and signed. Mme. Rue was considered particularly effective with uneducated women.

But naturally many refugees had already left the depots, and others were going directly to friends, acquaintances, or other institutions upon their arrival. It devolved on the Home Office to locate and interview potential witnesses among these Belgians. The Belgian Minister in London offered his assistance, but urged that the names of witnesses be suppressed. No one would come forward, otherwise. (The Belgian government had meanwhile, on September 26th, set up its own commission in London, under Sir Mackenzie Chalmers, to take evidence from refugees in the U.K. The commission issued its sole report at the end of December.) Barristers were recruited to interview those willing to provide evidence.

As is generally the case in collective activities, a few individuals undertook most of the work. Chief among these were Aitken and Edward Grimwood Mears. (R. E. Lomax Vaughn Williams also conducted a number of interviews, and J. H. Morgan, recently appointed Professor of Constitutional Law at University College London, traveled to the continent to collect information from British soldiers and from the diaries and

letters of dead or captured German troops.)[5] Aitken (1860–1917) was of a
type perhaps not extinct in Whitehall—the polymath civil servant equally
at home at conferences on reformatories and prostitution and in the British
Library and among the antiquarian book dealers in the Strand. A specialist
in Augustan literature, Aitken wrote biographies of Steele and Arbuthnot,
and published editions of works by Swift and Defoe, as well as Marvell,
Burns, and others. He had served as private secretary to the Home Office's
Permanent Undersecretary and had been associated for many years with
committees investigating abuses of various kinds. It was he who organized
the investigation, locating witnesses, contacting barristers, and arranging
the interviews. (In one memo, dated 14 October 1914, Aitken is identified
as the Chairman of a Committee appointed by the Home Secretary and
Attorney General to investigate allegations of atrocities.)[6]

On the last day of September, Aitken recruited Grimwood Mears
(1869–1963), a well-connected Inner Temple barrister. Mears proved to be
the most energetic of the Home Office investigators. He bombarded Aitken
with requests for more help. Belgian refugees were dispersed throughout
England and Wales. "Within the last eight days," Mears complained to
Aitken on October 19, "I have traveled 1500 miles and it is impossible for
me to do this as quickly as ought to be done and to carry on my practice at
the bar."[7] Would McKenna permit him, he asked, to use one of his assistants? "Speed is essential," Mears wrote on the 26th, and submitted a list of
eight barristers for McKenna's approval. "It is absolutely essential to have
at least 4 men 'on the road' every day for the next 2 or 3 weeks," he wrote
three days later, and provided more names.

There was a succession of frustrations: at South Sea Hospital only three
of eleven men on Aitken's list were actually there; at Wandsworth, not one
of twenty-nine people listed as being there were present. Aitken tried to
husband Mears' prodigious energy, dissuading him from going to Cardiff
to interview one witness – the evidence seemed to be based on hearsay –
and attempting to locate witnesses from important towns – like Andenne
– that were under-represented.[8]

On November 9, six weeks after his appointment, Mears circulated a
preliminary report on alleged German atrocities, based on more than eighty
signed statements. Its twelve pages discuss eleven separate charges. Mears
was cautious on some issues: no woman claimed explicitly to have been

raped, though there were several second-hand accounts, and he doubted that the Germans had intentionally fired on hospitals or stretcher-bearers. Nonetheless, the barrister was convinced that children had been bayoneted and mutilated, in most cases after they were already dead. Ten witnesses had reported seeing a total of seventeen such children. He found the testimony of five witnesses on this subject particularly compelling.[9]

◄‹·›►

"We were led to suppose that Mr. McKenna would appoint a Commission of Inquiry," a leader in the *Times* of 8 December 1914 complained. "Has any such body been appointed? ...The Commission appointed by the Belgian Government has issued a series of such reports which have profoundly impressed the opinion of all civilized communities. Why does not Mr. McKenna follow their example?" In fact, the "small committee" that would review the material collected by the Office of the Public Prosecutor and the Home Office barristers was already being assembled. On December 4th, Sir John Simon wrote to Bryce asking if he would be willing to chair it. Others were contacted during the next week and an official "warrant of appointment" was issued by Asquith on the 15th. Serving with Bryce were Sir Frederick Pollock, eminent jurist and legal historian (and nominal co-author of Maitland's seminal *History of English Law*), H. A. L. Fisher, historian (Napoleon was an abiding interest), warden of New College, and Vice-Chancellor of the University of Sheffield, two distinguished lawyers, Sir Edward Clarke and Sir Alfred Hopkinson, and Harold Cox, economist, mathematician, journalist, and former MP, who was then editor of the *Edinburgh Review*. Fisher, at forty-nine, and the fifty-five-year-old Cox were the youngest members, the rest being in their sixties and seventies. Sir Kenelm Digby was added on January 22nd and Mears and another barrister, W. J. H. Broderick, were named secretaries. Nearly all were Liberals, known and respected in Germany and the U.S. None had ever expressed the least animosity toward Germany.

As many commentators have pointed out, James Bryce, the seventy-six-year-old chairman, was a particularly inspired choice. Bryce had studied at Heidelberg, made his reputation with a book on the Holy Roman Empire, and had received honorary degrees from the universities of Jena and Leipzig. A scrupulous Gladstonian Liberal, he had opposed the Boer

War and had sought accommodation with Germany. No less important, Bryce had been an very popular ambassador to Washington for six years. The author of the preeminent work on the political system of the U.S., *The American Commonwealth*, Bryce proved to be congenial as he was erudite, and had numerous admirers among leading American intellectuals and politicians.[10] Bryce's imprimatur virtually assured his Committee's Report a favorable reception in the country where this mattered most.

In his letter to Bryce inviting him to serve, Simon explicitly acknowledged his motives in selecting the members: "the value of this investigation entirely depends upon the known impartiality and authority of those who compose the Committee..."[11] A statement of the "Terms of Reference" accompanying the invitations to Bryce and the other members established the scope of the Committee's activities: it was "to consider and advise on the evidence collected on behalf of His Majesty's Government as to atrocities committed by German troops during the present War....and to prepare a report showing the conclusion at which they arrive on the evidence now available."[12]

It was with this brief that, late in the day, Harold Cox took issue. On March 1, 1915, Cox urged that the Committee interrogate some of the witnesses whose depositions members had read. Otherwise, the Committee could only report that "We have read through a large number of printed statements furnished to us by persons appointed by the British Government. These statements profess to be a transcript of depositions made by British soldiers and Belgian refugees. Some of the statements appear to us on prima facie grounds to be incredible; others appear on similar grounds to be probably true; and we report accordingly." He noted specifically that in the report written by Sir Frederick Pollock, eighteen of the forty-five depositions the jurist drew upon were dubious. Cox was also disturbed by the equivocal comments by the examining barristers as to the veracity of some of the statements used by Pollock.[13]

After listening to Cox's reservations in committee, other members were not sympathetic. "He seems to require a far higher degree of probability than a court of justice ever gets, and to think that every statement of fact must be absolutely true or absolutely false," wrote Pollock[14] "If history had to be revised on his principles most of it would become blank, including every document not expressly cited by some contemporary." H. A. L. Fisher concurred. "His scruples seem to me to be excessive[,] for our evidence is far better both in quality and quantity than that upon which most of our histories have been build."[15]

As an MP, the impracticality of Cox's proposals, wrote his friend, the Liberal economist F. W. Hirst, "marked a defect in Cox's fine qualities, which often made it difficult for others to co-operate with him in public life."[16] Yet in retrospect, as demonstrated below, Cox's reservations were justified. The final report itself is unimpeachable, but the evidence published in Appendix A includes too many stories of dubious merit, and a number that are most likely outright inventions. Unlike in his brief and stormy political career, the principled editor in fact compromised with Bryce over his demands. Convinced on March 9 that he would be unable to sign the report, so fundamental were his differences with the majority, on March 11, after speaking with Bryce and Simon, he agreed to a series of brief interviews with the barristers, in lieu of recalling the witnesses. We cannot know what Bryce and Simon said, but it's likely they stressed the difficulty of locating and interviewing the refugees, especially given the need for the timely publication of the report. Bryce undoubtedly pointed out the original charge to the Committee, that it was to draw conclusions from evidence submitted to it, rather than to gather that evidence. The Chairman also agreed to alter the preface in order to define more accurately the Committee's activities and this no doubt helped placate Cox.[17]

In the end, however, the deficiencies of the Appendix A had at least as much to do with the way the Committee conceived of its mandate as with its failure to be more skeptical about individual depositions or to have itself re-examined witnesses.

The Belgian Commission of 1914 set out to determine exactly what had happened in the specific locations where atrocities were alleged to have occurred. While Part I of the Bryce Report summarizes the testimony by region (reflecting the grouping of the individual depositions in Appendix A), the Committee was more interested in making generalizations about German behavior in Belgium as a whole. Thus, Part II, preceding the conclusion, treats seven categories of war crimes, condensing Mears's eleven. These categories are organized under two heads, "treatment of the civil population" and "offenses against combatants." This global approach encouraged the Committee to accept stories of similar incidents that were said to have occurred in different parts of the country. The recurrence of these incidents, instead of raising skepticism, merely corroborated, for the Committee members, tendencies they observed in the behavior of the German Army. Stories like those of two young children found abandoned in a cart – alleged to have taken place in various locations in Brabant – ought to have alerted members that either they were hearing the repetition of a myth, or that, though the incident had indeed taken place in one location, the alternate accounts were inventions, the witnesses maintaining that they had seen something that they had in fact heard about second-hand.

In Tamines, 383 civilians were killed, in Dinant, 685. In Hofstade, a small town just south of Mechelen, even in the most dubious depositions, the total number of victims was only three or four, fewer than were actually murdered there. Yet the RBC provides testimony from no less than fifty-five witnesses about events in Hofstade. The Committee apparently believed that multiplying accounts of the same few horrific murders was preferable to verifying and documenting unprovoked mass executions elsewhere in the country.

But the fault was not entirely the Committee's. For obvious reasons, refugees from Wallonia tended to go south. In consequence, only three depositions from Andenne, two from Tamines, and five from Dinant (two of which were from witnesses who left before the 23rd) were published in the RBC. Even if the Committee staff was aware of the scale of the enormities that had taken place in these towns – as they do not seem to have been in the case of Tamines – they did not have the evidence to document the crimes. Thus the vicious acts of individual soldiers, despite the Committee's stated wish to de-emphasize these, were given a prominence in the Report that they did not merit.

Both Belgian *Commissions d'Enquête* had a third advantage. Information was often forwarded to the committees and interviews conducted by local notables. These individuals, whether or not they had legal training, were known to those providing direct testimony. Witnesses were less likely to fabricate the stories they told such individuals than they were to foreign barristers. The Belgian investigators, de facto and de jure, were also less credulous than the Home Office attorneys. Refugees claiming to have seen something first-hand were simply not pressed with sufficient vigor in the U.K. A higher degree of integrity among non-criminals was perhaps taken for granted in England.

Ultimately, however, the Bryce Report ought to be compared not only to those published by the *Commission d'Enquête*, but to its German counterpart. Just as the King of England and the Prime Minister never issued statements like those made in September by the Kaiser and Bethmann Hollweg claiming that wounded German soldiers had been mutilated by Belgian women and children, the conclusions of the Bryce Report are a model of probity and judiciousness compared to the summaries of events contained in the German White Book.

It is worth emphasizing that the four conclusions of the *Report on Alleged German Outrages* are entirely accurate: 1. "That there were in many parts of Belgium deliberate and systematically organised massacres of the civil population, accompanied by many isolated murders and other outrages." 2. That women and children were among the victims. 3. That German officers ordered "the looting, house burning, and the wanton destruction of property." 4. That civilians were used as shields, wounded prisoners murdered, and the Red Cross and White Flag abused.[18]

The report goes out of its way to exonerate the individual soldier. The distinction is drawn between "individual acts of brutality" and the deliberate killing of civilians in order to terrorize the population. While the former were "more numerous and more shocking than would be expected in warfare between civilised Powers, ...they differ in extent rather than in kind from what has happened in previous though not recent wars." They were the result of criminals within the ranks, widespread drunkenness, and the incitements to violence war provides.

Altogether different was the massacre of "the innocent inhabitants of a village because shots have been fired, or are alleged to have been fired."[19] The systematic use of terror reflected the depraved morals of Prussian officers. "The Spirit of War is deified. Obedience to the State and its War Lord leaves no room for other duty or feeling. Cruelty becomes legitimate when it promises victory." These beliefs did not originate with the German people, but were a specifically military doctrine that had "hypnotised" the ruling caste.[20] Though shaken by the manifesto "To the Civilized World" and other signs of the unanimity of support for the invasion on the part of German intellectuals, Bryce and other Liberals clung to the belief that the Germany they recalled from their student years – for Bryce, this was the Heidelberg of 1863 – still survived. The *Denker und Dichter* had simply been thrust aside by the amoral militarists in Berlin, obsessed with world power.

Bryce repeated in private letters his strong wish to believe that the reports he'd heard of war crimes were grossly exaggerated.[21] The Report also insists that members began with doubts as to whether there would be sufficient evidence to indict the German Army.[22] These claims cannot be dismissed out of hand.

Two additional points are worth making about the much-maligned publication. First, the Report significantly understates the killing of civilians. While the death toll in Andenne is estimated at 400 (262 were in fact killed), the only statement regarding the largest single massacre of the invasion, in Tamines, is the following: "A witness describes how he saw the public square littered with corpses..."[23] For Dinant, too, where 685 civilians were killed, there is no attempt at an accurate tally. Various figures, added together, come to 410.[24] And in Aarschot, where 169 civilians were murdered, only ten executions took place, according to the evidence the Report provides.[25]

A second point: while a certain number of claims are clearly fraudulent, it is impossible to dismiss out of hand some accounts of grisly events. Other sources simply do not provide sufficient details to corroborate or reject these descriptions, and the testimony is consistent, detailed, and plausible. The Report's many critics have conceded, on the one hand, that there were criminal elements in the German Army whose inhibitions were further reduced by alcohol, the experience of combat, the absence of authorities, etc., but then have gone on to argue that any mention of rape or a particularly vicious killing is sheer atrocity-mongering. Clearly there were many instances of rape in both Liège province and central Brabant, and there is unimpeachable evidence that in the house-to-house "cleansings" and in some formal executions, victims were bayoneted. Unquestionably, many Belgian men, and some women and children, were killed in a particularly brutal fashion.[26]

-<-+->-

The ultimate fate of the Committee's papers remains a mystery. The Committee promised in its introduction that the original depositions, some 1,200, would be placed in the custody of the Home Office and would be available to scholars after the war.[27] But when James Read wished to consult them in 1939, they could not be located. He suggested that this shed "an interesting light...on the value of the depositions."[28] (The loss was embarrassing to the British Government, especially after the U.S. Embassy and the State Department became involved. Bernadotte Schmitt, Read's advisor, had originally contacted Harold Temperley, co-editor of the pre-war British papers. These were two of the leading diplomatic historians of the twentieth century, with friends in high places. Frantic efforts ensued to find the papers.)[29] However, on August 13, 1942, after the publication of Read's book, Sir Stephen Gaslee, the Foreign Office librarian, managed to locate the missing depositions.[30] But some time afterward, the Committee's papers were destroyed.[31] No mention is made as to how this came about. It's possible a German rocket was responsible. If this was the case, the Germans (albeit unintentionally in the case of the Bryce Committee) managed to keep out of the hands of scholars documents from two of the three bodies investigating the war crimes of August 1914.

⊰⟶⟶⊱

I have assigned individual depositions in Appendix A of the RBC to one of the following five categories, based on my assessment as to the probability that what they describe actually took place: very likely (5); likely (4); possibly (3); not likely (2); probably a legend or invention (1). Of the latter, I have distinguished between those atrocity stories that ought to have been evident to interviewers and those that were plausible, however gruesome, but irreconcilable with other, more reliable evidence not available to the investigators. It goes without saying that there is a degree of subjectivity in any such assessment, and others might award a given deposition a different number. I have used the following criteria to evaluate the testimony: a) Is it consistent with other sources?[32] b) Is it consistent with other testimony in the RBC? c) Does it contain credible details? d) Does the voice of the witness inspire confidence – are events related with care and precision?

Perhaps the most significant conclusion of an examination of the testimony in the RBC is the divergence in credibility between the statements of Belgian soldiers and civilians. The former are consistently more willing than the latter to describe events that in all probability they either heard about second-hand or invented. One must take into account the fact that soldiers had opportunities to see grim tableaux that it was not possible for civilians to witness – scenes in isolated farmhouses and châteaux, on the road between villages, or in places where civilians had been driven out. Frequently these were alleged to have taken place in areas which the Germans had recently evacuated after heavy fighting – particularly in the areas of central Brabant reoccupied by Belgian troops during the First and Second Sorties. There is incontestable evidence from multiple sources as to the consequences of German retreats from the Liège forts, from the Sambre at Tamines, from the Meuse at Dinant, and from the Dender at Aalst, and it is reasonable to suppose that the Kaiser's troops did not behave differently in the villages south of Mechelen.

There is also this consideration: civilians were unquestionably mutilated. Everyone stabbed by a bayonet was mutilated, and many hundreds of Belgians suffered this fate. It is certainly possible that some victims, in defending themselves, had their wrists and hands slashed. It is possible that some women, stabbed in the chest, had their breasts cut. Rapes unquestionably occurred, some of the victims were killed, and some of the murderers were undoubtedly sadists.

What, then, distinguishes a myth? 1) Not only does it contain details shocking to the sensibilities of most readers, but it appeals to their emotions in a blatant and contrived manner. 2) The same incident is alleged to have occurred in different locations, or the scene is described by two or more witnesses with details that differ more dramatically than is plausible (even given the fact that large discrepancies can occur in the accounts of the same event provided by educated, well-intentioned witnesses). 3) Not only is there no evidence from other sources corroborating the account, but either a) the events themselves would have been witnessed by others who do provide evidence, or b) the body of the victim would have been discovered and his or her identity revealed and the nature of the injuries described in discussions of war crimes in that location by other sources.

The unenviable reputation of the RBC is, then, the direct result of including evidence from soldiers. In the section on the city of Liège and villages to its east, such testimony accounts for only 17% of the depositions. In the section on events in the Meuse and Sambre valleys, it is nearly the identical percentage, 16.6%. As a result, descriptions of events in these two regions are largely reliable. Testimony from Liège averages 3.8.

Without the evidence of soldiers, who average 2.16, civilians rate a 4.14. Three of the five horror stories from Liège that are clearly, or more than likely, inventions come from soldiers, including three of the four stories the dubious nature of which ought to have been obvious to investigators and Committee members.

A similar pattern is evident in the river valley towns in western Liège, Namur, and Hainaut attacked between August 20th and 23rd. The thirty statements from witnesses average 3.77. The five soldiers, however, average only 2.4; without their depositions, civilians witnesses rate 4.04. The incidents they describe were likely to have happened. Only two atrocity tales were recounted by witnesses from this region, one by a soldier. Neither would necessarily have been evident to the British interviewers.

As a general rule, the larger the town, the more reliable the testimony. Even within the region designated as the "Aarschot, Mechelen, Vilvoorde, Leuven Quadrangle," the scene of some of the worst of the alleged outrages, testimony from residents of Aarschot is of high quality. The thirty-eight depositions average 4.0. However, this includes evidence from twelve soldiers (31.6% of the total), who average only 2.4, exactly like their counterparts in the Meuse and Sambre section. Without them, the twenty-six civilians average 4.73, providing credible accounts that tally fully with all other evidence.

⤛⤜

It is a different story when one moves to Hofstade. It is worth considering events in and around this village of 1,512 residents, a little less than two miles south of Mechelen, because no less than fifty-five depositions in the RBC describe scenes witnessed there – exactly 50% more than Aarschot, in second place (with two additional depositions included that probably describe events in Hofstade), and more than from Leuven, Andenne, Tamines, and Dinant combined. Hofstade changed hands four times. Occupied by the Germans on August 24th, retaken during the First Sortie by the 6th Division the following day, it was overrun by the Germans on the 26th, then captured again by the Belgian 1st Division on September 10th, before once more falling into German hands. Brutality inevitably accompanied German retreats – many massacres were "punishments" – and it is not surprising that isolated individuals and families suffered.

Just over 85% of the Hofstade depositions were provided by soldiers. Not surprisingly, the testimony about events in this village is particularly untrustworthy: twenty-seven depositions (49%) were either deliberate fabrications or cannot be reconciled with other evidence. Of these, at least eight ought to have been apparent to the investigators. The average rating for all 55 depositions is 2.11, the eight civilians averaging 3.25. With one exception, the officers were only a little more reliable than their men, the five non-commissioned officers averaging 2.4 and the three commissioned officers 2.33.

What happened at Hofstade? According to the synopsis and the four affidavits published by the post-war Commission d'Enquête, along with the testimony of one of the residents interviewed by Bryce Committee representatives, unpublished depositions in the General State Archives, and two diaries in private hands, German soldiers, upon entering the village early on the morning of the 24th, set fire to about thirty buildings along Driesstraat. During this operation, a sixty-five-year-old widow was murdered by a bayonet or lance thrust, or shot, and two men were hurled into a burning house. (The sequence of events remains unclear. Other homes, as many as twenty, may have been burned over the next twenty-four hours along the Tervuursesteenweg, and it's possible that the men were burned to death and the woman stabbed or shot later in the day.) Some of the inhabitants who fled their burning homes, or were chased out by the arsonists, numbering about fifty and including women and children, were herded northward, where they were used as a screen against Belgian forces advancing from Mechelen. Some Germans propped their rifles on the shoulders of the residents while they fired, one witness reported. The hostages were then marched to Elewijt, where they were held captive in a school. They were joined by other families from Hofstade who were also conducted to Elewijt. One man was taken from the school and shot, though he vigorously protested his innocence. Another four men were executed outside a castle near Elewijt, Rubens' former summer home, where they were sheltering with their families. Needless to say, no one had fired on the Germans and no arms were found.[33]

A few of the 47 Belgian soldiers interviewed by the Committee staff about events in Hofstade report seeing a body that may have been that of the sixty-five-year-old widow — one officer estimated her age exactly. But none of them recount the events summarized above, or their aftermath. Instead, most of the soldiers' depositions describe one of several tableaux, in addition to various far-fetched atrocity tales. The latter feature young children, often with hands or feet hacked off, or, in one case, nailed to the side of a house with a bayonet and in another dangling from a string, pregnant women bayoneted in the stomach, etc. One of the most detailed of such tales, testified to by two soldiers, concerns an artilleryman who happened to be from Hofstade discovering the mutilated bodies of his family and then going mad. Belgian soldiers could certainly be as inventive as their German counterparts.

However, no less than eleven witnesses, including some non-soldiers, describe seeing a boy or, more often, a young man, who had been killed in a café or a dance hall adjoining a café. Several state that the body was still in a kneeling position, and/or with hands clasped, as if he were begging for mercy. Six other witnesses describe a young man murdered in a blacksmith's shop. Some of these, too, assert that he was in a position of supplication, though lying on his side. Three of these claim his hands were severed, one that they were mutilated. Two of the witnesses claiming to have seen the young man in the dance hall, including a witness identifying himself as a friend of the man, also state that his hands or arms were severed. Witnesses reporting seeing the young man in the café, however, all say that he was stabbed in the chest.

These murders are not mentioned in the RDE. Are they fabrications? Not necessarily. Reports submitted by the parish priest of Hofstade, Frans van Bosch and the vicar, Karel van Oosterwyck, and signed by the burgomaster, describe the murder of eighteen-year-old Frans Janssens, who was stabbed to death in the home of a blacksmith, Pieter-Frans Verschueren. A diary kept by Frans Janssens's father confirms the killing. There was a great deal of blood around, said the priest, who prayed over him, along with an army chaplain. The young man had been bayoneted repeatedly in the stomach, and his wrists were broken.[34] However, the blacksmith himself testified under oath on September 11th that the young man's hands had been cut off. And the man who buried him, twenty-four-year-old Guillaume Pepermans, testifying under oath as well, two days earlier, also stated than Janssens's hands had been severed. They were lying next to him when Pepermans was requested to carry the body of the young man, along with that of the widow stabbed in the back, to the cemetery. It is possible that Janssens, after he was seen by the priests, was moved by the Germans from Verschueren's forge to the dance hall and it was there that enraged soldiers cut off his hands. The two civilians interviewed by the Bryce Committee barristers who reported seeing a mutilated body in the dance hall identified the victim as Frans Janssens. The young man's right arm had been severed at the elbow, according to Jan Marien, his good friend, and his left hand cut off at the wrist. Both lay beside the body, which also had a chest or stomach wound.[35]

There is additional archival testimony concerning a child who may have been killed by the Germans, along with Lucia Cortebeeck van Hummel and Frans Janssens.[36] In any event, Frans Janssen, unaccounted for by the RDE, was certainly murdered by the Germans on the 24th, and it's likely his hands were later severed. The Bryce Committee witnesses who testified to seeing his mutilated body were not inventing atrocities.

Whatever may have happened in Hofstade, it was certainly to the advantage of the reports of both Belgian Commissions of Inquest that they did not include testimony from soldiers. It is likely, in consequence, that they overlooked a few brutal killings that took place in remote locations or in villages deserted by civilians. But the trade-off, both for the value of their evidence and the reputation of the commissioners, was a good one.

<-‹-›->

In the end, however, it is worth re-emphasizing not only that the conclusions of the Bryce Report are entirely correct, but that the report reminds us of what was so novel – and therefore so horrifying – about the German invasion. Civilians had been seized before and held as a pledge for the good conduct of the residents of a town or city – as happened during the Paris Commune – but this was regarded as a recent and barbaric innovation. What was unprecedented in wars between civilized nations was the mass execution of innocent noncombatants merely because it was alleged that shots had been fired in their village or town. Committee members were astonished and appalled that the victims were charged with no offense and were not condemned by any sort of tribunal.[37]

It is also startling to recall that a massive flight of refugees before an invader was a novelty in Western Europe. Eighteenth and nineteenth century wars did not displace populations on anything like the scale of 1914. That hundreds of thousands of Belgians abandoned their homes and fled into exile seemed to the Committee members to confirm the evidence they had reviewed. It takes some effort to appreciate the incredulity of Bryce and his colleagues, for what happened in Belgium in the middle of August was to become commonplace across the globe during the next four decades, and beyond.

APPENDIX II

Justice

Articles 227 to 230 of the Versailles Treat stipulated that the Allies had the right to try individuals, including the Kaiser, for violations of the laws and customs of war. (Along with the "war guilt clause," in Article 231, these were labeled in Germany the *Schmachparagraphen*, the shame paragraphs.)[1] But Belgians excepting justice for the victims of the August massacres would be sorely disappointed. Before they were betrayed by the seven judges at the Imperial Court of Justice in Leipzig in the early summer of 1921, they would be betrayed by the British, French, and Americans.

Preceding the retreats and concessions by the Allies, there was a bitter struggle at Versailles over the culpability of the Kaiser. Lloyd George, while he had never called for hanging the German Emperor, had nonetheless campaigned in November and December of 1918 on a platform of bringing Wilhlem II to justice. Not surprisingly, in the two Allied nations not devastated by war, and with an electorate less likely than elsewhere to vote strictly on class and religious lines, and more subject, therefore, to the influence of the press, indignation had focused on the Kaiser to a greater degree than in other Allied countries. Americans in particular like to personify their enemies, and "Kaiser Bill" was villified in the U.S. perhaps even more than in Britain. But a reaction to Creel Committees excesses set in rapidly among East Coast intellectuals and political elites, and it's not surprising that it was America that most vigorously opposed holding the German Emperor accountable. Whether or not it would have been useful to have tried the Kaiser (requiring, first, more serious efforts to extradite him from the Netherlands), the struggle consumed a great deal of the time and energy.

American delegates on the Commission on the Violation of the Laws and Customs of War, which first met on 3 February 1919, also torpedoed the efforts of French and British members to move quickly against suspected war criminals. Apart from believing that justice deferred was justice denied, the latter recognized that individuals would escape and evidence be destroyed if the Allies did not act at once, while they had leverage. The armistice of November 11, 1918 had to be formally renewed, and the British insisted that a condition of the next renewal be the turning over of those accused of war crimes.[2] Only the two Americans, Secretary of State Robert Lansing and James B. Scott, an authority on international law, opposed the Commission's decision, but Lansing was the Chairman and ruled the motion out of order.

The head of the British delegation, Sir Ernest Pollock, attempted an end run, persuading Arthur Balfour to raise the proposal in the Council of Ten. But Lloyd George was absent at this session and Balfour's defense of the need to amend the armistice terms was less than energetic. Woodrow Wilson dismissed the idea.

Lansing also repeatedly frustrated the efforts of the British and French delegates to set up an international tribunal to try those accused of war crimes. Though it was chiefly a trial of the Kaiser that Lansing sought to avert, he and Scott were steeped in the reigning positivist school of international law, and appeals to Natural Law, to traditional distinctions between just and unjust wars, they considered anachronistic. "The essence of sovereignty," Lansing announced, "was the absence of responsibility."[3] It made no difference whether sovereignty rested with a hereditary monarch or a democratically elected head of state. While there might be a "moral obligation to mankind," no super-national sovereignty existed. The nation state was bound by no rules except those it voluntarily consented to.

British and French delegates, however, continued to demand an international tribunal, arguing that in signing the Treaty of London and the Hague and Geneva Conventions, Germany had indeed committed itself to legal obligations it had then violated. Lansing was obliged to call the question, and lost the vote.

But he, in turn, bypassed the Committee – and with greater success than Pollock. Lansing announced on March 15th that the U.S. would agree to the tribunal, but would reserve the right to withdraw its judges from any trial it chose not to participate in.[4] This effectively torpedoed the proposal. The spectacle of American judges filing out of a courtroom because they objected to the charges would have undermined the proceedings.

Not content with this triumph, the American delegates submitted as well a minority report explicitly rejecting the High Tribunal, largely on the grounds that such a court was without precedent and might be abused in the future. National military tribunals would be acceptable, however, for soldiers accused of committing war crimes; "political sanctions" would have to suffice for the Kaiser, his Chancellor, and other government officials.[5]

Inevitably, the Council of Four (reduced from Ten in the interim, Belgium being among the excluded), came up with a compromise; inevitably, the compromise was not a happy one. Needing Lloyd George's support on several pressing issues, Wilson on April 19th agreed to trying the Kaiser, but solely for the violation of the treaty guaranteeing Belgian neutrality. He would not be accused of transgressing criminal law, but of having offended against "international morality and the sanctity of treaties," and would be arraigned before a special tribunal made up of one judge from each of the Four Powers, and Japan.[6] National or mixed military tribunals would try those accused of war crimes; there would be no international tribunal, no "crimes against humanity." The trials would take place in the victim's own country and the perpetrator, if convicted, would be sentenced according to existing codes. (If citizens of more than one country were victims, mixed tribunals would hear the cases.) Lloyd George, whose chief objective was simply to set in motion some mechanism for trying the Kaiser, agreed.[7][8] The compromise at least stipulated that the accused be extradited to the country where the crime had taken place. This key provision was soon to be gutted.

The agreement was embodied in Articles 227–230. The "shame paragraphs," revealingly, took on more importance in Germany than the territorial concessions or the reparations (the total of which had yet to be determined). After a long and stormy debate, the *Reichstag* accepted the treaty in June, by a vote of 237 to 138, but only with the proviso that Articles 227 to 231 not be made binding: they were an affront to German honor.[9] The Allies rejected the German initiative and issued an ultimatum: sign, the government was told, or hostilities would be resumed. The *Reichswehr* had already been consulted about the possibility of further resistance. Now

President Friedrich Ebert telephoned the Supreme Command with only three hours left before the deadline of the ultimatum. Hindenberg left the room, and it remained for General Wilhelm Groener, the man who had informed the Kaiser that he had to abdicate, to insist that further resistance was impossible. The *Schmachparagraphen* would have to be swallowed.[10]

Even more threatening than a resumption of the war for the fledgling left-center government were the alternative prospects of a Bolshevik revolution or a military coup, the Scylla and Charybdis confronting the SPD. (It got both, but the Freikorps rescued the government from the first and the trade unions from the second.) The British and French were hardly less anxious about these twin perils, and ultimately these fears undermined the resolve to prosecute war criminals. (It was at times the French and other times the British who led the retreat from the compromise. The French leadership was naturally more interested, in the end, in compensation and security rather than convictions.)[11]

The indignation in Germany aroused by the "shame paragraphs" was exceeded by the outrage over the list of those accused of war crimes, which was promptly labeled the "Black List." Among the 1580 names on the initial list (reduced from over 3,000) were Germany's leading generals, including von Hindenburg, von Falkenhayn, von Ludendorff, Prince Rupprecht, and von Kluck, all venerated as heroes. The German emissary, von Lersner, refused even to accept the list.[12] The socialist government was convinced it would fall if it ordered the extradition of these luminaries. "Leave me the means of maintaining order. Don't ask for these officers," Defense Secretary Noske pleaded.[13] While resentment against the "shame paragraphs" was orchestrated, if not manufactured, by the nationalist press, the outrage against the list was probably spontaneous, and spanned the political spectrum, apart from the Communists. The Army, naturally, was intransigent: never would a brother officer be turned over to the enemy. *Reichswehr* Commander Hans von Seeckt made plans to overthrow the government if it insisted on turning over the accused officers. An alliance was to be concluded with the Soviets, Poland would be dismembered, and then the Army would strike westward – a rehearsal for 1939 and a prelude to the collaboration of the *Reichswehr* and the Red Army in the 1920s.[14]

While some Allied diplomats and military intelligence officers felt the threat was exaggerated, London and Paris retreated. The list was reduced to 1,043, then to 854. When the French refused to delete any more names, the British, in early February 1920, after toying with various compromises, resolved to accept the German proposal that the accused should be tried in German courts. While those familiar with German attitudes toward the perpetrators and victims of war crimes in Belgium and France were appalled, the capitulation provoked little public outrage.[15] The French reluctantly acquiesced, yielding even to Lloyd George's insistence that a wholly new Inter-Allied Commission select the cases to be submitted to the Germans, members of the current Commission having proved too obdurate. The Belgians were not consulted.

The court that was to try the German defendants was the Criminal Senate of the Imperial Court of Justice, on which sat seven judges. The presiding judge, the Court's President, Dr. Karl Schmidt, made some effort to be fair — he was brusque with defendants who were obviously lying — and treated Allied witnesses with courtesy. Schmidt conducted the questioning. The ostensible prosecutor, who made no secret of the pain his job caused him, played a minimal role. The courtroom was packed with highly partisan crowds. Cheers and jeers repeatedly interrupted the proceedings. The defendants were regarded as national heroes and were mobbed by supporters on their way in and out of the courtroom.[16]

For the Belgian victims of August 1914, the Leipzig trials were an utter fiasco.

Of the more than 3,000 names of war criminals originally collected by the Allies, Belgium had submitted around 1,100. When the total number was reduced first to 1,043, and then, in January 1920, to 854, the Belgian total was slashed to 334.[17] The final capitulation came on February 13, when it was decided that only 45 individuals would face charges in Leipzig. Just fifteen of these men were accused of crimes against Belgians, and among them were individuals who had allegedly mistreated prisoners of war and abused civilians during the long occupation. Of those individuals who were implicated in the crimes of August 1914, all were involved in the massacre at Andenne. None would ever have to answer for his actions. Only one German would be put on trial for activities in Belgium, and he would be acquitted.

The unlucky German was Max Ramdohr, an officer in the Secret Military Police, who was accused of torturing children in the town of

Geraardsbergen (Grammont) in East Flanders during the occupation. Ramdohr was trying to obtain information about sabotage of the railway lines south of the town. The case had excited indignation in Belgium and the Ministry of Justice naïvely assumed it would likewise appeal to the sentiments of ordinary Germans. The officer's activities were illegal as well as immoral: according to Section 56 of the German Penal Code, no one under thirteen could be prosecuted for a crime. But there was a Catch 22: German law also forbade witnesses under thirteen from testifying under oath, and as several of the Belgians called to the stand were still underage, their evidence was disregarded.[18] Even those permitted to testify were accused of "strong bias" against their torturer, who, the court concluded, had "merely fulfilled his duty."[19] The children, the judges decided, had been influenced by stories of "alleged atrocities," and as a result, may have been victims of a mass delusion.[20]

As in all the other cases, the court took great pains to prove that the defendant was only following orders, always stipulating that it was not passing judgment on the justification for the orders. Evidence from Ramdohr's colleagues and superiors about his excellent character weighed heavily, and the court carefully documented inconsistencies in the boys' testimony about the times, frequency, and duration of their torture.[21] The accused was the son of a Leipzig physician, and the crowd in the courtroom was even more demonstrative than at other trials.

In the end, despite the Court's admission that "the accused, in his endeavor, commendable in itself, to carry out his instructions, employed measures which were legally forbidden," Ramdohr was acquitted.[22] The Belgians were outraged, and the delegation left Leipzig immediately. The German government was informed that Belgium would itself enforce articles 227–230, an empty threat without the power of extradition.

The French walked out as well. Their case against General Karl Stenger implicated the highest officer against whom charges were brought at Leipzig. Unlike the Belgian case, the overwhelming evidence that Stenger had ordered the murder of wounded soldiers and prisoners included testimony by German soldiers and officers — a few of whom refused to carry out the order, including Major Benno Crusius, himself a defendant. There was, however, no written order, and other officers in Stenger's brigade (apart from Crusius) swore that the General had merely made an off-hand comment that French soldiers who began firing from the rear after pretending to be wounded should be shot (as if captured soldiers would not have been disarmed). Major Crusius was found to be deranged, and was sentenced to two years for "misinterpreting" Stenger's comment.[23] (Interestingly, it appears that Stenger originally issued the order after being alarmed by random shots fired nearby following an engagement with the enemy.) Owing to the French prosecution, Stenger became a national hero. Thunderous applause followed the defiant speech with which he concluded his defense.

When the French walked out after Stenger's acquittal, a total of six Germans had been tried on French and Belgian evidence. Only one, Major Crusius, was convicted. The moral was obvious.

The British fared somewhat better.[24] Five of the six men tried on British evidence were found guilty, though their sentences were derisory.[25]

While the Solicitor General and other British representatives at the trials expressed their satisfaction with the outcome, despite the leniency of the sentences, the Leipzig verdicts were received with nearly as much indignation in London as in Brussels and Paris.[26] The trials were "an ignominious farce," in the view of a British general and former law professor charged with investigating war crimes. "To call it window dressing," he wrote, "would be to pay it too high a compliment."[27] "Cruelty was no crime when they inflicted it," concluded the secretary of the department that had monitored the treatment of British prisoners of war.[28]

Endnotes

PREFACE

1. Easily the two most influential dismissals of the events of August were Arthur Ponsonby's *Falsehood in Wartime* (London, 1928) and James Read's more scholarly *Atrocity Propaganda, 1914–1919* (New Haven, 1941). For detailed examinations of these two books see page 611–623 and 640–647 of the first edition of *Rehearsals*. So persuasive did academics find these tendentious investigations that no original research appeared on the subject in English until the mid-1990s. The contributions of two German scholars, Peter Schöller (*Der Fall Löwen und das Weissbuch* (Köln, 1958)) and Lothar Wieland (*Belgien 1914* (Frankfurt, 1984)), were ignored.

2. It is always disheartening to see one's work misrepresented, and this happened a couple of times. A reviewer in the *American Historical Review* declared that I believe in a German "national character" that is "innately barbaric." I don't, of course, and didn't state or suggest it anywhere in the book. A reviewer in the *English Historical Review* took a different tack, claiming I had not discussed subjects to which I had in fact devoted many pages. Among these were the movements of the German armies preceding the killings and recent work on the franc-tireur question. For a full response to these and other accusations by the two reviewers, the curious can click on the link on the following page: http://www.jefflipkes.com/_i_rehearsals_the_german_army_in_belgium_august_1914_i_64078.htm.

3. This perception of the war fueled the outrage at the perfidious Anglo-Saxons, who had betrayed their kith and kin for a scrap of paper.

4. E. St. Clair Stobart, "Within the Enemy's Lines," *Fortnightly Review* (1914), 670–684; H. Gibson, *A Journal from our Legation in Belgium* (Garden City, NY, 1917), 162–3.

5. Hamburg Institute for Social Research, *The German Army and Genocide* (New York, 1999), 8.

6. To take but one small contingency, had Wilhelm I died young and Friedrich III lived to a ripe old age, it is possible that public opinion in early 20th century Germany might have differed in subtle and perhaps not so subtle ways. The Anglo-German alliance negotiations of 1898–1902 might then have had a different outcome.

7. For a glance at the *Sonderweg* question, see section 5 of the Afterword.

8. J. Horne and A. Kramer, *German Atrocities 1914* (New Haven, 2000), 92–93. M. Abbenhuis, *American Historical Review* (June 2008, v. 113, n. 3), 930.

9. Along with a rejection of quantification was a disenchantment with an exclusive focus on deep structures and on the material world and demographics. "The Revival of Narrative: Reflections on a New Old History," *Past and Present*, n. 85 (Nov. 1979), 3–24, reprinted in *The Past and the Present Revisited* (London, 1987), 74–98.

10. *The Past and Present Revisited*, 88.

11. S. De Schaepdrijver, *English Historical Review*, (August 2009, v. 124, n. 509), 1002.

12. Horne and Kramer, *German Atrocities*, 2. Typical also is the observation of another historian: "In many ways, however, the accuracy of atrocity reports is less relevant to the cultural history of the war than the fact that they were widely disseminated and commonly believed. Regardless of whether these tales were literally 'true' (as some historians now claim) or merely the fantastic and cynical fabrications of Allied publicists, atrocities gave concrete meaning to the complex diplomatic issues that had brought about the conflict."(N. Gullace, "Sexual Violence and Family Honor: British Propaganda and International Law during the First World War," *American Historical Review* (v. 101, n. 3), 716.

13. Some German testimony has been drawn upon: *Die völkerrechtswidrige Führung des belgischen Volkskriegs*, the German White Book, a compendium of affidavits by officers and soldiers, along with captured war diaries and letters, and interviews with

prisoners of war by French interrogators, one published, one not.

PROLOGUE

1. According to the tables of the second, post-war Belgian Commission of Inquest, 5,946 individuals were killed by the Germans, apart from fatalities inadvertently caused by shellfire and other acts of war. The total number of structures burned is impossible to calculate, because several towns and villages reported only that "many buildings were burned," "three-quarters of all homes were destroyed," etc. With conservative estimates for what the numbers might have been in the latter cases, the total is 24,895. (This figure would appear to include almost exclusively buildings intentionally burned – no structures are listed as having been destroyed in Ieper, for instance – but in a few cases includes the results of bombardments intended to punish a town, as happened in Dendermonde.)

2. It is instructive to compare this film, released in 1996, with its 1964 predecessor, CBS News' "World War I." The latter documentary, narrated by a stern-voiced Robert Ryan, attempts to acquaint its audience with the strategic objectives of the general staffs, the major battles, the political and economic developments on the home front, and the significant turning points in the war. Jay Winters' successor, reflecting post-'60s sensibilities as well as the triumph of social history over military and diplomatic history, is far more preoccupied with the war's impact on representative individuals, especially on the home front. While students appreciate the detailed examination of the trees, the forest often vanishes. With the unsentimental S. L. A. Marshall as lead consultant, the earlier documentary provides a more accurate appraisal of the invasion of Belgium.

3. The book published as a companion to the PBS series does not improve on the documentary. "The old traditions also called for the end of [sic] a country's hostilities when its army was beaten on the battlefield," readers are informed, after a description of the fall of the Liège forts, when the entire Belgian Army was still stationed behind the Gete, awaiting the invader. "Belgium fought differently." The "sensitive and intelligent" Moltke is quoted as claiming, "'we are fighting for our lives and all who get in the way must take the consequences.'" "On that day," the authors continue, "a number of Belgian priests had been executed for encouraging resistance to the invasion. But the Belgians needed little encouragement from their priests, as snipers shot at German soldiers laden with 25 kg packs on their backs through fields and villages." The authors concede that the German Army "responded with an iron fist... The medieval town of Leuven was heavily shelled." (In reality, not a single shell hit the town, just as there is no evidence any priest encouraged armed resistance by civilians or any civilian fired on German soldiers.) The section concludes with a long, generalized descant by a German infantryman on the horrors of war. (J. Winter, B. Baggett, *The Great War and the Shaping of the 20th Century* (New York, 1996), 65, 66.

4. T. Woods, *The Politically Incorrect Guide to American History* (Washington D.C., 2004), 110, 111. Even some Belgian historians have no wish to enlighten their readers as to what happened in August 1914. The only reference to the killing of civilians in P. Belien's *A Throne in Brussels* (Exeter, UK, 2005) is the following: "A decade earlier the royal propaganda staff had appreciated how effectively Leopold II's adversaries had exploited pictures of children with their hands cut off. Now they concocted stories of German soldiers chopping off the hands of little Belgians and used these to win international sympathy for Albert's cause." (151–2.)

5. Nonetheless, see the conclusion of the Appendix for a discussion for one of the more likely cases of severed hands. There is evidence also that the infamous "crucified Canadian" may have existed. An inquiry was conducted by the British government after German protests following the unveiling of a bas-relief representing the soldier, entitled "A Canadian Golgotha," at a 1919 exhibition in Ottawa. At least two credible witnesses from different regiments independently confirmed under oath seeing a Canadian soldier on 23 April 1915 who had been attached to a barn door outside St. Julien with bayonets through either his wrists or hands. (This would have been the

day after the first German gas attack.) One man observed him on his left as he headed toward the front, the other on his right as he returned with wounded. (NA, FO 395/304.)

6. The first is the controversy ignited initially by Fritz Fischer's *Griff nach der Weltmacht* (euphemistically translated into English as *Germany's Aims in the First World War*) and then by his *Krieg der Illusionen (War of Illusions)*. The furor, it is important to note, was largely confined to Germany, where historians were apparently unfamiliar with Luigi Albertini's magisterial three volume history of the war's origins.

The most important document introduced in *Griff nach der Weltmacht* was Beth-mann Hollweg's "September Program," which revealed that the distinction between the "Annexationists" and their opponents was more verbal than real. The second book drew on new evidence from diaries, particularly that of Admiral von Müller, and dispatches from military representatives of southern German states, to show that Germany's leaders were long agreed on the necessity of a pre-emptive strike against France and Russia, and that civilians in government willingly accepted the role assigned to them, that of getting the socialists on board and keeping the British neutral. Despite the ire of his critics, the case against Fischer and his supporters Röhl and Geiss was less than overwhelming. The diary of the Chancellor's secretary was adduced to show that the Philosopher of Hohenfinow was well-intentioned but depressed and pessimistic in 1914. The diary had been tampered with after the war, unfortunately. More substantive criticisms were made of Fischer's explanation for the economic basis of German foreign policy.

In the *Sonderweg* controversy, historians of Germany from Weber and Veblen forward had argued that the long-standing boast of German uniqueness was essentially correct, but nothing to be proud of. A supine *Burgerstand* was to blame. Having failed to pull off a revolution like its English and French counterparts, the middle classes permitted themselves to be co-opted by reactionary Junkers. Some of the problems with this thesis were pointed out by two British historians, Geoff Eley

and David Blackbourn. However, even if it is conceded that the middle classes were able to achieve many of their "aims" without fighting under the banner of liberalism – advanced capitalism flourished, professionalization and educational and social reforms proceeded apace in the *Kaiserreich*, the middle class dominated local governments, etc. – and if we concede as well that the *Mittelstand's* British and French cousins were hardly impervious to aristocratic tastes and values – the argument that the German bourgeoisie was not liberal merely because it didn't have to be is not entirely persuasive. However, the germane question as far as understanding what happened in Belgium is not whether or not the middle class thrived under the Bismarckian state because it had managed to pull off a "silent revolution," but why it was so profoundly illiberal. Why, for example, were young middle-class Germans such zealous duelists, when dueling had died out in the rest of Europe, and why were duels so often fatal?(K. McAleer, *Dueling: The Cult of Honor in Fin de Siecle Germany* (Princeton, 1994); U. Frevert, *Ehrenmänner: Das Duell in der bürgerliche Gesellschaft* (München, 1991)) Why the torrent of blood-curdling pamphlets and articles from the late 1890s through the war years making the case for the inevitability and justice of Germany's *Griff nach der Weltmacht*, marrying Social Darwinism, *völkisch* ideology, and German Idealism? The authors were seldom Junkers, and not infrequently came from the ranks of the National Liberal Party. (The classic history of German Liberalism in English, James Sheehan's, *German Liberalism in the Nineteenth Century*, disposes of its subject in a mere 283 pages, without the notes. Leonard Krieger's no less celebrated *The German Idea of Freedom* runs to 470 pages before it knocks off in 1870, and seems longer. "The English Idea of Freedom" could be disposed of in about a third the length, whereas a comprehensive history of English Liberalism would require three times the pages of Sheehan's book.)

The third controversy, the notorious *Historikerstreit*, was set off by an essay by Ernst Nolte in 1986 rejecting the *Sonderweg* thesis, but not on the grounds that Hitler represented a radical break with the past.

Rather he was merely an imitator of the century's only true revolutionary movement, Bolshevism. Animated by legitimate fears of Soviet Communism, Hitler unfortunately copied its methods. Instead of exterminating "class enemies," he exterminated "racial" enemies, confusing Jews with Bolsheviks. Half-truths are half true. Communist murderousness was all too real and was reported, sometimes quite accurately, by the tens of thousands of Russian refugees in Berlin, and Jews were disproportionately represented in the leadership of the GPU and NKVD. But just as German voters did not suddenly awaken to the Bolshevik threat between 1928, when the Nazis received 2.6% of the vote, and 1932, when their total rocketed to 37.4%, so Hitler did not need to be instructed by Russians. His murderous hatreds were conceived in Vienna in the decade before the First World War, and executed when the opportunity presented itself during the Second.

The behavior of German voters also creates problems for the Goldenhagen thesis of 1996. Hilter's antisemitism was well known in 1928, but the NSDAP received a smaller percentage of the vote than the antisemitic parties of the 1890s, whose combined total peaked at 4.6% before declining dramatically, hardly evidence of an endemic "eliminationist" antisemitism that led inexorably to the Holocaust. While a potent strain of antisemitism persisted in Germany from the '90s, this does not explain the violence visited on non-Jewish civilians in neighboring countries during the 20th century, nor the behavior of Latvian, Lithuanian, and other "auxiliaries" during World War II.

7.   As human types, the lanky, lugubrious Philosopher of Hohenfinow and the dwarfish Propaganda Minister, haranguing crowds in a black leather jacket, could hardly be more unalike (though Bethmann never wrote a line of philosophy, while Goebbels, with a Ph.D. in literature, had studied the subject at Bonn and Heidelberg). But Bethmann could be nearly as disingenuous as *die giftige Kröte* (the poisonous toad). Compare the Chancellor's acknowledgment of the gravity of Austrian military action against Serbia in February 1913 (the impossibility of Russian acquiescence to the dismemberment of

that country) with his pretended obliviousness in July 1914. Compare the reports of French attacks on German forces and German civilians on August 2nd and 3rd with reports of Polish attacks against Germany on August 31, 1939. Compare his statement on September 6, 1914, that "young Belgian girls have torn out the eyes of defenseless wounded on the battlefield" with Goebbels' reports on the atrocities committed against German residents in Danzig (some of which actually occurred.) For further evidence of the Chancellor's deceitfulness, see the correspondence between Grey and Rumbold and Goshen in Berlin following the issuing of the "blank cheque" to Austria-Hungary on July 5 in J. W. Headlam-Morley (ed.), *The Outbreak of War, v. XI: Foreign Office Documents, July 28th–August 4th, 1914* (London, 1926), and compare the reports of the ambassador and secretary of the embassy with the Chancellor's dispatches prior to July 30th in M. Montgelas and W. Schücking, *Outbreak of War: German Documents Collected by Karl Kautsky* (New York, 1924), particularly numbers 323, 361, 385, telegrams 174, 181, and 187. For fuller discussions of the extent of German knowledge of Austria's plans, German incitement of Vienna, and misrepresentations of both to London, see Chapters 10 and 11 in L. Albertini, *The Origins of the War of 1914*, v. 2 (New York, 2005 [1952].), Chapters 4, 7, 17, and 22 in F. Fischer, *War of Illusions* (New York, 1975), and the pithy summaries by J. Rohl, "Germany," in K. Wilson, *Decisions for War, 1914* (New York, 1995), 27–54, and *1914: Delusion or Design* (New York, 1973), 21–77, and by I. Geiss, *July 1914* (New York, 1974), 361–75. In his correspondence with Vienna, Bethmann Hollweg's overriding concern is to manipulate world opinion, viz., to make it appear as if Russia is guilty of precipitating the war. (See numbers 323, 385, and 441, telegrams 174, 187, and 200, among others.) The German Ambassador is pointedly advised on July 28 "to avoid very carefully giving rise to the impression that we wish to hold Austria back," (number 395, telegram 192) and when he is finally asked to urge Vienna to accept Grey's "Halt in Belgrade" proposal, it is purely for cosmetic reasons, (number 441, telegram 200) and a message two hours later orders him to ignore this instruction. (number 450, telegram 202) Convinced that the *Westminster Gazette* was the official organ of the Liberal Government, Bethmann took extraordinary measures to get the newspaper to publish his toothless warning to Vienna on July 30 of a "world conflagration." (number 396, telegram 193) (British Library, Spender Papers, Ad. Ms. 46392) The cable may even have been drafted for British consumption.

8. For a recent discussion, see I. Hull, *Absolute Destruction: Military Culture and the Practices of War in Imperial Germany* (Ithaca, 2005).

9. It was unquestionably the invasion of Belgium that was responsible for the British entry into the war and the treatment of civilians that reconfirmed that decision and spurred enlistments. Had Britain not dispatched its army to the continent, the war, and the remainder of the 20th century, would certainly have taken a far different course.

10. See R. J. Rummel, *Death by Government* (New Brunswick, 1997). While the final totals need to be regarded with caution, the range of his estimates is impressive.

CHAPTER 1: AN ULTIMATUM

1. Many historians, following Albertini, incorrectly give his first name as Klaus. All foreign countries having diplomatic relations with Belgium, with the exception of the papacy, were represented by ministers rather than ambassadors and maintained legations rather than embassies.

2. B. Whitlock, *Belgium, A Personal Narrative*, v. 1 (New York, 1920), 1.

3. *Ibid.*, 3.

4. On the lack of co-ordination between the General Staff of the Army and the Admiralty, Chancellory, and Foreign Office concerning Germany's war plans, see G. Ritter, *The Schlieffen Plan* (Westport, CT, 1979), 89–96 and L. Albertini, *The Origins of the War of 1914*, v. 3 (London, 1952), 236–53. The German Ambassador to Britain, Prince Max Lichnowski, bitterly complained that he "was always left in ignorance about important events." (H. Young, *Prince Lichnowski and the Great War* (Athens, GA, 1977), 92.) Most military historians appear not to have been convinced by Terrence Zuber's claim that the Schlieffen Plan never existed until it was invented after the

war as an excuse for the German Army's failure to defeat the French in September 1914. (*Inventing the Schlieffen Plan* (Oxford, 2002)). See Chapter 2, note 50.

5. A. de Bassompierre, "La nuit du 2 au 3 aout 1914," *Révue des Deux Mondes* (Paris) 15 February 1916, 884–906, 890; A. Klobukowski, *Souvenirs de Belgique* (Brussels, 1928), 80–81.

6. Klobukowsi, 63–4.

7. Bassompierre, 891.

8. "The Belgian Grey Book," in *Collected Diplomatic Documents Relating to the Outbreak of the War* (London, 1915), 308–9.

9. Bassompierre, 892.

10. J. Crokaert, "L'Ultimatum allemand," *Le Flambeau* (Brussels) 31 March 1922, 305–30, 309.

11. *Ibid.*, 308–10.

12. For the same reason, and also not to offend the Belgians, the Foreign Ministry had earlier altered the demand by Chief of Staff General Helmut von Moltke that the Kingdom "take the side of Germany." "Benevolent neutrality," however pleasing a euphemism, was perfectly meaningless. Interestingly, the phrase that Bethmann-Holweg excised, "at the expense of France," was not in Moltke's original draft. It had been added by Wilhelm Stumm, Political Director of the Foreign Ministry. (Albertini, v. 3, 454.) The Wilhelmstrasse was redrawing the map of Europe well before the notorious "September program" of annexations.

13. M. Montgelas, W. Schücking, eds. *Outbreak of the World War: German Documents Collected by Karl Kautsky* (New York, 1924), 486.

14. Counterfactuals rapidly run into quicksand. France and Russia would certainly not have precipitated a war by invading Germany, had Germany not struck first. Russia, even after mobilization, was quite prepared to continue negotiations. For no country in Europe, apart from Germany, did mobilization mean immediate war. But if Germany had struck eastward, as pre-Schlieffen war plans had called for, and France had responded by launching an offensive into Alsace and Lorraine, it is more than likely that Britain would have stood aside at the outset. (Albertini III, 373; G.P. Gooch and H. Temperley, eds., *British Documents on the Origins of the War, 1898–1914*, v. XI (J. W.

Headlam-Morley, ed. (London, 1926), 180.)
With the defeat of Russia, France would
have been tempted to sue for peace.

15. Montgelas, *Outbreak*, 486.

16. Crokaert, 310.

17. M. Hurst (ed.), *Key Treaties for the Great
Powers, 1814–1914*, v. 1 (New York, 1972),
242. At the outbreak of the Franco-Prussian War, anxieties ran so high in London
that Gladstone drew up two new treaties,
one with each of the belligerents, pledg-
ing to cooperate in the defense of Belgium
should the army of the other country cross
its border. (Hurst, 455–8.) An expeditionary force of 20,000 was readied for such an
eventuality. (H. C. G. Mathew, *Gladstone,
1809–1874* (London, 1988), 184.) (Gladstone was especially alarmed by a memorandum Bismarck leaked to the London
Times at the outbreak of hostilities. Four
years earlier the French Ambassador to
Berlin had indiscretely committed to paper
a quid pro quo proposed by Napoléon III
whereby, in exchange for French recog-
nition of the union of the South German
states with Prussia, Bismarck would consent to France's annexation of Belgium.)
Gladstone's soaring rhetoric was recalled in
London and Brussels in 1914: "the day that
witnessed Belgium's absorption would hear
the death-knell of public right and public
law." The annihilation of Belgium would be
"the direst crime that ever stained the pages
of history." (E. Cammaerts, *Albert of Belgium* (New York, 1935), 95.)

Yet another treaty reinforced the country's sense of security, the Fifth Convention
of the second Hague Conference, issued in
1907, and treating in detail "the rights and
duties of neutral powers and persons." Not
only was the territory of neutrals inviolable
(Article I), but belligerents were "forbidden
to allow troops or trains of ammunition or
provisions" to cross their borders (Article
II). Article V admonished neutrals not to
tolerate the least violation of the treaty's
strictures, and Article X stipulated that any
measures taken to defend a nation's neutrality were not to be regarded as hostile
acts. (L. Friedman (ed.), *The Law of War:
A Documentary History* (New York, 1972),
325). The German Empire, which had
assumed Prussia's international legal obligations in 1871 and had signed the Hague

Conventions in 1907, was thus violating two
solemn pledges on the night of August 2nd.
The confidence of Belgians in these paper
guarantees was such that during various
debates in Parliament over the funding of
the Army and the forts, it was occasionally
suggested, only half in jest, that the country's sole defense should consist of posting
copies of the Treaty of London at all border
crossings.

18. Bassompierre, 893. Below was, in fact,
still agitated. Hugh Gibson, Secretary at
the American Legation, passed the German Minister on his return trip. Below was
sweating profusely and puffing mechanically on a cigarette, and failed to give Gibson his usual ceremonious greeting. (H.
Gibson, *A Journal from our Legation in Belgium* (Garden City, 1917), 9.)

19. The title "Prime Minister" was not used in
Belgium until after the war. The *chef du cabinet*, though he did not serve in parliament
and was not necessarily the leader of the
party with a plurality in the chamber of deputies (though he had secured the support of
the majority in parliament), nonetheless
performed most of the duties of that office.

20. Bassompiere, 894, 896; Crokaert, 313–14.

21. Bassompierre, 897.

22. These were first made use of by R. Dev-
leeshouwer, *Les Belges et le danger de guerre*
(Brussels, 1958). In 1981, M-R. Thielemans
and E. Vanderwoude reviewed the entire
controversy and the discussion that follows
owes much to their article "Les conseils des
ministres et de la Couronne du 2 auot 1914:
recherche méthodologique sur la valeur
des témoignages." *Histoire et Méthode IV*
(1981), 417–444.

23. General Selliers de Moranville, the army's
Chief of Staff, attempting to substantiate his
version of the military discussion, wrote to
all of the surviving members of the Crown
Council in 1921, soliciting their views on
the account published by his rival, General
Louis de Ryckel. Both generals had forgotten that they had crossed swords at the earlier meeting. Selliers was no doubt disappointed that so many members replied that
they had no recollection of the exchange.
(A. Selliers de Moranville, "Le Conseil de
la Couronne du 2 aout 1914," *Le Flambeau*
(Brussels) 21 August 1921, 449–69, 463–8.)

24. *Ibid.*, 458.

25. *Ibid.*, 458–9.
26. L. de Ryckel, Memoires (Brussels, 1920), 288; E Galet, *King Albert in the Great War* (Boston, 1931), 47.
27. Galet 35–48. The overly impetuous De Ryckel and the overly cautious Selliers were simultaneously relieved of their commands on September 6th. De Ryckel was sent to Russia as an attaché and Selliers was dispatched to the rear as inspector-general of the army. Control of the Belgian forces was now entirely in the hands of the King.
28. Galet, 46.
29. Tielemans and Vanderwoude, 440.
30. Crockaert, 318.
31. Tielemans and Vanderwoude, 433. Woeste, a Catholic convert, was the son of a Prussian diplomat.
32. *Ibid.*, 436. When told by the officer sent to fetch him that there was to be an emergency meeting of the Crown Council that night, Greindl had exclaimed, "What's going on? Are the British disembarking on our territory?" (*Ibid.*, 437).
33. Crokaert, 315.
34. *Ibid.*, 318.
35. Albertini, 463.
36. Crokaert, 323.
37. I. Wullus-Rudiger, *La Belgique et l' équilibre européen* (Paris, 1933), 120.
38. "Belgian Grey Book," *Collected Diplomatic Documents*, 311–312. Albertini calls it "the noblest document produced by the whole crisis." (Albertini, v. 3, 465)
39. Crokaert, 322.
40. *Ibid.*
41. *Ibid.*, 330.
42. *Ibid.*
43. *Ibid.*, 328.
44. Bassompierre, 899.
45. Mongelas, *Outbreak*, 511.
46. *Ibid.*, 519.
47. *Ibid.*, 554.
48. Whitlock, a novelist before he entered politics, vividly described the scene. Flags flapped from every building, wildly enthusiastic crowds surged along rue Royale as the King and his entourage made their way to the Palais de la Nation. The King dismounted and strode through the hall to the repeated cries of *"Vive le Roi."* Glancing at his wife and children seated on the dias behind him, adjusting his prince-nez, Albert declared that he now saw before him only one party. When he asked the deputies if they were prepared to defend "the sacred heritage of our ancestors," the entire audience leapt to its feet, arms raised, chanting, "Yes, yes, yes!" After reading the German ultimatum and the Belgian response and describing briefly the military situation, the King paused and looked out over the assembly. "I have faith in our destiny," he said solemnly. "A country which defends itself gains the respect of all. Such a country will not perish. God will be with us in this just cause! Long live independent Belgium."

"The mad, passionate applause breaks, all unrestrained now," Whitlock reported. "Handkerchiefs are waved, then pressed to weeping eyes... The King seizes his kepi, the Queen and the little princes rise, and the King stalks out, sword clanking; away on stern business now!

"And I find myself leaning over the balcony rail, a catch in my throat, my eyes moist.

"Then that stillness again in the chamber, intense, vibrant with emotion, the thrill of patriotism, the sense of tragedy..." (Whitlock, 59–61.)
49. Whitlock, 63–4.
50. *Ibid.*, 64.
51. Baron Beyens, *Germany Before the War* (London, 1916), 10.
52. Shortly before a birthday dinner for the Kaiser at Potsdam in January, 1904, the Emperor buttonholed the King. As Leopold listened incredulously, Wilhelm sketched for him the prospect of a revived Burgundian empire with the King at its head. French Flanders, Artois, the entire Ardennes might be his. "In the formidable struggle which will take place, Germany is certain of victory, but this time you will be obliged to choose. You will be with us or against us. If you are with us, I shall give you the Flemish Provinces which France took from you, in defiance of all right... You will become the sovereign of a powerful kingdom. Think of what I offer you and what you may expect." (Cammaerts, 108–9.) The King was appalled. He laughed nervously and then reminded the Kaiser that France had seized the provinces in the 17th century, and that some time had elapsed since then. But even if he were interested, he went on, neither his ministers nor Parliament would

ever consent.

The Kaiser was indignant at Leopold's lighthearted dismissal of the proposal, and especially at its contemptible grounds. A monarch was responsible only to God, not to ministers and parliaments, he told the King of the Belgians. If Belgium didn't side with Germany, he would be guided only by strategic considerations. The threat could hardly have been more explicit.

The other guests at dinner couldn't help noticing how upset Leopold looked and how sullen the Kaiser appeared. After dinner, the King took Chancellor von Bülow aside. "The Emperor has told me appalling things," he said gravely. "I rely on your good influence, your wisdom and your *savoir faire* to avoid great calamities." (B. Von Bülow, *Memoirs of Prince von Bülow*, v. 2 (Boston, 1931), 84.) So agitated was Leopold that on the way to the station he put on his Prussian Dragoons helmet backwards.

In December 1909, Leopold died and was succeed by his nephew, to the immense relief of most Belgians. Early the following year, King Albert paid a visit to Berlin. The burden of the Crown Prince's welcoming speech was how pleased Germans were that, with the marriage of the young king – a Hohenzollern on his mother's side – to a Bavarian princess, the two countries were so closely linked by the German blood of their sovereigns. (Beyens, *Germany*, 324.)

During the return visit in April, the Kaiser offered Albert some unsolicited advice. "Why grant so many audiences, and to men of no account?" he asked. "You have your policy – it is for them to follow it."

"My country and I, we make our policy together," Albert explained.

"But we Hohenzollerns are God's deputies," the Kaiser replied crossly. Albert was sufficiently nonplussed to confide the exchange to his Prime Minister. (T. Aronson, *The Coburgs of Belgium* (London, 1968), 166.)

In December 1912, King Albert's mother, the Countess of Flanders, died. The selection of her older brother, Leopold, a member of the Catholic branch of the Hohenzollerns, to occupy the vacant Spanish throne had eventually precipitated the Franco-Prussian War, even though he speedily withdrew his candidacy. The Countess's younger brother, Charles, had had better luck in the east: he had become King Carol of Rumania. When the Belgian Minister, Baron de Gaiffier, arrived at the Royal Palace in Bucharest to express his condolences on the death of the King's much-beloved sister, Carol felt moved to offer an undisguised warning to the diplomat. "Frankly, no account will be taken of your neutrality," he said. "The miracle of 1870 will not be repeated." The message was taken very seriously. It had come from a Hohenzollern. (Cammaerts, 132.)

The next warning Albert received was from a still more unimpeachable source, the Kaiser himself. Albert returned to Berlin in November, 1913. The occasion was a dinner in his honor following a visit to the Sixteenth Dragoons, headquartered at Lüneburg in Hannover. (Albert was an honorary colonel in the regiment.) Earlier in the year, the Belgian military attaché in Berlin, Major de Melotte had been sought out several times by General von Moltke. On each occasion the Chief of Staff wished to know exactly what Belgium would do in the event her territory was invaded. When told Belgium would defend her neutrality, Moltke pressed the major as to exactly what was meant by the phrase. (In response, King Albert approved a memorandum drafted by his friend and Military Adviser, Captain Galet. "We are resolved," Galet wrote defiantly, "to declare war at once on any Power which deliberately violates the smallest portion of our territory, to wage this war with the utmost energy and with the whole of our military resources wherever required, even beyond our frontiers, and to continue to wage war after the invader has vacated our territory, until the conclusion of a general peace." (Galet, 22–23) The memorandum did little to deflect skepticism in both Paris and Berlin.)

On November 6, 1913, there were three conversations before and after dinner, obviously co-ordinated. First the Kaiser spoke with the King, then Moltke spoke with Albert, and finally the Chief of Staff conferred once again with Major de Melotte. As the two monarchs toured Sans-Souci late in the afternoon, Wilhelm warned Albert that war with France was inevitable and imminent. France, the Kaiser claimed, wanted war. When the King attempted to convince him that this was quite untrue, Wilhelm reminded him of his Hohenzollern pedigree. He would do well to remember his ties to the Kaiser. There was no bribe this time.

After the meal, Moltke enlarged on the Kaiser's theme. "This time we must make an end of it," he told the King, "and your Majesty cannot imagine the irresistible enthusiasm which will permeate the entire German nation on 'The Day.'" The war would be terribly destructive – "the *furor teutonicus* will overrun everything" – but victory would never be in doubt, and the vanquished would suffer. Small nations would have to make choices, and Belgium would be well advised to join with the victor if it wished to preserve its independence, the Chief of Staff added, without a soupçon of irony.

Moltke then cornered de Melotte and reiterated and amplified on his warnings. (Baron Beyens, *Deux Années à Berlin, 1912–1914*, v. 2 (Paris, 1931), 47–53; J. Stengers, "Guillaume II et le Roi Albert a Potsdam en novembre 1913," *Académie royale des sciences, des lettres et des beauxarts de Belgique: Bulletin de la Classe des lettres et des sciences morales et politiques*, v. iv (1993), 234; Galet, 23.) The failure of the Belgian, French, and British General Staffs to anticipate a full-scale invasion across the Hesbaye plain is one of the great mysteries of the war. In the U.K. alone at least four articles in the major reviews provided persuasive evidence that such an invasion would take place.

53. Beyens, *Germany*, 334.

54. E. Waxweiler, *Belgium, Neutral and Loyal* (New York, 1915), 64–66; Beyens, *Germany*, 346.

CHAPTER 2: LIÈGE

1. The following account is based on a confidential letter (dated the Hague, 8 March 1917) from an anonymous officer who, on August 4, had monitored communications from two reconnaissance platoons despatched by General Leman and from border posts. The name of the recipient has been cut out. Sergeant Peiffer provided the details. (MFA, 285: II; see also L. van der Essen, *The Invasion and the War in Belgium* (London, 1917), 50, who gives the name of the second guard as Henrion.

2. Van der Essen, 50–52.

3. *Ibid.*, 48; *Collected Diplomatic Documents Relating to the European War* (London, 1915), 316.

4. Only about an hour earlier a hot-headed cavalryman, Antoine-Alphonse Fonck, was killed by a patrol of cyclists. Though the Belgian squadrons were under orders merely to observe German troop movement, Fonck fired on a group of uhlans outside Thimister, dispersing them. But cyclists nearby fired back. Today, he stares eternally eastward, his right hand shielding his eyes, in a statue commemorating his courage or folly. (J-L. Lhoest, M. Georis, *Liège, Août 14* (Paris, 1964), 82–85.)

5. An exception was the Hautes Fagnes resort of Francorchamps, where a number of vacationing Bruxellois were stranded when the train service was abruptly cut off. When a well-known attorney, a member of the Brussels Court of Appeals, Emil Laude, was among those massacred on the 8th, the news shocked his colleagues and others in the capital. (GSA, 305 (Francorchamps), Jaspars). Visé was also home to number of middle-class professionals and businessmen with ties to Liège and Brussels.

6. The stories of refugees had been routinely disparaged, Somville noted. Perhaps people would be more willing to believe the testimony of those who remained behind. Aware that the Germans, who were conducting an investigation of their own, were on his trail, Somville fled to the Netherlands in March of 1915, then sailed to England and published an account of what he'd been told, divided into sections covering crimes along the four invasion routes the Germans took. Somville was perhaps the most talented writer describing German war crimes in Belgium, and the events are recounted with a lacerating, Swiftian indignation. The vivid and moving vignettes are not always complete or reliable, however, but the book is nonetheless indispensable.

7. RDE 1, 24, 26–7. As mentioned, those not destroyed in Berlin were taken to Moscow. They are very slowly being returned to Brussels, along with many other files on Belgium seized by the Germans, but are not among the few that have been catalogued and are accessible.

8. J. Keegan, *Opening Moves, August 1914*

(London, 1971), 86.

9. E. Waxweiler, Belgium, *Neutral and Loyal*
    (New York, 1915), 209–1L; van der Essen,
    83–5; Somville, 12,. The offer was dis-
    patched to the U.S. Minister in Brussels,
    Brand Whitlock, and read: "The fortress
    of Liège has been taken by assault after a
    brave defense. The German Government
    most deeply regrets that bloody encounters
    should have resulted from the attitude of the
    Belgian Government; it is only through the
    force of circumstances that they had, owing
    to the military measures of France, to take
    the grave decision of entering Belgium and
    occupying Liège... Now that the Belgian
    Army has upheld the honor of its arms by
    its heroic resistance to a very superior force,
    the German Government beg the King of
    the Belgians and the Belgian Government
    to spare Belgium the further horrors of
    war. The German Government are ready
    for any compact with Belgium which can
    be reconciled with their arrangements with
    France. Germany once more gives her sol-
    emn assurance that it is not her intention
    to appropriate Belgian territory to herself,
    and that such an intention is far from her
    thoughts. Germany is still ready to evacu-
    ate Belgium as soon as the state of war will
    allow her to do so." (B. Whitlock, *Belgium,
    A Personal Narrative*, v. 1, (New York,
    1920), 89–90.)

    Whitlock was not beguiled by the apol-
    ogetic, almost pleading tone, and refused
    to transmit it: "No such offer should soil
    my hands," he wrote. (91) The Germans,
    who had hopefully concluded the origi-
    nal message with the sentence, "The U.S.
    Ambassador here concurs in this attempt
    at mediation by his colleague in Brussels,"
    were obliged to ask the Dutch to transmit
    the proposal.

10. Reply, 84.

11. In Acoz, a lieutenant testified that four dis-
    charged cartridges were found on a man
    named Boucher "or some name like this;"
    a second lieutenant was more positive about
    the name, and identified another individual
    as well, Bastin, though the cartridges and
    weapons, he claimed, were found nearby.
    Particularly damning, in the eyes of the offi-
    cers, was a receipt for a revolver found on
    the person of the priest in whose house the
    men were hiding. (DVF, 44–5.) The men,

who were executed along with the priest,
were, in fact, named Archange and Bour-
boux, and it was not difficult for the authors
of the Belgian Reply to demonstrate how
the testimony of the four officers who provided depositions about the events utterly
failed to support their assumptions. French
troops occupied the town and had requested
all civilians to leave (residents had been
marched in front of German troops to
shield them in a nearby town); Acoz was
abandoned, the doors locked, the windows
shuttered, as the Germans confirm. For
some reason the three unlucky men stayed
behind. Shots came from every house in
the main street and from a side street, the
officers testify, yet the three men were the
only residents located. The hundreds of
guns deposited in the town hall, with a
label on each, which the Germans took as
evidence of a franc-tireur arsenal, were of
course the weapons dutifully turned in to
communal authorities, as required by law
and as occurred in nearly every town and
village in eastern Belgium. The guerillas
of Acoz apparently launched their attack
without their weapons. The three victims
were interrogated, but their replies were
"unintelligible." No doubt they did not
speak German. One officer claims he found
discharged cartridges on one of the civilians, but it is clear from the testimony of the
others that it was soldiers unaccompanied
by an officer who located the men, and then
hauled them before the officers. Each witness, moreover, provides a different account
as to what the men were accused of by the
soldiers. Clearly, they were killed for hiding in the attic of a house that French troops
may have fired from. (Reply, 79–80)

The other occasion on which the Germans identified a franc-tireur is no less
dubious. Arthur Otto Hund, described
only as a reservist in the 12th Company of
the 178th Regiment, testified that he and
two comrades were fired on by the twelve-
year-old son of a lawyer named Adam. One
German was fatally wounded, and the boy
in turn was killed. He was identified by photos in the house in front of the garden where
the shootings occurred. A lawyer named
Adam did indeed own a home in Leffe, contiguous with Dinant. However, he and his
family fled over a week before the Germans

arrived; his only son was twenty-four years old in 1914. The youngest victim in Leffe, moreover, was fourteen years old. (DVF, 169–70; SN, quatrième partie, v. 2, 79–80.)

12. One of the best-documented cases was the trial of Father Joseph Dossogne, the curé of Hockay, near Francorchamps. A German sympathizer, the curé informed his interrogators that he had an old, rusted revolver in the presbytery. The gun had not been fired recently, two of three German witnesses summoned before the tribunal declared that they could not testify that they had seen the curé fire, and no one was hit by a bullet in the vicinity of the presbytery. But on the basis of one soldier's word that he had seen Father Dossogne fire a gun from the church's bell tower, the curé was condemned to death and executed the next morning. (GSA, Brussels: Memoires de Guerre 27/3 Inquest made by Commandant Charles Lemaire.) Similar sham trials were reported in Francorchamps, Herve, Battice, Leuven, and other places, where the accused were given the opportunity to hear the charges against them. (RDE, 420; Tiers and Gilbart, 91; Reply, 81; Anon. [H. de Gruben], *The Germans at Louvain* (London, 1916), 44–5.)

13. An exception was the contribution of a Belgian collaborator, Raf Verhulst, *The Question of the Belgian FrancsTireurs* (Brugge, 1930).

14. Verhulst, 56.

15. *Het Handelsblad* (Antwerp), August 6. Cited by R. Grasshof, *The Tragedy of Belgium* (New York, 1915), 44–45.

16. *Nieuwe Gazet* (Antwerp), August 8th, cited by Verhulst, 58.

17. An example: "Unfortunately, it is only too sad a truth, that the incited fury of the lowest classes led to frightful deeds. The proofs? We cannot serve the thirst for sensation with a cabinet of horrors; the equipment of the German army in this war still lacks test tubes, bottles, and Vickersheimer fluid enough to preserve for exhibition in the war museums the parts of human bodies that were cut off. Hospitals do not receive those that are dead. If Germany should be compelled to undertake a second campaign against the civilized nations of Western Europe, she will not neglect to provide in her organization these items of equipment

that are necessary in the case of such opponents." (Grasshof, 52) As the author was reminded by Belgian opponents, the German Army did not fail to bring a great many cameras. There are plenty of photographs of smiling Germans posing in front of ruined buildings, but none of mutilated corpses.

18. *Le Patriote* (Brussels), August 9th, Verhulst, 67.

19. *Le Patriote* (Brussels), August 14th, Grasshof, 48.

20. L. Mokveld, *The German Fury in Belgium* (New York, 1917), 88–9.

21. Verhulst, 40.

22. *Ibid.*, 40–41.

23. *Ibid.*, 60.

24. Reply, 13–15; J Horne and A. Kramer, *German Atrocities 1914: A History of Denial* (New Haven, 2001), 125–9. German investigators did locate instructions issued to some units of the non-active Garde in the days just before the invasion that could be interpreted as suggesting that more than police-work would be required of them. But there is no record of their being ordered into combat or any evidence that they ever fought German troops. (R. Oszwald, *Der Streit um den belgischen Franktireurkrieg* (Köln, 1931), 73–77, 232–3.) The experience of Georges Locus in Tamines is probably typical. "Each of us received a rifle with only one bullet. We were never taught how to shoot, and personally, I don't know how to. We hung onto our rifles until Tuesday evening [August 18]. Then they made us deposit them in the town hall and they were replaced by batons. For uniforms, we had a smock and an armband." (FSN, Tamines, Georges Locus.)

25. IWM, World War I Atrocities, journal of Miss J. H. Gifford, 93/22/1. (Generally, all cavalrymen were referred to as "uhlans" by witnesses, as all handguns were called "revolvers.") The cavalryman was buried by local peasants. When the Germans discovered the body, several civilians were executed. A fourteen-year-old boy was dragged from behind his mother and shot; another man was tied to a saddle head-down, and the horse was made to gallop in a circle. "Never, never, could I forget the horror of it all," a witness told the headmistress. (*Ibid.*)

26. R. Chambry, *The Truth About Louvain* (London, 1915), 19.

27. "Feldwebel C.", *The Diary of a German Soldier* (New York, 1919), 36–8. Anon., *A German Deserter's War Experience* (New York, 1917), 11–12.

28. RDE 1, 249, 220. The commander apologized to an *échevin* for the execution the following day. Even in the sergeant's account, no one saw the policeman fire nor was a gun found in his possession. Among the more convincing German affidavits in the White Book, see the descriptions of events in Polseur, Tintigny, and Champion in DVF, 8, 11–12; 19–23; 35–37.

29. B. Duhr, *Der Lügengeist im Völkerkrieg: KriegsMärchen* (München, 1915), 11; 11–15. Similarly, he contacted military authorities regarding the charges against the clergy, and these were also categorically denied.

30. F. van Langenhove, *The Growth of a Legend: A Study Based upon the German Accounts of Francs Tireurs and "Atrocities" in Belgium* (New York, 1916), 7.

31. K. Liebknecht, *The Future Belongs to the People* (New York, 1919), 27–8; H. Trotnow, *Karl Liebknecht* (Hamden, CT, 1984), 139.

32. Horne and Kramer, 246.

33. DVF, 244–5.

34. After the war, a book appeared making the case that 128 soldiers were killed by franctireurs. (A. Fonck, *Schrotschüsse in Belgien* (Berlin, 1931)). German critics were skeptical of this number at the time and subsequently. (L. Wieland, *Belgien 1914: Die Frage des belgischen "Franktireurkrieges" und die deutsche öffentliche Meinung von 1914 bis 1936* (Frankfurt am Main, 1984), 327–40.) An internal Foreign Ministry report claimed that 516 officers and men had been killed by civilians, but this was purely a "statistical analysis" and provided no evidence. The government decided that it was not worth publishing. (Horne and Kramer, 397.)

35. RBC, 48–9.

36. Langenhove, 298–307.

37. *Ibid.*, 304.

38. *Ibid.*, 305. To demonstrate his scrupulous objectivity, van Langenhove insisted on relying solely on German sources to refute atrocity allegations.

39. Horne and Kramer, 142.

40. *Ibid.*, 92. They are also indebted to the discussion of *die Franktireurpsychose* in Wieland, 23–31.

41. *Ibid.*, 138.

42. *Ibid.*, 119; A. Banks, *A Military Atlas of the First World War* (Barnsley, S. Yorkshire, 2001) 228–9; P. Haythornthwaite, *The World War One Source Book* (London, 1996), 63–5.

43. Horne and Kramer, 133.

44. *Ibid.*, 132.

45. The "Schlieffen Plan" may be something of a misnomer. But Terrence Zuber's intriguing *Inventing the Schlieffen Plan* (Oxford, 2002) remains controversial. Most military historians are not persuaded that the "Plan" was concocted after the war by generals attempting to protect their reputations and then embraced by foreigners as proof of German aggressiveness, or that the *Grosse Denkschrift* of December 1905 was merely a ploy to persuade the government to increase the size of the Army and represented a whimsical departure from Schlieffen's prior thinking. Exactly when the envelopment of the French Army became the strategic objective of the Imperial Army, when and why changes were made in the number of divisions allotted to the right wing, whether or not the army on the tip of that wing was required to proceed west of Paris, and other important questions are not relevant for our purposes. At some point before 1912, the OHL had adopted a war plan that required a massive invasion of Belgium and a rapid, wheeling advance to the south, and it is convenient to continue to refer to it by the name of the author of the famous *Denkschrift*.

46. N. Ascherson, *The King Incorporated* (New York, 1964), 49; D. Boulger, *The Reign of Leopold II*, v. 2, (London, 1926), 5. The descriptions of the forts that follow are derived from van der Essen, 39–40, 55–56, C. Bronne, "The Defence of Liège," *The English Review*, v. 20 (April 1915), 50–65; J. Buchan, *A History of the Great War*, v. 1 (Boston, 1922), 127–8.

47. Personal communications from David Heal, Colin Fenn, 22 May 2005.

48. de Gruben, 10.

49. This and the following paragraph are based on Keegan, 86–92; Haythornthwaite, 84; B. Tuchman, *August 1914* (London, 1980), 167.

50. The Austrians – that is, the Czechs – were

ahead of the Germans. The Skoda 305 mm, the Austrian counterpart of the Krupp goliath, moved on tank-treads and could be assembled in 45 minutes. (The original Krupp gun took six hours to set up.) Several of the Skodas had been lent to the German army by the Austrians. These, however, were manned by Austrian crews, and as the Empire had not declared war on Belgium – to Germany's chagrin, it failed to declare war even on Russia until August 6 – Vienna was unwilling to let its nationals take part in the invasion. (These scruples would be overcome by the time Namur was invested, though Austria, typically, only got around to declaring war four days after the Namur forts surrendered.) (H. Davignon (ed.), *Belgium and Germany* (London, 1915), 21–22; RVR I, xii–xiii.)

51. van der Essen, 73.

52. G. Somville, *The Road to Liège: the Path of Crime* (London, 1916). I have used Vers Liège: Le Chemin du Crime (Paris, 1915) to amend some of the translations. Somville, 74.

53. *Ibid.*, 74–5.

54. FR, Aprés-Guerre, 76, Soumagne, Melen; Somville, 73, 75, 125; Thier and Gilbart, 124–130, who state the massacres on the 6th took place later in the morning at 7 and 8 a.m.

55. RDE, 341, 608; Thier and Gilbart, 128, which gives the total killed as 128, including 73 from Melen.

56. RDE, 342. The following paragraphs are based on RDE, 25, 342, and Thier and Gilbart, 124.

57. Somville, 78.

58. *Ibid.*, 113.

59. *Ibid.*, 114, 124; RDE, 343.

60. *Ibid.*, 343; Thier and Gilbart, 181–2.

61. *Ibid.*, 181; Somville, 123, 124.

62. *Ibid.*, 119

63. RDE, 343.

64. *Ibid.*, 344.

65. Somville, 124.

66. *Ibid.*, 122–123; Thier and Gilbart, 182.

67. Somville, 114, 120, 123; Thier and Gilbart, 185.

68. Somville, 112; Thier and Gilbart, 145.

69. Thier and Gilbart, 142; Somville, 82–3.

70. Thier and Gilbart, 143.

71. *Ibid.*, 143–4. The following paragraphs are based on Warnier's written account as

reproduced in Thier and Gilbart.

72. Warnier's post-war memoir differs in some details from what she told Gustave Somville in late 1914 or early 1915. It is possible that she repressed some of the awful memories in the interim. It is also conceivable, though unlikely, that she repeated to the journalist what she'd been told by others, or even that she or Somville invented details. In any case, in Warnier's earlier account of the episode, she did not lose consciousness. She heard Nelly gasping for breath and then felt her die on top of her. She heard the screams of Mme. Naval as her husband was about to be shot and listened as the couple's five-year-old boy pleaded with the Germans: "Mr. Soldier, don't do anything bad to Papa. He didn't do anything. He's so good." (Somville, 85)

73. *Ibid.*, 86.

74. *Ibid.*, 86–87; Thier and Gilbart, 147.

75. Somville, 87.

76. RDE, 374.

77. The Germans behaved with incredible savagery at Barchon, massacring thirty-two in a population of 610. The victims ranged in age from one to ninety years old, and included eight girls and women. As at Soumagne and Melen, entire families were slaughtered. The killings commenced on the night of the 14th, six days after the fort of Barchon had surrendered. During the afternoon of the 14th, soldiers were drinking heavily, having pillaged a liquor warehouse. Around 9:00 p.m., residents heard a single gunshot, followed by a second, and then a burst of firing from the center of the village. Then their homes were invaded. An impressive arsenal of incendiary devices was deployed, and soon more than one hundred homes and buildings were on fire. There was no pretense of a trial, needless to say, and the only specific charge the curé heard was that civilians had killed a horse and wounded a soldier. A number of women and girls were raped, including a sixty-two-year-old woman; one girl, Thérèse Renier, was shot for resisting; another woman, Ida Froidmont Rensonnet was shot for protesting the execution of her son. (FR, 79, Visé, Barchon; RDE, 19–20, 339–41; Somville, 152–7; Thier and Gilbart, 16–23.)

78. A copy of the narrative written by the nuns is in the archive of the Diocese of Liège. It

contains a few passages omitted from the version published by the second Committee of Inquest. The extracts from the curé's diary, however, which are included within the sisters' report, are less complete and differ slightly from the excerpts published by Somville and by Thier and Gilbart, which are nearly identical. All three versions differ in turn from a more truncated transcription of the diary that appears in the *Rapports*. Extracts were also published in Reply, 101.

79. T. Ghuysen, *Historique de l' invasion a Blégny Trembleur* (Aubel, 1919), 7.

80. *Ibid.*, 7, 10.

81. RDE, 299; Somville, 157–8.

82. RDE, 298–9, 300; Somville, 158; Ghuysen, 10.

83. RDE, 300–301.

84. *Ibid.*, 303.

85. Somville, 158–9; RBC, 73.

86. Somville, 159; RBC, 73.

87. Other estimates of the group's number were considerably higher: 280, 296. (RBC, 73; Somville, 158.)

88. Thier and Gilbart, 35; Somville, 164.

89. RBC, 73.

90. *Ibid.*, 74.

91. Ghuysen, 18; FR, Visé, La guerre de 1914 à Blégny; Thier and Gilbart, 34–6; Somville, 163–5.

92. RDE, 306.

93. RDE, 311; Somville, 165–6.

94. RBC, 81–82; RDE, 311, 313.

95. RDE, 311. This was the second deliberate provocation witnessed by residents. On the 5th or 6th of August, a leading citizen observed an officer fire his revolver in the air and then whistle. He was immediately surrounded by soldiers shouting *"Man hat geschossen!"* (Somville, 162.)

96. RDE, 311. Earlier, on the 6th, Dr. Reidemester had identified as a German bullet the projectile he extracted from a mortally wounded soldier. He emphasized the fact to the officers present. When interrogated by the Germans the following February, he repeatedly stood by his claim, and demonstrated his familiarity with Belgian, German, and French bullets. (Somville, 161–2.)

97. RDE, 312.

98. *Ibid.*, 311.

99. Somville, 166.

100. *Ibid.*, 167.

101. *Ibid.*, 165.

102. The account that follows draws primarily on the report Fléchet himself submitted to the first Commission of Inquiry. This was issued as the Commission's 16th report on 10 May 1915 (the day the German White Book was released, coincidentally), along with a detailed narrative written by "a substantial inhabitant of Warsage" who wished not to be identified. (RVR 2, 29–45. Fléchet's statement was reproduced by the second Commission, RDE, 289–96.) The paragraphs below also draw on descriptions in Somville, 134–143, and Thier and Gilbart, 236–241.

103. RVR 2, 30, 40.

104. *Ibid.*, 43–4. According to one account, several civilians witnessed the shooting, and one woman was able to identify the soldier responsible, who was arrested by an officer. The "reprisals," however, continued unchecked. (Somville, 138).

105. RVR 2, 43.

106. *Ibid.*, 31.

107. Somville, 138. Within a couple of minutes soldiers faked another franc-tireur incident, according to witnesses. Another shot was discharged and a soldier perched on a munitions wagon fell dramatically to the ground. Soldiers prepared to invade the buildings opposite. But the ruse was too transparent, and an officer intervened, reprimanding the men. The "wounded" soldier scrambled to his feet, clambered aboard the wagon, and the detachment set off once again for Mouland.

108. RVR 2, 32.

109. Somville, 140.

110. RVR 2, 35.

111. *Ibid.*, 36.

112. Somville, 141.

113. Reports, 37.

114. *Ibid.*, 37–8.

115. *Ibid.*, 45.

116. Somville, 177–178.

117. RDE, 317.

118. Somville, 179. Istas may have survived. Thier and Gilbart make no mention of him.

119. RDE, 317.

120. Thier and Gilbart, 213.

121. RDE, 331, 334.

122. *Ibid.*, 329.

123. *Ibid.*, 338.

124. *Ibid.*, 337–9.

125. *Ibid.*, 330.

126. *Ibid.*, 316–317.
127. *Ibid.*, 317.
128. *Ibid.*, 331, 332.
129. *Ibid.*, 322.
130. Thier and Gilbart, 219.
131. *Ibid.*, 214–15.
132. *Ibid.*, 216–17; Somville, 180–1; RDE, 333.
133. Somville, 333.
134. RBC, 78.
135. Mokveld, 74–5.
136. *Ibid.*, 77–8.
137. *Ibid.*, 79.
138. *Ibid.*, 80–82.
139. Thier and Gilbart, 218–19.
140. Somville, 182. The prison camp was located near the *umlautlos* Munster in what was then the province of Hannover, not near the larger and better known Münster in Westphalia.
141. *Ibid.*, 182.
142. *Ibid.*, 183.
143. *Ibid.*, 184.
144. Whitlock, 197–8.
145. *Ibid.*, 198.
146. Mokveld, 84.
147. Somville, 168.
148. *Ibid.*, 169. A German captain did make an effort to recover the objects. He assembled his men and had them open their packs. Nine hundred eighty francs were discovered in a mess kit. (Thier and Gilbart, 288.)
149. Somville, 154–5.
150. Thier and Gilbart, 228–9; RDE, 388.
151. Somville, 171; Thier and Gilbart, 228–231.
152. *Ibid.*, 232.
153. Somville, 173.
154. RDE, 398, 390. According to another, more melodramatic, version, the sergeant killed himself.
155. Somville, 206–7.
156. *Ibid.*, 67.
157. *Ibid.*, 175–6.
158. *Ibid.*, 234.
159. Thier and Gilbart, 255. One of the most persistent myths about the Great War concerns the heroics of Ludendorff, who is supposed to have courageously pounded on the door of the Citadel at Liège and singlehandedly forced it to surrender. The Citadel in fact was undefended; it was not part of the system of forts protecting the Meuse crossings. The object of the forts was not to defend the city of Liège, but to deny passage to German troops.

160. *Ibid.*
161. *Ibid.*, 252.
162. Somville, 234.
163. Thier and Gilbart, 256.
164. RDE, 374, 380, 382; Somville, 209.
165. RDE, 374, 382, 384, 378.
166. GSA, 315 (Liège), Fléron.
167. Somville, 210.
168. RDE, 380–1; Somville, 235.
169. GSA, 315; RDE, 377–8; Somville, 211.
170. RDE, 379.
171. *Ibid.*
172. Somville, 215, 217; RBC, 83, 85–7.
173. *Ibid.*, 86, 87; Somville, 212.
174. RDE, 381–2.
175. *Ibid.*, 378. Somville, 212.
176. Thier and Gilbart, 253–4.
177. Someville, 214; RBC, 84.
178. Somville, 234.
179. *Ibid.*
180. GSA, 315, Bloustein.
181. RDE, 383.
182. Somville, 232.
183. RDE, 381–2.
184. Somville, 222–4
185. *Ibid.*, 227–8

CHAPTER 3: AARSCHOT

1. Reply, 107, 113. A major when he gave his deposition, Gilson was a captain at the time. An order to withdraw never reached him — two messengers transmitting it were killed — and when he saw other companies pulling back, Gilson believed he and his men were responsible for covering the Belgian retreat to the last man. C. Buffin, *Brave Belgians* (New York, 1918), 87–95.

2. RBC, 127, 130. When individuals testifying before the committee are identified by name, they have been taken from lists of witnesses in NA, HO 45/11061/266503/10 and/or /71.

3. GSA, 119 (Aarschot), Leemans; RBC, 127.

5. RDE, Book 2, 382. The Dean of Aarschot, Joseph Meeus, was upset about the firing, and informed the burgomaster, who raced over and told the commander that he was putting civilian lives in jeopardy. In his published deposition, the Dean states that he believed the soldiers didn't fire any more after this admonishment, though in unpublished testimony he suggested that Belgian troops may have used the tower to fire on the invaders at the height of the battle. (GSA, chemise 96, Meeus)

6. RDE, 10.
7. GSA, 119, Verlinden.
8. Reply, 117.
9. RBC, 130.
10. *Ibid.*, 126.
11. Reply, 114, 120.
12. GSA, 119, Van Praet.
13. RDE, 370.
14. RBC, 135, 143, 146.
15. *Ibid.*, 135.
16. RBC, 139; Reply, 114; GSA, chemise 93, Theeuws; J. Delhaize, *Châtiments sans Crimes, Crimes sans Châtiments* (Namur, n.d. [1920]), 105–6.
17. RBC, 125; Reply, 114, 117.
18. DVF, 93.
19. RBC, 132, 140.
20. *Ibid.*, 139.
21. GSA, 119, Thiere.
22. Reply, 117; RDE, 373.
23. RDE, 365.
24. *Ibid.*
25. *Ibid.*
26. RBC, 131.
27. RBC, 143; GSA, 119, Bols, Van Criechigen.
28. Reply, 117–118; GSA, 119, Tielemans.
29. GSA, 119, Leflot, Nijs, 93, Bruyninckx.
30. *Ibid.*, Meeus; RBC, 125.
31. GSA, 119, Marguerite.
32. L. Grondys [Grondijs], *The Germans in Belgium* (London, 1915), 13.
33. B. Whitlock, Belgium, *A Personal Narrative*, v. 1 (New York, 1920), 151–2. He told the same tale to *New York Tribune* correspondent R. H. Davies. (*New York Tribune*, 31 August 1914.)
34. Reply, 115; RDE, 369.
35. RDE, 371; GSA, 119, Terweduwe.
36. RBC, 132.
37. GSA, 119, Theeuws.
38. *Ibid.*, Nijs.
39. Reply, 114–115.
40. DVF, 95.
41. GSA, 119, Nijs.
42. Delhaize, 107.
43. Reply, 114, 115
44. RDE, 369.
45. DVF, 96.
46. *Ibid.*, 90.
47. *Ibid.*, 100.
48. Reply, 107.
49. DVF, 95–99; Karge believed he executed 88. Belgian authorities maintained that only 78 men were shot.

50. RDE, 375.
51. *Ibid.*, 375–6.
52. *Ibid.*, 376.
53. RBC, 134–5.
54. RDE, 377.
55. Reply, 115.
56. *Ibid.*; L. van der Essen, *A Statement about the Destruction of Louvain and Neighborhood* (Chicago, 1915), 3.
57. RBC, 129.
58. RDE, 377; Reply, 115.
59. RDE, 377.
60. GSA, 119, Bols.
61. Reply, 115.
62. *Ibid.*, 118.
63. *Ibid.*, 115.
64. RBC, 134.
65. Reply, 115.
66. *Ibid.*, 115, 116.
67. *Ibid.*, 115.
68. RBC, 134.
69. DVF, 97.
70. *Ibid.*, 95.
71. W. Schroeven (ed.), *Aarschot en de Oorlog, 1914–1918* (Aarschot, 1989), 3. J. Cuvelier, *La Belgique et la Guerre*, v. II, *L'Invasion Allemande* (Brussels, 1921), 262; the Commission of Inquest has a figure of 156 deaths (RDE, 679).
72. Reply, 114; RDE, 372.
73. RDE, 372.
74. *Ibid.*, 377.
75. PRW, Aarschot, Van Roey.
76. RDE, 45.
77. GSA, 119, Van Praet; RDE, 381–2.
78. RDE, 46.
79. DVF, 101.
80. *Ibid.*
81. RDE, 384.
82. Reply, 116; RVR 1, 21–22.
83. GSA, 119, Van Reusel.
84. RDE, 367–8.
85. *Ibid.*, 372–3.
86. *Ibid.*, 372.
87. GSA, 119, Cresens; RVR 2, 177.
88. GSA, 119, Van Hanke.
89. Reply, 113; PRW, Aarschot: handwritten report by Mevrouw Gustave Michiels-Corens; RDE, 370; RBC, 125.
90. RVR 1, 109.
91. RDE, 48; RBC, 153–9; Reply, 108.
92. RBC, 155.
93. *Ibid.*, 153.
94. *Ibid.*, 155.

95. *Ibid.*, 156; RDE, 53.

96. RDE, 48, 52; RBC, 156.

97. Reply, 117.

98. *Ibid.*, 122.

99. RBC, 146; RDE, 380, 384.

100. RDE, 383, 384; RBC, 145.

101. RDE, 48; GSA, 119, Van Praet.

102. RVR 1, 109–110.

103. Reply, 121. The following account is based on a report submitted by Father Simon Goovaerts, Reply, 121–127, and D. Andries, et. al., *Van Damiaangesticht tot Damiaaninstituut: 100 jaar Paters HH. Harten en hun onderwijs te Aarschot, 1890–1990* (Aarschot, 1992), 74–82.

104. Reply, 121, 123.

105. *Ibid.*, 123.

106. *Ibid.*, 124.

107. *Ibid.*, 125.

108. *Ibid.*

109. *Ibid.*, 126.

110. *Ibid.*

111. *Ibid.*, 121; RDE, 47; RBC, 147.

112. Reply, 119; RBC, 146–8; Delhaize, 112.

113. Reply, 119, 120; GSA, 119, Van Praet.

114. Reply, 119.

115. RDE, 380.

116. *Ibid.*

117. Reply, 120.

118. *Ibid.*

119. *Ibid.*

120. RDE, 378–9; RBC, 148, 159.

121. RDE, 380. Elsewhere she is listed as a servant. (PRW, Leuven: "Bodies Found or Exhumed in Louvain.")

122. PRW, Leuven: report on corpses buried in Van de Weyer Square; RBC, 140–141, 146, 148, 159; Reply, 121; Van der Essen, 4; RDE provides no figures.

123. RBC, 148; Delhaize, 113.

124. RDE, 381; RBC, 159.

125. Anonymous [Hervé de Gruben], *The Germans at Louvain* (London, 1916), 77–9.

126. P. Schöller, *Le cas de Louvain et le Livre Blanc allemand* (Leuven, 1958), 98–100.

127. *Ibid.*, 101–2.

128. *Ibid.*, 103.

129. *Ibid.*, 102.

130. H. Gibson, *A Journal from our Legation in Belgium* (Garden City, NY, 1917), 165.

131. *Ibid.*, 166.

132. *Ibid.*, 164.

133. *Ibid.*, 168.

134. B. Whitlock, *Belgium, A Personal Narrative,* v. 1 (New York, 1920), 188–9.

135. One Aarschot resident, taking refuge in a convent, was warned by an officer to avoid soldiers wearing a sign in the shape of an eight on their sleeves – "they were very dangerous." When a priest was escorted from the convent, he was surrounded by soldiers from a different regiment "to protect him from the '8s'." (GSA, 119, Theeuws). Overall crime rates for Germany, one historian has concluded, "are in line with other comparatively nonviolent northern European countries and are considerably below American rates in the same period." But violent crimes increased by some 44% during the three decades before the war, and, according to statistics from the *Vierteljahrshefte*, published by the Imperial Statistics Office in Berlin, and from the Home Office and Attorney General's Office, crime rates were in fact significantly higher in Germany than in the U.K. The annualized per-capita murder rate (including manslaughter) in the Empire, for example, was over 2 ½ times that of Great Britain. (E. Johnson, *Urbanization and Crime: Germany, 1871–1914* (Cambridge, UK, 1995), 230; H. Zehr, *Crime and Development in Modern Society* (London, 1976), 88.); T. Smith, *The Soul of Germany: A Twelve Years' Study of the People from Within, 1902–14* (New York, 1915), 348–351.)

136. RBC, 145.

137. Reply, 116, 117; GSA, 119, Leemans.

138. RDE, 49.

139. RBC, 154. The young women in Elewijt were Marie Dewit, daughter of a communal counselor, age 16 or 17, sixteen-year-old Marie Salus, also the daughter of a communal counselor, who was violated consecutively by three Germans, Marie van Wijn, 17, and a woman identified as the wife of a soldier, Jan Vrochen. The parents of the first three girls were kept at bay during the rapes. (GSA, 135 (Elewijt), Van den Wijngaerd.)

140. *Ibid.*, 150.

141. *Ibid.*, 151.

142. GSA, 119, Verhaegen; RDE 383; There is detailed, credible testimony of an attempt to rape a nun, Sister Ludovica, and a lay sister, Gabriella Petri, on September 18th, after the Germans reoccupied Aarschot (PRW, Aarschot).

143. PRW, Aarschot; PRW, Leuven: "The Case of Sister Rosa (Eugènie Grauls)." The Germans were understandably sensitive about the subject. Sister Rosa was threatened with prison if she spoke about her experience. A curé in Namur province, Arthur Tagnon, was imprisoned and fined in January 1915, charged with claiming nuns had been raped. Father Tagnon stoutly denied the accusation. When a German military chaplain had attempted to entrap him, after he had argued that priests had been executed without cause, Tagnon had said only that he'd heard rumors about nuns, but didn't know if they were true. (PRW, Namur.)

144. The Secretary to the First Commission of Inquiry, who visited Aarschot on September 11, reported that although "numerous assaults on women and girls took place," the victims and their families generally refused to answer any questions he asked. (RVR 1, 18.) The most detailed study of rape during the German invasion that I'm aware of was compiled by the British investigator J. H. Morgan for the town of Bailleul in French Flanders. The town was occupied for eight days in October 1914 by a regiment of Saxon hussars. "Cases of rape," reported Morgan, "were authenticated by sworn statements and by medical certificates." A leading physician in town, Dr. Bels, put the number as high as sixty. Officers and soldiers usually hunted in pairs, according to the report, gaining access to homes by claiming to seek billets or simply forcing the doors open. Most men were at the front. Those present were ordered away on some pretext, and threatened if they refused. The victims were often beaten and kicked, and, if they still resisted, menaced with revolvers. Some women were raped in the presence of their mothers or children. Several cases were described in detail; Morgan was convinced the evidence "would satisfy any court of law." Officers who were approached for protection just shrugged their shoulders. (NA, HO 45/11061/266503/7 "Summary of Inquiries in France")

145. Grondijs, 7.
146. Ibid., 8–9.
147. Ibid., 12.
148. R. S. Liddell, The Track of the War (London, 1915), 138.
149. Ibid., 146–7.

150. L. Mack, A Woman's Experiences in the Great War (London, 1915), 40–43.
151. Liddell, 138.
152. Grondijs, 18.
153. E. A. Powell, Fighting in Flanders (New York, 1914), 83–85.
154. Ibid., 85–88. Hugh Gibson had a remarkably similar encounter in Leuven on August 28th. When his car pulled up beside a little girl, "she burst out crying with fear, and we saw that she was in terror of her life. We called out to reassure her, but she turned and ran like a hunted animal." (Gibson, 170)

CHAPTER 4: ANDENNE

1. RVR 1, 35–6; there is a photo of the document in RVR 2, 165; SN, Part 2 (Le Siege de Namur), 68; E. Brognier, et. al., Andenne: le temps des libertés (1875–1975) (Andenne, 1993), 16, and in Anon., Andenne la Martyre (Andenne, 1919), 46. The text is reproduced in RDE 1, 466.
2. In Andenne itself, the report of the postwar Commission of Inquest lists 211 deaths (RDE, 610); other sources claim 218 (J. Cuvelier, La Belgique et la Guerre, v. 2, l'Invasion allemande (Brussels, 1921), 193) and 223 (SN, 9).
3. L. Mokveld, The German Fury in Belgium (New York, 1917), 149.
4. SN, 71.
5. Ibid., 70.
6. FSN, Andenne, Frère Réginald; RBC, 94–5; RDE, 99, 424. Abbé Louis Cartiaux, Dean of Andenne, listed five German grievances against residents of Andenne. He included the blowing up of the bridge, but omitted the ambushes of uhlan squadrons, more than likely the most significant act prejudicing the Germans. Also arousing suspicions were the holes civilians made to connect contiguous cellars, acting on the advice of the commander of the fort at Maizeret. Shells could fall in the vicinity of Andenne and civilians might need to escape their own cellars. According to the Dean, the invaders were further incited by loopholes made in some walls by Belgian soldiers ten days before the arrival of German troops. When the bridge was blown, a water line was damaged, and soldiers suspected that the sediment in the water flowing from some faucets was poison. In addition, some

lead pellets from hunting rifles were found in the streets. German soldiers had pillaged a gun shop whose weapons had not been taken to city hall, and had fired them in the streets, injuring at least one civilian, Auguste Henin. (FSN, Doyenné d'Andenne: Cartiaux.)

7. RDE, 460.

8. One, number 218, issued to Léon Delvigne for two cases of ammunition, one rifle and one carbine, and signed by the burgomaster on August 14, remains in the files of the first Belgian Commission of Inquest.

9. SN, 28–9; Reports, 87; Reply, 136.

10. RDE, 40, 432.

11. *Ibid.*, 432.

12. Reply, 136.

13. GSA, 417 (Andenne), Delvigne.

14. FSN, Cartiaux.

15. GSA, 417, Pirsoul; RVR 1, 87; Reply, 134–7; SN, 71.

16. DVF, 107.

17. SN, 83.

18. *Ibid.*, 36.

19. J. de Thier and O. Gilbart, *Liège pendant la grande Guerre*, v. 2, *Liège martyre* (Liège, 1919), 170.

20. RDE, 457.

21. FSN, "Fusillade de la Gare"; RDE, 459.

22. *Ibid.*, 462.

23. SN, 84; RDE, 459; Thier and Gilbart, 170–1.

24. SN, 84, 37–8; GSA, 417, Delvigne.

25. RDE, 104, 459, 462; Thier and Gilbart, 171.

26. RDE, 445.

27. GSA, 417, Vaesen, Magis.

28. Reply, 138. 29. RDE, 434.

30. *Ibid.*

31. *Ibid.*, 456; SN, 34.

32. RBC, 127, 130, 97.

33. Reply, 138. 34. RDE, 449.

35. GSA, 417, Pirsoul.

36. FSN, "Seilles."

37. SN, 34. In another version she was told, "Tomorrow we'll take care of your Andenne." (GSA, 417, Vaesen.)

38. SN, 34.

39. FSN, Frère Réginald; SN, 35. 40. RDE, 436, 440; SN, 93.

41. RDE, 437–8; SN, 39–41. Valentine's recollections differ slightly from her sister's. Soldiers may have fired on the group initially out of anger when some of the Warzées escaped. The Hautebise residents came across the bodies of two soldiers, not one, and they were propped up against a small flight of stairs leading to a garden. Valentine, unlike her younger sister, saw at once that the shot from the officer's pistol had blasted their mother's face off and exposed her brains. Returning soldiers shined a flashlight on the girls' faces to determine if they were still alive. Valentine testified that a cousin and his wife also survived the massacre. The sisters' wounds are described in *Andenne la Martyre*, 55.

42. RDE, 448.

43. *Ibid.*, 428–430; J. Delhaize, *Châtiments sans Crimes, Crimes sans Châtiments* (Namur, n.d.[1920]) 121–130.

44. Reply, 139.

45. RDE, 445–446; H. Davignon, *Belgium and Germany* (London, 1915), 67. Mme. Walgraffe recalled there being nine people altogether. (SN, 42)

46. SN, 42.

47. RDE, 458, 609.

48. *Ibid.*, 444; SN, 46.

49. RDE, 446; SN, 42.

50. RVR 1, 88.

51. Davignon, 67; RDE, 434, 442; Reply, 140.

52. RDE, 442–3.

53. SN, 44.

54. Reply, 129, 137; GSA, 417, Magis. According to other estimates, there were about 800 people altogether. (RDE, 106.)

55. FSN, Servais.

56. RDE, 453; SN, 76. I have not been able to determine the relationship between Major Bronsart von Schellendorf and the Prussian War Minister of the 1880s, Paul Bronsart von Schellendorf, or the German Chief of the Turkish General Staff (implicated in the Armenian massacres) and future Nazi Friedrich Bronsart von Schellendorf. The former famously predicted that "there will be many atrocities in the next war." (SN, 68, n. 1.) The family also produced the composer Hans Bronsart von Schellendorf.

57. SN, 47; GSA, 417, Magis; RVR 1, 89; Reply, 136.

58. RDE, 435.

59. FSN, Servais.

60. RDE, 445, 451; Reply, 89.

61. RDE, 447; GSA, 417, Pirsoul; Reply, 141.

62. SN, 49–50, 77–8.

63. *Ibid.*, 47.

64. RDE, 450; SN, 46–7.

65. GSA, 417, Magis; RDE, 450–1; SN, 50–1; RBC, 98.
66. RBC, 95–6.
67. Reply, 137.
68. RDE, 454. In other testimony, he says he observed the soldiers leaving the Place. (SN, 52)
69. RDE, 454–5; SN, 45, 52.
70. SN, 52.
71. RDE, 456.
72. *Ibid.*, 451. Comes eventually returned to the country, marrying a Belgian, Félix Delsupexhe, and settling for a time in Maizeret. Efforts to trace the couple there and in Andenne and Mayen have proved fruitless.
73. *Ibid.*, 449.
74. RDE, 453; Reply, 137; SN, 51. Others put the time of the order at around 11:00 a.m.
75. RBC, 98.
76. GSA, 417, Magis.
77. *Ibid.*; RBC, 99.
78. GSA, 417, Delvigne; two other residents reported this: GSA, 417, Montjoie; Reply, 136.
79. SN, 87.
80. GSA, 417, Pirsoul.
81. SN, 56.
82. *Ibid.* The names of the widows come from a list of victims, their age, profession, spouse, and residence in *Andenne la Martyre*, 49–53.
83. SN, 57.
84. "Martyrologe Phamaceutique," *Journal de Pharmacie de Belgique*, n. 4, 26 Jan. 1919, 58. "Everywhere we heard women wailing", reported a magistrate who emerged from hiding after 10:00. (Reply, 139.)
85. SN, 56.
86. SN, 53–4. As in other cases, however, one can never be sure of German motives. According to records in the city archives in Andenne, Noël had just turned 50 in August, 1914, and Arthur Bischoff, the soldier who signed Noël's pass, may have been acting out of nothing more than disinterested compassion. (Communication from P. Monjoie, archivist, 6 July 2005.)
87. SN, 68.
88. Reply, 134.
89. *Ibid.*
90. *Ibid.* 135; SN, 68. Other witnesses described the singing and piano-playing that accompanied the massacres. (GSA, 417, Delvigne). Wabnitz went on to offer some unwelcome testimony before a postwar

commission in Berlin. Bronsart and his own commander, Colonel Scheunemann, had told the company commanders of the Guards Reserve and Pioneer Battalions that "all men capable of bearing arms were to be executed on the spot" because they wanted "an example to be made" of Andenne. The soldiers were to use their bayonets; shooting might lead to more panicked firing by the troops and additional German casualties. Wabnitz insisted that he had seen no firing by civilians at any time. (J. Horne and A. Kramer, *German Atrocities 1914: A History of Denial* (New Haven, 2001), 33.)
91. FSN, Frère Réginald; SN, 69; RDE, 425–6.
92. SN, 41–2.
93. *Ibid.*, 63.
94. RDE, 445.
95. GSA, 417, Delvigne.
96. RBC, 98–99.
97. SN, 60; GSA, 417, Delvigne.
98. FSN, Cartiaux.
99. RBC, 99; Reply, 141; GSA, 417, Delvigne. A proclamation issued by the new commandant on the 28th was still more dire: "The least revolt on the part of the inhabitants will result in the burning of the entire town and the hanging of all the men." *Andenne la Martyre*, 47.
100. SN, 61.
101. *Ibid.*, 88–9.
102. RDE, 433, 434.
103. *Ibid.*, 433; SN, 63.
104. RDE, 433.
105. DVF, 111–12.
106. The carillon was sounded by the sacristan's mother to summon that official back to the bell tower, so he could turn over the keys of the church to the Dean of Andenne, Abbé Cartiaux. The Dean had been approached by two German soldiers, one of whom identified himself as an architecture student who wished to examine the interior of the church. As the keys could not be located, the sacristan's mother rang the bells, a long-standing signal that her son should return to the church. The tour was a success and the Dean was conversing with the two amiable soldiers in the square outside the church when firing erupted. (SN, 36; FSN, Cartiaux.)
107. DVF, 107.
109. *Ibid.*, 109–110.
110. *Ibid.*, 107.

111. RDE, 428.

112. DVF, 107.

113. *Ibid.*, 107–8.

114. RDE, 426, 454, 455.

115. DVF, 110. 116. RDE, 87–9.

117. RDE, 422; RVR 2, 61; SN, 62–3. Major von Bassewitz served in either the 3rd or 4th Prussian Guard Regiment.

CHAPTER 5: TAMINES

1. B. Whitlock, *Belgium, A Personal Narrative*, v. 1 (New York, 1920), 211–212.

2. C. Callwell, *Field-Marshall Sir Henry Wilson, His Life and Diaries*, v. 1, (New York, 1927), 165, cited by B. Tuchman, *August 1914* (London, 1962), 253.

3. B. H. Liddell Hart, *History of the First World War* (London, 1970), 43; A. Banks, *A Military Atlas of the First World War* (Barnsley, S. Yorkshire, 1989), 30–31.

4. Lanrezac's thirteen divisions were smaller than their German counterparts, with roughly 15,000 men each to the Germans' 17,000; significantly, an Imperial Army division also had twice as many guns, 72 to 36. (Banks, 34; Tuchman, 266–7.)

5. Cannae refers to the classic double envelopment performed by Hannibal's Carthagian troops against Rome in 216 B.C.; Schlieffen toyed with the strategy before his death.

6. The disastrous consequences of Moltke's emendations enabled some apologists for the German Army during the interwar period to argue that the Plan would have succeeded had it not been tampered with. The German Commander, having already reduced the Schlieffen right wing from a ratio of 8:1 to less than 3:1 over his left, now peeled off an extra corps to invest Antwerp, sent two off to Russia, and retained two more behind Rupprecht that were to have augmented the right wing. (Banks, 22; J. Stokesbury, *A Short History of World War I* (New York, 1981), 46; S. L. A. Marshall, World War I (New York, 1964), 58.) But even before the publication of Ritter's classic analysis of the Plan fifty years ago, most historians blamed the strategy, not its execution. Without motorized transportation, German troops were asked to march along the circumference of a circle the French could cross the chord of by train, in Liddell Hart's analogy. (G. Ritter, *The Schlieffen Plan, Critique of a Myth* (Westport,

Connecticut, 1979), 6.) This is quite apart from the Plan's disastrous political impact – ensuring that Britain would fight beside the French.

7. Lanrezac has been censured, in particular, for failing to permit at least one division of Franchet d'Espery's Ist Corps to fall on von Bülow's left flank as the Second German Army crossed the Sambre on the 23rd. The prospects certainly seemed excellent to Franchet and his staff, who pleaded with the commander to unleash them against the Prussian Guard Corps passing in front of them, oblivious to their presence. Spears bases his assessment in part on von Bülow's reluctance to pursue the retreating French. "Is it unfair to assume that the German Commander who paused and hesitated on the edge of an empty battlefield, might have called a halt to the whole advance had he been attacked with determination?" (E. Spears, *Liaison 1914* (New York, 1968), 161.) But Bülow, though certainly cautious, was in fact waiting impatiently for his colleague to the south, von Hausen, to cross the Meuse and cut off the retreating French. He had no wish to chase the enemy below Philippeville and Dinant, enabling him to escape the trap.

8. The original Plan XVII had naturally respected Belgium's and Luxembourg's neutrality, and the Fifth Army was to slide below the Duchy to support an attack by the two neighboring armies on Thionville and Metz.

9. E. Galet, *Albert, King of the Belgians, in the Great War* (Boston, 1931), 116–119; E. Cammaerts, *Albert of Belgium, Defender of Right* (New York, 1935), 156–7.

10. Spears, 130.

11. Francet d'Esperey has been credited with being an exception, (Tuchman, 272) making more careful preparations along the Meuse before being ordered north, but there's no evidence he dug trenches around Dinant, where the German Third Army had revealed as early as the 15th that it intended to cross the river.

12. SN, Part 3 *(Tamines et la Bataille de la Sambre)*, 75; RDE 1, 616. The figure includes neighboring villages.

13. In 1914 it was called, successively, rue de Velaine, rue de l'Hôtel de Ville, rue de la Station, and, after it crossed the Sambre, rue

de Falisolle. (A. Lemaire, *La Tragédie de Tamines* (Tamines, 1957), 9; SN, 76.) Today rue de l'Hôtel de Ville and rue de la Station are avenue Roosevelt and rue du Roi Albert, and rue de Falisolle is avenue des Français.

14. S. Alexandre, "Mémoire de la Grande Guerre 1914–1918 en Belgique: Le Massacre de Tamines, 22 aout 1914" *(http:// www. grandeguerre.net)*, 11.

15. As Tamines goes unmentioned in official German accounts, it is impossible to determine how many regiments of the Xth Army Corp's 20th division were attempting to cross the Sambre at Tamines on Friday the 21st. The 77th Hanoverian Reserve Infantry (called "Elisabeth") was responsible for the massacres. The 76th was also in Tamines on Saturday.

16. Lemaire, 185–6; SN, 79–80; 7. FSN, Tamines: Latteur, Frère Guillaume (Guillaume Plum). There was a rather pathetic "non-active" Garde Civique unit from Tamines, but it had been disbanded Wednesday evening, August 19th, after several days of guarding bridges.

17. RVR 1, 84; SN, 79–80; Alexandre, 13.

18. SN, 81, 80, 83; Lemaire, 185. "In spite of the danger, in spite of my pleas, in spite of my emphatic orders, the inhabitants insisted on 'taking a look.' It was thanks to the great prudence of our men that there were no victims among the population." Captain Gillieaux pointedly refuted the allegation of an Austrian colliery worker named Graf that appeared in Richard Grasshoff's *Belgiens Schuld*. Graf claimed he saw no soldiers or anyone else in uniform during the firing. (Grasshof, 87.) Graf's disingenuousness is transparent: he claimed to have seen a machine-gun shooting "dum-dum" bullets operated by civilians from a home near the Sambre bridge. Dum-dum bullets were not manufactured for machine-guns, and one would have to inspect a bullet closely to determine if it were indeed a dum-dum (a soft-nosed bullet that expands on striking an object). In any case, the two machine-guns covering the bridge were removed by French troops long before the Germans crossed. Graf also claimed that "Some days later I heard inhabitants brag how cleverly they had acted in shooting the Germans without being discovered." This would have been *after* the Saturday evening

massacre! It is inconceivable that anyone would have made such a claim in light of the consequences. Graf naturally does not mention any names. (Grasshof, 87–8.)

19. Lemaire, 177.

20. FSN, Frère Guillaume; Alexandre, 14.

21. SN, 85–6, 94–5. Another instance of déjà vu, in addition to the spectacle of hostages preceding attacking troops: the Germans tried, without success, to lower the national flag flying from the church tower at Alloux, the northern parish of Tamines. After a sergeant was unable to remove it, residents were told the tower would be destroyed by artillery if the hated symbol was not immediately hauled down. The curé was located, marched to the top of the clock tower at gunpoint, and the flag was pulled down. (GSA, 493 (Tamines), Hottlet.)

22. SN, 77, 85–6.

23. One heroic member, Pierre Lefeuvre, desperately defended route de Falisolle from the shelter of a château's narrow stone stairway, using the cartridges of his dead comrades. Fifty-eight Germans died in the vicinity of his redoubt. (SN, 97; FSN, undated letter from Rennes, signature illegible.)

24. The Battle of Tamines goes unmentioned in the official history of the war, *Der Welkrieg*, and in a number of other authoritative accounts of the campaign. A figure frequently cited by civilians was 2–3,000 German dead, an estimate possibly derived from the claim of a German officer haranguing hostages in Notre-Dame d'Alloux. The acting burgomaster, Émile Duculot, heard an officer mention 600 casualties, but he may have been referring to his own battalion or regiment. (Lemaire, 17; Alexandre, 14.)

25. FSN, Frère Guillaume.

26. SN, 81–3.

27. *Ibid.*, 82. Duculot was then made to deliver an ultimatum to the curé of Alloux that the Belgian flag had to be removed or the church tower would be shelled.

28. SN, 94–5; FSN, Arthur Paille, Widow Devillers.

29. SN, 98.

30. SN, 96; FSN, "Flore Garot" (5 pp; no author – Nieuwland?): "Stupefied, Evrard remained beside his wife's body for many hours, without daring to touch her." His paralysis may have saved him. He was

seized by soldiers and taken from his wife's side only after the mass execution.

31. FSN, *Documents Relatif à l'Histoire de l'Église de Belgique pendant la Grande Guerre,* by the Convent of the Sisters of the Immaculate Conception, Tamines, St. Martin's; J. Cuvelier, *La Belgique et la Guerre,* v. 2, *l'Invasion allemande* (Brussels, 1921), 202; RBC, 106; SN, 81, 143–4; Alexandre, 13.

32. Cuvelier, 205. 33. SN, 99.

34. *Ibid.,* 99–100.

35. *Ibid.,* 88, 95.

36. FSN, Germaine Desguin.

37. SN, 86–7; Cuvelier, 203.

38. The burgomaster's sister-in-law, Catherine Mage, a widow, was staying at the Guiots to care for her eighty-nine-year-old mother, Anastasie Jaumain, confined to her bed. Mme. Mage was not pleased that her sister had precipitously abandoned their mother when she fled with her husband. But late that night, some time after 2:00 a.m., when the retreating Germans set fire to the hotel, Mme. Mage herself failed to rescue the old woman. The last thing she saw as she fled the burning house was her mother jumping off the bed, "with a superhuman effort." (SN, 90.) Four days later, on a tip from a German soldier, survivors of the Saturday massacre were permitted to dig in Mme. Mage's rose garden, next door to her brother-in-law's hotel. "We discovered first the body of a pig...then a second pig...then a dog... and finally we saw a hand. Using a rope tied to the hand, we pulled out the corpse of a naked female. The body was considerably swollen. The head was crushed to a pulp and half-devoured. This was the mortal remains of Anastasie Jaumain." The naked body had been wrapped in a grey-checked tablecloth. The soldiers who despatched Mme. Jaumin had set the record for the oldest civilian killed in Tamines, just edging out the platoon responsible for the death of Mme. Thiry. (*Ibid*; FSN, Alexandre Warnier.)

39. SN, 87.

40. *Ibid.,* 88–9.

41. *Ibid.,* 88.

42. Alexandre, 14–15.

43. SN, 91.

44. *Ibid.*

45. *Ibid.,* 92.

46. FSN, Georges Locus.

47. Lemaire, 166, 174.

48. FSN, diagram by Jules Moussiaux; Lemaire, 160. Testimony naturally diverges on the numbers and formation of the soldiers in the square.

49. SN, 101–114.

50. *Ibid.,* 102.

51. *Ibid.,* 103.

52. *Ibid.,* 104.

53. *Ibid.*

54. Lemaire, 32–3.

55. GSA, 493, Hottlet.

56. J. Petit (ed.), "Les évènements tragiques d'août 1914 à Tamines," *Feuilleton de "Vers l'Avenir!"* (n.d.), récit de Sevrin, 13. Some German soldiers may have genuinely believed that Notre-Dames des Alloux had been designated as a safe haven. An officer from Lorraine who seemed well disposed toward the Seron family advised them to take refuge in the church. He was from a different regiment than the executioners. (J. Delhaize, *Châtiments sans Crimes, Crimes sans Châtiments* (Namur, n.d.[1920]), 204–6.)

57. Petit, de Roover, 11.

58. *Ibid.,* Vigneron, 10; FSN, Seron, Callebaut.

59. Petit, de Roover, 11.

60. Lemaire, 126–7.

61. GSA, 493, Loriaux-Leonard.

62. Lemaire, 147; SN, 105.

63. *Ibid.*; FSN, Seron.

64. P. Delandsheere (ed.), "Les Atrocités Allemandes: La Boucherie de Tamines" *XXieme Siecle* (Brussels), 29 December 1918 (récit de E. Callebaut), 4.

65. SN, 106.

66. Lemaire, 39 132, 147, 153; Delhaize, 209; GSA, 493, Lambotte.

67. SN, 106.

68. Petit, Firmin Sevrin, 13.

69. Lemaire, 144, 154; Petit, de Roover, 11. 70. SN, 137–51.

71. GSA, 493, Lambotte.

72. FSN, Seron.

73. Lemaire, 155.

74. Cuvelier, 207; RDE, 143, 478. Others naturally reported different versions. "You've fired on our soldiers" was the only sentence one victim could make out. (Petit, récit de Charles Guillaume, 13.)

75. Lemaire, 158.

76. Cuvelier, 207; Lemaire, 50, 69, 133, 146; FSN, Duculot, Seron.

77. SN, 110.

78. Lemaire, 50n.

79. FSN, Duculot.

80. FSN, Seron.

81. Petit, Bruyere, 15. He probably meant a section – about 22 men.

82. Petit, Thiry, 11. As the executioners were facing the Sambre, these would likely have been bullets from the machine-gun placed at the bottom of the steps leading up to the bridge, and from troops posted above it. Thiry's family, captured late in the day, was taken directly to Place St. Martin.

83. Alexandre, 17; Petit, de Roover, 11.

84. From the opening days of the war, German soldiers had shot unpopular commanders. What happened in Tamines, however, may have been the first instance of organized disobedience in the German Army in World War I, and the last before 1918.

85. Cuvelier, 207.

86. SN, 108.

87. *Ibid.*, 109.

88. *Ibid.*, 110.

89. RDE, 144; SN, 109 n.3; FSN, Seron; Petit, Tourneur, Gerard, Seron, 16–17; Cuvelier, 208; Lemaire, 54, 57, 65; Delhaize, 211.

90. Lardinois was uninjured during the fusilades. His father and two brothers also survived the shootings. A German soldier clambered on top of Lucien's older brother Louis. The Red Cross medic was trying to bayonet other survivors still writhing in agony. Louis Ladinois kept perfectly still, even when the soldier planted his foot squarely on the bullet wound in his back. "I felt acutely every thrust he delivered with the bayonet," the eighteen-year-old recalled. With the final blow, the victim cried out. It was Lardinois's father. (Lemaire, 51–2.)

91. RDE, 478.

92. Delandsheere, 5–6.

93. *Ibid.*, 7–8.

94. Lemaire, 65–7.

95. *Ibid.*, 67–9.

96. *Ibid.*, 69–71; FSN, report of the Convent of the Sisters of the Immaculate Conception, Tamines, St. Martin's.

97. Lemaire, 55.

98. RDE, 478.

99. Petit, Legrain, 15.

100. Lemaire, 159.

101. *Ibid.*, 58.

102. *Ibid.*, 163–5.

103. Delhaize, 214.

104. Lemaire, 137–8; FSN, Seron.

105. Delhaize, 215; FSN, Seron; Lemaire, 137–8.

106. Lemaire, 148–9.

107. Alexandre, 19.

108. SN, 117.

109. FSN, Locus: "I told myself: the French are returning; we're saved. Then there was total silence."

110. Lemaire, 86.

111. SN, 117.

112. *Ibid.*, 118.

113. *Ibid.*

114. *Ibid.*, 113.

115. RVR 1, 86.

116. Lemaire, 138; Delhaize, 215.

117. SN, 118.

118. *Ibid.*, 119; Cuvelier, 200.

119. SN, 119.

120. *Ibid.*, 118; RDE, 478.

121. SN, 119.

122. Lemaire, 165.

123. RBC, 107; SN, 111.

124. FSN, Lambotte.

125. SN, 136. Lemaire's figure is six. (205.)

126. Lemaire, 93.

127. Reply, 86.

128. Cuvelier, 216.

129. FSN, Lambotte. Lambotte did not live to see the realization of his vow. He was killed on 18 June 1918. He had been serving in the 12th Company of the 19th Regiment of the Line. Lambotte was eventually buried in his home town of Vitrival, a few kilometers south of Tamines. (Communication from Patrick de Wolf, 1 June 2005).

130. GSA, 493, Hottlet.

131. RVR 2, 120–1; Cuvelier, 216.

132. SN, 119.

133. Lemaire, 170.

134. Lemaire, 169–171. It was widely believed that Canon Crousse had successfully pleaded with the doctor for the lives of the remaining civilians, and that the doctor, in turn, had begged the commanding officer for mercy. (GSA, 493, Widow Barbier) In fact, the sympathetic sergeant, true to his word, had told Adolphe Seron around noon that there would be no more shootings. Everyone would be taken to Fleurus and liberated. (Lemaire, 138.)

135. SN, 119.

136. *Ibid.*

137. RVR 1, 86.

138. SN, 120.

139. GSA, 493, Loriaux-Leonard.

140. *Ibid.*

141. SN, 120; RVR 1, 86. According to one witness, the burgomaster of Velaine announced to the crowd and the German officers that he would assume responsibility for the refugees. (GSA, 493, Loriaux-Leonard.)

142. SN, 128.

143. Lemaire, 187.

144. Alexandre, 2; Lemaire, photograph following page 160.

145. This figure excludes the nine victims who were never identified. (SN, 121.)

146. Whitlock, 213.

147. SN, 136–7.

148. *Ibid.*, 122.

149. FSN, Convent of the Sisters of the Providence of the Immaculate Conception, Tamines – St. Martin. All subsequent quotations and information in this section, unless otherwise noted, come from this sixteen-page document.

150. FSN, Locus; SN, 123. Locus's story reveals how arbitrary fate could be on the 22nd. His home was among the last to be invaded: the soldiers were amazed to discover a man still at large. They shoved the barrels of their guns against his back, then an officer pressed a revolver to his temple. However, moments later a second officer abruptly signaled to him to go away. After a painful glance back at his family, he fled into the street.

151. SN, 135.

152. When it traverses Alloux, the street is called rue de Velaine, but further north it is called rue de Keumiee, and it is possible Deule conflated the two names. There is no rue de Vignées in the area, nor is there a nearby village (nor one anywhere in Belgium) called Vignées. There is a route d'Oignies paralleling the Sambre south of town, and a rue de Moignelée bisecting rue de l'Hôtel de Ville.

153. DVF, 50–51.

154. Lemaire, 117.

155. SN, 133.

CHAPTER 6: DINANT INTRODUCTION, LEFFE

1. DVF, 117: "On August 15, 1914, an operation of the German cavalry, in which, among other units, the 12th Jäger Battalion took part, led to the temporary occupation of the right bank of the Meuse. Owing to superior enemy forces, it was evacuated on the same day and numerous dead and some wounded were left behind."

2. Von Kircheisen, *Das Volkerringen, 1914–1915,* p. 438; cited by SN, Part 4 *(Le Combat de Dinant),* Book 2 *(Le Sac de la Ville),* 41. A recent commentator has also argued that the Germans lost the war on the Meuse rather than the Marne. (R. Citino, *The German Way of War: From the Thirty Years' War to the Third Reich* (Lawrence, Kansas, 2005), 211–17.)

3. SN, 29–30, 32; J. Cuvelier, *La Belgique et la Guerre,* v. 2, *l'Invasion allemande* (Brussels, 1921), 229.

4. SN, 35–6.

5. *Ibid.,* 38–9; RBC, 122. Among the wounded in the French victory was a young lieutenant named Charles de Gaulle.

6. SN, 41.

7. FSN, Dinant, Lamotte.

8. SN, 58.

9. RVR 2, 94.

10. SN, 43.

11. The account that follows is based largely on testimony in SN, 44–9.

12. Reply, 168.

13. RBC, 121–2.

14. SN, 49; RVR 1, 154.

15. J. Bédier, *How Germany Seeks to Justify her Atrocities* (Paris, 1915), 38.

16. DVF, 134, 200.

17. *Ibid.,* 133.

18. Nieuwland and Tschoffen make such a case. N. Nieuwland and M. Tschoffen, *The Legend of the "Francs Tireurs" of Dinant* (Gembloux, 1929), 41–46.

19. Reply, 190. This and the following testimony were provided in a series of interviews of 414 prisoners of war from the XIIth Corps by French prosecutors in Bordeaux. The Saxons were not very forthcoming. "The results, though satisfactory, might have been better. It is clear that there is too much reticence in the statements obtained," the chief investigator, Lieutenant Loustalot, concluded. (Reply, 169) Enlisted men were separated from officers and n.c.o.s; nonetheless, they all expected to be repatriated after the war and feared the consequences of speaking freely. Nor was

there any remorse over the massacre of 685 civilians. "It would show very little knowledge of German mentality to imagine that a single one of them, confronted with these horrors, felt any revulsion of conscience or any sentiment of revolt against officers so unworthy to be leaders. Not one of them had any thought of attacking or exposing his officer. But they very naturally excused themselves by pleading strict execution of the orders given to them in conformity with what the German considers the law of war." (Reply, 174) Testimony from prisoners was also collected by a war council in Montpellier under Captain Cruveillé. These depositions were never published.

20. "As to us," he added, "our company was never attacked by civilians." (Reply, 192.)

21. Reply, 201.

22. Ibid., 193.

23. Ibid., 198–9.

24. Ibid., 173.

25. Ibid., 177.

26. Ibid., 177.

27. GSA, 435 (Dinant), Cruveillé, Conseil de Guerre, 16ème Région de Corps, Montpellier.

28. SN, 50, 21, 116.

29. SN, 117.

30. FSN, A. Mathieu.

31. SN, 51–53; A. Banks, *A Military Atlas of the First World War* (Barnsley, S. Yorkshire, 1989), 30–31.

32. SN, 51.

33. Von Bülow, incidentally, may have been somewhat more skeptical, or candid, than his colleagues. Von Kluck and von Hausen fulminate against the civilian sharpshooters in their memoirs, as does Ludendorff; von Bülow doesn't mention them. Perhaps he was familiar with the suppressed German reports on Andenne and Tamines.

34. Nieuwland and Tschoffen, 47.

35. DVF, 170.

36. Nieuwland and Tschoffen, 53; SN, 79–80. Franz Adam, himself a lawyer, had fled across the Meuse with his family on the 22nd of August, and proceeded on to Yvoir.

37. SN, 282–326. The population of Dinant and its faubourgs was about 7,890 in 1914. (SN, 25.)

38. RDE 1, 612, which gives a different death total, 665. Nieuwland and Tschoffen provide a final count of 674 (92)

39. DVF, 161.

40. J. Cuvelier, *La Belgique et la Guerre*, v. 2, *l'Invasion allemande* (Brussels, 1921), 236.

41. GSA, 435.

42. *Ibid.*, SN, 262–3. The brothers did not resume production of the Abbey's famous beers. These were brewed again only after World War II, and not in Leffe.

43. FSN, Bullens-Jacquet; SN, 61.

44. FSN, Bullens-Jacquet.

45. SN, 62. According to another account, it was Jules who said, "Goodbye. We'll meet in heaven." "Yes, my boy. Have courage," replied his mother. (FSN, M. Delaey)

46. SN, 58.

47. DVF, 175.

48. Reply, 188.

49. Nieuwland and Tschoffen, 53.

50. FSN, M. Delaey; SN, 64.

51. FSN, Marette-Delvigne, Pieroux-Poncelet.

52. FSN, Bullens-Zwollen. His age is listed as fourteen in SN (289).

53. SN, 66.

54. RBC, 120; FSN, Lejeune; SN, 88.

55. FSN, A. Monin; SN, 67.

56. SN, 78.

57. SN, 74–75.

58. FSN, A. Monin; SN, 71–2.

59. FSN, A. Mathieu. 60. SN, 82, n. 1.

61. FSN, A. Mathieu; SN, 290–2.

62. FSN, Zwollen-Sanglier; SN, 82.

63. SN, 83.

64. *Ibid.*, 84.

65. DVF, 203, 204.

66. A couple of anti-Catholic incidents were also reported to the curé of Leffe when he returned in September. When an officer knocking on the door of a residence was told that the master of the house had been shot and its contents pillaged, he replied, "You owe this to your pig of a king, to your pigs of fathers, to pigs of priests and to your Catholicism. We've killed more than forty curés." Seeing two women in tears, another soldier called out them, "Don't blame us, but him over there" – and pointed to a crucifix on a chimney. (FSN, Curé of Leffe)

67. SN, 82.

68. FSN, Zwollen-Sanglier.

69. SN, 83.

70. *Ibid.*, 78–9.

71. *Ibid.*, 86–7.

72. J. Bédier, *German Atrocities from German Evidence* (Paris, 1915), 11.

73. French Ministry of Foreign Affairs, *Germany's Violation of the Laws of War, 1914–15* (London, 1915), 112.
74. FSN, Gourdinne-Blanchard.
75. SN, 92–5.
76. DVF, 205.
77. Anon., *Le Martyre de Dinant* (Dinant, 1920), 59.
78. Reply, 181.
79. *Ibid.*, 182.
80. *Ibid.*, 189.
81. GSA, 435, Cruveillé
82. RBC, 119.
83. FSN, Mathieu.
84. Reply, 192.
85. RBC, 120.
86. SN, 67.
87. FSN, Bullens-Jacquet; SN, 67.
88. FSN, Delaey.
89. SN, 68.
90. FSN, Monin-Haustenne 2; SN, 85.
91. Bédier, *German Atrocities*, 23.
92. *Ibid.*, 23–4.
93. French Ministry of Foreign Affairs, 157–8.
94. Reply, 181.
95. RBC, 407.
96. Reply, 179–80.
97. *Ibid.*, 180.
98. RBC, 409.
99. *Ibid.*
100. French Ministry of Foreign Affairs, 181.
101. *Ibid.*, 175–6.
102. Bédier, *How Germany Seeks to Justify her Crimes*, 17–19.
103. FSN, Ravet.
104. SN, 63.
105. RBC, 408.
106. *Ibid.*, 398.
107. French Ministry of Foreign Affairs, 159–60.
108. *Ibid.*, 179.
109. GSA, 435, Cruveillé.
110. Reply, 188.

CHAPTER 7: DINANT ST. JACQUES, ST. NICOLAS

1. SN, Part 4 *(Le Combat de Dinant)*, Book 2 *(Le Sac de la Ville)*, 108–9; Anon., *Le Martyre de Dinant* (Dinant, 1920) (LMD), 128–9.
2. SN, 110.
3. FSN, Dinant, Longville.
4. *Ibid.*; SN, 111–12.
5. *Ibid.*, 115; LMD, 130.
6. SN, 117–8.
7. DVF, 148–9.
8. *Ibid.*, 147–9.
9. *Ibid.*, 137.
10. FSN, Dinant, Herbecq; RVR, 2, 83; SN, 129, 135, 142 n2.
11. SN, 129 n. 3.
12. *Ibid.*, 134. Mme. Henquin in fact did not give birth until a month later.
13. RVR 2, 84.
14. SN, 132.
15. FSN, Altenhoven; SN, 136–7, 302.
16. SN, 139.
17. GSA, 435 (Dinant), Dizy, Toupiet. Another witness believed Firmin was bayoneted first, then shot. (SN, 141–2.)
18. LMD, 75; SN, 144.
19. *Ibid.*, 145.
20. *Ibid.*, 147.
21. *Ibid.*, 147, n. 6. Sasserath (1881–1958) went on to have a long and distinguished political career in Dinant, serving twice as burgomaster (1927–36, 1947–56), as a member of the provincial council (1925–35) and as a senator (1935–46). (C. Ferrier, "Léon Sasserath," http://www.wallonie-en-ligne.net/Encyclopedie/Biographies/Notices/Sasserath-L.htm.)
22. FSN, Leblanc-Vilain; LMD, 67, 71, 77, 87; RDE 1, 482, 488. His exact words, according to Anna Vilain, were "You can be reassured that nothing will happen to you. In the name of this officer, I give you my solemn vow." And the officer nodded in agreement.
23. SN, 147 n. 4. There is some confusion as to when Sasserath himself was released. Schmitz and Nieuwland indicate that he was taken home around 1:00 p.m., an hour before the general exodus. Yet when some individuals who were at the head of the crowd taken to the Tschoffen wall were pushed into the prison around 6:00 p.m., Sasserath was there to greet them. (SN, 158) It's likely he was obliged to remain, though his family may have been freed.
24. SN, 147. No other witness reports that Sasserath led the other captives out of the forge.
25. RVR 2, 84.
26. *Ibid.*, 85; SN, 149, 302.
27. FSN, Drion, Wayens; LMD, 95.
28. RBC, 123; SN, 149.
29. RVR 2, 85.
30. SN, 150; FSN, Wayens; LMD, 96.

31. RBC, 124.
32. LMD, 96.
33. SN, 150.
34. FSN, Drion.
35. RVR 2, 86–7.
36. SN, 183–4.
37. *Ibid.*, 151; RVR 2, 84; FSN, Jaumot.
38. FSN, Leblanc-Vilain, Devanelle-Février; SN, 151 n. 3; LMD, 56, 87.
39. FSN, Devanelle-Février.
40. FSN, Leblanc-Vilain.
41. LMD, 56.
42. SN, 152–3; LMD, 64, 69, 90.
43. LMD, 69.
44. FSN, Van Heden; SN, 153.
45. SN, 153.
46. LMD, 53.
47. SN, 154; LMD, 61, 69; FSN, Lenel-Lemineur; L. Gillet, *Récit Officiel d'un Rescapé* (Charleroi, 1919), 9.
48. LMD, 67; RDE, 489.
49. FSN, Jaumot, Collignon-Roba; LMD, 93; SN, 155.
50. RDE, 489.
51. FSN, Georges-Lebrun, FSN, Renard; LMD, 88; SN, 155–6, 156 n 1.
52. FSN, Van Heden, Thyrion-Mossiat; SN, 156; LMD, 69–70, 75. In other accounts the Germans themselves opened the door, following Mme. Drion's appeal.
53. SN, 158.
54. FSN, Thyrion-Mossiat, Jaumot.
55. RDE, 489.
56. FSN, Leblanc-Vilain; SN, 157, 160.
57. SN, 158.
58. FSN, Rénard.
59. FSN, Lenel-Lemineur.
60. SN, 158.
61. *Ibid.*, 159.
62. *Ibid.*
63. FSN, Biname; SN, 159–160.
64. FSN, Henry-Wasseige.
65. SN, 160.
66. RDE, 489.
67. LMD, 57, 90–1, 92.
68. *Ibid.*, 57.
69. *Ibid.*, 88; SN, 160.
70. SN, 160.
71. LMD, 57; SN, 163.
72. LMD, 92; SN, 163.
73. SN, 162–3, RDE, 485.
74. SN, 162.
75. *Ibid.*, 161.
76. *Ibid.*

77. RDE, 486, 489; LMD, 53. The officer addressing the victims was also described as a good-looking young man, no more than twenty-two or twenty-three. (LMD, 75)
78. SN, 162.
79. RDE, 483; SN, 162. Others reported similar comments. (LMD, 78)
80. SN, 164.
81. *Ibid.*, 165–6.
82. FSN, Georges-Lebrun.
83. SN, 164.
84. GSA, 435, Garnir; SN, 169 n. 2. Some four hundred saved themselves by hiding in the grottos of Rondpeine further north
85. FSN, Jassogne; SN, 169–170.
86. SN, 178–9.
87. *Ibid.*, 179.
88. Dr. Laurent independently confirmed his wife's testimony. (FSN, Laurent; SN, 180 n. 1.) A British-born Ursuline nun, Mother Marie-Grégoire, also observed German soldiers finishing off their wounded. (IWM, World War I Atrocities, 86/19/1.)
89. *Ibid.*, 179–180.
90. FSN, Laurent.
91. SN, 139 n. 1; 180.
92. *Ibid.*, 180.
93. *Ibid.*, 181.
94. This total does not include men who survived for up to a few hours, but then died of their wounds.
95. SN, 173–174.
96. SN, 174–5; RDE, 482; LMD, 79. The baron also sheltered the remnants of the Wasseige family. (FSN, Henry-Wasseige.)
97. SN, 177–8; RDE, 485–6; LMD, 53–55.
98. LMD, 58–60; SN, 175–6.
99. FSN, Van Heden; LMD, 82; SN, 177.
100. Gillet, 13.
101. FSN, Devanelle-Février.
102. FSN, Leblanc-Vilain.
103. *Ibid.*

CHAPTER 8: DINANT LES RIVAGES, NEFFE

1. DVF, 185.
2. *Ibid.*, 187.
3. *Ibid.*, 184.
4. *Ibid.*, 185.
5. N. Nieuwland and M. Tschoffen, *The Legend of the "Francs Tireurs" of Dinant* (Gembloux, 1929), 69.
6. DVF, 184.
7. SN, Part 4 *(Le Combat de Dinant)*, Book 2

(Le Sac de la Ville), 192.

8. *Ibid.*

9. DVF, 122.

10. SN, 221–2.

11. *Ibid.*, 221 n 1.

12. *Ibid.*, 193.

13. Anon., *Le Martyre de Dinant* (LMD) (Dinant, 1920), 142; SN, 193–4, n 3.

14. SN, 194.

15. *Ibid.*, 195.

16. *Ibid.*, 195–6; LMD, 139; RDE 1, 487–8.

17. SN, 196.

18. *Ibid.*, 197.

19. *Ibid.*, 198–200.

20. *Ibid.*, 201.

21. E. Bennett, *The German Army in Belgium* (New York, 1921), xi.

22. DVF, 184. Though the homes had been searched three times and all civilians rounded up, "the inhabitants opened up a murderous fire on the companies from all the houses and gardens and from the slopes of the mountains. Inside and outside the houses, men of all ages were firing, also innumerable women and even ten-year-old girls." (DVF, 183)

23. *Ibid.*, 187. According to this inventive Saxon officer, firing continued from the homes in Les Rivages even after the civilians had been mowed down against the Bourdon wall. Two franc-tireurs with ammunition in their pockets finally surrendered, and were duly executed. A woman with a revolver, however, was pardoned.

The compilers of the German White Book, Major Bauer and Dr. Wagner, were clearly nonplused at the murder of so many women and children. The bald lies of von Rochow and von Schlick were contradicted by too much evidence they themselves were intending to publish. The civilians being held by the Bourdon wall were hostages, Bauer and Wagner conceded. If franc-tireurs were firing on German troops, it was not these individuals who were doing the firing.

The authors made a half-hearted attempt to link the captives and their franc-tireur compatriots: when the hostages were shot, lo and behold, the firing ceased. The massacre was "evidently visible to the unseen franc-tirers" and the deaths chastened the guerillas. This was not a very satisfactory justification, however, and the authors conceded, in the end, that the gunfire directed against the pioneers constructing the bridge and grenadiers waiting to cross had resulted in "the greatest consternation and confusion. *As a result of this,* the male hostages assembled by the garden wall were shot."[italics mine] Chaos among the troops, then, was responsible for the massacre. (DVF, 123) What about the women and children? The authors claim they had been placed "somewhat further down the river." (*Ibid.*) How did they come to be killed? "A few women and children were also hit" because "in the general confusion, they had left their position and crowded together with the male hostages." Two annexes are cited, neither of which gives any evidence that this happened. (DVF, 126)

According to Sir James Edmonds, some members of Von Hausen's staff recognized the enormity of what had in fact transpired. "It will look bad in history," one of them observed. General von Hausen, however, was not perturbed. "We shall write the history ourselves," he replied. (J. Edmonds, *A Short History of World War I* (New York, 1968), 26.)

24. SN, 201.

25. *Ibid.*, 203.

26. *Ibid.*, 188.

27. Reply, 343.

28. SN, 208–9; Nieuwland and Tschoffen, 75; FSN, Dinant, R. Florin, L. Florin. Twenty residents, lying in the middle of the group, were uninjured.

29. SN, 213.

30. *Ibid.*; LMD, 154–5.

31. SN, 214; LMD, 153.

32. SN, 215.

33. *Ibid.*, 216.

34. *Ibid.*

35. *Ibid.*, 217.

36. *Ibid.*, 216–17.

37. FSN, R. Florin; SN, 219 n. 1.

38. *Ibid.*, 216; FSN, R. Florin; LMD, 148.

39. *Ibid.*, 148–9.

40. SN, 217 n.1.

41. *Ibid.*, 215; LMD, 157–8.

42. Nieuwland and Tschoffen, 76.

43. SN, 220.

44. FSN, L. Florin.

45. *Ibid.*

46. DVF, 122, 179–80.

47. SN, 222–3.

48. *Ibid.*, 225.

49. *Ibid.*, 226.

50. *Ibid.*

51. *Ibid.*

52. *Ibid.*, 258.

53. *Ibid.*, 250.

54. *Ibid.*, 251.

55. *Ibid.*, 259.

56. *Ibid.*, 260.

57. *Ibid.*, 267–8.

58. *Ibid.*, 261–2.

59. *Ibid.*, 264.

60. FSN, Dubois, 7.

61. SN, 265–6.

62. RVR 2, 96.

63. *Ibid.*

64. *Ibid.*, 97.

65. *Ibid.*

66. *Ibid.*, 98. He was able to get up later on and return to Dinant.

67. *Ibid.*, 99–100.

68. *Ibid.*, 100–101.

69. *Ibid.*, 101.

70. *Ibid.*, 103.

71. *Ibid.*, 104.

72. *Ibid.*, 93. Later, when he returned to Dinant, Tschoffen was told by General von Long-champs, Military Governor of Namur, that "the result of the inquiry I held was that no civilian fired at Dinant. But there may have been Frenchmen disguised as civilians who did, and then in the heat of battle one some-times goes further than one ought." While he appreciated the concession about the civilians, albeit belated, Tschoffen naturally rejected the hypothesis regarding French soldiers. (*Ibid.*)

73. E. Spears, *Liaison 1914* (New York, 1968), 153–4.

CHAPTER 9: LEUVEN PRELIMINARIES

1. Anon. [H. de Gruben], *The Germans at Lou-vain* (London, 1916), 5–7.

2. *Ibid.*, 7.

3. *Ibid.*, 8–9.

4. *Ibid.*, 9–10.

5. L. van der Essen, *The Invasion and the War in Belgium* (London, 1917), 47.

6. de Gruben, 10.

7. *Ibid.*, 12.

8. *Ibid.*, 13.

9. *Ibid.*

10. *Ibid.*, 14–15.

11. *Ibid.*, 16–17.

12. *Ibid.*, 21.

13. R. Chambry, *The Truth About Louvain* (London, 1915), 12–13.

14. RDE 2, 475.

15. *Ibid.*, 63, 415, 470; J. de Becker, "The Amer-ican College and the Great War," *American College Bulletin*, v. 13, n. 1 (1920), p. 5; GSA, Leuven, chemise 94, R. van Kerckhove.

16. RDE, 415.

17. Reply, 213, 267.

18. *Ibid.*, 267.

19. RBC, 243. When individual witnesses are identified by name, the source is the roster included in NA, HO 45/11061/266503/10 and/or /71.

20. Reply, 267.

21. RBC, 279, 280; RDE, 425, 475.

22. RBC, 279.

23. RDE, 416; Reply, 214.

24. Reply, 262.

25. RBC, 275.

26. Chambry, 12; Reply, 213.

27. de Gruben, 22–23.

28. Chambry, 15–17.

29. Reply, 254; GSA, chemise 94.

30. Reply, 214.

31. RBC, 267.

32. Reply, 248.

33. RBC, 246.

34. Reply, 244. This officer and the previous one must have arrived late in the evening, as the massacres in Aarschot commenced around 7:00 p.m. Belgian time on the 19th. The conversations could have taken place on a subsequent day, as troops continued streaming through Leuven, though seldom lodging overnight.

35. De Gruben, 25.

36. RDE, 64–5. The notice read as follows:

    INHABITANTS

We don't make war against citizens but only against the enemy army. Despite this German troops have been attacked in great numbers by persons not belonging to the army. They have committed *acts of the most gruesome cruelty* not only against combat-ants but also against our wounded and our doctors who were seeking protection under the red cross.

To prevent these brutalities in the future, I order the following: …

In the case of a single weapon found in no matter what home or that any hostile act is committed against our troops, our transports, our telegraphic lines, our railways or that anyone gives asylum to franc tireurs, the guilty and the hostages that will be arrested in each village will be shot without pity. …

I will give no pardon!

The General commander-in-chief

37. De Gruben, 26. Manteuffel was not installed until the 22nd.

38. L. Grondys [Grondijs], *The Germans in Belgium: Experiences of a Neutral* (London, 1915), 49.

39. Reply, 213–14, 246, 267.

40. *Ibid.*, 214.

41. RDE, 481.

42. *Ibid.*

43. *Ibid.*, 416, 482.

45. *Ibid.*, 482.

46. *Ibid.*, 417.

47. *Ibid.*, 482.

48. *Ibid.*, 425–6.

49. Reply, 240.

50. PRW, Leuven, Report of Abbé Tuyls; Reply, 260.

51. RDE, 475–6.

52. RBC, 275.

53. GSA, *chemise* 92, G. Bomans.

54. Reply, 261, 269–70; RBC, 243; GSA, 93, L. F. Lemaire. 53. RDE, 416.

55. *Ibid.*, 425.

56. *Ibid.*, 476.

57. Reply, 278.

58. RBC, 244.

59. Chambry, 63–65.

60. GSA, 27.

61. RDE, 427, 447–8; Reply, 249.

62. RDE, 394; Reply, 281. It is not likely that the hospitals were evacuated in anticipation of casualties from the First Sortie, the assault on German defensive positions by the Belgian Army. The only clash between German and Belgian forces on the 24th began late in the day, and was a diversionary attack by the 5th Division toward Willebroek, some 22 miles northwest of Leuven. The hospitals in Brussels were far closer.

63. RDE, 504.

64. Chambry, 20–21. Chambry stated the story under oath.

65. Reply, 241, 249, 269.

66. *Ibid.*, 241.

67. RDE, 491.

68. Reply, 281.

69. PRW, Blauwput.

70. RDE., 100.

71. *Ibid.*, 101.

72. Reply, 281.

73. RDE, 101.

74. *Ibid.*

75. *Ibid.*

76. *Ibid.*, 102.

77. *Ibid.*

CHAPTER 10: LEUVEN FIRE AND SWORD

1. RDE 2, 476; Reply, 246, 254; RBC, 246. (When individual witnesses are identified by name, the source is the roster included in NA, HO 45/11061/266503/10 and/ or /71.) DVF, 305; P. Schöller, *Le cas de Louvain et le Livre Blanc allemand* (Leuven, 1958), 38–40.

2. GSA, Leuven, *chemise* 94, Verbruggen.

3. RBC, 240; DVF, 249.

4. GSA, Leuven, 93, de Brieuz.

5. DVF, 251.

6. RDE, 684.

7. DVF, 251, 255, 259.

8. *Ibid.*, 262.

9. *Ibid.*, 263.

10. *Ibid.*

11. *Ibid.*, 293, 309.

12. *Ibid.*, 264.

13. *Ibid.*, 264, 265–6, 271.

14. Reply, 264; RDE, 394. The most significant, a rocket fired into the Oude Markt, is described below.

15. Reply, 245.

16. *Ibid.*, 236.

17. DVF, 308. Ordered to find lodging for his company's officers, the paymaster of Reserve Railroad Construction Company 11 discovered that all the rooms in Stationsplein were already occupied by officers of other units.

18. RDE, 500.

19. *Ibid.*, 466–7.

20. Reply, 261.

21. DVF, 288–9.

22. *Ibid.*, 305–6.

23. *Ibid.*, 253.

24. *Ibid.*, 261.

25. *Ibid.*, 302.

26. *Ibid.*, 262, 263–4, 265, 271, 272, 273.

27. *Ibid.*, 263.

28. *Ibid.*, 252.

29. *Ibid.*, 253.

30. *Ibid.*, 259.
31. *Ibid.*, 251.
32. *Ibid.*, 272.
33. Schöller, 95.
34. *Ibid.*, 94. This testimony was given in 1921, before an investigative tribunal established under the Ministry of War, in lieu of extraditing to Belgium officers accused of war crimes. (Schöller, 80–82.)
35. *Ibid.*, 94.
36. *Ibid.*
37. *Ibid.*, 95.
38. GSA, Leuven, 94, Verbruggen.
39. GSA, Leuven, 32, Verhelst; Schöller, 96; RDE, 70; Anon. [H. de Gruben], *The Germans at Louvain* (London, 1916), 41–2.
40. PRW, Leuven, van Steenberghe; RDE, 77–8, which gives the husband's name as Pierre.
41. RDE, 513; Reply, 241, 251.
42. Reply, 246.
43. *Ibid.*, 243.
44. RBC, 254.
45. RDE, 467.
46. RBC, 244.
47. GSA, Leuven, 33, Tuyls.
48. DVF, 255.
49. *Ibid.*, 253.
50. Report compiled by the Commander-in-Chief of the Belgian Army, *The War of 1914, Military Operations of Belgium* (London, 1915), 40–1; L. van der Essen, The Invasion and the War in Belgium from Liège to the Yser (London, 1917), 180–1. E. Galet, *Albert, King of the Belgians, in the Great War* (Boston, 1931), 139. "The first day's experience confirmed only too well the estimate we had made of the fighting capacities both of our leaders and our troops – in other words, of the real worth of the Army," Galet, Albert's chief military advisor, bitterly concluded. "Now all illusions had been dispelled." (*Ibid.*)
51. RDE, 512–13.
52. DVF, 251, 253.
53. *Ibid.*, 253.
54. *Ibid.*, 251.
55. L. van der Essen, *The Invasion*, 189; A. Fuglister, *A Neutral Description of the Sack of Louvain* (Concord, NH, 1929), 8.
56. Reply, 241. Von Sandt was presented to General von Boehn, the senior commander in Leuven, and asked if he was willing to swear under oath that civilians had fired on

his men. When he promptly did so, this may have sealed the town's fate. (DVF, 254.)
57. RBC, 257–8.
58. DVF, 242.
59. *Ibid.*, 274.
60. *Ibid.*, 232, 233, 243.
61. *Ibid.*, 257, 262, 264, 265, 277.
62. *Ibid.*, 244, 246, 249.
63. *Ibid.*, 249; Schöller, 58.
64. DVF, 244.
65. *Ibid.*, 259, 246, 302.
66. *Ibid.*, 236.
67. *Ibid.*, 229. It declares these losses to be those of "the Staff of the General Command" alone, but includes the names of officers serving with various units throughout the city. The corpses of sixteen German soldiers were recovered from Van de Weyer square, in front of the station, in January 1915, when communal authorities received permission to exhume the bodies of victims. (Reply, 282.) The square, named after a leader of the Belgian revolution, signer of the 1839 Treaty of London and the country's first Foreign Minister, was renamed Martyrs' Square (Martelarenplein) after the war.
68. *Ibid.*, 245.
69. *Ibid.*, 278.
70. De Gruben, 33–4.
71. DVF, 253.
72. *Ibid.*, 289.
73. Reply, 253.
74. L. Grondys [Grondijs], *The Germans in Belgium: Experiences of a Neutral* (London, 1915), 55–56.
75. *Ibid.*, 55–56.
76. RBC, 258.
77. RDE, 395; GSA, Leuven, 94, Verbruggen.
78. Reply, 252.
79. *Ibid.*, 242 n. 1.
80. *Ibid.*, 242.
81. DVF, 241, 261, 267, 272, 290.
82. RBC, 264.
83. *Ibid.*, 275–276, 271.
84. Grondijs, 37, 51; Reply, 271; RDE, 445–6, 515.
85. Reply, 264.
86. RDE, 394.
87. RBC, 264.
88. *Ibid.*, 269.
89. Grondijs, 49.
90. RBC, 279–80.
91. RDE, 477–8.

92. *Ibid.*, 69.
93. R. Chambry, *The Truth About Louvain* (London, 1915), 21–23.
94. J. de Becker, "The American College and the Great War," *American College Bulletin*, v. 13, n. 1 (1920), 7.
95. Chambry, 23–25.
96. Reply, 252. Information on professors comes from *Annuaire de l'Université Catholique de Louvain, 1914*.
97. De Gruben, 32–34.
98. Reply, 242–3.
99. RDE, 476.
100. *Ibid.*, 477–8.
101. *Ibid.*, 478.
102. Grondijs, 39.
103. *Ibid.*
104. *Ibid.*, 42.
105. *Ibid.*, 48.
106. *Ibid.*, 45.
107. *Ibid.*, 49.
108. H. Davignon, *Belgium and Germany* (London, 1915), 55.
109. Grondijs, 49.
110. *Ibid.*, 44.
111. De Gruben, 11; RBC, 268; Chambry, 26.
112. RDE, 480.
113. *Ibid.*, 410.
114. *Ibid.*, 428.
115. *Ibid.*
116. *Ibid.*, 512.
117. B. Whitlock, Belgium, *A Personal Narrative*, v. 1 (New York, 1920), 192–3.
118. Revealingly, Manteuffel didn't bother questioning the gendarme who was sent to fetch him. It was only en route back to the Stadhuis that the policeman revealed that there had been reports of civilians firing on soldiers. (DVF, 244.)
119. RDE, 463.
120. *Ibid.*, 417–18.
121. *Ibid.*, 420.
122. Other witnesses heard a figure of 25 million. (RDE, 463, 465.)
123. *Ibid.*, 418.
124. *Ibid.*, 459.
125. *Ibid.*, 463.
126. *Ibid.*, 459–60.
127. *Ibid.*, 429.
128. *Ibid.*, 419.
129. *Ibid.*, 460.
130. *Ibid.*, 419, 430.
131. *Ibid.*, 430.
132. *Ibid.*

133. DVF, 257.
134. RDE, 420.
135. *Ibid.*, 431, 451.
136. DVF, 257.
137. RDE, 480.
138. De Gruben, 96–97.
139. RDE, 480; De Gruben, 95–98; RBC, 268; PRW, Leuven, List of bodies found or exhumed in Leuven.
140. RDE, 431.
141. *Ibid.*, 420.
142. *Ibid.*, 500–1.
143. *Ibid.*, 420, 502.
144. *Ibid.*, 460.
145. *Ibid.*, 436.
146. *Ibid.*, 421.
147. *Ibid.*, 420–1.
148. PRW, Leuven, a two-page report Schmit wrote for Cardinal Mercier; RDE, 421.
149. RDE, 422.
150. *Ibid.* Baron Orban de Xivry came to the same conclusion: "He struck me as weak and hesitant." (*Ibid.*, 436.)
151. *Ibid.*, 435.
152. *Ibid.*, 480.
153. De Gruben, 89.
154. L. Mokveld, *The German Fury in Belgium* (New York, 1917), 121.
155. *Ibid.*
156. *Ibid.*, 122.
157. *Ibid.*, 127.
158. *Ibid.*, 129.
159. Grondijs, 45.
160. P. Delannoy, "The Library of the University of Louvain," *The Nineteenth Century*, v. lxxvii, n. 459, (May 1915), 1061–1071. Most of the information in this and the following four paragraphs is derived from this article, by the university's chief librarian, along with additional information from M. Derez, "The Flames of Louvain: The War Experience of an Academic Community" in H. Cecil and P. Liddell, *Facing Armageddon* (London, 1996), 617–27.
161. RDE, 73.
162. PRW, Leuven-St Michel.
163. *Ibid.*, Leuven, Devijver. *(Rapport des événements de Louvain 26 août et jours suivants. Faits observés au vieux-Marché)*
164. *Ibid.* A graduate in commercial sciences, the twenty-seven-year-old Devijver was studying at the Higher Institute of Philosophy in Leuven. He would go on to teach economics at Trinity College. (Communication

from Father Paul Janssens, 27 February 2007.)

165. Reply, 281.

166. GSA, Leuven, 33, Slagmelder

167. Anon. ("Dr. of Physics and Mathematics"), *An Eyewitness at Louvain* (London, 1914), 3–4.

168. PRW, Leuven, Devyver. The professor watching from the roof of the college also observed a fire engine at the north end of the square "protecting the approaches to the Stadhuis." (*An Eyewitness*, 4.). It is safe to assume that the anonymous Josephite Father mentioned by Abbé Aloijsius van den Bergh, emissary of the Prince-Archbishop of Vienna, was Devyver.

169. RDE, 73; de Gruben, 94.

170. Fulgister, 15.

171. PRW, Leuven, Report of Abbé Tuyls; Leuven-St. Michel.

172. Reply, 271. Professor Georges Bruylants, President of the Belgian Academy of Medicine, recklessly ventured into the Oude Markt at 4:00 a.m. and then twice afterwards. Several houses on the western side of the square were still in flames. A sentry, reeking of gin, told him soldiers had been fired on from University Hall. Bruylants imagined that a quarrel had broken out in one or more of the cafés in the Oude Markt, and the men had retreated to opposite ends of the square, sniping at each other.

173. PRW, Leuven-St. Pieters; Fulgister, 15–17; de Gruben, 92–3; Grondijs, 39–40; *An Eyewitness*, 4.

174. RDE, 463.

175. *Ibid.*, 461.

176. De Gruben, 93.

177. RDE, 464.

178. Reply, 277–8; RDE, 392.

179. IWM, World War I Atrocities: 86/19/1. "I have learned quite a lot about bullet wounds," she noted drily.

180. GSA, Leuven, 92, Schadts.

181. Chambry, 29–30.

182. *Ibid.*, 49; Reply, 284; GSA, Leuven, 94, Bruylants.

183. RDE, 75.

184. PRW, Leuven, eleven-page typed ms, probably by Father Claes; Reply, 286.

185. PRW, Leuven, Tuyls; Leuven, List of bodies found or exhumed in Leuven; RDE, 77, 453–4 (where Jean Mahy is mistakenly referred to as Adolphe, another victim).

186. RDE, 241.

187. RBC, 245–6.

188. De Gruben, 44–5. Some kind of impromptu court martial may have met at the station, but there is very little testimony about it, either Belgian or German. The only soldier describing the proceedings was a young volunteer driver with a vivid imagination, Richard Gruner, who claimed to have served as the tribunal's translator. He estimated that eighty to one hundred civilians were shot "according to martial law," including ten to fifteen priests (one of whom had a loaded revolver which had just been fired). His two depositions, the longest in Appendix D, are completely unreliable. For one thing, only five priests were killed in Leuven and surrounding communities; none brandished a loaded revolver. (DVF, 293–8.)

189. De Gruben, 45.

190. RDE, 81–2; RBC, 246.

191. GSA, 94; RVR 2, 178–80. Several soldiers expressed their disgust cryptically to Belgian civilians. And after order was restored in town, some high-ranking Germans visiting the ruins, including the Chancellor, expressed privately their dismay over the behavior of their troops on the 25th and 26th.

192. French Ministry of Foreign Affairs, *Germany's Violations of the Laws of War, 1914–1915* (London, 1915), 187–8; J. Bédier, *How Germany Seeks to Justify her Atrocities* (Paris, 1915), 45–6.

193. De Gruben, 36–40.

194. *Ibid.*, 50.

195. RDE, 422.

196. De Gruben, 50–1.

197. *Ibid.*, 397.

198. *Ibid.*, 472; De Becker, 9.

199. RDE, 478–9.

200. *Ibid.*, 479.

201. Reply, 262.

202. *Ibid.*, 253.

203. Chambry, 40.

204. Grondjis, 51–2.

205. Reply, 262.

206. RDE, 396.

207. De Gruben, 74–5.

208. *Ibid.*, 72–3.

209. *Ibid.*, 73.

210. *Ibid.*, 76–7.

211. *Ibid.*, 85–7.

212. *Ibid.*, 90–1.

213. *Ibid.*, 92–3. Ironically, Hervé de Gruben would go on to serve as Belgium's Ambassador to Germany following the Second World War.

214. Mokveld, 141.

215. *Ibid.*

216. *Ibid.*, 115–117.

217. *Ibid.*, 128.

CHAPTER 11: LEUVEN EXODUS

1. Reply, 245. Information on faculty members comes from *Annuaire de l'Université Catholique de Louvain, 1914.*

2. RDE 2, 508.

3. Reply, 253.

4. RDE, 493–4.

5. Anon. ("Dr. of Physics and Mathematics"), *An Eyewitness at Louvain* (London, 1914), 5–6.

6. Reply, 263.

7. *Ibid.*

8. RDE, 473. Another cleric provided a still different version: "At the beginning of the war we laughed when French newspapers spoke of the invasion of barbarian hordes. Those who, like us, have seen the conduct of the Germans at Leuven now know what to expect. Genseric's methods were no different. After the burning of the Library and the University, the barbarians can no longer have a word to say against Khalif Omar for burning the Library at Alexandria. And all in the name of German culture!" (*An Eyewitness*, 6–7)

9. *An Eyewitness*, 6.

10. *Ibid.*, 7.

11. Reply, 263.

12. RDE, 473–4. See the more detailed account in J. de Becker, "The American College and the Great War," *American College Bulletin* (v. 13, n. 1) (1920), pp. 13–14.

13. B. Whitlock, Belgium: *A Personal Narrative* (New York, 1920), 151–2.

14. L. Grondys [Grondijs], *The Germans in Belgium: Experiences of a Neutral* (London, 1915), 59, 74.

15. Whitlock, 154–5.

16. *Ibid.*, 155.

17. *Ibid.*, 159–160.

18. Grondijs, 26.

19. *Ibid.*, 62.

20. RDE, 467–8.

21. Grondijs, 64–5.

22. *Ibid.*, 72.

23. *Ibid.*, 75.

24. RDE, 468.

25. *Ibid.*, 469.

26. Grondijs, 81.

27. Reply, 251.

28. PRW, Leuven, Gevangenneming van Pater Raynerius Snel, Minderbroeder.

29. RBC, 245. When individuals providing testimony have been identified by name, this has been made possible by logs in NA, HO 45/11061/266503/10 and/or /71.

30. PRW, Leuven, Snel; Leuven, Father François Neyens, curé of St. Joseph's; [Laurent Noël], "Narrative of a Professor of Louvain," *The Hibbert Journal* (v. 13, n. 2) (Jan. 1915), 282–3; Reply, 251–2; L. van der Essen, *A Statement about the Destruction of Louvain and Neighborhood* (Chicago, 1915), 20; L. van der Essen, *Some More News about the Destruction of Louvain* (Chicago, 1915), 1.

31. Reply, 250; Van der Essen, *Statement*, 20.

32. Reply, 245.

33. *Ibid.*, 251.

34. *Ibid.*

35. Noël, "Narrative...", 282–3.

36. R. Chambry, *The Truth About Louvain* (London, 1915), 41.

37. *Ibid.*, 44–5.

38. Reply, 245.

39. Chambry, 52–7.

40. RBC, 251–2.

41. RBC, 251.

42. *Ibid.*

43. *Ibid.*, 246

44. *Ibid.*, 246–7. The details as to the timing of the arrest differ in the two accounts he provided.

45. Reply, 254.

46. RBC, 247.

47. Reply, 255.

48. RBC, 247; Reply, 255.

49. GSA, Leuven, *chemise* 36.

50. RBC, 247–8.

51. *Ibid.*, 248.

52. *Ibid.*, 240.

53. Reply, 247; RBC, 240.

54. L. van der Essen, *The Invasion and the War in Belgium from Liège to the Yser* (London, 1917), 180–4; E. Galet, *Albert, King of the Belgians, in the Great War* (Boston, 1931), 139–143.

55. RBC, 241.

56. Reply, 275; see also the account in [Anon.], *A South American Priest in Belgium* (London, 1915) (reprint of article in *La Tribuna* (Paraguay) 24 February 1915).
57. *Ibid.*
58. GSA, Leuven, 94, Rémy; RBC, 242; Reply, 246. Some of the men were given the choice of standing, kneeling, or lying down.
59. GSA, Leuven, 94, Rémy; RBC, 242; Reply, 246–7, 275.
60. RBC, 242.
61. GSA, Leuven, 94, Rémy.
62. Reply, 247.
63. RBC, 258.
64. *Ibid.*, 259.
65. *Ibid.*, 260.
66. *Ibid.*
67. *Ibid.*
68. *Ibid.*, 261.
69. Reply, 248–9.
70. RBC, 265.
71. Reply, 246; RBC, 265.
72. RDE, 516.
73. RBC, 265.
74. RDE, 498, 516; De Becker, 8; Reply, 282.
75. PRW, Bovenlo, Naerhuysen.
76. PRW, Leuven, De Strycker.
77. RBC, 261; [Anon.], *A South American Priest...*, 5.
78. PRW, Leuven, Report on Corpses Summarily Buried in Van de Weyer Square.
79. Whitlock, 149–50.
80. *New York Tribune*, 31 August 1914.
81. RDE, 496.
82. *Ibid.*, 497.
83. *Ibid.*
84. *Ibid.*, 498.
85. *Ibid.*, 432; RBC, 265.
86. RDE, 432.
87. Reply, 246.
88. RDE, 433.
89. *Ibid.*, 434.
90. *Ibid.*, 494.
91. RBC, 277; Chambry, 33. Like their counterparts throughout Western Europe, the Civic Guard was a largely middle-class volunteer militia – one had to purchase one's uniform, and these were not cheap. The men generally drilled once a month, but the Civic Guard was more a fraternal organization than a National Guard corps in the U.S. sense – there was likely to be more parading than putting down riots or dealing with municipal emergencies.

92. Chambry, 33–4; Van der Essen, *Statement*, 16.
93. Reply, 265; GSA, Leuven, 33, Tuyls.
94. RBC, 277; Van der Essen, *Statement*, 17.
95. RBC, 276, 278; Van der Essen, *Statement*, 19.
96. RBC, 274.
97. Van der Essen, *Statement*, 18; Reply, 264.
98. Reply, 264; RBC, 278.
99. Reply, 265; RDE, 508.
100. RBC, 252.
101. *Ibid.*, 253. In fact, the residents must have been provided with some water; the trip, with the layover in Aachen, lasted over four days.
102. RDE, 517.
103. GSA, Leuven, 33, Tuyls.
104. RDE, 464.
105. *Ibid.*, 464–5.
106. PRW, Leuven, Huypens.
107. Reply, 265.
108. RBC, 253.
109. GSA, Leuven, 33, Tuyls.
110. RDE, 507.
111. RBC, 253; Reply, 266.
112. Reply, 266; RDE, 517–18, 519.
113. RDE, 517–518.
114. *Ibid.*, 517.
115. *Ibid.*, 508.
116. *Ibid.*, 509.
117. RBC, 254; Reply, 266; GSA, Leuven, 33, Tuyls. Rosaries had been confiscated soon after the men had arrived in Munster, but, if Pastoor Huypens' experience was typical, some Catholic soldiers provided the Belgians with replacements. (PRW, Leuven, Huypens)
118. GSA, Leuven, 33, Verhelst; RBC, 254.
119. RDE, 507.
120. *Ibid.*, 506.
121. *Ibid.*, 507.
122. *Ibid.*, 518.
123. Reply, 267; RDE, 507; GSA, Leuven, 33, Tuyls.
124. Reply, 267.
125. RBC, 271; Reply, 257.
126. RDE, 506.
127. Reply, 257.
128. RBC, 255.
129. PRW, Leuven, Huypens; RBC, 271.
130. RBC, 271.
131. In most accounts, the mob in Köln, which one witness estimated at about 4,000, was menacing. "They made all kinds of gestures

to show us that we were going to be shot or hanged," recalled Alphonse Wijnants. (Reply, 261) But in one instance, when a woman held up one of her young children, "a hush came over the crowd." (RBC, 248) Another witness spoke of some of the faces in the crowd thronging the street as "more humane" than elsewhere. (Reply, 257)

132. RBC, 256.
133. *Ibid.*, 261–2, 263, 272; Reply, 255, 259, 261.
134. Reply, 255.
135. RBC, 272.
136. *Ibid.*, 256.
137. Reply, 255, 256; RBC, 270.
138. Reply, 256.
139. RBC, 256, 262, 263.
140. *Ibid.*, 262.
141. *La Roumanie*, Bucharest, Sept. 5–18, 1914, cited by Anon. [H. de Gruben], *The Germans at Louvain* (London, 1916), 69n.
142. Reply, 259; RBC, 272.
143. Reply, 259.
144. RBC, 263.
145. Reply, 259.
146. *La Roumanie*, Bucharest, Sept. 5–18th, 1914, cited by de Gruben, 70n.
147. Reply, 259.
148. RBC, 256.
149. *Ibid.*, 272.
150. *Ibid.*, 256–7.
151. *Ibid.*, 257; Reply, 260. Like Van Steenbeeck, Father Huypens was also told to flee by soldiers guarding him, prior to the trip to Munsterlager. At first he thought they were sincere, but heard the click of a rifle being loaded nearby and turned them down. They were furious, and beat him as they returned him to Wezemaal. (PRW, Leuven, Huypens)
152. RBC, 273; Reply, 256, 261.

CHAPTER 12: LEUVEN AFTERMATH

1. RDE 2, 453.
2. *Ibid.*, 448; Reply, 282.
3. RDE, 449.
4. *Ibid.*
5. *Ibid.*, 450.
6. *Ibid.*, 452.
7. L. Mokveld, *The German Fury in Belgium* (New York, 1917), 135.
8. RDE, 453.
9. Anon. [H. de Gruben], *The Germans at Louvain* (London, 1916), 89.

10. Reply, 251.
11. RDE, 448.
12. *Ibid.*, 450–1. On his return to Germany, Sonnenschein published an article in a leading Catholic paper absolving the University and the clergy from any responsibility for "the trouble" at Leuven. But he did not venture any criticisms of the German Army, needless to say. ("In Löwen," *Kölnische Volkszeitung*, 10 September 1914; cited by De Gruben, 95.)
13. RDE, 405, 410.
14. *Ibid.*, 457.
15. Reply, 282; PRW, Leuven, Report on Corpses Summarily Buried in Van de Weyer Square. Bart Mokveld overheard the colonel say, "It's incomprehensible that this should be the outcome when one knows how well educated and cultured our nation is!" (Reply, 282.)
16. PRW, Leuven, Report on Corpses.
17. RDE, 411.
18. *Ibid.* Monsigneur Ladeuze, Rector of the University, never heard Lubbert express an opinion about the events of the 25th and 26th. The assistant civilian commissioner, Herr Kreuter, however, abandoned his initial preconception that residents had fired on the troops. "We'll never know the truth about the events in Leuven," he confided to the Rector. (*Ibid.*, 470.)
19. *Ibid.*, 408.
20. *Ibid.*, 456.
21. *Ibid.*, 479–80.
22. *Ibid.*, 456.
23. PRW, Leuven, Parijs.
24. RDE, 480.
25. *Ibid.*, 494–5. Beaudrin calls him a captain, but he refers to himself as *Oberleutnant*.
26. *Ibid.*, 520.
27. *Ibid.*, 521.
28. *Ibid.*
29. *Ibid.*, 521–2.
30. *Ibid.*, 522.
31. *Ibid.*, 495.
32. *Ibid.*
33. *Ibid.* On Reinbrecht, see also B. Lefebvre, S.J., *L'Abbaye du Mont César à Louvain et les Incendiaires allemands de 1914* (Brussels, 1920).
34. *Ibid.*, 454.
35. Gibson would go on to have a distinguished career with the State Department. The son of a Los Angeles banker, he was the first

American diplomat to attend the prestigious *École Libre des Sciences Politiques* in Paris – quite fortuitously. As a twenty-year-old visiting France with his widowed mother, when their baggage failed to materialize in Calais before their ship was to sail, Gibson announced that it was quite all right – he preferred to return to Paris and study there. Gibson is memorialized by the cocktail bearing his name. (Ironically, the original "Gibson" was pure water – a second drink made him tipsy – and the obliging bartender inserted a pickled onion to distinguish the ersatz martini from the gin and vermouth variety.)(P. C. Galpin, ed., *Hugh Gibson* (New York, 1956), 28, 159.

36. H. Gibson, *A Journal From Our Legation in Belgium* (Garden City, NY, 1917), 154.
37. *Ibid.*, 156–158.
38. *Ibid.*, 159–160.
39. *Ibid.*, 161.
40. *Ibid.*, 162–163.
41. *Ibid.*, 163.
42. *Ibid.*, 164.
43. *Ibid.*, 164–5.
44. *Ibid.*, 165.
45. *Ibid.*, 166, 168.
46. *Ibid.*, 169.
47. *Ibid.*, 170.
48. B. Whitlock, *Belgium: A Personal Narrative* (New York, 1920), 188–9, 293; Belgians who learned of the episode were especially indignant. (Reply, 276, 280.)
49. Gibson, 171–2.
50. Whitlock, 295.
51. *Ibid.*, 295–6.
52. GSA, Leuven, *chemise* 92,Workman.
53. Reply, 249.
54. *Ibid.*, 253.
55. RBC, 267.
56. R. Chambry, *The Truth About Louvain* (London, 1915), 73–77.

CHAPTER 13: EXPLANATIONS

1. Horne and Kramer, *German Atrocities*, 132. The authors concede that the men were made "receptive" by prior warnings and that "during the main invasion the part played by the military command became much more pronounced." When "the main invasion" commenced is not made clear.
2. *Ibid.*, 152–3. The novel was *Volk wider Volk*, the second in a trilogy by the future Nazi apologist Walter Bloem. Speculating about

the influence of novels is clearly hazardous. One would not want to infer from the popularity of the Austrian Bertha von Suttner's *Die Waffen Nieder!* that most Austrians and Germans were pacifists.

3. Students were taught how Stein, from his Moscow exile, called for a popular uprising against the French, and how, when the Prussian monarch Friedrich Wilhelm came round, he demanded that "every son of the fatherland participate in this battle for honor and freedom." (cited in J. Sheehan, *German History, 1770–1866* (Oxford, 1989), 315.) Andreas Hofer, the anti-French guerilla leader in the Tyrol, was honored as a latter-day Wilhelm Tell, and the peasants and workers who rushed to join the *Landwehr* (the Prussian Garde Civil) were hailed as the liberators of the nation. Positive images of civilian marksmen were enshrined as well in Schiller's *Wilhelm Tell* itself and in Weber's *Der Freischütz*, one of the most popular plays and one of the most popular operas in Germany.

4. See, for example, the frequent articles by Edith Sellers in the *Fortnightly Review* and *Contemporary Review* and the admiring books by American commentators like Elmer Roberts and Price Collier.

5. According to the recollections of veterans at a meeting of the Florida Citrus Chapter of the Veterans of the Battle of the Bulge, 12 February 2005, this was the chief preoccupation of military authorities. Fraternization, of course, meant having sex with German women. The pamphlet did instruct officers to have their men carry their weapons and wear their helmets at all times, to "walk in groups of not less than two," and to disarm all civilians. One soldier was warned not to eat anything found in a home after house-to-house combat, as it might be poisoned. Otherwise there was no suggestion that troops had anything to fear from German civilians, except for the corruption of their morals and venereal disease.

6. While the morality of the strategic bombing campaign can be debated, it is simply not analogous to the two invasions by infantry forces being compared. Belgian civilians were not killed as part of a campaign to disable the production of war materiel for an army that had conquered a dozen countries and enslaved and massacred millions.

7. E. St. Clair Stobart, "Within the Enemy's Lines," *Fortnightly Review* (1914), 670–684.

8. According to the *Berliner Zeitung am Mittag* of August 5, sixty-four "spies" were seized by unruly mobs on August 3rd. "Among others who were 'captured' and threatened with death by the raging crowd on the Potsdamer Platz were: a pensioned Prussian major...; a surgeon in the Landwehr, a high official from the Courts of Justice; and lastly, a pensioned Bavarian army officer who, on account of his stature, was thought to be a Russian. A drunken shop-assistant egged on the crowd against this last suspect, so that his life was really in danger..."(Cited in T. F. A. Smith, *What Germany Thinks* (New York, 1916), 93. Another hair-raising experience, this time in Frankfurt, was recounted by R. S. Nolan, who was mistaken by a mob for a Russian in disguise. (R. S. Nolan, "Germany Today," *Nineteenth Century* (14 October 1914), 783.) No one was killed in Berlin on this day, but the official rumor that French officers in disguise were transporting gold to Russia in motorcars resulted in several unlucky motorists and passengers being shot to death.(Smith, 94–101.)

9. G. McClellan, "How Germany Looks to George B. McClellan," *New York Times* 26 Sept. 1915, (Sunday Magazine), 5. This belief, as noted, was based on documents discovered in Brussels reporting on two inconclusive conversations between British and Belgian military authorities regarding ways in which the two armies might coordinate operations following a German invasion. In 1911, the talks were suspended without any agreement; the Germans pushed ahead with their invasion plans. (In fact, German ingenuity in doctoring the reports found in the Brussels archives was probably superfluous. "England is a disgusting hypocrite," proclaimed the Governor General's wife, Baroness von Bissing, to an American visitor. "It is a pleasant joke of theirs, about our invading Belgium first, but I know that the English and French were there before us." (E. D. Bullitt, *An Uncensored Diary from the Central Empires* (New York, 1917), 79.) Among other notable examples of paranoia was the conviction of Eric von Ludendorff, de facto ruler of Germany for most of 1916–18, that Jews and Freemasons were responsible for the setback at the Marne in September 1914. (A. Mombauer, "Myths and Realities of Germany's 'Fateful Battle,' *The Historian*, v. 68, n. 4, 765–6.)

10. "The charge of treachery," concluded the Danish theologian J. P. Bang, "is nothing but hysteria... The German conceptions of Edward VII and Sir Edward Grey are... purely fantastic." (J. Bang, *Hurrah and Hallelujah: The Teaching of Germany's Poets, Prophets, Professors and Preachers* (New York, 1917), 214.) See also the Orwellian definitions of "encirclement," "benevolent neutrality," and "localization of the conflict," current in Germany in July. The first meant that Germany would not be able to attack in the west without risking a counterattack in the east, and vice versa, the second meant that the rights of neutrals as defined by the Fifth Hague Convention of 1907 would be abrogated and Germany's treaty obligations ignored, and the last meant that Austria would have a free hand to incorporate Belgrade into the Empire, distribute other regions of Serbia to Bulgaria, Greece, and Albania, and install a puppet regime in the remainder of the country.

11. Notwithstanding the dubious caveat that "one man's terrorist is another man's freedom fighter," the legal definitions of terrorism in the United States are unexceptionable. The Code of Federal Regulations stipulates that terrorism is "the unlawful use of force and violence against persons or property to intimidate or coerce a government" (28 CFR, Section 85) and Title 22 of the United States Code, Section 2656f(d) states that "the term 'terrorism' means premeditated, politically motivated violence perpetrated against noncombatants..."

12. cited in Somville, xi.

13. GSA, 119 (Aarschot), Thiere.

14. RDE, Book 1, 460.

15. RBC, 97; Reply, 138; RDE I, 449; GSA, 417 (Andenne), Pirsoul, Vaesen; FSN, Seilles, Andenne, Frère Reginald; SN, Part 2, 34–35.

16. RDE 1, 379; RVR 2, 94; SN, Part 4 *(Le Combat de Dinant)*, Book 2 *(Le Sac de la Ville)*, 41, 58; FSN, Dinant, Lemotte.

17. SN, Part 3 *(Tamines et la Bataille de la Sambre)*, 72, 130.

18. Reply, 241, 249, 269; RDE 2, 504; R. Chambry, *The Truth About Louvain*

(London, 1915), 20–21.

19. RDE 2, 100–102, 491; PRW, Blauwput. Several residents noted the odd behavior of officers taking their leave when put on the alert at 8:00 p.m. "With tears in his eyes," one told Englebert Cappuyns, "'We shall not meet again, so it is goodbye.'" (E. Cappuyns, *Louvain: A Personal Experience* (Kingston-on-Thames, 1915), 13.)

20. RDE 1, 374, 380, 456; SN, Part 2, 34; RBC, 97; Reply, 138; GSA, 417 (Andenne), Pirsoul; RDE 2, 476; Reply, 256, 254; RBC, 246; P. Schöller, *Le cas de Louvain et le Livre Blanc allemand* (Leuven, 1958), 38–40; DVF, 268; GSA, Leuven, chemise 94, Verbruggen.

21. RVR 2, 56.

22. RDE 1, 311; Somville, 162.

23. RDE 1, 344.

24. *Ibid.*, 322. An entry from the diary of Sgt. Reinhold Koehn, 2nd Battalion of Engineers, iiird Army Corps reads as follows: "During the night of the 15th–16th in the town of Visé, Engineer Gr. sounded the alarm. Everyone was shot or taken prisoner, and the houses burned down." No franc-tireur attack is mentioned. (French Ministry of Foreign Affairs, *Germany's Violations*, 163–5.)

25. Reply, 84, 127; Somville, 31–5; J. Thier and O. Gilbart, *Liege Pendant La Grande Guerre*, v. 2 (Liege, 1919), 189, 191; Anon., *A German Deserter's War Experience* (J. Koettgen, trans. and ed.) (New York, 1917), 8.

26. GSA, 119 (Aarschot), Theenws, Nijs; DVF, 95.

27. SN, Part 2, 36; Thier and Gilbart, 170.

28. RDE, Book 1, 434.

29. *Ibid.*, 378.

30. DVF, 251, 255, 259, 262–266, 271; Reply, 245, 264; RDE 2, 395.

31. Reply, 243; RBC, 257–8.

32. GSA, Leuven, chemise 32, Verhulst; RDE, Book 2, 70; Reply, 242–3; Schöller, 96; Anon. [H. de Gruben], *The Germans at Louvain* (London, 1916), 41–2.

33. PRW, Leuven, Devyver, *Rapport des événements de Louvain 26 août et jours suivants. Faits observés au Vieux Marché.*

34. RDE 1, 466; RVR 1, 35. In fact, 262 civilians were massacred in Andenne.

35. J. H. Morgan, (trans. and ed.), *The German War Book*, translation of *Kriegsbrauch im Landkriege* (London, 1915), 52.

36. *Ibid.*, 55.

37. *Ibid.*, 120, 122. This quotation does not accurately characterize Wellington's orders.

38. *Ibid.*, 121.

39. *Ibid.*, 140.

40. *Ibid.*, 122.

41. Viz., "war is an act of violence which in its application knows no bounds. ...To introduce into the philosophy of war itself a principle of moderation would be an absurdity."

42. Morgan, 4.

43. I. Hull, *Absolute Destruction: Military Culture and the Practices of War in Imperial Germany* (Ithaca, 2005), 124; RVR 1, xxiv.

44. Reply, 117–118; GSA, 119 (Aarschot), Tielemans.

45. RDE 2, 370; Reply, 113.

46. RDE 1, 450.

47. RVR 1, xxvi; GSA, Leuven, 92, G. Bruylants, *"Incendies des Boulevards de Tirlemont intérieur et extérieur."*

48. Bédier, 11; RBC, 409.

49. There are a number of stories of officers restraining enraged soldiers, particularly from lynching priests. "I'm master here!" yelled Menne in Aarschot. "Who's master here?" shouted von Manteuffel in Leuven. In both cases it was clerical captives who were being menaced. The officer who liberated the priests from the Lovenjoel pigsty was also obliged to protect them from his troops, as did the lieutenant assigned to guard the curé of Neffe. Unheeded shouts and whistles were reported in both Aarschot and Leuven during the initial outbreak of violence, and, two days later, officers in the latter town struggled with soldiers in the Stationsplein intent on shooting the women and children who had just arrived from Aarschot. Most of the White Book testimony of Lieutenant Telemann, one of von Manteuffel's staff officers, concerns his efforts on the night of the 25th to prevent soldiers from igniting buildings. *Oberarzt* Porst was similarly engaged.

   On the other hand, some soldiers clearly resented orders to shoot unarmed civilians, and there is evidence of sporadic insubordination in various places, and possibly organized resistance in Tamines. (Officers, too, for that matter, did not disguise their unhappiness with the orders of superiors, at least in Andenne. One of the regiments in town was the 28th Pioneers, and its engineer officers had not expected that their men would be required to bayonet non-combatants. Officers grumbled in Leuven as well.) In the end, however, the vast majority of Belgian victims were killed by troops acting under orders, and it was not ordinary soldiers who issued these, however eagerly they obeyed them.

50. J. Witcover, *Sabotage at Black Tom: Imperial Germany's Secret War in America, 1914 –1917* (Chapel Hill, 1989), 3–28, 152–172, 321. German agents and sympathizers committed nearly two hundred other acts of sabotage against the U.S. before the two nations went to war, including bombing the U.S. Capitol. At one point anthrax was sent from Germany to poison horses and mules that were to be shipped to Europe.

51. Concerning Chirol, Chancellor von Bulow wrote in a secret memorandum, "On the whole it is certain that opinion in England is far less anti-German than opinion in Germany is anti-English. Therefore those Englishmen like Chirol and Saunders [Chirol's successor as the *Times's* Berlin correspondent] are most dangerous for us, who know from their own observation the depth and bitterness of German antipathy against England." (V. Chirol, *Fifty Years in a Changing World* (New York, 1928), 284–5; see also E. Grey, *Twenty-five Years,* v. 2 (New York, 1925), 49.

52. The work of foreign historians who studied in Germany before the war, though inevitably dated and sometimes tendentious, tends to be undervalued as well, including that of J. E. Barker, J. A. Cramb, W. H. Dawson, B. Schmitt, and R. Usher. Among journalists familiar with the Fatherland, the books and articles of E. J. Dillon and J. McCabe are still worth looking at.

53. *Les origines du Pangermanisme, 1800–1888* (Paris, 1915), *Le Pangermanisme continental sous Guillaume II, 1888–1914* (Paris, 1915), *Le Pangermanisme colonial sous Guillaume II* (Paris, 1916), *Le Pangermanisme philosophique, 1800–1914* (Paris, 1917). Among others are collections by William Archer, J. P. Bang, Bruce Dickins, Alexander Gray, Ford Maddox Hueffer, Otfried Nippold, and Wallace Notestein and Elmer Stoll, and, after outbreak of the Second World War, Aurel Kolnai and W. W. Coole and M. F. Potter (W. Kulski and M.

Potulicki). An earlier book, from 1908, by "Vigilans sed Aequus" (W. T. Arnold) also quotes and summarizes Pan-Germanist literature, as does Leo Maxse's 1914 collection of articles published in the *National Review,* and books by André Chéradame and Paul Vergnet, and an additional pamphlet by Charles Andler.

54. A survey of Berlin booksellers by Professor Deissmann reported that *Zarathustra* was the book most frequently purchased, along with Faust and the Bible, by soldiers heading off to war. A special edition of 150,000 copies with durable covers was prepared for men in the trenches. (W. Archer, *Gems (?) of German Thought* (New York, 1917), 21; S. Aschheim, *The Nietzsche Legacy in Germany* (Berkeley, 1992), 135.) Nietzsche, of course, was no patriot, and his English defenders were able to pick quotations virtually at random from *Ecce Homo* savaging Prussia, Wilhelmite culture, and the German people. Nonetheless, his influence was hardly a calming one: "You say it is the good cause that sanctifies even war. I say unto you: it is the good war that sanctifies any cause. War and courage have accomplished more great things than love of one's neighbor." (*Zarathustra,* "War and Warriors," in W. Kaufmann (ed.), *The Portable Nietzsche* (New York, 1968), 159.). For recent contributions to the long debate over Nietzsche's legacy, see J. Golomb and R. Wistrich (eds.), *Nietzsche, Godfather of Fascism?: On the Uses and Abuses of a Philosophy* (Princeton, 2002). Haeckel's contribution will be considered very briefly below. Far and away the leading Darwinian in Germany, his *Welträtsel* (*Riddle of the Universe,* 1899), a popularization of his philosophy, Monism, sold over one hundred thousand copies its first year and half a million by 1933. For discussions of his influence, see D. Gasman, *The Scientific Origins of National Socialism: Social Darwinism in Ernst Haeckel and the German Monist League* (London, 1971), A. Kelly, *The Descent of Darwin: The Popularization of Darwin in Germany, 1860–1914* (Chapel Hill, NC, 1981), and M. Hawkins, *Social Darwinism in European and American Thought, 1860–1945* (Cambridge, 1997).

55. "Among contemporary historians," wrote the distinguished philosopher Friedrich Paulsen before the war, "Treitschke has

exercised the greatest influence upon the political thought of the rising generation. With the characteristic vehemence of his eloquence he preaches the maxim that the State is power, and war is its first, most elementary function." (cited by W. H. Dawson, "Some Memories of Treitschke," *Nineteenth Century* (January 1915), 156.) Though his methodology was no longer in vogue, many of Germany's leading historians were Treitschke's students or disciples – Delbrück, Lamprecht, Meinecke, Weber. Those who had sat at his feet went on to teach the men who became Germany's generals, statesmen, and civil servants, and those who taught, in turn, in the nation's *Gymnasia* and *Oberrealschulen*. There are many reports of his spellbinding oratory and the passionate response it evoked. Virtually the sole dissenting voice in Germany was that of Otto Umfrid, an obscure Evangelical pastor from Stuttgart, whose *Anti-Treitschke* was published by the tiny German Peace Society. A. Dorpalen's *Heinrich von Treitschke* (New Haven, 1957) is still the best treatment in English. The military historian Hans Delbrück, who succeeded Treitschke as editor of the influential *Das Preussische Jahrbücher*, was perhaps his most important disciple.

56. On this eccentric polymath, see G. Field, *Evangelist of Race* (New York, 1981) and R. Stackelberg, *Idealism Debased: From Volkish Ideology to National Socialism* (Kent, Ohio, 1981).

57. F. M. Hueffer, *Between St. Dennis and St. George* (London, 1915), 30, 32.

58. In the *Critique of Aesthetic Judgment*, the author of *Perpetual Peace* wrote, "Even where civilisation has reached a high pitch, there remains this special reverence for the soldier... War itself, provided it is conducted with order and a sacred respect for the rights of civilians, has something sublime about it, and gives nations that carry it on in such a manner a stamp of mind all the more sublime, the more numerous the dangers to which they are exposed and which they are able to meet with fortitude. On the other hand, a prolonged peace favours the predominance of a mere commercial spirit and with it a debasing self-interest, cowardice, and effeminacy, and tends to degrade the character of the nation." Wilhelm von Humboldt, the Prussian Education Minister celebrated as an early libertarian, wrote that "the influence of war upon the character of a people is one of the most profitable phenomena for the perfecting of the human race." (*Ibid.*, 259.)

59. *Ibid.*, 33–4.

60. G. Lowes Dickinson, *The European Anarchy* (New York, 1917), 62–3. Dickinson was quoting with approval the Belgian Ambassador, Baron Beyens, by no means a Germanophobe.

61. E. Haeckel, *Riddle of the Universe* (London, 1900), 277. Spencer's *Social Statics* appeared in 1851, so it does him an injustice to regard him merely as a popularizer of Darwin. Nonetheless, he reformulated his beliefs in light of *Origin of the Species*.

62. K. Wagner, *Krieg*, (Berlin, 1906), 153, cited in W. Archer, *Gems (?) of German Thought* (New York, 1917), 141.

63. F. von Bernardi, *Germany and the Next War* (New York, 1914), 18, 34.

64. J. Gerard, *My Four Years in Germany* (New York, 1917), 77–8.

65. R. Vansittart, *The Black Record of Germany* (New York, 1943), 75–6.

66. *Ibid.*, 77.

67. "International Law" in [A. Hausrath, H. Treitschke], *Treitschke: His Life and Works* (London, 1914), 166.

68. What induces a State to declare war, apart from "the slightest insult to its honor"? It is the discovery, Treitschke declares, that "its existing treaties have ceased to express the relative strength of itself and another treaty-State." If it can't convince the other nation to cancel the treaty, "then has come the moment for the 'legal proceedings' customary between nations, that is, for war.... Personal greed plays no part in such an act," he added disingenuously. (*Ibid*, 167.) No one did more to convince Germans to begin "legal proceedings" against England than did Treitschke.

69. *Ibid.*, 169.

70. viz., Novalis's demand that "the citizen should pay his taxes as he gives presents to his lover." (R. Aris, *The History of Political Thought in Germany* (London, 1965), 279.

71. "*Rat*," Gerard explained, "means councillor, and is a title of honour given to anyone who has attained a certain measure of success or standing in his chosen business

or profession. For instance, a businessman is made a commerce *Rat*; a lawyer a justice *Rat*; a doctor, a sanitary *Rat*; an architect or builder, a building *Rat*; keeper of the archives, an archive *Rat*; and so on. They are created in this way: first a man becomes a plain *Rat*, then, later on, he becomes a secret *Rat* or privy councillor; still later, a secret court *Rat* and, later still, a *wirklicher*, or really and truly secret court *Rat*... But see the insidious working of the system. By German custom the woman always carries the husband's title. The wife of a successful builder is known as Mrs. Really Truly Secret Court Building *Rat* and her social precedence over the other women depends entirely upon her husband's position in the *Rat* class." Needless to say, "Mrs. Second-Lieutenant von Bing" takes precedence over "Mrs. Manufactory-Proprietor Schultze" even if the latter is "an old lady noted for her works of charity" and the former is "only seventeen years old." (J. Gerard, 113, 114.)

72. Notable among a great number of such books are A. Kolnai, *The War Against the West* (London, 1938), P. Viereck, *Metapolitics* (New York, 1941), R. D'O. Butler, *The Roots of National Socialism* (London, 1942), L. Snyder, *German Nationalism: the Tragedy of a People* (Harrisburg, PA, 1952), H. Kohn, *The Mind of Germany* (New York, 1960), F. Stern, *The Politics of Cultural Despair* (New York, 1961), G. Mosse, *The Crisis of German Ideology* (New York, 1964), and R. Stackelberg, *Idealism Debased* (1981). De Lagarde was of interest to the early generation of critics as well.

73. E. Reich, *Germany's Swelled Head* (London, 1907). The ubiquity of nationalist sentiments amazed and amused foreigners. In 1900, Ford Maddox Hueffer found himself walking in a public garden in Germany with a friend. He admired the oleanders, cypresses, immaculate lawns, and classical statues. He noted the signs on the benches: *"Nur für Kinder"* and then *"Schulkinder verboten."* Sitting down in front of a pool of water, he observed some schoolchildren playing with toy boats and painting something on a strip of calico. After dozing off for a few minutes, he noticed that what he'd imagined was a mural was in fact a banner on which the children had carefully painted the words *"Unser Zukunft ist auf den Wasser."* (Our Future is on the Water) The children were barely old enough to write. (Hueffer, *Between St. Dennis and St. George*, 64.) The *Flottenverein*, whose slogan this was, was founded by forty-four individuals in 1898. On the eve of the war it had well over 300,000 members; some estimates range much higher. (R. Chickering, *We Men Who Feel Most German* (London, 1984), 205; T. Smith, *The Soul of Germany* (New York, 1915), 304.)

Sometime in the '90s, shops selling imported goods began bearing the name *"Kolonialwaren,"* just as warehouse workers began to be called *"Kolonialwarenhändler."* The first time he noticed such a sign, in gilt letters, Heuffer had just purchased French claret, English cigarettes, and Spanish olives and had been assured they were *"echt französisch, "echt englisch"* and *"echt spanisch."* (*Ibid.*, 61.) Meanwhile, conscientious officers worked diligently to combat the corrupting influence of foreign cultures within the Fatherland. On a visit to the Rhineland, Hueffer found himself sitting on the verandah of his hotel one afternoon when the commanding officer of a nearby garrison drove up. The man summonsed the hotel's owner. Pointing to a sign with the word "Garage," he announced that if the word were not changed, the hotel would be placed out of bounds for all his officers and men. The next day the sign was replaced by one that read *"Kraftwageneinstellraum"* (power-wagon-standing-in-room). (F. M. Hueffer, *When Blood is Their Argument: An Analysis of Prussian Culture* (New York, 1915), 271.)

74. J. Bang, *Hurrah and Hallelujah* (New York, 1917), 22.

75. "The fate that Belgium has called down upon herself is hard for the individual, but...the destinies of the immortal great nations stand so high, that they cannot but have the right, in case of need, to stride over existences that cannot defend themselves, but live as parasites..." wrote the eminent Heidelberg historian Hermann Oncken in *Süddeutsche Monatshefte* (September, 1914)(cited by W. W. Coole and M. F. Potter (eds.), *Thus Spake Germany* (London, 1941), 208–9). The French and British, needless to say, were not bereft of national

pride. But in neither case did it threaten the stability of Europe. No informed historian now believes that *revanchiste* sentiments drove French foreign policy in the decade before the war. British pride in the Empire was based on impressive accomplishments, however they may be judged today. (British writers were more moved by the fact that India's population had doubled under English rule and that only about 65,000 European troops were required to govern its nearly 300,000,000 people than they were by Clive's exploits.) And feelings about the Empire did not preclude significant concessions to Germany. (There were almost continuous negotiations from 1890 to 1914, when agreement was finally reached on the thorny Bagdad Railroad question.)

76. H. Heine, "Concerning the History of Religion and Philosophy in Germany" in *The Romantic School and Other Essays* (New York, 1985), 243.

77. G. Santayana, *The German Mind: A Philosophical Diagnosis* (New York, 1968). J.H. Muirhead demurred: Haeckel, not Hegel, was the culprit. (*German Philosophy in Relation to the War* (London, 1915). But the prolific Leonard Hobhouse, among others, counterattacked (*Questions of War and Peace* (London, 1916), *The Metaphysical Theory of the State* (London, 1918), and the war undoubtedly accelerated the reaction against British Idealism. See S. Wallace, *War and the Image of Germany: British Academics, 1914–1918* (Edinburgh, 1988), 43–57. Hervé de Gruben, along with many other Belgian intellectuals, also blamed German war crimes on the Hegelian deification of the State. (H. de Gruben, *The Germans at Louvain* (London, 1916), 115.) A colleague of Fichte's saw the way the wind was blowing as early as 1796: "God forbid that Fichte should be persecuted or else there might very well emerge a Fichtianity a hundred times worse than Christianity." (Cited by G. A. Kelly, *Idealism, Politics and History* (Cambridge, 1969), 187–8.)

78. See, for example, the final three paragraphs of the second speech in *On Religion: Speeches to its Cultured Despisers* (Cambridge, 1988), 53–4.

79. Anon., *Why Germany Will Be Defeated* (Letchworth, 1915), 15.

80. *Ibid.*, 15, 14. "In all classes the adult population is quite indifferent to religion," wrote Fritz Berolzheimer in *Moral und Gesellschaft* (cited by T. F. A. Smith, *The Soul of Germany* (New York, 1915), 74.) Smith and other commentators believed that Germany's high crime rate compared to the U.K. was a direct consequence. Based on figures from the *Vierteljahrshefte*, published by the Imperial Statistics Office in Berlin, and statistics from the Home Office and Attorney General's Office, the annualized per-capita murder rate (including manslaughter) in Germany was 2.6 times that of the U.K. for the period 1901–1912, the illegitimacy rate 2.5, the divorce rate 14.4 and the abortion rate 23 times that of the U.K. (Smith, *Soul*, 348–351.)

81. Smith, *Soul*, 79.

82. Anon., *Why*, 20–21.

83. L. Macdonald, *1914* (New York, 1988), 215. A popular cartoon depicted a grinning British soldier taking aim at a cowering German and telling him, "Got mittens, have you? Well, here's socks!"

84. Bang, 79; A. Hoover, *The Gospel of Nationalism* (Stuttgart, 1986), 135.

85. Friedrich Lange in *Tägliche Rundschau*, cited by Reich, 42.

86. "Though the warrior's bread be scanty, bring Thou daily death and tenfold woe unto the enemy. Forgive... each bullet and each blow which misses its mark! Lead us not into the temptation of letting our wrath be too tame in carrying out Thy divine judgment! Deliver us and our Ally from the infernal Enemy and his servants on earth. Thine is the kingdom, the German land; may we, by aid of Thy steel-clad hand, achieve the power and the glory." (Bang, 42–3.) A dictum of the Kaiser was frequently quoted: "Our German nation shall be the rock of granite on which the Almighty shall finish His work of civilising the world." Writers such as de Lagarde, Bonus, and Kaftan worked heroically to found a Germanic Christianity in the Fatherland.

87. Cited by Archer, 78–9.

88. G. Williamson, *The Longing for Myth in Germany* (Chicago, 2004), 109–10.

89. *Ibid.*, 105. Luther, according to the Heidelberg Romantics, had merely resurrected ancient paganism. He had restored a religion that gave direct access to God

in nature. The Romantics brushed aside the argument that Luther's bibliolatry was in fact a revolt against an institution that had accommodated itself all too readily to pagan myths. Luther took a lot of heat from those seeking the roots of State terrorism. Justification by faith alone provided a slippery slope, in their view. (See M. Tuker, "Religions and the War," *Nineteenth Century* (Dec. 1914), 1318–1330; A. W. G. Randall, "Aspects of Teutonism: The 'German God,'" *Fortnightly Review*, (v. 98, n. 586, 623–643; McGovern, *From Luther to Hitler*, 30–35.). Others thought the problem was the late conversion of Germany to Christianity and the fact that Roman civilization had stopped at the Rhine. Some clergyman, however, thought the problem was not that German Christianity was pagan, but that it was "Judaistic." (G. Frodsham, "What is Wrong with German Christianity," *Nineteenth Century* (May 1915), 1084–1091. Randall also suggested this.)

90. *"Was ist das Deutschen Vaterland?"* asks the poem's narrator and repeatedly rejects the responses, replying *"O nein! nein! nein!/ Sein Vaterland muss grösser sein"* (Oh no, no, no. His Fatherland must be larger.) In the end, it was to extend "As far as the German tongue sounds/ And God sings songs in heaven,"and for Arndt "the German tongue" was very broadly defined. Punch in 1870 published a parody: "What is the German Fatherland?/Now, children, take your maps in hand,/And see if you can tell me what/The German Fatherland is not." Arndt's influence was as powerful in 1915 as in 1815. In making the case for incorporating Belgium into the *Kaiserreich*, its Governor, General von Bissing, quoted the poet. (*General von Bissing's Testament* (London, 1917), 21.

91. This is not to imply any simplistic correlation between a lack of faith and barbarism. Few Englishmen were more moral than the Cambridge agnostics of the late nineteenth century, though the same cannot be said of their children. What replaced Christianity was critical. But there can be no question that a far greater percentage of the population in Germany rejected Protestantism than in Britain, and on different grounds. Rather than being converted by Darwinism, most English atheists abandoned

Christianity because they found the concept of heaven and hell immoral. (S. Budd, *Varieties of Unbelief: Atheists and Agnostics in British Society, 1850–1959* (London, 1977).)

EPILOGUE

1. Ministry of Justice, War Crimes Commission, *War crimes committed during the invasion of the national territory, May 1940* (Liège, 1946), 17, 29.

2. *Ibid.*, 30. He believed the shelling commenced earlier than witnesses in town reported.

3. *Ibid.* 34. The town may also have been shelled by batteries in Kessel-Lo. (*Ibid.*, 27.) The inscription read "Furore Teutonico Diruta; Dono Americano Restituta." (Destroyed by German Fury; Restored by American Gift)

4. *Ibid.*, 30–31. The Germans more than tripled the amount of destruction they had wrought in 1914, incinerating some 880,000 volumes, along with hundreds of manuscripts and the 811 incunabula that the University had collected since 1919. (C. Coppens, M. Derez, J. Roegiers, *Leuven University Library, 1425–2000* (Leuven, 2005), 320.

5. Ministry of Justice, *War Crimes*, 25.

6. *Ibid.*, 26.

7. *Ibid.*, 33.

8. *Ibid.*, 19, 24.

9. *Ibid.*, 21.

10. W. Shirer, *Berlin Diary* (New York, 1941), 359. In the rooms in the Stadhuis once occupied by von Manteuffel and his staff, Shirer saw maps, notepads, beer bottles, and biscuit tins hastily abandoned by the British. "In each room, under the sweeping Renaissance paintings on the walls, disheveled mattresses on which the British slept. Most of them bloodstained, as if in the last days they were used not to sleep on, but to die on." (*Ibid.*) Shirer toured the abandoned town. He noted the stone inscriptions on the library from various American donors, mostly schools and universities. "I look for the famous inscription about which there was so much silly controversy (it doesn't sound quite so silly today)." (*Ibid.*, 356.) For a detailed account of the destruction of the library in 1940, see W. Schivelbusch, *Die Bibliothek von Loewen* (Munich, 1988), 171–181.

11. W. Coolrick, O. Tanner, *The Battle of the*

Bulge (Morristown, NJ, 1979), 178–80; T. Dupuy, *Hitler's Last Gamble: The Battle of the Bulge, December 1944–January 1945* (New York, 1994), 233; C. MacDonald, *A Time for Trumpets: The Untold Story of the Battle of the Bulge* (New York, 1985), 560–1, 566–7; H. Cole, *The Ardennes: the Battle of the Bulge* (Washington, D.C., 1965), 650; P. Schrijvers, *The Unknown Dead: Civilians in the Battle of the Bulge* (Lexington, KY, 2005), 252–4.

12. For accounts of the massacres at Stavelot and Bande, see Schrijvers, 40–9, 249–52. See also Coolrick, 118, and MacDonald, 575–6. Schrijvers estimates that about 2,500 Belgian civilians were killed during the German counter-offensive, about one-third in Allied bombings. (Schrijvers, xiv, 359.) Civilians were once again told by German soldiers that "the innocent must pay for the guilty." (*Ibid.*, 44.) Though unlike in 1914, there had been a resistance movement between 1940 and 1944, the SS was no more scrupulous in the punishments it meted out than at Oradour-sur-Glane. Some 13,000 civilians had already perished in the eighteen days of fighting in 1940 before the government surrendered, and another 2,622 during the liberation of the country in the summer of 1944. An additional 6,500 civilians were killed that year by Allied bombings. (V. Malinson, *Belgium* (New York, 1970), 115, 121–2.) (Malinson's total for civilian victims during the Battle of the Bulge is 1,205, excluding bombing victims.)

13. Textbooks and encyclopedias still quote wildly inflated figures, borrowed from Goebbels, who increased the highest estimate tenfold. For an informed discussion of the numbers, see F. Taylor's thorough and judicious *Dresden, Tuesday, February 13, 1945* (London, 2004), 443–8. Another recent treatment in English, based on U.S. and British sources, comes to similar conclusions, M. De Bruhl, *Firestorm: Allied Airpower and the Destruction of Dresden* (New York, 2006); see also P. Addison and J. Crang (eds.), *Firestorm: The Bombing of Dresden, 1945* (Chicago, 2006); N. Longmate, *The Bombers: The RAF Offensive Against Germany, 1939–45* (London, 1983); USAF Historical Division, Research Studies, *Historical Analysis of the 1415 February 1945 bombings of Dresden*. See as well

R. Evans, *Lying About Hitler: History, the Holocaust, and the David Irving Trial* (New York, 2001), 149–184.

14. See pages 293–4.

15. About 900 Belgian airmen and ground personnel served with the RAF. Nearly half were members of three all-Belgian fighter squadrons, but some were attached to Bomber Command and may have participated in the February raids. (R. Allen, *Churchill's Guests: Britain and the Belgian Exiles during World War II* (Westport, CT, 2003), 126.)

16. R. W. Emerson, "Compensation," in I. Edman (ed.), *Essays by Ralph Waldo Emerson* (New York, 1951), 74.

17. Estimates of the deaths range from about 556,000 to 3.2 million for Poland alone. Rummel concludes that the total was in the vicinity of 1.6 million, but does not reveal how he arrived as this number. (R. Rummel, *Death by Government* (New Brunswick, NJ, 1997), 306. De Zayas estimates a total of 2,111,000, but his figures also ought to be taken with caution. (A. de Zayas, *The German Expellees: Victims in War and Peace* (New York, 1993), 150. (The book was also published also under the title *A Terrible Revenge*).

18. K. Marx, *The Eighteenth Brumaire of Louis Bonaparte* in L. Feuer (ed.), *Marx and Engels: Basic Writings on Politics and Philosophy* (Garden City, NY, 1959), 320.

19. Anyone seriously interested in the question of the war's origins will naturally want to consult the published diplomatic correspondence of the European Powers. I. Geiss's *July 1914* (New York, 1967), a condensation of his two-volume *Julikrise und Kriegsausbruch, 1914*, provides a selection of the most important dispatches, with acute introductions. Valuable article collections include W. Laquer and G. Mosse (eds.), *1914: The Coming of the First World War* (New York, 1966), H. W. Koch (ed.), *The Origins of the First World War* (London, 1972), R. J. W. Evans and H. Pogge von Strandmann (eds.), *The Coming of the First World War* (Oxford, 1988), and K. Wilson (ed.), *Decisions for War, 1914* (New York, 1995). A. Mombauer, *Origins of the First World War: Controversies and Consensus* (London, 2002) and M. Hewitson, *Germany and the Causes of the First World War* (Oxford, 2004)

provide recent summaries of the state of play. Helpful short annotated bibliographies are provided by J. Remak, *The Origins of World War I*, 2nd edition (Ft. Worth, TX, 1995) and H. Herwig (ed.), *The Outbreak of World War I* (Lexington, MA, 1991). Of the shelves of volumes published on the causes of the war, there is still one indispensable work, Luigi Albertini's three-volume study, *The Origins of the War of 1914*.

20. Cited by Brian Bond, *The Unquiet Western Front* (Cambridge, 2002), 77.

21. It is certainly possible that Germany would have launched wars in 1905 and 1909 if France and Russia, respectively, had not capitulated. It was not prepared to do so in the second Moroccan crisis of 1911, however, nor in the fall of 1912, following the first Balkan War. Diplomatic papers from that period indicate, incidentally, that the Kaiser and his ministers were fully aware of the strategic importance Russia attached to maintaining the independence of the Balkan states. The Kaiser was leery of intervening. "*Under no circumstances* will I *march against Paris and Moscow* on account of Albania and Durazzo," he telegraphed his Foreign Minister on 9 November 1912, . He refused to gamble "with the very existence of Germany," the Kaiser wrote a few days later, merely because "Austria does not want to have the Serbs in Albania or Durazzo... The German Army and people could not be placed at the direct service of the whims of another State's foreign policy. The alliance did not pledge Germany to support Austria unconditionally in cases of friction over the possessions of others." (J. Rohl, *The Kaiser and his Court: Wilhelm II and the Government of Germany* (Cambridge, 1994), 168, 169; L. Albertini, *The Origins of the War of 1914*, v. 1 (New York, 2005 [1952]), 399–400.) But in June of 1914, when the German Ambassador in Vienna assumed that the same policy was in force and urged caution on the Austrians, he was roundly denounced by the Kaiser. The change of heart probably dates from late November 1912. At the infamous "War Council" of 8 December 1912, the Chief of the General Staff, von Moltke, welcomed the Kaiser's new bellicosity: "I believe war is unavoidable and the sooner the better," he announced. Admiral Tirpitz, State Secretary of the Naval Office, however, urged a delay

for tactical reasons – it would be best to wait until the Kiel Canal was completed in July 1914. Von Moltke conceded that it would be helpful to prepare public opinion for war by launching a press campaign against Russia. This was begun and a new Army Bill drafted. (Rohl, 162–89.)

22. It is worth recalling the actual cause of the war: Austria's insistence on conducting an investigation of the Sarajevo assassination on Serbian soil. The Serbs accepted all other demands in the ultimatum, including suppressing "any publication that incites hatred or contempt" of Austria-Hungary, eliminating any school text making unflattering references to the Dual Monarchy, and firing any teacher, army officer, or bureaucrat who had expressed criticisms of the Viennese government, the Dual Monarchy to provide names. However, an Austrian investigation within Serbia would violate the Serbian Constitution and criminal law statutes, Belgrade argued. It was willing, though, to permit the International Tribunal at the Hague or a conference of Great Powers to negotiate the precise role Austrian officials would play in a Serbian investigation of the assassination. "Given goodwill, everything could have been settled at one or two sittings" of such a conference, declared Prince Max Lichnowski, the German Ambassador in London. (M. Lichnowski, *Heading for the Abyss: Reminiscences* (London, 1928), 74.) He had represented Germany at the London Conference of Ambassadors only a year and a half earlier, and had helped resolve much thornier conflicts resulting from the First Balkan War. The Central Powers had every reason to feel satisfied with the outcome: Serbia was denied access to the Adriatic and Albania was created as an Austrian vassal state. In the end, well over ten million people died because Austria-Hungary, supported by Germany, claimed that its dignity would be compromised were it to permit an international body to negotiate the role its officials would play in an investigation of the Archduke's assassination. (The Kaiser demurred. "A brilliant achievement in a time limit of only forty-eight hours!" he wrote of the Serbian reply. "It is more than one could have expected! A great moral success for Vienna; but with it all reason for war is gone... After

that I should never have ordered mobilization!" (Albertini, vol. 2, 467) Anticipating such a response, Bethmann Hollweg withheld the Serbian text from the Kaiser for nearly forty-eight hours. "A mere hint from Berlin would have decided Count Berchtold to content himself with a diplomatic success, and to accept the Serbian reply," wrote Lichnowski. "This hint was not given.") (Lichnowski, 74.) Ironically, any international investigation would have discovered what the Austrian investigator had failed to unearth – that Serb officials were aware of the plot to kill the Archduke and had taken inadequate measures to forestall it.

23. Needless to say, this does not imply that France and Russia were guiltless. Russia, in the first place, mobilized prematurely, providing Germany with a *casus belli* (though provoked by the entirely correct conclusion that this time Germany intended to go to war). France, though intentionally deprived of taking any initiative in the July Crisis by the timing of Austria's ultimatum, had done nothing earlier (in the fall of 1912, for instance), to pressure Russia into exercising caution in the Balkans. When Europe was poised on the brink of war at that time, it was Austria and, especially, Russia that voluntarily pulled back.

24. When conditions were similar in World War II, as on the Italian peninsula, the campaign was nearly as frustrating as operations on the Western Front. However, there is no question that much incompetence was displayed, particularly in the first two years of the war. On the other hand, the notion that all General Staffs were totally unprepared for trench warfare in 1914 is a myth. Every Army conducted detailed studies of the frustrating stalemates that made the U.S. Civil War, the Russo-Japanese War, the Boer War, and the Balkan Wars so bloody and costly.

25. Haig's competence will be forever debated. There is no doubt that, apart from a repellant personality, he remained, like most Allied generals, wedded for far too long to a doctrine of the offensive that over-emphasized the "morale" of the infantry and was indifferent to "wastage," willing to accept staggering losses. His HQ ignored relevant information down to the Spring of 1918, and, in consequence, prolonged operations

that should have been terminated weeks earlier. Even in November of 1918, Army intelligence was misinformed about German capabilities. However, Haig did not dictate strategy or tactics to his commanders and the best of them were able to apply lessons learned during the war's first years.

26. Among the many books that provide a more balanced and nuanced assessment of the war the Allies waged are Paddy Griffith, *Battle Tactics of the Western Front* (New Haven, 1994), G. Hartcup, *The War of Invention: Scientific Developments, 1914–18* (London, 1987), R. Pryor and T. Wilson, *Command on the Western Front: The Military Career of Sir Henry Rawlinson, 1914–1918* (Oxford, 1992); S. Robbins, *British Generalship on the Western Front, 1914–18: Defeat Into Victory* (London, 2005); G. Sheffield, *Forgotten Victory* (London, 2001); G. Sheffield and D. Todman, *Command and Control on the Western Front: The British Army's Experience, 1914–1918* (London, 2004); A. Simpson, *The Evolution of Victory: British Battles on the Western Front* (London, 1995); J. Terraine, *To Win a War, 1918: The Year of Victory* (London, 1978) and *White Heat: The New Warfare, 1914–1918* (London, 1982); T. Travers, *The Killing Ground: The British Army, the Western Front, and the Emergence of Modern Warfare* (London, 1987) and *How the War Was Won: Command and Technology on the Western Front, 1916–1918* (London, 1992).

27. Foch famously proclaimed, "This is not a Peace. It is an Armistice for twenty years." (A. Sharp, *The Versailles Settlement: Peacemaking in Paris, 1919* (New York: 1991), 189.) As Michael Fry notes, "Revisionism has flourished to an extent that it has virtually institutionalized a paradox – to defend the 1919 settlement would be revisionist." (M. Fry, "British Revisionism," in M. Boemeke, G. Feldman, E. Glaser, *The Versailles Treaty: A Reassessment After 75 Years* (Cambridge, 1998), 565.) For an insightful overview of the mounting hostility to the Treaty in Britain and the U.S. after 1919, see G. Martel, "A Comment," *Ibid.*, 615–636.

28. S. Marks, "Smoke and Mirrors,"Boemeke, et. al., *The Treaty of Versailles*, 345, n. 33. Prior estimates had ranged from 60 to 100 milliard, according to Marks.

29. S. Marks, *Innocent Abroad: Belgium at the*

Paris Peace Conference of 1919 (Chapel Hill, 1981), 180. Despite the depredations of the invaders and the destruction along the front in Flanders, only about 5% of the nation's farmland was ruined, although the Germans had stripped the countryside of virtually all livestock and farm equipment. Belgium, however, was the most industrialized country on the continent and its leading industries suffered catastrophically. The spinning industry was entirely eliminated and coal, iron and steel production were decimated. Compared to prewar levels, production in the various metallurgic industries ranged from one-twentieth to one-seventh in 1918. Altogether, Belgian industrial output stood at around 15% of prewar levels. About three-quarters of the nation's workforce was still unemployed when the Treaty was signed. (Marks, 172–80.)

30. M. Trachtenberg, "Reparations at the Paris Peace Conference," Journal of Modern History, v. 51, n.1 (1979), 40. At one point the chief French negotiator proposed a figure of 124 milliard ($31). (Ibid., 39.)

31. S. Marks, "The Myths of Reparations," Central European History, v. 11, n. 3 (1978), 236. For a detailed discussion of the negotiations, and a persuasive case for French moderation, see M. Trachtenberg, "Reparations at the Paris Peace Conference," 24–55, and M. Trachtenberg, Reparation in World Politics (New York, 1980), 58, 63. While putting forward more modest claims initially, British representatives pressed for certain war costs to be included – severance payments to families of mobilized men and pensions for widows and orphans and for the dependents of injured soldiers. Its territory had sustained minimal damages from German shelling and bombing (though 1,265 civilians were killed) and the territory of other combatants from the Empire, India, Canada, Australia, and New Zealand, was untouched by war. The Lansing Note of November 5, the basis for the Armistice agreement, appeared to exclude reimbursement for war costs, including pensions. The Note held Germany liable "for all damage done to the civilian population of the Allies and their property by the aggression of Germany by land, by sea and from the air." (The final phrase was requested by Britain in lieu of "by the invasion of

Belgium and France.")(E. Mantoux, The Carthaginian Peace (Pittsburgh, 1964), 98.) Keynes, with characteristic extravagance, suggested that the reinterpretation of the language of the Lansing Note, which Germany duly accepted, represented "a breach of engagements and international morality comparable...[to] the invasion of Belgium." (J. M. Keynes, The Economic Consequences of the Peace, v. 2, The Collected Writings of J. M. Keynes (London: Macmillan, 1971), 40.) Keynes's hyperbole aside, it would certainly have been preferable for the British to have abided by the letter of the November 5th Note, however politically difficult, and renounce repayment for war costs. The belief that Lloyd George demanded payment for pensions because of domestic pressures has been challenged by M. Trachtenberg and A. Lentin, among others, who note that Lloyd George was in a strong position at home and in fact did not consult public opinion during the negotiations at Paris. ("Reparations at the Paris Peace Conference," 53; "Comment," Boemeke, Feldman, Glaser, The Treaty of Versailles, 223–7.) See also M. Trachtenberg, "Versailles After Sixty Years," Journal of Contemporary History, v. 17, n. 3 (1982), 487–506.

32. S. Marks, "The Myths of Reparations," 237. Bethmann Hollweg's acknowledgment of German guilt occurred in his speech to the Reichstag announcing the invasions of Luxembourg and Belgium. Collected Diplomatic Documents Relating to the Outbreak of the European War (London, 1915), 438.

33. The Weimar government claimed to have paid 67 milliard gold marks in the end ($16.75 billion), but by bookkeeping tactics that would have made an Enron accountant blush. Eight and a half milliard was claimed for destruction of war materiel, 1.2 milliard for the value of work performed by German p.o.w.s (with no deduction, naturally, for the work performed by the far greater number of Allied prisoners), and an additional 3.5 milliard was credited to "industrial disarmament." The government also failed to deduct the value of the forced labor requisitioned from Belgium or the goods seized by the Army in occupied territories in 1914 and after. Germany also claimed the interest on its loans as reparations payments. The subterfuges of the German government

outraged the few commentators familiar
with them. (Mantoux, 152–4; R. C. Long,
The Mythology of Reparations (London,
1928) 103–4; G. Borsky, *The Greatest Swin-
dle in the World* (London, 1942); R. Vansittart, *Lessons of My Life* (New York, 1943),
125–148.

34. Payments were reduced to less than half
of what had been called for by the London
Schedule of Payments of May, 1921, precipitating a flow of funds from American investors. (B. Kent, *Spoils of War* (Oxford, 1989),
384–5. Between 1925 and 1930, Germany
made annual payments of 1.1 to 2.5 milliard
gold marks, representing between 1.8 and
3.3% of its GDP (2.4%, on average).

35. Marks, *Innocent Abroad*, 197–203.

36. *Ibid.*, 200–204. The $500 million repre-
sented a "priority payment," though it took
much cajolery, and American pressure,
before Belgium finally received even this
sum – more than six years after it had been
pledged. It is difficult to calculate exactly
how much more the country received, but
the total came to no more than 25% of the
damages claimed by the government.

37. S. Schuker, *American "Reparations" to Germany, 1919–33: Implications for the Third
World Debt Crisis* (Princeton, 1988), 63;
Mantoux, 146–7. Mantoux estimates that
short-term and long-term debts totaled
about 21 million.

38. The Versailles Treaty in fact required Germany to tax its citizens at a rate comparable to that of the Allied countries, as did
the Dawes Agreements. These stipulations
were ignored. Thanks largely to inflation,
Germany's internal debt in 1930 was only
about 6% of Great Britain's. (Borsky, 67.)

39. Schuker, 120. While America was lending
money so promiscuously, it was insisting
on repayment of all Allied debts incurred
during the war, which totaled, in gold
marks, about 74 milliard ($18.5 billion), of
which approximately 59 milliard ($14.75 bil-
lion) was owed to the U.S. (Sharp, 99.)

40. B. Mitchell, *European Historical Statistics,
1750–1970* (New York, 1978), 411.

41. M. Trachtenberg, *Reparation in World Politics*, 66–7; Schuker, 16–17; Mantoux, 115,
117, 163; Borsky, 33, 68; Mitchell, 411. Using
other indices, the percentage would have
been 7.38 for the final years of the decade.

42. It was also paid off without flooding its

creditors with cheap goods, the bête noir
of Versailles Treaty opponents in the 1920s.
(If the "transfer problem" was exaggerated,
Germany still required a trade surplus to
finance its reparations.) Nor was France
credited with surrendered assets in Alsace
and Lorraine and other kinds of losses that
inflated the German contribution.

43. H. Herwig, *The First World War: Germany
and Austria–Hungary, 1914–1918* (London,
1997), 384.

44. F. Fischer, *Germany's War Aims in the First
World War*, 104–5. Britain is not mentioned
in the memorandum, except implicitly. It
would cede territory to enable Germany to
create "a contiguous Central African colonial empire." Russia's fate would be considered later. The case for retaining all of Belgium and incorporating it into the Kaiserreich was made eloquently by its Governor
General. (*General von Bissing's Testament:
A Study in German Ideals* (London, 1917).)

45. Sharp, 106–127.

46. While the *Wehrmacht* ran Poland, until 25
October 1939, 531 towns and villages were
burned and 16,376 people were killed in 714
mass executions. After the transfer to civilian rule, another 19,792 Poles were killed
in 769 operations resulting in the murder
of ten or more. In at least 21 villages, more
than one hundred residents were massacred.
By the war's end 45% of doctors and den-
tists, 57% of attorneys, 40% of professors,
30% of technicians, and 18% of the clergy
had been killed. (R. Lukas, *The Forgotten
Holocaust: The Poles Under German Occupation, 1939–1944* (Lexington, KY, 1986), 3,
5–7, 37.

47. He may have been influenced by his affection for the beleaguered German economic
representative Carl Melchior, along with
his embarrassment before his Bloomsbury
friends at having lent support to the war.
Apart from his motives, the contemporary reader cannot help but be struck by
Keynes's breathtaking hubris. He casually
made projections for a national economy
that a responsible contemporary economist,
with ten gigabytes of data and a 2 gigahertz
processor, would be reluctant to hazard
for the next quarter's earnings of a single
company.

48. This is not to say, of course, that the Treaty
was without flaws and the behavior of the

Allies was irreproachable. Some of the criticisms made by Smuts and Keynes were legitimate: the initial cash payments and payments in kind ought to have been lower, the requirement that Germany build ships for the Allies moderated, the Polish borders redrawn, a somewhat larger army permitted, and various "pinpricks" eliminated, such as the forbidding of fishing in the Baltic. Had the U.S. been willing to forgive Allied debts, Belgium, France, and Britain would have been able to reduce reparations totals at the outset, rather than piecemeal and by default. Britain ought not to have pressed for any war costs, and forgiveness of its debts might have been the quid pro quo that would have enabled Lloyd George to forego these. France in the end was less worried about reparations than security, and Britain and the U.S. ought to have addressed its legitimate concerns, however politically difficult. (Ironically, Wilson's faith in the League of Nations and horror of balance-of-power politics had the same impact as Britain's skepticism about the League and its desire to maintain a balance of power in Europe – the abandonment of the French.) The Allies are often faulted for continuing the naval blockade for five months after the Armistice. But British warships, remaining at their stations to deter Germany from resuming the war, did not seize food shipments, which in fact crossed the Atlantic. Germany, however, resisted surrendering temporarily its merchant marine to transport supplies, an Allied condition, and insisted on paying in gold specie, which the French opposed (believing it would reduce reparations). (S. Bane, R. Lutz (eds.), *The Blockade of Germany After the Armistice* (New York, 1972), 24–5, 41–3, 184–197, and passim; C. P. Vincent, *The Politics of Hunger* (Athens, OH, 1985), 77–123).

49. For the case that it began at Versailles, see A. Lentin, "'Appeasement' at the Paris Peace Conference" and K. Robbins, "The Treaty of Versailles, 'Never Again' and Appeasement" in M. Dockrill and J. Fisher (eds.), *The Paris Peace Conference, 1919: Peace Without Victory?* (London, 2001), 51–66 and 103–114; and A. Lentin, *Lloyd George, Woodrow Wilson and the Guilt of Germany: An Essay in the Prehistory of Appeasement* (Leicester, 1984).

50. General John J. Pershing was convinced that Germany would use the armistice to rearm and, when ready, would resume the war. He lived to see his fears realized. "There can be no conclusion to this war until Germany is brought to her knees," he declared in November 1918. (F. Vandiver, *Black Jack: The Life and Times of John J. Pershing*, v. 2 (College Station, TX, 1977), 981.) Friends and associates had never seen him so enraged as when he learned of the Armistice terms. (G. Smith, *Until the Last Trumpet Sounds* (New York, 1998), 200–1.) There may have been some self-reproach in his anger. Meeting at Senlis on 25 October 1918 with Haig, Pétain, and Foch to discuss the terms of the armistice, Pershing, unaware of his government's position and suffering from flu, had failed to push for unconditional surrender. He advocated this forcefully soon after in a long statement to the Supreme War Council. (Vandiver, 982–3; F. Palmer, *John J. Pershing, General of the Armies* (Westport, CT, 1970 [1948], 334.) On his 85th birthday, in 1945, Pershing received the following telegram from President Truman: "This should be one of the happiest of your many birthdays, as you remember that this time we went all the way through to Berlin, as you counseled in 1918." (Vandiver, 1096.)

51. J. Wheeler-Bennett, *The Nemesis of Power: The German Army in Politics* (New York, 1967), 31. Complementing the myth of the "November criminals" who overthrew the *Kaiserreich* and signed the Armistice, was the myth of the "September incompetents" – notably Chief of Staff von Moltke and Lieutenant Colonel Hentsch, who snatched defeat from the jaws of victory in 1914 by being irresolute, pessimistic, and unimaginative, and, above all, in von Moltke's case, by not adhering to Schlieffen's Plan. Perhaps no one decision was as fatal to Europe's future as Wilson's resolve to conclude an armistice only with the government of a German republic, imposing on it the stigma of defeat rather than on the Kaiser and Hindenburg. It is also significant that the President refused to tour the devastated regions of France, as Clemenceau urged, or to visit Aarschot, Dinant, or Visé. (He did come to Leuven to receive an honorary degree.) Nor did Wilson find

the time to pay his respects to U.S. troops, whether in barracks, hospitals, or cemeteries. The President did not wish unpleasant realities to cast a shadow on his vision of a just peace.

NOTES TO AFTERWORD

1. R. Lukas, *The Forgotten Holocaust: The Poles Under German Occupation, 1939–1944* (Lexington, KY, 1986), 3, 5–7, 37.

2. Hitler repeatedly alluded to his famous "prophesy" of January 30, 1939, and by October 1941 was declaring, "By exterminating this pest [the Jews], we shall do humanity a service of which our soldiers can have no idea."(S. Friedlander, *Nazi Germany and the Jews, 1939–1945: The Years of Extermination* (New York, 2007), 273.) Goebbels took up the refrain the following month: "[Jewry] is now gradually being engulfed by the same extermination process that it had intended for us..."(*Ibid.*, 276.) This is essentially the thesis of Jeffrey Herf's *The Jewish Enemy* (Cambridge, 2006), which also emphasizes the activity of Otto Dietrich, director of the Reich Press Office, operating independently of Goebbels and with daily access to Hitler.

3. A great number of scholars have discussed the roles of fear and greed in the Holocaust, but some recent books on these subjects have received considerable attention, apart from Herf's *The Jewish Enemy*, notably Götz Aly's *Hitlers Volksstaat* (2005), translated as *Hitler's Beneficiaries* (2006), Adam Tooze's *The Wages of Destruction* (2006), and Saul Friedlander's monumental *Nazi Germany and the Jews: The Years of Extermination, 1939–1945* (2007). In another controversial and widely reviewed book, *Fear* (2007), Jan Gross analyzes the greed behind the fear that triggered the pogroms in post-war Poland: the ancient blood libel enabled Poles to retain confiscated property.

4. It is part of a larger literature on messianic political movements. Notable contributions include E. Kedourie, *Nationalism*; J. Talmon, *The Origins of Totalitarian Democracy* and its two successors; G. Mosse, *The Nationalization of the Masses*; J. Billington, *Fire in the Minds of Men*; M. Burleigh, *Earthly Powers* and *Sacred Causes*; N. Cohn, *The Pursuit of the Millennium*; E. Voegelin, *Political Religions* and *From Enlightenment*

to Revolution; for its more benign British incarnation, see, among other works, T. J. Wright, *The Religion of Humanity: Comtean Positivism in Victorian Britain*; M. Oakeshott, *Rationalism in Politics*, S. Letwin, *The Pursuit of Certainty*; B. Knights, *The Idea of the Clerisy in the Nineteenth Century*; and, for the perennial debate on Mill's sacralization of politics in particular, J. Hamburger, *John Stuart Mill on Liberty and Control*, J. Carlisle, *John Stuart Mill and the Writing of Character*, L. Raeder, *J. S. Mill and the Religion of Humanity*.

5. That German nationalism was inspired by and inextricably linked to Protestantism was a recurring theme in the work of the great 19th century Prussian historians Droysen, Sybel, and Treitschke, and was repeated ad nauseum by journalists, politicians, pastors and theologians after 1870. See H. W. Smith, *German Nationalism and Religious Conflict: Culture, Ideology and Politics* (Princeton, 1995), 27–34; A. Hoover, *The Gospel of Nationalism: German Patriotic Preaching from Napoleon to Versailles* (Stuttgart, 1986), 40–42. For Ranke, see J. Toews, *Becoming Historical: Cultural Reformation and Public Memory in Early Nineteenth-Century Berlin* (Cambridge, 2004), 372–418.

6. This was the year Adalbert Falk, Minister of Education, was dismissed and a rapprochement reached with Ludwig Windthorst, the Center Party leader, and the new pope, Leo XIII. Some historians argue that it only ended in 1887, with the repeal of most, though not all, of the anti-Catholic legislation. The ban on Jesuits remained in force until 1917 and the Pulpit Paragraph persisted until 1953. This forbade discussion by clergy of political issues "in a manner endangering public peace." (M. Gross, *The War Against Catholicism: Liberalism and the Anti-Catholic Imagination in Nineteenth Century Germany* (Ann Arbor, Michigan, 2004), 255). The *Kulturkampf* began by secularizing schools, but in May 1873, it set educational requirements for the ordination of all priests and ministers, and then, a year later, began expelling clerics who had not been certified. Soon a third of Prussian parishes were without a priest and many were in jail, including the Primate of Poland.

7. For anti-Catholicism after Bismarck, see R. Ross, *Beleaguered Tower: The Dilemma of*

Political Catholicism in Wilhelmine Germany (Notre Dame, 1976), 1–32.

8. Beginning in the late 1890s, there was a proliferation of European-wide conferences, congresses, and exhibitions. Brussels, already with ambitions of becoming the capital of Europe, was the site of a number of these. Every summer more than 20,000 German families vacationed on the Belgian coast.(E. Waxweiler, *Belgium Neutral and Loyal: The War of 1914* (New York, 1915), 2.) It was cheaper than the Riviera and more *gemütlich* than Normandie. Some villages—Blakenberghe, Heyst, Knocke, Westende—became virtual German colonies in July and August. Many thousands of Germans lived in Belgium year-round; there were at least 5,000 seeking to leave Brussels at the outbreak of the war.(B. Whitlock, *Belgium: A Personal Narrative*, v. 1, (New York, 1920), 86.) In Antwerp, the colony had its own social clubs, choral societies, gymnasia, churches, Masonic lodges, newspapers, and schools.(J. Claes, "Belgium Before the War" in J. Claes, et. al., *Life and Death in Belgium, by Ten Belgian Journalists in Exile* (Sydney, 1917), 33.) The German schools in Brussels and Antwerp attracted a large number of Belgian students as well, so impressive was the reputation of Teutonic educational methods. For some time it had been considered highly desirable for Belgian scholars, and almost obligatory for scientists, to have studied at a German university. Even among Walloons, Heidelberg, Bonn, and Berlin had acquired more cachet than the Sorbonne. Eventually German undergraduates trickled west to study with the students of the illustrious emeriti of German universities. Journals—including some published jointly by German and Belgian scholars—and conferences insured a continuous exchange of ideas and friendships between scholars in the same discipline.

Belgian and German socialists also collaborated closely. Emile Vandervelde, the venerable leader of Belgian socialism, was president of the Second International at the outbreak of war. Trade unionists from both countries mingled at these and other conferences, and Belgian socialists and non-socialists alike conscientiously studied German experiments in state-funded health, unemployment, and retirement insurance, and reported on municipal services in model cities like Frankfort and Dusseldorf.

German penetration of Belgian markets and competition in exports was naturally not welcomed by all. There were widespread complaints, particularly in Antwerp, about unfair practices. After the outbreak of war, the large and wealthy German colony there was also accused of various subversive activities.(Claes, "Belgium Before the War," 31–37.) Nonetheless, contacts between urban Belgians and Germans in all walks of life were extensive and largely amiable in the two decades before the war.

9. For Schönerer and Austrian Pan-Germanism, see A. Whiteside, *The Socialism of Fools* (Berkeley, 1975)

10. Gross, 283. The introduction ("Who are the Elders?") to the most widely circulated English translation of the most influential anti-Semitic tract, *Protocols of the Elders of Zion*, begins, "This is a secret which has not been revealed. They are the Hidden Hand," and goes on to quote Disraeli: "The world is governed by very different personages from what is imagined by those who are not behind the scenes."(V. Marsden (trans.) *The Protocols of the Meetings of Learned Elders of Zion* (Houston, 1934), 7.)

11. As others have noted, subsequent ethnic cleansing campaigns cannot be compared to the Nazi project to eliminate Jews from Europe: Jews were to be removed from countries no Germans had ever lived in or intended to live in.

12. The curtain raiser is usually held to be the dissolution of the Catholic Section of the Prussian Ministry of Culture in June of 1871. The head of the Section was accused of encouraging the teaching of Polish in Posen.(R. Healy, *The Jesuit Specter in Imperial Germany* (Boston, 2003), 57.

13. J. Harris, *A Study in the Theory and Practice of German Liberalism: Eduard Lasker, 1829–1884* (Lanham, Maryland, 1984), 49.

14. Healy, 67. For more on Lasker, Jews, and the Jesuit Law, see Gross, 258–267. Gross reveals the extent to which the *Kulturkampf* was a Liberal crusade, the contribution of the progressive middle-classes to German unification. (Bismarck was more preoccupied with the perceived political threat posed by the Center Party.) Gross further

argues that the *Kulturkampf* did not represent a betrayal of core Liberal beliefs in individual rights and tolerance, as is sometimes assumed. Rather, Liberals insisted that freedom and social progress required energetic action by the state to combat the influence of the Church. German Liberals were no more libertarian than their British and American counterparts would be a century later.

15. David Blackbourn, "Roman Catholics, the Center Party, and Antisemitism in Imperial Germany," in H. A. Strauss (ed.), *Hostages to Modernization: Studies in Antisemitism, 1870–1933* (Berlin, 1993), 111. There was of course much antisemitism in the Church itself in the '70s. Apart from traditional accusations dating back to the Church Fathers, liberalism was identified with Jews, who were blamed for the *Kulturkampf*, and the Depression of 1873 elicited renewed outbursts against Jewish capitalists. Jews were especially linked by Catholic polemicists to Freemasons, still another group inspiring rampant paranoia.

16. For the lone, but influential, British version, see Carlyle, particularly *Sartor Resartus*, *Frederick the Great*, and *Latter Day Pamphlets*. However, the Sage of Chelsea's admiration for "captains of industry" owed nothing to Germany, and certainly found few takers there. (There is a fainter echo of German motifs in Coleridge.) Other English and Scottish intellectuals went into the import business, naturally, and by the end of the century there were British Idealists, Historicists, Nietzscheans, and Wagnerians. But no one is now referred to as "the English Hegel," any more than there is a "German John Stuart Mill."

17. Healy, 7. Pater Filuzius, with the help of a Frenchman and a socialist, plots to murder the spinster's rightful heir, Gottlieb Michael, representing the innocent and naive German. The trio is thwarted, and wind up being hurled onto a dung heap. (*Ibid.*, 24, 70; Gross, 236–7).

18. W. Arndt, (ed. and trans.) *The Genius of Wilhelm Busch: Comedy of Frustration. An English Anthology* (Berkeley, 1982), 41.

19. cited by J. Katz, *The Darker Side of Genius: Richard Wagner's Antisemitism* (Hanover, New Hampshire, 1986), 35.

20. Katz, 115.

21. Katz, 33. Wagner had, of course, generous Jewish patrons, including Meyerbeer, the target of his 1850 pamphlet, and there were several Jewish musicians in his entourage. For discussions of Wagner's antisemitism, see, in addition to Katz, M. Weiner, *Richard Wagner and the Antisemitic Imagination* (Lincoln, NB, 1995), M. Brener, *Richard Wagner and the Jews* (Jefferson, NC, 2006), H. Zelinsky, *Richard Wagner: Ein deutsches Thema, 1876–1976* (Vienna, 1983), and P. Rose, *Wagner: Race and Revolution* (New Haven, 1992) and *Revolutionary Antisemitism in Germany from Kant to Wagner* (Princeton, 1990), among others. Rose makes the case that Wagner's intellectual development is misrepresented when it is bifurcated into "liberal, democratic" and "racist, nationalist" phases. The two were of a piece. The antisemitism of the radical Left has a long pedigree. However, the attempt to show, by Rose, Zelinsky and others, that Wagner's operas are permeated by the antisemitism he gave vent to in essays, letters, and conversation has not convinced most musicologists.

22. Rose, *Wagner*, 373.

23. E. Newman, *The Life of Richard Wagner*, v. 3, (New York, 1941), 517.

24. Newman, *Ibid.*, v. 4 (New York, 1946), 72.

25. However, the *Kulturkampf*, he felt, had been a clumsy blunder. Chamberlain hoped German Catholics would increasingly ignore the siren-call of the Vatican, and defended the creation of an "affirmative action" chair for Catholics at University of Strassburg.(G. Field, *Evangelist of Race: The Germanic Vision of Houston Stewart Chamberlain* (New York, 1981), 308.)

26. L. Poliakov, *The History of Anti-Semitism*, v. 4, *Suicidal Europe, 1870–1933*, 58, 294.

27. "All religions that depart from the true Christian religion are *ex opere operato*, that is, teach 'this I will do, and that will please God.' But one must hold fast to the rule that every *opus operatum* is idolatrous. Whatever the papists taught was *opus operatum*. At all events, their rules and regulations remind me of the Jews, and actually very much was borrowed from the Jews."(T. Tappert (ed.), *Luther's Works*, v. 54, *"Table Talk"* (Philadelphia, 1967), 436–7.) The author of the classic biography of Luther in English famously wished that his subject

had died before he published "On the Jews and their Lies" in 1543.(R. Bainton, *Here I Stand* (New York, 1950), 379.) The level of the invective in this pamphlet has to be read to be believed; see especially the fourth section. (F. Sherman (ed.*) Luther's Works, v. 47, "The Christian in Society"* (Philadelphia, 1971), 121–307.) But Luther lived another three years, writing additional antisemitic tracts and castigating Jews in letters and conversations. As with Jews, his attacks on the "The Robbing and Murdering Hordes of Peasants" in 1525 had been preceded by milder sentiments.(See R. Schultz, ed. *Luther's Works, v. 46* (Philadelphia, 1967), 45–56. ("These are strange times," Luther admits near the end of the tract, "when a prince can win heaven with bloodshed better than other men with prayer!"*(Ibid.,* 54.) The attack had been preceded by the conciliatory "Admonition to Peace," just as his attack on Jews had been preceded, two decades earlier, by the conciliatory "Jesus Christ was Born a Jew," which blamed the Church for the Jews' continued resistance to message of the Gospels.) But the failure of the Jews to now convert and the peasants' insistence on taking subversive Old and New Testament passages literally caused the splenetic Reformer to redirect some of his fury from the Church to those who had disappointed him. The Luther-to-Hitler case owed much, of course, to German scholarship of a century earlier, which clearly differentiated the two forms of Protestantism. Whether or not the doctrine of predestination infected its believers with "the spirit of capitalism," Calvinism and other Western European heresies fostered a different set of attitudes toward secular authorities, toward the law, and toward commerce and banking, as well as toward the Old Testament and Jews, which were to have repercussions subsequently. (Similarly, French racialist thinking, that of Gobineau and Renan, was not antisemitic, in contrast to versions flourishing east of the Rhine.) There can also be no denying that the movement Luther founded contributed both to the protracted weakness of Germany, in dividing it politically and religiously (though this is hardly what he intended), and to the keen resentment this weakness occasioned. As to Luther's

antisemitic writings, however, while one can say they "anticipated" or re-enforced Nazi beliefs, they were probably without much influence from the late 17th to the late 19th centuries, reproduced only in editions of his collected works, and not even cited by Eisenmenger, the most important German antisemite before Duhring.

28. Ministére des affaires etrangéres, *Belgium's Martyrdom* (reprinted in *Current History* (New York, 1918), 517.

29. H. Pirenne, *Belgium and the First World War* (Wesley Chapel, FL, 2014), 162.

30. B. Whitlock, *Belgium: A Personal Narrative*, v. 2 (New York, 1920), 365.

31. Ministére, *Belgium's Martyrdom*, 517.

32. Using the CPI, and over $64 billion using nominal GDP per capita.

33. The operation was directed by two agencies under the Ministry of War. A consortium of German firms responsible for the work made 1,433,000 marks in profit during the first nine months of the demolitions. (Pirenne, *Belgium*, 188–194.)

34. As noted, the real scandal of Versailles was the treatment of the Belgians, not the Germans. Promised "privilege" and "priority"—that their claims would be met first, and would include the country's war costs—the Belgians would have received neither had it not been for the insistence of Colonel House, and in the end recovered less than a quarter of the cost of the damages inflicted by the Germans.(S. Marks, *Innocent Abroad: Belgium at the Paris Peace Conference of 1919* (Chapel Hill, 1981),183–195.)

35. On von Bissing's designs, see the long memorandum published after his death by M. W. Becmeister in *Das Grössere Deutschland* and *Bergisch Märkische Zeitung* in May 1917 and translated as *General von Bissing's Testament* (London, 1917). The Governor General told the Chancellor that he "knew of no means available to a civilized state to extract labor from people unwilling to give it."(F. Passelecq, *Déportation et Travail Forcé des Ouvriers et de la Population civile de la Belgique occupée, 1916–1918* (Paris, 1928), 441. He further argued that the deportations would violate international law, unless the work was non-war-related, and would offend neutrals. But then, overcoming these unpatriotic scruples, he suggested that the government might get around the Hague

Conventions by claiming that the deportations were necessary to maintain public order.

36. The initiative to force Belgians to work in German factories came from leading industrialists like Walter Rathenau, the AEG chief in charge of wartime economic planning, and Carl Duisberg, director of Bayer. Hindenburg and Ludendorff were more than happy to oblige.

37. For a summary, see RDE, v. II, 67–115 and Pirenne, *Belgium*, 157–185. The most complete information on German tactics comes from documents abandoned in the district of Nivelles, located midway between Brussels and Charleroi. The scenes outside the centers were memorable, family members shouting, sobbing, and trying to hand over packages, the captives singing *La Brabaçonne* and *La Marseillaise*, and chanting that they would not sign the labor contracts. Naturally many individuals were seized mistakenly—students, rentiers, small businessmen and shopkeepers, and workers who were employed. They were told they could file complaints from the detention camps in Germany. See also the detailed eyewitness account in *The Daily Telegraph* of December 13, 1916 reprinted in A. Toynbee, *The Belgian Deportations* (London, 1917), 88–95.

38. RDE, v. II, 179. Priests remonstrating with the soldiers were struck with rifle butts and called "dirty Catholics."

39. *Ibid.*, 24–5.

40. The Emperor was ostensibly responding to a plea from Cardinal Mercier and other prominent Belgians. (Pirenne, *Belgium*, 182.)

41. He is accused of exaggerating the extent to which ordinary Germans escaped paying for the war. While corporate tax revenues rose more rapidly than revenues from taxes on wages, this merely reflected soaring business profits; the share of the national income going to working class Germans declined. Indeed, real wages declined, Aly's critics argue, for he failed to factor in inflation. Adam Tooze in particular condemns the argument that payment for the war was deferred by borrowing. Goods and "services" required by war have to be paid for in the present, by the transfer of resources from consumption. Money used to purchase bonds can't be used again. The percentage of war costs borne by Germans versus foreigners is the exact opposite of what Aly claims, according to Tooze: ordinary Germans subsidized 70% of the war costs, not 30%. In response, Aly argues that declines in consumption were partially offset by the flow of goods sent by soldiers from occupied territory, and that these did indeed sustain morale, as did financing the war by credit rather than taxation: through 1942 bond purchasers were confident they would be reimbursed by revenue from further German conquests.(For a summary of some criticism, see A. Mierzejewski, "The Latest Phase of Germany's Effort to Master its Nazi Past" H-Net German 15 September 2005, (http://h-net.msu.edu/cgi-bin/logbrowse.pl?trx=vx&list=H-German&month=0509&week=c&msg=T-4Vz9eCQ0vqppY%2bZMH64hg&user=&pw=); A. Tooze, "Economics, Ideology and Cohesion in the Third Reich: A critique of Goetz Aly's *Hitlers Volksstaat*"available at http://www.hist.cam.ac.uk/academic_staff/further_details/tooze-aly.pdf; G. Aly, *Hitler's Beneficiaries: Plunder, Racial War, and the Nazi Welfare State* (New York, 2006), 327–332.

42. Aly, 136.

43. *Ibid.*, 136–7.

44. *Ibid.*, 138–141.

45. *Ibid.* 156–7.

46. M. Foote, *Resistance: European Resistance to Nazism, 1940–1945* (New York, 1977), 257; V. Mallinson, *Belgium* (New York, 1970), 121–2.

47. L. Nicholas, *The Rape of Europa* (New York, 1994), 143–4.

48. *Ibid.*, 85, 143–4; P. Harclerode and B. Pittaway, *The Lost Masters* (New York, 2000), 15.

49. "When he first heard of the murders..., Wilhelm was almost euphoric about what he considered a 'splendid opportunity' for taking action. He immediately drafted a telegram ordering the East Asian squadron to occupy Jiaozhou Bay." J. Schrecker, *Imperialism and Chinese Nationalism: Germany in Shantung* (Cambridge, Massachusetts, 1971), 33. The fact that the missionaries were Catholic was an added bonus.

50. The Boxers, actually the Boxers United in Righteousness, succeeded other charismatic

anti-Christian movements in which members were trained in the martial arts and practiced rituals to make them, they believed, invulnerable. Severe flooding and then drought in the northern provinces, and the famine and lawlessness that followed, increased membership, as did mass unemployment among bargemen and others affected by the European steamboats and railroads. A particularly acute source of resentment was the legal protection afforded converts by missionaries.

51. P. Cohen, *History in Three Keys: The Boxers as Event, Experience, and Myth* (New York, 1997), 311. A Japanese consular official was also killed.

52. W. Schroeder (ed.), *Das persönliche Regiment: Reden und sonstige öffentlich Äusserungen Wilhelms II* (Munich, 1912), 40–42 (trans., Richard Levy). The famous speech was recorded by a single reporter from a local newspaper who knew shorthand. Other papers published the heavily censored version released by the Chancellor.

53. Shrecker, 136.

54. C. Tan, *The Boxer Catastrophe* (New York, 1955), 145.

55. D. Preston, *The Boxer Rebellion: The Dramatic Story of China's War on Foreigners that Shook the World in the Summer of 1900* (New York, 2000), 306. The behavior of the German troops shocked and offended the British. Col. J. M. Grierson, who was to have commanded II Corps of the BEF in 1914, then serving on the staff of General von Waldersee, sent a long, confidential memo to the Undersecretary of State for War on 24 July 1901 complaining about the "imperious demands" of the Germans and "their arrogant and high-handed manner," and concluding that "of all our Allies in China, they were the most difficult to get on with, not even excepting the Russians... and I am convinced that it is the opinion of every British Officer, both naval and military, who has served in China, that they are our most bitter and implacable rivals."(NA, Lansdowne Papers, 800/119.)

56. I. Hull, *Absolute Destruction: Military Culture and the Practices of War in Imperial Germany* (Ithaca, 2005),10–11; J. Bridgman, *The Revolt of the Hereros* (Berkeley, 1981), 12.

57. Hull, 56.

58. *Ibid.*, 28.

59. *Ibid.*, 29.

60. *Ibid.*, 31.

61. Bridgman, 19.

62. Hull, 47. See also J. Bridgman and L. Worley, "Genocide of the Hereros" in S. Totten, *et. al* (eds.), *Century of Genocide: Eyewitness Accounts and Critical Views* (New York, 1997), 3–40.

63. M. Kitchen, *The German Officer Corps, 1890–1914* (Oxford, 1968), 206.

64. He was accompanied to jail by two colleagues, but then released.

65. Kitchen, 202.

66. The above account is based on Kitchen, H.-U. Wehler, "*Der Fall Zabern von 1913/14 als Verfassungskrise des Wilhelminischen Kaiserreichs,*" *Krisenherde des Kaiserreichs, 1871–1918* (Göttingen, 1970), 70–88, and D. Schoenbaum, *Zabern 1913: Consensus Politics in Imperial Germany* (London, 1982). The latter offers a somewhat more upbeat conclusion.

67. After May 1915, subs that did surface to give advance warning to their target, it must be noted, risked being sunk by naval vessels disguised as merchantmen, though the Q-ships were not very effective compared to depth charges, and subs that surfaced in front of the decoys normally did so to use their deck guns and conserve torpedoes, not to save lives.

68. This happened following the sinking of the "Llandovery Castle," a clearly-marked hospital ship, on June 27, 1918 by U-boat 86.(NA, ADM 1/8611/158; C. Mullins, *The Leipzig Trials* (London, 1921), 107–134.) See Appendix II.

69. A committee of enquiry after the war determined that 1,265 civilians living in the UK were killed by airships, bombers, and naval vessels, and 3,490 injured.(NA CAB 24/85 GT 7806.)

70. Catholics taking an oath of loyalty to the King were permitted to own and inherit land, and laws targeting priests were repealed.

71. "The Wreck of the Deutschland" by Gerard Manley Hopkins. The nuns' destination was America, but other nuns, priests, and members of religious orders fled to Britain.

72. W. Rubinstein, *A History of Jews in the English Speaking World: Great Britain* (London, 1996), 95.

73. *Ibid.*, 120.

74. *Ibid.*, 313–14.

75. Nor is there a chapter on Italy. R. Levy, *Antisemitism in the Modern World* (Lexington, Massachusetts, 1991).

76. *H.M.S. Pinafore* opened in 1878, two years after the Ring cycle. Gilbert and Sullivan's first collaboration took place during the year the foundation stone was laid for the Bayreuth *Festspielhaus*, 1871.

77. The belief that one German death was sufficient justification for mass killing—or war—was hardly unique to Dr. Berghausen. The murder of a German diplomat in Paris was the pretext for the *Kristalnacht* pogrom, just as the *Anschluss* was to have been provoked by the murder of von Papen, the Ambassador, and the invasion of Czechoslovakia by the assassination of a German diplomat in Prague. The killing of a single German soldier at Gleiwitz (actually a Silesian opponent of the regime killed by lethal injection) was the casus belli for World War II. Hitler understood that for most of his countryman, the murder of one German would be an acceptable pretext for launching his armies.

78. The controversy was ignited by Rudolf Hochhuth's 1963 play *The Deputy*. See, among other works, G. Lewy, *The Catholic Church and Nazi Germany* (1964), S. Friedlander, *Pius XII and the Third Reich* (1966), J. Cornwell, *Hitler's Pope* (1999), S. Zuccotti, *Under His Very Windows: The Vatican and the Holocaust in Italy* (2000), M. Phayer, *The Catholic Church and the Holocaust* (2000), and, for sympathetic treatments, P. Blet, *Pius XII and the Second World War: According to the Archives of the Vatican* (1999) and R. Rychlak, *Hitler, the War, and the Pope* (2000). For more polemical approaches, see D. Goldhagen, *A Moral Reckoning* (2002) and D. Lapin, *The Myth of Hitler's Pope* (2005).

79. After the war, he did not hesitate to excommunicate all communists, even as he lobbied for clemency for Nazi war criminals. The counterfactual argument that protests by the Pope would have accomplished nothing and may have harmed the Jews is not persuasive, any more than is the argument that the bombing of the rail-lines or crematoria at Auschwitz would have been counterproductive. It is hard to imagine how either

initiative would have resulted in a worse outcome than the failure to act. The Vatican was exceptionally well informed about the scope of the Final Solution.

80. Diplomats from Britain and the U.S. had been withdrawn shortly after the loss of the Vatican's temporal power in 1870 and France had broken relations in 1905.(J. Pollard, *The Unknown Pope: Benedict XV and the Pursuit of Peace* (London, 1999), 89. For a more critical take on the Pontiff, see D. Zivojinovic, *The United States and the Vatican Policies, 1914–1918* (Boulder, Colorado, 1978). It was the Normans who defended the papacy from the middle of the 11th century to the first quarter of the 13th, while France became the most formidable menace to Rome in the 14th century, kidnapping one pope and installing French successors in Avignon, then backing French candidates during the Great Schism. But by the early 16th century the country again became the champion of Holy See until the Revolution, resuming the role in 1815 down to the Third Republic.

81. The total of 45 clergymen who were executed includes members of religious orders, lay brothers, and seminarians.(A. Mélot, *Le Martyre du Clergé Belge* (Paris, 1915), 10, 15, 16–17, 21–2.)

82. When the Papal nuncio, who had fled, returned to Brussels and was briefed, he wrote the Vatican Secretary of State, "One would be tempted to say that an order circulated among the troops to massacre, destroy and terrorize the population throughout their passage."(J. Horne and A. Kramer, *German Atrocities*, 268.)

83. *Ibid.*, 270.

84. The German Church had a pretty good idea as to what had happened. Matthias Erzberger, the Center Party politician who was in charge of foreign propaganda, confessed that "It has been proven beyond doubt, including by the testimony of German officers, that there have been cases of gross pillage, that many houses were set on fire without due cause, and that many Belgians were executed, without a judgment or without their guilt being shown."(*Ibid.*, 275.)

85. *Ibid.*, 269. Baudrilliet edited a book of essays condemning the German invasion from a Catholic standpoint, *The German War and Catholicism* (Paris, 1915).

86. See A. Rossino, *Hitler Strikes Poland*

(Lawrence, Kansas, 2003) for an account of how the 1939 Blitzkrieg itself anticipated the brutality of the 1941 invasion of the Soviet Union.

87. And occasionally in the West, the most notable case being Oradeur-sur-Glane near Limoges.

88. Among the exceptions would be those cases where the NKVD murdered their prisoners before they pulled out, following the German invasion of the Soviet Union. These were routinely blamed on the Jews, who were accused either of collaborating with or merely sharing the ethnicity of the killers, for it was believed that Jews ran the organization. But the killing of prisoners inspired revenge by local populations as a rule, not Germans.

89. M. Steinberg, "The *Judenpolitik* in Belgium within the West European Context: Comparative Observations" in D. Michman (ed.), *Belgium and the Holocaust: Jews, Belgians, Germans* (Jerusalem, 1998), 202–6; B. Moore, *Victims and Survivors: The Nazi Persecution of Jews in the Netherlands, 1940–1945* (London, 1997), 20, 37. Alternative figures for native Belgian Jews are 4,341 of 65,696, or 6.6%.(B. Moore, *Victims*, 37.) Jews in France fared better still: "only" 20–27% were sent east. But about 44% of foreign Jews were deported, nearly the same percentage as in Belgium. Some 56% of Jews in France were citizens, about 17% of whom were deported, compared with the approximately 23% of Jewish Belgian citizens who were deported. Belgian officials had clearly indicated, according to the SS, that "they only wanted to take care of the Jews who were Belgian nationals." The Belgian people, however, sheltered Jews of all nationalities, at great risk. About 4% of the deportees survived Auschwitz. (*Ibid.*, 214, 219)

90. Very effective organizations for spiriting British servicemen, and then downed American and British flyers, to safety were established during the Second World War, drawing on the experience, and sometimes the personnel, of the networks with which Edith Cavell and Gabriel Petit were involved. The underground press was also revived, and flourished. Eight papers called themselves *La Libre Belgique*, after the most famous clandestine journal of the first

occupation.(P. Lagrou, "Belgium" in B. Moore (ed.), *Resistance in Western Europe* (Oxford, 2000), 39.) Valuable information on German troop movements was also passed to the British.(M. Foote, *Resistance: European Resistance to Nazism, 1940–1945* (New York, 1977), 254–7.)

91. Three members of the Resistance accomplished this, armed with one pistol, a pliers, and a hurricane lantern covered with red paper. Five Jews were liberated. But, inspired by the rescue attempt, two hundred twenty-six others escaped before the train reached Germany, though ninety were recaptured and twenty-six killed. The train was guarded by sixteen soldiers. For a detailed account, see M. Schreiber, *Stille Rebellen* (Berlin, 2001).

APPENDIX I

The Report Of The British Committee On Alleged German Outrages (RBC)

1. *The Daily Mail*, 16 September 1914. The investigation might not take the form of a commission, he added.

2. Oxford University, Bodleian Library, Western Manuscripts, Bryce Papers, 247–8 (Bryce).

3. NA, HO 45/266503/5.

4. NA, HO 45/11061/266503

5. The War Office was enlisted to provide testimony from wounded British soldiers being treated at London hospitals. Not surprisingly, the results were disappointing. British troops were not operating in the areas of Belgium in which massacres took place, and were unlikely to have encountered refugees. Instances of mistreatment of wounded British soldiers was "exceptional," one officer wrote. However, several soldiers reported seeing Germans firing out of Red Cross wagons and exposing prisoners to direct fire. (NA, HO 45/266503/5; 266503/-.)

6. NA, HO 45/266503/7.

7. NA, HO 45/266503/5.

8. At McKenna's insistence, Mears was asked to be one of the two secretaries to the Bryce Committee when it was formed in December. Serving as a secretary to high-powered committees proved to be his métier, earning him a knighthood in 1917. After his work investigating the German outrages, Mears filled a similar role on committees

investigating the Dardanelles campaign and the Irish Rising of 1916. After the war, he joined the staff of Lord Reading, ambassador to the U.S., and wound up a High Court Chief Justice in India, where he also headed the law faculty at Allahbad University.

9. NA, HO 45/266503/10.

10. He impressed royalty and workers alike. "I like Mr. Bryce," Queen Victoria was reported to have remarked. "He knows so much and is so modest." A Nevada miner concurred: "Ole man Bryce is all right," he was overheard telling a companion. (H. A. L. Fisher, *James Bryce*, New York, 1927), v. 1, 295; v. 2, 3.)

11. Bryce, Simon to Bryce, 4 December 1914.

12. *Ibid.*

13. *Ibid.*, Cox to Bryce, 1 March 1915. Bryce himself had originally wished to interrogate witnesses. In reply, Simon had conceded that the Committee might hear evidence if it wished, "but the matter has been so prepared that they can pass a judgment on it without themselves undertaking the work of interrogation." (*Ibid.*, Simon to Bryce, 8 December 1914.)

14. *Ibid.*, Pollock to Bryce, 6 March 1915.

15. *Ibid.*, Fisher to Bryce, 11 March 1915.

16. F. Hirst, "Harold Cox," *Dictionary of National Biography, Supplement*, v. 55, (Oxford, 1940), 196.

17. He had criticized three statements that misrepresented the Committee's oversight of the investigation.

18. (*Report of the British Committee on Alleged German Outrages* (RBC) (Australia, 1915), 66.)

19. RBC, 44, 48–9.

20. *Ibid.*, 49.

21. K. Robbins, "Lord Bryce and the First World War, *The Historical Journal* v. 10, n. 2 (1967), 259. "It is my impression," wrote Fisher, "that Bryce approached this great body of evidence with a real hope and expectation that the Committee would be able if not to return a verdict of acquittal, at any rate to reduce within a small compass the burden of the charge..." (Fisher, v. 1, 133.)

22. RBC, 10.

23. *Ibid.*, 19, 20.

24. *Ibid.*, 22–3.

25. *Ibid.*, 28.

26. See Chapter 15 of the first edition for a detailed examination of the most sophisticated attempt to discredit the Bryce Report merely on the grounds of the brutality of the killings, as described by witnesses. There are a number of letters and depositions in the archives of the first *Commission d'Enquête* that provide plausible testimony of mutilations that cannot be discredited by the RDE or the parish archives. For example, Comte Harold de Hemptinne of Gent reported entering Zemst at 3:00 a.m. on the 26th and discovering the partially burned body of a resident whose legs had been severed above the knee, another body, also burned, whose legs and arms had been cut off, and the body of a boy younger than 14 which was riddled with bayonet wounds. Of the 15 civilians from Zemst who were killed, the RDE gives the names of five of the six shot at Eppegem, and seven of the remaining nine killed in the village, but provides details of the death of only one of these, who was murdered a month later. The one deposition from Zemst, by the burgomaster, mentions seeing two men shot and one burned alive. There is no parish report from Zemst. Unless one believes as a matter of faith that it was impossible that the Germans ever dismembered the bodies of individuals they killed, as they did to Charles Naus in Dinant and to Marie-Pauline Verleysen in Leuven, there is no basis for rejecting de Hemptinne's sworn and signed deposition. (GSA, 177, Zemst.)

27. RBC, 5.

28. J. Read, *Atrocity Propaganda, 1914–1919* (New Haven, 1941), 206. Many subsequent writers have echoed Read's accusation of bad faith.

29. NA, FO 370/587 L 1185/152.

30. NA, FO 370/587 L1185/170.

31. NA, HO 45/11061/266503. Bryce's own papers, according to his sister's executor C. H. Hartman, "would prove a powder magazine even now, if it were to fall into the wrong hands... There are innumerable extremely indiscreet letters from statesmen and public men of all nationalities." (Hartman to Gaslee, 8 May 1940. NA, FO 370/595.) It is not clear how many of the potentially embarrassing letters were destroyed before the collection was transferred to the Bodleian in 1946.

32. As noted, however, not only was it not the

purpose of the RDE to verify the testimony in the RBC, but the objectives of the Belgian report – the prosecution of criminal officers – and its methods meant that it would not provide affidavits describing the kind of evidence for which the Bryce Report was to be denounced – reports of the discovery, often in isolated locations, of victims who had been brutally murdered. An examination of events in Hofstade below reveals the limitations of the RDE.

33. RDE, 138, 552–5; RBC, 179. The two diaries are by Jan Janssens, dated 6 February 1915, and by three nuns of the Zusters van Maria convent in Leuven who ran a school in Hofstade. Sister Maria Dorothea Aerden was the mother superior and head mistress. They were consulted with the kind permission of Staf Floridor of Hofstade.

34. PRW, Mechelen-Zuid, Hofstade. Jan Janssens, Frans's father, was prevented from seeing his son's body by a soldier who threatened him with his bayonet, then beat him with his rifle butt.

35. GSA, 148, Hofstade; RBC, 193–4; NA HO 45/11061/266503/70. Marien and Janssens are named in the Committee's records, but not, of course, in its published report, where the later is identified only as "J." The eighteen-year-old victim worked in a sand quarry, Marien testified. General Deruette, an aide de camp of the King and commander of the 20th mixed brigade, also saw the bodies in the dance hall. The widow was on a stretcher, but the young man – the general guessed he was 15 or 16 – was covered by a sheet. It was Deruette who ordered that the bodies be buried, as they were starting to reek. An incurious regimental surgeon also spotted the two victims, but he stated that he "was not able to ascertain the injuries of the two bodies," though he "was told they had received bayonet wounds." (GSA, 148, Hofstade.)

36. In addition to an older woman and an eighteen-year-old, whom he identified as "Verschuere," Major General Maes reported seeing the bodies of a woman and her son, a boy of about fourteen. An artilleryman with the 20th mixed brigade, Alberic Rolin, also testified to seeing the bodies of a mother and child, but he gave their ages as 40 and 5. The boy had been stabbed six times. (GSA, 148, Hofstade). A patrol of three grenadiers, Sergeant Jonkers, Corporal Pollijn, and Private Vermeren, also reported coming across a boy killed by bayonet blows. They thought he was seven years old. (GSA, Hofstade, chemise 64.)

37. RBC, 45.

APPENDIX II

1. The clause (which was drafted by the Commission for the Reparations for Damages rather than the body charged with investigating the war's outbreak), merely assigned responsibility to Germany for the losses and damages inflicted on its enemies. This hardly struck Allied diplomats as controversial: who else, after all, had invaded and devasted Belgium, Northern France, and Serbia? A subordinate clause noted that the damages had resulted from "the aggression of Germany and her allies." (A. Sharp, *The Versailles Settlement: Peacemaking in Paris, 1919* (New York, 1991), 85–7.) The German Chancellor himself had acknowledged that the invasion of Belgium was "a wrong... which we will try to make good as soon as our military aims have been attained." ("The German White Book," *Collected Diplomatic Documents Relating to the Outbreak of the European War* (London, 1915), 438.

2. J. Willis, *Prologue to Nuremberg: The Politics and Diplomacy of Punishing War Criminals of the First World War* (Westwood, CT, 1982), 209, 70. The Germans killed outright nearly as many British as French civilians. A Committee of Enquiry into Breaches of the Laws of War, under Sir John MacDonell, determined that 498 civilians had been killed by airships, 619 by bombers, and 148 by sea bombardments, 1,265 deaths in all, with a total of 3,490 injuries. (NA, CAB 24/85 GT 7806.) The committee carefully sought to calculate how many of the casualties were the result of a deliberate campaign of terror, and how many were the consequences of attacks on legitimate military targets. But both political and legal considerations mitigated against prosecuting those responsible even for what the majority of the committee regarded as terrorist bombing. (Not surprisingly, representatives of the Royal Air Force were the strongest opponents of holding the Germans culpable.) Similarly, two of the "atrocities" that had excited the most outrage in Britain also went unpunished.

The Committee determined that Edith Cavell's sentence was in fact justified under German law. The Government also decided not to prosecute the Admirals who had condemned to death Captain Charles Fryatt as a quid pro quo with the French, who the British did not wish to see bringing charges against the commanding generals. (CAB, p. 424; Willis, 128.) (It was Fryatt's execution that originally moved the British government to resolve to prosecute war criminals after the war. The captain of an unarmed frigate, Fryatt was accused by the Germans of ramming a submarine that was preparing to sink his vessel, *Brussels*. (That same day, 28 March 1915, another u-boat sank a British liner, drowning 104 passengers and crew.) When he was subsequently captured, the "franc-tireur of the sea" was executed. Nurse Cavell helped British soldiers stranded behind German lines escape to the Netherlands.) This decision also obviously removed from prosecution those who had authorized U-boat attacks on merchant vessels. Thus the war's single greatest atrocity, from the British and American perspective, the sinking of the *Lusitania*, would go unpunished. However, individual commanders who had torpedoed hospital ships were still liable.

3. Willis, 74.

4. Lansing characterized his threat as a "high explosive" and, to heighten its impact, arranged that he would be summoned away from the committee immediately after delivering it. (Willis, 74–5.)

5. Lansing was uncompromising, rejecting even a French proposal to try the accused under German law as it existed in 1914. (Willis, 73.)

6. P. Mantoux, *The Deliberations of the Council of Four*, v. I (Princeton, 1992), 187–197; Willis, 80.

7. In the judgment of Willis, the historian of the Leipzig trials, the decision was regrettable. "Such a trial would have established a new precedent in international law regarding the responsibility of national leaders. The charges would not, however, have been of an ex post facto character, for the Hague conventions contained relatively clear standards for the conduct of war." (Willis, 81.) This was the position of the Belgian government. (RVR I, xxxiii.)

8. The Council of Four first took up the issue of trials in April 1919. Debate centered on the fate of the Kaiser, as the individual ultimately responsible both for the breach of Belgian neutrality and the war crimes that followed. ("Suppose," Lloyd George argued, "the Kaiser alone, in peace time, had crossed the frontier of Belgium with gun in hand and had fired on the inhabitants: the first Belgian policeman on the spot would have had the right to arrest him and to have him hanged; and because, instead of doing it himself, he sent a million men into Belgium, he should go unscathed?")(Mantoux, 189.) The British Prime Minister had initially declared that it was a matter of indifference whether or not the All Highest was tried, as long as he was punished by exile (to a more remote and forbidding location than the Netherlands), à la Napoleon. Soon Lloyd George came around to Clemenceau's position that a formal trial was imperative. ("The violation of law in the case of Belgium was so flagrant that the conscience of the peoples would not be satisfied if that act were treated in any other way than as a crime against public law.")(*Ibid.*, 189.) Wilson, who had already expressed his reservations about the possibility of convicting those high up in the chain of command – "nothing is easier than to destroy the trace of orders given" (*Ibid.*, 188) – expressed his disapproval of trying the Kaiser for violating treaties. To do so would be to "lower ourselves to the level of the criminal by abandoning principles of law." "Political precautions" – exile, presumably – should suffice. "The worst punishment," Wilson concluded, "would be public opinion." "Don't count on it," Clemenceau replied acidly. (*Ibid.*, 190.) Lloyd George, conflating the massacres and the breach of Belgian neutrality, continued to press for a trial. "I would bring him to trial solely for violation of the Treaty of 1839. The tribunal would hear witnesses who would explain how the treaty was violated, who would recall the atrocities committed in Dinant, in Leuven, and I would then say to the court: 'Judge!'" (*Ibid.*, 190.) Orlando, however, supported Wilson: there were no precedents for trying heads of state. Clemenceau, the only non-lawyer among the four (he was trained as a physician), argued passionately for

creating new precedents. (*Ibid.*, 193.) The issue was rendered moot when the Netherlands refused to surrender the Kaiser and the Allies opted not to pressure the Dutch government (by threatening, for example, to award the Schelde estuary to Belgium). A quixotic attempt by Tennessee National Guard officers to kidnap Wilhelm was foiled by the Dutch police. 9. E. Eyck, *A History of the Weimar Republic*, v. I (New York, 1967), 101–2. Germany agreed to abide by the findings of an international tribunal composed of judges from neutral countries on condition that its own courts reserved the right to sentence those convicted and that Allied citizens also be subject to trials.

10. *Ibid.*, 104.

11. In August 1919, Clemenceau was prepared to waive articles 228–230 in exchange for additional reparations; six months later his successor Millerand refused to compromise on the trials not in the interest of justice, but because Germany's failure to comply would furnish the pretext for delaying indefinitely the evacuation of the occupied territories in Germany. (Willis, 116, 123.)

12. J. Morgan, *Assize of Arms: The Disarmament of Germany and her Rearmament, 1919–1939* (New York, 1946), 169. It was despatched by courier to the Foreign Office.

13. Willis, 119.

14. Willis 122; R. Vansittart, *The Mist Procession* (London, 1958), 251.

15. Willis, 123; Morgan, 173.

16. C. Mullins, *The Leipzig Trials: An Account of the War Criminals' Trials and a Study of German Mentality* (London, 1921), 35, 40, 42, 44.

17. Willis, 119–120, 226; Morgan, 169; S. Marks, *Innocent Abroad: Belgium at the Paris Peace Conference of 1919* (Chapel Hill, 1981), 348. With the reduction in numbers, the Belgian prosecutors decided to focus on two towns, so as not to offend either Flemish or Walloon sensibilities. Aarschot and Andenne were selected because they had received much less attention than Leuven or Dinant.

18. Mullins, 136–51.

19. *Ibid.*, 140.

20. *Ibid.*, 141.

21. He was "exceedingly correct, ...quiet and deliberative, ...a man of refined sentiments." (*Ibid.*, 148).

22. *Ibid.*, 149.

23. *Ibid.*, 165–7. From testimony, it is fairly clear that Crusius's "derangement" consisted of his acute discomfort with the order and with the resistance of his men. The French had conducted a thorough investigation of the killings, and had abundant evidence of the brigade order from German diaries, letters, and p.o.w. testimony. (French Ministry of Foreign Affairs, *Germany's Violations of the Laws of War, 1914–15* (London, 1915), 49–54) Several other massacres of prisoners were credibly documented by the French. (*Ibid.*, 28–75.)

24. The Germans were clearly aware of the growing hostility of Britain's intelligentsia to the Versailles settlement, the reluctance on the government's part to pursue Articles 227–230, and an increasing disenchantment with the French. A creditable performance in the British cases might further divide the Allies, and terminate the trials. There was much more co-operation and mutual respect, if not camaraderie, between the German judges and lawyers and their British counterparts. Members of the Belgian delegation had refused to shake hands with the Germans.

25. Having just acquitted a submarine commander for torpedoing a hospital ship, the *Dover Castle*, on the grounds that he was only following orders (incredibly, subs were permitted to sink hospital ships under certain conditions), the Germans themselves indicted the captain of another u-boat who had not only sunk a clearly marked hospital ship, the *Llandovery Castle*, well outside the permitted zone for such actions, but had then turned his guns on the survivors, killing everyone aboard two lifeboats (another escaped in the darkness, after three of its passengers were interrogated on the U-boat). The captain apparently believed the *Llandovery Castle* was transporting eight American aviators. It was after he recognized his mistake that the captain attempted to kill all survivors. He then altered his log-book and swore his two lieutenants to secrecy. (Mullins, 103–5.) (The testimony of British officers held captive on the sub was damning. One told about the great excitement on board when the hospital ship was sighted and identified. "I suppose you know it is a hospital ship you have sunk," another told the captain after 13 or 14 shells

had been fired. "Yes, the *Llandovery Cas-tle*," he replied.)(NA, ADM 1/8611/158) The captain was living in Danzig, beyond the reach of German authorities, but his two lieutenants, Dittmar and Boldt, were arrested. Though they refused to testify, citing their oath, witnesses on the subs confirmed the testimony of those in the surviving lifeboat. The two officers were convicted of failing to disobey orders that were manifestly illegal and sentenced to four years imprisonment. As members of the public rushed up to commiserate with the two heroes, whose actions had been defended in court by an admiral, among others, a secret organization of Freikorps soldiers made plans to free the victims. This was accomplished within two years. Other convicted Germans did not require the services of the O.C. Two brutal prison-camp commanders, responsible for hundreds of deaths, were freed on medical grounds after serving three and five months. And in 1928, the convictions of Dittmar and Boldt were reversed by the State Court. (Willis, 140–141, 146.)

26. Mullins, 10–13, 224–234; Willis, 139.
27. Morgan, 173.
28. Vansittart, 251.

Bibliography

ARCHIVES

NOTE: Reference numbers for documents consulted at the General State Archives before the completion of the new inventory by Pierre-Alain Tallier in 2001 and the microfilming of the holdings have been changed to correspond to the new numbering system, except for those from Leuven. The dossiers of the first Commission d'Enquête for this town are presently missing and I have referred to them by their original, pre-inventory chemise numbers. I have also occasionally used the old numbers to cite other depositions or communications that were not for some reason transferred to the designated chemise for the locality in which the events they describe took place. I have not, however, verified that every document I've cited from the original folders and to which I've assigned a new number is actually to be found in the new chemise for that village or town.

Testimony collected by the second, post-war Commission d'Equête was removed from Brussels by the Germans some time between June 1940 and September 1944. It included detailed questionnaires filled out by witnesses or interviewers. Those that survived the war were taken from Berlin by the Russians in 1945, along with other Belgian documents. These are being very slowly returned from Moscow to the Royal Museum of the Army and Military History in Brussels. Unfortunately, no files from the towns and villages covered in this book are currently available to scholars. The original depositions from the British Committee on Alleged German Outrages, reported missing in 1939, were located in 1942, but were subsequently destroyed, possibly by a German V1 or V2 rocket.

General State Archives (Algemeen Rijksarchief/Archives Générale du Royaume)
> Inventaires 298: Inventaire des archives de la Commission d'Enquête sur la Violation des Règles du Droit des Gens, des Lois et des Coutumes de la Guerre (1914–1926)
> Mémoires de la Guerre 27/3 Inquest made by Commandant Charles Lemaire Papiers Schollaert-Helleputte, 124

Royal Museum of the Army and Military History (Koninklijk Museum van het Leger en de Krijgsgeschiedenis/ Musée Royal de l'Armée et d'Histoire Militaire)
> Fonds 85–4, 185–14, 14a, Boxes 87, 116, 5301, 5302

Ministry of Foreign Affairs, Brussels
> Boxes 285 I, II, 298 V

Diocesan Archive, Liège
> Fonds Rutten

Archdiocesan Archive, MechelenBrussel
> Parish Reports on World War I, Dekenijen Leuven, Mechelen-Zuid

Diocesan Archive, Namur
> Fonds Schmitz-Nieuwland

National Archives of the United Kingdom
> ADM 1/8611/158; CAB 24/72, 24/85, 24/111; FO 370/587, 372/495, 395/147, 395/304; HO 45/11061/266503; MUN 5/78; T 1/12292, 102/20; WO 161/178.

Imperial War Museum
Atrocity Stories, World War I
77/60, 85/32, 86/19, 88/26, 92/10, 93/22, 95/25, 97/27.

Bodleian Library, Oxford University
Western Manuscripts Collection
Bryce Papers, 239, 247–8; Fisher Papers, 60, 61

OFFICIAL REPORTS AND PAPERS

Commission d'Enquête sur les Violations des Règles du Droit des Gens, des Lois et des Coutumes de la Guerre, *Rapports* (Suppléments au *Moniteur Belge*) (22 reports issued individually between 28 August 1914 and 28 October 1915) / Official Commission of the Belgian Government, *Reports on the Violation of the Rights of Nations and of the Laws and Customs of War in Belgium*, 2 vols. (London, 1915)

Commission d'Enquête sur les Violations des Règles du Droit des Gens, des Lois et des Coutumes de la Guerre, *Rapports et Documents d'Enquête*, premier vol., tomes 1 et 2 (Brussels, 1922–23)

War Crimes Commission, Ministry of Justice, *War Crimes Committed During the Invasion of the National Territory, The Destruction of the Library of the University of Louvain* (Liège, 1946)

La Campagne de l'armée belge (31 Juillet 1914 1er Janvier 1915) d'après les documents officiels (Paris, 1915) / Commander-in-Chief of the Belgian Army, *Military Operations of Belgium* (London, 1915)

Le Livre rouge allemand: un document écrasant. Les atrocités allemandes: texte complet du rapport offciel de la commission instituée en vue de constater les actes commis par l'ennemi en violation du droit des gens (Paris, 1915) / French Ministry of Foreign Affairs, *Germany's Violations of the Laws of War, 1914–15* (London, 1915)

Collected Diplomatic Documents Relating to the Outbreak of War (London, 1915)

Committee on Alleged German Outrages, *Report of the British Committee on Alleged German Outrages* (Sydney, Australia, 1915)

G. P. Gooch and H. Temperley (eds.), *British Documents on the Origins of the War, 1898–1919*, vol. 11, J. W. Headlam-Morley (ed.)

Imperial War Ministry, Imperial Ministry of Foreign Affairs, *Die völkerrechtswidrige Führung des belgischen Volkskriegs* (Berlin, 1915)

M. Mongelas, W. Schücking (eds.), *Outbreak of the World War: German Documents Collected by Karl Kautsky* (New York, 1924)

Der Weltkrieg, 1914 bis 1918, Bearbeitet im Reichsarchiv: Die militärischen Operationen zu Lande (Erster Band): Die Grenzschlachten im Westen (Berlin, 1925)

NEWSPAPERS AND JOURNALS

Le XXième Siècle
L'Indépendance Belge
L'Étoile Belge
Blackstone's
Contemporary Review
Edinburgh Review
English Review
Fortnightly Review
Hibbert Review
National Review
Nineteenth Century and After
Quarterly Review
Daily Mail
Daily Express

The Times
Morning Post
Daily News and Leader
Daily Chronicle
Westminster Gazette
New York Times
Chicago Tribune

BOOKS AND PAMPHLETS (PRIMARY)

Anonymous:

Vigilans sed Aequus [W. T. Arnold], *German Ambitions as they affect Britain and the United States of America* (New York, 1908)

Verax [F. Bonnet] *Truth: A Path to Justice and Reconciliation* (London, n.d. [c. 1926])

[Bernhard Dernburg, et. al.], *Truth About Germany: Facts About the War* (New York n.d., [1914])

[Richard Grelling], *J'Accuse* (New York, 1915)

[Hervé de Gruben], *The Germans at Louvain* (London, 1916)

Feldwebel C., *The Diary of a German Soldier* (New York, n. d., 1919)

A Prussian, *Why Germany Will be Defeated* (Letchworth, 1915)

An Eye-Witness at Louvain (London, 1914)

The German Army from Within (New York, 1914)

A German Deserter's War Experience (New York, 1917)

The Horrors of Louvain by an Eye Witness (London, n.d.)

Le Martyre de Dinant, 5th ed. (Dinant, 1920)

Andenne la Martyre (Andenne, 1919)

Andler, Charles, *Les origines du pangermanisme, 1800–1888* (Paris, 1915),

–, *Le pangermanisme continental sous Guillaume II, 1888–1914* (Paris, 1915),

–, *Le pangermanisme colonial sous Guillaume II* (Paris, 1916)

–, *Le pangermanisme philosophique, 1800–1914* (Paris, 1917)

Andler, Charles and E. Lavisse, *German Theory and Practice of War* (Paris, 1915)

Archer, William, *Gems (?) of German Thought* (New York, 1917)

Bang, J. P., *Hurrah and Hallelujah: The Teaching of Germany's Poets, Prophets, Professors and Preachers* (New York, 1917)

Barnes, H., *In Quest of Truth and Justice: Debunking the War Guilt Myth*, (Chicago, 1928)

–, *Selected Revisionist Pamphlets* (New York, 1972)

Baudrillart, Alfred (ed.), *The German War and Catholicism* (Paris, 1915)

Bédier, Joseph, *German Atrocities from German Evidence* (Paris, 1915)

–, *How Germany Seeks to Justify her Atrocities* (Paris, 1915)

Berden, Louis and G. Verdavaine, *Pictures of Ruined Belgium/Visions de la Belgique Détruite* (London, n.d.)

Bernhardi, Friedrich von, *Germany and the Next War* (New York, 1914)

Bevan, Edwyn, *German Social Democracy During the War* (London, 1918)

Beyens, Baron Eugène Louis, *Germany Before the War* (London, 1916)

–, *Deux Années à Berlin, 1912–1914*, 2 vols. (Paris, 1931)

Bülow, Prince Bernhard von, *Memoirs*, 2 vols. (Boston, 1931)

Bilse, Lieutenant [Fritz von der Kryberg], *A Little Garrison: A Realistic Novel of German Army Life Today* (New York, 1904)

Bissing, Moritz von, *General Von Bissing's Testament: A Study in German Ideals* (London, n.d.)

Blucher, Evelyn, *An English Wife in Berlin* (New York, 1920)

Bourdon, Georges, *The German Enigma* (London, n.d.)

Buffin, Charles, *Brave Belgians* (New York, 1918)

Bullitt, Ernesta, *An Uncensored Diary from the Central Empires* (New York, 1917)

Cammaerts, Emile, *Through the Iron Bars* (London, 1917)

Cappuyns, Englebert, *Louvain: A Personal Experience* (Kingston-on-Thames, 1915)

Chamberlain, H. S., *The Ravings of a Renegade: Being the War Essays of Houston Stewart Chamberlain* (London, n.d.)

Chambry, René, *The Truth About Louvain* (London, 1915)

Chéradame, André, *The Pangerman Plot Unmasked* (New York, 1917)

Chirol, Valentine, *Fifty Years in a Changing World* (New York, 1928)

Chomondeley, Alice [Elizabeth von Arnim], *Christine* (New York, 1917)

Chot, Jean, *La furie allemande dans l'entre-Sambre-et-Meuse* (Charleroi, 1919)

Collier, Price, *Germany and the Germans from an American Point of View* (New York, 1913)

Coole, W. W. and M. F. Potter [Wladistan Kulski and Michal Potulicki], *Thus Spake Germany* (London, 1941)

Cramb, J. A. *England and Germany* (New York, 1914)

Cuvelier, Jacques, *L'Invasion allemande*, vol. 2 of *La Belgique et la guerre* (Paris, 1921)

Dane, Edmund, *Hacking Through Belgium* (London, 1914)

Davignon, Henri (ed.), *Belgium and Germany* (London, 1915)

Davis, Richard H., *With the Allies* (London, 1915)

Dawson, William H., *Germany and the Germans* (London, 1894)

–, *What is Wrong with Germany?* (London, 1915)

Delhaize, Jules, *Châtiments sans Crimes, Crimes sans Châtiments* (Namur, n.d. [1920])

Demartial, Georges, *La Guerre de 1914, Comment on mobilisa les consciences* (Paris, 1922)

Dernburg, Bernhard, *The Case of Belgium* (New York, n.d.)

–, *Search-Lights on the War* (New York, 1915)

Dickins, Bruce, *Germany's War Mania: The Teutonic Point of View as Officially Stated by her Leaders* (London, 1915)

Dillon, E. J., *Ourselves and Germany* (London, 1916)

Duhr, Bernhard, S. J., *Der Lügengeist im Völkerkrieg: Kriegs-Märchen* (München, 1915)

Durkheim, Emile, *L'Allemagne au dessus de tout* (Paris, 1915)

Essen, Léon van der, *The Invasion and the War in Belgium from Liège to the Yser* (London, 1917)

–, *A Statement About the Destruction of Louvain and Neighborhood* (Chicago, 1915)

–, *Some More News about the Destruction of Louvain* (Chicago, 1915)

Fonck, Alfons, *Schrotschüsse in Belgien: Die Ergebnisse einer Untersuchung über die Franktireurfrage* (Berlin, 1931)

Fulgister, Albert, *A Neutral Description of the Sack of Louvain* (Concord, NH, 1929)

Gaffney, T. St. John, *Breaking the Silence: England, Ireland, Wilson and the War* (New York, n.d. [c.1930])

Gallinger, Auguste, *The Counter-Charge: The Matter of War Criminals from the German Side* (München, 1922)

Gamarra, M., *A South American Priest in Belgium* (London, 1915)

Gerard, James, *My Four Years in Germany* (New York, 1917)

Ghuysen, Theophil, *Historique de l'invasion à Blégny-Trembleuer* (Aubel, 1919)

Gibson, Hugh, *A Journal from our Legation in Belgium* (New York, 1917)

Gillet, Leon, *Récit Officiel d'un Rescapé* (Charleroi, 1919)

Golenvaux, Fernand, *Les premiers jours de la Guerre à Namur, Août 1914* (Namur, 1935)

Grasshoff, Richard, *The Tragedy of Belgium: An Answer to Professor Waxweiler* (New York, 1915)

Grondys [Grondijs], L. H., *The Germans in Belgium: Experiences of a Neutral* (London, 1915)

Harrison, Austin, *The Kaiser's War* (London, 1914)

Harrison, Frederic, *The German Peril* (London, 1915)

Hazard, Paul, *Un examen de conscience de l'Allemagne: d'après les papiers de prisonniers de guerre allemands* (Paris 1915)

Heney, T. W., et. al. (ed.), *Life and Death in Belgium by Ten Belgian Journalists in Exile* (Melbourne, 1917)

Hillis, Newall, *German Atrocities: Their Nature and Philosophy* (New York, 1918)

Hobhouse, Leonard, *The Metaphysical Theory of the State* (London, 1918)

Houtte, Paul van, *The PanGermanic Crime: Impressions and Investigations in Belgium during the German Occupation* (London, 1915)

Hueffer, Ford Maddox, *Between St. Denis and St. George* (London, 1915)

–, *When Blood is Their Argument* (London, 1915)

Jacobsen, Wojcieck, *En marche sur Paris avec l'armée prussienne du Général von Kluck* (Brussels, 1937)

James, Henry, *Within the Rim and Other Essays* (London, 1918)

Jannasch, Lilli, *German Militarism at Work: A Collection of Documents* (London, 1926)

Jaspaers, Gustave, *Les Belges en Hollande, 1914–1917* (Amsterdam, n.d.)

Joffre, Maréchal Joseph, *Charleroi et la Marne* (Paris, n.d. [1928])

Johannet, Rene (ed.), *Pan-Germanism versus Christendom, the Conversion of a Neutral: Being an open letter by M. Emile Prum* (London, 1916)

Kennedy, J. M., *The Campaign round Liège* (London, 1914)

Klobukowski, A., *Souvenirs de Belgique* (Brussels, 1928)

Kurth, Godefroid, *Le Guet-apens prussien en Belgique* (Paris, 1919)

Langenhove, Fernand van, *The Growth of a Legend: A Study Based upon the German Accounts of Francs-Tireurs and "Atrocities" in Belgium* (New York, 1916)

Lasswell, Harold, *Propaganda Technique in World War I* (Cambridge, MA, 1971 [1927])

Lemaire, A., *La Tragédie de Tamines* (5th ed.) (Tamines, 1957)

Le Queux, William, *German Atrocities: A Record of Shameless Deeds* (London, 1914)

Lhoest, Jean-Louis and Michel Georis, *Liège, Août 14* (Paris, 1964)

Lichnowski, Max, *Heading for the Abyss: Reminiscences* (London, 1928)

Liddell, R. Scotland, *The Track of War* (London, 1915)

Liebknecht, Karl, *"The Future Belongs to the People": Speeches Made Since the Beginning of the War* (New York, 1918)

Mack, Louise, *A Woman's Experiences in the Great War* (London, 1915)

Maeterlinck, Maurice, *Les Débris de la guerre* (Paris, 1916)

–, *Le bourgmestre de Stilemonde* (Paris, 1919)

Mantoux, Paul, *The Deliberations of the Council of Four*, v. 1 (Princeton, 1992)

Massart, Jean, *Belgians under the German Eagle* (London, 1916)

–, *The Secret Press in Belgium* (London, 1918)

Mattern, Johannes, *Alleged German Atrocities: England's Most Effective Weapon* (Chicago, 1915)

Maxse, Leopold, *"Germany on the Brain" or, the Obsession of "A Crank"* (London, 1915)

Mayence, Fernand, *l'Armée allemande à Louvain et le Livre Blanc: traduction et réfutation de la partie de le Livre Blanc relative au sac de Louvain* (Leuven, 1919)

–, *The Legend of the "Francs Tireurs" of Louvain: A Reply to the Report of Dr. Meurer, Professor at the University of Würzburg* (Leuven, 1928)

Melot, Auguste, *Le Martyre du Clergé Belge* (Paris, n.d. [1915])

Mercier, Cardinal Désiré, *The Voice of Belgium, Being the War Utterances of Cardinal Mercier* (London, 1918)

–, *Cardinal Mercier's Own Story* (New York, 1920)

Mokveld, L., *The German Fury in Belgium* (New York, 1915)

Morgan, J. H., *German Atrocities: An Official Investigation* (London, 1916)

–, *The German War Book: Being "The Usages of War on Land" (Kriegsbrauch im Landkrieg) issued by the Great General Staff of the German Army* (London, 1915)

Muirhead, J. H., *German Philosophy in Relation to the War* (London, 1915)

Mullins, Claud, *The Leipzig Trials: An Account of the War Criminals' Trials and a Study of German Mentality* (London, 1921)

Munro, Dana, et. al., *German War Practices, Part 1: Treatment of Civilians* (Washington, D.C., n.d.)

Nieuwland, Dom Norbert and Maurice Tschoffen, *The Legend of the "Francs Tireurs" of Dinant* (Gembloux, 1929)

Notestein, Wallace and Elmer Stoll, *Conquest and Kultur: Aims of the Germans in Their own Words* (Washington, D.C., 1918)

Oszwald, Robert, *Der Streit um den belgischen Franktireurkrieg: Eine kritische Untersuchung der Ereignisse in den Augusttagen 1914 und der darüber bis 1930 erschienenen Literatur unter Benutzung bisher nicht veröffentlichten Materials* (Köln, 1931)

Passelecq, Fernand, *The Legend of the Francs-Tireurs' Warfare in Belgium* (Le Havre, 1915)

–, *Essai critique et notes sur l'alteration officielle des documents belges* (Paris, 1916)
–, *La réponse du gouvernement belge au livre blanc allemand* (Paris, 1916)
–, *Truth and Travesty: An Analytical Study of the Reply of the Belgian Government to the German White Book* (London, 1916)
–, *The "Sincere Chancellor"* (London, 1917)
Ponsonby, Arthur, *Falsehood in Wartime* (London, 1928)
Powell, E. Alexander, *Fighting in Flanders* (New York, 1914)
Prum, E. M, *Le Veuvage de la Verité: Une réponse aux Catholiques Allemands* (Amsterdam, 1916)
Raemaekers, Louis, *Raemaekers' Cartoons, with Accompanying Notes by well-known English Writers* (New York, 1916)
–, *Kultur in Cartoons, with Accompanying Notes by well-known English Writers* (New York, 1917)
Reich, Emil, *Germany's Swelled Head* (London, 1907)
Roberts, Elmer, *Monarchical Socialism in Germany* (New York, 1913)
Santayana, George, *The German Mind: A Philosophical Diagnosis* (New York, 1968 [1915])
Schmitt, Bernadotte, *England and Germany, 1740–1914* (Princeton, 1916)
Schmitz, Jean and Norbert Nieuwland, *Documents pour servir a l'histoire de l'invasion allemande dans les provinces de Namur et de Luxembourg*, 7 vols (Brussels, 1919–24)
Schryver, Charles de, *Liège pendant la guerre* (Liège, n.d.)
Smith, Thomas F. A. *The Soul of Germany: A Twelve Years Study of the People from Within, 1902–14* (New York, 1915)
–, *What Germany Thinks: The War As Germans See It* (New York, [1916])
Soete, Pierre de, *The Louvain Library Controversy: The Misadventures of an American Artist, or "Furore Teutonico Diruta: Dono Americano Restituta"* (Concord, NH, 1929)
Sombert, Werner, *Händler und Helden: Patriotische Besinnungen* (München, 1915)
Somville, Gustave, *The Road to Liège: the Path of Crime* (London, 1916)
Spears, Edward, *Liason 1914* (New York, 1968)
Struycken, A. A. H., *The German White Book and the War in Belgium: A Commentary* (Edinburgh, 1915)
Thier, Jules de and Olympe Gilbart, *Liège pendant la grande guerre*, tome 1, *Liège héroique*, tome 2, *Liège martyre* (Liège, 1919)
Topham, Anne, *A Distant Thunder: Intimate Recollections of the Kaiser's Court* (New York, 1992 [1914]
Toynbee, Arnold, *The German Terror in Belgium* (London, 1917)
–, *The German Terror in France* (London, 1917)
–, *The Belgian Deportations* (London, n.d.)
Usher, Roland, *Pan-Germanism* (Boston, 1913)
Vansittart, Robert, *The Lessons of My Life* (New York, 1943)
–, *The Black Record of Germany – Past, Present and Future?* (New York, 1944)
–, *The Mist Procession* (London, 1958)
Verhulst, Raf, *The Question of the Belgian Francs Tireurs: Belgium Before the World Tribunal* (Sint-Andries, 1930)
Vergnet, Paul, *La France en danger: l'oeuvre de pangermanistes: ce qu'ils sont...ce qu'ils peuvent... ce qu'ils veulent* (Paris, 1913)
Viereck, George, *Spreading Germs of Hate* (New York, 1930)
Waxweiler, Emil, *Belgium, Neutral and Loyal* (New York, 1915)
Weiss, Andre, *The Violation by Germany of the Neutrality of Belgium and Luxemburg* (Paris, 1915)
Whitehouse, J. H., *Belgium in War: A Record of Personal Experiences* (Cambridge, 1915)
Whitlock, Brand, *Belgium, A Personal Narrative*, 2 vols. (New York, 1920)
Whitman, Sidney, *Teuton Studies* (London, 1895)

BOOKS (SECONDARY – SELECTED)

Albertini, Luigi, *The Origins of the War of 1914*, 3 vols. (London, 1952)
Anderson, Pauline, *The Background of Anti-English Feeling in Germany, 1890–1902* (New York, 1939)
Aris, Reinhold, *History of Political Thought in Germany from 1789 to 1815* (London, 1965)
Aronson, Theo, *The Coburgs of Belgium* (London, 1968)
Ascherson, Neil, *The King Incorporated* (New York, 1964)

Aschheim, Steven, *The Nietzsche Legacy in Germany* (Berkeley, 1992)

Aveneri, Shlomo, *Hegel's Theory of the Modern State* (Cambridge, 1972)

Baldwin, Peter, *Reworking the Past: Hitler, the Holocaust, and the Historians' Debate* (Boston, 1990)

Balfour, Michael, *The Kaiser and His Times* (New York, 1972)

Banks, Arthur, *A Military Atlas of the First World War* (Barnsley, 2001)

Bass, Gary, *Stay the Hand of Vengeance: The Politics of War Crime Tribunals* (Princeton, 2000)

Beiser, Frederic, *Enlightenment, Revolution, and Romanticism: The Genesis of Modern German Political Thought, 1790–1800* (Cambridge, MA, 1992)

Belien, Paul, *A Throne in Brussels* (Exeter, 2005)

Berghahn, Volker, *Germany and the Approach of War* (New York, 1973)

Best, Geoffrey, *Humanity in Warfare: The Modern History of the International Law of Armed Conflicts* (London, 1980)

Blackbourn, David and Geoff Eley, *The Peculiarities of German History: Bourgeois Society and Politics in Nineteenth Century Germany* (Oxford, 1984)

Boemeke, Manfred, Gerald Feldman, Elisabeth Glaser (eds.), *The Versailles Treaty: A Reassessment After 75 Years* (Cambridge, 1998)

Boemeke, Manfred, Roger Chickering, Stig Förster (eds.), *Anticipating Total War: The German and American Experiences, 1871–1914* (Cambridge, 1999)

Bond, Brian, *The Unquiet Western Front: Britain's Role in Literature and History* (Cambridge, 2002)

Bossenbrook, William, *The German Mind* (Detroit, 1961)

Boulger, Demetrius, *The Reign of Leopold II*, vol. 2 (London, 1925)

Buchan, John, *A History of the Great War*, vol. 1 (Boston, 1922)

Buitenhuis, Peter, *The Great War of Words: British, American, and Canadian Propaganda and Fiction, 1914–1933* (Vancouver, 1987)

Butler, Rohan, *The Roots of National Socialism, 1783–1933* (London, 1941)

Cammaerts, Émile, *Albert of Belgium, Defender of Right* (New York, 1935)

Carsten, F. L., *A History of the Prussian Junkers* (Aldershot, 1989)

Cassirer, Ernst, *The Myth of the State* (New Haven, 1946)

Ceadel, Marin, *Pacifism in Britain, 1914–1945* (Oxford, 1980)

Cecil, Hugh and Peter Liddell (eds.), *Facing Armageddon* (London, 1996)

Cecil, Lamar, *Wilhelm I*, vols. 1 and 2 (Chapel Hill, 1989, 1996)

Chickering, Roger, *Imperial Germany and a World without War: The Peace Movement and German Society, 1892–1914* (Princeton, 1975)

–, *We Men who Feel most German: A Cultural Study of the Pan German League, 1886–1914* (Boston, 1984)

Citino, Robert, *The German Way of War: From the Thirty Years' War to the Third Reich* (Lawrence, Kansas, 2005)

Cohen, Warren, *The American Revisionists: The Lessons of Intervention in World War I* (Chicago, 1967)

Coppens, Chris, Mark Derez, and Jan Roegiers, *Leuven University Library, 1425–2000* (Leuven, 2005)

Craig, Gordon, *The Politics of the Prussian Army* (Oxford, 1955)

–, *Germany, 1866–1945* (New York, 1978)

Crozier, E. *American Reporters on the Western Front, 1914–1918* (Oxford, 1959)

Fisher, H. A. L., *James Bryce*, 2 vols. (New York, 1927)

Dockrill, M. and J. Fisher (eds.), *The Paris Peace Conference, 1919: Peace Without Victory?* (London, 2001)

Dorpalen, Andreas, *Heinrich von Treitschke* (New Haven, 1957)

Doerries, Reinhold, *Imperial Challenge: Ambassador Count Bernstorff and German American Relations, 1908–1917* (Chapel Hill, 1989)

Eley, Geoff, *Reshaping the German Right: Radical Nationalism and Political Change after Bismarck* (New Haven, 1980)

Essen, Leon van der, *A Short History of Belgium* (Chicago, 1920)

Evans, Richard, *Rethinking German History: Nineteenth Century Germany and the Origins of the Third Reich* (London, 1987)

–, *Rereading German History : From Unification to Reunification* (London, 1997)

Fay, Sidney, *The Origins of the World War*, 2 vols. (New York, 1928)

Field, Geoffrey, *Evangelist of Race: The Germanic Vision of Houston Stewart Chamberlain* (New York, 1981)

Fischer, Fritz, *Germany's Aims in the First World War* (New York: Norton, 1967)

–, *World Power or Decline* (New York, 1974)

–, *War of Illusions: German Policies from 1911 to 1914* (New York, 1975)

–, *From Kaiserreich to Third Reich: Elements of Continuity in German History* (London, 1986)

Friedman, Leonard, *The Law of War: A Documentary History* (New York, 1972)

Frevert, Ute, *Ehrenmänner: Das Duell in der bürgerliche Gesellschaft* (München, 1991)

Galpin, P., *Hugh Gibson, 1883–1954: Extracts from his Letters and Anecdotes from his Friends* (New York, 1956)

Galet, Emil, *King Albert in the Great War* (Boston, 1931)

Gasman, Daniel, *The Scientific Origins of National Socialism: Social Darwinism in Ernst Haeckel and the German Monist League* (London, 1971)

Geiss, Imanuel, *July 1914: The Outbreak of the First World War: Selected Documents* (New York, 1974)

Grimsley, Mark and C. J. Rogers (eds.), *Civilians in the Path of War* (Lincoln, Nebraska, 2002)

Gross, Michael, *The War Against Catholicism: Liberalism and the AntiCatholic Imagination in Nineteenth Century Germany* (Ann Arbor, 2004)

Gruber, Carol, *Mars and Minerva: World War I and the Uses of Higher Learning in America* (Baton Rouge, 1975)

Haste, Cate, *Keep the Home Fires Burning* (London, 1977)

Hawkins, Mike, *Social Darwinism in European and American Thought, 1860–1945* (Cambridge, 1997)

Herwig, Holgar, *The First World War: Germany and AustriaHungary, 1914–1918* (London, 1997)

Helmreich, Jonathan, *Belgium and Europe: A Study in Small Power Diplomacy* (The Hague, 1976)

Hewitson, Mark, *Germany and the Causes of the First World War* (Oxford, 2004)

Horne, John and Alan Kramer, *German Atrocities 1914: A History of Denial* (New Haven, 2001)

Howard, Michael, *The Franco-Prussian War: The German Invasion of France, 1870–1* (New York, 1990)

Hull, Isabel, *Absolute Destruction: Military Culture and the Practices of War in Imperial Germany* (Ithaca, 2005)

Hurst, M. (ed.), *Key Treaties for the Great Powers, 1814–1914*, 2 vols. (New York, 1972)

James, Harold, *A German Identity, 1770–1990* (New York, 1989)

Jarausch, Konrad, *The Enigmatic Chancellor: Bethmann Hollweg and the Hubris of Imperial Germany* (New Haven, 1973)

Keegan, John, *Opening Moves, August 1914* (London, 1971)

Kelly, Alfred, *The Descent of Darwin: The Popularization of Darwinism in Germany, 1860–1914* (Princeton, 1981)

Kelly, George A., *Idealism, Politics and History: Sources of Hegelian Thought* (Cambridge, 1969)

Kennedy, Paul, *The Rise of AngloGerman Antagonism, 1860–1914* (London, 1980)

Keynes, J. M., *The Economic Consequences of the Peace*, v. 2, *The Collected Writings of J. M. Keynes* (London, Macmillan, 1971)

Kitchen, Martin, *The German Officer Corps, 1890–1914* (Oxford, 1968)

Knightley, Philip, *The First Casualty: The War Correspondent as Hero and Myth-Maker from the Crimea to Kosovo* (Baltimore, 2000)

Kohn, Hans, *The Mind of Germany: The Education of a Nation* (New York, 1960)

Krieger, Leonard, *The German Idea of Freedom* (Chicago, 1957)

Lentin, A., *Lloyd George, Woodrow Wilson and the Guilt of Germany: An Essay in the Prehistory of Appeasement* (Leicester, 1984)

Luebke, Frederick, *Bonds of Loyalty: German Americans and World War I* (De Kalb, 1974)

Malinson, V., *Belgium* (New York, 1970)

Marks, Sally, *Innocent Abroad: Belgium at the Paris Peace Conference of 1919* (Chapel Hill, 1981)

McAleer, Kevin, *Dueling: The Cult of Honor in Fin-de-Siècle Germany* (Princeton, 1994)

McGovern, William, *From Luther to Hitler* (Boston, 1941)

Messinger, Gary, *British Propaganda and the State in the First World War* (Manchester, 1992)

Mantoux, Etienne, *The Carthaginian Peace* (Pittsburgh, 1964 [1952])

Mosse, George, *The Crisis of German Ideology* (New York, 1964)

Nipperdey, Thomas, *Deutsche Geschichte, 1866–1918, Band II, Machstaat vor der Demokratie* (München, 1992)

Novick, Peter, *The Noble Dream: The "Objectivity Question" and the American Historical Profession* (Cambridge, UK, 1988)

Peterson, H. C., *Propaganda for War: The Campaign against American Neutrality, 1914–1917* (Norman, OK, 1938)

Pirenne, Henri, *Belgium and the First World War* (Wesley Chapel, 2014)

–, *Histoire de Belgique des origines à nos jours*, vol. 4 (Brussels, 1952)

Ramm, Agatha, *Germany, 1789–1919* (London, 1981)

Read, James, *Atrocity Propaganda, 1914–1919* (New Haven, 1941)

Renouvin, Pierre, *The Immediate Origins of the War (28th June – 4th August 1914)* (New Haven, 1928)

Ritter, Gerhard, *The Sword and the Scepter: The Problem of Militarism in Germany*, vol. II: *The European Powers and the Wilhelminian Empire, 1890–1914* (Coral Gables, FL, 1970)

–, *The Schlieffen Plan: Critique of a Myth* (Westport, CT, 1979)

Röhl, John, *The Kaiser and his Court: Wilhelm II and the Government of Germany* (Cambridge, 1994)

–, (ed.), *Delusion or Design? The Testimony of Two German Diplomats* (New York, 1973)

Rubenstein, Shimon, *German Atrocity or British Propaganda?: The Seventieth Anniversary of a Scandal: German Corpse Utilization Establishments in the First World War* (Jerusalem, 1987)

Sanders, M. L. and Philip Taylor, *British Propaganda During the First World War, 1914–1918* (London, 1982)

Schaepdrijver, Sophie de, *La Belgique et la premier Guerre mondiale* (Brussels, 2012)

Schivelbusch, Wolfgang, *Die Bibliothek von Löwen* (München, 1988)

Schlesinger, J., et. al, *The Birtley Belgians*, 5th ed. (Durham, UK, 2003)

Schmitt, Bernadotte, *Germany and England, 1740–1914* (Princeton, 1916)

–, *The Coming of the War, 1914*, 2 vols. (New York, 1930)

Schöller, Peter, *Le cas de Louvain et le Livre Blanc allemand: Étude critique de la documentation allemande relative aux événements qui sont déroulés à Louvain du 15 au 28 août 1914* (Leuven, 1958)

Schrijvers, Peter, *The Unknown Dead: Civilians in the Battle of the Bulge* (Lexington, KY, 2005)

Schuker, Steven, *American "Reparations" to Germany, 1919–33: Implications for the Third World Debt Crisis* (Princeton, 1988)

Sheffield, Gary, *Forgotten Victory: The First World War: Myths and Realities* (London, 2002)

Sharp, Alan, *The Versailles Settlement: Peacemaking in Paris, 1919* (New York, 1991)

Smith, Helmut Walser, *German Nationalism and Religious Conflict: Culture, Ideology and Politics* (Princeton, 1995)

Snyder, Louis, *German Nationalism: The Tragedy of a People* (Harrisburg, PA, 1952)

–, *Roots of German Nationalism: The Sources of Political and Cultural Identity, 1815–1976* (New York, 1978)

Sontag, Raymond, *Germany and England: Background of Conflict, 1848–1894* (New York, 1969 [1938])

Squires, James, *British Propaganda at Home and in the United States* (Cambridge, 1935)

Stackelberg, Roderick, *Idealism Debased: From Volkish Ideology to National Socialism* (Kent, Ohio, 1981)

Stengers, Jean, *L'action du roi en Belgique depuis 1831: pouvoir et influence: essai de typologie des modes d'action du roi* (Paris, 1992)

Stern, Fritz, *The Politics of Cultural Despair: A Study in the Rise of the Germanic Ideology* (Berkeley, 1989 [1961])

–, *The Failure of Illiberalism: Essays on the Political Culture of Modern Germany* (New York, 1992)

Swartz, Martin, *The Union of Democratic Control in British Politics During the First World War* (London, 1971)

Stromberg, Roland, *Redemption by War: The Intellectuals and 1914* (Lawrence, KS, 1982)

Thielemans, Marie-Rose and Emile Vandewoude, *Le roi Albert: au traverse ses lettres inedités, 1882–1916* (Brussels, 1982)

Thomas, Daniel H., *The Guarantee of Belgian Independence* (Kingston, RI, n.d.)

Trachtenberg, Mark, *Reparation in World Politics* (New York, 1980)

Trotnow, Helmut, *Karl Liebknecht: A Political Biography* (Hamden, CT, 1984)

Tuchman, Barbara, *August 1914* (London, 1980)

Ungern-Sternberg, Juergen and Wolfgang von, *Der Aufruf 'An die Kulturwelt!': Der Manifest der 93 und die Anfänge der Kriespropaganda im Ersten Weltkrieg* (Stuttgart, 1996)

Vagts, Alfred, *A History of Militarism* (New York, 1959)

Viereck, Peter, *Metapolitics: The Roots of the Nazi Mind* (New York, 1965)

Wallace, Stuart, *War and the Image of Germany: British Academics, 1914–1918* (Edinburgh, 1988)

Wehler, Hans-Ulrich, *The German Empire, 1871–1918* (Leamington Spa, 1985)

Welch, David, *Germany, Propaganda, and Total War, 1914–1918* (New Brunswick, 2000)

Wende, Frank, *Die belgische Frage in der deutschen Politik des Ersten Weltkrieg* (Hamburg, 1969)

Wertheimer, Mildred, *The Pan-German League, 1890–1914* (New York, 1924)

Wheeler-Bennett, John, *The Nemesis of Power: The German Army in Politics* (New York, 1967)

Wieland, Lothar, *Belgien 1914: Die Frage des belgischen "Franktireurkrieges" und die deutsche öffentliche Meinung von 1914 bis 1936* (Frankfurt, 1984)

Williamson, George, *The Longing for Myth in Germany: Religion and Aesthetic Culture from Romanticism to Nietzsche* (Chicago, 2004)

Willis, James, *Prologue to Nuremberg: The Politics and Diplomacy of Punishing War Criminals of the First World War* (Westport, CT, 1982)

Wilson, Keith (ed.), *Forging the Collective Memory: Government and International Historians through Two World Wars* (Providence, R.I., 1996)

–, *(ed.) Decisions for War, 1914* (New York, 1995)

Witcover, Jules, *Sabotage at Black Tom: Imperial Germany's Secret War in America, 1914–1917* (Chapel Hill, 1989)

Wittke, Carl, *German-Americans and the World War* (Columbus, OH, 1936)

Wohl, Robert, *The Generation of 1914* (Cambridge, MA, 1979)

Wullus-Rudiger, I. *La Belgique et l'équilibre européen* (Paris, 1933)

Young, Harry, *Prince Lichnowski and the Great War* (Athens, GA, 1977)

Ypersele, Laurence van, *Le Roi Albert: Histoire d'un mythe* (Ottignes, 1995)

Zuckerman, Larry, *The Rape of Belgium: The Untold Story of World War I* (New York, 2002)

ARTICLES

"A Blond Beast," "Nietzsche," *English Review*, v. 18 (Oct. 1914), 392–6.

Archer, William, "The Germans in Belgium," *Quarterly Review*, v. 236, n. 468, 191–205.

Bassompiere, Alfred de, "La nuit du 2 au 3 août 1914," *Révue des Deux Mondes* (Paris), 15 February 1916, 884–906.

Becker, Jules de, "The American College and the Great War, Part I," *American College Bulletin*, v. 13, n. 1 (Jan. 1920), 3–26; Part II, v. 14, n. 2 (Jan. 1921), 49–66.

Bronne, Charles, "The Defence of Liège," *The English Review*, v. 20 (April 1915), 50–65.

Cammaerts, Emile, "Belgium's War Aims," *Nineteenth Century*, v. 84 (Nov. 1918), 825–834.

Chirol, Valentine, "Origins of the Present War," *Quarterly Review*, v. 223, n. 441, 415–449.

Crokaert, J., "L'Ultimatum allemand," *Le Flambeau* (Brussels), 31 March 1922, 305–30.

David, Camille, "Dinant la Morte," *Contemporary Review*, v. 108 (Aug. 1915), 212–219.

Davignon, Henri, "German Methods of Penetration in Belgium Before and During the War," *Quarterly Review*, v. 225, n. 446, 130–147.

Dawson, William H., "Some Personal Memories of Treitschke," *Nineteenth Century*, v. 77 (Jan. 1915), 151–158.

Delandsheere, P. (ed.), "Les atrocités allemandes: La Boucherie de Tamines" *Le XXième Siècle* (Brussels), 29 December 1918.

Delannoy, Pierre, "The Library of the University of Louvain," *Nineteenth Century*, v. 77, n. 459 (May 1915), 1061–1071.

Derez, Mark, "The Flames of Louvain: The War Experience of an Academic Community" in H. Cecil and P. Liddell, *Facing Armageddon* (London, 1996).

Fox, Frank, "Belgium on the Rack: A Bystander's Testimony," *Nineteenth Century*, v. 77 (Jan. 1915), 42–51.

Frodsham, Bishop George, "What Is Wrong With German Christianity?", *Nineteenth Century*, v. 77 (May 1915), 1084–1091.

Gullace, Nicole, "Sexual Violence and Family Honor: British Propaganda and International Law during the First World War," *American Historical Review*, v. 102, n. 3 (June 1997), 714–747.

Harris, Ruth, "The 'Child of the Barbarian': Rape, Race and Nationalism in France during the First World War," *Past and Present 141* (1993), 170–206.

Hatch, Ernest, "Belgian Refugees in the United Kingdom," *Quarterly Review*, v. 225, n. 446, 188–214.

Herwig, Holgar, "Clio Deceived: Patriotic Self-Censorship in Germany after the Great War," in K. Wilson (ed.), *Forging the Collective Memory* (Providence, R. I., 1996).

–, "The Immorality of Expediency: The German Military from Ludendorff to Hitler," in M. Grimsley and C. J. Rogers (eds.), *Civilians in the Path of War* (Lincoln, Nebraska, 2002).

Horne, John and Alan Kramer, "German 'Atrocities' and Franco-German Opinion, 1914: The Evidence of German Soldiers' Diaries," *The Journal of Modern History* v. 66, n. 1 (March 1994), 1–33.

Jacobs, E. A., "Les 'Oubliés': Le rôle de la Garde civique en août 1914," *Le Roi Albert et ses soldats: expositon organisée à l'occasion du 50e anniversaire de l'inauguration du Musée de l'armée par Sa Majesté le Roi Albert, le 22 juillet 1923: Bruxelles, Musée royal de l'armée et d'histoire militaire, 26 octobre 18 novembre 1973.*

Jesse, F. Tennyson, "From Behind the Front," *English Review*, v. 18 (Nov. 1914) , 492–500.

Kocka, Jurgen, "German History before Hitler: The Debate about the German Sonderweg," *Journal of Contemporary History*, v. 23, n. 1, 3–16.

Leclere, Léon, "La Belgique à la veille de l'invasion," *Revue d'Histoire de la Guerre Mondiale* (July 1926), 193–216.

Lehmann, Hartmut, "Germany: 'God Our Old Ally,'" in W. Hutchison and H. Lehmann (eds.), *Many are Chosen: Divine Election and Western Nationalism* (Minneapolis, 1994).

Marks, Sally, "The Myths of Reparations," *Central European History*, v. 11, n. 3 (1978), 231–255.

Mayence, Fernand, "The Belgian Rejoinder," *Current History* (July 1928), 566–71

McClellan, George, "How Germany Looks to George B. McClellan," *New York Times* 26 September 1915, (Sunday supplement), 5.

–, "How I Found Belgium Under German Rule," *New York Times*, 10 October 1915, 46 (Sunday supplement), 1.

Meurer, Christian "The Blame for the Sack of Louvain: The Case for the Germans," *Current History* (July 1928), 556–566.

[Noël, Laurent] "Récit d'un Professeur de Louvain," *Hibbert Journal*, v. 13 (Jan. and April, 1915), 272–83, 889–92.

–, "The Soul of Belgium," *Hibbert Journal*, v. 13, 233–42.

Nolan, R. S., "Germany Today: Some Experiences and Impressions of a Civil Prisoner of War," *Nineteenth Century*, v. 76 (October 1914), 782–792.

Peemans, Françoise, "Tensions dans les relations belgo-vaticanes en 1914–1918: La conciliation difficile des nationalismes et des intérêts catholiques en Europe," *Risorgimento*, 21 (1979), 173–94.

Petit, J. (ed.), "Les événements tragiques d'août 1914 à Tamines," *Feuilleton de "Vers l'Avenir!"* (n. d.)

Randall, A. W. G., "Aspects of Teutonism: The 'German God,'" *Fortnightly Review*, v. 98, n. 586, 622–643.

Recouly, Raymond, "Les Heures tragiques d'Avant-Guerre," *La révue de France* (1 Sept. 1921), 31–40.

Robbins, Keith, "Lord Bryce and the First World War," *The Historical Journal*, v. 10, n. 2 (1967), 255–77.

St. Clair Stobart, E. "Within the Enemy's Lines," *Fortnightly Review*, v. 97, n. 580, 670–684.

Selliers de Moranville, A., "Le Conseil de la Couronne du 2 août 1914," *Le Flambeau* (Brussels), 21 August 1921, 449–69.

Shadwell, A., "German Hate, Its Causes and Meaning," *Nineteenth Century*, v. 77 (May 1915), 987–1003.

Sheridan, R. B. C., "The Vatican and the War: The Pope, Orthodoxy, and the Allies," *Nineteenth Century*, v. 78 (October 1915), 862–869.

Stengers, Jean, "Guillaume II et le Roi Albert à Potsdam en novembre 1913," *Académie royale des sciences, des lettres et des beauxarts de Belgique: Bulletin de la classe des lettres et des sciences morales et politiques*, v. 4 (1993), 227–253.

Thielemans, M.-R. and E. Vandewoude, "Les conseils des ministres et de la Couronne du 2 août 1914: récherche méthodologique sur la valeur des témoignages," *Histoire et Méthode*, 4 (1981), 417–444.

Trachtenberg, Mark, "Reparations at the Paris Peace Conference," *Journal of Modern History*, v. 51, n. 1 (1979), 24–55.

–, "Versailles After Sixty Years," *Journal of Contemporary History*, v. 17, n. 3 (1982), 487–506.

Tuker, M. A. R., "Religions and the War," *Nineteenth Century*, v. 76 (December 1914), 1318–1330.

Vandervelde, Emile, "La Belgique d'Aujourdhui et la Belgique de Demain," *Nineteenth Century* (April 1915), 797–802.

Watson, Foster, "The Humanists of Louvain," *Nineteenth Century*, v. 76 (October 1914), 765–775.

Wilson, Trevor, "Lord Bryce's Investigation into Alleged German Atrocities," *Journal of Contemporary History* 14 (1979), 369–83.

Illustration Credits

The author has attempted to contact all holders of the copyright to the visual material contained in this publication. Any copyright-holders who believe that illustrations have been reproduced without their knowledge are asked to contact the publisher. The numbers below refer to the pages on which the illustrations appear.

brothers Arnou, made for the University of Leuven in August 1914, K.U.Leuven Archives.

470 Photograph. Collection Rik Uytterhoeven in City Archives Leuven. Taken from M. Ceunen and P. Veldeman (eds.), *Aan onze helden en martelaren. Beelden van de brand van Leuven (augustus 1914)* (Leuven, 2004), 64.

482 Postcard. Collection Jeff Lipkes.

518 Photograph. Private Collection Peter Tayhon. Taken from M. Ceunen en P. Veldeman (eds.), *Aan onze helden en martelaren. Beelden van de brand van Leuven (augustus 1914)* (Leuven, 2004), 254.

Index

Lightning Source UK Ltd.
Milton Keynes UK
UKOW05f1827250716

279214UK00008B/100/P

9 780989 099363